A Guide to Architecture in the
ADIRONDACKS

Published by Adirondack Architectural Heritage
1745 Main Street
Keeseville, NY 12944
www.aarch.org

Design, editing and production by Adirondack Life, Inc.
www.adirondacklife.com

Cover photo by Nancie Battaglia
Back cover photo by Richard Longstreth
Maps by Paul Davidson

This publication is made possible, in part, by a grant from

Furthermore:
a program of the J.M. Kaplan Fund

Longstreth, Richard
A Guide to Architecture in the Adirondacks

Manufactured in the United States

10 9 8 7 6 5 4 3 2 1

CIP data is on file with the Library of Congress

ISBN
978-0-96-703885-8

A Guide to Architecture in the
ADIRONDACKS

Richard Longstreth

In memory of Cuthbert Russell Train,
without whom I would never have gotten to know
the Adirondacks.

CONTENTS

CONTENTS

FOREWORD

The Adirondack region is best known for its incredible natural resources—millions of acres of wild and forested land, rugged mountains, miles of rivers, and thousands of lakes and ponds—much of which is constitutionally protected in the Adirondack Forest Preserve. Less well known and appreciated are the region's historic sites, its architectural treasures, and the many small communities that embody nearly 250 years of settlement and enterprise here.

When Adirondack Architectural Heritage (AARCH) was founded in 1990, our first advocacy effort was to take up the cause of preserving Camp Santanoni, a state-owned historic Great Camp in the Essex County town of Newcomb. As focused as we were on the preservation and public enjoyment of Santanoni, we were equally committed to shining a light on the broad and diverse architectural legacy of the Adirondacks and to help make the preservation of this heritage central to the region's identity and prosperity.

This interest in heralding the diverse wealth of architecture here is reflected in almost everything we do as an organization. The first slide lecture we took on the road, which has been given in more than seventy-five locations around the region, was *There's More to Adirondack Architecture than Great Camps*. Our annual offering of day-long public educational outings are rife with the ordinary and the unusual, taking people to industrial communities like Lyon Mountain, Tahawus, Corinth, and Newton Falls; or to explore late 20th-century places like a Cold War–era missile silo, theme parks, ski chalet developments, roadside architecture, a "back-to-the-land" community, and a cluster of young farmers and entrepreneurs near Keeseville. We've also brought people to the maximum security prison at Dannemora, learned about the rich tradition of children's camps, examined the work of individual architects, and have done so on foot and by train, bicycle, and canoe.

One of our greatest joys is the unexpected communication we get when an individual directs our attention to some obscure place we've never heard of or asks for our help to preserve a threatened historic building not on our radar. These communications have often led to new advocacy efforts or have been the impetus for new adventures, including to a private pedestrian suspension bridge, an outdoor amphitheater, stone ruins and heaps of shoe leather at a former tannery site, a "million dollar dam" in the pine barrens, a cluster of Lustron homes, a suffragette's grave, and cottages inspired by Japanese architecture, to name just a few.

So we were incredibly pleased to have found, in Richard Longstreth, a true kindred spirit, with a similar passion for the variety of architecture and communities that we have. To his passion and natural curiosity, Professor Longstreth brings his substantial experience as an architectural historian and author, an impressive background in the preservation field, nearly forty years of exploring the Adirondacks, and his own individual sense of what is worthy of our attention, admiration, and good stewardship.

We hope that this book will be a means by which readers can explore the towns, villages, and rural roads of the region and see its astonishing variety of special places, large and small, familiar and little known, old and new. But this endeavor is not just about the thrill of discovering new places. It's also about greater appreciation and understanding and, central to our mission, a greater individual and collective sense of stewardship for our architecture and communities, ultimately comparable to the affection and protection we feel towards the region's natural resources.

The publication of *A Guide to Architecture in the Adirondacks* was supported by a number of institutions and individuals, to whom we are deeply grateful. Adirondack Architectural Heritage received a generous grant from Furthermore, a program of the J. M. Kaplan Fund. Funding for this project also came from a 2017 Local Heritage Grant from the Champlain Valley National Heritage Partnership.

Individual support for this publication came from: Anne Adams-Laumont, Sanders and Sally Berk, Brian and Janet Bliss, Courtney Iglehart, Annette Merle-Smith, James Morley, Anthony Pell, Mason Snyder and James Sams, Elizabeth and William Stewart, Nicholas Taylor, Fairman Thompson, and Philip Winterer.

Many more photographs of the buildings, landscapes, and structures covered in this guide will soon be available online to AARCH members. Check the AARCH website for a notice.

We hope you enjoy *A Guide to Architecture in the Adirondacks.*

Steven Engelhart

Executive Director
Adirondack Architectural Heritage
www.aarch.org

Interior, main lodge, Camp Santanoni.

ACKNOWLEDGMENTS

Credit for the idea of creating a guide to architecture in the Adirondacks goes to Adirondack Architectural Heritage (AARCH) and particularly to its director, Steven Engelhart, who has long understood the value such a publication could have in furthering an appreciation and understanding of the built environment in the region. The idea was pursued for over a decade, and while many AARCH supporters were enthusiastic about the prospect, the lack of staff time and funds to undertake such a venture conspired to keep it in the realm of a vision. After completing a major book and a host of smaller pieces, I decided to offer my services pro bono to prepare the manuscript. Doing so has led to a remarkable adventure.

Many people contributed in significant ways to the book's development. Among those who provided information on individual properties are: Jana Atwell, David and Joyce Anteau, Perry Babcock, Margaret Bartley, Sally Berk, Bridget Blinn, Noras Burke, Janet and Robert Cabat, Kevin Callahan, Jamie Campbell, Stephen Cermek, Murri Chase, Bob Conway, Francis Cocozza, Andrew Crossier, Jim Dillon, Sarah Disney, Christine Dixon, Peter Donnelley, Kathy Dorman, Louis Falzerano, Sharal Falzerano, Linda Favata, Conrad Fleischman, Jay Foggerty, Christopher Fox, Bob Frederick, Megan Funk, Carol Gehrig, Tony Goodwin, Shanna Graham, George W. Greene, Robin Gucker, Alison Haas, Robert W. Hammond, Ernest Ippisch, Skip Izzo, Judy Jones, Richard Kagey, Dave Langston, David LeBar, Hillarie Logan-Dechene, Bryan McDonald, Steven McFarland, Mary McGowan, Mark McMurry, Dolores Marinelli, Sister Connie Messitt, Wester Miga, Connie Southmayd Morrison, Mike Orday, Paul Provost, Carly Randy, Ray Rios, Phyllis Rogers, Donald Roessler, Amy Sabattis, Lauel St. Onge, Dawn Revette, William S. Saxton, Bridgit and Rolf Schulte, Auype Shaheen, Mike Sheridan, Tom Silabski, Maurice Southmayd, Jackie Strasser, Jim Sullivan, Neil Surprenant, Randy Teetz, Al Turner, Steven Vassar, Naj Wikoff, Gary Wilson, and Mary Sue Wolson.

A number of town historians and other public officials were very helpful in sharing information they had gathered and in some cases researched for me: Jeanne Barley (Town of Russia clerk), Eleanor Brooks (Bleecker), Ron Bruno (Willsboro), Rachael Clothier (Corinth), Gail Cramer (Northville), Janet Cross (Elizabethtown), Jean Dickerson (Lewis), Peg Edwards (Village of Lake Placid), Priscilla Edwards (Edinburg), Jean Grimm (Fine, retired), Therese Brannon Haley (Minerva), Sharon Hewston (Jay), Joan Hundson (Crown Point), Paula Johnson (Russia), Donna Lagoy (Chester), Elizabeth LaMoria (Moriah), Margaret Mannix (Village of Lake George), Peg Masters (Webb), Colleen Murtagh (Horicon), Joseph Provoncha (North Hudson), Beverly Reid (North Elba), Amanda Seeley (Morehouse), Jo Ann Smith (Johnsburg), Marilyn Van Dyke (Queensbury), Abby Verner (Long Lake), Carolyn Walker (Stratford), Anne Weaver (Lake Pleasant), and William Zullo (Hamilton County, retired)

The directors and other staff members of numerous historical societies, museums, and libraries were also of invaluable assistance, including: Lisa Adamson (Lake George Historical Society and Museum), Todd Bailey (Historic Saranac Lake), Elizabeth Brelia and June Venette (Anderson Falls Heritage Society), Dale Burnett (Hopkinton Historical Group), Delbert Chambers (Town of Warrensburg Museum of Local History),

Loris Clark (Schroon–North Hudson Historical Society), David Cranston (Hadley-Luzerne Historical Society), William Dolback (Ticonderoga Historical Society), Franklin Historical and Museum Society, Karen Glass (Keene Valley Library), Carol Haber (Essex County Historical Museum), Rita Kwetchian (Friends of Lyon Mountain), Kate Lewis (Town of Webb Historical Association), Peg Mauer (Goff-Nelson Memorial Library, Tupper Lake), Jerold Pepper (Adirondack Museum), Karen Rappaport (Wells Memorial Library, Upper Jay), Joan Rock (Putnam District #1 Schoolhouse Museum, Putnam), Michelle San Antonio (North Creek Railroad Depot Museum, North Creek), Nancy Shaw (Minerva Historical Society), Jennifer Tufano (Lake Placid–North Elba Historical Society), and Michele Tucker (Adirondack Research Room, Saranac Lake Free Library).

Special thanks also go to Nancy Hadley, director of the member archives at the American Institute of Architects in Washington, D.C., who graciously responded to my numerous requests for biographical material on deceased architects who had done work in the Adirondacks. Russ Quade, former curator of the files of the National Register of Historic Places and National Historic Landmarks at the National Park Service in Washington, facilitated my probing of that invaluable resource, now inaccessible. Additional repositories from which I benefited include George Washington University's Gelman Library, the Architecture and McKeldin libraries at the University of Maryland, and the Library of Congress.

Other people provided material and guidance as well: Jeanne Barley, Bryan Burke, Stephen Cermek, Edward Comstock, Richard Cook, Matthew Foley, William Preston Gates, Carole Gehrig, Elizabeth Lambeth Gereau, Michael Griffin, David Hislop, Mary Hotaling, William Johnston, William Krattinger, Chester Liebs, Nils Luderowski, Tom Lynch, Connie Prickett, Deanne Rehm, David and Betsey Thomas-Train, Caroline Welsh, Mark Wilcox, and William Wilkins.

The material gathered with the help of many people and much additional information found in books, articles, brochures, manuscripts, newspapers (often through Proquest and New York Historical Newspapers databases), and historic photographs and prints was supplemented by five summers of fieldwork. Driving over 25,000 miles (within the Blue Line), I was able to examine the work included in this book firsthand, often on several occasions, selecting it from many more examples that merit our attention as well. Philip Anderson and James Jacobs, James A. Figg III, Douglas and Tita Hyland, Michael and Rosemary Sulzbach, and deTeel Patterson Tiller provided exceptional company on some of these forays.

I am eternally grateful to those who gave their time and expertise to review a draft of the manuscript and provided an array of important suggestions for its improvement: Edward Comstock, Howard Kirschenbaum, Philip Terrie, and Diana and John G. Waite. Christopher Fox, Jay Higgins, David Hislop, Mary Hotaling, and Peg Masters read portions of a draft and were likewise of invaluable assistance. Paul Davidson deserves a round of applause for his superb work in preparing the maps that are essential to this guide.

The extensive files and library at the office of Adirondack Architectural Heritage in Keeseville greatly facilitated my research, and I am grateful to the AARCH staff, especially Mary-Nell Bockman, who has done more than one can imagine to help in the book's production. My deep appreciation also goes to Bonnie DeGolyer, Virginia Siskavich-Bosley, and Ellen Ryan for their assistance. Throughout the six-year preparation and production of this guide, Steven Engelhart has been a continuous source of ideas, information, and encouragement. The AARCH board, too, offered its vigorous support of the project. It has been a great pleasure to work with Elizabeth Folwell at *Adirondack Life*, who did a superb job of copyediting the manuscript and helped guide this project into reality in many others ways. Thanks, too, goes to her assistant, Niki Kourofsky, and to Marty Kilburn for his skillful work in meeting the myriad challenges to laying out a book of this complexity.

I have had the good fortune to be a seasonal resident of the Adirondacks since 1978, due to my wife, Cinda Train Longstreth, whose father, the late Cuthbert Russell Train, shortly after World War II purchased the 1898 Keene Valley house in which we now reside. He loved the mountains and knew them well. Without his foresight and enthusiasm I would never have been in a position to learn about the places about which I have had the privilege to write in this book.

A Note on the Illustrations

The great majority of images used in this book were taken by me between June 2012 and August 2016. I used a Nikon D90 camera body with a Nikon DX 18-105mm lens. Concurrently, I shot most of the same material with a Nikon F camera, using a 35mm pc lens and Ilford Delta 100 black-and-white film. Discs from the former and negatives and contact sheets from the latter are archived at AARCH's offices in Keeseville. In a few instances I relied on 35mm color slides taken by me using the same Nikon F camera and 35mm pc lens beginning in the 1980s. These include the images accompanying: CH 4, PH 1a, WP 21, WI 4, KS 20, AF 15, LP 14, SL 27i, PS 3, PS 5, SN 2, SN 3, TL 3, BE 1, LO 7, RL 7, and BG 2.

In the course of my research I shot some 2,300 digital images—far more than needed for the published guide. Many of these will be posted, in the same order as entries appear in the book, on a special website that is part of the Society of Architectural Historians' vast image bank (SAHARA) of buildings, landscapes, and communities worldwide and can be accessed by AARCH as well as SAH members.

Many of the historic images used in the Introduction and the introductory paragraphs of each section are taken from postcards, prints, photographs, or 19th-century books in my possession. A number of images are from postcards formerly in the collection of Edward Comstock of Saranac Lake, who kindly allowed me to photograph them in 2015. They are now in the Special Collections division of the library at St. Lawrence University. These include: I-1, I-2, I-3, I-5, I-6, I-8, I-10, I-15, I-16, I-17, I-18, I-27; 4-5; 5-5; 7-5; 8-3; 9-4, 9-5; 10-1, 10-2, 10-4, 10-6; 11-3, 11-4; 12-4, 12-7, and the image accompanying OF 1.

Yet others are from the Prints and Photographs Division of the Library of Congress. Most were taken by the Detroit Photography Company in the early 20th century: I-4, I-19, I-24, I-25, I-28; 1-3, 1-5, 1-7; 4-4; 9-1, 9-3, 9-6, 9-7, 9-8; 12-3, 12-6, and the image accompanying LG 8. The image accompanying TA 2a was taken by Jet Lowe for the Historic American Engineering Record and is likewise available online through the same archival source.

The photograph on page iv is courtesy of Nancie Battaglia; that on page 46 is courtesy of Spencer Morrissey. Figure 5-1 is courtesy of the New York State Office of Parks, Recreation, and Historic Preservation; 5-4 courtesy of the Penfield Foundation; 7-1 courtesy of AARCH; NE 2 courtesy of Bill Killon; and IL 3 by Robert Benson, courtesy of Sally and Sanders Berk.

A GUIDE TO THIS GUIDE

Most architectural guides focus on a community or a metropolitan area. Some address work in a county; yet others, most notably the Society of Architectural Historians' Buildings of the United States series, cover an entire state in one or two volumes. There are guides to college and university campuses, to municipal parks and park systems, and to certain building types such as railroad stations. But how does one cover a region such as the Adirondacks? Using the **Adirondack Park** to delineate that area is both a logical and instructive solution. The park is a legally defined geographic entity with boundaries that appear on most maps. While encompassing a multitude of political jurisdictions, the physical complexion of the park is in part shaped by the "forever wild" provisions established by the state constitution in 1894 and by numerous legislative measures enacted thereafter. Since 1885, state-owned lands in the Adirondacks have been called the **Forest Preserve**. Beginning in the early 1970s, the **Department of Environmental Conservation (DEC)** has held jurisdiction over how those lands are used, and the **Adirondack Park Agency (APA)** has held similar authority over the use of privately held property. By virtue of its landscape—much of it wild, most of the rest developed at low densities—the Adirondacks is a reasonably coherent area. Even portions of the park that seem quite different, most notably the Champlain Valley, are closely tied historically to the mountainous lands farther west.

Thus, throughout the book, **Adirondacks, Adirondack Park, park**, and **region** are used synonymously. Since its establishment in 1892, the park has been expanded on a number of occasions, most recently in 1972, but references to it in the text all entail the current size of six million acres. The boundary of the park has long been known as the **Blue Line**, a reference to the color used to delineate it in early (and many later) maps.

Throughout New York State, as in New England, the term **town** refers to the same kind of local jurisdiction as township does in mid-Atlantic states. In the Adirondacks, the area encompassed by each of the eighty-nine towns that lie—entirely or partially—within its boundaries is predominantly rural or undeveloped. In many cases, large portions of a town are part of the Forest Preserve. Most concentrated settlements are politically integral components of towns and are known as **hamlets**. Some hamlets have the same name as their towns (Essex and Indian Lake, for example). Eleven settlements are separately incorporated as **villages**. A few villages and hamlets straddle two or more towns (Au Sable Forks, Keeseville, Saranac Lake). I have adhered to this official nomenclature instead of more common parlance throughout the text to avoid the confusion that might otherwise occur. The only exception is using generic terms such as mining town or company town, where employing "company hamlet" could seem forced.

In selecting buildings, structures (bridges, fire towers, etc.), and landscapes (gardens, golf courses, cemeteries) for inclusion in the guide, I have generally followed the criteria used for the National Register of Historic Places—criteria that have become accepted nationwide. Design, use of building materials, structural configurations, and functions served are all central determinants. In the case of landscapes, the manipulation of topography, use of plant materials, salient artificial features (paths, fences, walls), and (for cemeteries) presence of noteworthy monuments.

Space limitations, however, preclude being as inclusive as National Register criteria permit, and omission from this guide does not mean that a property lacks historical significance. I have also not included properties that are noteworthy for their associational attributes (with an important individual, organization, or event) unless their physical qualities are also of interest. Archaeological sites are likewise excluded unless at least some of their significance is evident aboveground, as with the earthworks at Fort Ticonderoga or the remnants of Fort St. Frédéric at Crown Point. Properties that have been conspicuously altered in ways that substantially detract from their historic qualities are omitted unless the alterations themselves contribute to the work's significance.

A further limitation is excluding work, no matter how significant, that cannot be seen from a public road and is not otherwise publicly accessible. Thus the guide does not list most camps (private residences) unless they are on public land (Santanoni, Debar Pond Lodge), are accessible through regularly scheduled tours (Sagamore, White Pine), or owned by institutions and can be visited by arrangement. For all privately owned properties that are listed, inclusion in this guide should in no way be construed as an invitation to trespass. The rights of owners, including privacy, should be observed at all times.

The guide is organized in twelve sections, each with its own map and historical introduction. Those sections were determined by grouping concentrated settlements—which encompass the great majority of listings—into logical clusters. The communities in a given section are sequenced in an order conducive to touring, but many users of this guide will want to develop their own itineraries based on interests, points of origin, and paths of travel. As the map showing the entire area reveals, for example, Section 1 abuts Sections 4 and 5 as well as Section 2. Thus, before setting out, it is wise to plan a route that suits individual circumstances. The maps drawn for each section and for the larger communities are diagrammatic, and while approximating actual configurations should not preclude the use of the USGS or road maps available in print or electronically.

For individual entries I have generally used the historical name of the property except in cases where it has long been known by its current name. I have given the name of the architect or builder whenever possible. Architects based outside the Blue Line have the location of their office set in parentheses. Architects and other designers with offices in the Adirondacks are covered in brief biographies at the end of this volume. Two entries resist the sectional format: fire towers, which are accessible only by foot, and the Adirondack Northway (I-87), which runs through numerous jurisdictions within the park between Lake George and Keeseville. Both have separate listings located after the Introduction and before Section 1.

Information contained in the entries draws from a wide variety of sources, including: historical books and articles, historic resource surveys, historic maps, historic photographs, period and current newspapers, period trade magazines, museum and historical society archives, the research of numerous town historians and others who have an interest in local heritage, nomination forms to the National Register of Historic Places and National Historic Landmarks Program, interviews with current and past property owners, and site visits to all listed properties, most of them on more than one occasion. I have striven for accuracy; however, as in any project that must rely on an array of secondary sources, new information will inevitably come to light. I am eager to learn of any such findings and would appreciate being contacted at **rwl@gwu.edu**.

While this guide was undertaken for Adirondack Architectural Heritage and benefited from frequent consultations with, and review by, the director and some members of the board, the format and content are my own. The views expressed herein are in no way to be construed as representing official ones of AARCH, its board, or its membership.

LIST OF COMMUNITY ABBREVIATIONS

Adirondack - **AD**

Atwell - **AT**

Au Sable Forks - **AF**

Bakers Mills - **BS**

Batchellerville - **BA**

Beaver River - **BV**

Benson Mines & Star Lake - **BE**

Big Moose - **BG**

Bleecker - **BC**

Bloomingdale - **BM**

Blue Mountain Lake - **BK**

Bolton Landing - **BL**

Boquet - **BO**

Brant Lake - **BR**

Brooks Bay - **BB**

Caroga Lake - **CA**

Chestertown - **CH**

Childwold - **CI**

Chilson - **CN**

Clemons - **CL**

Clintonville - **CT**

Conklingville - **CK**

Corinth - **CO**

Crown Point Center &

Crown Point - **CP**

Dannemora - **DN**

Diamond Point - **DP**

Duane - **DU**

Eagle Bay - **EB**

Edinburg - **ED**

Elizabethtown - **EL**

Essex - **ES**

Fine - **FI**

Fish House - **FH**

Friends Lake & Loon Lake - **FL**

Gabriels - **GA**

Grant - **GR**

Hague - **HA**

Harkness - **HK**

Hoffmeister - **HF**

Hopkinton - **HO**

Huletts Landing - **HL**

Indian Lake - **IL**

Inlet - **IN**

Ironville - **IR**

Jay - **JA**

Johnsburg - **JH**

Keene - **KN**

Keene Valley &

St. Huberts - **KV**

Keeseville - **KS**

Lake Clear - **LC**

Lake George - **LG**

Lake Luzerne & Hadley - **LL**

Lake Placid - **LP**

Lake Pleasant &

Speculator - **SP**

Lake Vanare - **LV**

Lewis - **LE**

Long Lake - **LO**

Loon Lake - **LN**

Lower Chateaugay Lake - **LW**

Lyon Mountain - **LM**

Mayfield - **MA**

McKeever - **MK**

Minerva - **MN**

Mineville & Witherbee - **MV**

Moriah Corners - **MC**

New Russia - **NA**

Newcomb - **NE**

Newton Falls - **NF**

Nicholville - **NI**

North Creek - **NC**

North Elba - **NL**

North Hudson - **NH**

North River - **NR**

Northville - **NV**

Ohio - **OH**

Old Forge & Thendara - **OF**

Olmstedville - **OL**

Onchiota - **ON**

Oswegatchie - **OS**

Otter Lake - **OT**

Owls Head - **OW**

Paul Smiths - **PS**

Peasleeville - **PE**

Pecks Park - **PP**

Piercefield - **PI**

Piseco Lake - **PL**

Port Henry - **PH**

Port Kent - **PK**

Pottersville - **PV**

Putnam Center - **PT**

Raquette Lake - **RL**

Ray Brook - **RB**

Riparius - **RI**

Saranac Lake - **SL**

Schroon Lake - **SH**

Sevey - **SV**

Silver Bay &

Sabbath Day Point - **SB**

Standish - **SD**

Stony Creek - **SC**

Stratford - **SO**

St. Regis Falls - **SI**

Tahawus - **TA**

Ticonderoga - **TI**

Town of Clare - **CR**

Town of Lyonsdale - **LY**

Town of Santa Clara - **SR**

Town of Saranac - **SA**

Tupper Lake - **TL**

Upper Jay - **UJ**

Upper Saranac Lake - **SN**

Valcour - **VA**

Vermontville - **VT**

Wadhams - **WD**

Wanakena - **WN**

Warrensburg - **WA**

Wells - **WS**

Westport - **WP**

Wevertown - **WV**

Whallonsburg - **WH**

Willsboro - **WI**

Wilmington - **WM**

Woodgate - **WT**

MAP OF THE COUNTIES

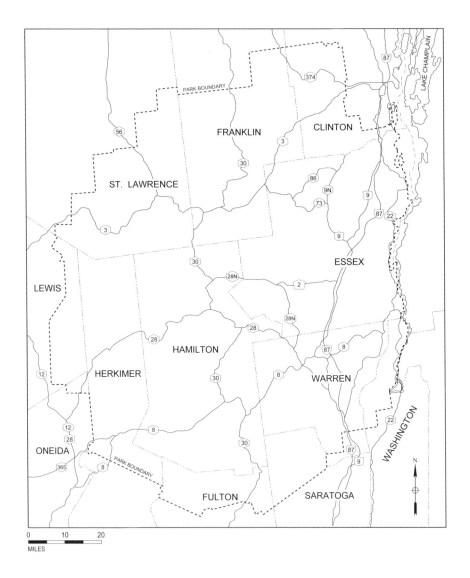

MAP OF THE SECTIONS

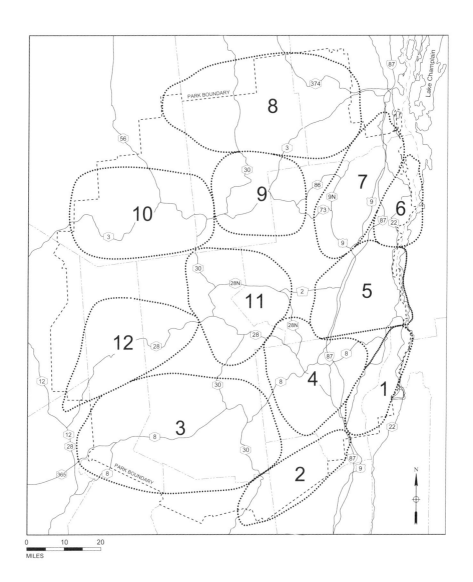

INTRODUCTION

The Adirondack Park encompasses an enormous area—5,927,600 acres—roughly one-fifth of the state of New York and about equal in size to the state of Vermont. It is bigger than any national park in the contiguous forty-eight states and larger than Yellowstone, Glacier, Yosemite, and Grand Canyon national parks combined. It includes two counties in their entirety (Essex and Hamilton); significant portions of six others (Clinton, 46 percent; Franklin, 68 percent; Fulton, 60 percent; Herkimer, 60 percent; St. Lawrence, 34 percent; and Warren, 90 percent); as well as smaller portions of four more (Lewis, 20 percent; Oneida, 2 percent; Saratoga, 28 percent; and Washington, 19 percent). Within these jurisdictions lie sixty-one entire towns and portions of twenty-eight more. Some 2,800 lakes and ponds are found within the park's borders, along with 1,500 miles of rivers fed by an estimated 30,000 brooks and streams. Collectively, these form the headwaters of five major drainage basins: Lake Champlain, and the Black, Hudson, Mohawk, and St. Lawrence rivers. Unlike national and conventional state parks, much of the land within the Adirondack Park is privately held. About 2.7 million acres (nearly 50 percent) comprise the state-held Forest Preserve. Privately owned land that is protected by working forest or scenic easements entails another 50,000 acres. With the exception of the much smaller Catskill Park, no other place officially designated as parkland in the United States affords so rich a mixture of wild lands and those that have been manipulated by humans.

Still, the great majority of the Adirondacks remains undeveloped and most of the rest is rural. The year-round population was somewhat over 130,000 in 2010 (a 30,000 increase over 1900), less than that of Syracuse. The largest community, the village of Saranac Lake, held just over 5,400 people in 2010, and only twelve others had populations of over 1,000. Saranac Lake is one of merely eleven incorporated communities. The park's population nearly doubles during the summer months, with some 110,000 seasonal residents. Both contingents have been overwhelmingly white, 97 percent in the case of year-round inhabitants. The relatively small parts of the region that enjoy a substantial tourist trade can feel crowded at peak periods, especially July and August, hosting many of the estimated ten million visitors yearly.

* * * * *

Settling in the Adirondacks was no easy matter. Visions of large-scale territorial development abounded; none came to fruition. Following the Seven Years War, when British control of eastern North America became uncontested, some members of the New York colonial elite harbored plans to extend the manorial system of land ownership that defined much of the lower Hudson River Valley to encompass parts of the Adirondacks. Very little was known about this "great northern wilderness," most of which had yet to be explored, let alone settled. Among the most ambitious plans were those held by Sir William Johnson, who in 1739, after receiving 86,000 acres south of the Mohawk River from his uncle, began acquiring more land to the north, and in 1769 received an additional 100,000 acres in a royal grant. Johnson commissioned a country house (1748), which still stands, near the later community of Johnstown, and in 1765 had a retreat, Mount Joy, erected along the Sacandaga River in the southeastern Adirondacks. He encouraged settlement in the Sacandaga Valley, but relatively little had occurred before the Revolution, when his holdings were confiscated.

While of humbler origins, William Gilliland, a former British soldier, began to acquire land in Essex County from his savings and his wife's dowry, claiming over 60,000 acres by 1775. He, too, sought to attract settlers to cultivate his land, but the subsequent military actions in the Champlain Valley took their toll, and he was all but ruined when, ironically, Benedict Arnold claimed he was a traitor. The most ambitious land assembly was the work of Joseph Totten and Stephen Crossfield, who formed a partnership in 1771 to acquire property encompassing much of what became Hamilton County as well as portions of Essex, Herkimer, and Warren counties. Within a few years they had amassed some 1.5 million acres for their investors, but the venture collapsed during the Revolution since most of their clients were Loyalists.

After independence, the appeal of the Adirondacks among speculators intensified. Beginning in 1789 a number of large patents (land grants to individuals) were issued, including the Nobleboro Patent (40,000 acres in Herkimer County), Arthurboro Patent (more than 43,000 acres in Hamilton County), and a patent to Jonathan Lawrence (more than 35,000 acres in southern Hamilton and Herkimer counties). None of these ventures led to substantial settlement. Similarly, the ongoing urge to establish manors spurred little permanent change. James Caldwell's enterprise along the southwestern shores of Lake George, begun in the 1780s; Charles Frederick Herreshoff's venture to develop lands held by his father-in-law, John Brown of Providence, during the 1810s around the later community of Old Forge; and Andrew Morehouse's efforts to create agricultural hamlets and manufacturing centers at Piseco Lake and Hoffmeister in the 1830s all ended in failure. Among the early settlement builders, John Thurman was the exception, owing in large part to his own substantial investment in milling operations during the 1790s and 1800s on his holdings along the Hudson River in what would later become Warren County. Still, the land he was instrumental in developing never coalesced into communities of substantial size.

INDUSTRY

Agriculture

Early landlords and speculators alike viewed the Adirondacks' potential for economic gain in then conventional terms, with agricultural development providing the basis for settlement and growth. So did the state legislature, which passed a bill affording a seven-year tax relief if homesteaders established themselves in the region for at least that same period. In 1786, a 650,000-acre Old Military Tract was demarcated in Essex and Franklin counties where Revolutionary War veterans could receive land in lieu of scrip. But several factors stymied any wholesale transformation of the wilderness. Thin soil that was laden with glacial deposits, long harsh winters and hence a short growing season, and the absence of readily accessible markets all discouraged developing a viable agricultural economy. The largest area that was suited to farming lay along Lake Champlain, where early efforts to develop the land were hindered by the military engagements during the War of 1812. The lure of cheap land there subsequently brought a number of settlers, the great majority of them from New England. Some newcomers remained, but many soon moved to more fertile lands in the Mohawk and St. Lawrence valleys or still farther west.

The opening of the Champlain Canal, connecting Lake Champlain's southern end with the Hudson River, in 1823 created opportunities for agricultural exports, apples, potatoes, and wool among them. But the primary impetus for agricultural growth there was the emergence of the iron industry. Feeding those who mined the hills and manned the forges provided the crucial instrument for turning a subsistence occupation into a profitable one. Clearing the land for fuel (charcoal) not only opened new areas for agriculture, it provided farmers with supplemental income as lumberjacks during the otherwise lean winter months. Between the 1820s and 1850s, portions of Warren, Essex, and Clinton counties developed into prosperous agricultural territory, not just along Lake Champlain, but in the Boquet, Ausable, Saranac, Schroon, and Hudson valleys as well.

Elsewhere, too, industry stimulated agriculture. Tanning served that purpose in portions of Warren County. Small pockets of good farmland in North Elba (Essex County) and Gabriels (Franklin County) grew during the second half of the 19th century to service the burgeoning resorts for well-heeled visitors as well as the mounting numbers of tuberculosis patients who came for the "cure." In the southern Adirondacks, along the Sacandaga River in Saratoga and Fulton counties, farming endured from the early 19th to the mid-20th centuries, although it never reached significant proportions. In Hamilton County, agriculture remained a subsistence operation. Many parts of the Adirondacks supported no agricultural activity at all save for small household plots. Irrespective of the scale at which they worked, most Adirondack farmers secured additional income by operating sawmills, cutting timber, making potash (from hardwood ashes), and producing maple sugar and syrup. Diversification was often key to survival.

The nature of crops raised and livestock kept in the Adirondacks has varied over time. Merino sheep were raised extensively in the Champlain Valley between the 1810s and 1830s. The wool trade rebounded during the Civil War, but then sharply declined. Staple crops such as corn enjoyed much longer periods of planting. Dairy products grew significantly by the late 19th century in the northeastern Adirondacks, and the buildings associated with this production remain among the most conspicuous in that area. Many fields tended into the mid-20th century have since lain fallow or are used only for growing hay. In recent years some derelict farmland has been resuscitated for organic operations encompassing both crops and livestock.

Logging, Tanning, and Paper Making

While agriculture has always been a supporting industry, logging was for many decades a primary engine of the Adirondack economy, and for a while it was the dominant force. During the 1820s and 1830s cutting timber for building lumber, furniture, and implements became a large-scale operation in New York State. Glens Falls grew into a major milling center; eventually Albany became the largest lumber port in the East. By the 1830s, the insatiable demand for pine had depleted the woodlands along the Hudson River south of the Blue Line. Even before then, loggers had begun to penetrate the Adirondacks in search of an even more desirable softwood, spruce. These activities steadily grew not just along the upper Hudson as far north as Newcomb, but also along the Sacandaga and Schroon rivers. Timber was cut as far as six miles from a river during the fall and especially in the winter when snow enabled the logs to be hauled by horse- or ox-drawn sleds to the water's edge.

3

This crop was then "driven" downstream in spring, when currents were the strongest. The drives could last up to two months and involve as many as sixty men.

Lumberjacks and log sled. (early 20th-century postcard)

Logs on frozen river, probably the Hudson, awaiting spring thaw. Photograph by Henry M. Beach. (early 20th-century postcard)

During the mid-19th century lumbering had spread to other parts of the region. The Saranac River, flowing to Plattsburgh, on Lake Champlain, was one of the first to be designated as a public highway through 1846 legislation crafted to facilitate log drives. (Such designations elsewhere in the Adirondacks had begun in the early 19th century.) Logging began in earnest along the Moose River in the southwestern Adirondacks during the 1860s, after the completion of the Black River Canal to Carthage. New York State was the nation's largest lumber producer according to the 1850 census. But cutting logs and sending them downstream to mills beyond the Blue Line did little to stimulate local growth. Logging camps were by their very nature impermanent. The commercial operations that undertook these ventures were

Jim Weston's logging camp, near Bascout Pond, St. Lawrence County. (early 20th-century postcard)

owned and managed outside the Adirondacks. Log drives to their plants remained common through the 1920s, and the last two occurred on the Moose River in 1948 and on the Hudson in 1950. But by the 1870s manufacturing plants began to be developed within the Blue Line that had a significant impact on local development patterns.

Just as in New England, sawmills proliferated in the Adirondacks during the early decades of settlement, but these were almost entirely small-scale operations tailored to meeting local needs, and they were part of a rural landscape, not an urban one in embryo. More substantial operations took hold in a few communities, most notably in Warrensburg and Ticonderoga in the 1850s. However, a development of greater consequence for portions of the eastern, southern, and western Adirondacks was the emergence of tanning as a large-scale operation during the same decade. By the 1880s about half of the 112 tanneries in the park were sizable plants. For each hide, twelve times its weight in hemlock bark, which provided the tannin, had to be gathered. Enormous timberland holdings were necessary to supply a substantial tannery, which, for economic reasons, needed to be close to that source. The process was also labor intensive, spurring the development of communities to a

Sawmill on Ausable River, Keene. (early 20th-century photograph)

far greater extent than lumbering or small-scale milling. Building and operating a tannery as well as its attendant infrastructure required large sums of capital, bringing a new level of investment to the region.

Although almost every Adirondack tannery had ties to leather brokers or shoe manufacturers in New York and Boston, the plants and their owners were locally based. Warrensburg, Lake Luzerne, Chestertown, North Creek, Stony Creek, Minerva, Pottersville, Wevertown, Wells, Wheelerville, Bleecker, Piseco, Fine, and St. Regis

Garner Leather Works, Lake Luzerne, begun 1868, closed 1909; Edward Garner house in foreground. (ca. 1880s print)

6

Falls, among other settlements, could credit tanning with their rise as established communities. The boom proved short-lived, however. The rapid rate at which hemlocks were used quickly depleted forests within a manageable radius of tanneries, most of which lasted no more than twenty years. The industry suffered from abrupt decline during the 1880s, never to recover.

An equally dramatic change occurred after the Civil War with the rise of manufacturing pulp paper. The process of using spruce instead of relatively scarce poplar trees was introduced to the United States by German immigrants Albrecht and Rudolf Pagenstecher at an experimental plant in Lake Luzerne in 1869 and shortly thereafter moved downstream to Corinth and organized as the Hudson River Pulp & Paper Company. In 1881 Clayton Delano established a similar plant at Ticonderoga. Seventeen years later both were absorbed into a new conglomerate, International Paper Company. Within this framework, the Corinth plant became an industry leader. Other major mills opened at Willsboro in the mid-1880s, Newton Falls in 1896, Piercefield in 1898, and at Au Sable Forks in 1902. The quest for pulp had an enormous impact on Adirondack forests. Between 1890 and 1910 nearly twice as many trees were cut as had occurred in the previous four decades.

Paper plants required substantial workforces, and the communities in which they were located were primarily industrial ones. Newton Falls and Piercefield were in fact created to serve their respective mills. The softwoods for making pulp paper broadened the range of timber that could be cut: small, short, and bent trees unsuited for lumber were of no lesser value for this purpose than tall, straight ones. The intensity of logging operations for pulp swiftly eroded the supply. By the early 20th century half of the pulp processed in the state came from Canada. Industry innovations during the 1940s and 1950s allowed plants to use hardwoods; 60 percent of pulp was so produced in New York State in 1963. But by that point the business had declined some 30 percent from its early 20th-century peak. At the same time, several Adirondack plants were long-lived: the one at Au Sable Forks ran until 1958 and that at Willsboro until 1965. The flagship plant at Corinth lasted until 2002, and the Newton Falls operation extended into the 21st century, while International Paper erected a new plant at Ticonderoga in 1971 that continues to operate.

Development in the western Adirondacks was also fostered by large-scale lumber mills, which began to be built in the 1880s. Railroads, which did not penetrate the Blue Line until the mid-1870s, enabled the economical transportation of lumber from remote sites to major markets. But such ventures required considerable outlays of capital, as lines had to be built and maintained. Several important ventures of this kind were initiated between 1882 and 1911; routes were carved through the wilderness from St. Regis Falls to Tupper Lake, from Childwold to Cranberry Lake, and two from Star Lake to Newton Falls and Wanakena. Logging on an industrial scale for lumber, just as for pulp, could not be sustained for long, however. Competition arose from the vast scale of operations in the northern Midwest and Northwest as well as from Canada. But even without this pressure, Adirondack timber was being felled at around fourteen times its rate of growth during the early 20th century. The forests around Wanakena were depleted in little over a decade. Most mills at Tupper Lake and St. Regis Falls closed during the 1910s or 1920s. Cranberry Lake's mill closed in 1927. By the post–World War II era, extracting timber from the great forests of the park had become a comparatively minor activity.

Sawmill, New Bridge, St. Lawrence County. (early 20th-century postcard)

Mining and Processing Minerals

For well over a century the mining of iron ore and the manufacturing of iron and iron products figured significantly in the region's development. Combined, they were key instruments not only in establishing many communities, but also in sustaining them. The discovery of large and numerous deposits of high-grade magnetite ore not long after the War of 1812 attracted both entrepreneurs and capital. Through the first half of the 19th century operations generally were small; they combined mining ore and making iron, with the manufacturing equipment located not far from the place of extraction. Most of these ventures were situated in the Champlain Valley around Ticonderoga, Crown Point, and Port Henry; along the Ausable River between Clintonville and Jay; and along the Saranac River. The Boquet and Schroon rivers also had pioneering works. On the other hand, the operation begun in the early 1830s by Archibald McIntyre lay in a wilderness area near Henderson Lake, far removed from existing settlement. Though remoteness continually curtailed McIntyre's efforts, the industry thrived in many other locations. The opening of the Champlain Canal in 1823 and the imposition of a stiff tariff on imported iron a year later contributed to the boom. At least eighty forges were built along the Ausable and Saranac rivers alone between 1820 and 1833; iron production in Essex and Clinton counties escalated from $58,000 in 1820 to over $400,000 fifteen years later.

The great majority of Adirondack iron was forged at bloomeries, where after being crushed and washed, the ore was cooked in hearths, then hammered into billets (blooms) that could be sent to manufactories. Each cooking hearth was small enough to be managed by a single skilled person. Blast furnaces were more complicated to operate. Ore had to be dumped into the top of the furnace tower, where it was blasted, reduced to molten iron, and then separated from the slag residue. Both bloomeries and blast furnaces required enormous quantities of charcoal to stoke their fires. As much as 7,000 acres of hardwood forest was cleared annually to serve a plant; an estimated 200,000 to 250,000 acres were cleared for the purpose in the Adirondacks.

ADIRONDACK VILLAGE.

Community of Adirondac for Adirondack Iron & Steel Company, begun 1830s. (mid-19th-century engraving)

Through the 1840s most of the iron produced was for local consumption; thereafter, the Adirondacks became a significant supplier to a much greater market. With its emergence as a major iron manufacturing center, Troy greatly stimulated iron production in the Adirondacks, just as Glens Falls served as a primary receptacle for Adirondack timber. The demands of the Civil War prompted extensive rebuilding and expansion of plants. By the 1880s, Adirondack companies were producing roughly 10% of the nation's iron. Significant growth occurred, too, in the manufacture of iron products in Keeseville and Au Sable Forks. As ironmaking became a large operation, many old plants closed, and in some cases the property was acquired by new, more capitalized businesses. James and John Rogers developed one of the region's biggest iron enterprises by purchasing companies at Au Sable Forks, Black Brook, and Jay beginning in the late 1830s and controlling virtually all operations in that area by 1870. Similarly, George D. Sherman and S. H. and J. G. Witherbee started to assemble a number of mines and plants around Port Henry in 1851, dominating the trade in the lower Champlain Valley within three decades.

But after the mid-1880s, many iron enterprises started to decline. Newer and larger steel mills in western Pennsylvania and the Great Lakes provided stiff competition. The discovery of huge ore deposits around Lake Superior and the use of coal instead of charcoal as fuel placed the Adirondacks at a geographic disadvantage. The depression of the mid-1890s dealt a severe blow to the industry across the board. By 1905 even large operations such as the Rogers brothers' had closed. Only Witherbee, Sherman & Company and the Chateaugay Ore & Iron Company at Lyon Mountain remained viable businesses. In fact, both enterprises expanded during the first two decades of the 20th century owing to a rise in demand for their high-grade ore and by shipping that ore to mills elsewhere. The Chateaugay company, which had not been established until the early 1870s, also benefited by leasing its vast holdings to the Delaware & Hudson Railway, which was able to invest heavily in infrastructural improvements. Still, both plants were antiquated by the 1930s, when the Depression forced them to cease operations for most of that decade. Both were saved when Republic Steel took over their plants in anticipation of wartime needs. Under Republic's tutelage, the blast furnaces that remained at both plants were demolished; all the ore was exported. Republic kept its Adirondack plants going well past World War II. More than any other factor, it was a decline in the industry nationwide that led to the closing of Lyon Mountain in 1966 and the former Witherbee, Sherman mines five years later.

World War II also gave new life to Benson Mines, in the far northwestern Adirondacks near Star Lake. While operations there began in 1889, they proved short-lived, with only sporadic extraction occurring over the next quarter century.

BIRDS EYE VIEW OF BENSON MINES N.Y. FROM THE STORE.

Benson Mines, Star Lake, begun 1889. (early 20th-century postcard)

The mine was purchased by the federal Defense Plant Corporation in 1941 and leased to the Pittsburgh-based Jones & Laughlin Steel Company, which acquired the property soon after the return of peace and developed it into the largest open-pit quarry for magnetic iron ore in the world by 1950. Benson proved an important laboratory for rendering low-grade ores for steel, and it remained in operation until 1978, well after its venerable forebears in the eastern Adirondacks.

Wartime needs also initiated the extraction of titanium oxide near the site of McIntyre's early ironworks. After the United States entered World War II, the federal government appropriated land for an open-pit mine, an attendant plant, and a community to house the workforce. A railroad line was extended from North Creek to service the isolated facility. Constructed and run by National Lead Company, based in New York, the plant continued operations until 1989.

Two active mines remain within the Blue Line. The Barton Mines Company extracts garnet on Ruby Mountain near North River in the central Adirondacks. The first operation began in 1878, when Henry Hudson Barton, owner of a coated abrasives business in Philadelphia, began to mine garnet on Gore Mountain. In the process of that work he discovered the deposit of industrial-grade garnet was so vast—in fact, it is the world's largest—that he purchased the better part of the mountain in 1887. The ore was shipped to Philadelphia for processing until the company erected a plant onsite in 1924. Barton garnet became the standard for industrial abrasives in woodworking, metalworking, and glass grinding. The company continued operations there until 1978, when it moved to nearby Ruby Mountain, which Barton had acquired along with the rival North River Garnet Company in 1928. Today the mine is the leading producer of the world's abrasive garnet.

The other mine lies near Willsboro and opened in 1949 for the extraction of wollastonite, a reinforcing agent for paper, paint, plastics, ceramics, roof finishes, and many other products. Under the auspices of the Cabot Corporation during the 1950s it became the nation's largest producer of wollastonite and remains one of only two such places in the United States. Now under the ownership of NYCO Minerals, this and one other plant, which is also in New York State, generate about a quarter of the wollastonite produced annually worldwide.

Like the felling of timber, the extraction of minerals in the Adirondacks attained major industrial proportions during the late 19th and early 20th centuries, but that scale did not continue for long. By the 1950s adequate supplies of raw materials could no longer be mined in economically sustainable ways. The operations that survive at Ruby Mountain and near Willsboro not only proved to be exceptions, they will likely continue to contribute to the Adirondack economy. At the same time, both are small enterprises compared to those devoted to iron decades earlier.

RECREATION

Wilderness Camping

The appeal of the Adirondacks as a place to visit for recreational purposes began not long after the region's natural resources started to be extracted for material wealth. During the first half of the 19th century the region attracted a largely male audience for sport—the opportunity to fish and hunt as part of a vigorous, outdoor expedition—and for its scenic attractions.

These pursuits were tied to the rise of travel among the affluent to experience nature beginning in the 1820s. A fishing party took place in the Adirondacks as early as 1814, and a number of clubs devoted to angling were formed between the 1830s and 1850s, most of them making treks in southern parts of the region. Newspaper accounts made such ventures well known among urban dwellers. Charles Fenno Hoffman wrote engagingly for the *New York Mirror* in 1837 about his camping trip, which took him to the remote reaches of what are now Henderson Lake and Indian Pass in Essex County. During the next decade the Reverend Joel T. Headley wrote about his expedition to the High Peaks and Long Lake in serial form, then gathered the accounts in *The Adirondacks; or Life in the Woods* (1849), which suggested preserving the region as wild land for the regenerative qualities it possessed.

Male camping parties seeking isolated parts of the Adirondacks became more than an occasional phenomenon during the 1850s. These expeditions necessitated guides who knew the territory and could take care of the considerable logistics involved. In places where farming proved of limited return, and with logging limited seasonally, serving as a guide afforded a welcome source of income. Even in this ephemeral way, lacking any well-established infrastructure, recreation began to emerge as a consequential part of the Adirondack economy. But roughing it was not

Lakeside camping party. (early 20th-century postcard)

for everyone. After the Civil War, a book by another divine, William H. H. Murray, *Adventures in the Wilderness; or Camp-Life in the Adirondacks* (1869), triggered an onslaught of visitors, especially to the areas he depicted around Long and Raquette lakes. The rush proved short-lived. Murray's stirring descriptions of wild land were no match for the elementary accommodations, difficulty of access, and the hordes of insects common to the region. Without at least some of the creature comforts to which

Twin-cell lean-to camp, with sportsman and guide. (early 20th-century postcard)

well-heeled urbanites had become accustomed, the appeal of unbridled nature had its limits. Four years before the release of Murray's book, Charles Loring Brace had written a stirring editorial in the *New York Times*, incanting preservation of the wilderness so it could become a "Central Park for the World," apparently without contemplating the fundamental differences between the two places.

Commercial Accommodations

The influx of sportsmen soon required more than temporary campsites. Early settlers were quick to provide visitors with food and overnight lodging en route to the wilds. But the demand for less confining quarters quickly arose. During the 1850s a number of "wilderness" hotels were constructed in remote areas as bases for hunting and fishing parties. Rustic Lodge on Upper Saranac Lake (1850), Martin's on Lower Saranac, and Hunter's Home on Loon Lake (both 1852) were among the pioneering ventures. In less than a decade, Paul Smith, who had built the Loon Lake establishment, relocated at Lower St. Regis Lake, erecting a hotel that would become one of the most famous in the Adirondacks. Such rudimentary buildings continued to be erected in remote parts of the Adirondacks through the 19th century. Two were built at Blue Mountain Lake in the mid-1870s, and the Red Tavern Hotel (1879–80), erected in a still-isolated part of the town of Santa Clara to serve overland travelers as well as sportsmen, continues to perform the latter function.

After the Civil War the demand for accommodations extended beyond sporting parties to include families with a desire to stay for a protracted period. The growing embrace of nature and the related admiration for picturesque landscape among the well-to-do and middle class helped transform the Adirondacks into a pleasure ground of national repute. Besides a growing array of newspaper accounts and books extolling the beauties of the region, paintings by some of the country's foremost artists, including Thomas Cole, Asher B. Durand, and Samuel Colman, as well as the English émigré Arthur F. Tait (whose work was perhaps best known through Currier & Ives prints), brought the stunning visual attributes of the Adirondacks to a sizable audience. Guidebooks, issued annually by photographer-entrepreneur Seneca Ray Stoddard, began to appear in 1874; Edwin R. Wallace started to issue his own in the next year.

All the publicity generated a market that spawned the construction of dozens of resort hotels in the Adirondacks during the last three decades of the 19th century. Some, such as the Beede House (1876) in the heart of the High Peaks south of Keene Valley, possessed both the rugged simplicity of a wilderness hotel and amenities of a resort so that hunting, fishing, and hiking were supplemented by tennis, walking, and even relaxed conversations on the porch. But many others offered a more pampering atmosphere. Paul Smith's reputation grew through a series of four enlargements to the main building of his establishment between 1875 and 1898 as well as numerous other recreational facilities on the grounds. A similar transformation occurred at the Prospect House on Upper Saranac Lake, which began as an elementary lodging place around 1864, was enlarged as the Saranac Inn about a decade later, and continued to be aggrandized into the 1920s. The trend toward erecting posh resorts actually started more or less concurrently with the wilderness inn, most notably with Lake George's Fort William Henry Hotel (1854–55, 1868–69), which sought to rival the finest hostelries at Saratoga Springs. Creating a resort of comparable standing in more isolated areas was later pursued, most famously with

Source of the Hudson in the Indian Pass. *(mid-19th-century print)*

the Prospect House at Blue Mountain Lake (1880–82).

Abundant luxury amid the wilds proved uneconomical, however. More typically the most prestigious Adirondack resort hotels of the late 19th century were comfortable and accommodating—with tennis, boating, and, later, golf—but not extraordinarily opulent. Between 1870 and 1900 Bolton Landing, Elizabethtown, Lower Saranac Lake, and, especially, Lake Placid emerged as premier resort communities, all boasting large and distinguished hotels. Schroon Lake, Ausable Chasm, Westport, Keene Valley, Loon Lake, Inlet, Canada Lake, Star Lake, and Old Forge were among the other places where establishments of this type figured prominently. Most had a lakefront orientation, but in places such as Wilmington, Elizabethtown, Keene Valley, and Ausable Chasm, the mountain scenery or unusual natural features were the principal attractions. After 1900, resort hotel building in the Adirondacks decreased sharply. Some well-established hostelries continued to expand, but few new buildings were undertaken and those that were generally replaced ones destroyed by fire.

For people of somewhat lesser means and others who wished to avoid the rituals of hotel life, the Adirondacks contained numerous small, informal establishments where families and individuals alike could sojourn for a few days, weeks, or the season.

Beede House, Keene Valley, 1876 (right), 1885–86 (left), burned 1890. (ca. 1886–89 photograph by Seneca Ray Stoddard)

Many were houses adapted or enlarged to take care of seasonal visitors. Others were purpose-built, but remained domestic in scale and character, sometimes with cabins scattered around common dining and lounge facilities. As with sizable resort hotels, lakes frequently determined their location. Many others were situated along rivers or in meadows as rural getaways, partaking in the region's varied landscape. Such places have generally been overlooked in historical studies, but warrant attention as retreats for countless Adirondack vacations during the 19th and a good portion of the 20th centuries.

Mountain Home, Hoffmeister vicinity, late 19th century. (early 20th-century postcard)

15

The demise of the hotel as a vacation mainstay in the Adirondacks was fostered by a number of factors, including a greater mobility induced by automobiles and improved roads. The car enabled shorter, more frequent trips, a more informal routine, and the ability to travel on a lower budget. The subsequent Depression hurt even some of the most venerable hotels. There was also growing competition from a new form of overnight accommodation, commonly referred to as cabins, courts, and, by the post–World War II era, motels. Those establishments attracted the budget conscious, but they also appealed to others who eschewed formality and enjoyed convenience. Such places increased flexibility, permitting families to visit many parts of the region by staying at a succession of places. A number of modest cabin complexes could be found along major routes within the park by the late 1920s, and development of this kind continued into the mid-20th century. By the late 1950s larger, more commodious motels began to appear in tourist centers such as Lake George, Ausable Chasm, Lake Placid, Saranac Lake, and Old Forge, where they might accommodate guests for a week or more. Such places were also built in other sizable communities along heavily traveled routes, most notably at Tupper Lake.

Nor' West Bay Motel, Bolton Landing. (ca. late 1950s postcard)

Another important alternative to the resort hotel here was the dude ranch, around twenty-eight of which were developed in Warren County between the 1930s and 1950s. Unlike their western counterparts, these establishments catered to young single persons on a tight budget. This audience found the dude ranch an attractive setting for informal socializing and outdoor recreation. Some establishments were converted farms, others purpose-built, but irrespective of origins a western theme generally prevailed in setting and activities. The season typically ran from late spring well into the fall—longer than many resort enterprises. The first dude ranch may have been developed by Vern and Lu Walter on French Hill in Thurman, but the most prominent figure in advancing the concept was schoolteacher-turned-developer Earl Woodward, who began Northwoods, an informal cabin community at

Stony Creek Dude Ranch, Stony Creek, established 1930s. (ca. 1930s postcard)

Lake Vanare, in 1928. Within a few years an existing residence was converted into a lodge for a dude ranch, which became the enclave's hub. Woodward expanded on the idea at Hidden Valley Ranch nearby, which opened in 1939 and became a model for a number of subsequent ventures. Painted Pony Ranch (begun 1945–47), in many ways inspired by Woodward, started the trend of orienting dude ranches to families, and in 1952 also inaugurated rodeos to entertain guests and many others from the area. During the late 1940s and 1950s other dude ranches became more family-oriented as well. Ridin-Hy (begun 1940), near Warrensburg, expanded to function year-round in 1975. By that time many dude ranches had closed, as potential customers demanded ever more amenities. The few that remained open were able to do so only by emulating more ambitious resorts.

A new form of accommodation has enjoyed popularity in recent decades, the bed-and-breakfast, which combines aspects of the small, informal hotels that once proliferated in the Adirondacks and the tourist homes that were common in towns along highways nationwide prior to the interstate system. The entrepreneurial individuals and couples who have created these places have often gravitated to 19th- and early 20th-century houses of some distinction and have taken pains to repair and retain their salient features. In cases where the dwelling is too large to attract a family and is in a community too small to warrant more office space, the bed-and-breakfast conversion has likely saved the building. Elizabethtown, Warrensburg, Keene Valley, Westport, Schroon Lake, and Lake Luzerne are among the communities that have benefited from these transformations.

Clubs

By 1900 a small number of clubs had emerged as important destinations for their generally well-heeled members who wished to spend extended time in the Adirondacks. The tradition of male-only fishing clubs leasing land that began in the mid-

17

19th century continues to the present. Clubhouses were (and are) typically small log or wood-frame buildings, utilitarian in character and with few amenities. The idea of a male retreat dedicated to fishing assumed a new dimension with the formation of the Adirondack Club in 1877, which leased a vast tract from McIntyre's Adirondack Iron & Steel Company, including both the Upper Works and, some seven miles to the south, the Lower Works. Rechristened the Tahawus Club in 1901, the organization held some 75,000 acres, using the Upper Works as its headquarters. When the National Lead Company, which had established a titanium mine nearby during World War II, took over the acreage in 1947, the club reorganized again, moving to the Lower Works site, where an 1877 building was revamped as a main lodge with few major physical changes.

Overlooking the Hudson in a remote location north of the hamlet of Minerva, the North Woods Club was founded in 1887 as another male preserve. Like the Tahawus Club it has always been a small organization, with seldom more than fifty members. Fishing, hunting, and hiking were (and are) the primary pastimes in a largely virginal landscape made famous through the paintings of one of its early members, Winslow Homer. Around the turn of the 20th century some members erected rustic cottages near the three-story log boardinghouse, forming an enclave that has changed relatively little since.

Some distance to the north, the Adirondack Mountain Reserve (AMR) was also formed in 1887, as a stockholders' organization to protect the Lower and Upper Ausable lakes and the High Peaks that surround them from logging. Fishing and camping (with guides) on the lakes were the primary uses. Hiking was also part of the equation, and in contrast to other Adirondack preserves, the public was allowed access to mountain trails. Hunting was forbidden. Habitués of the nearby Beede House, who took over that establishment in 1890, were the driving force behind the AMR. When their enterprise failed, the hotel building (reconstructed also in 1890) became the clubhouse, and a subsidiary of the AMR, the Ausable Club, was established to run it. A number of cottages had been erected in the vicinity over the previous decades. The club also boasted a golf course, tennis courts, and a bowling green for members less inclined to the rugged diversions of the reserve. From the start, the Ausable Club was a family organization, maintaining many of the social dynamics of life at the Beede House and other resort hotels.

At the opposite end of the park, near Old Forge, the Adirondack League Club (ALC) was a far more ambitious venture. Formed in 1890, it initially boasted 91,000 acres that included dozens of lakes. Along the shores of three, land was allocated for a lodge and member camps. The principal lodge, on Little Moose Lake, was enormous, but more than at the Ausable Club, social interaction occurred primarily at the camps, eighty of which had been constructed by 1921. Member architects William S. Wicks of Buffalo and Augustus D. Shepard of New York were responsible for the designs of most buildings before 1930, giving a strong sense of continuity to the three lakeside enclaves. Forestry was integral to the enterprise from the start. Bernhard E. Fernow, who would later become director of the USDA Division of Forestry, was a charter member. The ALC sought to provide a model for managing timberlands in the Adirondacks and also depended upon the revenues generated from logging to help support its sprawling physical plant.

While each of the major Adirondack clubs was a singular institution in its development and complexion, the Lake Placid Club was the most conspicuously different in several respects. It was formed in 1895 by librarian-entrepreneur Melvil Dewey, who controlled all aspects of the club's operation until his death in 1931. In its first three decades the club grew to unprecedented size with some 10,000 acres, most of which were not kept as forest, but instead used for five clubhouses, innumerable cottages, three golf courses, dozens of tennis and squash courts, a ski jump, boathouse, concert hall and amphitheater, and nearly forty farms. While other clubs were remotely sited and in some cases completely isolated from public view, the Lake Placid Club's main campus was prominently anchored to Mirror Lake, much like the grand hotels that had propelled the village of Lake Placid into the limelight. Dewey also instituted sports during the winter of 1904–05 to keep his burgeoning campus occupied for much of the year. His son, Godfrey, secured Lake Placid as the site of the 1932 Winter Olympics, and the club's leadership played an important role in the 1980 sequel. That same year the club closed its doors, overburdened by its enormous real estate holdings and a weak institutional structure left in the wake of its eccentric founder. While the Tahawus, North Woods, Ausable, and Adirondack League clubs are well-preserved physical vestiges of their development during the 19th and early 20th centuries, little but the golf courses and a few private cottages remain of the Lake Placid Club.

Camps and Cottages

Boardinghouses, hotels of all stripes, motels, dude ranches, and clubs large and small accommodated many of those who visited the Adirondacks, but individually owned seasonal residences have comprised an increasingly large component of the recreational landscape since the late 19th century. At least until the 1950s these have taken one of two prevalent forms: camp and cottage. Both types are more based on ideas than any specific set of physical characteristics. "Camp," as it is used in the region, connotes a retreat, generally of wood construction that is rustic in appearance, but also elementary in its components. The idea is an outgrowth of the makeshift campsites created by guides to house hunting and fishing parties beginning in the mid-19th century. But in reality, camp can mean one of numerous kinds of dwellings in the Adirondacks. Many year-round residents have camps that are small, utilitarian cabins used on summer weekends and for hunting. For seasonal residents camp can mean shelter as basic as a lean-to, a great enclave of multiple buildings, and anything in between. Rustic design qualities are considered important attributes to a camp; however, some dwellings that would look perfectly at home in a fashionable suburb are called camps. A camp is what is called a camp.

"Cottage" may not be a widely used term today, but from the second quarter of the 19th until the mid-20th century it was part of common parlance throughout the United States. Initially "cottage" referred to a rural dwelling of somewhat modest dimensions. But this term, too, came to enjoy wide referential parameters. Blue-collar houses constructed in 19th-century Chicago were (and are) commonly called cottages, but so are the enormous summer houses erected at the turn of the 20th century in Newport. In the Adirondacks, as in most resort areas of the country, cottage generally connoted a seasonal dwelling that could be ornamental or quite plain, rustic or otherwise, perhaps more commodious and finished than many camps, but still somewhat informal in character and neither particularly large nor pretentious.

Taking the idea of camp beyond an impermanent outpost of tents and perhaps a lean-to to an enclave of rustic buildings that provided some of the comforts of

Unidentified hunting camp. (early 20th-century postcard)

home and served as a destination in its own right, suitable for women and children as well as adult males, was to a large degree the work of William West Durant at Raquette Lake, beginning with his own Pine Knot (1877–78 and later). Durant deserves some of the credit, too, for expanding the idea to include very grand enclaves on their own lakes—Camp Uncas (1893–95) and Sagamore Lodge (1897–98). But by that point camps large and otherwise were becoming fixtures in many parts

Unidentified camp compound. (early 20th-century postcard)

of the Adirondacks. Some of the most ambitious examples could be found on Lower and Upper Saranac lakes as well as near Paul Smith's hotel on Upper St. Regis and Spitfire lakes. The lakes along the Fulton Chain, Big Moose Lake, Piseco Lake, Blue Mountain Lake, Long Lake, Tupper Lake, and Lake Placid all sported sizable camps, many of them highly individualistic in nature. Modest camps existed in many other places, including Mount Arab, Eagle Crag, Cranberry, Star, Little Wolf, Loon (in Warren County), Canada, Pleasant, Paradox, Eagle, and Brant lakes, among them. Some camps were situated on their own lakes, some of them the nexus of vast preserves such as Trophy Lodge at Brandreth Park (1885), Forest Lodge at Ne-Ha-Sa-Ne Park (1892), and Camp Santanoni (1892–93).

Cottages were just as old as camps in the Adirondacks, but not as prevalent for seasonal residences. Keene Valley had one of the earliest, Brook Knoll Lodge (1875), an eccentric log structure banked into a mammoth boulder, but in its form was a variation on the antebellum cottage designs of Andrew Jackson Downing and Alexander Jackson Davis. Cottages, if seldom made of logs, became the standard seasonal dwelling in Keene Valley and Elizabethtown. They were also the convention for Loon Lake in Franklin County and along the Lake Champlain shore in Westport and elsewhere. They could likewise be found at a few lake communities in the southern Adirondacks, notably Lake Luzerne and Caroga Lake. Cottages were built on the northern shores of Lake George at communities such as Silver Bay, Hague, and Huletts Landing. The big houses that extended from Lake George village to Bolton Landing, on the other hand, were more akin to country places around New York, Philadelphia, or Boston and do not seem to have been accorded a specific term during their heyday. Elsewhere in the eastern Adirondacks, some seasonal residents appropriated old farm dwellings for their summer sojourns, a trend that has gained added currency in recent decades.

Since World War II, seasonal dwellings and, with the enactment of new building codes, winterized houses used seasonally have proliferated in the Adirondacks. The great majority of these dwellings are modest in size and situated along lakefronts. Many portions of Great Sacandaga Lake are lined with such places, as are a number of southern lakes that experienced little development in earlier years. A few developments catering to middle-income families such as Ausable Acres, in Essex County, have been created amid interior woodlands, though the efforts of conservation groups and zoning within the Blue Line has precluded large-scale residential tracts. In recent years expansive and generally pretentious new "camps" have been constructed on lakes and in isolated interior locations alike.

Children's Camps

Given the topography and climate, it is hardly surprising that the Adirondacks became home to numerous children's camps during the early 20th century. Sending children to camp gained favor among well-to-do and middle-class families as a means of building character, fostering socialization skills, nurturing teamwork as well as sportsmanship more broadly, and developing an appreciation for nature. From an early date, too, efforts were made to enable some children from households of lesser means to partake in the experience. For boys, especially, summer camp was further seen as an antidote for the pampering worlds of privileged urban and suburban life—as an instrument for cultivating self-reliance and manliness. The emergence of new camps in the Adirondacks for boys and, only to a slightly

Unidentified boys' camp. (early 20th-century postcard)

lesser degree, for girls, rose steadily and swiftly. At least four such establishments existed in 1900; fifteen were added over the next decade; fifty-six during the 1910s. The peak was reached in the 1920s, with around seventy-seven new camps, followed by a gradual decline through the 1960s, when twenty-three camps were founded.

Children's camps in the Adirondacks varied considerably in complexion. Some were formed by religious groups, others by educators, and still others by Boy or Girl Scout councils. Coeducational camps began in the 1910s and enjoyed considerable popularity from the 1940s through the 1960s. Some were run as extensions of boarding schools, with classes an integral part of the routine; some espoused the philosophy of progressive education; many featured competitive sports, while others concentrated on hiking and similarly rugged outdoor activities. Some were elementary in their physical plants, with tents pitched on the ground as sleeping quarters; others were equipped with bunkhouses and large pavilions for dining and indoor activities. During the mid-20th century several children's camps were given, or acquired at little cost, enormous private camp complexes such as Eagle Island and Prospect Point on Upper Saranac Lake, at a time when these places were seen as white elephants. A few camps—most notably Meadowmount, founded in 1944 near Lewis—specialized in training gifted musicians, adapting an expansive country place as its quarters. Many camps were short-lived. On the other hand, Camp Dudley, which was formed in 1884 and moved to the shores of Lake Champlain near Westport in 1903, is the oldest children's camp in continuous operation in the United States. Camp Pok-O-Moonshine, outside Willsboro, opened in 1905 and is still run by descendants of its founder. Of over 330 camps established here between 1890 and 2000, more than sixty are ongoing concerns, one of the largest concentrations in the country. Besides introducing many children and their parents to the Adirondacks, these institutions have benefited the local economy through employment, goods and services purchased, and, in many cases, taxes.

Unidentified boys' camp. (early 20th-century photograph)

Camping and Campgrounds

During the 20th century camping grew beyond the realms of sporting expeditions and children's pastimes into a widespread phenomenon for families and groups of friends. Camping obviated the costs of a resort or other commercial accommodations, but this activity also became highly appealing as an escape from everyday life by having a relatively close relationship with nature. Camping assumed two basic forms: one could be quite rugged, the other measurably less so. The first was to a degree an offspring of the 19th-century sportsmen's treks. Hikers (without a guide) could spend two days or longer traversing mountains, setting up camp along the way. The development of lightweight canoes in the late 19th century also facilitated such trips by water. The less strenuous way to camp was to drive to a campground designed to accommodate a number of parties.

Into the early 20th century state officials were generally unconcerned with the demands of tourism in the Adirondacks and many of them remained hostile or indifferent to the concept of protecting wild lands in the Forest Preserve. Policy began to change with the appointment in 1915 of George du Pont Pratt as the first head of the Conservation Commission (reorganized as the Conservation Department in 1927 and again as the Department of Environmental Conservation in 1970). Pratt embraced both forestry and the idea of keeping some land in a wild state. However, he was also an advocate for camping and helped found the Boy Scouts of America. If the park was to have a future, he believed, it had to have a solid public constituency that state-owned lands served. As part of his campaign to build a permanent network of steel fire towers, which was launched in 1917, Pratt established a trail-building program so that the public could have ready access to the mountaintops from which the towers rose. Basic camping facilities—lean-tos, fireplaces, and outhouses—were

23

also constructed. Two years later he began to acquire land specifically for public recreational purposes. Concurrent with the surge in state parks outside the Blue Line,
the Conservation Commission expanded its trail network and began to develop a
number of sizable campgrounds that were readily accessible to motorists.

Whereas limiting the degradations of industry in the Adirondacks had been considered the state's primary mission in earlier years, the development of compatible
facilities for tourism now became the focus. Twenty large campgrounds were operating in the Adirondacks and Catskills by 1927, when nearly 37,000 people reg-
istered at them. Demand soon outstripped supply. Three years later, campground
registrations had swollen to almost 268,000. During the Depression, with the aid
of federal dollars and labor, campsites began to be created in remote, undisturbed
portions of the Forest Preserve. A new surge in campground development occurred
after World War II, by which time construction focused on large facilities rather
than small ones in isolated areas. By 2000 the state operated forty-five such places
in the Adirondacks, accommodating some 1.3 million people annually.

Golden Beach campground, Raquette Lake. (ca. 1930s postcard)

Winter Sports
Winter sports began to emerge in an organized fashion in the Adirondacks at the
turn of the 20th century and some grew to enjoy widespread popularity within a few
decades. Perhaps the first facility to cater to such activities was the Hotel Ampersand, which opened on Lower Saranac Lake in 1888, and, unlike other Adirondack
resorts at that time, operated year-round. In the nearby village of Saranac Lake the
Pontiac Club inaugurated the Winter Carnival nine years later, with hockey, speed
skating, and ski jumping among the contests. Devised in part to entertain the burgeoning contingent of tuberculosis patients quartered in that community, the event
also enabled the healthier of those so afflicted to participate. Many of the professionals and others who serviced what had by then become the largest settlement
in the Adirondacks also found the Winter Carnival a source of enjoyment, whether

as players or spectators. The Lake Placid Club's inauguration of winter sports during the 1904–05 season was the most ambitious such program in the early 20th century. To various forms of skating the club added tobogganing and skiing: downhill on Mount Whitney and cross-country on other portions of its extensive landholdings.

The 1932 Winter Olympics in Lake Placid gave a great boost to the public's perception of the Adirondacks as a winter playground. The enormous indoor arena, then only matched by facilities in the largest U.S. cities, became a permanent home for training in hockey and figure skating as well as a place to skate for fun.

Olympic Arena interior, Lake Placid, 1931–32. (ca. 1930s postcard)

The bobsled run at Mount Van Hoevenberg helped introduce a new sport to the nation and has been an important center for competition ever since. The games also gave the Adirondacks its finest ski jumps.

In the years that followed, downhill skiing came to enjoy widespread popularity in many parts of the country. Skiing clubs were formed throughout New York State, and the Adirondacks became their primary destination. A number of clubs spearheaded the cutting of ski trails, sometimes with the help of the Civilian Conservation Corps. A Schenectady-based club inaugurated the first ski train in 1934, disembarking at North Creek to ski the slopes of Gore Mountain. The idea proved infectious: soon such trains made regular trips not only to North Creek, but Ticonderoga, Old Forge, and Lake Placid. At first, skiers were trucked to the mountain's back side, from which they could use several downhill runs. But soon a lift comprised of nothing more than an elementary rope tow was erected at a North Creek slope, the first in the state. The hiatus that occurred during World War II was followed by a boom at mid-century. Skiing became more a family affair as the young singles who had pioneered the slopes prior to the war got married and now brought their children.

Forty-six private-sector slopes lay through many sections of the park in 1948, when the state entered the equation with its Whiteface Ski Center. The facility was

OLYMPIC BOB RUN. LAKE PLACID, N.Y.   1855

Mount Van Hoevenberg Olympic Bobsled Run, North Elba, 1930. (ca. 1930s postcard)

poorly located and was replaced a decade later by the nearby Little Whiteface Ski Center. The latter facility at once became a popular attraction not only for skiers, but also for summer tourists eager to ride the gondolas and partake in the spectacular views. In 1964 the state also developed a new facility on Gore Mountain, reviving North Creek's appeal as a ski center. However, skiing in the Adirondacks

Gore Mountain Ski Center, North Creek, as proposed. (early 1960s postcard)

experienced a pronounced decline during the 1970s, and many slopes closed, unable to compete with new resorts and the powdery snow in the West. Still, over a dozen centers remain in operation or have been restored in recent years. Gore and White-face mountains remain important destinations. Other facilities include ones near Old Forge, Tupper Lake, Speculator, Newcomb, Saranac Lake, and Chestertown.

TRANSPORTATION

Waterways

Until the mid-19th century, rivers, lakes, and oceans provided the principal means of long-distance transportation in the United States, and it was for navigating those bodies of water that most of the investment and technological innovation occurred. In the Adirondacks, Lake Champlain had been a primary route of communication during the colonial period; its strategic importance was why the lake was such con-tested territory during the Seven Years and Revolutionary wars. Thereafter the lake became a vital inland waterway for trade. John and James Winan, who had worked with Robert Fulton on his *Clermont*, relocated to Burlington, where they built the *Vermont* in 1809, the second commercial steamboat in the country. Still the lake re-mained isolated from most major markets; nearby portions of Canada had the most accessible population centers and had the greatest demand, especially for timber and potash. The situation changed profoundly with the completion in 1823 of the Champlain Canal, connecting to the Hudson River. The canal was the catalyst for the eastern Adirondacks' iron industry, and for the expansion of stone quarrying; sheep raising; growing apples, grain, and potatoes; and purveying dairy products. The canal also allowed those who resided within reach of Lake Champlain access to an array of downstate goods previously available only at great cost. No other project was so im-portant to the Adirondack economy until the arrival of railroads half a century later.

The canal also generated a boom in boat building at several lakeshore communi-ties. Steam craft grew steadily in numbers for passenger and some cargo service, but canal boats became the most ubiquitous conveyances. By the 1830s a hybrid was developed in the form of a canal boat that, once on the lake, had masts that could be raised and, with sails unfurled, would function as a schooner. This inno-vation lowered the time and cost of transport, avoiding the transfer of goods from sailing craft to canal boats at Whitehall or the need for a steam tug to maneuver canal boats on the lake. Concurrently passenger steamboats grew ever larger and more luxurious. The Champlain Transportation Company emerged as the industry leader and gained a monopoly on passenger service by 1835. On the lake's Vermont side railroads began to compete with boats of all kinds in the 1850s. The building of the Delaware & Hudson line along the Adirondack lakeshore two decades later proved devastating to the boat operations that depended upon transporting iron ore. Steam craft continued to ply the waters into the mid-20th century, but as an increasingly ancillary form of conveyance. Thereafter car ferries remained as the lake's primary commercial carriers.

Throughout the second half of the 19th century and well into the 20th, steam-boats afforded the primary means of travel on numerous lakes within the Adiron-dacks. For cottage and camp owners, for hotel guests, for all those who serviced these establishments, and for sightseers as well, commercial boats were indeed the only viable means of access to many of their destinations. Lake George had the most extensive steamboat operations. A company was chartered for the purpose as early

Steamer Horicon *leaving dock at Lake George. (early 20th-century photograph)*

Steamer Doris *on Placid lake. (early 20th-century photograph)*

as 1817, but it was not until after the Civil War, when the Champlain Transportation Company extended its monopoly to Lake George, that efficient service was instituted, accelerating lakeside development.

By the late 19th century, small steamers were operating on many Adirondack waterways, including Raquette, Star, Cranberry, Placid, Blue Mountain, Schroon, and the Chateaugay lakes, as well as those that comprised the Fulton Chain.

Roads

Of all the transportation infrastructural systems that existed during the 19th century, roads remained the most primitive. A highly localized approach to road-building projects was an English inheritance that became pervasive throughout the empire's North American colonies and was maintained for over a century after independence. Giving local jurisdictions authority to finance, build, and maintain roads was in part perpetuated by the strong, ostensibly democratic, resistance to centralized authority. The New York state government committed to some financial assistance for the development of major road projects in the early 19th century; however, the financing of the Erie Canal and heavy subsidies to fledgling railroads led to provisions enacted in 1846 that constrained the legislature from making significant investments in transportation. As a result, rural roads were just adequate enough to be passable in good weather, leaving the population served by them isolated for a good portion of the year. In the Adirondacks the situation was more acute owing to the paucity of settlements, jobs, and in many cases the region's distance from a nurturing market economy.

The few local jurisdictions within the region during the early 19th century were generally in no position to undertake public works of any significance no matter how substantial their benefits might be to growth. Initially the state legislature allocated some resources to construct a few key routes to stimulate development with the anticipation that tolls charged would defray ongoing expenses. One of the first and most important was the Great Northern Turnpike, chartered in 1805, which extended from Hudson Falls to the Canadian border along a path similar to US 9 in the 1920s and the Adirondack Northway (I-87) some four decades later. This road connected Lake George, Warrensburg, Chestertown, Schroon Lake, Elizabethtown, and Keeseville—all of which became key centers in the region's development. The Military Turnpike, chartered in 1808, took a challenging mountainous route from Westport to Saranac Lake to encourage settlement by veterans of the Revolutionary War and, later, the War of 1812 at a time when land was one of the few major assets the state government had at its disposal.

Among the most ambitious of such undertakings was the Port Kent and Hopkinton Turnpike, connecting Lake Champlain with the St. Lawrence Valley at Nicholville. With nearly $26,000 authorized by the state legislature, the seventy-five-mile road was constructed through a largely wilderness area between 1829 and 1832. Though isolated (the route still passes through mostly unpopulated areas between Black Brook and St. Regis Falls), the turnpike played a major role in transporting timber and iron during the winter months when packed snow gave it a hard surface, and it was crucial in developing the Ausable Valley

Old Military Road, Essex County. (early 20th-century photograph by Kathleen McClelland)

as an industrial area. On the other hand, most of the traffic occurred near both ends of the turnpike, and in 1835 the toll system was abandoned, with the road reverting to the jurisdictions through which it passed. By that time, the turnpike system was proving incapable of generating the revenue necessary to maintain it.

Within a decade a new entrepreneurial realm emerged with the construction of plank roads. New York State was quick to adopt methods that began to be used in Canada around 1840. The state's first plank road, connecting Salina to Syracuse's Central Square in 1844, was also the first in the nation, and New York remained the national leader, with some 3,500 miles constructed. Laying "planks" comprised of squared logs around eight feet long set on log rails (sills) was believed to provide a durable platform for travel even in rainy periods and to enable relatively smooth rides irrespective of all but the most adverse weather. Like the turnpikes before them, tolls were charged for passage. One of the earliest of these ventures in the Adirondacks opened in 1845 from Westport to Elizabethtown, the Essex County seat and also a nascent industrial center. Following the passage of a bill with favorable provisions for forming private-sector plank road companies, a nine-mile road was built along the path of the Great Northern Turnpike from Glens Falls to Lake George. Through separate companies it was soon extended to Warrensburg and then to Chestertown. The growth of the iron industry in the northeastern Adirondacks led to the construction of a number of plank roads, including one twenty-four miles in length along the Saranac River (1849), a four-mile road from Au Sable Forks to Black Brook (1850) to upgrade the deteriorating Port Kent and Hopkinton Turnpike, and one with a steep ascent from Port Henry to Mineville (1851). But soon plank roads lost their appeal as their wooden components deteriorated much faster than anticipated. As with the earlier turnpikes, income failed to keep pace with cost.

Through the second half of the 19th century Adirondack roads remained in generally poor condition, and even in dry seasons many fledgling settlements were isolated much of the time. Rivers within the park were fine for log drives and generating power, but none of them were truly navigable. Occasionally private enterprise

Rural road, Northville vicinity. (late 19th/early 20th-century postcard)

30

would undertake road improvements, as Thomas C. and William West Durant did, beginning in 1878, to the long stage route from North Creek to Blue Mountain Lake to provide some comfort to visitors. Paul Smith may have done similarly for the stage line he operated to his hotel all the way from Westport and, later, from Au Sable Forks. But until the interwar decades of the 20th century the only way to traverse most portions of the Adirondacks in a manner that was both dependable and did not tax passengers' endurance was by railroad.

Railroads

For eighty years railroads were vital to advancing the Adirondack economy. They were a boon to the iron industry, allowing some operations to emerge as major centers of production. Without railroads iron mining in the region would have ended long before 1900. Railroads facilitated the large-scale cutting of timber in the western Adirondacks, though this surge was relatively short-lived. Railroads also enabled the manufacturing of lumber and wood products within the Blue Line. Railroads were essential for titanium mining at Tahawus for nearly a half century, and they remain necessary for papermaking at Ticonderoga and the processing of wollastonite at Willsboro. But if railroads have been the lifeline of industry, they also greatly bolstered recreational pursuits in many parts of the region at least until World War II. From the private varnish of the very rich that gathered by Raquette Lake to the ski trains that brought thousands of young people of more moderate means to North Creek and Old Forge, the railroad revolutionized the meaning of accessibility in the Adirondacks.

The first line actually to enter the park was Thomas C. Durant's Adirondack Railway, which he envisioned as traversing the region to link the Mohawk and St. Lawrence valleys. Work got under way on the first section, from Saratoga Springs to North Creek, in 1864, but it was not completed until 1871. Durant and his partners had insufficient funds to continue the project farther, and he turned his attention to exploiting the line for the development of the family's vast holdings around Blue Mountain and Raquette lakes—a venture spearheaded by his son, William West Durant.

The Delaware & Hudson Railway purchased Durant's line in 1889 as part of an expansion program north of the Mohawk Valley that began eighteen years earlier, when it leased in perpetuity the Rensselaer & Saratoga Railroad's line from Albany to Whitehall. The following year, 1872, the D&H took over the Montreal & Plattsburgh and Whitehall & Plattsburgh railroad companies (organized in 1852 and 1866, respectively), neither of which had managed to lay much track. Work progressed swiftly thereafter, with the line that traversed the western shore of Lake Champlain to Canada opening in 1875. This project proved to be a greater stimulus to development than Durant's endeavor since it ran through a rich agricultural area and tapped the burgeoning iron industry around Port Henry. Four years later the D&H moved to strengthen its new ties to iron ore extraction by forming the Chateaugay Railroad to take over a state-built line running west from Plattsburgh to the prison at Dannemora and extend it to the fast-growing mine at Lyon Mountain. Subsequently, the company pushed the line farther to Loon Lake in 1886 and Saranac Lake the following year. These latter projects were not as much tied to the prospects for industrial expansion as they were to the area's newly developing resorts and the emergence of Saranac Lake as a center for the treatment of tuberculosis patients. The further extension of this line to Lake Placid in 1893 bolstered its importance as

Adirondack Railway along Hudson River near North Creek. (ca. 1870s photograph)

a carrier of seasonal residents and visitors.

By that point the D&H had serious competition from the railroad constructed by William Seward Webb, which, despite the fact that it ran through large wilderness areas, was completed in less than two years (1891–92). After Webb purchased the small, narrow-gauge Herkimer, Newport & Poland Railway, which ran north from Utica, he converted it to standard gauge and extended the line to the vicinity of Old Forge, thence to Tupper Lake. Farther to the northeast, at Lake Clear, a spur was constructed to Saranac Lake, but the main line continued—very close to the Chateaugay's for a stretch—to Malone, the Franklin County seat, well north of the Blue Line. Webb quickly exited the enterprise, leasing it to the New York Central a year after the line's completion. While it never played an important role in stimulating industry, the line did much to enhance resort development along the Fulton Chain and Big Moose Lake—places where Webb was a major landholder—as well as around Blue Mountain Lake, the Saranac lakes, Lake Placid, and Paul Smiths. By the 1920s as many as 2,000 people took the New York Central to the Adirondacks on a summer Friday.

A number of relatively short railroad lines were built primarily for transporting logs, lumber, and other wood products. The first was undertaken by John Hurd in 1883 to tap the rich timberlands in Franklin County south of St. Regis Falls, where he erected a sizable mill. Six years later the line was extended to Tupper Lake, where he constructed the largest sawmill in the state. While chartered in 1883 to access ore deposits near Star Lake, Byron Benson's Adirondack & Carthage Railroad did not reach its destination until 1889. Within fifteen years the line sprouted two extensions, the first to service a large paper mill at Newton Falls (1894), and the second to support an equally ambitious lumbering operation at Wanakena (1902). A decade later William L. Sykes's Adirondack Lumber Company constructed what would soon be called the Grasse River Railroad, running west from the New York Central's line at Childwold to Conifer, a mill town he developed. In 1917 Sykes extended the line to Cranberry Lake, where he erected another mill. All three lines eventually had myriad spurs to facilitate tapping virgin forest. All three also carried passengers, and indeed fostered seasonal developments at Cranberry and Star lakes. It was not long, however, before the railroads' dominance in Adirondack travel began to be challenged by automobiles, trucks, and other motor vehicles moving along a system of highways that rapidly improved during the interwar decades.

Highways

The deplorable condition of Adirondack roads began to change during the first two decades of the 20th century as part of a statewide improvement program. The demand for such measures swelled after 1900 to facilitate the transportation of agricultural products, to counter the effects of rural isolation (rural free delivery had been instituted by the U.S. Postal Service in 1896), and to make the countryside more accessible to pleasure seekers. New York State led the nation in appropriating $100 million for road construction through two bond issues in 1905 and 1912. Monies augmented these funds through the Federal Aid Road Act of 1916, which allocated dollars to states on a matching basis. The state highway commission was established in 1907, the Department of Highways two years later, and a professional engineer was put in charge of operations in 1919. The numbering of state and local routes was established in 1921, four years before the U.S. Bureau of Public Roads created the national system of highways. In two decades the responsibility for constructing and maintaining roads had, to a significant degree, shifted from local authorities to a professional state bureaucracy—a shift that would be more or less completed by the eve of World War II.

Wilmington High Falls Road, Essex County. (ca. 1910 photograph)

Within the Blue Line, a growing number of business leaders realized the value of road improvements for tourism—some affluent visitors were undertaking ambitious "motor trips" to reach their camps or just to explore rural areas—and for the large-scale enterprise of treating tuberculosis patients. An Adirondack Good Roads Association was formed in Saranac Lake in 1910 to lobby for the cause. By 1920 many portions of Warren, Essex, Clinton, and Franklin counties were relatively well served by hard-surfaced roads, and others could be found, such as that from Utica to Raquette Lake. Far more extensive improvements were undertaken over the next two decades, with the creation of a region-wide network of all-year roads. Many existing routes were straightened and widened as well as graded for higher speeds (a process greatly enhanced by the introduction of the bulldozer in 1928). Legislation passed in 1921 facilitated improving roads on state land within the park.

Some roads that had always been marginal were transformed, as, for example, the mountainous path connecting Keene Valley with North Hudson, which was developed as a major new route to accommodate those attending the 1932 Winter Olympics. Still, due to the restrictions placed on the Forest Preserve, only a few entirely new roads were constructed after 1915, most notably completing the last

State road, later US Route 9, North Hudson. (ca. early 1920s postcard)

leg of the route from Old Forge to Saranac Lake, that from Indian Lake to Speculator, providing circuits around the south and north shores of Great Sacandaga Lake, and the scenic route up Whiteface Mountain. To help finance such work, Governor Franklin Roosevelt successfully pressed for a two-cent gasoline tax in 1929 and did much to foster rural road improvements under the New Deal agencies he created as president.

After World War II the state allocated enormous sums to compensate for deferred maintenance and to make further improvements. The road network that exists today in the Adirondacks was for the most part in place by the mid-1950s.

The construction of new roads in the region was curtailed by concerns for preserving public lands in their natural state and by large-scale private-sector landowners who shared that concern or wished to keep forests for logging. The principal exceptions were for new local roads on private land created for residential development, much of it seasonal.

The Adirondack region was profoundly affected by the building of high-speed, limited-access highways. First among these was the New York State Thruway, the major portion of which was built between 1954 and 1956. The Thruway dramatically cut driving times to the Adirondacks for people coming from downstate or farther south as well as from areas to the west. Likewise, access from New England was markedly improved by construction of the Massachusetts Turnpike and its Thruway connection, which opened in 1959. Thereafter, these routes were directly linked to the Adirondacks with the construction of the Northway (I-87) in 1960–67, which enabled those residing in the New York and Boston metropolitan areas to reach the park in a half-day's drive. Two later interstate routes—89 in Vermont and 81, extending north from Binghamton to the Canadian border—have also contributed to ease of access.

4—Approaching Lake George from the South, Lake George, N. Y.

US Route 9, approaching Lake George. (late 1930s postcard)

CONSERVATION

Greater access to and passage throughout the Adirondacks by motor vehicles gave a new impetus to conservationists to protect lands—state- and privately held alike—within the park. Those efforts were predicated on concerns and legislative measures that had taken root as early as the mid-19th century, more or less at the same time as industry and recreational pursuits were emerging as significant forces in the region. While conservationists have always focused on preserving the land in a natural or near-natural state, they have affected the complexion of the park as much as all the forces of development combined. Surveying the region in its totality today one could indeed argue that conservation has been the overwhelmingly dominant factor in determining the character of the landscape. Settled areas are diminutive compared to the vast expanses of unimpaired forest, bogs, lakes, and rivers within the Blue Line.

Among the earliest concrete steps to protect wild lands in the Adirondacks were privately held preserves established primarily for the enjoyment of their owners. Brandreth Park, in Hamilton County north of Raquette Lake, was the first, dating to 1851. Still in the hands of Brandreth descendants it contains some 26,000 acres. Eight years later Paul Smith created a preserve of nearly 19,000 acres for use by his hotel guests. The most intense period of such endeavors occurred between the late 1880s and late 1890s and included the Adirondack Mountain Reserve, with some 40,000 acres by 1910; the Adirondack League Club, with over 91,000 acres (peaking at 128,000); William Seward Webb's 115,000-acre Ne-Ha-Sa-Ne Park (1890) near the Brandreth holdings; Robert Pruyn's 12,900-acre Santanoni Park (1892) near Newcomb; Edward Litchfield's Litchfield Park (1893) of over 12,000 acres between Tupper and Long lakes; and William C. Whitney's Whitney Park of nearly 73,000 acres adjacent to the Brandreths. By 1904 such preserves occupied over 800,000 acres, more than one-third of the privately held property in the Adirondacks.

Acquiring large tracts of land for personal enjoyment was bolstered by the 1871 Act of Private Parks and Game Preserves, which allowed owners to fence and post their land prohibiting trespass. An amendment enacted five years later stiffened the penalties. These provisions angered a number of early settlers who viewed the forest as common land that provided food and timber essential for their subsistence. In at least one case, a preserve owner appears to have been killed owing to his aggressive policy against nearby residents coming on his property.

Following the state's measures to protect preserves, it ceased selling land that had reverted to the public domain due to default on taxes in 1883. A considerable amount of acreage was available in this way because, after securing the timber they desired, logging concerns often abandoned the property. In contrast to earlier decades, when selling state land was the primary object, the government now began to stockpile its holdings. Adirondack land in the public domain rose from 17,000 acres in 1871 to some 500,000 fourteen years later, which would later form the nucleus of the Forest Preserve. The year following its establishment in 1872 the Commission on State Parks recommended that 1,730,000 acres be allocated for park purposes and that state-held land be set aside until creating such a park could be consummated. That same year a member of the commission, Verplanck Colvin, was appointed superintendent of the Adirondack Survey, the first systematic program to prepare an accurate recording of the region's land, a project that lasted for well over a decade. Giving up his legal career to lead the effort, Colvin was an unabashed advocate for creating a park that, he believed, would be an East Coast counterpart of Yosemite. Such a place would afford "a perpetual and refreshing summer resort for our people, and a vast natural and healthful pleasure ground for our youth." He asserted, "Preservation of the timber and the conservation of the waters" would "secure to the state vastly increased wealth, importance and power."

Pressure from an expanding array of interests for protecting the natural attributes of the Adirondacks and also the mounting fear that soil erosion and other effects of logging would despoil the waters, and thus the economy, in the Mohawk and Hudson valleys eventually prompted the legislature to act. In 1883 a law was passed that prevented the state from any further sale of land (save in Oneida County). Two years later the Forest Preserve Act established the Forest Commission and was perhaps the earliest governmental measure in the United States crafted in recognition that the nation's vast natural resources were indeed limited. Though far less than the park commission had advocated a decade earlier, dedicating 607,098 acres of state-owned land comprised an impressive initial step. Just what would happen to that land, scattered in hundreds of separate parcels, not to mention other land in the region, remained an open-ended issue, however. The quest for pulpwood intensified the threat, and the state government's habitual partiality to business interests was no comfort among those who advocated for more definitive measures. In 1890 the legislature did resolve to enlarge the Forest Preserve through purchasing additional land, and two years later the Adirondack Park, encompassing some 2.8 million acres of both public and private land, was established. Its boundary became known as the Blue Line.

Provisions for really protecting state land finally occurred in 1894, with a new state constitution stipulating, in Article VII, Section 7 (Article XIV, Section 1 since 1938), that the Forest Preserve shall "be forever kept wild as forest lands. They shall not be leased, sold or exchanged, or be taken by any corporation, public or private, nor shall the timber thereon be sold, removed or destroyed." After nine years of remaining in a vulnerable state, the Forest Preserve became an entity, albeit a fragmented one, that enjoyed greater protection than most natural landscapes in the world. A Forest Preserve Board was created in 1897 to oversee land and acquire more, amassing 530,674 additional acres by 1900, which nearly doubled the preserve's size. The successor Forest, Fish & Game Commission was more modest in its purchases: 157,905 acres between 1901 and 1910; 43,862 acres over the following decade. The gains of the 1890s were not matched until 1950. The park itself was substantially enlarged—by 1.25 million acres in 1912, at which time privately held land within the Blue Line was declared part of the park for statutory purposes. An additional 1.1 million acres were added in 1931. Much smaller areas were added in 1956 and 1972.

At the same time the park faced many challenges, none of which was greater than repeated drives to amend the constitution to allow the Forest Preserve to be logged. Advocates argued for applying forestry practices that would avoid the excesses of the past. They also believed that so doing would sustain forest production over an extended period of time. The Association for the Protection of the Adirondacks, the first private-sector organization of consequence to advance the conservationist cause in the region, countered the loggers' initiative. Founded in 1902 by a group of rich seasonal residents, the group initially focused on ways to prevent forest fires, but soon set its sights on upholding the integrity of Article VII's "forever wild" mandate. Even though logging advocates made a concerted effort to change that provision during the state constitutional convention of 1915, the arguments of the association for retaining the Forest Preserve in an undisturbed state prevailed. A second attempt at dilution came during the 1938 constitutional convention, again to no avail. Midway between those assaults, in 1924, the state legislature passed a bill that profoundly affected the landscape throughout the park. At a time when motoring was becoming a widespread phenomenon, the law prohibited billboards and other forms of outdoor advertising within the Blue Line except for signs on the property they heralded. So sweeping a provision curtailing what reformers derided as "roadside blight" had little if any precedent in the United States.

The protection of wild lands, locally and nationally, entered a more activist phase beginning in the early 1930s. In the Adirondacks, the leader was Paul Schaefer, who since childhood had spent summers at his family's small cabin at Bakers Mills in northwestern Warren County. He was a lifelong hunting enthusiast, but also was inspired by Colvin's writings to preserve the wildness that still pervaded much of the land within the Blue Line. Through the Association for the Protection of the Adirondacks he assembled a coalition that proved consistently effective among many constituencies to stave off threats to what was now Article XIV. During the mid-20th century he led campaigns that defeated proposals to construct more than thirty dams in the Adirondacks, and in 1953 his coalition secured an amendment to Article XIV that prevented flooding of any part of the Forest Preserve for the purposes of regulating a river's flow. Schaefer saw damming as the first step in preparing for intense recreational development, as it had been in the Sacandaga Valley after the large earth dam had been built there in the late 1920s. "The Adirondack Forest Preserve," he declared in 1952, "is not intended to be an area for commercial exploitation, nor is it intended to be a highly developed playground or a manicured park....It is not a place for concrete bathing pools, luxurious hotels, or superhighways." His advocacy extended for more than sixty years, ending only with his death in 1996 at age eighty-eight.

Among Schaefer's early allies was Bob Marshall, son of the distinguished constitutional lawyer Louis Marshall, who led the defense of Article VII, Section 7 in 1915. Like Schaefer, the younger Marshall came to embrace the Adirondacks as a youth, in this case at the family's grand camp at the Knollwood Club, on Lower Saranac Lake. Early in his career Marshall rose to prominence as a forester and in 1935 was one of eight founders of the Wilderness Society (others included Aldo Leopold and Benton MacKaye). Marshall died only three years later, at age thirty-eight, but left much of his inherited wealth to the organization, allowing it to continue a mission that was little understood at that time. After World War II the group focused on creating national legislation that would protect wild portions of federal land. The chief architect of what would become the Wilderness Act of 1964 was Howard Zahniser, the society's executive secretary since 1945. Zahniser was introduced to the Adirondacks by Schaefer, and soon after joining the Wilderness Society staff he purchased a cabin near Schaefer's at Bakers Mills. In drafting the Wilderness Act, Zahniser drew liberally from the provisions of the state constitution that protect the Forest Preserve. While he died shortly before the legislation was signed into law, his legacy protected over nine million acres (now over 109 million) of federal land. Zahniser was perhaps the most important figure to bring conservation practices nurtured in the Adirondacks to the forefront of national policy.

An unanticipated challenge to the efficacy of the state constitution occurred in 1967 when Laurance Rockefeller released a report he had commissioned from Conrad Wirth, recently retired director of the National Park Service. Rockefeller's proposal was for an Adirondack Mountain National Park in the High Peaks encompassing some 1.72 million acres, nearly a third of which comprised private land that would be acquired by eminent domain. The initiative created a firestorm of protest. Conservationists viewed it as a serious attack on the Forest Preserve as it would open some of the region's most dramatic wild landscapes to unprecedented public access and call the validity of Article XIV into question. Seasonal residents were infuriated over the prospects of losing their prized retreats. Year-round residents considered it the most egregious example to date of outside decision-makers (a Rockefeller no less!) treating their land as if they never existed, even though villages would have remained as inholdings.

Criticism was so fervent and widespread that neither federal nor state officials dared pursue the matter, but the incident underscored the fact that the park was in danger of rapid and dramatic change; measures beyond those of the state constitution were warranted if the region was to retain its natural integrity. The year after his brother's stillborn plan, Governor Nelson Rockefeller appointed the Temporary Study Commission on the Future of the Adirondacks, a citizens group charged with delineating a comprehensive approach to planning—and stewardship—of public and private land alike. After the commission's initial foundering, Rockefeller appointed Harold K. Hochschild as the new chair. Scion of a rich mining family, longtime seasonal resident, founder of the Adirondack Museum, and by that time perhaps the most active advocate for conservation within the Blue Line, Hochschild steered the commission away from the longstanding alliance between state government and business interests in the Adirondacks. The commission's report, issued in 1970, called for adding a substantial amount of acreage to the park, which was consummated two years later. But the most sweeping recommendation entailed creating a detailed zoning plan for all privately held land, to be developed and administered by a new entity, the Adirondack Park Agency (APA), and an equally detailed land-use plan for the Forest Preserve. Subsequently, Hochschild worked effectively behind the scenes in Albany to ensure the bill adopting his commission's recommendations was passed.

Issued in 1973, the APA's Private Land Use and Development Plan has five categories. Two percent of the land was designated as "hamlets," where the most intense development could occur, and another 3 percent as buffer zones ("moderate-intensity use areas"), allowing one building per 1.3 acres. Eight percent of the land was allocated for "low-intensity use areas" (one building per 3.2 acres), but the lion's share of land was divided into "rural use areas" (one building per 8.5 acres) and "resource management areas" (one building per 42.7 acres) "to preserve the natural resources and open-space character of the park." Opposition was fierce, particularly among year-round residents who regarded the measures as an unwarranted infringement on property rights. An inexperienced and under-funded APA staff, overwhelmed by the volume of requests for development and by local hostility, exacerbated the problem for some years.

At an early stage, too, the APA was challenged by two unprecedented proposals for large-scale residential development. In 1971, plans were unveiled by real estate developer Louis Paparazzo for Ton-Da-Lay, a community in the Franklin County towns of Altamont and Santa Clara to accommodate from 44,000 to 64,000 seasonal residents. While Paparazzo asserted that 90 percent of the land would remain undeveloped, the scheme was eventually defeated in the courts, primarily on the grounds that its ongoing infrastructural demands would far outweigh any economic benefit to the larger area. A similar fate befell plans unveiled in 1972 by the Horizon Corporation of Tucson to create a seasonal community of 36,000 people in St. Lawrence County on the western edge of the park.

The ferocious response to the APA during its initial years, as well as the many environmental challenges facing the park, spurred the formation of the Adirondack Council in 1975. Established by an alliance of regional and national groups, with Hochschild a leading proponent, the organization was set up to lobby and litigate. It would keep watch over environmental conditions in the park and defend the APA's planning program, but also keep watch over the actions of that agency, the Department of Environmental Conservation, and other government entities to ensure they acted in the public interest.

Issued in 1972, the State Land Master Plan had two major categories for the Forest Preserve: "wilderness" (45 percent)—land of primeval character only visited, without intervention, by humans—and "wild forest" (51 percent)—areas that could withstand higher levels of human use. Small areas were designated to accommodate such uses as overland travel and administration and, later, for historic properties. The primary sources of contention in this plan, administered by the DEC, are how many areas can accommodate motorized access and recreation and, to a much lesser degree, how many sites should be designated as historic. The precedent for such designation was established in 1992 as part of the protracted effort to preserve Camp Santanoni, which had been transferred to the state twenty years earlier.

The Santanoni acquisition was the pilot project of a new chapter of the Nature Conservancy, the Adirondack Conservancy Committee. Founded in 1971, this organization has focused primarily on purchasing land suitable for the Forest Preserve and holding it until the state is able to consummate its purchase. The 12,500-acre Santanoni tract was considered an impressive gain for the Forest Preserve by virtue of its size as well as its natural attributes. By 2004 the conservancy and the affiliate Adirondack Land Trust (1984) had helped protect 282,000 acres, including 128,000 acres turned over to the state and 70,000 acres held in easement. In recent years the conservancy has undertaken two major projects, acquiring the 161,000-acre Finch, Pruyn & Company lands in 2007 and the 14,600-acre Follensby Pond lands in the following year. In the former instance, the conservancy has retained 92,000 acres for sustainable logging. The state has purchased the remaining land in increments, beginning with 21,000 acres in 2013. While much smaller, the Follensby Pond acquisition encompasses a landscape long renowned for the 1858 encampment of eminent intellectuals, including Ralph Waldo Emerson and Louis Agassiz.

In recent years efforts to protect the Adirondacks have often been more conciliatory than the confrontations of the 1970s and 1980s. Preserving Camp Santanoni demonstrated that historic resources could be retained without a detrimental impact on the Forest Preserve. The Adirondack Council has joined the Nature Conservancy in accepting sustainable logging practices on privately held land. At the same time controversies remain over recreational uses of state land and over the nature of seasonal development on private land, driven by the belief persistent among local politicians and business leaders that the Forest Preserve inhibits economic development. Still, the Adirondacks is now more often portrayed as a place that is enriched by the intertwining of human development and wild lands than as a place where wildness is spoiled by human occupation or a place where human endeavors are shackled by the restraints of conservation.

ARCHITECTURE

The Adirondacks does not possess a distinct architecture, and, contrary to some assertions, there is certainly no such phenomenon as an Adirondack Style. During the first half of the 19th century buildings erected in the region primarily embodied characteristics drawn from practices common to those parts of New England and to a lesser extent contiguous portions of New York State whence most early settlers came. Migrating builders were principal agents of transfer, but it is also likely that some reasonably well-off settlers brought ideas about what they wanted for a house or other building based on previous experiences in, say, central Connecticut, southern Vermont, or the lower Hudson Valley.

After the Civil War, building patterns in the Adirondacks began to follow broader, national trends owing to the proliferation of literature on design. Plan books for houses, stables, and even commercial buildings and denominational guidelines for churches affected local building practices, as did the tendency toward standardization in the design of such buildings as railroad stations and schoolhouses. Greater mobility for people and circulation of mass-produced materials also tended to break down regional barriers. Many buildings in the Adirondacks looked like counterparts in many other parts of the United States—at least the Northeastern United States—by the century's end.

Yet when viewing them as parts of a larger landscape, the effects of architecture in the Adirondacks could differ from the character of many surrounding areas of New York and New England. The distinctions could arise from a paucity of resources—people having less money to spend on building; builders with a more limited repertoire; building supply companies with fewer inventory choices. Such factors may explain buildings that were somewhat plainer than counterparts in more populous areas. Conservatism—in taste and in spending—that can be prevalent in many rural areas may have contributed as well. Then there were the vagaries of the regional economy. The milling of lumber that propelled the rapid growth of Tupper Lake at the turn of the 20th century, for example, created a landscape that looked like industrial boom towns of the period in other parts of the country. Similarly, such commercial centers as those of Lake George and Lake Placid catered in large part to a seasonal crowd and thus even in their heyday seemed less imposing and permanent than counterparts where prosperity could be enjoyed year round. Such qualities are difficult to enumerate in precise terms, but the small size, relative isolation, and mercurial economic fluctuations of many Adirondack settlements made them appear—and often still make them appear—somewhat different from those in surrounding areas.

On the other hand, during the late 19th and early decades of the 20th century, an increasing number of the Adirondacks' most prominent buildings—banks, churches, hotels, libraries, schools, store blocks, and sizable residences—were designed by outsiders in ways that transcended localisms. Many distinguished New York City architects were chosen by clients who wanted work well above the ordinary, including Grosvenor Atterbury; Don Barber; Alfred Bossom; J. C. Cady; Delano & Aldrich; C. P. H. Gilbert; Thomas W. Lamb; Guy Lowell; Addison Mizner; Jacob Wray Mould; John Russell Pope, Renwick, Aspinwall & Renwick; R. H. Robertson; and Richard Michell Upjohn. Other leading architects hailed from Boston (Andrews & Jacques, Hartwell & Richardson), Philadelphia (Wilson Eyre, Wilson Brothers), and Albany

(A. W. Fuller, Thomas Fuller, and R. W. Gibson). In recent decades, too, nationally known architects have been secured for important institutional and public buildings (Ann Beha, Hellmuth Obata Kassbaum, Perry Dean Rogers) and also for residences (Edward Larabee Barnes, Joseph Biondo, Bohlin Cywinski Jackson, Centerbrook, David Childs, Peter Gluck, Steven Holl, and Philip Johnson). (Most houses designed by the latter group cannot be seen from public roads and are thus not included in the guide.) Many other firms have contributed as well, including over sixteen from New York, as well as from Albany, Cortland, Glens Falls, Gloversville, Newburgh, Plattsburgh, Port Washington, Queensbury, Rensselaer, Rye, Saratoga Springs, Troy, Utica, Watertown, and White Plains. Outside the state, architects have hailed from Boston, Newark, Toronto, and Burlington and Warren, Vermont.

The character of such work varies greatly depending upon the nature of the project, the period in which it was done, and, often, the architect. Upjohn's Adirondack churches or the Wilson Brothers' hotels of the Gilded Age were hardly regional specific although they were well attuned to their settings. Likewise any number of consolidated schools designed by downstate architects during the interwar decades manifested state standards for facilities, layout, and appearance. On the other hand, in designing camps or cottages, Atterbury, Lamb, Mizner, Pope, and Robertson, among others, each pursued varying rustic forms of expression that could be closely associated with, if not unique to, the Adirondacks. In that pursuit they were adhering to an idea that had already been given concrete form by a gifted amateur, William West Durant, at his ingenious early log and bark-clad camps at Raquette Lake; by artisan-guides, who assisted him and worked on their own, designing decorative embellishments and furniture; and by a pioneering transplant architect, William L. Coulter, who was the first to establish a practice of any consequence based in the Adirondacks.

Coulter and his successor, William G. Distin, as well as Buffalo architect William S. Wicks and a New Yorker, Augustus D. Shepard, both of whom worked extensively at the Adirondack League Club, developed readily discernible personal styles for their rustic camps. At the same time they were part of the mainstream of eclecticism at the turn of the 20th century that encompassed a wide variety of forms of expression. The character of a given design depended upon size, function, site, budget, and client needs. That Distin designed an English Gothic–inspired church or a Roman classical bank, on one hand, and rustic log camps on the other was not an indication of conflict or discord, but simply a reflection of the elasticity and a catholic approach that were then a bedrock of eclecticism in American architecture. His camps were not part of a regional style, per se, but rather were developed using a mode of expression that responded to specific regional circumstances. The same holds true for some of the best recent residential architecture, which can be properly understood within a broader modernist framework.

Heritage

Much of the historic landscape of the Adirondacks has been lost. In contrast to many parts of New England or elsewhere in New York State, little remains of industrial complexes save in a few communities such as Mineville and Witherbee, Lyon Mountain, and Newton Falls. Even there, most of the industrial structures have been demolished. Bridges of any vintage are hard to find, in part because the state highway department is one of the greatest users of salt for roadways in the United States.

Many agricultural buildings have been lost in recent decades. On the other hand, the Adirondacks has retained an especially rich array of small, independently owned motels dating between the 1930s and 1960s, many of which enjoy a strong repeat clientele. More broadly, with a terrain and climate that is resistant to intense development, Adirondack communities have changed less than many counterparts that are close to urban areas. Driving through the Adirondacks is often like stepping back in time in terms of the scale and texture of development. In recent years there has been a growing consciousness of the historical importance of the region's built environment. Twenty years ago a number of the properties contained in this guide were threatened with demolition, neglect, or degradation. Adirondack Architectural Heritage has done much to alter the situation, as have numerous activists, property owners, developers, and others sympathetic to local heritage. Yet many places remain vulnerable. The pages that follow will, I hope, stimulate greater awareness of the built environment within the park and broaden efforts to protect it in the years ahead.

*   *   *   *   *

Azure Mountain fire tower, Franklin County, 1918.

Fire Towers

The thirty-one fire towers that survive at their original locations within the Blue Line (twenty on public land; eleven on private land) are for the most part well removed from established communities. Few of them are seen, but most are accessed, from public roads. Yet these prefabricated steel structures of standardized design are important emblems of heritage for many visitors and long-term residents whose family members and/or friends were connected with their operation. More broadly, these structures manifested a new level of state stewardship for the park and, nationally, they represent one of the most ambitious programs to establish a comprehensive system of permanent fire observation posts during the first quarter of the 20th century.

A proliferation of forest fires in the Adirondacks, with especially large ones in 1903 and 1908, propelled major amendments to the Forest, Fish and Game law in 1909. Those changes included giving the state financial responsibility for fire protection outside of population centers within the park. They also restricted practices among railroad companies and logging operations that had generated a number of fires. Finally, the provisions called for the establishment of a fire patrol service and the building of wooden observation towers as instruments of preventing conflagration. This program was modeled after a successful one implemented in Maine four years earlier, and it soon gained further impetus from objectives of the newly formed Forest Service division of the U.S. Department of Agriculture. Gifford Pinchot, that agency's first director, set the agenda based on his belief that forests could only be conserved (and used, whether for recreational or commercial purposes) by the suppression of fire—an objective that gained considerable momentum following the destruction of some three million acres of timberland in the Northwest in 1910.

The great majority of New York State's fire towers were situated in and around the Adirondacks and Catskills. Forty-nine towers could be found statewide by the close of 1913. Two years earlier, fire wardens were rechristened forest rangers, and soon the newly formed Ranger School at Wanakena [WN 2, Section 10] began to supply the corps with well-trained personnel who directed the fire observation program. Implementing that program led to a dramatic reduction in the toll taken by fire.

From 1916 to 1925, the need for long-lasting facilities that also provided shelter to observers during harsh weather led Forest, Fish and Game's successor, the Conservation Commission, to replace the wooden towers with the steel ones that remain today. All of these structures were manufactured by Aeromotor Company of Chicago, an enterprise founded in 1888 to produce windmills, pumps, and water tanks that grew into one of the nation's largest manufacturers of these staple farm implements. The company was making fire towers as early as 1914 and received endorsement from the Forest Service two years later. For over half a century Aeromotor manufactured thousands of fire towers for federal and state forestry departments. New York State appears to have had one of the more aggressive programs using this product before the mid-1920s. The initial towers were Aeromotor's LL-25 models, with the observation deck reached by a ladder; soon, however, the somewhat heavier-frame LS-40 model was used, with a stair replacing the ladder—a change made in response to the towers' overnight popularity with hikers. Both types were adaptations of Aeromotor's windmill derricks, with light weight, battered (inward-sloping), modular steel frames that were cross-braced to form a truss. Height was determined by how many of these units were used. The observation deck was enclosed in a steel cab, generally seven feet square, with glazing to provide shelter from the elements. The location of a fire could be pinpointed by a device known as the Osborne Firefinder, developed by the Forest Service in 1911 and first installed in the Adirondacks at the Poke-O-Moonshine tower seven years later. The information was then relayed by telephone from observers to rangers. Teams of horses dragged components of these structures from roads to the highest elevation they could negotiate. At that point work crews hauled the material to the summit, where they assembled the tower with relative ease in around ten days. With free labor the cost of a tower averaged $530. Wooden cabins, situated nearby or at least within walking distance, were provided for fire observers. A standardized design for these habitations was inaugurated in 1922; refinements were introduced to the

Stillwater Mountain fire tower, 1917, with Osborne Firefinder in foreground.

plans in 1928 and 1936, with some minor modifications thereafter.

The DEC began to close the towers in 1971 as aerial surveillance proved a more cost-effective means of identifying fires and modern forestry practices significantly reduced the fire threat. Grassroots campaigns arose in many communities, pressuring the DEC to preserve towers rather than dismantle them. The Adirondack Mountain Club and other hiking groups joined the initiative since the towers had always been popular destinations among their constituents. (In a number of cases tree cover prevents hikers from gaining any view from a summit; the fire tower affords a welcome reward. Even when summit views are plentiful, fire towers can enrich the experience.) Adirondack Architectural Heritage has played an instrumental role in assisting new, locally based fire tower organizations and in coordinating their efforts.

As of June 2016, twelve towers—Mount Arab and Azure, Blue, Hadley, Hurricane,

Kane, Owls Head, Pillsbury, Poke-O-Moonshine, Rondaxe (Bald), Stillwater, and Vanderwhacker mountains—have been restored by friends groups, often with assistance from the DEC. Another three—St. Regis, Wakely, and Woodhull mountains—are in the process of being so rescued. Yet five more are now maintained for visitors by the DEC—Belfry, Lyon, Snowy, Adams, and Goodnow mountains. The remaining three have been adapted for use as communication towers. Goodnow and Blue mountains have restored observers' cabins. Several towers lie within a mile of public roads; most require a longer hike with adequate preparations for the trip. John P. Freeman's *Views from on High* (Adirondack Mountain Club, 2011) provides an informative guide to towers in both the Adirondacks and Catskills.

Two fire towers appear elsewhere in this guide. That at Whiteface Mountain was dismantled and reassembled in 1971 at the Adirondack Museum, in Blue Mountain Lake [BK 1, Section 11]. Parts of two others—from Kempshall and West mountains—were used to create the tower at the Adirondack History Center Museum, in Elizabethtown [EL 4, Section 6]. The Tooley Pond Mountain tower was reassembled at Cathedral Rocks near the Ranger School in Wanakena.

Adirondack Northway near exit 34, Poke-O-Moonshine mountain in background.

Adirondack Northway

Extending 175 miles from Albany to the Canadian border, nearly half of the Adirondack Northway (I-87) runs within the Blue Line between Lake George and Keeseville, a distance of 79 miles. Tied to the New York Thruway, the major portion of which was completed in 1956, and to Canadian Expressway 15, which leads to Montreal, the Northway is an important link in the national network of high-speed, limited-access highways. Conceived in 1957, the same year the National System of Interstate and Defense Highways was inaugurated, and built in stages between 1960 and 1967, the Adirondack Northway was the first toll-free component of that system in the state. The project was intended to spur recreational development and economic growth along its path and also improve access to what was then the Plattsburgh Air Force Base, a Strategic Air Command facility. Local lore credits Arthur L. Bensen, owner and operator of Frontier Town children's theme park in North Hudson [NH 3, Section 5], for persuading Governor Nelson Rockefeller to name the highway (few interstates built as part of that system were given such names) to underscore the route's role as a gateway to the Adirondacks. No single project has had a greater impact on the park, before or since.

Adirondack Northway overpasses at exit 31 spanning State Route 9N.

In several respects the Northway is a singular work within the interstate system. Since portions of the route cross the Forest Preserve, an amendment to the state constitution was required to build it. There was little public argument over the need for the Northway, but some controversy arose over its optimal path. In 1959 the state legislature approved the plan that would eventually be constructed, one that more or less followed the course of US 9, a path that had been used to connect Albany and Montreal since the early 19th century, and one that would traverse only 254 acres of Forest Preserve. The Citizens' Northway Committee was formed in opposition, advocating an alternative route that would run outside the Blue Line from Glens Falls to Whitehall; thence close to Lake Champlain through Ticonderoga, Crown Point, Port Henry, Westport, and Essex; and then inland to Keeseville. The committee's argument that this path would not intrude on the Forest Preserve gained the support of many environmentalists; however, in the November 1959 plebiscite for amending the constitution, the state-supported route was the one voters approved.

Construction began in 1960; five years later segments north and south of the Blue Line were completed. The last portion opened in late August 1967. The total cost was about $208 million. Since that final segment traversed mostly forested land (both public and private), unusual measures were taken to ensure that the intrusion would be minimal. Unlike most interstate highways, the Northway within the Blue Line responds to the existing topography. Major grading was necessary, but was much less invasive than interstate highway configurations in many topographically challenging areas. With the Northway the effect is generally harmonious with the terrain. Attention was paid to capturing views; more than many roads in the Adirondacks the Northway affords an engaging, if passive, means to observe an ever-varying landscape. Restrictions were instituted to curb motorist-oriented development around intersections, most of which offer few or no services. The experience remains almost entirely one of traveling through a natural world in pronounced contrast to most interstate routes, which have often generated nodes of intense commercial building. Overpasses and other components of the original infrastructure were generally simple and straightforward in design, complementing, but not competing with, the natural landscape. They are gradually being replaced by less visually sensitive structures.

The Northway made the Adirondacks far more accessible from population centers in much of the Northeast and as a result brought new impetus for residential and recreational development. For those concerned with preserving the region's abundant natural attributes, the challenges were now expanded beyond the Forest Preserve to the park as a whole.

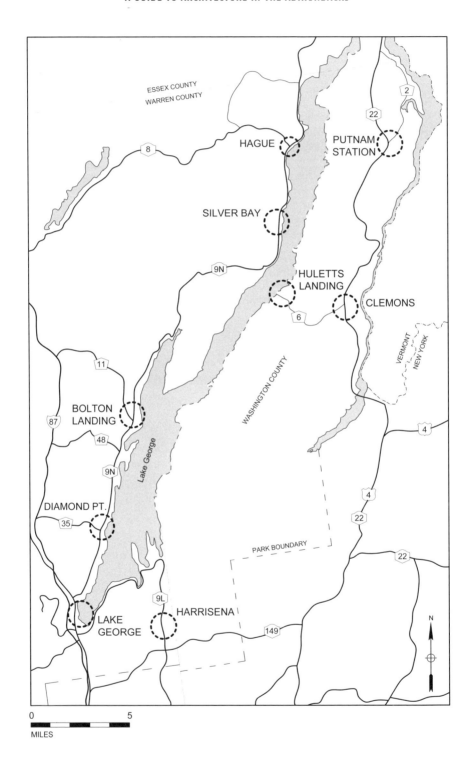

ESSEX COUNTY
WARREN COUNTY

2

22

8

HAGUE

PUTNAM
STATION

SILVER BAY

9N

HULETTS
LANDING

6

CLEMONS

VERMONT
NEW YORK

WASHINGTON COUNTY

11

87

BOLTON
LANDING

48

9N

Lake George

4

DIAMOND PT.

35

4

22

PARK BOUNDARY

22

9L

HARRISENA

LAKE
GEORGE

149

N

0   5

MILES

1
LAKE GEORGE

SITUATED IN THE SOUTHEASTERN CORNER OF THE ADIRONDACKS, the area around Lake George, encompassing portions of Warren and Washington counties, is one of contrast and extremes. Thirty-two miles long, occupying some forty-four square miles, and harboring nearly 200 islands, the lake is enormous and most of it is framed by mountains that come close to the shoreline, affording a degree of visual drama not found elsewhere on a comparable scale.

Lake George: The Narrows with Black Mountain and Bolton, and the Hummock in the Foreground. *(steel engraving by Samuel Valentine Hunt after William Richards Miller, mid-19th century)*

Much of the acreage around the lake is part of the Forest Preserve, and the great majority of the other land adjoining the lake's eastern side remains undeveloped. But privately held land on the west side, especially toward the lake's southern end, includes some of the most intensely developed property within the Blue Line. Farming once was a mainstay along the slopes between the villages of Lake George and Bolton Landing, on the rolling terrain that extends southeast from the lake in the Town of Queensbury, and in the lower Champlain Valley beyond the mountain ridges to the lake's east. Most of the occupied acreage, however, has been devoted to recreational pursuits. Accommodating tourists and seasonal residents has been the mainstay of the area's economy since the mid-19th century.

LIKE LAKE CHAMPLAIN, LAKE GEORGE LIES ALONG THE STRATEGIC AXIS between New York City and Montreal and was hotly contested territory during the Seven Years

War. In 1755 the British established an encampment at the lake's southern end as a staging ground to attack the French at Fort St. Frédéric [PH 1b, Section 5], and the commanding general, Sir William Johnson, rechristened what had been Lac du Saint Sacrement as Lake George in his king's honor. Johnson never got to Lake Champlain, but he did attain a resounding victory in the Battle of Lake George. Johnson saw the need for more permanent quarters and commenced constructing Fort William Henry in 1755 near the site of his camp [LG 7]. The French, too, began to construct a new and far more ambitious outpost, Fort Carillon [TI 1, Section 5], on Lake Champlain not far from the northern end of Lake George. The new British compound succumbed to attack by France's Indian allies two years later. Following their subsequent victory in 1759 the British concentrated military forces on Lake Champlain.

Lake George remained virtually uninhabited until the end of the 18th century. It was still in this near-virginal state when Thomas Jefferson visited in 1791, remarking: "Lake George is without comparison, the most beautiful water I ever saw...its water limpid as crystal, and the mountain sides covered with rich groves."

Concurrently, a wealthy Albany merchant, James Caldwell, had a different vision. During the 1780s he secured some 1,500 acres, which he intended to develop in the fashion of an English manor. He recruited tenants to cut timber, build sawmills, and cultivate the land. Some development had occurred by the 1820s, concentrated around a settlement that bore his name, which was later incorporated as a village. Caldwell remained the official name until 1903, when Lake George was substituted. (The Town of Lake George was officially Caldwell until 1962.) Lumbering and farming became the most prevalent pursuits. Yet the grand plan proved short-lived. The idea of tenancy was unpopular, and owing to the harsh climate, enterprises were mostly limited to a short season. Caldwell and his son, William, were late to see the area's tourism potential, and they never gave it a high priority. Well before William's death in 1848, his hopes of creating a great estate had evaporated.

Farther north, agriculture also took hold in the Town of Bolton, the oldest on the lake, formed in 1790 after settlers began to arrive, most of them from New England. Farming was done on the hillside, well above a body of water that was still traveled by Indians who were less than receptive to what they considered encroachment by whites. Agrarian settlement also extended south from what would become the Town of Ticonderoga along the valley that paralleled, but was removed from, Lake George's northern reaches. The most extensive agricultural activity occurred beyond the mountains framing the lake's eastern side in Washington County's Town of Putnam, where settlement began in the 1780s amid rolling terrain similar to western New England whence many of the newcomers came. During the early 19th century farming also flourished near Warren County's eastern edge south of Lake George in the Town of Queensbury.

But it was Lake George's spectacular setting, which then seemed to have few rivals in occupied North America, coupled with its relative proximity to major population centers in New York and New England, that led to recreation as the primary economic engine by the mid-19th century. Lake George lay less than twenty-five miles north of Saratoga Springs and slightly farther from Ballston Spa, the premier watering places in the Northeast, and excursions to the lake became increasingly common by the 1820s. The Romantic sensibilities of well-heeled city dwellers were captivated by descriptions from James Fenimore Cooper's *Last of the Mohicans* (1826), which depicted the sack of Fort William Henry by the Huron. The following year Thomas Cole painted an enormous canvas based on the novel, and the lake itself became a favorite subject of Hudson River School artists over the years that followed. Lake George village emerged not just as a pioneering resort community in the Adirondacks, but also an early tourist destination in the United States. Access was greatly improved by the construction of a plank road from Glens Falls in 1848, and much more so by a spur of the Delaware & Hudson Railway from Albany to Plattsburgh, which was completed in 1875.

James Caldwell had converted his house to an inn in 1818, and several substantial hotels could be found along the lake's southern rim by the 1830s. However, it was the Fort William Henry Hotel (1854–55) that set the tone for Lake George (both village and lake) as a grand resort. A New York entrepreneur and architect, Thomas Thomas, established the stock company that financed the venture, and it was probably Thomas and son Griffith who designed the great edifice.

Fort William Henry Hotel (I), 1854–55, 1856, burned 1894. (mid-19th-century engraving)

Located next to the site of the British fort that was its namesake and that Cooper had made famous, the hotel rose three stories, with a two-story colonnade extending across much of its lakefront elevation of 235 feet. It was aggrandized further in 1868–69, increasing its capacity to some 900 guests, and was festooned with lavish, High Victorian embellishments that gave it palatial overtones. Few resort hotels in the United States could match its opulence; with its realization Lake George indeed rivaled Saratoga Springs in lavish accommodations and afforded a far more dramatic setting. Especially after the additions to the Grand Union Hotel in 1874, Saratoga's Broadway was an urban oasis of leisure, dense and bustling like its New York City namesake. The Fort William Henry, on the other hand, turned its back to the road, facing the lake and the mountains amid cultivated grounds. The grand hotel succumbed to fire four decades later, and was replaced by a smaller, more reserved, but no less elegant building (1910–11). Loosely inspired by Italian Renaissance sources, it was designed by New York architect Henry Janeway Hardenbergh, who had gained renown for his pioneering apartment houses as well as the Waldorf, Astoria, and Plaza hotels. The new plant also boasted an extensive waterfront development, with a casino framed by colonnades.

Fort William Henry Hotel (I), as remodeled, 1868–69. (early 20th-century photograph)

Fort William Henry Hotel (II), 1910–11, demolished 1969. (ca. 1910s photograph).

During the 1880s the hamlet of Bolton Landing (so named in 1882), some nine miles to the north, started to compete with Lake George village as an exclusive summer destination. This community and others along the lake were now reached with relative ease by craft of the Lake George Steamboat Company. Chartered in 1817, with James Caldwell one of the directors, the enterprise remained elementary and undependable for several decades. It was taken over by the Champlain Transportation Company in 1868, and two years later was leased to the Delaware & Hudson. Service became increasingly frequent and amenable, catering to a swelling number of vacationers wishing to stay on upper portions of the lake.

Bolton Landing ranked among the most popular destinations and by the Gilded Age had the highest concentration of hotels on the lake. All of these were eclipsed by the Sagamore Hotel (1882–83). Situated in a park-like landscape on Green Island,

Steamer Sagamore *at Silver Bay, Lake George. (early 20th-century photograph)*

just off the main shore, the Sagamore was a rambling affair, less pretentious than the Fort William Henry, but no less well appointed and accommodating. Destroyed by fire a decade after it opened, the Sagamore was rebuilt in 1893–94 on an even more expansive scale. It lasted twenty years and was not fully replaced until an entirely new facility was constructed in 1929–30, which rejuvenated the island as a locus of activity for the wealthy [BL 11].

Hotel life was not the only option. By 1880, the picturesque lakefront acreage that lay between the communities of Lake George and Bolton Landing began to be developed with sizable houses, primarily for rich New Yorkers. The scale and elaborateness of these summer retreats tended to increase into the early 20th century, some reaching palatial proportions. In their character, the houses along what was dubbed Millionaires' Row were a predictably eclectic lot that differed little from those found in the most elegant country places around New York City. No attempt was made to develop designs that embodied the special qualities of Lake George, and in this respect they were worlds apart from the grand, rustic camps being constructed in many parts of the interior Adirondacks. Only the theatrically medievalizing Lake George Club (1908–09), rising above an arched motorboat portal at its center, and a no less ebullient, island-hopping lodge built for Spencer and Katrina Trask (1907–08) suggest the potential for architecture that endeavored to engage the specialness of a place.

Erlowest, Edward Morse Shepard house, Lake George, 1898, altered. (early 20th-century postcard)

If this southwestern part of Lake George emerged as the most extravagantly developed, it later became the most subject to change. Sweeping improvements to roads, including the establishment of US Route 9 through Lake George village during the interwar decades, made the area much more accessible to a broad segment of the public. The decline of resort hotels as destinations for prolonged stays, coupled with the Depression, rendered establishments such as the Fort William Henry less financially viable. The economy, along with the institution of graduated income and rising inheritance taxes, also rendered many grand lakefront houses white elephants. During the post–World War II era, the explosion of travel by a new middle class with more income, leisure time, and mobility than many people of previous generations intensified the shift from a chain of exclusive enclaves to a popular mass resort. Lake George village had always catered to people of lesser means than those who could afford the Fort William Henry. Several relatively modest establishments such as the Arlington and Worden hotels (ca. 1870s) lined the principal thoroughfare, Canada Street.

By the 1950s, however, Canada Street was well on its way to becoming an avenue of motels. Even the Fort William Henry was replaced by a motel with the same name in 1969. Farther north, one estate after another was replaced by clusters of cabins or motels, many of them retaining access to the lake. Bolton Landing managed to keep some of its former aura. A scattering of grand houses remains—as restaurants, condominiums, or even in their original capacity—but places appealing to the budget-conscious abound as well. The acreage from Lake George to Bolton Landing reportedly has more rooms for rent than can be found in all the rest of the Adirondacks.

North of Bolton Landing lies the Tongue Mountain Range, rising on a peninsula that, along with interior land, never attracted development and has long been part of the Forest Preserve. Silver Bay and Hague developed much more modestly than those communities farther south and have been subject to far less change.

Arlington and Worden hotels, Lake George, ca. 1875–76; burned 1978. (early 20th-century photograph)

Silver Bay grew around a large but hardly pretentious hotel, the Silver Bay House. The hostelry opened in 1899, but several years later became a facility of the YMCA, expanding to a campus of mostly rustic buildings that continues to operate with remarkably little modifications to its century-old fabric [SB 2]. Hague emerged as a crossroads hamlet much earlier, before 1800, and began to attract visitors by the mid-19th century. Thanks to improvements in steamboat service it later boasted at least eight hotels and also became a center for numerous low-key summer residences.

Huletts Landing, the most prominent resort community on Lake George's eastern shore, was first settled by Revolutionary War veteran David Hulett around 1804 with a land grant for service. Successive generations of the family continued to farm there. Philander Hulett built a steamboat landing in 1870 as he was converting the family house into Hulett's Hotel. Eight years later a second hostelry, the Lakeside Inn, was erected under the auspices of John W. Hall. Over the next several decades numerous cottages were built well beyond the hotel, hugging the shore for more than two miles to the north and about a mile to the south. After fire destroyed the first hotel a replacement, the New Hulett House, opened in 1916, continuing service as a nexus for the community. Three decades later it was deemed obsolete and was demolished in 1948. The appeal of nearby residential areas, however, never waned.

* * * * *

HARRISENA

Town of Queensbury, Warren County

Named for Moses Harris Jr., who did extensive surveys of the environs after the Revolution, this small community still gives ample evidence of its rural origins and development through the 19th century, with a number of farmhouses from the century's first half scattered along the upland road that forms its spine. Historically the area is more closely tied to the agricultural lands in Queensbury to the south than to the developed communities on Lake George.

HS 1 WINDRIDGE, GEORGE W. BRAYTON HOUSE
1593 Ridge Road (NY 9L); ca. 1870–75

By far the most elaborate farmhouse remaining in the area, Windridge employs a traditional three-bay, side-hall plan rendered in the then fashionable Second Empire mode, with mansard roof and an abundance of ornamental details. To its side lies a sizable barn of the same period, with the owner's initials worked into the slate roof.

HS 2 HARRISENA COMMUNITY CHURCH
1616 Ridge Road; 1866–69, A. Henderson, builder (Quebec province)

More reserved, but scarcely less extravagant, this house of worship was funded by Moses Harris's grandson John, himself a wealthy landowner, to honor his wife's wishes for an Episcopal church in their community. The Harrises were members of

the St. James Episcopal Church in Lake George [LG 9], which started construction the same year and was rendered in a similar Anglican-inspired Gothic Revival mode. But Harris reputedly drew his inspiration from a church he had seen in Canada and hired the builder of that church to erect this in the same vein, complete with Canadian limestone. Sadly, the first service was Harris's own funeral, and after his wife's death the church closed for thirty-five years. In 1918 the Ladies' Aid Society reopened the church for the summer, but it was little used until the formation of the Harrisena Community Church in 1947 in response to suburban growth in the area.

HS 3 JOHN J. HARRIS HOUSE
1645 Ridge Road; ca. 1830s

John Harris's residence is likewise reserved, rendered in a chaste Greek Revival mode, but has a configuration that makes it distinctive: a two-story central section, with a recessed entry porch, flanked by single-story wings. This arrangement could occasionally be found in antebellum houses in the eastern Adirondacks and drew from a more common, but still not widespread, practice in northern New England.

HS 4 RIDGE TERRACE RESTAURANT
2172 Ridge Road; ca. 1915; additions ca. late 1940s

The core of what was originally named the Little Brown Cabin ranks among the earliest known roadside ventures of log construction within the Blue Line. It was built by a German-American, Hans Braun, shortly before U.S. entry into World War I. This structure remains intact and serves as the main dining room. After World War II it was purchased by Henry Dietch, who erected the encasing structure and gave the restaurant its present name.

end. Motels, filling stations, convenience stores, restaurants, miniature golf courses, souvenir shops, and a variety of other functions catering primarily to a summer trade line this thoroughfare with little interruption save for an occasional public building. The lake's southern shore was developed

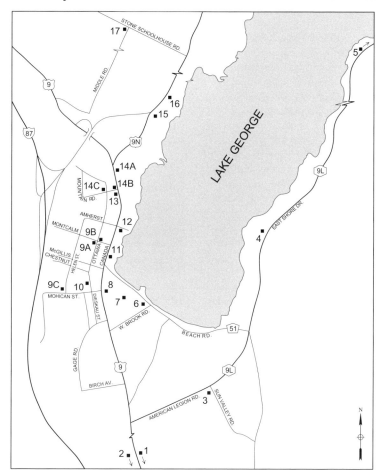

LAKE GEORGE

Town of Lake George, Warren County

Lake George village is perceptually defined by Canada Street (US 9)—an expansive commercial strip that begins well to the south of the Blue Line in Glens Falls and continues to the village's northern

as a beach in 1948–49, where the excursion vessels of the Lake George Steamboat Company—reputedly the oldest continuously operating transportation business in the United States—take on passengers for tours. Farther east some of the character of southside lake development during the late 19th and early 20th centuries still prevails. Just west of Canada Street extend blocks occupied by village residents that likewise retain much of the feeling of a community enjoyed by earlier generations. With a village population of 906 and a town population of 3,515 in 2010, Lake George remains the largest community in the area.

LG 1 MAGIC FOREST THEME PARK

US 9 and Bloody Pond Road; 1963 and later

This vintage children's playground, once one of several themed attractions along this stretch of US 9, was developed by Arthur Gillette, who ran carnival shows from 1944 to 1956. After starting two amusement parks, he opened what was originally called Christmas City, USA in 1963. The parameters of the enterprise were expanded following the first season and within a few years the name was changed to Magic Forest. Beyond the parking lot the grounds rank among the most densely wooded of their kind in the state. The fantasy "houses" were designed for the park, but the **Chapel in the Woods**, a log structure probably dating to the 1920s, was moved from Rensselaer. Most of the rides and the abundant (over 1,000) fiberglass figures, including what is purportedly the world's largest Uncle Sam, were purchased from other parks and fairgrounds by Gillette's son, Jack, who took over operations in 1979. Today Magic Forest is a rare showcase of mid-century amusement park attractions.

LG 2 PIRATE'S COVE ADVENTURE GOLF

2115 Canada Street (US 9); 2000–01

Part of a chain operation that began in 1997 on US 9 south of the Blue Line, Pirate's Cove characteristically features natural elements (including a pond, waterfall, and extensive vegetation) as a counterpoint to fabricated ones to form a highly scenographic display. Nearby, at the intersection of Canada Street and NY 9N, **Goofy Golf** (1972), originally also a unit in a chain, shows what had earlier been the industry

norm, with greater reliance on hardscape and models of storybook characters. Just to the north of Pirate's Cove lies the last remaining restaurant operating under the name Howard Johnson, once a defining chain restaurant company that was pervasive in the Northeast.

LG 3 LAKE GEORGE ELEMENTARY SCHOOL

Sun Valley Road at NY 9L; 1966–68, Crandall Associates, architects (Port Washington, N.Y.), Charles Whitney, partner-in-charge; Sargent, Webster, Crenshaw & Foley, associate architects (Syracuse)

The rise in town residents resulting from the post–World War II boom in tourism and other businesses farther afield eventually led to the construction of a separate elementary school. Among mid-century examples in the Adirondacks, this is of unusually distinguished design. To accommodate new teaching methods, instructional space was arranged in an open plan, forming four clusters.

LG 4 WIAWAKA CENTER FOR WOMEN

3778 East Shore Drive (NY 9L); 1870s; 1900s (accessible by prior arrangement)

The oldest buildings in this complex,

Mayflower and **Rose** cottages, were constructed in 1873 for New Yorker Francis Crosby's Crosbyside House. Opened around 1850, the hotel ranked among the oldest and most celebrated on the lake. In contrast to the Fort William Henry Hotel, Crosbyside possessed a relatively intimate, domestic atmosphere commensurate with its remote location. Crosby was himself the proprietor and around 1876 had a commodious residence (now called **Fuller House**) erected on the premises. The property was purchased in 1902 by Spencer and Katrina Trask and George Foster Peabody, rich summer residents, who established the Girls Friendly Society to enable working-class women to enjoy a fulfilling holiday. While the hotel burned in 1905, the compound continued to serve its new purpose. Three years later the Trasks commissioned **Wakonda Lodge**, a rustic lakeside center for artists and writers. The complex also included the **House of Trix** (ca. 1904), constructed as a boathouse and converted to a recreation hall, as well as a second **boathouse** and a caretaker's house, **Pine Cottage** (both ca. 1907). This unusual enclave continues to serve as a retreat.

LG 5 MOUNTAINSIDE LIBRARY
3090 East Shore Drive (NY 9L); 1894

This unpretentious building is one of a number of privately operated libraries in the Adirondacks funded by seasonal residents for public use. Some monies may have come from the Carnegie Corporation as well.

LG 6 DELAWARE & HUDSON RAILWAY STATION
Beach Road (CR 51) near West Brook Road (CR 69); 1909–11, Ludlow & Peabody, architects (New York)

Plans were under way to replace the 1880s station before the adjacent Fort William Henry Hotel, which the Delaware & Hudson had recently bought, was destroyed by fire in 1909. With a land-mark tower, the new station bespoke its role as the portal to a fashionable resort and complemented the vaguely Italian-inspired design of the rebuilt hotel. After rail service was discontinued, the depot was acquired by the Lake George Steamboat Company in 1961, continuing its role as a transportation facility. Two of that company's boats are worth noting: The *Mohican* (II) was constructed in 1908 by the Baldwin Shipyard at the lake's northern end. It was streamlined in 1946–47, only to be remade in a more traditional manner twenty years later. The *Lac du Sacrement* is of recent vintage but modeled on the Hudson River Day Line's early 20th-century steamer *Peter Stuyvesant*.

LG 7 FORT WILLIAM HENRY RECONSTRUCTION
Beach Road (CR 51) and West Brook Road (CR 69); entered from Canada Street (US 9); 1955–57, Distin & Wareham, architects

Built in 1755–57 under the direction of Major General William Johnson following his victory over French forces at the Battle of Lake George, Fort William Henry scarcely survived its completion. English troops surrendered to a vastly superior French and Indian force in August 1757, only to endure extensive casualties while being led to Fort Edward farther south. The log fort was burned after its evacuation. Both the battle and the later massacre assumed legendary proportions. With the construction of the Fort William Henry Hotel, the fort's site was left undisturbed and eventually developed as a park. Albany real estate broker Henry Veeder formed a stock company to purchase the property in 1952 and two years later commissioned archaeologist Stanley Gifford to excavate the land to provide a basis for reconstructing the fort. As realized the structure seems to have been conceived as much for its touristic appeal as for its historical attributes, with gift shop, snack bar, and restaurant integral parts of the interior.

LG 8 FORT WILLIAM HENRY HOTEL GARAGE

48 Canada Street (US 9); ca. 1890s

What was apparently built to accommodate hotel stages and, perhaps, the horses that pulled them, was by the early 20th century modified for patrons' automobiles. Remarkably, the building survives, with little change to its exterior. While utilitarian in function, its design is decorous, suggesting the stables of a great country place. Many resort hotels created such facilities in the early 20th century, but this is the only one known to survive in the Adirondacks.

LG 9 CHURCHES

If the wealth of a community can be judged by its houses of worship, these three edifices are telling examples. With a congregation that was established in 1810, members of the **First Presbyterian Church (a)** were sufficient in number and in funds to erect an edifice in 1855–56 at 71 Montcalm Street that befitted the now well-established community. Accommodating summer visitors may also have entered the equation, and it is likely that all three complexes benefited from their largess. Cattycorner at 172 Ottawa Street, **St. James Episcopal Church (b)** (1866–67) is more modest in size, but no less conspicuous by virtue of its design—a textbook example of Gothic Revival as propounded by Ecclesiologists in England and their Episcopal brethren in the United States. The designer was probably the Reverend Robert Fulton Crary, who was a catalyst in

advancing "proper" Gothic church architecture in the eastern Adirondacks. Not to be outdone, Roman Catholics built a more imposing Gothic house of worship, **Sacred Heart Church (c)** (1874–75), at a more commanding elevation (40–50 Montcalm Street). Here the **rectory** is no less ambitious, suggestive of a residence in a stylish 1920s suburb, even though it was constructed in 1947, the work of architects Myers & Crandall of Glens Falls.

LG 10 WOODBINE MOTEL

75 Dieskau Street; ca. 1870s; mid-20th-century additions and alterations

While hostelries in the Adirondacks and other resort areas nationwide generally excluded African-Americans until rather late in the 20th century, the Woodbine was an exception. Adapting a Victorian house that was moved from Canada Street in 1926, the operation began in 1935 under the auspices of Samuel McFerson, who, after taking title in 1950, added a motel to the premises. The Woodbine was a place of entertainment as well, with Cab Calloway, Ella Fitzgerald, and other luminaries performing there.

LG 11 POST OFFICE
180 Canada Street (US 9); 1935, Louis A. Simon, Supervising Architect of the Treasury (Washington, D.C.)

The exterior is a revealing example of the tendency that took hold during the 1930s among a number of architects to develop designs that were traditional in their form and composition, but minimalist in detail and abstract in effect, with few, if any, overt references to historical precedent.

LG 12 WARREN COUNTY COURTHOUSE
290 Canada Street; 1845–46, front addition 1877–78, Thomas Fuller, architect (Albany), Winfield S. Sherwood, builder (Glens Falls); additions 1890, 1896

Lake George served as the county seat from 1815 until 1963, when the offices were moved to new quarters south of the Blue Line. The core of the current building replaced one erected in 1817–18, which burned in 1843. The addition of the 1870s defies its relatively modest dimensions to form a striking Gilded Age interpretation of civic authority. Born and trained in England, the architect immigrated to Canada in 1857. Two years later he was awarded the commission for the parliament buildings in Ottawa. Subsequently he won the competition for the capitol in Albany, relocating to that city to supervise the project. Additional competition entries included a successful one for San Francisco's mammoth city hall. Fuller ranked among the foremost architects of major public buildings in North America. He returned to Canada in 1881 as chief architect to the dominion. After the courts vacated, the building became home to the Lake George Historical Association and Museum in 1963.

LG 13 LAKE GEORGE JUNIOR HIGH SCHOOL
381 Canada Street; 1925–26, Edward Shepard Hewitt, architect (New York); addition (new auditorium and gym) 1953, Milton Lee Crandall, architect (Glens Falls); additions 2002, Conservation Design & Research, architects (office location unknown)

The result of an extensive school consolidation and expansion campaign that occurred in rural parts of the state during the interwar decades, this school, which originally included all grades, is an especially telling example. The exterior achieves a balance between the reserve of the Georgian vocabulary that inspired it and the lively composition that entails more window area than wall. The building afforded facilities seldom found in the region's earlier schools, including a gymnasium in one wing and an auditorium in the other. These two spaces had much larger replacements in a rear addition of 1953 that, despite its bulk, is rendered in a compatible vein. Recent additions have likewise sought to connect to earlier portions in a coherent manner.

LG 14 MOTELS
Within a few blocks lie several motels that provide a revealing cross-section of three decades of the type's development.

Sullivan's Wigwam Motel at 410 Canada Street was a complex of log cabins (two of which remain) and a restaurant built prior to World War II. Owner John Hugh Sullivan began to update the premises in 1965, designing a building inspired by the Thunderbird Motel in Miami, and rechristening his establishment O'Sullivan's Motel (a). Around 1969 guest rooms were added adjacent to the owner's residence on the second level and a new range of rooms built on the south side. The house fronting the Admiral Motel (b) at 401 Canada Street was likely built in the 1920s; the motel ranges were added in several stages during the 1950s and perhaps 1960s. At 1 Old Post Road, the Lido Motel (c) is a compact building of a thoroughly modernist cut (the pipe railings were recently replaced) wrapped around two sides of a swimming pool, much like some West Coast apartment compounds of the period. The Brookside Motel (d), at 504 US 9, began as a cluster of cabins, perhaps as early as the late 1920s, a number of which remain at the property's rear. Others were replaced by ranges of rooms, fronted by the proprietor's office and residence, probably in the 1950s.

LG 16 ALPINE VILLAGE
3054 Lake Shore Drive (NY 9N); late 1930s; ca. 1946–47, Earl Woodward, developer

With a scattering of log cabins set around a rustic lodge, Alpine Village represents the beginning of the transformation of Millionaires' Row into a chain of popular vacation complexes. Initial components were built

LG 15 EVELLEY, CHARLES JOHN PEABODY HOUSE
Lake Shore Drive (NY 9N) at I-87 exit 22 extension; 1912, Ludlow & Peabody, architects (New York)

Built for a partner in Spencer Trask's brokerage firm, Evelley replaced a house that burned the previous year and was part of a family compound. An assertive if not entirely disciplined interpretation of English Tudor manor houses (here with an incongruous tower) embodies the showiness that characterized many of the dwellings of Millionaires' Row. Among the largest of such places, it is a rare survivor and the more unusual in that it can be readily seen from the road.

for the Burgmeyer brothers on the site of a ca. 1890 house that burned in the mid-1930s. After World War II the property was purchased by Earl Woodward, an entrepreneur who had been instrumental in the development of Lake Vanare [Section 2] into a center for dude ranches. Woodward, who had embraced log construction for over a decade, added some of the cabins and may have been responsible for the lodge as well. Thereafter, Woodward concentrated on this part of Lake George, buying estates and building cabin groups targeted to economy-minded tourists.

LG 17 CALDWELL SCHOOL DISTRICT SCHOOL #2 (STONE SCHOOLHOUSE)
Stone Schoolhouse and Middle roads; 1880

During the second half of the 19th century rural schoolhouses in the Adirondacks and most other parts of the Northeast were of elementary wood-frame construction, with few embellishments. Located in what was once a farming area, this building was a conspicuous exception. It is not only a masonry structure, but supports such stylish components as a jerkinhead roof (clipped at the gable ends), cross gables, and a decorated bell tower. The meager funds usually available for such building may have been augmented by seasonal residents whose lakefront houses lay nearby. It has been sensitively converted into a residence.

Stone was also used in the 1887 **Bolton School District School #1** in Bolton Landing (4553 NY 9N), but this building is of a much simpler design.

DIAMOND POINT
Town of Lake George, Warren County

DP 1 UNION EVANGELICAL CHURCH
3699 NY 9N, 1876–79

A small hamlet set around a "T" intersection, Diamond Point developed as a service community for summer residents near this midpoint between Lake George village and Bolton Landing. The size and accomplished Gothic design of the Union Evangelical Church, prominently sited at the principal intersection, suggested it may have been at least partially funded by summer residents for use by them and townsfolk alike.

DP 2 HILL VIEW LIBRARY
3717 NY 9N; 1901, J. Dickson Hunter, architect (New York)

A seasonal resident, New Yorker Jane Keyes Hamilton, established the library for public use in 1899. Soon thereafter she commissioned an architect friend to prepare plans for a purpose-built facility. His design possesses a massiveness popularized by the libraries of Henry Hobson Richardson over a decade earlier, while it also conveys the intimacy of a small cottage.

DP 3 OLYMPIAN MOTEL
3716 NY 9N; ca. early 1960s

The motel as an affordable resort is exemplified in this building's U-shaped arrangement, its open end oriented to the lake and a swimming pool in the center of the court. Though turning its back to the highway, the building nevertheless presents a memorable image from that vantage point, with its court entered through a portal surmounted by a cartoon-like chalet.

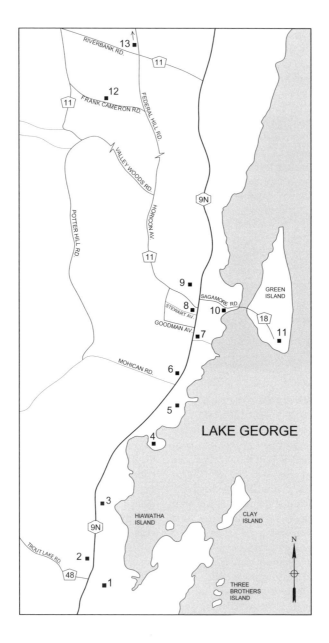

BOLTON LANDING
Town of Bolton, Warren County

Situated along a narrow strip of land between the lakeshore and steep hills, Bolton Landing developed in a linear fashion extending over some three miles. The community has the highest incidence of grand summer houses to survive on Lake George and the only major resort hotel built prior to World War II that is still operating in the

Adirondacks. It also harbors many newer, more economical tourist destinations. The hamlet's commercial center has become a crowded enclave of boutiques. Though subsumed by later buildings, evidence of development from the first half of the 19th century can be found as well. From the shoreline and especially from higher elevations, Bolton Landing offers some of the most spectacular views, including the Tongue Mountain Range just to the north and the expanse of uninhabited mountains across the lake to the east.

BL 1 VILLA MARIE ANTOINETTE GATEHOUSE
4590 NY 9N; 1919–20, Frederick H. Roosa, architect (New York)

Though the main house was demolished in 1953, the gates and portal lodge give some indication of what was among the most pretentious estates along Millionaires' Row. The place was commissioned by William Gerard Beckers, a German immigrant who made his fortune in New York from innovations in the dye industry. Despite the name he bestowed upon the place, which he used year-round, Beckers seems to have been inspired by sea- and lakeside villas in northern Italy; his concoction was rendered the more exotic with a spirited use of Spanish allusions as well. In 1943 his pleasure ground was sold to Harry K. Thaw, the notorious assassin of architect Stanford White.

BL 2 REYNOLDS-GATES HOUSE
4617 NY 9N; ca. 1830; porch probably mid- to late 19th century

This former farmhouse was built for Elijah Reynolds, who settled in Bolton in 1808, and suggests the level of prosperity some attained within a couple of decades of their arrival. Subsequently it was occupied by Jonathan Gates, co-owner of a nearby general store, who married Reynolds's adopted daughter, Zilpha, in 1873. The house remains in the hands of descendants. The ninety-acre farm was sold to Beckers for his Villa Marie Antoinette [BL 1] in 1919, and the house was moved across the road. It is a rare survivor of the town's early period of development.

BL 3 NORTHWARD HO! LAKESIDE RESORT
4648 NY 9N; ca. early 1960s; later additions

Among the many motels along NY 9N, this one is unusual in the extent of its lawns, in separating automobile parking areas from many of the units, and in its modernist design for both the ranges of attached units and the freestanding cottages.

BL 4 MARCELLA SEMBRICH STUDIO
4800 NY 9N; 1922–24, Arthur Mannix, architect (New York)

Situated on a wooded peninsula facing a cove, this low-key building served as the instructional headquarters of a famous diva from the late 19th and early 20th centuries. Born in Poland, Sembrich debuted at the Metropolitan Opera on the second night of its inaugural performance in 1883. She returned to Europe, but also appeared regularly at the Met. Moving to the United States in 1897, she directed the vocal departments at the Juilliard School of Music and at Philadelphia's Curtis Institute. Beginning in 1915, summers were spent teaching at Lake Placid. In 1922 she rented Bay View, a lavish Gilded Age pile, which she purchased at the end of the season and soon remodeled. After World War II, ten acres of the property were sold, some of it to Earl Woodward, the principal developer of Lake Vanare [Section 2], for two cabin groups. The remaining land was deeded to the newly formed Marcella Sembrich Memorial Association, which maintains the studio as a museum.

BL 5 MOHICAN LODGE, WILLIAM K. BIXBY HOUSE
4860 NY 9N; 1901–02, Wilson Eyre, architect (Philadelphia)

Commanding an expansive site, Mohican Lodge was commissioned by the president of the St. Louis–based American Car & Foundry Company. Bixby originally intended to adapt the Mohican House, Bolton's earliest hotel, for his residence, but determined that its physical condition warranted constructing a new dwelling. The circumstances under which he turned to Eyre, one of the nation's most talented and well-known architects of country houses, are unclear. Eyre lived up to his reputation with a spirited and unorthodox interpretation of 18th- and early 19th-century American sources, including three giant, Ionic porticos that articulate a cruciform plan. The house remains in the family, but can be glimpsed from the roadway.

BL 6 ST. SACRAMENT EPISCOPAL CHURCH
4879 NY 9N; 1867–69, Richard Michell Upjohn, architect (New York)

A straightforward but striking design well suited to a "country" church in a fash-ionable resort, plans for St. Sacrament were prepared by the son of Richard Upjohn, considered then and now as the foremost architect of religious buildings of his generation. Here, the younger Upjohn effectively translated his scheme for the Church of the Holy Comforter on Staten Island (1865) into masonry.

Nearby are two wood-frame houses of worship that are more representative of such edifices in the region. **Blessed Sacrament Catholic Church** (1890), at 4924 NY 9N, has served as the Bolton Historical Museum since 1971. **Emmanuel United Methodist Church** (1900–04), at 17 Stewart Avenue, like the 1904 Presbyterian church in Wanakena [WN 1] and the now altered Methodist church in Long Lake, was based on a plan by Philadelphia architect Benjamin D. Price for the Methodist Board of Church Extension's *Catalogue of Architectural Plans* (1889).

BL 7 BOLTON FREE LIBRARY
4922 NY 9N; 1903; additions 1971–72, 2001

Established 1901, this privately operated institution retains a low profile. Its two rear additions were designed to appear as one with the original building.

BL 8 BOLTON BEANS
4967 NY 9N; 1946; Worcester Lunch Car Company, designer and fabricator (Worcester, Mass.); moved 1989

This diner and its predecessor have complicated histories. The current establishment originally was located in Providence, Rhode Island, then in Plainfield and subsequently in Foxboro, Massachusetts. It found its present home in 1989 as Julie's

Service Diner, replacing the Miss Bolton Diner. The latter was built in 1937 as an interurban rail car running from Saratoga to Warrensburg, then operated as the Bill Gates Diner in Bolton Landing from 1949 to 1981. That car was donated to the Adirondack Museum in 1989, and in 2005 was loaned to the Champlain Valley Transportation Museum, in Plattsburgh.

BL 9 BOLTON CENTRAL SCHOOL
26 Horicon Avenue (CR 11); 1928–29,
J. Russell White, architect (Albany); wings
1974–75, Crandall Associates, architects
(Glens Falls); additions 1999–2000

Resting on a site carved out of the hillside high above the hamlet's commercial center, Bolton's school is an imposing edifice, with many elements scaled to have visual impact when seen from a distance. Costing $265,000, the building resulted from the consolidation of the town's nine school districts. Nearby on Horicon Avenue at 2nd Street lies a predecessor, the former **Union Free School**, which was by far the largest in the town when built in 1898. Comparing the two underscores the dramatic scope of change brought by consolidating districts within a single jurisdiction.

BL 10 WILLIAM REIS HOUSE
44 Sagamore Road (CR 18) at lakefront;
1906, 1917, Hiram F. Seeman, stonemason

Perhaps the most extravagant boathouse on the lake, this was built to quarter the pleasure craft of William Reis, who

spent the summers at the nearby Sagamore Hotel from 1901 to 1914. After the hotel burned Reis remodeled the building for his seasonal residence. It was inherited by son George Reis, champion speedboat racer, and occupied by him until 1962. It now functions as a bed-and-breakfast.

BL 11 SAGAMORE HOTEL
110 Sagamore Road; 1921–22, Ernest Stiles
(Lake George) and Robert H. Rheinlander
(Glens Falls), associated architects; exten-
sive additions and alterations 1929–30,
Harold Field Kellogg, architect (Boston); later
additions

The third hotel to bear the name Sagamore was only completed after a prolonged period. The drive to rebuild after the second Sagamore burned in 1914 met resistance from stockholders and the enterprise was reorganized. The new leadership called for a more modest and intimate building with just thirty rooms. Called Sagamore Club Hotel, it was not opened until the early 1920s. Only a few years later investors led by William Beckers [BL 1] and William Bixby [BL 5] successfully argued for a much more ambitious facility and convinced Karl Abbott, head of a major hotel corporation, to run it. The result was a complete transformation—a sprawling wood-frame pile organized on a butterfly plan to optimize lake views and cross-ventilation. Despite its great size, many aspects of the Colonial Revival design carry domestic overtones, while the giant, semi-circular portico on the southeast face and the tower (vaguely alluding to that of Independence Hall) at the entrance bespeak its institutional role. Even though the new Sagamore opened at the onset of the Depression, the venture proved a success. During the 1980s the physical plant was expanded to accommodate conventions and business retreats.

BL 12 SAGAMORE GOLF CLUB

55 Frank Cameron Road, off Federal Hill Road (CR 27); 1927–29

With an informal Tudorish clubhouse and a stunning course designed by famed golf architect Donald J. Ross, the club was formed as a private venture, but was taken over by the Sagamore Hotel in 1938.

BL 13 FEDERAL HILL FARM, JAMES TUTTLE HOUSE

433 Federal Hill Road (CR 41); late 18th century and later

No complex in the Town of Bolton more vividly conveys the importance agriculture played along the upper slopes during the 19th century. While the origins of this farm date before 1800, the elegant, five-bay house sporting Greek Revival details probably was built in the 1830s–40s, and the adjacent barn in later decades.

SABBATH DAY POINT
and
SILVER BAY

Town of Hague, Warren County

SB 1 GRACE MEMORIAL UNION CHAPEL

Sabbath Day Point Road, off NY 9N; 1885, William B. Tuthill, architect (New York)

An intricate design in the Queen Anne–inspired free style of the period, this modestly sized house of worship was funded by summer residents exclusively for seasonal use. Tuthill, a prominent New York architect who designed Carnegie Hall, donated his services, suggesting that he, too, may have frequented the area or at least was friends with the sponsors. Not long after the chapel's completion, its landscape began to be embellished as a park with ornamental trees.

SB 2 SILVER BAY ASSOCIATION FOR CHRISTIAN CONFERENCES AND TRAINING

Silver Bay Road, off NY 9N

This remarkable complex of late 19th- and early 20th-century buildings had serendipitous origins. Silas Paine, a rich New Yorker and a senior executive of the Standard Oil Company, had attended a religious retreat at Sabbath Day Point in 1888. He fell in love with the area and built a sizable house not far to the north. When learning that the adjacent farm was

designed by White Plains, New York, architect Franklyn Edwards, who worked extensively for the Y and did several other facilities on the Silver Bay campus.

Wedged into the hillside nearby, the **Helen Hughes Memorial Chapel (c)** (1921–22) makes a forceful statement despite its modest size through a manipulation of form that is as abstract as it is evocative of English medieval precedent. Designed by the Boston firm of Allen & Collins, well known for their ecclesiastical work, it was built in memory of New York Governor Charles Evans Hughes's daughter, who died at age twenty-eight in the influenza epidemic of 1918 and had been a rising star in the YWCA. As the YMCA expanded its facilities, it did so incrementally, keeping the scale relatively modest and the character of the campus informal. **Munn Hall (d)** (1913–14) illustrates the pattern as an unassuming shelter for meetings named to honor John P. Munn, chair of the Railroad Department of the International Committee of the YMCA. It was the work of New York architect Louis E. Jallade, who, like Edwards, contributed significantly to Silver Bay's appearance.

to be developed as a hostelry that would serve alcoholic beverages, he bought the land and erected the Silver Bay House. In 1902 the YMCA brought 1,000 people to the establishment to found the Young People's Missionary Movement. Delighted with the spiritual nature of the gathering, Paine leased the whole premises to the organization for the following two summers and sold it to the Y as a place for summer retreats in 1905. Several years later, Silver Bay played an instrumental role in the founding of the Boy Scouts of America. It still serves its original function—a rare resort enclave that has experienced little change for over a century.

The original portion of the **Silver Bay House (a)** (1898–99) and its seamless addition of a quarter century later (1925–28), the work of Troy architect William E. Clark, provide an unusual glimpse of an intact resort hotel from the period, both inside and out. In this respect, it bears affinity with the Ausable Club, in Essex County [KV 7, Section 7].

Constructed in 1905–07 and rebuilt with slight modifications after a fire in 1908–09, the YMCA's **Auditorium (b)** vies with the former hotel as a centerpiece of the campus. The shingled exterior is at once low-key and grand, its great, trussed meeting hall punctuated by a tall, five-bay gathering of windows on the east side, its corner punctuated by a latter-day campanile. The building was

Farther up the hillside lies **Forest Lodge**, also known as **Hepbron Hall (e)**, an expansive, yet simple, rustic pile that was built for Paine in 1901–02 to accommodate people

whose budgets precluded staying at the hotel. An otherwise plain exterior is given a lively composition by partially exposing its wood frame, with the panels so formed embellished by false cross-bracing. Nearby, the **See Memorial (f)** (1909–10) achieves a sophisticated effect through a more structurally suggestive interplay of exposed studs and window frames, using an exterior construction technique that had become popular for the interiors of Adirondack rustic buildings. Possibly the work of Louis Jallade, this music center and his **Fisher Gymnasium (g)** (1916–17) use the stud pattern to give rhythm and discipline to the overall effect. The hulking form of the latter building is tempered by the stud and window-cluster wall treatment to be more compatible with other campus buildings. The facility was later named for physician George Fisher of the Y's Physical Training Department and a national advocate for physical fitness. Set in a cove on the shoreline, Silver Bay's **boathouse (h)** (1906–07), by Franklyn Edwards, includes a recreation area above the boat slips, employing on an institutional scale what was a typical coupling of functions for the boathouses

of private camps. Inspired to a degree by the work of Henry Hobson Richardson, Edwards's **Richard C. Munn Hall (i)** (1901) is an essay in cobblestone designed to house Paine's extensive collections of hymnals, sacred music sheets, flora and fauna of the region, and local historical documents. It was sold to the Silver Bay Association in 1917 to accommodate a library and classrooms for a boys' school that operated off-season between 1918 and 1934. Munn Hall was converted to conference rooms in 1973. Across the road lies the **general store (j)** (ca. 1904–05), also by Edwards, erected for Paine to accommodate everyday needs of hotel guests and to house staff members. It has continued to serve that function ever since. Another utilitarian facility, which is now the **Earl W. Brandenburg Memorial Administrative Center (k)**, is probably the oldest building on the campus, constructed as a barn around the 1880s. With a major addition in 1906 and alterations in 1948 and 1983, it has served a variety of functions, including a laundry, tailor shop, post office, barbershop, classroom building, and now administrative offices.

HAGUE

Town of Hague, Warren County

HA 1 HAMLET CENTER

Although the hamlet has lost its steamboat landing and hotels, it still gives suggestion of its role as a hub for vacationers. Most conspicuous in this regard are the **Hague Baptist Church (a)** (1912–13), a workmanlike exercise in cobblestone at 9832 NY 8, and the **Church of the Blessed Sacrament (b)** (1923–24) at 9790 NY 8, which speaks to the once sizable Roman Catholic population here. **Ruah**, the house built for artist **Henry Wilson Watrous (c)** around the turn of the 20th century at 9221 NY 9N, ranks among the more ambitious seasonal residences in the vicinity.

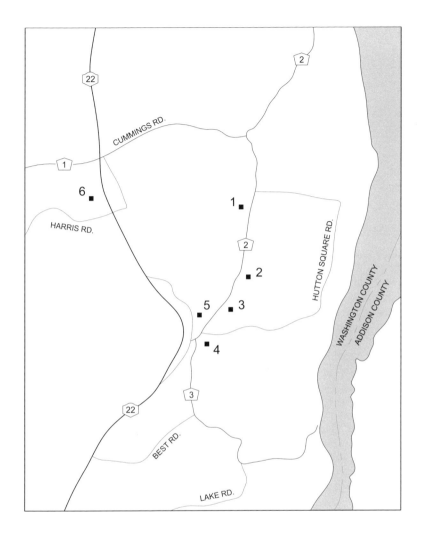

PUTNAM CENTER
Town of Putnam, Washington County

While one of the earliest towns in the Adirondack Park to be settled, beginning around 1782, Putnam remains small, with a population of 645 in 2010. Remnants of the agricultural landscape prevail today, with little new development occurring for well over a century. Putnam Center is a classic, small, northern New England settlement from the antebellum period, where the principal house of worship stands well apart from other functions, the commercial core consists of only a few buildings, and farmsteads punctuate the environs beyond.

PT 1 PUTNAM UNITED PRESBYTERIAN CHURCH
365 Lower Road (CR 2); 1853–57

The form of Putnam's Presbyterian church is one used by Congregationalists and other Protestant denominations in New England from the late 18th through the mid-19th centuries. But the setting, overlooking a valley and framed by a steep hill to the rear, is unusual. Adding to its dramatic backdrop is the forceful scale given to the façade by a giant portico, with a high pitch to its pediment. The congregation was organized in 1803, and the first church edifice (1806–17) as well as a second, masonry one (1838) were situated on what became the burial ground adjacent to the present building.

On the property abutting the road lies the Church School District School #1 of 1880, the fourth on this site. Closed in 1928, it was converted to a residence. Some eight decades later it began to be restored for use as a local history center. Despite is proximity to the church, the two institutions were never affiliated. Farther south of Lower Road is Meadow Knoll Cemetery, a good example of a modest rural burial ground from later in the 19th century.

PT 2 WILLIAM HUTTON HOUSE
146 Lower Road (CR 2); 1834

This substantial, if unadorned, five-bay house, presumably constructed of stone quarried nearby, attests to the prosperity of some local farmers within several decades of settlement. Other examples include the **McLaughlin house** at 88 CR 3, built two years later with finely laid stone walls of rough-cut slabs. On the same road (at No. 126) is the brick **P. Hutton house**, which probably dates from the 1830s or 1840s.

PT 3 PUTNAM CENTRAL SCHOOL
126 Lower Road (CR 2); 1928; addition 1934–35, Carl W. Clark, architect (Cortland, N.Y.); additions 1990s

School consolidation occurred in areas without sizable population centers as well as in larger communities like Lake George and Bolton. The modest size of this building and its auditorium addition, which continue to serve the entire town, underscore the low density of Putnam's settlement.

PT 4 CHICKIE'S GENERAL STORE
Lower Road (CR 2) and CR 3; probably late 19th century

Whereas a front porch was a conventional appendage to general stores built during the late 19th and early 20th centuries, Chickie's has a shallow recess at ground level. Otherwise it is typical of rural mercantile establishments of the period.

PT 5 PUTNAM TOWN HALL
Putnam Center Road and Lower Road (CR 2); 1854

The aspirations of town residents were

sufficient in the mid-19th century to erect Putnam Academy, a private-sector response to the rudimentary conditions then common in most rural schools. The institution did not last long; the building has served as a town hall for most of its life. Still, the exterior has experienced relatively little change, making it a rare survivor.

PT 6 PUTNAM LOG CHAPEL
NY 22 between Putnam Center Road and CR 1; 1933–34, Rev. J. S. Vance, designer; addition 1992–93

This rustic building was not intended to attract tourists, but rather planned by the rector of Putnam's Presbyterian church as a nondenominational house of worship for the "poor" families residing in the western part of the town.

CLEMONS
Town of Dresden, Washington County

CL 1 ADIRONDACK COUNTRY CABINS
14157 NY 22; ca. 1940

The route connecting Ticonderoga and

Whitehall to the south has never been heavily traveled. This modest cabin cluster, built for Leo Benjamin, is among the last vestiges of roadside enterprise between the two communities and provided what were once rather spacious accommodations.

HULETTS LANDING
Town of Dresden, Washington County

HL 1 MOUNTAIN GROVE MEMORIAL CHURCH AND CEMETERY
Land's End Road, west of Huletts Landing Road (CR 6); church 1922–23

Set in a clearing surrounded by mature trees, the simple cobblestone-faced building gives its setting sharp focus. The cemetery was originally a private burial ground for the Hulett family. Henry W. Buckell, owner of the New Hulett House, donated the land, and he did likewise for adjacent **Our Lady of the Assumption Catholic Church** at 226 Lands End Road, built in 1901.

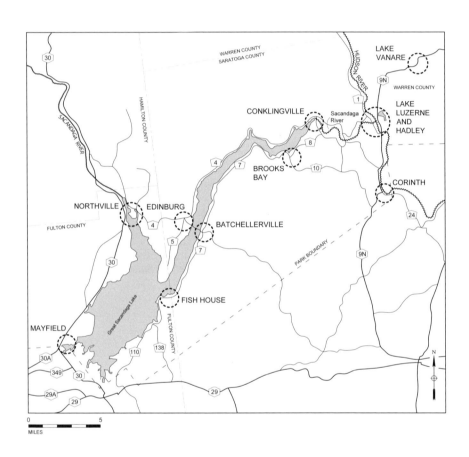

2
GREAT SACANDAGA LAKE

LIKE LAKE GEORGE, GREAT SACANDAGA LAKE makes a convenient geographic feature for a section of this guide. But in contrast to Lake George, the communities on or near this extensive body of water have little or no historical ties to it for the simple reason that Great Sacandaga is an artificial waterbody, created by a dam in 1930. Rather, with two exceptions, the development of these communities should be considered in terms of two rivers, the Hudson, which flows by Lake Luzerne, Hadley, and Corinth, and the old Sacandaga, along which Northville, Edinburg, Fish House, Batchellerville, Brooks Bay, and Conklingville developed. Lake Vanare, the northernmost community in this section, emerged as a resort outpost of Lake Luzerne and, to a lesser extent, of Lake George village. The southernmost community, Mayfield, grew as an extension of Gloversville and Johnstown, two industrial centers that lie outside the Blue Line.

THE EASTERN PART OF THE SACANDAGA RIVER VALLEY, which is now the lake, and the area where that body of water meets the Hudson were among the earliest places to be permanently settled in the Adirondacks. At the confluence of those rivers, the hamlet of Lake Luzerne (formed as Fairfield in 1792; renamed Luzerne in 1808 and Lake Luzerne in 1963) began to develop after the Seven Years War. Little growth occurred until the early 19th century, when lumbering became a significant business. This area was probably the first within the Adirondacks to be targeted for its timber, owing to its proximity to the lumber manufacturing center of Glens Falls and the ease with which logs could be floated down the Hudson to mills there.

Rockwell Falls Fiber Company paper plant, Hadley, 1878, with Lake Luzerne (background) at confluence of Hudson and Sacandaga rivers. (early 20th-century photograph)

Tanning became a significant staple of the economy with the establishment of the Raymond & Ely plant in 1867, which was purchased the following year and soon expanded by the New York–based Thomas Garner & Company. Industrial development was facilitated by the arrival of Thomas C. Durant's Adirondack Railway—the first to extend into the park—in 1869. That same year brothers Albrecht and Rudolf Pagenstecher, who had come from Germany via Massachusetts to manufacture pulp paper by a process they imported, established the Hudson River Pulp & Paper Company. Their experimental Luzerne plant was the first in the country to use U.S.-made machinery and also the first to employ spruce bark, which abounded in the area, rather than aspen. While they soon moved operations to Corinth, where the water flow was stronger, other plants opened in Hadley and Lake Luzerne, including the Rockwell Falls Fiber Company and the Union Bag & Paper Company.

By the late 19th century, the readily available supplies of timber were nearing depletion. Garner's plant closed in 1909. Well before then, Lake Luzerne had attracted tourists by virtue of its picturesque setting. George T. Rockwell opened a hotel in the 1820s and continued to expand it for several decades. But the major attraction became the Wayside Inn, which was built in 1869 and greatly aggrandized around the 1880s on a twenty-acre site with numerous cottages embellishing the campus. The Wayside and a growing number of summer houses were oriented to the lake after which both hamlet and town were named. That body of water lay to the east of, and on higher ground than, the Hudson, enabling a natural buffer between industrial and recreational activities. While Lake Luzerne never approached Lake George's renown, it nonetheless became a resort of considerable fashion toward the century's end.

Wayside Inn, Lake Luzerne, 1869, ca. 1880s, burned 1938. (early 20th-century postcard)

In contrast to Lake George, Lake Luzerne's appeal as a resort had substantially waned by the mid-20th century. However, a new kind of recreational facility, the dude ranch, emerged to fill the void. A concentration of such places lay along NY 9N in the northern part of the town at Lake Vanare. The key figure behind this phenomenon was Ohio native Earl Woodward, who came to the Adirondacks in 1920 and eventually got into real estate development. He began to purchase land around Lake Vanare in 1927 and the following year started to create a community of cabins scattered around a lodge [LV 2]. Christened Northwoods, the project was targeted to middle-income families. Thereafter, Woodward picked up on the idea of a dude ranch as a means of providing an informal, outdoor-oriented atmosphere that appealed to young, single city dwellers. Northwoods Lodge became an experiment for this venture, and in 1939 he opened nearby Hidden Valley Ranch as a full-fledged operation [LV 4]. Woodward directly and otherwise stimulated other dude ranches and complementary enterprises along 9N; by the late 1940s it had the highest concentration of these rustic retreats in the Adirondacks and perhaps in the eastern United States.

International Paper Company, Palmer Falls Mill, Corinth, begun 1870. (1930s photograph)

Some four miles south of Lake Luzerne hamlet, the village of Corinth grew into a significant industrial center. The area was first settled in the 1770s, and the town established in 1818. As at Lake Luzerne, lumbering was a major base for the economy in the first half of the 19th century, but the community's boom took place after the Hudson River Pulp & Paper Company moved there in 1870. The relocation to a former woolen mill occurred because Palmer Falls, the highest on the Hudson at eighty-seven feet, provided a superior source for waterpower. (The falls, however, were not dammed until 1914, when development in reinforced-concrete technology made such a structure feasible.) Arguably the birthplace of modern paper manufacturing, the plant made substantial contributions to integrating the processes of making pulp and manufacturing paper, and it remained a center for innovation in devising larger, faster, and more efficient machinery. The scale of the operation and its rate of expansion is suggested by the consumption of 16,000 tons of pulpwood a day in 1880 and 70,000 eight years later. In 1898, the business was one of sixteen that merged to form International Paper Company, and the Corinth plant soon became the largest of its kind in the world. The business dominated the community through the 20th century, but the village boasted other industries as well, including the Cluett, Peabody & Company shirt factory, which operated from 1899 until 1975. Although it is now bereft of major businesses, Corinth has sustained a substantial population (2,559 in 2010) because it is within commuting distance of Glens Falls.

Along the Sacandaga River, most communities supported logging operations early on and maintained an agrarian base through the 19th and into the 20th centuries, but some spawned manufacturing on a modest scale as well. Conklingville was the largest settlement at the river's eastern end. It emerged as a small industrial center during the second half of the 19th century, with a tannery, sawmills, and woodworking factory, but was in decline by the century's end. Beecher Hollow in the Town of Edinburg attracted settlers as early as the 1790s and subsequently harbored such enterprises as carriage making. Across the river, Batchellerville had a woodenware mill as early as 1837 and three more by 1870. To the south, the tiny hamlet of Fish House was founded in 1752, the first community to be settled in the Town of Northampton under the aegis of Sir William Johnson, whose immense estate included much of the Sacandaga Valley. To satisfy his angling pursuit he built a retreat named Fish House (perhaps referring to the renowned Schuylkill Fishing Company in Philadelphia). While the hamlet's name was not officially changed until 1961, it had long been known by Johnson's appellation.

Sacandaga Park, Northville vicinity, begun 1880s. (early 20th-century postcard)

Northville, located at a bend in the Sacandaga where it turned north toward Lake Pleasant [Section 3], was first settled in the late 1780s and grew rapidly as a village after 1830, supporting a tannery, four mills for making mittens, a metallic binding company, a lumber mill, a large knitting mill in 1891, and a textile machinery works in 1912. Manufacturing was stimulated by the arrival of the Fonda, Johnstown & Gloversville Railroad in 1875, which connected the village to the Mohawk Valley and two of Fulton County's largest industrial centers. The railroad line lay across the river, as did Sacandaga Park, which was established as a Methodist meeting camp in the early 1870s and was later transformed into a large resort, complete with its own amusement park. With a population of 1,099 in 2010, Northville survives as a town of commuters and those who cater to lake-generated recreation.

Farther south, the Town of Mayfield was established in 1793, but efforts to develop the area extended from the 1760s, when much of the land was held by Sir William Johnson and was subject to his initiatives for settlement. The area proved conducive to agriculture. Lumbering and limestone quarrying were also pursued. During the mid-19th century, glove making became an important industry that endured into the 1960s, rendering Mayfield part of the economy that drove the much larger manufacturing center of Gloversville not far to the south.

The construction of the Conklingville Dam in 1927–30, which created Great Sacandaga Lake, transformed the river valley and its economy. Twenty-two miles long and an average of three miles wide, this body of water is second to Lake George in size. Such a project had been discussed since the late 1860s, but it was the frequent spring flooding in Albany and nearby Hudson River communities that brought the matter to a head. A particularly devastating flood in 1913 eventually led the state legislature to approve the project. Cost was the major hurdle, and the plan approved in 1925 called for 95.5 percent of the expenditure to be paid by industries that would benefit from a vigorous water supply year-round and also from the hydroelectric power the dam would generate. Albany, Troy, Rensselaer, Watervliet, and Green Island—the municipalities most affected by the perennial flooding—would cover the remainder of the outlay. The logistics were formidable. Some 1,137 land parcels, covering around 27,000 acres, had to be purchased, and 12,000 acres of timberland cleared. Those buildings in hamlets and on farms that were not moved by their owners had to be destroyed. Twenty-four cemeteries with 3,872 graves had to be relocated. Sixty-eight miles of road had to be abandoned, and forty-three miles of highway constructed on higher ground.

Creating the largest man-made reservoir in the state at a cost of over $24 million was justified as a flood-control measure, but it was also planned as a major recreation center—a place that would attract short-term vacationers and seasonal residents alike. The new roads around the lake's perimeter were designed as pleasure drives, following the hillside contours, and allowing ample space when possible for building cabins and more substantial vacation houses. Residential development was meager during the Depression, but by the 1950s began to increase. Proximity not only to cities on the upper Hudson, but also to those in the Mohawk Valley bolstered the lake's popularity. Today the lake has what is probably the most fully developed waterfront in the Adirondacks, but it is one comprised almost entirely of single-family residences—at least 8,000 of them. Commercial establishments, including motels, are unusually scarce. Unlike lower Lake George, Sacandaga's residential development attains a middle ground between the extremes of large houses and modest hostelries. On the other hand, while much of the acreage beyond Sacandaga's lakeshore development remains sparsely inhabited or wild, none of it is included in the Forest Preserve.

*   *   *   *   *

81

LAKE VANARE

Town of Lake Luzerne, Warren County

The hamlet of Lake Vanare actually has three lakes, all of them artificial. Vanare (pronounced van-R and named after a prominent Lake Luzerne resident), on the west side of NY 9N, was created in the 1920s as an instrument for recreational development. Entrepreneur Earl Woodward sought to complement that effort, with lakes Allure and Forest for his Northwoods tract on 9N's east side. Restaurants and other businesses that catered to dude ranch visitors, and often competed with those establishments, grew up along the highway. Most of these buildings remain intact, though few now serve their original functions. The roads at Northwoods are among the most telling of the informal atmosphere Woodward sought to create.

in front so that dude ranch riders could stop for a meal. Probably not long after World War II the building was enlarged at the rear with an enormous space for dining and special functions. The room was spanned by trusses, comprised of large tree trunks, and yet more such members were used for the walls. A second addition expanded the space to the north, and it was probably at this time that the widest tree trunks were used as posts to support the trusses above them. The effect rivals that of even the most elaborate private camps from the turn of the 20th century in its baroque rusticity. Despite its structural fanfare, the Hitching Post has lain vacant most of the time since the 1980s. The current owner, wanting it to see a better future, plans to begin the revival by opening it for special occasions.

LV 1 HITCHING POST RESTAURANT
NY 9N southwest of Northwoods Road; 1939; later additions

Built for a Danish-American entrepreneur, Sven Munck, the original portion of "the Most Unique Log Cabin in the Adirondacks" appears to have been patterned after the main lodge, built more or less concurrently at Woodward's nearby Hidden Valley Dude Ranch [LV 4], and may have been constructed by the same crew. Besides a restaurant, the establishment included a bar and a few rooms upstairs for overnight guests. A stable was on the premises, and there was a hitching post

LV 2 NORTHWOODS DEVELOPMENT
Northwoods Road, off NY 9N; begun 1928, Earl Woodward, developer

In 1928 Earl Woodward bought some 1,800 acres, most of it on the south side of 9N, for what he envisioned as a residential enclave that enabled middle-class people to partake in the pleasures of the Adirondacks. Besides damming a brook to create two connected lakes, he set aside 600 acres to remain in its natural state for walking and riding. The cabin sites were modest (⅝ of an acre), but the terrain remained forested, affording privacy as well as a rustic atmosphere. Near 9N, an existing farmhouse was remade as a lodge, which opened ca. 1931–33, and several guest cottages were built adjacent to it. Woodward rebranded the establishment a **dude ranch** in the mid-1930s, erecting a **stable** across the road. Through the decade, Woodward built thirty-nine log **cabins** and nine frame ones with "brainstorm" siding (with the lower edge left irregular). No two dwellings were identical, but most were executed in a consistent manner. A one-story **farmhouse** (at 87 Northwoods Road) from the early 19th century was also incorporated in the development. The ranch closed in 1960 and the lodge burned in 2012. Most of the enclave, however, has experienced little physical change.

LV 3 PAINTED PONY RANCH
746 Howe Road; lodge 1945–47, cabins 1947–49, George Breitenbucher, architect (New York); rodeo complex at 703 Howe Road

In the middle of World War II a young printing executive, Walter Isaacson, gave up his career in New York to start a dude ranch, the kind of resort he rightly judged would only increase in popularity with the return of peace. After a futile search for property, he met Earl Woodward, who guided him to a decaying farmstead near Northwoods. Isaacson bought it, some adjacent land from Woodward's friend Sven Munck, and eventually more property from Woodward himself. The main lodge was patterned after Woodward's Hidden Valley Ranch, and a number of men who had worked for the developer helped Isaacson construct the building, using logs cut on the property. Woodward also convinced Isaacson to build his own furniture. Unlike many other dude ranches at that time, Painted Pony began to cater to families. Isaacson also inaugurated rodeos, which continue to operate even though the ranch itself closed in 1996.

LV 4 HIDDEN VALLEY DUDE RANCH
97 Hidden Valley Road; 1939 and later, Earl Woodward, developer (some buildings visible from road; campus accessible through prior arrangement)

When it opened, Hidden Valley became Woodward's signature project and the main lodge an icon for Adirondack dude ranches. A number of cabins straddle the hillside to the north and east, making an informal campus of log structures that could accommodate 125 guests by the late 1940s. The main lodge has been much altered; some of the cabins have been modified; and new facilities have been added since 1993, when the property was purchased by Paul Newman and local philanthropist Charles R. Wood for the Hole in the Wall (now Double H) Ranch, a camp dedicated to children with life-threatening or debilitating illnesses.

LV 5 KASTNER'S CABINS
188 Hidden Valley Road; ca. late 1930s–40s

A lakeside range of cabins sheathed in board-and-batten siding that has changed little since it was constructed, Kastner's is an increasingly rare survivor of a once ubiquitous type of modest resort.

LAKE LUZERNE and HADLEY
Town of Lake Luzerne, Warren County, and Town of Hadley, Saratoga County

A well-tended, verdant community, Lake Luzerne gives little overt indication of its past either as an industrial center or as fashionable resort. While it has lost many of its 19th-century landmarks, what remains still provides clues of the hamlet's dual heritage. Situated directly across the Hudson, Hadley is considerably smaller. It, too, serviced river-oriented industries and also was a transportation hub, with bridges spanning both the Hudson and Sacandaga rivers at an early date and a depot for Thomas C. Durant's Adirondack Railway.

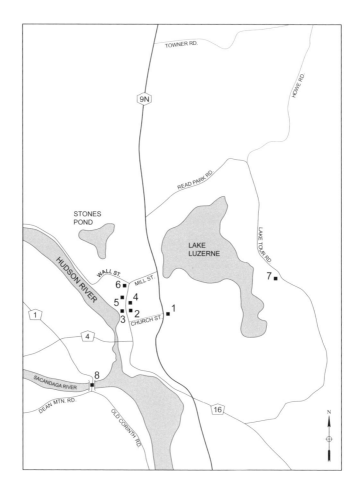

LL 1 ST. MARY'S EPISCOPAL CHURCH
220 Lake Avenue (NY 9N) and Church Street; 1874–75, Jacob Wray Mould, architect (New York)

A rigorously disciplined and highly original composition by one of New York's most creative architects of the mid-19th century, St. Mary's is a telling reminder of the hamlet's stature as an industrial hub and a resort. Born and trained in England, Mould arrived in New York in 1852. As an assistant to Frederick Law Olmsted and Calvert Vaux, he designed the ornament for structures in Central Park, and with Vaux he designed the initial portions of the Metropolitan Museum of Art and the American Museum of Natural History.

The **Rockwell Falls Presbyterian Church** (1882; burned and rebuilt 1922) at 7 Rockwell Street still retains much of its Gilded Age vigor. In contrast, the **United Methodist Church** (1852) at 24 Main Street is a conventional Greek Revival design, enlivened somewhat by an exuberant entry porch added in the late 19th century.

LL 2 BENJAMIN CLAPP BUTLER HOUSE
28 Main Street (CR 44); ca. 1870s

A major contributor to building St. Mary's Church, Butler had one of the more ornamental houses in the hamlet.

LL 3 ROCKWELL HOTEL COTTAGE
37 Main Street; 1832; later additions

Part of George T. Rockwell's campaign to enlarge and update his hotel included erecting four cottages, of which this is the sole survivor. His daughter, Elizabeth Rockwell Windsor, resided here during the summers until 1972. The cottage was then occupied by her niece, Miriam Hamon, who bequeathed it to the historical society. After a major fire in 2002, the building was sold to the town, which rehabilitated it as a visitor center.

LL 4 EDWARD GARNER HOUSE
38 Main Street; ca. 1880s

Garner chose to build his fashionable house immediately adjacent to his leather works, an offshoot of the tanning business run by his father. Edward's granddaughter Frances Garner Kinnear donated the house to the Hadley-Luzerne Historical Society in 1982 for use as its quarters.

LL 5 GARNER LEATHER WORKS POWERHOUSE STACK
Main Street; ca. 1880s

The Garner plant straddled both sides of Main Street to take advantage of fast-moving water descending from the lake to the Hudson. Eventually a powerhouse was add-

ed to the complex, and when the works was demolished in 1922 its stack was retained as a reminder of this key regional industry.

LL 6 GAILEY HILL SCHOOL DISTRICT SCHOOL NO. 2
Main, Mill, and Wall streets; 1865, Warren Hall, builder

Originally on Gailey Hill Road, the school operated until the district consolidation in 1937. Forty years later it was donated to the Lions Club and moved to 15 Main Street. In 2004 it was moved again to the present location and restored to an appearance more suggestive of the early 20th century than the mid-19th.

LL 7 LUZERNE MUSIC CENTER
203 Lake Tour Road; ca. 1920s–30s and later (accessible by prior arrangement)

This complex of simple cabins was built in several stages as Camp Tekakwitha by the Catholic Youth Organization of the Albany Diocese. Established in 1915 on Brant Lake [Section 4], the operation was moved to Lake Luzerne during the interwar decades. Since 1980 it has served as a training camp for gifted young musicians.

LL 8 HADLEY BOW BRIDGE
Old Corinth Road at Sacandaga River; 1885, Berlin Iron Bridge Company, designer and fabricator (East Berlin, Conn.)

The first bridge at this location dates to 1813 and provided a strategic connection between the Adirondacks and more rapidly settling areas to the south. The same year that bridge burned, in 1885, it was replaced by the current structure. A design-determining stipulation was that the single pier and abutments of the earlier bridge be used to reduce construction costs. The result was a two-span, wrought-iron structure, with a parabolic (or lenticular) truss. The bridge is the only remaining example of three such structures known to have been erected in the United States with the deck at mid-height of the trusses, an arrangement that added lateral stiffness and precluded end posts at the portals. Construction of NY 9N bypassed the bridge in 1932, and it was closed fifty-one years later. In 2000 it became the focus of a preservation effort that succeeded in returning it to its original use.

Just to the west stands the much higher **Delaware & Hudson Railway bridge,** an early 20th-century replacement of the original one of 1869. Both used Pratt trusses (with vertical posts set in compression and diagonal bracing set in tension) placed below the deck to span the river. The juxtaposition of highway and railroad bridges is a poignant reminder of the priority long given to the latter form of transportation.

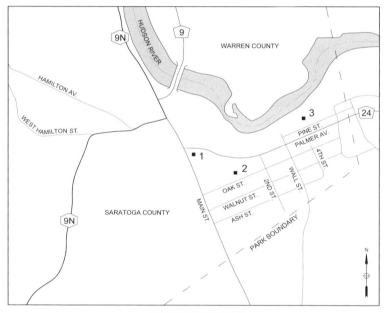

CORINTH
Town of Corinth, Saratoga County

In contrast to Lake Luzerne, Corinth gives every appearance of having been an industrial center even though the plants themselves have gone. And unlike Ticonderoga [Section 5], whose economy was also driven by International Paper Company at the turn of the 20th century, Corinth has few distinctive buildings. On the other hand, residential development was mostly comprised of single-family houses that, however modest, were built at a relatively low density, giving a sense of spatial openness not always found in working-class communities of the period.

CO 1 FIRST BAPTIST CHURCH

Main Street and Palmer Avenue, southeast corner; 1897–98, Robert Newton Breeze, architect (Saratoga Springs, N.Y.)

A handsome variation on Richardsonian Romanesque, the church was strategically placed at a major intersection on the main thoroughfare between the commercial center and the residential blocks beyond. It was vacated around 2000 due to a dwindling congregation.

CO 2 CORINTH CENTRAL HIGH SCHOOL

105 Oak Street; 1935, J. Russell White, architect (Albany); additions 1957–59, John C. Ehrlich, architect (Geneva, N.Y.); later additions

Ehrlich's large, one-story addition gave the school a new entrance and a new staging area, where a canopy supported by bent steel I-beams provides shelter as well as a strong compositional counterpoint to the reserved building behind it. Nearby are the twin former **Union Free schools nos. 2 and 3** (both 1908) at 333 Main Street and 611 Palmer Avenue, respectively, which operated until around 2000 and are good examples of their period.

CO 3 INTERNATIONAL PAPER COMPANY, PALMER FALLS MILL ADMINISTRATION BUILDING

Pine Street at 4th Street; early 20th century

Despite the size and importance of International Paper's Corinth plant the administrative headquarters was quite small and never experienced significant changes. While the plant was demolished in 2010–11, this building was spared and given to the town the following year. It is maintained for civic occasions and other events.

CONKLINGVILLE

Town of Hadley, Warren County

CK 1 COMMUNITY CHURCH OF CONKLINGVILLE

North Shore Road (CR 4) at Walter Maxfield Road; 1845, moved late 1920s

Though most of the hamlet of Conklingville was demolished in preparing for the dam [CK 2], a few buildings were moved to higher ground. What was originally the First Christian Church is the most noteworthy in terms of the attempt to preserve a sense of community. Though much altered, the building still conveys a clear sense of its original appearance as a modest rendition of the temple form popular for Greek Revival houses of worship in the antebellum period. Just above, on Cemetery Road, lies another relocated building, constructed in the early 20th century as a four-room schoolhouse. Though now vacant, it was long used for church-related activities.

CK 2 CONKLINGVILLE DAM AND ELMER J. WEST ELECTRIC STATION

CR 8 at North Shore Road (CR 4); 1927–30, Edward H. Sargent, chief engineer for the dam; S. J. Groves & Son Company, builders, E. J. Cox, engineer (Minneapolis)

Originally defining the eastern end of Great Sacandaga Lake at the narrowest section of the valley, the dam itself is hardly dramatic in appearance. Geological conditions precluded a reinforced-concrete structure. Instead it is of semi-hydraulic, earth-filled construction, with a sliced granite core and rock cover. Rising 95 feet and spanning a distance of 1,100 feet, it stands like an elongated pyramid, 650 feet wide at the base, 45 feet at the top. Rock cliffs on the north side allowed construction of a concrete siphon spillway that is nearly as long as the dam itself and was the largest of its kind at the time of construction. The spillway connects to the electric power plant, which was built by New York Power & Light Corporation. Farther east, **Stewart Dam**, on South Shore Road [CR 7] below its terminus at North Shore Road, was constructed after World War II and is of more modest dimensions.

CK 3 LYNWOOD BAPTIST CHURCH
4291 South Shore Road (CR 7); 1869–70,
David Hyde, builder

Built for a congregation formed in 1826, this temple-front Greek Revival church stands in isolation, with the community it once served dispersed by the lake. It replaced an 1842 edifice that was the work of the same builder. The congregation disbanded in 1952, but was revived in 1990.

EDINBURG
Town of Edinburg, Saratoga County

Edinburg has always been a scattered rural community, rendered more so by the creation of Great Sacandaga Lake. On the north side the small, clustered settlement of Beecher Hollow comes as close to a hamlet center as any segment of the town.

ED 1 OLD TRAIL INN
232 North Shore Road (CR 4); ca. late 19th
century; additions and alterations
mid- to late 20th century

A classic roadhouse, this building, perhaps originally part of a farm, was moved in the late 1920s from the lake's path to its present site, where it has since functioned as a tavern.

ED 2 BEECHER HOLLOW

Beecher Hollow is a remarkably well-preserved small, linear, rural enclave developed mostly between the 1820s and 1850s. Brothers Arad and Leonard Copeland came from Vermont in 1815, purchasing Ely Beecher's sawmill and carriage business. They also traded as wheelwrights, metalworkers, and makers of cabinets, furniture, and coffins. **Leonard Copeland** constructed the wood-frame **house (a)** at 83 North Shore Road [CR 4] five years later and substantially enlarged it around the 1840s. Next door, at 81 North Shore Road, **Arad Copeland's** equally commodious brick **dwelling (b)** dates to 1832.

Arad also farmed, and the diminutive (35-foot-long) **covered bridge (c)** opposite his house was erected in 1879 to facilitate getting livestock to pasture on the high ground above Beecher's Creek. The brothers' **carriage shop (d)** was built by them around 1828 and remains remarkably intact. **Ely Beecher**, who with his wife came from across the river at Fish House in 1802, at various times served as postmaster and ran a general store out of his modest **residence (e)**, which was begun soon after his arrival. Located at the intersection of North Shore and Old Military roads, it was expanded to the rear around 1824, and its center section was given a second story in 1891. On the west side of the same intersection, **John Barker's hardware and general store (f)** (1847) is far larger and more imposing with its giant portico—a rare element for a building of this type—attesting to the community's prosperity. It reputedly served as a way station on the

laid vertically in angled projection, as if architectural sculpture.

Underground Railroad. Descendants operated the establishment until 1890 and it continued as a store until 1945. The **Beecher Hollow School (g)** (1860), on CR 4 just north of CR 98, replaced a crude log structure; after closing it served as the town hall from 1931 to 1970. Five years later it opened as the town's historical museum. Situated

ED 4 ROSSLYN HOUSE, FRANK MARVIN SINCLAIRE HOUSE
523 Sinclair Road; 1919–20

Brooklynite Frank Sinclaire spent summers on his family's farm at Fish House, across the Sacandaga River. In 1910 he married Marie Meta Bischoff, whose father owned Schenley Liquor Distillery. Sinclaire worked for his father-in-law and eventually took over the business. He closed the plant with the onset of Prohibition and retired. The imposing house he erected outside Northville was on part of the family farm, most of which was flooded by the lake a decade later.

The adjacent farmhouse to the southwest, probably dating to the 1840s or 1850s, was occupied by a member of the **Beecher** family in 1868 and may have been built by him. The porch and rear wing were perhaps added by Frank Sinclaire's sister, Lucy, who resided there during the 20th century. Just to the rear is a building known as **Truax School District School No. 3**, which was located near the Sacandaga River and moved to its current site to avoid destruction by the lake.

at a major intersection (CRs 4 and 98), which connects Beecher Hollow to Batchellerville and Northville, the **Edinburg Methodist Church (h)** (1836–37) provides a major focal point to the community.

ED 3 EDINBURG COMMON SCHOOL
4 Johnson Road and CR 4; 1986–88, John D. Smith, architect (Burnt Hills, N.Y.)

A sprawling box is given visual discipline and interest through the simplest of means, with window bands bounded by courses and punctuated by solar panels

NORTHVILLE

Town of Northampton, Fulton County

Northville's character suggests it has long enjoyed prosperity. Sizable, decorous houses, churches, and other buildings are found in considerable number, while the scale and sense of intimacy of the place evokes the best associations with a small town. Long a river community, Northville is now the major center for Great Sacandaga Lake. Northville is a mostly intact example of a settlement whose core had fully developed by the early 20th century.

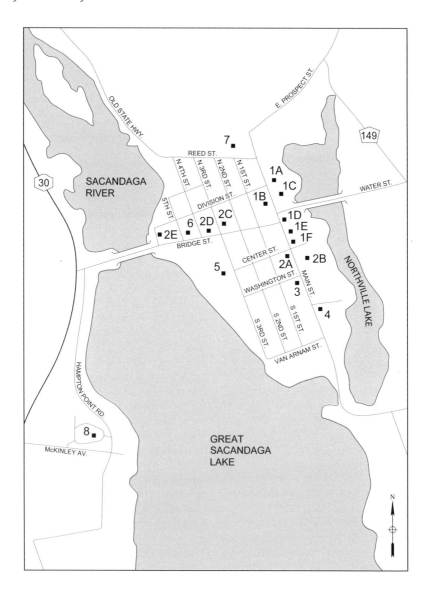

NV 1 MAIN STREET COMMERCIAL BUILDINGS

Extending two blocks, Northville's business center is a good representative of its kind. The functional configuration, however, is unusual, with stores and offices lining one side of Main Street and a small hotel and houses the other. The **store buildings (a)** at 118 and 120–22 N. Main are good examples of the wood-frame retail architecture of the late 19th century—a type that was once common to the region and many other places. The **Northville House (b)** at 131 N. Main was constructed in 1813 as a residence for James Lobdell, and was later converted to a hotel by Jacob van Arnam. Additions were followed by further changes after a fire in 1898. The business ceased operation in 1951. The **Allen and Palmer Block (c)** at 112–14 N. Main was erected in 1885 as an investment by the owners of the community's leading hardware store. The 1914 **Willard Brothers Block (d)** at 114–16 S. Main was constructed for the R. G. DeWitt Company variety store. Later the J. J. Newberry Company occupied the space, and it is now the Northville 5-10-25 Cent Store—an unusual example of functional continuity over a period of 100 years. The **Wright Block (e)** (ca. 1890–91) at 118–20 S. Main was built for Franklin Wright, a leading physician, whose office was on the second floor. Finally, the 1895 **Cole Building (f)** at 128–30 S. Main was a speculative investment of a pioneer lumberman and contained a lodge hall in addition to stores.

NV 2 TURN-OF-THE-20TH-CENTURY HOUSES

The late 19th and early 20th centuries were clearly a period of economic growth

for Northville, whose elite concentrated their houses on South Main and Bridge streets, the two major thoroughfares. Collectively these houses offer an illustrative cross-section of design modes in popularized form that enjoyed widespread use nationally. Surviving examples are numerous, some of them still residences; others serve compatible commercial functions. The **George N. Brown house (a)** at 201 S. Main probably dates to the late 1890s, its exterior a liberal mixing of Queen Anne and Colonial Revival motifs. Its owner was the first president of the Northville Bank and served as town clerk. The **John Resseguie house (b)** (1888) at 252 S. Main boasts an array of Eastlake details. **Ray Hubbell** commissioned a **house (c)** of more reserved design at 381 Bridge around 1890. He and his partner, James Cole [NV 1f], started the Globe Metallic Binding Company for oil- and floorcloth in 1880 and three years later also made gloves. Hubbell

served as the Town of Northampton supervisor. Across the intersection, at 401 Bridge, the **William G. Harris house (d)** (1908) is similarly restrained. The 1903 **house** of **John A. Willard (e)**, a lumber baron, vice-president of the Northville Bank, and town supervisor as well, ranks among the community's most ambitious in its size and restless play of forms that take advantage of its prominent site at 641 Bridge, overlooking the Sacandaga River. Another **Resseguie house (f)** (ca. 1880) was moved in 1912 from a presumably more prominent location to its current one at 141 N. First Street.

NV 3 FIRST UNITED METHODIST CHURCH
301 S. Main Street at Washington Street; 1871–72

Reputedly designed by its pastor, Cabot M. Clark, in a chaste, round-arch mode ultimately derived from northern Italian Romanesque precedent and one favored by many Methodist congregations during the mid-19th century, the church has its worship space on the second floor—an arrangement Methodists had frequently employed since the 1830s. While very different in form and composition, the **Gordon B. Mosher Memorial Education Center** (1961) at the rear is a good example of a compatible addition.

NV 4 GIFFORD'S VALLEY SCHOOL NO. 9
412 S. Main Street; ca. 1856

This one-room building originally lay some two miles from the village, on Giffords Valley Road, where a school had operated since 1813, and no doubt represented a substantial improvement over its predecessor. Classes were conducted there until 1930, by which time it was seen as an antique. In 1990 the building was moved for restoration and use as Northville-Northampton Historical Museum.

NV 5 NORTHVILLE CENTRAL SCHOOL
1315 Third Street; 1931–33, Carl W. Clark architect, (Cortland, N.Y.); additions 1949–50, Clark

As with many other communities in the

Adirondacks and elsewhere, consolidating rural schools into a central facility represented a quantum leap, not just in size, but also in the range of instruction and activities. Workshops, an auditorium for plays and concerts, a library, a gymnasium, and athletic fields all contributed to the change. Instruction now extended through twelfth grade, accreditation for which the town secured in 1910. School consolidation was a key measure by which the importance of villages and even some hamlets came to play a significant role in the lives of the rural population. Clark's elegantly simple composition gives a low-key presence to a major civic function.

NV 6 ST. FRANCIS OF ASSISI CATHOLIC CHURCH
501 Bridge Street; 1922–23, Ogden & Gander, architects (Albany)

St. Francis looks to basically the same historical sources as the Methodist church [NV 3], but is more precise in its allusions and traditional in its configuration. Like many Roman Catholic churches of the late 19th and early 20th centuries, it stands as a memory image of the old countries whence many congregants came.

NV 7 UNITED PRESBYTERIAN CHURCH
161 Reed Street at First; 1857; spire replaced by tower 1930

This Greek Revival, temple-front design represents a building form widely embraced by a number of Protestant denominations in the Northeast during the antebellum period. While added seventy years later, the tower is rendered fully in the spirit of mid-19th-century work.

NV 8 SACANDAGA PARK
McKinley and Pine avenues and Canoe Circle between Hampton Point Road and NY 30; 1880s and later

What became one of the major vacation communities in the Adirondacks began as a Methodist tent camp meeting in the early 1870s. When the Fonda, Johnstown & Gloversville Railroad completed its line to Northville in 1875, it acquired a large adjacent tract and began to develop a cottage colony, which soon was called Sacandaga Park. In some cases the company just sold lots; in others, it built and rented the dwellings. To boost business further, the railroad erected the Adirondack Inn in 1889. A major fire nine years later destroyed much of the compound, but the railroad rebounded by greatly expanding its holdings and intensifying development. Hundreds of cottages and three hotels were built into the 1920s, and an amusement park constructed on a nearby island. Additional fires took their toll in 1912 and 1918. Creating Great Sacandaga Lake obliterated the island and some other components as well (a number of cottages were moved to higher ground). The railroad sold its remaining interest in 1952. Still, Sacandaga Park encompasses a rich array of late 19th- and early 20th-century summer cottages lining narrow streets in the camp meeting tradition.

MAYFIELD
Town of Mayfield, Fulton County

Bypassed by NY 30, the village of Mayfield is a small residential community, suggestive of its industrial past, and continues as a satellite of the Gloversville-Johnstown area.

MA 1 POUR JIM'S FAMILY RESTAURANT AND TAVERN
2399 NY 30 and N. Main Street; ca. 1930s
A classic roadhouse of the interwar de-cades, this watering hole was probably built not long after the highway it fronts was developed as a major automobile route into the Adirondacks.

MA 2 MAYFIELD SCHOOL
27 School Street; 1939, Walter Brown van Dresser, architect (Gloversville, N.Y.); later additions
A very long front elevation is given scale by being treated as a series of slightly receding pavilions. Recent additions complement the original building in an understated manner.

MA 3 OLIVER RICE HOUSE
328 Riceville Road, off SR 30; ca. 1790; ca.
1810; later additions and alterations

A sequestered reminder of Mayfield's 18th-century origins, this house was built for a Revolutionary War veteran who came to Mayfield from Connecticut in 1789. The original one-story dwelling lay across the road and was moved to serve as a rear ell (service wing) to the ca. 1810 house either at that time or during the next several decades. The main block of the house reflects Rice's rise as a farmer, millwright, and postmaster. At the same time it is conservative in configuration, with major spaces arranged around a central chimney—a plan that prevailed in New England during the 17th and first half of the 18th centuries, but would have seemed dated by the early 19th. Between 1924 and 1936 an entry porch was added and the roof of the ell raised. Before then a second, southern, entrance was made and portions of the interior reconfigured. The house remained in the hands of descendants until 1988 and is now home to the Mayfield Historical Society—a rich document of nearly two centuries of occupancy by a single family.

FISH HOUSE
Town of Perth, Fulton County

FH 1 NORTHAMPTON METHODIST CHURCH
1605 South Shore Road (CR 117); 1859–60

While portions of this tiny hamlet were submerged by Great Sacandaga Lake, significant buildings survive. Foremost among them is this handsome example of a Greek Revival, temple-front house of worship, which has been carefully restored by its congregation.

FH 2 CLARK S. GRINNELL HOUSE
122 Old Fish House Road; early 19th centu-
ry; additions and alterations 1841

Grinnell served in the state assembly for a dozen years. Financed by his father-in-law, Alexander St. John, this temple-front house is unusual in its one-story pedimented porch.

FH 3 NORTHAMPTON SCHOOL DISTRICT SCHOOL NO. 6
1624 South Shore Road; 1908–09, Frederick
L. Comstock, architect (Gloversville, N.Y.)

Replacing a one-room school of 1867, this modest two-room building represents efforts to improve rural educational facilities in the era before consolidation. Classes were held there until 1958. It now serves as a community center.

FH 4 GODFREY SHEW HOUSE
1632 South Shore Road; 1784; later
additions

German immigrant Gottfried Shoe was recruited by Sir William Johnson to participate in the development of his vast manorial estate. By 1772 Shoe had Anglicized his name to Shew and had erected a cabin on a 100-acre farm at Fish House. The current house manifests his success in the venture. The entrance porch probably dates to the mid-19th century. To the rear lies a carriagehouse built around 1885.

BATCHELLERVILLE
Town of Edinburg, Saratoga County

BA 1 BATCHELLERVILLE PRESBYTERIAN CHURCH
South Shore Road (CR 7), just east of the Sacandaga Bridge; 1867, Norman Hickock, builder; later additions and alterations

Following the development of Great Sacandaga Lake, little remains of this once thriving industrial hamlet. A covered bridge spanned the river here in 1844 to connect eastern portions of the town to those on the western side and to the Town of Northampton beyond. A much longer steel bridge was completed in 1931 to accommodate the breadth of the lake. In turn, this was replaced in 2012 by one of less distinguished design. The most prominent building left in the hamlet is this church, which was moved when the lake was created. The temple-front building is embellished with a few simple Greek Revival details, all set at a monumental scale. A different vocabulary was employed for the tower, which may be a later addition. The windows and the interior configuration were altered following the move.

Adirondacks during the early decades of the 20th century. Its tongue-in-cheek name emanates from the circumstances of its construction. Gray lived with his mother and stepfather, whose house was moved to higher ground while preparations were made for the lake. Once relocated, Gray built this simple dwelling to the rear.

BB 2 DAVID RAYFIEL HOUSE
1288 Kathan Road; 1958, George Lawrence Moore, architect (New York)

Avant-garde modernism seldom found its way into the repertoire of seasonal domestic architecture in the Adirondacks. This house is among the rare exceptions. The client, a prominent screenwriter and collaborator with Sydney Pollack, considered it his primary residence, and it was where he wrote most of his screenplays, including *Three Days of the Condor*. Little is known about the architect he selected.

BROOKS BAY
Town of Day, Saratoga County

BB 1 HI-N-DRI, IRA ("ADIRONDACK IKE") GRAY CAMP
996 West Mountain Road, south of South Shore Road (CR 7); ca. 1930–31

Built for a well-known woodsman, this camp is a good example of the modest seasonal residences that abounded in the

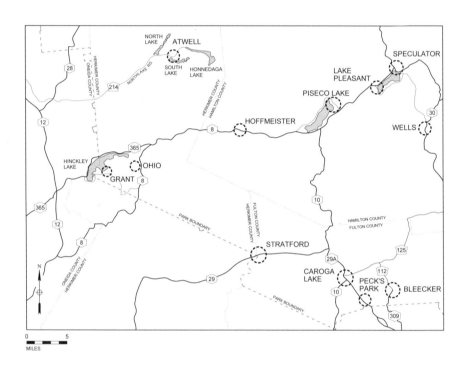

3

SOUTH-CENTRAL LAKES

NO SINGLE BODY OF WATER DEFINES THE EXTENSIVE AREA covered in this section, which includes portions of Fulton, Hamilton, and Herkimer counties. A number of lakes—including Peck, Caroga, Canada, North, Piseco, and Pleasant—lie within the territory. Hinckley Reservoir, the result of damming West Canada Creek, sits on the western edge of this area, and upper portions of the Sacandaga River run near its eastern boundary. Most of the communities developed around these natural features. But settlement was at least equally predicated on a series of long-traveled roads, especially what are now NY 8, 10, 29A, and 30, which traverse large amounts of uninhabited land. These highways connect what is otherwise a miscellany of places, most of which have little or no relationship to one another.

WITHIN THE BLUE LINE, SETTLEMENT ALONG ROUTES 10 and 29A in the towns of Johns-town and Caroga began between the late 18th and mid-19th centuries, with lumbering and tanning the two principal bases for the economy. As early as the 1870s, however, recreation emerged as an important, and eventually dominant, source of revenue. A resident of Johnstown, John Peck started to buy land nearby in the Town of Bleecker in 1842 to exploit its great supply of timber. Following his death in 1888, son Albert Taylor Peck acquired additional tracts that totaled some 5,000 acres to develop a resort around the lake that bore the family name. Around 1911 two dams erected by the Mohawk Hydro-Electric Company enlarged the lakes, necessitating moving many of the cabins along its shores. Peck's Park, as it is known, continued to be operated by descendants through the 20th century.

Auskerada Hotel, Canada Lake, 1892–93, burned 1921. (early 20th-century postcard)

Along with Peck's Park and Sacandaga Park [Section 2], Canada Lake was another early resort development targeted to the middle class. In 1865 William Claflin bought 20,000 acres of forestland to supply his tannery in nearby Wheelerville, but he left the lake area untouched, building a hotel along its shore in 1866 and platting the land around the lake the following year. Nearly thirty years later Alfred Dolge, owner of a piano-parts factory in Dolgeville, gave new life to Claflin's project, but went bankrupt in 1898. Undaunted, Cyrus Durey bought the enterprise, now boasting some forty cottages, in 1904. Canada Lake's primacy as a resort began to be challenged as early as 1878, when John Sherman commissioned the Caroga Lake Hotel two miles to the south. Other modest hostelries were erected, and by the early 20th century cottages could be found along the shore. Caroga Lake's biggest attraction became Sherman's Park [CA 3], a pleasure ground begun in the early 1920s. At the shore and continuing to the southwest lies one of the largest bathing beaches in the Adirondacks. Nearby in Wheelerville, Durey sought to augment his lumber operation by developing the Caroga Recreation Park, which was to include an airstrip to accommodate tourists' planes. Instead it became a golf course, the first six holes of which were completed in 1925.

Beach, Caroga Lake. (1930s postcard)

To the east, though not far from Peck Lake, the tiny hamlet of Bleecker never adapted when the extensive forestland was cleared by the late 19th century, remaining an isolated outpost. A tannery was established there during the mid-19th century and by 1878 the settlement boasted a hotel, church, school, two sawmills, a second tannery, store, broom-handle factory, and twenty-three houses, of which very little remains. West on NY 29A, the larger and more long-lasting community of Stratford benefited from both East Canada Creek, along which mills began to be erected as early as 1806, and land that was more suited to farming.

Farther north, along NY 10 and 8 to the west, most of the land is part of the Forest Preserve and settlement is sparse. The hamlet of Hoffmeister, containing the majority of the Town of Morehouse's eighty-six residents in 2010, underscores the difficulties that those who sought to develop the area have experienced since the early 19th century. In 1834 Rensselaer van Rensselaer began to acquire large tracts for development, but soon lost interest. The following year Andrew K. Morehouse succeeded in getting the town that bears his name formed, where Hoffmeister became the major settlement. It never succeeded in attracting industry, however, remaining an area of small farms, scattered not far from the main road (later NY 8). In 1837 Morehouse began to create a village at the head of Piseco Lake in the adjacent, newly formed Town of Arietta, as the centerpiece of what he envisioned as a sort of fiefdom. He erected a sawmill, several stores, machine shop, and even a brick manufactory, but the people who had been lured to operate the enterprises soon balked at Morehouse's rigid contracts. His hamlet was nearly deserted by 1847. Tanning revived the economy in the 1870s; however, as occurred throughout the Adirondacks, the supply of hemlock was exhausted within a few decades. Tourism proved a more stable economic base by the late 1870s. Several modest hotels were constructed near the lake in the latter decades of the 19th century, and, by the early 20th century, camps—some quite modest; others grand—appeared on the lakeshore in considerable number. Still the year-round population of Arietta was only 304 in 2010.

Osborn House, Lake Pleasant, 1901, demolished 1969. (early 20th-century postcard)

Some four miles to the east along NY 8 lies the hamlet of Lake Pleasant, bordering a lake of the same name, and Sacandaga Lake (a natural lake not to be confused with Great Sacandaga Lake in Section 2). Settlement began there as early as the 1780s, and when Hamilton County was formed in 1816, Sageville, as the hamlet was then called, was designated the governmental seat. The community remained small for most of the century, with some modest agricultural and lumbering activities; however, remoteness, poor soil, and short growing seasons limited these endeavors. Timber cutting picked up toward the century's end, but the major boost came from recreation. The Pleasant Lake Club Park was established around 1899, along the lines of earlier plans for Canada Lake. A number of other hotels were constructed on the lakeshore into the early 20th century. The lake's southern shore was developed with sizable summer houses in the 1890s. The expansive lakefront was also conducive to the creation of children's camps, starting in the early 20th century. At the lake's northeastern corner the village of Speculator, which was in-corporated in 1925, had emerged well before then as a principal base for recreation-al development, with both hotels and summer residences.

To the south, along the East Branch of the Sacandaga River at the rural commu-nity of Griffin, is the site of one of the largest tanneries in the Adirondacks, which flourished between the 1870s and 1890s. Farther south on the East Branch lies the hamlet of Wells, in what was the earliest settled area in this section. Formed in 1805, the community developed into a small industrial hub, with extensive lumbering and several tanneries by the mid-19th century. One of the tanneries was later converted to a veneer works, expanding to lumber in the early 20th century, and in recent years has been imaginatively adapted as an artist's studio and sculpture park [WS 4].

Adirondack Lumber Company plant, Wells, ca. 1918, altered. (ca. 1920s postcard)

*   *   *   *   *

100

PECK'S PARK
Town of Johnstown, Fulton County

PP 1 SCHOOL BUILDING
104 Peck Lake Road, off NY 29A; ca. early 20th century

Now a local history museum, this one-room schoolhouse is said to date from 1857, when John Peck did erect such a building in the area; however, its appearance suggests the facility was perhaps extensively remodeled or, more likely, built anew at the turn of the 20th century.

CAROGA LAKE
Town of Caroga, Fulton County

Though it has lost its hotels, the mostly seasonal settlement around Caroga Lake remains one of the largest resort developments in the southern Adirondacks, with some 2,000 residences on its shores. The eastern portions of this development give some indication of what such places were like a century ago.

CA 1 MAPLE TREE KNOLL RESTAURANT AND LOUNGE
2794 NY 10; mid-19th, early 20th centuries; later additions

Situated well to the south of the hamlet amid a once agricultural area, this house may originally have been part of a prosperous farm. Very little is known about its history save what is indicated by the building itself. The original (east) section is a three-bay, temple-front house probably built between the 1830s and 1850s. Around the 1920s it was aggrandized, probably as a country retreat, with the former façade now subordinated to a long south elevation, enunciated by a seven-bay porch, the center three bays of which project farther as a temple-front porte-cochere. Since the 1950s it has housed a restaurant.

CA 2 SUMMER COTTAGE
East side of NY 10 between Lake and Grove avenues, behind store building; early 20th century

Behind a vacant commercial building lies an uninhabited cottage of a kind widely used in the Adirondacks and other vacation areas of the country during the early 20th century. Many of these modest shelters were prefabricated as kits that could be easily transported to and erected at their destinations. Unlike most examples, this cottage appears little changed.

Nearby, along **West Shore Drive**, can be found a number of good examples of somewhat larger two-story cottages from the turn of the 20th century.

CA 3 SHERMAN'S PARK
NY 10 and West Shore Drive; 1921 and later

101

A rare surviving example of its type more generally, this small enclave began with a two-story **bathhouse and dancehall** erected by Frank Sherman. With well-known bands playing on weekends, the attraction proved popular enough to construct other amusement facilities in the following years, when a **Ferris wheel** and **carousel** were added. After World War II, a **frozen custard stand** was erected near the entrance. Sherman died in 1955; his son continued the operation for another fifteen years. The subsequent owners declared bankruptcy in 1989. The park remains intact, but unused.

CA 4 NICK STONER INN
1810 NY 10; mid-19th century; 1927

This hulking watering hole started as a barn at the Wheeler, Claflin Company's Wheelerville tannery. Its recasting was part of Cyrus Durey's plans to develop the Caroga Recreational Park. Lying opposite the golf course, it was originally called Caroga Recreation Club House. Later, the establishment was renamed to honor a regional hero and well-known Adirondack trapper.

BLEECKER
Town of Bleecker, Fulton County

BC 1 BLEECKER COMMUNITY CHURCH
CR 112; 1865–66, Karl Gutha and George Ort, builders

Driving on CR 112 to Bleecker affords some sense of the isolation that once characterized many Adirondack settlements. Located about two miles above the now vanished hamlet center, what was originally St. John's Lutheran Church is of an elementary nature that suggests the limited means of a congregation that was nonetheless determined to create a sense of permanency in what remained a near-frontier environment. Maintaining the institution proved challenging. The church closed in 1921 when its congregation relocated to Gloversville. Twenty-four years later it reopened as the Bleecker Community Church and in 1950 began affiliation with the Mayfield Methodist Church.

STRATFORD
Town of Stratford, Fulton County, and Town of Salisbury, Herkimer County

SO 1 HELTERLINE HOUSE
6166 NY 29A; ca. 1850s

Straddling two towns, this bifurcated hamlet retains many aspects of its 19th-century development. Among the most interesting dwellings is this house, built in a simple Italianate mode, but with an unusual sheathing treatment that alternates panels of horizontally and vertically laid boards articulated by battens.

SO 2 LIGHTHOUSE BAPTIST CHURCH
6178 NY 29A; 1861

This classic example of mid-19th-century Baptist church design played a key role in solidifying its congregation. Formed as the Stratford Baptist Church in 1809, the assembly split in 1848, but elected to reunite the year after the new edifice was built.

HOFFMEISTER
Town of Morehouse, Hamilton County

HF 1 FARMSTEAD
NY 8, just east of Post Office; ca. mid-19th century

The history of this complex, which appears to be one of the oldest in the area, remains to be documented. It was likely erected at a time when at least a small number of settlers shared Andrew K. Morehouse's visions of a prosperous agricultural area. The five-bay, one-and-one-half-story house may have been built in two stages and is a good example of early farm dwellings in the central Adirondacks. To the east lies a carriagehouse and barn. During the early 20th century it was purchased by Gordon and Margaret Dealing, who for many years ran a store, gas station, and garage on the premises.

HF 2 GEORGE ABBOTT HOUSE
727 NY 8; ca. mid-19th century and later

Originally this house may have been part of a farmstead. It appears to be the product of at least three construction campaigns, of which the front "wing" is perhaps the oldest. The three-bay, gable-end main block may well have been added a decade or so later. The porches were appended thereafter.

HF 3 MOREHOUSE UNITED METHODIST CHURCH
NY 8; ca. late 1850s

A diminutive version of the Stratford Baptist Church [SO 2], this modest building has long been the hamlet's most prominent landmark. It was probably constructed shortly before the Civil War as the Union Congregational Church and has been the only house of worship in Morehouse since the 1870s. Later it was taken over by the Methodist Episcopal Church, which was formed in 1881. In recent decades the edifice has served as quarters for the Morehouse Historical Society.

HF 4 JOHN SCHRINER HOUSE
NY 8, just west of United Methodist Church; ca. 1870s–80s

The farmhouse that by the early 20th century was occupied by John Schriner is a regularized version of the Abbott house [HF 2], with a two-story main block, side wing, and porch all probably constructed at the same time. The barns lay directly across the road. Long vacant, the house will likely be demolished.

HF 5 FLOYD KREUZER HOUSE AND RESTAURANT
Leon's Road, off NY 8; 1929, Floyd Kreuzer, designer and builder (best viewed from NY 8)

A descendant of Henry Kreuzer, who managed the Central Hotel, the town's first, from 1890 until it burned in 1924, Floyd Kreuzer drew inspiration from the *Mayflower*, and sought to replicate it at his roadside establishment. Oriented to the original path of NY 8, the building is a rare survivor of the tendency to fashion commercial outlets after unlikely objects—from watercraft to animals—to attract motorists. It is now a residence. During the 1920s Route 8 became a major entry to the Adirondacks from Utica, Rome, and other parts of the central Mohawk Valley.

103

HF 6 GRAY ROCKS
163 Mountain House Road; late 1860s

Long known as Gray Rocks, this pioneering sportsmen's hotel in the area was erected for F. W. Kassing. Beyond serving visitors, the establishment harbored town meetings for several years over the following decade. While of a configuration that became commonplace for such establishments in the mid-19th century, this example is probably the most intact in the Adirondacks.

OHIO
Town of Ohio, Hamilton County

HF 7 BRANT MOUNTAIN CLUB
End of Erb Road, off NY 8; ca. 1870s–80s

Having long served as quarters for a hunting club, this house was part of a farmstead developed by the Brant family and bears close resemblance to the Schriner house [HF 4]. While the front has experienced some modifications, the basic form and much of the character of the house remain intact. The porch is of recent vintage, but replaced one that similarly extended across the front.

OH 1 OHIO UNITED METHODIST CHURCH
104 Church Street off NY 8; ca. 1847

Most of the Town of Ohio is part of the Forest Preserve, but the tiny hamlet of the same name lies on the southwestern fringe of the park amid an area that for much of the 19th and 20th centuries was used for cultivating potatoes and grazing. As at Hoffmeister, the church has long been a major landmark, even though it is of even smaller dimensions. Some of its elements were likely added at a later date.

GRANT
Town of Russia, Herkimer County

GR 1 GRANT HOTEL
121 Stormy Hills Road, west of intersection of CRs 84 and 90; before 1865, additions and alterations 1889

Some two miles to the west along what was West Canada Creek and has been transformed as Hinckley Reservoir is the small resort community of Grant. Originally called Booth's Hotel, this establishment (and the hamlet) was renamed following Lincoln's assassination. Operating until around 2006, it is a rare surviving example of an early Adirondack hostelry.

ATWELL
Town of Ohio, Herkimer County

AT 1 STATE HOUSE
2831 North Lake Road; 1882

North Lake was created in 1857 as a reservoir to ensure consistently adequate water levels for the Erie and Black River canals. Significant changes in the reservoir's own levels, coupled with the dam's failure in 1869, led the state Canal Corporation to construct a superintendent's house onsite

by 1875. Apparently the edifice was poorly built, necessitating its replacement by the present structure. While vacant for some years, the house has experienced relatively little change.

PISECO LAKE
Town of Arietta, Hamilton County

PL 1 ARIETTA SCHOOL DISTRICT SCHOOL NO. 2
193 Higgins Bay Road, off NY 8; 1906

This modest school was built for children of those serving the growing number of camps on Piseco Lake. Erected on a new site to replace an 1850 school, the building's design is more decorous than the norm, with a bracketed hood over the entry and a bell tower atop its pyramidal roof.

PL 2 BONNIE BRAE HOTEL
176 Higgins Bay Road, off NY 8; mid- to late 19th century

Configured much like Gray Rocks [HF 6] and the Grant Hotel [GR 1], this once common example of a simple Adirondack hostelry was likewise built in stages. The earliest section was probably constructed in the 1820s as a house for Eli Rudes, who opened it to sportsmen. Between around 1857 and 1890 it was operated as an inn by son Daniel Rudes, and continued to function in that capacity in the hands of others well into the 20th century.

PL 3 IRONDEQUOIT INN
471 Old Piseco Road; 1850s; additions 1892, 1914

What is now an unusually low-key resort began in 1892 as the Irondequoit Club Inn under the auspices of C. Albert Doubleday of Montclair, New Jersey. He purchased the land, which contained a two-story 1850s farmhouse, from the Adirondack Timber & Mineral Company. In preparing for his venture, Doubleday had an annex built and an existing building moved to the site to serve as a kitchen. A second story was added to the kitchen in 1914. Otherwise the complex has experienced little modification.

PL 4 OXBOW INN
1803 NY 8; mid-19th century and later
This classic roadside establishment began as a residence in the mid-19th century. Soon it was operating as a boarding-house run by the Henry Rogers family and catering to sportsmen. The western end is the original portion; the lower, two-level segment to the east was probably added in the late 19th century. The building has undergone many 20th-century alterations as a popular restaurant and bar.

LAKE PLEASANT
and SPECULATOR
Town of Lake Pleasant, Hamilton County

Though having served as the county seat since 1837, the hamlet of Lake Pleasant has little in the way of a concentrated center. The cluster of county buildings stands more or less in isolation. No vestiges remain of the hotels that once were situated at this western end of the lake; however, a number of the early lakefront cottages are nearby on South Shore Road. The contiguous village of Speculator has always been

an unpretentious resort, its lakeshore lined with generally modest seasonal houses. The village has no major attractions for tourists today, only places supporting the needs of seasonal residents. The lake itself is best seen approaching from the south along NY 8 and 30.

SP 1 MOUNTAIN VIEW HOUSE
2993 NY 8; 1880 and later
Like the Oxbow Inn [PL 4] the Mountain View House is another outgrowth of the area's popularity among sportsmen. Begun by Peter Weaver in 1880, it was gradually expanded to include more accommodations, a bar, general store, and later a filling station. Little altered for more than a century, the building remains in the family, though it is no longer used for commercial purposes.

SP 2 TAMARACK CLUB
2369 NY 8 at Tamarack Road; ca. 1938
Malcolm Atterbury, son of a president of the Pennsylvania Railroad, and his wife, the former Ellen Ayres Hardies of Amsterdam, New York, developed a complex for evening entertainment. The Tamarack Playhouse offered nine plays per season and movies during three weekdays, while the club provided dancing, meals, and other refreshments. The Atterburys booked a high level of talent from urban centers. Among those who performed there were a young Kirk Douglas and Karl Malden. After World War II, the property was sold; the club continuing in its entertainment capacities, the playhouse as a movie theater. The latter burned in 1956; the former continued for some years but is now vacant.

SP 3 HAMILTON COUNTY GOVERNMENT CENTER

NY 8 and South Shore Road; Courthouse, 1928–29, Walter Brown van Dresser, architect (Gloversville, N.Y.); Jail, begun 1847, James Moffit, mason; addition 1938–40, J. Russell White, architect (Albany); later additions

Replacing the original facility of 1843, the courthouse exudes a commanding presence, despite its relatively modest dimensions, with a giant portico, cupola, and other motifs of the Colonial Revival mode then in its height of popularity for public buildings. The former jail, at the southern end of the range, is a rare surviving example of its type from the antebellum period. When a local builder failed to meet his contract, mason James Moffit, who had come from Schenectady, was hired to execute the project. That building was expanded with a near-duplicative addition some ninety years later.

SP 4 DERLOCH, JOHN L. HILL HOUSE

203 South Shore Road, ca. 1891–92; alterations and additions ca. early 1920s

A prominent Brooklyn attorney, Hill was among the first to establish a summer residence on the lake. The original design was a fanciful Victorian concoction, with a two-tier porch wrapping around two sides of a three-story mass. In 1918 the property was acquired by David W. Chalmers, and it was probably he who raised the roof and colonialized the house inside and out. Set on a gently sloping site with a broad lawn extending to the lake, Derloch boasts a spectacular view, though its open landscape is more typical of the Hudson River Valley than the Adirondacks. The late 19th-century barn and stable complex remains intact across the road. Above lies a reservoir built to supply fresh water.

SP 5 BEARHURST, HERMAN MEYROWITZ HOUSE

116 South Shore Road; 1894–95

A spirited assemblage of log and shingle sheathing, punctuated by stonework, this summer house is a reminder that many rustic retreats built on Adirondack lakeshores at the turn of the 20th century were accommodating and costly but far from the grand camps that have become emblems of the region. It is now operated as Bearhurst Lakeside Cottages.

SP 6 CAMP TEKOA
117 Page Street; 1934 and later

The original portion of the complex was built as Civilian Conservation Corps (CCC) Camp S-90 for Company 1028. The only one of its kind left in the state and probably one of the few to remain so intact anywhere in the country, it survived after its closure in 1942 by being turned over to the Cornell Cooperative Extension associations in Fulton, Montgomery, Oneida, and Warren counties for a 4-H camp. A number of additional buildings were erected thereafter. That operation closed in 2004, but the compound has been sensitively rehabilitated as a camp for children with special needs and their families.

SP 7 LAKE PLEASANT TOWN HALL
2885 NY 8; 1894

Most Adirondack town halls are simple affairs, and this is a good example of one from the late 19th century. It served as the town library between 1937 and 2003 and now is the town museum.

SP 8 MELODY LODGE
Old Indian Lake Road, off NY 30; 1912 and later

Standing on Page Hill north of the village center, this building started as a music school for girls under the auspices of Marie Van Hoose. It soon was converted to a summer house and in 1937 was purchased by Frances and Hamilton Chequer of Speculator for a restaurant and lodging. It continues in its former capacity.

SP 9 ZIESER'S RESTAURANT AND ROOMS
2967 NY 30, early 20th century and later

Built as an annex to the Sturges House (1858) located across the road, it has been transformed by a number of mid-20th-century alterations and is a classic highway eating establishment of that period.

SP 10 GRAHAM'S HOTEL
2871 NY 30; 1923; later moved to present location

Now Pleasant Point Country Inn, this is a vintage early 20th-century hostelry of modest proportions that, in its basic form and character, is little different from predecessors from the second half of the 19th century, such as those at Hoffmeister [HF 6], Grant [GR1], and Piseco Lake [PL 1]. The building was originally located on a side street across NY 30.

WELLS
Town of Wells, Hamilton County

WS 1 GRIFFIN HUNTING CAMP
NY 8, 2.8 miles east of NY 30; 1883

Northeast of Wells, this former boardinghouse was built for Morgan & Company amid the boom of the industrial community of Griffin, which held one of the largest tanning operations in the Adirondacks. Six years after its construction Henry J. Girard purchased the building and converted it to a hotel. However, the tannery closed around

1891, and most of the boomtown that had grown up with it lay vacant. Soon materials were taken from many of the buildings for new construction in Wells hamlet. Apparently Girard's Hotel remained in business for a while and was later purchased for a gun club. The building is not only an unusual survivor, it is the most intact remnant of its community and is also one of the few Adirondack hunting camps of any vintage that can be readily seen from the road.

WS 2 WELLS BAPTIST CHURCH
1443 NY 30; 1845

Much of the 19th-century residential fabric of this hamlet remains, as does this key landmark, the earliest extant church in Hamilton County. Not long after completing the edifice, the congregation foundered, and counterparts in Saratoga Springs and Glens Falls had to come to its financial assistance. The church has been inactive since 1949, but, like many such places in the Adirondacks, the building has been kept as an important embodiment of community. Long owned by the Hamilton County Historical Society, it was purchased in 2012 by a couple who have sensitively rehabilitated it as a community center.

WS 3 SUSPENSION BRIDGE
Northville–Lake Placid Trail, over west branch of Sacandaga River, .2 mile south of end of North Creek Road, 9 miles west of NY 38, via Algonquin Road; 1962

Well known to long-distance hikers,

this steel pier and cable, double-span pedestrian suspension bridge is an engaging latter-day example of what was once a relatively common type. The iron suspension bridge at Keeseville is the most spectacular surviving example in the Adirondacks [KS 1b, Section 7]. A splendid wooden one could be found in Wanakena [WN 1, Section 9] until a flood destroyed it in 2014; however, it has since been rebuilt.

WS 4 SACANDAGA RIVER SCULPTURE PARK
1293 NY 30; late 19th and early 20th centuries; converted to studio and park 1987 and later

The one contemporary art park within the Blue Line, this complex has a storied past as an industrial plant. Three tanneries occupied the site, beginning in the mid-19th century. After the plant had lain vacant for some years it was purchased and adapted as a veneer works under the auspices of the Schults Manufacturing Company in 1899. After several iterations it was partly destroyed by fire in 1917, only to be developed anew by Charles B. Hanley as the Adirondack Lumber Company. That business lasted over sixty years. Then in 1987 John Van Alstine, an internationally known sculptor, purchased the property and modified the remaining buildings as his home, studio, galleries, and display grounds for his large-scale work. The epic dimensions and rugged character of Van Alstine's creations afford a fitting complement to the property's unusually long history as an industrial site.

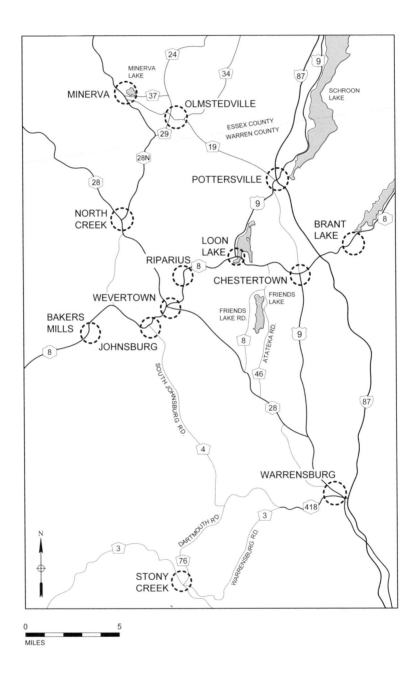

MINERVA
MINERVA LAKE
24
34
9
87
SCHROON LAKE
37
OLMSTEDVILLE
ESSEX COUNTY
WARREN COUNTY
29
19
28N
POTTERSVILLE
28
9
NORTH CREEK
BRANT LAKE
8
LOON LAKE
RIPARIUS
8
CHESTERTOWN
WEVERTOWN
FRIENDS LAKE
FRIENDS LAKE RD.
BAKERS MILLS
JOHNSBURG
8
9
8
ATATEKA RD.
SOUTH JOHNSBURG RD.
46
28
87
4
WARRENSBURG
418
3
DARTMOUTH RD.
WARRENSBURG RD.
N
3
76
STONY CREEK

0   5
MILES

110

4
UPPER HUDSON RIVER

PERMANENT SETTLEMENT CAME TO MOST OF THE COMMUNITIES along portions of the upper Hudson and lower Schroon rivers between the 1780s and 1810s; many who settled there were given land grants in recompense for service in the Revolutionary War or War of 1812. Besides farming, lumbering became a major economic base during the first half of the 19th century, and tanning gave development a significant boost thereafter. Functionally, then, these communities formed a network that was one of the principal suppliers of forest-based products to the state's manufacturing centers. Warrensburg and Chestertown also benefited from locations along what had been the principal route between Albany and Montreal since the turn of the 19th century.

Tannery and other plants along Schroon River, Warrensburg. (mid-19th-century engraving)

SITUATED THREE MILES EAST OF WHERE THE TWO RIVERS INTERSECT, Warrensburg (Warrensburgh until 1894) was by far the most important locus of industry. Settlement began there as early as the 1780s, and the town was formed in 1813. Capitalizing on a seventy-foot drop in the Schroon River, several mills were erected before 1820. Over the next four decades the economy began to diversify. A sizable tannery was established in 1830 and later expanded, especially after its purchase by B. P. Burhans & Sons in 1860. Albert C. Emerson started his lumber company in 1855, which grew to be the area's principal supplier. Wagon and sleigh makers, cabinet shops, and a sash-and-blind factory were among the other businesses operating by 1860. With them came an influx of Irish and Canadian immigrants. Access to markets was boosted by construction of a nine-mile plank road to Lake George in 1847–48.

Additional large enterprises emerged after the Civil War, starting with the Warrensburgh Woolen Mill in 1873, which, after an 1891 reorganization, operated until 1950. The Empire Shirt Factory began production in 1879, with one of Albert Emerson's sons, Louis, as co-owner, but it was soon acquired by Louis's brother James. The expanding plant went through two more purchases, continuing to operate into the early 1970s. James Emerson was also one of four men to form the Schroon River Pulp Company in 1892. Situated two miles west of the hamlet, it differed from other local plants in having a large masonry structure, which operated into the late 1970s, when it had to be abandoned after extensive flooding. While these substantial complexes were long-lived, Warrensburg had lost a number of other industries earlier in the 20th century.

Main Street, Warrensburg, showing at left Colonial Arms hotel, 1880s, 1890s, 20th century, demolished 1994; Floyd Bennett Memorial, 1929–31, at right. (1950s postcard)

Extending north from the Schroon River on higher ground, downtown Warrensburg boasted a number of sizable commercial blocks by 1900. It also harbored several hotels catering to growing numbers of tourists. Most notable among them was the Adirondack Hotel, which began as a tavern in 1825, but was rebuilt and expanded several times during the 1880s and 1890s. Remade again as the Colonial Arms following its purchase by Albert L. Emerson (James's son) in 1939, it remained a community landmark until 1994, when it was demolished for a chain store. Areas outside the hamlet began to be developed for children's camps in the 1920s and for dude ranches by the end of the next decade.

Although the origins of Chestertown, some ten miles to the north, were similar to those of Warrensburg, the hamlet never became a major industrial center. Robertson, Faxon & Company's tannery operated there from 1849 to 1898, and a marble works started in 1872, but much of the land between the two settlements

112

Chester House, Chestertown, ca. 1810, ca. 1850s, and later, demolished 1955. (early 20th-century postcard)

was used for agricultural purposes once it had been logged. During the mid-19th century Chestertown also began to attract visitors. The Chester House was built around 1810 and greatly enlarged some four decades later as a three-story edifice with two tiers of porches. The Rising House opened around 1881 [CH 8]. Four miles to the northeast at the head of Brant Lake, tourism started to supplement small tanneries in the late 19th century, with a number of visitors returning to build lakeside cottages. But the area's growth as a resort was centered two miles west of Chestertown at Friends and Loon lakes. The former spawned at least six hotels, all of them relatively small, between 1888 and 1900, while the latter became home to the Loon Lake Colony in the 1920s [FL 2, FL 5]. Access to all these places was greatly facilitated by Thomas C. Durant's Adirondack Railway, which reached the Hudson River less than two miles west of Loon Lake in 1870. The station, called Riverside and now known as Riparius, was a point of embarkation, from which stages ran not just east toward Chestertown and Brant Lake, but also to Schroon Lake [Section 5] via Pottersville to the northeast and to Johnsburg and Wevertown to the west. The railroad was also the likely catalyst for the formation of a Methodist camp meeting directly across the river from the depot in 1873 [RI 1].

Beyond the Hudson Valley, in southern Essex County, the area around the small hamlets of Olmstedville and Minerva began much like Chestertown. Extensive lumbering occurred there during the 19th century, but once land was cleared, farming followed, much of it on a subsistence level.

Farther up the Hudson, little permanent settlement occurred until the mid-19th century. North Creek was essentially a lumber camp until Milton Sawyer built a tannery there in 1852. North Creek also was the unintended terminus of Durant's railroad twenty years later and thus became a major staging ground for sportsmen

113

An Adirondack Stage, *location unknown. (early 20th-century photograph)*

and tourists going to Indian, Blue Mountain, and even Long lakes. The railroad further encouraged local enterprises with substantial saw- and woodworking mills established after its arrival. In 1878 Henry Hudson Barton came to North Creek in search of garnet for making abrasives. At neighboring Gore Mountain, he found what was later determined to be the largest deposit and highest quality of garnet in the United States. After thorough exploration, he bought much of the mountain in 1887. H. H. Barton & Sons became not only a major mining operation, but the leading manufacturer of abrasive paper used for woodworking, metalworking, and glass grinding. A production mill was built onsite in 1924, replacing the previous one in Philadelphia. Four years later Barton acquired the nearby North River Garnet Company, a competitor since 1893, and also Ruby Mountain, where Barton's new operation (replacing the original one) opened in 1983.

If Gore Mountain was a font of mineral wealth, it also became a magnet for winter vacations. Inspired by the success of the 1932 Winter Olympics in Lake Placid [Section 9], the Gore Mountain Ski Club was formed, opening its first trail in March 1934. Within two years as many as 3,000 skiers would come for a weekend, a large number of them by train. The far more ambitious Ski Center was developed in the early 1960s under the auspices of the state conservation department.

To the south, the hamlets of Wevertown and Johnsburg evolved much like Olmstedville and Minerva. After extensive timber cutting, the land developed mostly as modest farms. Wevertown supported a tannery between 1833 and 1885, a major impetus for its development, and a sawmill that became an important lumber supplier for the area in the 20th century [WV 1]. Johnsburg did not have industries of lasting import, but was home to a tourist hotel from the late 19th to the mid-20th centuries [JH 1]. West of Warrensburg, settlement was pioneered by John Thurman, who began to acquire over 25,000 acres in 1788. Along the Hudson, he erected a distillery, a woolen mill (soon converted to a cotton mill), and a calico-printing

114

Alpine ski lift, North Creek. (1930s postcard)

works during the mid-1790s, but none of these ventures was long-lived. Thurman succeeded in attracting people to the area, but otherwise he joined others whose vision of building an empire in the Adirondacks soon evaporated. West of Thurman's enterprises lies Stony Creek, initially settled in 1795 and sparsely occupied, except for lumbering operations, during its first half century. The situation changed in 1852 when John Bowman came from Vermont to build a tannery and a sawmill, purchasing some 6,000 acres to supply them. A broom factory was also established, but none of these businesses lasted into the 20th century. Like many other hamlets in the area, Stony Creek retained its rural character and had little besides modest farming operations.

* * * * *

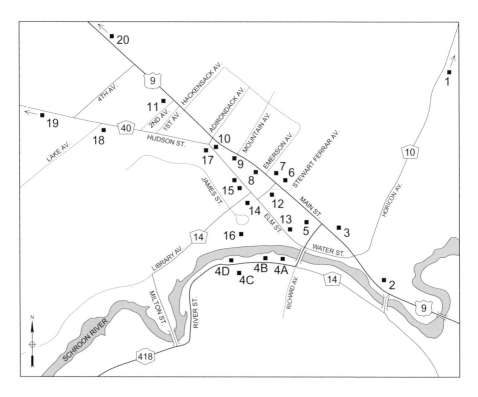

WARRENSBURG

Town of Warrensburg, Warren County

With a population of just over 3,000 in 2010 the hamlet of Warrensburg and surrounding area ranks among the largest in the Adirondacks, and while it no longer harbors any large-scale businesses, it lies within easy commuting distance of employment centers farther south in Warren and Saratoga counties. By the mid-20th century Warrensburg also emerged as a major gateway to the central Adirondacks—Minerva, Newcomb, Long Lake, Indian Lake, and Blue Mountain Lake among the destinations. The hamlet possesses an architectural richness commensurate with its position as an industrial hub during the 19th and early 20th centuries. Yet recent decades have not been kind to much of that legacy. The traditional commercial center on Main Street has for the most part been lost, and many of the commodious houses that lined that street have gone as well. In their place lies an assemblage of late 20th-century commercial buildings that form a conspicuously discordant tone to what was once an elegant, tree-lined thoroughfare. On the other side of and paralleling the Schroon, River Street, the principal path along which industrial development occurred in the late 19th century, has likewise lost some key components, and the fate of others is tenuous.

WA 1 WARREN COUNTY HOME AND WARREN COUNTY FAIRGROUNDS
Horicon Avenue (CR 10) and Schroon River Road; 1865 (stone building), Peter Buell, builder; additions 1879, 1883; barns and other agricultural buildings mostly early 20th century

Two hundred acres were purchased for

the Warren County Home in 1826, not long after it became a county responsibility in New York State to house the poor. The facility was soon constructed on fertile lands along the Schroon River east of the hamlet. By 1860, however, it was considered inadequate, and $2,500 was appropriated to erect a stone building to house fifty-four people. Occupants worked the farm, which supplied many of their needs. With its focus long directed to the elderly, the home operated until 1981, when it was replaced by the Countryside Residence across the road. The residential buildings were sold and redeveloped as apartments; the county retained the barns and other outbuildings for its fairgrounds.

WA 2 JOHN MIXTER BLACKSMITH SHOP
3728 Main Street (US 9); ca. 1840; ca. 1892

An unusual survivor of its type, Mixter's commodious shop has had its upper story modified for residential use. It now serves the Warrensburg Chamber of Commerce.

WA 3 EPISCOPAL CHURCH OF THE HOLY CROSS
3764 Main Street (US 9); 1864–65, Rev. Robert Fulton Crary and Frederick O. Burhans, designers; Albert Allen, builder; rectory 1886; addition 1911

Rev. Crary, rector of St. James Church in Lake George [LG 6b, Section 1], who initiated Episcopal services locally in 1861 and was an advocate of developing churches

along Anglican lines, supplied sketches for Holy Cross. He was aided by Burhans, the son of and a partner with a wealthy parishioner. Built of local granite, the church is an accomplished rendition of the Gothic Revival mode as adapted for congregations of modest size.

WA 4 MILL DISTRICT

Though much has been lost in recent decades either through demolition or remodeling, some portions of the hamlet's industrial center remain. The only intact component of the **Empire Shirt Company factory (a)** is one section, long vacant, of a linear plant (1870 or later) that straddled the Schroon River and River Street (CR 418) west of Richards Avenue. (Another component of the plant, directly across River Street, has been extensively altered in recent years.) The former **gristmill (b)** at 100

River Street was built by Dudley Farlin in 1824 and sold the following year. The plant went through a series of modifications and owners, including Benjamin Burhans, operating until 1967. It was rehabilitated as a restaurant in 1976. Across River Street is the grain and feed plant built in 1917 for **T. J. Smith & Son (c)**, a rare example of its kind in the region. Vacant since around 2000, **Herrick's Variety Store (d)** at 134 River Street was initially built in 1893. With a number of additions and alterations, it is a reminder that many of the people who lived on the south side of the Schroon and worked in the plants patronized neighborhood merchants.

WA 5 THE ELMS, GRAY-BURHANS HOUSE
3785 Main Street (US 9); ca. 1840 and later

Built for Thomas S. Gray, this Greek Revival house was purchased by Benjamin Peck Burhans a decade or so later. Burhans came to Warrensburg in 1836, acquiring controlling interest in a large tannery, which he operated with Gray. In 1860 Burhans and his son, Frederick, took over the business, and it was at about that time he also acquired Gray's house, adding a tower and other Victorian embellishments. He erected an even more lavish masonry Italianate villa for Frederick nearby in 1865, which was demolished slightly less than a century later. The Elms was purchased by Philip and Ethel Roberts in 1949 and renamed the Colony House. They established a gift and craft shop on the premises and soon thereafter built an adjacent motel, catering to tourists who came to the Adirondacks by automobile.

WA 6 DANIEL HOWARD HOUSE
3822 Main Street; ca. 1865–66

Set far back from the street, this wood-frame Italianate villa was perhaps inspired by the grander one that was being, or had just been, built for Frederick Burhans. Similarly, too, this was a gift of physician Eliakin Howard to his son, Daniel, after the latter had graduated from Albany Medical College in 1865. The building served as home and office for Daniel and his physician partner, James Goodman. It is now the Seasons Bed & Breakfast.

WA 7 RICHARDS-EMERSON HOUSE
3826 Main Street; ca. 1830s and later

Relatively few houses so conspicuously manifest the accumulations of divergent building campaigns. Constructed for Samuel Richards as a temple-front Greek Revival house, it was purchased in 1855 by Albert C. Emerson, owner of a major lumber company and other businesses, when he married Abigail Woodward. Subsequently Emerson added a northern section with a bulky mansard-roof tower around the 1870s. After Emerson's death in 1888, son Louis remodeled the entry (having one of the pillars removed to gain an unobstructed view from newly installed plate-glass window) and added a second portico to the south face. In 2000–01 it was rejuvenated to serve as the Emerson House Bed & Breakfast.

WA 8 MILES THOMAS HOUSE
3847 Main Street; 1873

Arriving from the Town of Bolton in 1854, Thomas built up a major retail business in clothing and general merchandise. The house he commissioned attests to his success. While it has no tower or other such prominent feature, it is (and was) among the most embellished dwellings along Main Street. It was purchased by the town in 1978 and now serves as a senior citizens' center.

WA 9 EMERSON NATIONAL BANK
3853 Main Street; 1926–27

Founded in 1884 by Albert C. Emerson and his son, Louis, the community's leading bank was run by members of the family

until 1963. This classical brick building, the bank's first purpose-built quarters and one of the most impressive of its kind in the Adirondacks, physically related as much to Main Street's grand residential area as to the business center. It is now a branch of the Glens Falls National Bank.

WA 10 FLOYD BENNETT MEMORIAL PARK AND BANDSTAND
Main, Elm, and Hudson (CR 40) streets; 1929–31, Paul Gurney, architect (Chicago)

At the hamlet's major intersection, in the heart of what was once the commercial center, this structure was created for concerts and civic events—a project carried out by a local citizens group. It honors a native son who was raised on a subsistence farm. Bennett became a Navy airplane mechanic and later a pilot. He assisted Commander Richard E. Byrd in his 1925–26 Arctic expedition—the first flight to the North Pole. He died of pneumonia after a rescue expedition in 1928. Also a native son, Gurney moved to Chicago after attending Cornell University's School of Architecture. From 1934 to 1969 he served as chief architect for Montgomery Ward, designing retail outlets that became fixtures of many commercial centers nationwide.

WA 11 LEWIS BENJAMIN THOMSON HOUSE
3921 Main Street; 1908–09, W. K. Lawrence, architect (Glens Falls, N.Y.)

Born on a farm near Warrensburg, Thomson began his career buying and selling livestock, eventually becoming one of the largest cattle dealers in the area. He also became a successful real estate broker for farm property. In the early 1890s he joined Albert H. Thomas in establishing a major pulp and lumber business. His expansive house, a late iteration of the popularized Queen Anne mode with some Colonial Revival details, has been meticulously restored inside and out and operates as the Cornerstone Victorian Bed & Breakfast. Adjacent to the north at 3927 Main, the **John G. Hunt house** (before 1876) was rendered in a simpler version of Queen Anne through an extensive remodeling of 1888. The house also boasts a period stable. Across Main Street the grand **Bonnie Brae Villa** (1865, late 19th century) burned in 1980; however, its large **stable and barn complex** remain, albeit in derelict condition, toward the property's rear.

WA 12 FIRST PRESBYTERIAN CHURCH
2 Stewart Farrar Avenue; 1836; additions and alterations 1887–88

A simple Greek Revival church was expanded and thoroughly recast in a slightly Gothic vein that failed to overcome the bulky form of the original building.

WA 13 CARETAKER'S HOUSE
19 Elm Street; 1865

To complement Frederick O. Burhans's grand Italianate house, this modest dwelling was fashioned as a Gothic cottage in a manner popularized by Andrew Jackson Downing.

119

WA 14 RICHARDS LIBRARY

36 Elm Street at Library Street; 1900, A. W. Fuller, architect (Albany); matching rear addition 1911; gutted by fire 1914 and rebuilt 1915; new rear addition and interior alterations 2006–13, JMZ Architects (Glens Falls, N.Y.)

Sisters Mary Richards Kellogg and Clara Richards conceived and financed Warrensburg's library on property inherited from their grandfather, and it was probably they who selected a prominent Albany architect to prepare the plans. Fuller's design is a somewhat updated version of nationally known ones by Henry Hobson Richardson from the 1880s.

WA 15 ELM STREET HOUSES

Though not as large as their Main Street counterparts, many of the houses on the first block of Elm Street are noteworthy counterparts of a somewhat later vintage. The two at **42 and 44 Elm** are among the most interesting. The former was designed in a simplified version of the popular Queen Anne mode, with an imaginative use of decoration for its gable ends. The latter possesses the same basic form, but sports a rather lavish array of Colonial Revival motifs. Both date from around 1905. The former was the work of local builder Jim Hall; the latter probably also came from his hand.

WA 16 WARRENSBURG CENTRAL SCHOOL

1 James Street; 1941–43, J. Russell White, architect (Albany); addition 1963–64, Milton Lee Crandall, architect (Glens Falls, N.Y.), Charles T. Whitney and William Boulton Bird, associate architects (Saratoga Springs, N.Y.); later additions

Unlike many schools built in the Adirondacks during the drive for consolidation in the interwar decades, this sprawling facility is not situated on a main street, but on a cul-de-sac at what was then Warrensburg's western edge. The location allowed ample space for building and athletic fields alike in a community where land values were relatively high, and it also lay within walking distance of most neighborhoods—from those of the elite to the working class. White was well known for his schools in northern New York, including ones in Indian Lake, North Creek [NC 4], and Corinth [CO 2, Section 2].

WA 17 STEPHEN GRIFFING II HOUSE

2 Hudson Street (CR 40); early 19th century; main block ca. 1855; rear wing 1911; alterations 2014–15

Born in Thurman, Griffing purchased the Adirondack Hotel, which he operated from 1838 to 1846. He subsequently became a prominent lumberman and built

tanneries in Johnsburg (1877) and Wells (1880). He bought a relatively modest, one-and-one-half-story house across Main Street from the hotel and aggrandized it with a sizable, temple-front addition around 1855. The dwelling remained in the family until 1979 and later served as a restaurant. In 2014–15 it underwent extensive rehabilitation under new ownership and operates as Merrill Magee Inn.

WA 18 ASHE'S HOTEL
85 Hudson Street; 1836; ca. 1889

What began as a boardinghouse was purchased by Henry Ashe and his father James in 1888 and considerably enlarged to its present form. They re-christened the establishment the Agricultural Hotel owing to its proximity to Warren County Agricultural Society fairgrounds. Later Henry's son Maurice bestowed his family's name on the establishment. It remained under Ashe ownership until 1972.

WA 19 CAMP ECHO LAKE
Hudson Street and Fish Hatchery Road; 1925 and later

Founded in 1946 by Bill and Edith Medine and Archie and Bea Kaplan, educators from Brooklyn, this children's camp is actually an agglomeration of three complexes. The

Main Village opened in 1925 as Echo Lake Tavern (later Echo Lake Lodge), a campground for adults. It included an administration building that had been a farmhouse and eleven bunkhouses, to which the Medines added another thirty that they had purchased elsewhere the same year they acquired the camp. A **recreation hall** was added in 1955. The **Senior Village**, or **Lodge at Echo Lake**, was originally Indian Head Camp, which opened in 1926 as a family resort with housekeeping cottages and a recreation hall. It was incorporated as part of Camp Echo Lake in 1982 and is used by adults. **Alumni Village** was purchased by the Medines from the Noble family, who had run it as a resort with stables since the 1920s.

WA 20 TUMBLEHOME BOATSHOP
684 NY 28; 1950s, rehabilitation and addition 2012, Mike Rice of MacMillan Design & Construction, designers and builders (Chestertown, N.Y.)

This pair of buildings well illustrates the potential of rehabilitation to enhance the character of utilitarian structures while retaining virtually all of their original components. The two were built at about the same time by independent parties to house and repair heavy equipment. The one lying to the north now contains offices and the boat repair shop, while the other, with a spirited front addition, serves as the sales facility. The company specializes in antique boat restoration and in building new ones along vintage lines.

CHESTERTOWN
Town of Chester, Warren County

While it has lost the Chester House, long its principal hotel, most of Chestertown conveys a good sense of how a small hamlet developed during the 19th and early 20th centuries. Bypassed by the Northway, commercial enterprises along US 9 languished over the last several decades; however, recent efforts have been made to make the center attractive to vacationers.

up to thirty guests. A lodge was erected in 1948; it burned in 1982 and was quickly rebuilt. Other guest accommodations were improved during the 1950s and 1960s, with twenty-five cabins constructed on the south side of the basin that extends from the lake to the equestrian area. During the 1960s, nine "chalets" were built on the north side. To compete with the other thirty dude ranches in Warren County, by the late 1950s Ridin-Hy assumed more of a family orientation. A rodeo began in 1976, and cross-country skiing was added the following year as the camp was transforming into a year-round operation.

CH 1 RIDIN-HY RANCH RESORT
Burnt Hill Road, 2.5 miles north of CR 11, Warrensburg; 1940; most buildings post-1950
One of the few Adirondack dude ranches developed during the mid-20th century that is still in operation, Ridin-Hy affords a good sense of what such places were like at that time. Located on the site of a girls' summer camp (Camp Arcady in the Pines), the establishment was inaugurated by New Yorker Ed Carstens, the son of German immigrants, who had fallen in love with the Adirondacks on his first visit at age twelve. Situated on Lake Sherman, the ranch offers swimming and other water activities to supplement horseback riding. Initially there were twelve cabins housing

CH 2 CHESTERTOWN CENTRAL SCHOOL
6307 Main Street (US 9); 1933–34, Carl W. Clark, architect (Cortland, N.Y.)
Although most Adirondack consolidated schools of the interwar decades employed a Georgian-inspired vocabulary for their exteriors, this one loosely draws from Tudor precedent. It has been adapted to serve as the town hall and library, with little change to its original interior.

CH 3 CHESTER HIGH SCHOOL
6339 Main Street; 1913
Built when the town began offering instruction at the secondary level, this wood-frame building stands in sharp contrast to the large, more accommodating

central school of two decades later [CH 2]. Subsequently it housed a glove factory, store, and finally the town government before that function was moved to the recently vacated central school in the 1990s. It now serves as a restaurant and ice cream parlor.

CH 4 EPISCOPAL CHURCH OF THE GOOD SHEPHERD

6343 Main Street; 1883

A spirited interpretation of English Gothic sources, this building exemplifies the Episcopalian pursuit of effectively translating a masonry tradition into simpler, wood-frame construction that was affordable for small, nascent congregations.

CH 5 CHARLES FOWLER HOUSE

6347 Main Street; ca. 1837; later additions

A prosperous merchant, farmer, and large-scale landowner, Fowler came to Chestertown shortly before he commissioned this decorous Greek Revival house. In 1906 it was purchased by Harry Downs, proprietor of the nearby Chester House. The porches appear to have been added

around that time. The house remained in the Downs family until 1987; it is now the Chester Inn Bed & Breakfast.

CH 6 CAROL THEATER

102 Riverside Road; 1931, Ward Grover Shippey, architect (Glens Falls, N.Y.)

This reserved, Georgian-inspired mixed-use building—its theater supplemented by stores and apartments in the front section—was commissioned by local entrepreneur Walter Wertime, who some seven years earlier had commissioned Shippey to design the Tudorish (and now much altered) Wertime Building, which lies adjacent at 6353 Main Street.

CH 7 REMINGTON BLOCK

6369 Main Street; 1893

Chestertown's commercial buildings testify to the widespread use of wood rather than masonry construction for such work in many Adirondack communities through the 19th century. The fire that destroyed the dry goods store of W. H. & J. B. Remington Company did not curtail the owners from building anew with the same materials. It has recently been rehabilitated as the Bullhouse restaurant. Other wooden store buildings have survived at **6375 Main Street** and **25** and **23 Church Street**.

CH 8 RISING HOUSE HOTEL

6372 Main Street; probably mid-19th century, later additions and alterations

Chestertown's other hotel was built as a residence in the mid-19th century and was purchased in 1882 by Jonathan Rising, who expanded it into a hotel, with a two-tier porch defining its front. A third story and side porches were added somewhat later, as was a new dining room wing at the rear. The Rising House operated into the mid-20th century. In more recent years it has been stripped of its appendages and now contains apartments.

CH 9 UNITED METHODIST CHURCH
11 Church Street (CR 43); 1867, addition and rectory 1890–92
Replacing a church erected in 1835, this building has its worship space on the second floor, a configuration favored by many Methodists during much of the 19th century. When the nearby Presbyterian church closed in 1918, that congregation joined the Methodists to form what became the Community Church in 1946.

CH 10 ST. JOHN THE BAPTIST CATHOLIC CHURCH
63 Riverside Street at Church Street; 1936–37, Gander, Gander & Gander, architects (Albany)
The Catholic congregation first purchased the Methodists' former building, which soon burned, was rebuilt, and then was replaced by a new edifice in 1886. The present masonry structure is a subdued and consciously modern interpretation of English Gothic sources. Seasonal residents in the area helped fund the project.

CH 11 THURSTON-HASKELL HOUSE
19 Landon Hill Road (CR 68); early 19th century, later additions
Reputedly built as a stagecoach stop

on the road to Montreal, the original portion of this building was operated by Hobby Mead. Two owners later, Milton and Thankful Sawyer enlarged the premises during their tenure from 1853 to 1865, and it was probably at this time that the building assumed something approximating its current appearance. After the Civil War, it became a residence for the Thurston and Haskell families.

BRANT LAKE
Town of Horicon, Warren County

Like Speculator [Section 3], Brant Lake is not the location of major tourist attractions, but rather a seasonal place defined by lakeside residences and children's camps. Owing to its location and proximity to the Northway, Brant Lake is also a place of more year-round habitation. Intimate in scale and informal in character, the area retains many of the attributes that attracted people in the summers a century ago.

BR 1 CHURCHES
Standing side by side at the lake's western end, **St. Paul's Episcopal Church (a)** (1890) and **St. Teresa of Avila Catholic Church (b)** (early 1920s) at 6596 and 6606 NY 8, respectively, are good examples of houses of worship built for seasonal communities at the turn of the 20th century. St. Paul's may have been based on a design by Boston architect H. M. Stephenson illustrated in George Shinn's *Church Architecture* (1882).

BR 2 HEINTZELMAN LIBRARY
6615 NY 8; 1907
This tiny facility was named in honor of longtime summer resident Emily Heintzelman, who died soon after she gave 150 books to the forming institution. Trustees of her estate subsequently donated the land. Constructed of cobblestones, with much of the structure extending over the lake, the building embodies the kind of

idiosyncrasies that render seasonal architecture distinctive and memorable. After a quarter century it became the library for the Town of Horicon. Since 2001 it has served as a repository of historical materials.

BR 3 STUART (?) HEINTZELMAN HOUSE
End of Brant Estates Road, off NY 8; ca. 1900s

This large stone-and-shingle house on Brant Lake was probably built for Stuart Heintzelman, son of Emily and Civil War veteran General Samuel P. Heintzelman. Stuart was also an Army officer, who devoted much of his career to military instruction and became a major general in 1931. The house is a telling example of astylar design of a kind popular during the Arts and Crafts Movement, here with two stories sheltered under an immense gable roof and resting on a rustic stone ground-story base.

BR 4 SUNSET MOUNTAIN LODGE
7294 NY 8; 1873; additions 1892, 1924

The first hostelry on the lake, Sunset Mountain Lodge was preceded by an elementary log structure named Trout Pa-

vilion that was built for Benjamin Hayes in 1860. It was constructed anew as the wood-frame Brant Lake Club thirteen years later. Additions followed in 1892 (Bass Pavilion on Brant Lake) and in 1924. During its long life, the hotel was instrumental in developing the lake as a resort.

FRIENDS LAKE and LOON LAKE
Town of Chester, Warren County

FL 1 HOUSE
Friends Lake (CR 8) and Atateka (CR 48) roads; ca. mid-19th century

Little is known about this small Greek Revival house aside from its unorthodox configuration, with a story-and-a-half portico (without a central column) fronting a two-story central section and one-story wings and rear ell.

FL 2 CHESTERTOWN FARM
935 Friends Lake Road; ca. 1860s; additions ca. early 1890s

The mostly wooded rolling terrain around Friends Lake hardly suggests that it was once the home to half a dozen hotels, except for what is now Chestertown Farm. Constructed as a farmhouse during the late 1860s or early 1870s, it was built for Timothy Murphy, who came from Ireland and eventually settled in Chestertown, working in the tannery. With his brother Eugene, he bought a 100-acre tract for a farm, which grew to more than twice

that size by 1882. A decade or so later the dwelling was expanded and opened as the Lake View House, which operated as a hotel until the late 1930s. Timothy Murphy's sons were instrumental in furthering the area's reputation as a resort. One built the Loon Lake House; another, the Atateka House; and a third the Friends Lake Inn, which still stands, much altered, at 963 Friends Lake Road.

FL 3 JOHN CHANDLER HOUSE
5408 US 9 and SR 8; ca. 1840s

This commodious, if simple, Greek Revival farmhouse sits at the southeastern edge of Loon Lake. In 1901 it was bought by Alfred Vetter, who ran it as Vetter's Villa, a boardinghouse, presumably for seasonal visitors. As part of the Loon Lake RV Park, it continues to serve a transient constituency.

FL 4 PRIORY RETREAT HOUSE
End of Priory Road, off Pine Notch Road, off US 9 and NY 8, Loon Lake; 1977–79

This unusual assemblage, filled with ad-hocisms inside and out, was designed as a monastery, the Priory of St. Benedict, by an unidentified architecture student from Rensselaer Polytechnic Institute, in Troy, and built with the help of volunteers on the site of a farm. Falling on hard times, the facility was converted in 1986 to a retreat for people of all faiths.

FL 5 ALP HORN MOTEL
5064 NY 8, Loon Lake; ca. early 1920s and later

This establishment began as the Loon Lake Inn, which was probably built in the early 1920s for Lester Pettigrew, a former New York City policeman, and his wife, who operated the place until after World War II. Advertisements boasted a billiard parlor and dance hall, as well as a tennis court. By 1930, there were also cottages, and four years later it was called the Loon Lake Colony. The log building that is now the motel's centerpiece was likely a key component of that development. Some of the cabins were remade as the current motel in the 1960s; other components were demolished.

RIPARIUS
Towns of Johnsburg and Chester, Warren County

RI 1 RIVERSIDE CAMP MEETING
End of Hudson River Drive, off NY 8; late 19th and early 20th centuries

The most concentrated settlement in the tiny hamlet of Riparius is the cluster of buildings initially developed under the auspices of the Riverside Camp Meeting Association. That group was founded in 1873, three years after the railroad's arrival, by Methodists from the Town of Johnsburg. Initially a tent camp, the compound grew into a circle of cottages around a tabernacle during the late 19th and early 20th centuries—a pattern characteristic to Methodist camp meetings. In 1912 it was rechristened the Riverside Grove Association and functioned as a church camp for young people—a program that lasted over half a century. Later it assumed its original role as a faith-based summer colony. While many of the cottages have been altered, the basic form and character of the ensemble make it a good example of its type.

RI 2 RIPARIUS BRIDGE
NY 8 at Hudson River; 2003

A wooden suspension bridge (Center Bridge) was constructed in 1872 where what later became NY 8 crosses the Hudson, enabling Riparius to serve as a staging ground to resorts and other communities. Following county purchase in 1919, the bridge was replaced by one with steel camelback trusses, which remained in use into the early 21st century. Sentiment for that structure led the state Department of Transportation to erect a new bridge in 2003 that is somewhat reminiscent of its forebear in form if not in dramatic effect.

RI 3 DELAWARE & HUDSON RAILWAY STATION
CR 1, off NY 8; 1913–14

On the Hudson's west side, this station replaced that erected by the Adirondack Railway Company in 1872. Before construction began the old station was moved not far to the south and subsequently was modified to serve as a **freight building**. It is now an artist's studio. The station closed in 1956. A campaign to restore the building was launched in 1995; four years later it reopened for the Upper Hudson River Railroad, which now carries tourists between Saratoga Springs and North Creek.

RI 4 RIVERSIDE DISTRIBUTION COMPANY
CR 1 south of NY 8; 1916

The railroad attracted brewer D. G. Yuengling, who owned a camp at Brant Lake, to Riparius, where he erected one of his many breweries in 1892. The plant was sold only five years later, and in 1902 became the Riverside Distributing Company, purveying beer, ale, soda, and spring water. After a fire destroyed the complex, it was rebuilt in concrete. Quarters for offices and sale took a traditional mercantile form, but with poured concrete walls rather than of wood. The distribution building is of a more advanced design, with a reinforced concrete frame and terra cotta infill panels—an unusual example of this kind of construction in the Adirondacks. Headed by W. J. and J. F. McCarthy and Joseph Martin, the operation continued well into the mid-20th century.

RI 5 AUTOMOBILE GARAGE
4646 NY 8; ca. mid- to late 1920s

Riparius's importance as a transportation hub expanded after World War I when improvements were made to NY 8, which eventually became the primary southern trans-Adirondack route for motor vehicles. This early garage no doubt catered to travelers, but also may have provided cars for vacationers who arrived in the hamlet by train. In recent decades it has housed an antiques store, but now lies vacant.

POTTERSVILLE

Town of Chester, Warren County

PV 1 WELLS HOUSE HOTEL
US 9 and Olmstedville Road (CR 19); 1898

Pottersville's primary role as a way station for tourists and others headed for Schroon Lake or points north is manifested in this establishment. The original hotel was built around 1845 for Joseph Hotchkiss and Joshua Collar as a stage stop. It was enlarged by Marcus Downs, proprietor from 1860 to 1869. Downs also rebuilt it in 1898 after the building was destroyed by fire. Judging from appearances the new hostelry was probably patterned after its mid-19th-century predecessor. It was rehabilitated in 2003–05, but now lies vacant—a rare survivor of its kind.

PV 2 THE "N" ON MOUNTAINSPRING LAKE
105 Nicholsville Road, off US 9; 1898 and later

Troy, New York, surgeon Calvin E. Nichols built the Shingle Style house that is the focal point of this complex as a summer residence on a 550-acre tract, complete with its own lake. During the 1920s the carriagehouse was converted for guests. The economic constraints of the following decade spurred the modification of other outbuildings for rent, with the main house assuming some of the functions of a commercial lodge as well as a family residence. The enclave evolved into a modest cabin colony that is still run by descendants and has changed little for over seven decades.

OLMSTEDVILLE

Town of Minerva, Essex County

OL 1 FIRST METHODIST CHURCH
Olmstedville Road (CR 29), east of Church Road; ca. 1893–94

A crossroads hamlet, Olmstedville retains much of its character as a 19th-century rural center. The Methodist church replaced an 1848 edifice that burned. In its form the building is more suggestive of an Episcopal house of worship than the boxy mass characteristic to numerous Methodist churches of the 19th century. Closed in 1975, it now serves as the Minerva Historical Society.

OL 2 MCGUIRE-SULLIVAN STORE AND HOUSE
Irishtown Road (CR 24) and Main Street (CR 29); ca. 1850s and later

Grain merchant Thomas McGuire's store boasted a decorous Greek Revival façade that has since been modified. The attached dwelling is set back from the road and was likely added around the 1870s. Across Main

Street lies a substantially altered **general store** that was probably built on speculation around the 1870s–1880s by local carpenter Henry Dornburgh. It was occupied by a succession of merchants before purchase by Frederick T. Johnson in 1939. He ran his business there for at least thirty years.

OL 3 MINERVA CENTRAL SCHOOL
1466 Main Street (CR 29); 1936, Carl W. Clark, architect (Cortland, N.Y.); addition 1960, W. Parker Dodge Associates, architects and engineers (Rensselaer, N.Y.); small rear addition 1966, Maurice J. Finnegan, Jr., architect (Syracuse, N.Y.); major addition and remodeling 1992, Richard Jones, architect (Queensbury, N.Y.)

A rare instance where Art Deco motifs were used on an Adirondack school, the building was sensitively rehabilitated in 1992, when a complementary addition, including a new main entrance, was constructed to the west.

OL 4 IRISHTOWN

A mile and a half north of Olmstedville, Irishtown is not a hamlet so much as a remnant of mid-19th-century agricultural settlement and a small iron mining operation. Just west of CR 24 on CR 37 lies the **Irishtown School** of 1860, which replaced a log structure of some twenty years previous. Last occupied in the 1930s, it was relegated to serve as a storage facility until it was donated to the Minerva Historical Society around 1997 and subsequently restored. Adjacent is **St. Mary's Church**, begun in 1848—probably the first Roman Catholic church to be initiated within the Blue Line. It was, however, rarely used after the building of St. Joseph's Catholic Church

at Olmstedville in 1871. Nearby to the north at 401 CR 24 is a good surviving example of a mid-19th-century **farmhouse**, enveloped by a somewhat later porch.

MINERVA
Town of Minerva, Essex County

MN 1 REXFORD-DORNBURGH HOUSE
151 Morse Memorial Highway (CR 30); ca. 1849, Jordan Rexford, builder; later additions

This unusually complete mid-19th-century farmstead was constructed for and by builder Jordan Rexford and sold to carpenter Henry Dornburgh in 1854. The one-and-one-half-story Greek Revival house, with a porch wrapping around two sides, fronts a tavern wing, added later by Thomas Murphy. The woodshed and barns are also attached, following a traditional practice found among many New England farmsteads. Nearby lie a blacksmith shop and later garage.

MN 2 MORNINGSIDE CAMPS AND COTTAGES
67 Longs Hill Road (CR 37); ca. 1838 and later

Absolom P. Morse, lumberman, farmer, and first supervisor of the town, had his house constructed around 1838 at what was once known as Morse's Corners. At the turn of the 20th century, son Orson P. Morse, who served as a member of Verplanck Colvin's Adirondack survey party, added a long rear extension in two stages,

effectively doubling the house's size, and also added a porch wrapping around two sides. The dimensions of the building and the extent of its porch suggest that it may have served as a boardinghouse for vacationers as well as a family residence. The place was named Morningside following its purchase by Baptist minister Frank La-Bar and his wife in 1914. During the Depression, their son, Frank Jr., built ten log rental cabins along newly created Minerva Lake at the property's northern end. Additional units were constructed later. The enterprise remains in the family.

MN 3 MINERVA BAPTIST CHURCH
NY 28N and Morse Memorial Highway (CR 30); 1848, Jordan Rexford, builder; additions 1884, 1932

As was the case in many other rural areas, the church did not occupy its own building until well after it was formed—in this instance the waiting period lasted over four decades. A bell tower was added in 1884, but the major change came in 1932 when a new sanctuary was erected at right

angles to the old one, which was, in turn, converted to a Sunday school and social room. The arrangement allowed both spaces to be joined for special occasions, while giving the ensemble an idiosyncratic, accretive appearance.

NORTH CREEK
Town of Johnsburg, Warren County

In recent years North Creek has capitalized on its rich architectural heritage as a railhead, its recreational opportunities, and its strategic setting along a primary path to the central Adirondacks to develop a lively tourist trade extending over much of the year. A bypass for NY 28 was constructed in the late 1960s, sparing the community's core from the pressures of highway-oriented development. Much of the hamlet's 19th- and 20th-century fabric remains and has become increasingly appreciated.

NC 1 CONRAD MARSHOCK HOUSE
330 Byrnes Road, 1.5 miles west of NY 28N; ca. 1896

The circumstances contributing to this unorthodox house have yet to be fully documented. The exterior possesses many attributes common to sizable wood-frame houses of the late 19th century; however, a number of details, especially the panels under the window bays, are of an individualistic nature, suggesting the hand of a builder who was allowed (or asked) to create effects of his own invention. The house never appears to have had a porch, an odd omission for the period and particularly for a dwelling in a rural location. There is also no evidence of the house having once been part of a farm; it did have an orchard, but was primarily a place of retreat.

NC 2 MARY ("MELISSA") PARSONS HOUSE
63 Main Street (CR 77); ca. 1893; later addition

North River lumberman James Ordway left Parsons, his housekeeper and mistress, much of his fortune. A few years after his death in 1890 she commissioned one of the largest residences in the hamlet. Although the details are different, they share some of the elementary and unorthodox qualities of the Marshock house [NC 1]. The rear section appears to be an early 20th-century addition. Behind lies a two-story stable and carriagehouse. Next door at 57 Main Street stands a good example of a modest Greek Revival **house**, built probably in the 1840s–50s.

NC 3 FIRST BAPTIST CHURCH AND UNION CEMETERY
93 Main Street; 1853; later alterations

A simple but sizable building, the presence of which is the more pronounced with the adjoining, but organizationally unrelated, cemetery begun around the same time.

NC 4 JOHNSBURG CENTRAL SCHOOL
165 Main Street; 1925–26, J. Russell White, architect (Albany); north wing 1952–53; south wing 1962–63; later additions 1994–95, 2005–06

The result of district consolidation, this school building is prominently sited along North Creek's principal street close to residential blocks.

NC 5 NORTH CREEK NATIONAL BANK
244 Main Street; 1926–27

Perched on a high point at the southern end of the business center, this bank exudes solidity and permanence, enlivened slightly by the mannered treatment of its classical front. It is now a branch of Community Bank.

NC 6 MAIN STREET COMMERCIAL BUILDINGS

North Creek's business center is distinguished from many others in the Adirondacks in the extent of two-tier porches that front its commercial buildings. These appendages were generally applied to such work in warmer climates. Some exceptions could be found in the Adirondacks. What precipitated their extensive use here is unknown. As a group, these buildings manifest a continuity of use as much as appearance.

William Noxon and Alfred Braley, who established a partnership in 1888, erected the **Braley & Noxon hardware store (a)** at 256 Main Street seven years later. The second story (for rental offices originally, now rental space) and porch were added in the early 20th century, at which time the roof was given its pyramidal form. The **Waddell Building (b)** at 262 Main was erected in the 1900s in a single construction campaign.

Nathan and Millie Baverman's clothing store (c) at 282 Main dates to 1903. It is now Izzy's Market & Deli. The adjacent commercial building (d) at 284 Main was erected around 1892 for use as the town hall and theater, as well as for mercantile purposes. It has always harbored a pharmacy at ground level. Smith's Restaurant and Bakery (e) at 296 Main (1924) operated

as a family enterprise for some seventy years. It, too, continues its original function, though under a new name.

NC 7 DELAWARE & HUDSON RAILWAY STATION
5 Railroad Place, off Main Street; 1872

While North Creek was the northern terminus of Thomas C. Durant's Adirondack Railway Company line, the tracks were extended in 1944 to serve the titanium mine at Tahawus [Section 11]. The line remained active until 1989. Passenger service reopened with the Upper Hudson River Railroad in 1998 and the full sixty-mile segment to Saratoga Springs was opened for the Saratoga & North Creek Railway. The station is the earliest surviving in the Adirondacks and was in near ruinous con-

dition before restoration as a local history center was begun in 1994. The environs offer a now unusual railroad landscape from the first half of the 20th century, including the engine house (1943–44, 1950, 1957), turntable (1943–44), and tool house. To the north of the station lies the shed-like freight house, built in 1903, the second on that site. This is the depot to which Theodore Roosevelt was taken from the Tahawus Club [Section 11] following the assassination of William McKinley in 1901.

NORTH RIVER
Town of Johnsburg, Warren County

NR 1 NORTH RIVER UNITED METHODIST CHURCH
13th Lake Road, .9 mile from NY 28; 1847

The development of upland farming in this remote area is evidenced by this church, which served as a community centerpiece. The building's size and elementary character underscore the challenging circumstances under which it was built.

NR 2 JACOB DAVIS HOUSE
Old Schoolhouse Road, 1 mile from NY 28; ca. 1880s

Isolation seems to have been pursued by Davis in locating his house. A successful peddler who traded in North Creek as well as Indian and Blue Mountain lakes, he had acquired sufficient profits by 1881 to purchase a substantial and scenic mountain tract. Like the Marshock and Parsons houses [NC 1, NC 2], this dwelling departs from conventions of the period. All these dwellings suggest the hand of a local builder, who was either ignorant of or ignored the plan books that then had a pervasive influence on residential design nationally. The dwelling was rehabilitated in the early 2000s as the Cedarwood Bed & Breakfast.

Nearby at 42 Old Schoolhouse Road lies a **two-room school** (1900) that is similar to one built in 1895 at Blue Mountain Lake [BK 5, Section 11] and stands as a reminder that the environs were once more developed than they are today.

WEVERTOWN
Town of Johnsburg, Warren County

WV 2 TOWN OF JOHNSBURG COMMUNITY CENTER
2370 NY 28; 1913

Built as an Odd Fellows Hall and moved in 1931 to make room for highway improvements, this building of straightforward design achieves prominence primarily by virtue of its size and its location in a sparsely settled area. It was later purchased by the town government.

WV 3 WADELL-ELDRIDGE HOUSE
2362 NY 28; ca. 1870

A three-bay Italianate dwelling, complete with cupola, suggests a level of wealth gleaned from harvesting timber during the 19th and early 20th centuries. It was built for Robert Wadell, lumberman and town supervisor, who also served in the state assembly. Later it was occupied by the Wadells' daughter, who married Lemon T. Eldridge, proprietor of the hamlet's general store.

WV 1 PHILIP MOSTON SAWMILL
Dillon Hill Road, off NY 8; 1888–89

Though it lies at the intersection of two major Adirondack roads, Wevertown has always been a tiny hamlet, harboring a few functions important to a rural area. The oldest sawmill in the region (and indeed one of a very few remaining) was built by Philip Moston, using timbers from the tannery he had purchased, along with a dam. It operated until the mid-20th century and was revived in 1979 as a hydroelectric plant serving the T. C. Murphy Lumber Company, one of the area's major suppliers of hardware and building materials.

WV 4 ST. CHARLES BORROMEO CATHOLIC CHURCH
2349 NY 28; 1875

St. Charles Borromeo was one of three Catholic churches erected in Warren County on the initiative of Father James A. Kelly, pastor at Warrensburg, in this case to serve the swelling number of French-Canadian and Irish immigrants attracted by the tannery and lumbering operations. Though it now harbors Beaver Brook Outfitters, catering to outdoor sports enthusiasts, the building's striking Gothic-inspired exterior remains unchanged.

WV 5 JAMES DWYER HOUSE
2209 NY 28; ca. 1965 and later

A modernist A-frame dwelling, perhaps initially intended for seasonal use, has received one or more additions that present more traditional associations, making the overall effect an accretive one.

JOHNSBURG
Town of Johnsburg, Warren County

JH 1 JOHN DUNN HOUSE
1782 S. Johnsburg Road (CR 57); ca. 1845 and later

This temple-front Greek Revival house would have been an unusually ambitious undertaking for so remote a location in the mid-19th century. Dunn's wife was a granddaughter of John Thurman, who was instrumental in settling the area. The Dunns occupied the premises until 1890. Some sixteen years later, it was converted to a modest resort hotel by George and Mae Smith, who operated the establishment as Smith's Adirondack Inn at least until 1943. It was likely during the Smiths' ownership that the two-tiered side porch was added. It is currently undergoing renovations that will return it to residential use.

JH 2 JOHNSBURG METHODIST EPISCOPAL CHURCH
1798 S. Johnsburg Road; 1838–43 and later

Adjacent to the north, the Methodist Episcopal Church took five years to construct. The first builder, Sumner Nelson, failed to complete the work, and in 1841 John Hodgson was contracted to complete the project. The bell tower was added in 1892; the windows installed eight years later. Otherwise, the building embodies the conspicuous plainness many Methodists admired during the first half of the 19th century.

JH 3 CHARLES NOBLE HOUSE AND GENERAL STORE
3468 NY 8; 1879 and later

A now rare survivor of its kind, this building's projecting front section clearly housed mercantile operations. Noble may have resided on the second floor, adding the large east wing as his business flourished. The porch fronting this section probably dates from the 1920s.

BAKERS MILLS

BS 1 MATESKARED, HOWARD ZAHNISER HOUSE
End of Edwards Hill Road, off NY 8; 1940s

High above the tiny hamlet of Bakers Mills a young couple, Pansy and Harold Allen, erected a cabin during the 1940s adjacent to her parents' farm. After World War II, the Allens decided to locate in the valley below. Zahniser purchased the property in 1946. Based in Washington, D.C., he had recently become executive secretary of the Wilderness Society and would later be the principal architect of the 1964 Wilderness Act. By that time he was considered among the greatest conservationists of his generation. Zahniser grew attached to the area through his friend, conservationist Paul Schaefer, who had a cabin nearby. After he acquired the property, Zahniser named it after the first names of his four children and added a front porch that afforded a sweeping view of the valley. Sheathed in wood planks and asphalt shingles, the house is an embodiment of rusticity in the elementary, rather than cultivated, sense and a fitting retreat for so passionate a devotee of wildness.

STONY CREEK
Town of Stony Creek, Warren County

SC 1 TENEMENT HOUSE
45 Hadley Road (CR 12); ca. 1850s

One of the most remote communities in Warren County, Stony Creek bears ample evidence of its earlier role as a hub of lumbering, tanning, and related enterprises. The one surviving building associated with the tannery developed by John Bowman is this tenement house that was likely built around the time he established his business in 1852.

SC 2 STONY CREEK INN
Roaring Branch and Hadley roads; 1904–05

Nearby, this hostelry was built as the Collins House after its predecessor, the Cedar Creek House (1869–70), was destroyed in a flood. It soon began catering to tourists and later became an important social center for guests at nearby dude ranches, where drinking and dancing were initially discouraged.

SC 3 FLOYD WINSLOW GENERAL STORE
2 Warrensburg Road; 1897

Cattycorner to the inn (both roads change names at the intersection), this general store has an unusually ornate two-tier porch, the upper portion of which likely fronted its owner's residence. It now lies vacant. At 30 Harrisburg Road **Emerick's Emporium**, the initial portion of which was constructed around 1858 and is now substantially altered, has a rare surviving assemblage of service and storage buildings at its rear.

SC 4 UNITED METHODIST CHURCH
33 Warrensburg Road, 1856–59 and later

Though no longer in regular use, the Methodist Church remains a well-preserved example of a simple Greek Revival house of worship. The bell tower was added in 1874.

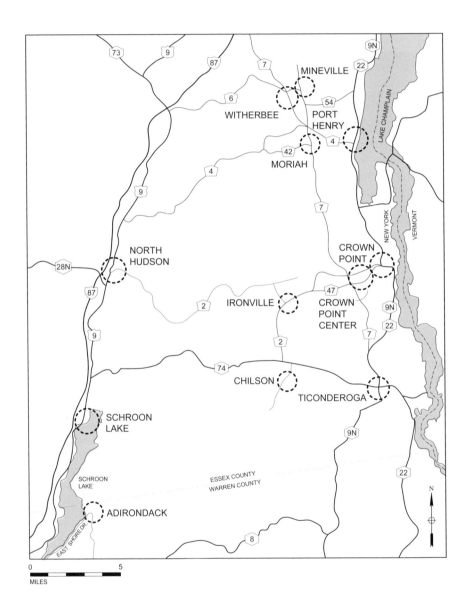

5

LOWER LAKE CHAMPLAIN VALLEY and INTERIOR

STRADDLING THE SHORE OF LAKE CHAMPLAIN AND EXTENDING WEST to the Schroon River, this portion of the eastern Adirondacks, all of it lying within Essex County, has four substantial population centers, three of which—Ticonderoga, Crown Point, and Port Henry—emerged as industrial hubs during the 19th century. Much of the interior area had the timber and iron that were essential for development of those lakefront communities. By contrast, recreational pursuits have long formed the primary economic base for the fourth population center, Schroon Lake.

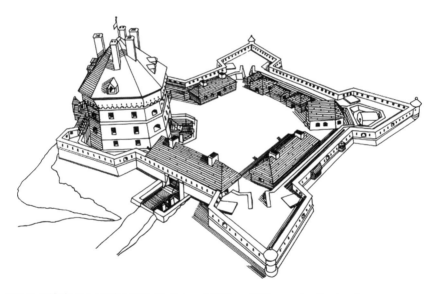

Fort St. Frédéric, Crown Point, 1733–37, destroyed 1759, ca. 1762; reconstruction drawing.

WELL BEFORE PERMANENT WHITE SETTLEMENT OCCURRED, LAKE CHAMPLAIN, as a key part of the axis from New York to Montreal, was a strategic path in the 18th-century struggles for control of North America. The French seized the advantage early on, with the construction of Fort St. Frédéric at Crown Point (1733–37) and Fort Carillon (1755–59) at Ticonderoga. Carillon became an important battleground in the Seven Years War, repelling a major British offensive in 1758, only to succumb a year later. Fort St. Frédéric was abandoned shortly thereafter in what amounted to a humiliating retreat. To help ensure Lake Champlain would never again be subject to "foreign" occupation, the British built a huge new fort at Crown Point, which never saw combat. Fort Ticonderoga (the rebuilt Carillon), on the other hand, was the site of a stunning British surrender to Ethan Allen and Benedict Arnold in 1775, three weeks after the first fighting at Lexington and Concord. Its cannon were subsequently transported overland, in the dead of winter, to support the newly formed Continental Army's campaign to wrest Boston from British troops. Both forts surrendered under General John Burgoyne's 1777 offensive and were abandoned after the Revolution. Fort Ticonderoga was soon plundered for its materials, but was rescued and preserved as a ruin in the 1820s—perhaps the first time such action was taken in the United States. Work started on re-creating the fort in 1909, marking another pioneering venture, in this case for a major historical reconstruction.

Ticonderoga at Sunset. (*engraving by Benson Jon Lossing, ca. 1850*)

Permanent settlement occurred along Champlain's shores after the Revolution, but did not gain significant ground until the first decades of the 19th century. Early residents were primarily from New England in search of acreage of their own, fostered in many instances by land grants to Revolutionary War and War of 1812 veterans as recompense for service. Most settlers likely came with the intention of farming, but save for areas near the lake and portions of interior river valleys, poor soil and a harsh climate precluded extensive cultivation. Other arrivals saw business opportunities in anticipation of future growth. Allen Penfield and Timothy Taft came from Vermont in 1807 and established a store several miles inland from the lake at what became Ironville, while Job Howe settled in Crown Point a decade later, constructing a gristmill, sawmill, and dam, embarking on what developed into a lucrative building practice. Crown Point was the earliest town to form, in 1788. From its expansive territory were carved out the towns of Ticonderoga and Schroon (1804), Moriah (1806), and others farther afield.

Population growth was primarily propelled by the prospects of industry. La Chute River, connecting lakes George and Champlain, had two falls near its eastern end in what became the hamlet of Ticonderoga, and modest manufacturing enterprises were established there not long after 1800. The opening of the Champlain Canal in 1823 markedly altered the area's potential for trade, allowing ready access to major markets all the way to New York. Ticonderoga became the setting for multiple enterprises, including tanning and making boats, cloth, cabinets, and wagons. Sixteen sawmills operated along La Chute between 1800 and 1850. Seemingly limitless supplies of timber helped make lumbering and the manufacture of wood products the dominant base of the local economy. Operations boomed during the decades after the Civil War, greatly facilitated by the opening of the Whitehall & Plattsburgh (later the Delaware & Hudson) Railroad as far north as Port Henry in 1871. Clayton Delano and Clark Ives established a major plant for the fabrication of sash, doors, and blinds in 1871, and ten years later they developed a pulp mill. After a series of expansions and mergers, that plant became part of the newly formed giant, International Paper Company, in 1898—an operation that grew to occupy much of the hamlet center until the 1970s.

While International Paper long dominated the local economy, other operations played important roles in Ticonderoga's prominence as an industrial center. Iron-making was a significant business through the mid-19th century. Nearby graphite mines were opened in the 1830s. The New York–based Butler & Clough teamed up with American Graphite in 1863 and was sold to what became John Dixon & Company a decade later, emerging as the largest consumer of and dealer in graphite worldwide; pencils bearing the Ticonderoga name became ubiquitous.

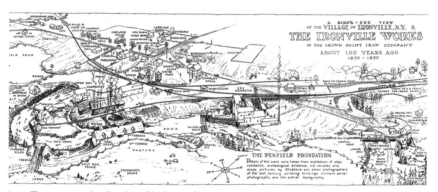

Ironville, *reconstruction drawing of its late 19th-century state.*

Crown Point developed into an important center for iron mining and manufacturing. An ore bed was discovered in 1818, and several beds in the area were working by 1823. Three years later Penfield and Taft found a major deposit and in 1828 erected a forge near their store at what would soon become the hamlet of Ironville. The ore was tested in New York and Washington, where it was determined to be of exceptionally fine quality, especially for making ships' chains. Samples were sent to Joseph Henry of Albany for his electromagnetic experiments. In 1831 Penfield and Taft built a magnetic ore separator, for which Henry supplied an electromagnet—perhaps the first use of electricity for industrial purposes in the country. The Ironville operation expanded in the 1840s following its reorganization as the Crown Point Iron Company with Penfield and his new partners Charles and John Hammond. Production rapidly grew during the 1870s. The company was again reorganized in 1872, now run by Charles Hammond's sons, John and Thomas. Concurrently an enormous deposit in the wilderness to the west began to be mined, leading to development of a boom community, Hammondville. In less than a decade the Hammondville mine became the tenth-largest in ore extraction in the United States. The Ironville plant was further enlarged and two large blast furnaces were erected on the shores of Lake Champlain in the hamlet of Crown Point. A narrow-gauge railroad connecting the new plant with Ironville and Hammondville was operating by 1893.

The boom did not last long. Depletion of minerals and a depression in iron prices during the 1890s led to bankruptcy by the decade's end. The Crown Point plant was purchased by American Steel & Wire Company in 1901, using ore from elsewhere, but it was soon closed, and the facility was demolished in 1905. The town's population declined by two-thirds between 1880 and 1920. Without much subsequent growth, Crown Point and tangent Crown Point Center remain modest communities, with abundant evidence of their 19th-century settlement.

Port Henry, N.Y., Main Street.

Main Street, Port Henry. (early 20th-century postcard)

Port Henry and its satellite communities remained an important mining center for a substantially longer period. Lying within the Town of Moriah, Port Henry became a staging center for lumber operations, capitalizing on roads along the lakeshore, a ferry to Vermont, and the Champlain Canal. While an ore bed was opened in 1828, scant mining occurred for some years. Following the establishment of the Port Henry Iron Company in 1840, however, growth was swift, soon rivaling operations at Crown Point. By 1860, the Port Henry area was among the leading iron centers in the region. Cedar Point, part of the flatlands on the hamlet's southeastern side, developed as a locus for manufacture, with foundries and furnaces.

The mid-19th century was a boom period in iron mining, driven by the purchase of several operations by the brothers S. H. and J. G. Witherbee and George D. Sherman.

Witherbee, Sherman & Company expanded operations at Cedar Point and also exploited ore deposits at Mineville, several miles to the northwest, then considered among the richest in North America, with ore of such high grade that it eventually commanded a significant share of the Eastern market. By the 1880s Mineville became a sizable company town, with a population of 2,000, developed by Witherbee, Sherman in a predictably hierarchical manner that also considered ethnic divisions between older groups (Irish, French-Canadians, Germans, and Scandinavians) and newer ones (Polish, Lithuanians, Italians, and Spanish). Soon after a company reorganization in 1900, acreage to the west was developed as a separate community, Witherbee, for those of eastern and southern European origin.

Port Henry not only served as the center for administration, manufacture, and transportation, but also as home of what became a substantial elite. The tone was set by the lavish houses of the Witherbees and Shermans [PH 18], the company's grand office building overlooking Cedar Point [PH 5], churches the moguls supported, and what was perhaps the best appointed library in the Adirondacks when it opened in 1887 [PH 7], a gift of George D. Sherman. Port Henry boasted tree-lined streets, a public park, and an imposing, if compact, commercial core. Conditions were far more elementary in Mineville and Witherbee; however, by the 1900s, the company began to improve housing with substantial concrete-block dwellings that were heralded as models of their kind.

Witherbee, Sherman & Company blast furnace, 1922, demolished late 1920s. (1920s postcard)

If Witherbee, Sherman's mining towns were better than many in the 1920s, other company infrastructure failed to keep pace. Most of the raw ore was sold to manufacturers elsewhere. Attempts to build a state-of-the-art blast furnace at Cedar Point in 1922 overextended company resources. The Depression worsened conditions, and the mines remained closed for much of that decade. With antiquated machinery and deteriorated mines, company officials approached Republic

Steel for a twenty-five-year lease, which was consummated in 1938. Republic substantially upgraded facilities and revived business, propelled by demand from the defense build-up and World War II. Republic also made improvements in worker services and living quarters. Then, in 1957, corporate officials started to sell this housing stock, most of which was purchased by occupants. By that time, a decline in the steel industry was felt nationwide and Republic began slowing operations, closing the mine for good in 1971, nearly three-quarters of a century after production had ceased at Crown Point.

Frontier Town, North Hudson, begun 1951–52. (ca. early 1960s postcard)

Witherbee, Sherman owned some 30,000 acres of interior land in 1900, acquired for its mining potential and for the timber required to sustain iron production. The Crown Point Iron Company held around 20,000 acres for the same reasons; the Hammondville mine, after all, had proven to be essential for that operation's continued existence. These circumstances, coupled with the rugged terrain beyond the Champlain Valley, left most of the interior land sparsely settled, if occupied at all, until the narrow valley of the Schroon River. That path had been the primary overland route from Albany to Montreal since the early 19th century. With the advent of motor vehicles over a hundred years later, it was the designated corridor for US 9 and, in the 1950s, for the Adirondack Northway (I-87). Tiny hamlets along that axis, such as North Hudson, were settled at the turn of the 19th century for small industries, but their economies were primarily sustained from logging—cutting hardwoods to make large quantities of charcoal for iron furnaces—until most accessible timber was depleted around the century's end. Accommodating motorists between the 1920s and 1950s spawned a scattering of cabin clusters, motels, and other roadside services, but never in concentration. A pioneering children's theme park, Frontier Town, opened in 1953, was the only major tourist attraction.

To the south, where the Schroon Valley widens, lies reasonably fertile land, much of the acreage originally cut for timber. This area, too, became the setting for some small-scale agricultural production during the first half of the 19th century. But where the river widens to become Schroon Lake, the surrounding land was primarily utilized to attract seasonal visitors as early as the 1850s. Extending some nine miles in length, and framed by mountains, hills, and flatlands, Schroon Lake was heralded as among the most scenic in the Adirondacks. Basic accommodations soon were supplemented by lavish ones, most notably the Leland House, which opened in 1872 in the hamlet that bears the lake's name. Like a number of fashionable Adirondack hotels, the appeal of the Leland House lay in part in its remoteness.

Leland House (II), Schroon Lake, 1915, burned 1938. (ca. late 1910s/1920s postcard)

Guests could travel by train up the Hudson River on Thomas C. Durant's Adirondack Railway as far as Riparius [Section 4], then take an arduous stage ride for twelve miles to Pottersville, and finally embark on a steamer up the lake. After fire destroyed the Leland House in 1914, a much larger establishment was built on the site, only to suffer fire again twenty-four years later. The operation continued after repairs until 1952. Other resort hotels—the Schroon Lake House, Lake House, and Windsor House among them—were erected in the early 20th century along the western lakeshore, most of them in response to the much easier access afforded by paved highways. Shortly after 1900, new owners of the Leland House broke precedent by allowing Jewish guests, a practice shunned by most hoteliers in the Adirondacks until decades later. Other Schroon Lake establishments followed suit, giving the community a unique reputation for openness. The most ambitious hostelry was the complex developed as the Scaroon Manor Resort, which opened in 1920 on the lake several miles south of the hamlet.

Besides the Leland House, the hamlet of Schroon Lake harbored many more modest tourist establishments—boardinghouses and, in the late 1920s, a cabin colony [SH 5], as well as motels in later years. Along the US 9/I-87 corridor, only Lake George village surpassed Schroon Lake for its array of visitor accommodations during the mid-20th century. Since then, the range has been expanded with a number of children's camps and religious retreats. By far the most ambitious of these facilities are those of the Word of Life Ministries, which began as an island-bound youth camp in 1947 and has expanded to encompass a number of lakefront compounds. Until recent decades, Schroon Lake never boasted a large number of cottages or private camps, but Paradox and Eagle lakes to the east, along the principal route to Ticonderoga (NY 74), have spawned such development since the late 19th century.

Settlement is sparser on Schroon Lake's eastern shore. The small hamlet of Adirondack (originally Mill Brook) was the earliest community, which grew up around a tannery built in 1849. Tourism began with the opening of the three-story Wells House in 1872. By the time it burned a quarter-century later, the area was beginning to attract seasonal residents who commissioned relatively modest lakeshore cottages. During the second half of the 20th century, the rate of building of vacation houses and even some apartment complexes has increased dramatically, much of it between Adirondack and the lake's southern end.

* * * * *

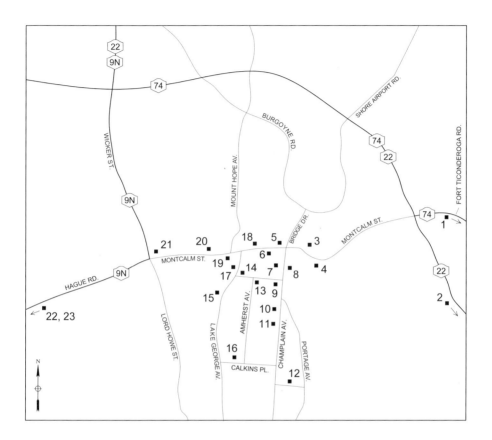

TICONDEROGA

Town of Ticonderoga, Essex County

Although it has long ceased to be an industrial center and most of the physical evidence of industry no longer exists, the sizable hamlet of Ticonderoga (population 3,382 in 2010) retains much of the building fabric that it had in its peak years of economic prosperity. The principal thoroughfare, Montcalm Street, retains a number of late 19th- and early 20th-century commercial buildings as well as some conspicuous gaps. The center also boasts an array of civic and institutional buildings from the same period. Most residential areas are intact, with a rich variety of vernacular house forms, predominantly

of wood-frame construction. If many residents must now commute elsewhere to work, Ticonderoga, which never seems to have been a gritty industrial community in the usual sense, remains a generally well-tended place, with generously sized house lots set on varied terrain on either side of La Chute River.

Since the first years of its reconstruction, Fort Ticonderoga has attracted tourists, who first came by steamer, then by train, and by the 1920s in ever-increasing numbers by automobile. But while it has long been one of the major visitor destinations in the Adirondacks, Ticonderoga never developed as a tourist center, owing in part to the longevity of International Paper Company's sprawling plant in the community's heart.

145

TI 1 FORT TICONDEROGA, GARRISON GROUNDS

Fort Ticonderoga Road (NY 74); entrance just east of railroad tracks

The area occupied by the fort, earthworks, and a variety of support facilities in the 18th century is one of the most storied cultural landscapes in North America. Long before any permanent settlement, this peninsula was possibly the site of Samuel de Champlain's bloody encounter with the Iroquois in 1609. Construction of Fort Carillon on the site, beginning in 1755, marked the apex of French intrusion into territory also claimed by Great Britain. The work of an inexperienced French military engineer, Marquis Michel Chartier de Lotbinière, the fort was of the square, four-bastion type developed in the 17th century by Sébastien le Prestre Vauban, which set the international standard for defense against artillery siege for over 100 years. The 1758 Battle of Carillon was the greatest victory the French achieved in North America during the Seven Years War, prolonging the conflict by another year at great cost to the British. Rather than allow their enemy to capture the fort during the successful siege of 1759 by the British, the French garrison blew up the powder magazine and set fire to the barracks. The British subsequently undertook the necessary repairs to house a garrison there. The 1775 capture by Ethan Allen and the Green Mountain Boys and the logistically implausible transfer of cannon from the fort to Boston were signature acts of audacity among those fighting for independence.

Following the Revolution, the fort was abandoned and in 1785 the land deeded first to the Regents of the University of the State of New York and then in 1803 to Columbia and Union colleges. Seventeen years later it was purchased by William Ferris Pell, a rich New York merchant, whose parents had held title to one of the colonial manors (much of Westchester County) and had fled to Canada during the Revolution. With the return of peace William Ferris Pell resettled in the United States and restored much of the family fortune. The historical associations of the site and of the ruined fort, which had lain derelict since the end of the war and soon began to be mined for building materials, were the likely factors spurring the purchase. Pell protected the fort with a fence and began to build a summer house (Beaumont) nearby. Aside from Sir William Johnson [Section 2], Pell was likely the first person of means to realize a seasonal residence in what is now the Adirondack Park. At that time probably no other American could boast of a country place with an actual ruin—a very historic one at that—on the grounds. The house soon burned, but was replaced by another, named the Pavilion. During the 1830s, son Archibald took over management of the place. After he was killed when firing a cannon in 1839, the dwelling became a hotel. His father died the following year, and for the next several decades the property was a genteel, if by later standards rather modest, resort. The fort, as well as its lakeside orientation, was the primary appeal. Pell descendants refused to sell the property, even though it had experienced considerable decline by the century's end.

The fort's national importance spawned three bills, drafted between 1888 and 1906, for the federal government to purchase it as a national shrine. Yet another attempt, announced at a clambake held on the Pavilion grounds in 1908, included a presentation by Alfred Bossom, an English émigré architect based in New York, to reconstruct the fort. Among those in the audience were William Ferris Pell's great-grandson, New York broker Stephen H. P. Pell, and his new bride, Sarah. Stephen (who had a longstanding interest in the fort and already harbored notions of restoring it) and Sarah were able to convince her father, Col. Robert Means Thompson, to pledge $500,000 to the project. Stephen moved quickly to purchase his relatives' shares in the property. Work began in the spring of 1909 on the officers' (west) barracks, inaugurating a project that was unprecedented in its scope for the United States. In preparing plans, Bossom combed archives in England, France, Canada, and the United States for material and returned to England to find artisans best suited to construct the tile roofs and other key components of the complex. Work continued until 1915 and resumed on some of the fortifications during the 1920s. Completion of the soldiers' (south) barracks occurred in 1931, when the property was formally transferred to the non-profit Pell Family (now Fort Ticonderoga) Association. Finally, the eastern bastion and wall were reconstructed in 1940. To furnish the two buildings, Stephen Pell rapaciously acquired weapons, documents, paintings, prints, and many other artifacts associated with the fort and with 18th- and early 19th-century military history, amassing what has become a collection of international importance.

Concurrent with the initial reconstruction work, the Pells "restored" the Pavilion as their summer residence, adding expansive gardens, an enormous garage, and other buildings. The acreage occupied by the fort and sites of military engagement—the Garrison Grounds, as they were called—were cultivated in a manner consonant with a great early 20th-century country place, boasting elaborate 18th-century English iron gates and a new gatehouse, a deer park, and cultivated fields. At various times, memorials were erected along the main approach to the fort, and what became the Log House was erected to accommodate visitors. The combination of public historic site and private rural estate was as unorthodox as was the idea of the reconstruction itself at the time it was undertaken.

After the death of the Pells' youngest son, John H. G. Pell, the Pavilion ceased to be used and suffered from neglect. The gardens were carefully restored in 1997–2001, and plans are under way to rehabilitate the house and other buildings in the vicinity. A major addition to the fort itself, at the site of the 18th-century storehouse, was built in the 2000s as a year-round educational center. Interpretation has expanded in recent years to a broader, more detailed and nuanced presentation of the 18th century and now also the complex history of the place under Pell family tutelage.

As reconstructed, **Fort Ticonderoga (a)** proper consists of the **West Barracks**, two **West Bastions** (arrow-like projections from the square plan), and **West Ramparts** (earth-filled walls in between the bastions), reconstructed in 1909–12; the **South Barracks**, reconstructed in 1914–15 and 1930–31; the **South Bastion**, reconstructed in 1919–23; the **North Demilune** (or **Ravelin**, semi-bastion, rising in front and independent of the wall), reconstructed in 1929–30; the **North Terreplein** (level areas on the ramparts between the outer wall and inner parade ground), reconstructed in 1930–33; the **East Terreplein**, reconstructed in 1940—all according to Alfred Bossom's plans. The **Deborah Clarke Mars Education Center** was built in 2003–08 on 18th-century walls excavated and consolidated during the mid-1920s, with plans prepared by Tonetti

147

Associates, architects, of New York.

Working in the tradition of 19th- and early 20th-century English church restorers, Bossom took his oversight of the reconstruction assiduously, determined to create an authentic iteration of the colonial outpost. It is doubtful if one could find a more thoroughly conceived enterprise for reviving a historic site in the United States prior to World War I. Perhaps only Stanford White's reconstruction of the burned Rotunda at the University of Virginia (1896–98) rivaled the care with which Bossom exercised his deference to the past. New masonry work, much of it using stones recovered from the site, was laid on existing foundations (English and French) and as much of the surviving walls was retained as possible. At the same time, the building elevations and interiors are interpretative, reflecting contemporary arts-and-crafts sensibilities as much as the practical considerations of 18th-century military engineering. Bossom supervised the work until about 1915, and that done over the next several decades generally followed his plans. However, Bossom (and presumably the Pells) did not envision a full reconstruction of the South Barracks, which was eventually undertaken out of a pressing need to display the ever-growing abundance of artifacts collected by Stephen Pell. New demands for exhibition and meeting space led to the Mars Education Center, the exterior of which was based on recently discovered evidence of the French storehouse that had been blown up in the face of the advancing British army in 1759. While unorthodox, this reconstruction strategy adds a new, yet fully compatible, twist to that taken by Bossom and his clients a century previous. On the other hand, the Mars Center's interior is entirely new in design.

The **Log House (b)** (1923, 1925) stands as an early example of a genre of tourist-oriented buildings purveying food, souvenirs, and crafts along American highways from the 1920s into the post–World War II era.

While expanded several times during the interwar decades, the Log House remains intimate in scale and folksy in character, and it is now a very rare example of this once-popular type of roadside attraction.

The **Pavilion (c)** was built in at least four stages. The two-story center block, with a Tuscan portico and the original rear service wing, dates to around 1827. The north end block appears to have been an earlier building moved to the site and modified about two years later; the same process occurred to create the matching south end block around 1832. The connecting hyphens, originally with open, colonnaded walkways, were added around 1838. The resulting five-part composition had enjoyed popularity in Anglo-American circles for nearly a century; however, the details of its configuration, with cell-like bedrooms in the hyphens bracketed on either end by what may have been more public spaces, are reminiscent of the ranges Thomas Jefferson designed at the University of Virginia. An 1858 account attributes the design to Glens Falls builder Beecher Higby, but no corroborating evidence has been found.

Stephen and Sarah Pell's "restoration," orchestrated by Alfred Bossom in 1908–09, actually appears to have been quite faithful to the house as of the late 1830s. A new service wing was built to be more in keeping with the original form than the larger, mid-19th-century replacement when the building operated as a hotel. The ca. 1880 porches on the end blocks were retained probably because they were thought to be part of the early design. The Pells' program called for extensive landscape improvements, with an enormous vegetable and cutting garden as well as a more formal flower garden—intended to evoke the 18th-century **Jardin du Roi** that had occupied much of the Pavilion site and known from the early 20th century on as the **King's Garden**—as well as orchards, new drives, a

tennis court, and a gazebo. Bossom was responsible for the garden walls and attached teahouse (1911–12), while the gardens were the work of New York landscape architect Marion Cruger Coffin (1921). In 1910 the Pells' young sons were given play quarters of their own, dubbed the **Y-D House** ("Yes, Do"—as opposed to the frequent admonitions of "No, Don't" in the Pavilion). Bossom described his log structure as being "in the manner of the original homes of the settlers…, who built under the protection of the walls of Fort Ticonderoga"—a comparison for which he had no basis. Bossom also designed what then must have been the most elaborate **automobile garage** in the Adirondacks, constructed in 1912–13, along

with a new entrance drive from the northeast. This drive and the connecting lower approach road were lined with ash trees, which, now in advanced age, form a majestic approach to the family portion of the Garrison Grounds.

Stephen Pell's uncle, Howland Pell, who had for some time been resident manager of the property, retained acreage for a dwelling of his own, which he called the **Block House (d)** (1909–10), another work of Bossom's. In arresting contrast to the Pavilion, this bristling pile was fashioned as if it were a remnant of some ancient military outpost. Long vacant, the building now lies in ruin.

No component of the early 20th-century work on the grounds is more indicative of their dual role of public museum and private preserve than the 1912 **gatehouse (e)**, again from Bossom's hand. This portal and the scenic drive beyond suggest entering a great country place, while the motifs of the gatehouse play off those Bossom developed for the reconstructed fort. The iron gates that once enunciated the entrance were acquired in 1913 following the demolition of Enfield House in Middlesex, the English manor for which they were made. The gates now lie outside the King's Garden, serving as a pedestrian portal between the Pavilion and the fort.

While not a part of the Garrison Grounds, the **Thompson-Pell Research Center (f)** at 30 Fort Ticonderoga Road has served as offices and archives for the fort since it was rehabilitated in 1989–92 under the direction of Ann Beha Associates, architects, of Boston. Built in 1931–32 for AT&T at the substantial cost of $60,000 as a repeater station to amplify telephone calls, this building boasts an unusually suave design for so utilitarian a function. Stylistically it bears affinity to the work of the prominent New York–based firm of Voorhees, Gmelin & Walker, which designed many telephone company buildings in the Northeast during the period.

TI 2 FORT VIEW HOTEL
325 NY 22; ca. 1874; later alterations

Strategically located at what was originally known as the Fort Ticonderoga station of the Delaware & Hudson Railway and at the southern terminus of Lake Champlain steamboats, this modest hostelry once served both tourists and business travelers. Later, the D&H erected a station in the hamlet proper [TI 8] and also one just north of the fort grounds.

TI 3 TICONDEROGA PULP & PAPER COMPANY OFFICES
137 Montcalm Street; 1888; addition ca. 1910

All that remains of the sprawling Ticonderoga (later International) Paper Company complex is this decorous administrative building that now serves as a local museum. It was built eleven years after Clayton Delano organized the company and shortly following a major expansion of the plant. The operation's size can be gleaned from the adjacent park that has taken its place. The only other remnant is the **Frazier Bridge** (1892–94), crossing La Chute River at the end of Frazier Bridge Drive. Bridges have existed at this location since 1822 and served an essential function of connecting workers with their plants. The bridge became so integral to the industrial infrastructure that it was purchased by International Paper in 1925.

TI 4 TICONDEROGA COMMUNITY BUILDING
132 Montcalm Street; 1927–28, Max Westhoff, architect (Springfield, Mass.)

Native son Horace Augustus Moses, who in his youth migrated to Massachusetts, amassed a fortune in paper-making there, forming Strathmore Paper Company in 1911. Moses gave this elaborate building to accommodate a wide range of civic functions, including space for municipal government and police, family court, draft board, and chamber of commerce. An auditorium and kitchen lie on the second floor,

while the basement was used as a recreation center. With the exception of Saranac Lake [SL 8, Section 9] no other community in the Adirondacks has benefited from so comprehensive a public facility.

TI 5 TICONDEROGA NATIONAL BANK
123 Montcalm Street at Champlain Avenue; 1927–29, A. S. Miller, architect (Brooklyn); now Champlain National Bank

Ticonderoga's prosperity and urban aspirations by the late 19th and early 20th centuries are still evident in its main commercial thoroughfare. This corner bank ranks among the largest built in the Adirondacks, and its somewhat abstract and ahistorical Beaux-Arts composition is among the most sophisticated.

TI 6 ROWELL & SHATTUCK DRY GOODS STORE
116 Montcalm Street; 1887

Rowell & Shattuck, the largest emporium

in the community when it opened, was for the most part unrivaled in its size within the Blue Line until recent decades. By 1900 it was one of a number of four-story commercial buildings that defined Ticonderoga's downtown. All the others have been lost, and this once grand emporium stands vacant. Across the street at 119 Montcalm, the **Gilligan & Stevens Block** is a more typical example for Ticonderoga. The initial (west) section of 1882 boasts an ornate central bay and other embellishments; the five-bay addition (1884–85) is somewhat more restrained.

standardized elements that could be used in varied combinations. This depot shares many attributes with that at Riparius [RI 3, Section 4]. It replaced a more utilitarian building constructed in 1891, when a spur line was extended into the heart of the burgeoning community. It now serves as quarters for the Evelyn C. Burleigh Center, a social services agency.

TI 9 H. G. BURLEIGH HOUSE
135 Champlain Avenue; 1894, C. C. Remington, builder; addition 1905, S. B. Remington, builder

A spirited, if provincial, rendition of Queen Anne motifs popular in the late 19th century, the Burleigh house ranks among the largest in Ticonderoga. Its owner began to amass his fortune operating canal boats in the 1860s, built the Burleigh House hotel a block away in 1876, and later served in the state assembly and the U.S. Congress. Following his death in 1900, Burleigh's daughter remodeled the original wood-frame house with a substantial addition similar to the 1890s portion save for its substitute of concrete block for stone.

TI 7 UNITED STATES POST OFFICE
169 Champlain Avenue; 1936–37, Louis A. Simon, Supervising Architect of the Treasury (Washington, D.C.)

Part of a massive public buildings construction campaign during the Depression, this post office was one of thirteen similar designs realized in the state. It is rendered in a restrained but decorous Colonial Revival vein characteristic to many such New Deal facilities. Characteristic, too, is the lobby mural inspired by local events, in this case *The Exhortation of Ethan Allen*, painted by Frederick Massa in 1941.

TI 8 DELAWARE & HUDSON RAILWAY STATION
170 Champlain Avenue; 1913–14

Unlike some major railroads of the era, the D&H does not appear to have used any stock design for its small ("country") stations. The company did, however, develop

TI 10 EPISCOPAL CHURCH OF THE HOLY CROSS
129 Champlain Avenue; 1885–86, Fuller, Wheeler & Prescott, architects (Albany)

Although modest in size, this house of worship was designed in a fashionable free style by a prominent Albany firm and is conspicuously located along one of the hamlet's major streets across from the park that was once the home of the Ticonderoga Academy.

TI 11 NEW YORK STATE ARMORY

123 Champlain Avenue; 1934–35, William E. Haufgaard, NYS Department of Public Works (Albany)

Another product of the New Deal public buildings programs, this facility was erected to house the Ticonderoga division of the National Guard, which was organized in 1926. Both institution and building spoke to the village's prominence in the region. The guard vacated in 2003; the building now is home to community services.

TI 12 MORTIMER FERRIS HOUSE

16 Carillon Road; 1911, William A. Gale, builder

Ferris, who was prominent in both civic and business affairs, commissioned a Colonial Revival design of the sort that was especially fashionable in eastern Massachusetts, whence he came in 1904. Gale was one of Bossom's foremen during the fort's reconstruction.

TI 13 ST. MARY'S CATHOLIC CHURCH

12 Father Jogues Place; 1888–92; 1943–44; 1959–60

A robust, if chaste, interpretation of English Gothic precedent, St. Mary's upstaged what had been the most prominent Catholic church on the New York side of the lake: St. Patrick's in Port Henry [PH 13]. The two communities harbored the largest Catholic populations in Essex County, and the cost of the Ticonderoga church, some $50,000, attested to its congregation's size and devotion. While suffering two major fires, the exterior and most of the basic interior forms remain intact.

TI 14 CLAYTON DELANO HOUSE

25 Father Jogues Place at Lake George Avenue; 1857; extensive additions and alterations ca. 1890

A substantial but basic and boxy Italianate house of the mid-19th century was enlarged several decades later to form a spirited, accretive assemblage. The driving force behind the Ticonderoga Pulp & Paper Company, Delano was arguably the key figure fostering the community's boom during the Gilded Age. His dominance was longstanding; he retired at age eighty-three in 1919, forty-two years after he organized the company.

TI 15 TICONDEROGA PULP & PAPER COMPANY HOUSES
301–31 Lake George Avenue; 1919–21, William A. Gale, builder
   Across from Delano's house begins a range of dwellings erected for his lieutenants. Delano had sold the land to his company in 1905; construction started right after his retirement. The designs are standardized, with exterior variations to enliven the streetscape. A smaller group of houses, also built for the company by Gale, lie nearby at 322–38 Amherst Avenue (1921–23).

TI 16 TICONDEROGA HIGH SCHOOL
5 Calkins Place between Lake George & Amherst avenues; 1928–30, Tooker & Marsh, architects (New York); burned 1933; rebuilt 1933–34 according to original plans; gymnasium 1958; addition 2008–10, CSARCH, architects (Newburgh, N.Y.), Douglas Dickinson, partner-in-charge.
   One of the grandest school buildings— in appearance and facilities—within the Blue Line, this pile vigorously celebrated Ticonderoga's colonial past in its motifs. The auditorium has a capacity of 1,000 people, allowing it to serve as the area's primary public gathering place. The recent addition is an object lesson in design compatibility, enabling the earlier building to remain dominant, while being a distinguished scheme in its own right. The architect, appropriately, was a graduate of the school. Nearby, at Carillon Road and Champlain Avenue, lies the former **Alexandria School** built in 1896 by S. B. Remington and similar to counterparts in Corinth [CO 2, Section 2] and Bolton Landing [BL 9, Section 1].

TI 17 ACME PAD COMPANY FACTORY
171 Lake George Avenue; 1893, S. B. Remington, builder
   The hamlet's last remaining industrial building of any size, this unadorned, three-story plant was typical of printing mills locally and farther afield. It has had a difficult history. Acme Pad Company was

taken over by a competitor the same year it opened, and that company soon failed. The building temporarily served as a public school, then harbored a variety of manufacturing functions.

TI 18 BLACK WATCH MEMORIAL LIBRARY
101 Montcalm Street; 1905, Fuller & Pitcher, architects (Albany); rear addition 2009

A diminutive but prominent building, this library was in large part the result of a campaign led by the secretary of the local historical society, F. B. Richards, who successfully secured a $5,000 grant from the Carnegie Corporation, and then got an additional $2,000 from another source for a memorial room dedicated to the Black Watch, a Scottish Highland regiment that fought gallantly in the 1758 Battle of Carillon.

TI 19 SILAS B. MOORE GRISTMILL
218 Montcalm Street; 1879–80; rear addition by 1886; front altered 1896

Though somewhat modified in later years, the salient physical features of this wooden gristmill fronted by a store building remain intact—a rare surviving example of a once common type. It has been occupied by Agway since 1961.

TI 20 FRANK CLARK HOUSE
331 Montcalm Street; 1921, Frank and Rollen Clark, builders

This sizable bungalow, with walls (and even balustrades) of fieldstone, is a fitting testament to the masonry skills of its owner and principal builder.

TI 21 TICONDEROGA HISTORICAL SOCIETY
6 Moses Circle at intersection of Montcalm and Wicker (NY 9N) streets; 1925–26, Max Westhoff, architect (Springfield, Mass.)

Another civic gift to his hometown by Horace Augustus Moses, this building was based on measured drawings made by architect John Sturgis of the Thomas Hancock house (1734–37) in Boston—one of the most lavish in colonial New England—shortly before it was demolished in 1861. This was the first known instance where such documentation was used to record a threatened historic building in the United States. Moses enticed the previously homeless New York State Historical Association to accept the building as its headquarters, buoyed by a $100,000 endowment, in his effort to perpetuate "American trends in History and the Fine Arts," as well as to bolster Ticonderoga as a visitor destination. The organization remained there for half a century. As Moses's community building [TI 4] enunciated the eastern entrance to the village, so this replica was part of an even more ceremonious western portal for motorists, with the (now demolished) Moses-Luddington Hospital (1923) rising on the hill to the west—all punctuated by a traffic circle with the **Liberty Memorial** (1921–24) by the distinguished New York sculptor Charles Keck. The monument makes overt reference to engagements at or near the fort, with figures representing a Native American, a French soldier, a Highlander in the British Army, and a Green Mountain Boy.

TI 22 VALLEY VIEW CEMETERY AND CHAPEL
NY 9N, 4.9 miles south of Moses Circle; chapel 1901

Though portions of the cemetery date to the early 19th century, its pervasive character was reshaped by picturesque sensibilities after 1900. Situated on high ground, the unadorned stone chapel is the key focal point, its over-scaled (and crenellated) tower serving as a prominent beacon. Horace Moses was president of the cemetery board and, with his uncle, donated the funds for the building.

TI 23 COOK HOUSES

Straddling the Ticonderoga-Hague town line, this pair of large, chaste federal-period brick houses was built for brothers Mortimer and William Cook, who were among Ticonderoga's early settlers and became successful lumbermen. The two houses are similar in design. Mortimer's residence (ca. 1824) at 5 NY 9N (Ticonderoga) has a more elaborate entry surmounted by a fanlight (the porch is a later addition), a motif repeated above. William's house at 9996 NY 9N (Hague) was built some two years earlier.

TI 24 INTERNATIONAL PAPER COMPANY PLANT
568 Shore-Airport Road (CR 43); 1967–71

One of a few major industrial developments made in the Adirondacks since World War II, this plant was constructed in part to increase pulp and fine-paper production capacity. Its creation was also due to pressures from both the states of New York and Vermont to address the pollution of the in-town complex, which a federal study revealed to be equivalent to that found in a city of 315,000. Along with the Barton Mines Ruby Mountain plant at North River of 1980–83 (not publicly accessible) and the NYCO wollastonite plant at Willsboro [WI 11, Section 6], this is a rare example of a longstanding Adirondack industry surviving on a substantial scale.

CHILSON

Town of Ticonderoga, Essex County

An outpost settlement dating from the early 19th century, Chilson endured through supplying timber to the ironmaking operations at Ironville, Crown Point, and even Mineville. By the late 19th century the economy was also sustained by supporting the modest summer enclave on Eagle Lake at the end of Putts Pond Road.

CN 1 HAMLET CENTER
Putts Pond Road (CR 39), off NY 74

Today, the hamlet retains a revealing array of the modest civic components of a very small rural settlement. The **Community Cemetery (a)** began as a burial ground in 1832 and came under the direction of the Methodist Church in 1898. Adjacent lies the **Community Building (b)**, a no-frills gathering place dating from the 1920s. Across the road is the **Fred Stowell Memorial Ball Field (c)**, a vintage remnant of baseball's pivotal role for young adults as well as children in the region. Farther southwest is the **United Methodist Church (d)**, constructed in 1893 as a lodge (Patrons Hall) and converted in 1897–98 into the Union Christian Church, to which the belfry was added in 1899—an elementary edifice that in its little-altered state is becoming increasingly rare.

IRONVILLE

Town of Crown Point, Essex County

This crossroads hamlet is an extraordinary survivor of a rural community from the second quarter of the 19th century; very little has been added since. What survives suggests a modest agricultural center, not part of the burgeoning industrial plant that gave its residents their wealth and in its heyday enjoyed a wide-ranging market. Penfield Pond, dammed to create waterpower for the operation along Putts Creek, and some foundations along the stream south of the settlements are among the scant indications of the iron-making here. Dedicated to preserving the site, the Penfield Foundation was established in 1962, and this grassroots initiative can be credited with keeping what remains so wholly intact.

IR 1 HAMLET CENTER
Creek Road (CR 2) at Penfield Road
The oldest and most prominent building in the community is the **Allen Penfield house (a)** at 703 Creek Road, a fine wood-frame Federal-period house that reflects its owner's Vermont origins. It was built in 1828, concurrent with the erection of the first iron forge. The front porch is among the later additions. To the rear lie a barn and smokehouse, both erected around 1828, and a carriagehouse dating to 1877. To the west lies the **Eleazer Harwood house (b)** at No. 697, a gable-end Greek Revival dwelling of a kind common to northern New England and the eastern Adirondacks.

It dates to the 1840s, but the heavily scaled porch may be a later addition, as certainly is the side wing. Across the street at nos. 702 and 700, respectively, are the **Parsonage (c)**, a smaller version of the Hardwood house, and the **Second Congregational Church (d)** (1842–43), an ecclesiastical rendition of the same mode.

IR 2 McKERNAN HOUSE
Hogback Road (north side), 1.5 miles west of Penfield Road; early to mid-19th century
Proceeding north on Penfield Road one can get a sense of the extent of land cleared to provide charcoal for the forge at Ironville. A number of the farms developed on this acreage survive, though most are no longer agriculturally active. Of special interest is this one-and-one-half-story house, which appears to date from the 1850s, with a side wing of squared logs that is likely older.

CROWN POINT CENTER
and
CROWN POINT

Town of Crown Point, Essex County

A small, linear hamlet situated in the Putts Creek Valley, Crown Point Center connected the older one of Crown Point with Ironville and farming areas to the west. Nearby to the east, the hamlet of Crown Point, like Ironville, belies its industrial past. Settlement emanated at a crossroads (now NY 9N and CRs 2 and 45) and

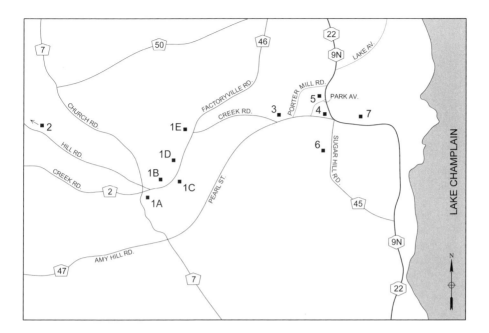

what eventually became a public park. A number of early to mid-19th-century components survive, but the community has also suffered from an employment base that was lost over a century ago and the fact that much of its development lies along a heavily traversed highway.

CP 1 CROWN POINT CENTER

At a key juncture of east-west (CR 2) and north-south (CR 7) routes lies **McCabe's store (a)** at 439 Middle Road, a little-changed rural emporium with a decorated parapet in all likelihood dating to the late 19th century. The attached house probably was added in the 1920s. In the heart of the hamlet at 1665 Creek Road is a larger commercial building, probably built as the **Baker & Wy-** man dry goods and grocery store (b) during the mid-19th century. It has long served as the **Fort Frederick International Order of Odd Fellows**. Nearby, at 1682 Creek Road, is the **United Methodist Church (c)**, a substantial Greek Revival edifice, probably erected around the 1840s, with an ornate late 19th-century porch. From the latter period, too, is the iron gate and fence of **Fairview Cemetery (d)** across the road. Farther east at 1765 Creek Road lies the octagonal **C. P. Forbes house (e)** dating from the 1850s. This building form was popular in many parts of the state, but this is the one known domestic example in the Adirondacks.

CP 2 GLENWOOD
555 Breed Hill Road; ca. late 1880s

This dwelling apparently was built under the auspices of Port Henry ironmonger and entrepreneur George D. Sherman. Its ornate design in the stylish Queen Anne mode, the equally ambitious carriage-house and stable to its rear, and the absence of any of the accouterments of a farmstead corroborate with local lore that

157

it was built as a remote sanctuary for one of his mistresses, known as "Black Sal."

CP 3 J. G. BREVOORT HOUSE
1971 Creek Road (CR 2); ca. 1840s–50s

A vigorously detailed, temple-front house, it was built for a prosperous farmer and mill owner.

CP 4 HAMLET GREEN
Creek Road, Park Avenue, and NY 9N

What at first glance might suggest an early 19th-century New England green actually dates from many decades later. The land initially was donated in 1893 to the Congregational church that fronts it by Juba Howe, the son of a prominent builder, and by Charlotte Hammond, widow of General John Hammond. The illusion of an early green is furthered by the fact that both families had resided on adjacent property since the 1820s, and their houses appear to have been built to partake of that open space. During the 20th century the church gave the property to the town.

The **Charles Hammond house (a)**, 2076 Creek Road at NY 9N, is an imposing brick residence in the Greek Revival mode. The dwelling marks its original owner's ascendancy as a prosperous merchant and lumberman, who would within a few years become a founding partner of the Crown Point Iron Company. Upon arriving at the fledgling community, he worked for Job Howe as a foreman to oversee the clearing of land and building a dam. In 1822 he joined with Howe, Eleazer Harwood, and Allen Penfield to form C. F. Hammond & Company for cutting and transporting timber and operating the store that would soon rise across the road. Howe built Hammond's house in 1837. In 1883 it was given by Hammond's son and two surviving daughters to the Congregational church and called Hammond Chapel. A portion was used as the town's library until 1929.

One of the oldest surviving buildings of its kind in the Adirondacks, the **C. F. Hammond & Company store (b)** across the street at 2073 Creek Road was constructed by Howe in 1827 to purvey general merchandise. Initially it was operated by Charles Hammond, who was joined by his brother John the following year. After the building was sold in 1871, it continued to serve its original function under the aegis of Barker & Wyman, expanding their Crown Point Center operations. From the 1940s to the 1970s it was a Grand Union market.

Sometime between 1886 and 1873 Charles Hammond spearheaded erecting the adjacent **Soldiers Monument (c)** to commemorate Civil War soldiers on land owned by his brother. Even at this early date, the Hammonds may have been contemplating the transformation of the open land beside their store to a public space.

A quarter century after its founding, the **First Congregational Church (d)** was given its land by Job Howe, who was a member of the congregation and served as the builder in 1829–33. His façade appears inspired by designs of Asher Benjamin, the Boston-based architect and prolific author of pattern books during the early 19th century. The church front was modified and the portico added after 1860.

To the north of Hammond's store a wood-frame building lies at 2793 NY 9N. It was constructed in two sections, one of which may have been a house erected by Job Howe around 1826. But the overall appearance suggests its fabric dates primarily from the mid-19th century, when it served as the **Masonic Hall (e)**.

After settling in Crown Point in 1818, **Job Howe** built mills [CP 5], dammed Putnams Creek, acquired extensive timberland, and became a proficient builder. His 1826 **house (f)** at 29 Park Avenue and NY 9N was likely the first masonry dwelling in Crown Point. It has experienced some later additions and other modifications.

CP 5 PORTER'S MILL
NY 9N at Putnam Creek; 1820s, Job Howe, builder; numerous later additions

At the core of this much-altered mill lies one of the oldest structures of its kind

remaining in the Adirondacks. It continued to operate as a gristmill until recent years and now lies vacant.

CP 6 ELMER BARKER HOUSE
225 Sugarhill Road (CR 45); ca. 1870s

An unusually elaborate High Victorian house for the Adirondacks, it was built as the residence for the owner of the town's principal store [CP 2b].

CP 7 CROWN POINT CENTRAL SCHOOL
2758 NY 9N; 1927–28, Coffin & Coffin, architects (New York); additions 1960, 1967, 1984, 1989

What was originally a school building of modest size was given a commanding presence by a Doric portico surmounted by an imaginatively detailed cupola and spreading, one-story wings—an assemblage that underscores the spirited interpretation of historical precedents characteristic of eclectic design of the early 20th century.

PORT HENRY
Town of Moriah, Essex County

The aura of a hamlet (population 1,194 in 2010) that had lost the major portion of its economic base by the mid-20th century is mitigated somewhat by the engaging array of architecture that remains at

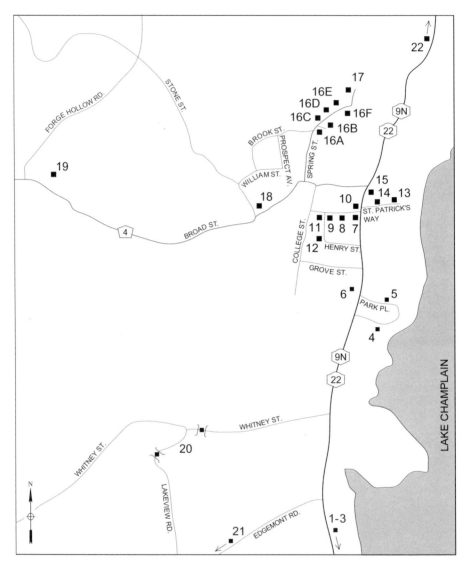

this spectacular site, one of the few places where the Adirondack foothills and Lake Champlain converge. Until the late 19th century almost all development occurred on relatively low ground not far from the lake, though the railroad inhibited much in the way of lakefront orientation. Houses of the mine owners, churches, commercial buildings, and industrial facilities all existed in proximity, joining to form a landscape that also possessed an orderly civic presence embellished by abundant street trees. Toward the century's end a younger generation of elite erected houses at higher elevations with panoramic views of the Champlain Valley. A majority of Port Henry's buildings from these prosperous decades remain, most of them intact.

PH 1 CROWN POINT STATE HISTORIC SITE
Off Bridge Road at Lake Champlain, Crown Point

Though lying within the Town of Crown Point, the northern part of the peninsula on which this property is located lies nearer to Port Henry, is closely tied visually, and its current state was to a degree shaped by Port Henry interests. In 1910, according to a contemporary account, Witherbee, Sherman gave twenty-five acres of land encompassing "ruins, which are perhaps the most extensive and best preserved of any in this country" for purposes of a public park, with the stipulation that the State of New York preserve them in their current form. How much this beneficence was made in competition with the Pells at Fort Ticonderoga is uncertain. The requirement that the ruins not be restored suggests an agenda in deliberate counterpoint to the sister fort's reconstruction.

While Fort Ticonderoga's significance today hinges on its many historical layers, **Fort Crown Point (a)** (1760–63) arguably affords the best evidence—both architectural and archaeological—of a major work of 18th-century military engineering in this country. It is also among the largest built by the British (or any other colonial power) in North America, designed to harbor over 100 cannon and 4,000 men. Construction began on the new fortifications, with timber and earth ramparts embracing stone buildings set in a parade ground three

times the size of that at Ticonderoga, under the direction of General Jeffrey Amherst, who had driven the French from the lake in 1759. Soon thereafter troops garrisoned at the site were instrumental in defeating the French at Montreal. While the Champlain Valley was no longer the scene of hostilities, work continued on the fort until the signing of the Treaty of Paris in 1763, leaving it partially unfinished.

A devastating fire in 1773 rendered the buildings useless, but the garrison remained. Two years later, the fort was captured by a detachment from Benedict Arnold and Ethan Allen's band the day after they had secured Fort Ticonderoga. Cannon and munitions were moved to the latter site. Before they recaptured Ticonderoga in 1777, the British army secured Crown Point and remained there for the war's duration. As at Ticonderoga, the land was later deeded to Union and Columbia colleges. The first purchaser stipulated in his subsequent sale that there be no "waste by tearing down any of the ramparts or walls or carrying away any of [their] material," but the difficulties of transporting stone over the lake to either the settlement at Port Henry or to adjacent rural areas of Vermont may have inhibited pillage more than any other factor.

Foundation walls and some earthworks remain of **Fort St. Frédéric (b)** (1733–37), among the most ambitious outposts built by the French in the Champlain Valley. The work of Gaspard-Joseph Chaussegros de Lery, chief engineer in New France, the complex was a hybrid, with a five-story redoubt, used by the French as isolated defenses designed to fend off surprise attacks, placed in one corner of a square, four-bastion fort. The structure proved its worth for staging raids on either side of the lake and discouraging British incursion into Canada. It was never intended, however, to resist a full-blown artillery siege. After the British finally captured Fort Carillon in 1759, the French withdrew from Crown Point, destroying several components of the fort in the process. While most of the complex remained, it was demolished once work was under way on the much larger British facility.

PH 2 CHAMPLAIN MEMORIAL LIGHT-HOUSE
Off Bridge Road at Crown Point State Campground; 1858; 1910–12, Dillon, McLellan & Beadel, architects (New York); sculptures by Carl A. Heber (New York) and Auguste Rodin (Paris)

In commemorating the Champlain tercentenary, New York joined forces with Vermont to encase the 1858 lighthouse at Crown Point in an elaborate classical veneer, with overscaled elements designed to have a strong visual impact from a distance. Rodin's bronze bust "La France" was a gift of the French government. The light was deactivated in 1930, following completion of the adjacent Lake Champlain Bridge.

PH 3 LAKE CHAMPLAIN BRIDGE
End of Bridge Road at Lake Champlain, Crown Point; 2009–11, HNTB Corporation, designers and engineers (New York), Theodore Zoli, principal-in-charge

The idea for a bridge over the lake was advanced as early as 1923, owing to the surge in the use of motor vehicles for touring. A temporary commission was established in 1926 to explore the possibilities and the site was selected seven months later. New York assumed 60 percent of the cost; Vermont, 40 percent. Construction began in 1928 and the bridge opened the following year. Designed by the Boston engineering firm of Fay, Spofford & Thorndike, the structure was the first American bridge with trusses spanning the channel that were of cantile-

ver construction. It also served as national prototype for continuous-truss technology, adapting methods used for railroad bridges to long-span highway bridges. After a concerted, bi-state effort to save it, the original bridge was demolished in 2009 due to structural weaknesses in its concrete piers. The toll collector's office and house adjacent on the New York side remains, designed by one D. Jackson, in association with the bridge's engineers.

A substantial effort was made to have the replacement bridge as structurally inspired and the effect as lyrical as its predecessor. The principal engineer, a leader in his field nationally, grew up not far away in Schroon Lake and his grandfather had worked on the Northway. Zoli's design was for a modified network-tied arch, with inclined hangers at numerous intersections to make the arch function like a truss. Among the scheme's innovations are the "V" supports above the concrete piers and cross cabling that was inspired by covered-bridge trusses.

PH 4 DELAWARE & HUDSON RAILWAY STATION
Park Place; 1888, possibly S. Gifford Slocum, architect (Saratoga Springs)

Replacing the original (1871) station, this building was far more decorous and expensive than its predecessor or any other such depot in the Adirondacks at that time. The project was funded by George D. Sherman, whose offices lay just to the north [PH 5]. Loosely drawing from the example of H. H. Richardson, the design bears stylistic affinity to, and was constructed concurrently with, the library that Sherman also gave to the hamlet [PH 8].

PH 5 WITHERBEE, SHERMAN & COMPANY OFFICE BUILDING
38 Park Place; 1875

Perhaps the most ornate building in the Adirondacks when it was completed, overlooking the railroad line, the manufactories, and the wharves on Cedar Point, Witherbee, Sherman's business house was an ebullient proclamation of the firm's

rapid ascendancy as the dominant iron company in the region and a significant force in the field more broadly. Inside, space was organized around a grand circular stair. Adjacent to the east lies the carriagehouse, built concurrently to accommodate the owners' rigs even though they lived only a short distance away. Later it was used as a company laboratory, then a firehouse. Both are remarkable survivals. The former is now the Moriah Town Hall, while the latter is occupied by the town's historical society. Separating them from the railroad station is a small park, intended for public recreation, fairs, and military demonstrations.

PH 6 S. L. MORRIS HOUSE
4267 Main Street (NY 9N); before 1876

While of modest dimensions, the elaborateness of this dwelling makes it a fitting complement to the Witherbee, Sherman offices across the street. Nearby at 4279 Main lies **George D. Sherman's** mid-19th-century **house**, much of the fabric of which remains intact even though it has sustained numerous alterations.

PH 7 FIRST NATIONAL BANK OF PORT HENRY
4307 Main Street; 1908

Like the Morris house, the lavishness of this bank building's exterior appointments belies its modest size. It is now a branch of the Glens Falls National Bank.

PH 8 SHERMAN FREE LIBRARY
20 Church Street; 1887–88, S. Gifford Slocum, architect (Saratoga Springs); rear addition 1907–08

George D. Sherman not only gave the building to the village, but also some 2,500 books and an endowment, which covered the cost of an addition that doubled the facility's size. Both sections form a single space that extends to the ridge of the roof, creating a memorable interior that has experienced little change. Like the railroad station [PH 4] and the Mount Moriah Presbyterian Church across the street [PH 10], the design is inspired by H. H. Richardson's work, but is far from derivative.

PH 9 HENRY'S GARAGE
10 Church Street; 1910–11, Earl Henry, designer

While hardly exuding a civic presence, this three-story garage attests to Port Henry's wealth in the early 20th century. It was built for C. W. Henry and his sons, Rau, Earl, and Harold, as a sales and service facility for automobiles, but also to service carriages. With a massive reinforced-concrete frame and concrete-block infill walls made with tailings from the Witherbee, Sherman mines, the building's design was prepared by Earl Henry as his

senior thesis at Rensselaer Polytechnic Institute, in Troy. The operation closed in 1969; portions of the building now serve the local fire department.

PH 10 MOUNT MORIAH PRESBYTERIAN CHURCH

19 Church Street at Main; 1888, probably S. Gifford Slocum, architect (Saratoga Springs); Sunday school and parlor addition 1913

When the parish outgrew its 1853–55 church, the new building was in large part funded by the Witherbees and Shermans. Among the hamlet's Richardsonian buildings, this is the most vigorous and confident interpretation.

PH 11 FIRST METHODIST CHURCH

6 Henry Street; 1872–73, William L. Wollett, architect (Albany)

A grand, if boxy, Gothic edifice, with its

worship space on the second floor, this church was likely conceived to rival St. Patrick's nearby [PH 13], which was receiving its tower and other additions at about the same time. Parishioners included a number of the hamlet's richest residents, J. G. Witherbee among them. It is now occupied by the Lake Champlain Bible Fellowship.

PH 12 CHRIST EPISCOPAL CHURCH

10 Henry Street; 1872, S. S. Woodcock, architect (Boston)

Built concurrently with the Methodist church, this Episcopal house of worship is much smaller, but also more sophisticated in its use of Gothic elements. It was funded in part by R. F. and J. H. Reed of Boston, industrialists involved with the Bay State Furnace Company at the north end of the village.

PH 13 ST. PATRICK'S CATHOLIC CHURCH

17 St. Patrick's Way; 1849–54; extensive alterations and additions (including bell tower) ca. early 1870s; rebuilt after 1897 fire in 1898–99

The first church established in Port Henry (1840), St. Patrick's began as a modest wood-frame building, which was replaced by the more substantial core of the present edifice. After the Civil War it was transformed into a landmark by additions to accommodate the village's swelling Catholic population. The 1890s post-fire renovations included moving the main entrance to the west side, the altar to the east, two sacristies, and stained-glass windows.

Across the street is **Ledgeside**, house of **F. S. Witherbee**, built before the Civil War and extensively remodeled (or remade) in the 1870s in an ornate manner complementing the company offices. The extensive front gardens were removed for a supermarket in 1957. Much of the 19th-century building remains, despite numerous disfiguring changes.

PH 14 MISS PORT HENRY DINER
5 St. Patrick's Way; ca. 1927, Ward & Dick-inson Company, designer and manufacturer (Silver Creek, N.Y.); moved to Port Henry 1933

Originally located in Glens Falls, this is reputedly among the oldest and most intact examples of the company's work and is a rare survivor. Ward & Dickinson pioneered in the use of the monitor roof (extending above the main roof and glazed on the sides). The mobility of their products was made clear by the use of small wheels cut into the body of each of its cars.

PH 15 MAIN STREET COMMERCIAL BUILDINGS
4314–30 Main Street (NY 9N)

This range of five commercial buildings is among the most urban in character to be found in the Adirondacks and manifests Port Henry's importance as a business center during the late 19th and early 20th centuries. The **Harlan Building (a)** (ca.

1881) at 4314 Main was constructed as a modest speculative venture with several store units. Its neighbor at 4316 Main **(b)** dates to the early 1880s as well and is a rare example of a stamped-iron façade in the

region. Use of this veneer was popular elsewhere in the country because of the ornamental qualities that were possible at a low cost. The **Lee House hotel (c)** at 4318 Main actually began as a residence for John A. Lee in 1874. During the 1880s it was enlarged as a three-story hotel. Under a new owner, the footprint doubled and a fourth story was added in 1911. Closed seventy years later, the building was renovated in 1985 as housing for the elderly.

Probably the largest and most elaborate commercial building in the Adirondacks when it was erected, the **Van Orum & Murdock Block (d)** (1874) at 4322 Main is typical of many erected in larger communities during the Gilded Age and was a harbinger of Port Henry's ascendancy. W. T. Foote made his fortune from mining investments and then put his money into real estate. The **Foote Block (e)** (ca. 1911–12) at 4326–30 Main was his most ambitious project. It replaced the ornate Lewald Opera House (ca. 1880) after that pile was destroyed by fire. The pent roof (a shallow, lean-to projection, much like a canopy) that used to extend below the parapet has been removed.

PH 16 SPRING STREET HOUSES

Little is known about this group of fashionable houses, constructed for some of the hamlet's well-to-do along a short, dead-end street that offers a panoramic view of the Champlain Valley. The houses at **48** and **52 Spring Street (a** and **b)** are compact renditions in the Queen Anne mode and date to around 1890. That at **59 Spring (c)** is of slightly later vintage (ca. 1900), sporting some Queen Anne vestiges, here subordinated to a dominant square mass capped by a pyramidal roof and simple, Colonial Revival details. The house at **65 Spring (d)** has the massing associated with the Shingle Style, but also Colonial Revival details and likely dates from around 1900 as well. The **M. H. Pease house** at **74 Spring (e)** predates 1876 and is typical of gable-end dwellings from the mid-19th century. Across the street the **S. F. Murdoch house** at **71 Spring (f)** may be even earlier.

PH 17 PORT HENRY LIGHT, HEAT & POWER COMPANY WATER TOWER
End of Spring Street; 1916, Chicago Bridge & Iron Works Company, manufacturers (Chicago)

This vintage steel tower was built as a surge water tank with capacity of 11,000 gallons. It is an unusual remnant of early municipal infrastructure in the Adirondacks.

PH 18 LEDGETOP, WALTER C. WITHERBEE HOUSE
10 Stone Street at Broad; ca. 1892–93, Frank T. Cornell, architect (Brooklyn)

Some seven years after Walter C. Witherbee took over Witherbee, Sherman, he commissioned a Shingle Style fantasy of a kind more associated with grand summer houses of the Gilded Age than with residences in town. The family occupied it for about fifty years. It was sold to the Town of Moriah in the early 1940s, thence to the American Legion in 1946 and Knights of Columbus in 1969. The latter group sealed off the upper floors and demolished the barn. Finding a suitable use for the building has been a challenge since it was returned to the town in 1992. Currently a new owner is repairing the exterior; most of the interior finishes were stripped prior to the sale.

PH 19 MORIAH UNION CEMETERY
Broad Street (CR 4) at Forge Hollow Road; laid out 1850s

Among the myriad burial grounds in the Adirondacks, this comes closest to embodying the picturesque ideals of rural cemeteries found on the edges of many American cities beginning in the 1830s. Being of sizable acreage, removed from the village, non-denominational, and generously landscaped, Moriah Union was clearly part of that movement, albeit with less variation in roadways and topography than leading examples. It boasts a rich array of funerary monuments from the 19th and early 20th centuries.

PH 20 LAKE CHAMPLAIN & MORIAH RAILROAD BRIDGES
Whitney Street, .5 mile west of Main; and Lakeview Avenue, .1 mile south of Whitney; 1909

Chartered in 1867 and built over the next two years by Witherbee, Sherman and the Port Henry Iron Company, this short line originally had wooden rails, which were replaced by steel ones four years later. The railroad ascended over 1,400 feet, traversing little more than five miles between Cedar Point and Mineville. These two concrete bridges upgraded the infrastructure and were emblematic of the enterprise's importance. They are now the primary surviving evidence of this crucial component of the local mining industry's infrastructure.

PH 21 EDGEMONT, SARAH McCARTHY HOUSE
284 Edgemont Road; 1900

After Glenwood [CP 2], George D. Sherman had Edgemont built for another mistress, and he himself reputedly resided here for a while. Like Glenwood, it is unusually fashionable for a rural setting, in this case rendered in a late Queen Anne mode with some Colonial Revival details.

PH 22 EARLY MOTELS

North of Port Henry, near the Lake Champlain shore at 4978 NY 9N, the recently renamed **Mitch's Place (a)** is an assemblage of early cabins for motorists that clearly were built at different times during the interwar decades. Some were apparently located on the lakeshore and were moved by Pat Paterson, who operated the complex as Paterson's Cottages. **Nelson's Cottages (b)** at 5046 NY 9N appears to be of the same vintage, sited away from the road, facing a broad lawn and a commanding view of the lake.

MORIAH CORNERS
Town of Moriah, Essex County

Occupying high ground to the west of Lake Champlain, this crossroads hamlet has most of the town's oldest buildings. It appears to have continued its role as an ag-

ricultural center well into the 20th century, bearing scant indication of the intensive mining not far to its north.

MC 1 MORIAH UNITED METHODIST CHURCH
639 Tarbell Hill Road (CR 42); 1885–86

Replacing the edifice that burned in 1884, this stylish building would have been at home in a well-heeled residential area of a much larger community and suggests the wealth that existed in the hamlet. Moriah Corners also attracted seasonal visitors who stayed at the Hotel Sherman, a commodious resort dating from the mid-19th century run by members of George D. Sherman's family.

MC 2 A. KIDDER HOUSE
638 Tarbell Hill Road; early 19th century; wing ca. mid-19th century

A classic gable-end, Federal-period New England design, this house was perhaps the most prominent in the hamlet when it was erected. The side wing is somewhat later and may have been moved to the site.

MC 3 MORIAH BAPTIST CHURCH
634 Tarbell Hill Road; 1828; alterations and tower 1874

This church is a good example of the hulking, box-like forms popular among some Protestant denominations during the mid-19th century. The last Baptist service there was in 1951. It now serves as the Daisy Morton Methodist Church.

MC 4 SHERMAN BLOCK
622 Tarbell Hill Road; 1907
As part of an effort to make his family's hamlet a showplace, George D. Sherman erected a business building that would have been at home in downtown Port Henry, but still comes as something of a surprise in this crossroads settlement. At the same time, the architectural vocabulary is more that of the Gilded Age than of the Progressive Era. Originally the building contained a general store, drug store, barbershop, and post office as well as a doctor's office and substantial quarters for Sherman's independent business activities. It now lies mostly vacant.

MC 5 LEWIS-POWELL HOUSE
2597 Center Road (CR 7); early to mid-19th century, alterations ca. late 1870s–1880s
What may have been a simple gable-end house was aggrandized for a town physician, G. H. Powell, with the intent of making it a hospital. The result is an eccentric Victorian fantasy of memorable character.

MINEVILLE and WITHERBEE
Town of Moriah, Essex County

While almost the entire aboveground industrial infrastructure has gone, the adjacent hamlets of Mineville and Witherbee are highly evocative of their past as company-owned settlements. As was common in such places, early housing in Mineville was of a crude, makeshift nature. With expanding operations at the turn of the 20th century, Witherbee, Sherman attracted an influx of eastern and southern European labor. Management decided to create a separate enclave for them, named Witherbee, which straddled the other side of the valley. The mines lay in between. Expansion and redevelopment contributed to a major change in the community as a whole. Beginning soon after 1900, Witherbee, Sherman's general manager, Sheldon Norton, who had formerly worked for a cement company, began to experiment with concrete blocks for building. His ventures were so successful that this material became the predominant one used by the decade's end. Utilizing the otherwise superfluous iron tailings, which possessed a high-grade aggregate, added to the appeal of this method. Construction costs were about the same as those utilizing lumber, but the expenditures for maintenance were much lower and the fire hazard markedly less. The volume of production was such that the company ran its own plant for manufacturing concrete blocks and bricks. All the work was done under the supervision of the company's chief engineer, Edmund Lefevre, and purchasing agent, Arthur Hodgkins. Ample space was provided for vegetable gardens adjoining each house, and there was at least one barn for employee livestock. The labor climate was far from tranquil, however. Before World War I, Witherbee, Sherman

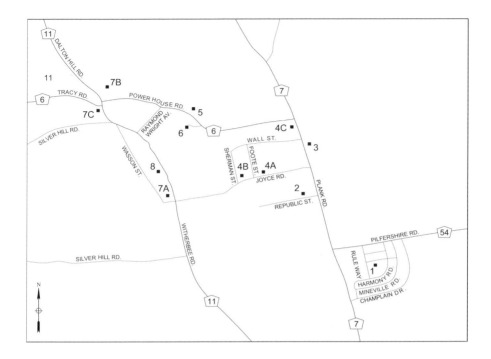

sought to appease workers by building more houses, more outbuildings for animals, and giving some families indoor plumbing for the first time.

While now occupied by retirees, persons living on public assistance, or others who must commute to work—a population now roughly the same as Port Henry's—the residential fabric of Mineville and Witherbee remains intact, forming an impressive spectrum of working-class housing and a veritable catalogue of patterns used for concrete blocks.

MV 1 GROVER HILLS SEMI-DETACHED HOUSES
Development bounded by Plank (CR 7) and Pilfershire (CR 54) roads and Champlain Drive; 1942, William G. Distin, architect

With resurgence in demand for high-grade ore during World War II, a new wave of growth came to the community. The housing shortage was such that the National Housing Administration planned some 900 units in Mineville, less than half of which were realized. Financing and construction were a cooperative venture between Republic Steel and state and federal authorities. Containing 316 semi-detached dwellings, Grover Hills, one of two tracts, was named after the first Moriah soldier to die in the conflict.

MV 2 MANAGERS' HOUSES
Plank Road and Republic Street; ca. 1900s and later

An enclave of semi-detached and free-standing, single-family houses, some built

169

using concrete blocks, others of wood, the group is clearly distinguished from miners' dwellings in size and decorous character.

MV 3 CONGREGATIONAL CHURCH
3174 Plank Road; 1875

This exuberant wood-frame High Victorian Gothic edifice was built for congregants comprised mostly of farmers and lumbermen, who broke away from the church at Moriah Corners. The area was emerging as a mining center at that time. It now serves as a residence.

MV 4 MINEVILLE CONCRETE-BLOCK WORKERS' HOUSES

An array of **freestanding, single-family houses (a)** on generously sized lots was built around 1908 for workers in Mineville. These were divided into several groups, varied in form as well as details, and situated at 503–05 Joyce Road, 423–33 Foote Street, and 37–39 Wall Street. Several **semi-detached houses (b)** were constructed some two years later on generously sized lots at 3–5, 4–6, 9–11, 10–12, and 16–18

Sherman Street. They are similar in plans, but have varied roof forms. A 1909 **store (c)** that once served these and other dwellings in the vicinity makes imaginative use of concrete elements for its second-story porch, fronting the proprietor's living quarters. It stands little altered but underutilized at 3217 Plank Road.

MV 5 WITHERBEE, SHERMAN & COMPANY OFFICE BUILDING
Office Road off Power House Road; 1907, addition 1945

To address its expanding operations the company erected an office building on site to supplement its headquarters in Port Henry. Like the employee housing, it is constructed of concrete blocks. Originally a broad stair ascended from the main road to the front door. Adjacent lies the former **health center**, which was converted from a blacksmith shop to an infirmary in 1910–11. Above lies a wood-frame **boardinghouse**.

MV 6 WITHERBEE MEMORIAL HALL
Power House Road (CR 6); 1893, possibly Frank T. Cornell, architect (Brooklyn)

Built by F. S. and W. C. Witherbee in memory of the company's founders, this great stone and wood-frame building cost $70,000 and provided a wide spectrum of facilities for miners and their families. It included a kindergarten, cooking school, sewing club, lending library, savings bank, hospital, auditorium for lectures and social events, clubrooms, billiard room, and meeting rooms. In the early 20th century it also housed some young, newly arrived miners and in 1913 housed strikebreakers. In 1970 it was sold to the Veterans of Foreign Wars, which continues to occupy the building. The wood-frame elementary school (1906–07) and concrete-block high school (1916–17) once lay adjacent to the west.

MV 7 WITHERBEE CONCRETE-BLOCK WORKERS' HOUSES

Along Witherbee Road, the main route connecting Port Henry with Elizabethtown, the county seat [Section 6], Witherbee, Sherman erected a series of large **multi-**

unit houses (a), including quadraplexes at nos. 201–03 and 213–15 (ca. 1916) and nos. 232–34 and 233–35 (ca. 1910); triplexes at nos. 205–07 and 206 (ca. 1916); and semi-detached houses at nos. 240–42 and 245–47 (ca. 1915). A number of these buildings were designed for single men. Similar dwellings line Wasson Street, running parallel to the west. A group of four **rowhouse blocks (b)** from ca. 1913 stands some distance away at 57–75 and 62–76 Dalton Hill Road (CR 70). Each has slightly different

details as part of the company's effort to vary the residential landscape, as well as to address different housing needs. In between on Norton Road lies a block of **detached** and **semi-detached houses** as well

as **flats** (one unit atop the other) known as **Bridal Row (c)** erected for higher-level employees between 1906 and 1914. Those on the west side of this short street are reputedly the first concrete-block dwellings built by the company.

MV 8 ST. MICHAEL'S CATHOLIC CHURCH
40 Wasson Street (faces Witherbee Road); 1911–12, Seymour R. Burdick, architect (Rutland, Vermont)

Also constructed of concrete block is the church built for Poles and other recent immigrants who were unwelcome among those of Irish and other northern European origins in Mineville. Witherbee, Sherman gave the land for a nominal price and funded the building's construction.

NORTH HUDSON
Town of North Hudson, Essex County

Always a sparsely settled community, North Hudson was a logging area for much of the 19th century, but lost two-thirds of its population between 1880 and 1930 owing to the demise of the iron industry farther east and depletion of forests. As US 9 became a major automobile route, some accommodations were developed along this corridor, but have been closed since construction of the Northway (I-87) in the 1960s.

NH 1 GERO HOUSE
Ensign Pond Road (CR 4), 1 mile east of Caza Turn Road; ca. 1880s

A good example of a relatively modest

seasonal cottage of a kind once numerous in the Adirondacks, this wood-frame dwelling is unusually intact.

"participate" in events, was an instant success. The following year Disney Studios did some filming on site as reconnaissance for Disneyland's Frontierland.

NH 2 VACANT MOTELS

Built in two stages during the late 1940s and 1950, the **Beacon Light Motel (a)** at 3095 US 9 has a range of cabins (ca. late 1940s) supplemented by one of connected units and a flared-front lobby as a centerpiece (ca. mid-1950s). A small lighthouse used to rise beside the highway as an advertising motif. Farther south at 3209 US 9 is the former **McNichol's Motel**, which is a good example of a cabin group that included a restaurant and service garage developed during the 1930s and probably later as well.

NH 3 FRONTIER TOWN

Motel and restaurant, US 9, .6 mile south of Blue Ridge Road (CR 2); site of village and cafeteria, Blue Ridge Road at exit 29 of I-87; 1951–52 and later

By far the largest business operating in North Hudson during the 20th century was this early theme park, which ran for nearly 50 years. Conceived by a Staten Island telephone lineman, Arthur L. Bensen, as the basis for a second career, the 150-acre site, once a farm, was secured after a protracted five-state search. Bensen laid out his simulated frontier community in 1951 and with the help of lumberjacks, a carpenter, and an electrician, constructed twelve log buildings. Opened on July 4, 1952, the park, where visitors were encouraged to

Bensen's compound was the product of frequent expansion. Prairie Junction, a "cowboy town," was added in 1953 and enlarged the next year. Horseback riding, riding a stagecoach, and rodeos ranked among the new activities. Eventually Bensen acquired around 100 horses and a farm in Wadhams to stable them off-season. In 1969 a sawmill was built to house a 100-year-old steam engine, and later a forge that had been on the property since 1857 was "restored."

Bensen ran the park until 1983. Subsequent mismanagement led to its closure two years later. Frontier Town was reopened in 1989 by new owners, but closed for good in 2004. While many of the attractions have been obscured from public view, some can be seen, including a large **motel** and adjacent **restaurant**, probably dating from the mid- to late 1950s, which remain vacant along US 9, and an even more conspicuous A-frame, multi-purpose **visitor facility** built in the mid-1960s to attract Northway motorists.

NH 4 FARMHOUSE

688 Johnson Pond Road (CR 2), 3.5 miles east of US 9; probably mid-19th century

This modest, one-story dwelling of a kind once common in the Adirondacks still has an extended rear barn—a configuration that had been widely used in New England since the 18th century and was subsequently employed in contiguous parts of New York. A former rural **schoolhouse**, probably from the late 19th century, stands along the road .2 mile to the west at Johnson Pond.

NH 5 BRUCE'S STORE
3433 Blue Ridge Road (CR 2), 2.3 miles west of I-87; ca. 1880s–90s
A good example of a small rural mercantile building, long operated by Myron Bruce as general store and post office, this modest outlet served the largely vanished hamlet of Blue Ridge.

NH 6 ELK LAKE LODGE
End of Elk Lake Road, 5 miles north of Blue Ridge Road; 1903–06 and later
Elk Lake Lodge is an unusual instance where a place developed for sportsmen in the 19th century has continued as a resort into the 21st century. Not long after it was created by damming the East and West inlets in the mid-19th century, Elk Lake became a destination for the former group owing to its remote wilderness setting. By 1878 Myron Bruce from Blue Ridge [NH 5] was running an inn there. Henry Pellitier Jones developed Hunter's Rest nearby a decade later. He also constructed **Elk Pond House**, using vertically laid logs, an unusual method in the region. In 1919 Emily Alice Darling built two **cottages** nearby (now part of the lodge), indicating Elk Lake's broadening appeal. Its success as a low-key resort was in large part the result of a later owner, Richard Ernst. In 1963 he acquired some 11,000 acres around the lake from the Finch, Pruyn Paper Company to preserve the lodge's spectacular natural setting. Ernst added new **cottages** and a large **dining hall** (1967) overlooking the lake.

SCHROON LAKE
Town of Schroon, Essex County

The hamlet of Schroon Lake continues to serve as the center for the myriad seasonal residents and tourists who come to the lake's shores. In character, this small community retains much of its informal charm. For some eight miles south along the lake's west side can be found an assortment of motels, campgrounds, children's camps, and faith-based retreats. Single-family cottages and camps, most of them built in recent decades, line portions of the east side

SH 1 THE TAVERN, SALLY MILLER SMITH HOUSE
2005 US 9, 1.9 miles north of NY 74, Schroon Falls; early 19th century; ca. 1927
Built as a sizable federal-period farmhouse that at some point in the 19th century also functioned as a tavern, the oldest part of this sprawling wood-frame pile attests to the prosperity of this once agricultural area of the Schroon Valley as well as to the longstanding importance of the north-south route it fronts. The house was in sorely neglected condition when it was acquired around 1927 by an heiress from Waterbury, Connecticut, whose father owned a brass factory and husband, Ralph Hubert Smith, had inherited a brass-button plant. Sally Smith had spent childhoods nearby on Paradox Lake, and this is one of several properties she later purchased in the area. She remade what she dubbed The Tavern in a highly unconventional form, predicated on frequent entertaining, with

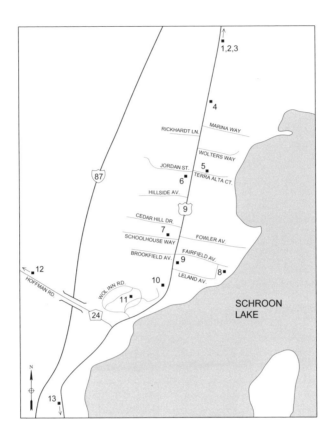

an enormous, eight-bay rear extension, at the far end of which lies the dining room, with living room above and tap room below. In between on the second floor extends a range of guest rooms, configured more as if they were in a hotel than in a residence. Despite its size, the addition's interior maintains an intimate scale, its design rendered in a manner then considered to be "early American." After Smith's death in 1952 it became a hostelry, with a small motel (since demolished) added to the south. Since 1981 it has been run as the Silver Spruce Inn.

SH 2 PARADOX LAKE HOUSE
167 NY 74, Severance; ca. 1900, Irving W. Tyrell, builder

A now rare example of the many modest resort accommodations built in the Adirondacks during the 19th and early 20th centuries, its tall mass departing from the more usual configuration of an oversized house.

SH 3 HOUSE

331 NY 74, Severance; probably late 19th century

Overlooking the western end of Paradox Lake, this cottage is a good representative of numerous moderate-sized seasonal residences erected within the Blue Line and elsewhere in the country during the Gilded Age. The complexity of its form suggests it may have been constructed in at least two stages.

SH 4 ROWE'S LAKE BREEZE MOTOR COURT

1328 Main Street (US 9); early 1950s

Built for Charlotte and George Rowe, this complex illustrates the persistence well after World War II of the cabin form for overnight accommodations in situations where central heating was not needed.

SH 5 TERRA ALTA

Main Street and Terra Alta Drive; ca. 1927–29, Montgomery Ward & Company designer and manufacturer of cabins; later additions to many cabins

An unusual and remarkably unchanged cabin colony, Terra Alta was built for seasonal residents (not short-term tourists) of modest income by an Italian immigrant, Joseph Giannini, who had already built the Schroon Lake Department Store and the Strand Theater [SH 9]. The complex occupies seventeen acres of former pastureland between US 9 and the lake at the northern edge of the hamlet. With thirty-five cabins (all but one of which remain), the complex included an icehouse (later converted to a recreation center), tennis court, and service garage. Responding to the sloping site, the layout is in oblong rings around a central open space to accommodate gatherings. Giannini planted scores of pine trees to create a semi-forested setting. Following his death in 1953, Martin Starfield of Brooklyn, who had managed the place since 1939, acquired the property. Ownership remains in his family. Over its more than eighty years of operation, Terra Alta has combined aspects of a resort hotel, motel, and summer camp to provide a distinctive setting for guests, most of whom still rent for a one- to two-month period.

SH 6 ARLINGTON

1183 Main Street at Jordan Street; 1880–81

This is another rare survivor in the recreational sphere, in this case of a summer boardinghouse.

SH 7 SCHROON LAKE CENTRAL SCHOOL

1125 Main Street opposite Fowler Street; 1935–36, Carl W. Clark, architect (Cortland, N.Y.)

Perhaps it was in response to its location in a prominent resort community that contributed to this school's exterior being among the more decorous of the period to be found within the Blue Line.

SH 8 LELAND HOUSE ANNEX
54 Leland Avenue; 1880

Festooned with porches to take full advantage of its lakefront location, this fanciful annex to the first Leland House is a poignant reminder of what was once Schroon Lake's finest hotel.

SH 9 STRAND THEATER
1102 Main Street; 1922; alterations 1937

Erected by Joseph Giannini for local motion picture exhibitors Clara and Arthur Richardson, the building also contained two stores and some rooms for overnight guests. In 1937 it was purchased and extensively remodeled by the Rossi Brothers. It continues as one of the few remaining movie houses in the Adirondacks.

SH 10 SHEEHY'S TAVERN
1071 Main Street; ca. 1937, possibly Ward Grover Shippey, architect (Glens Falls, N.Y.)

A stage-set "Tudor" façade marks this watering hole built for Ed Sheehy and for many years operated as Blasdell's Restaurant and Tavern. Though later than other works by Shippey in the area, this building's front has many of the characteristics of his style.

SH 11 BROWN SWAN CLUB
1027 Main Street; 1917, Ward Grover Shippey, architect (Glens Falls, N.Y.)

In contrast to the large resort hotels of the era, brothers P. E. and P. T. Rice developed their establishment with a less formal lodge enframed by sizable cottages (now gone) "to maintain a select patronage," suggesting that, unlike most Schroon Lake hostelries at that time, this "club" excluded Jews. It boasted a nine-hole golf course and riding stable among other amenities. It continues to serve as a hotel, now for the Word of Life Ministries. Just below, at 1051 Main Street, lies the **Yellow Coach Motel**, also by Shippey, which was originally part of the complex, housing a tavern, gift shop, and post office. It remained little changed on the exterior until it was sheathed in wood in 2015.

SH 12 UNION MEETING HOUSE
Potash Hill and Hoffman roads, 5.3 miles west of US 9; 1843

A rare surviving example in the Adirondacks of a mid-19th-century combination rural church and school, built to serve the remote settlement of Loch Muller. Just to the east lies a vacant and deteriorating farmhouse little changed from when it was built in the mid-19th century.

SH 13 SEAGLE MUSIC COLONY
999 Charley Hill Road, 2.5 miles west of US 9; theater and cottages 1922, Ward Grover Shippey, architect (Glens Falls, N.Y.)

The oldest summer training program for singers in the United States was established in 1915 by Oscar Seagle, an internationally

known baritone, in Hague [Section 1]. Seagle then taught at the Brown Swan Club [SH 11] and purchased two Charley Hill farms in 1922. The 19th-century **barn** on one property was enlarged as an **auditorium** for teaching and concerts, and sheathed in a fanciful half-timber mode inspired by cottages Seagle and his wife admired in England. The school was continued by family members following Seagle's death in 1946, and additional enlargements were made to the main building soon thereafter. Much of that building had to be reconstructed in 1950–51 after structural failure during a heavy snowstorm.

ADIRONDACK
Town of Horicon, Warren County

AD 1 ADIRONDACK GENERAL STORE
899 East Shore Drive; ca. 1855 and later
    Still thriving as a general store, this es-

tablishment was built to serve workers at the nearby tannery. An early proprietor, George W. Lee, was also involved in lumbering and real estate development in the community. When he left in 1866 the store was taken over by Thomas Wells, son of the tannery's original owner. Six years later it was purchased by Jesse Bush, son of the tannery's subsequent co-owner. The building has gone through a series of additions, and its general appearance suggests major changes were made during the early 20th century. At various times the establishment also harbored the post office, a boardinghouse upstairs, and a machine shop at the rear.

AD 2 ADIRONDACK SCHOOL
911 East Shore Drive; ca. 1908
    This two-classroom building illustrates the effort to improve rural schools in places that were too remote for, or whose residents were opposed to, consolidation. It remained in operation until 1951, and now serves as a community center.

AD 3 UNION CHURCH
Church Street; 1881
    Built from local donations, this very simple, and very late, iteration of a Greek Revival church was the product of contest and compromise. Benjamin Wells, who developed the tannery, was adamant that a Baptist church serve the nascent community, but others opposed him. The outcome was to erect a house of worship to be used alternatively by Baptists and Methodists and, at other times, used by additional denominations. It is now owned by the Horicon Historical Society.

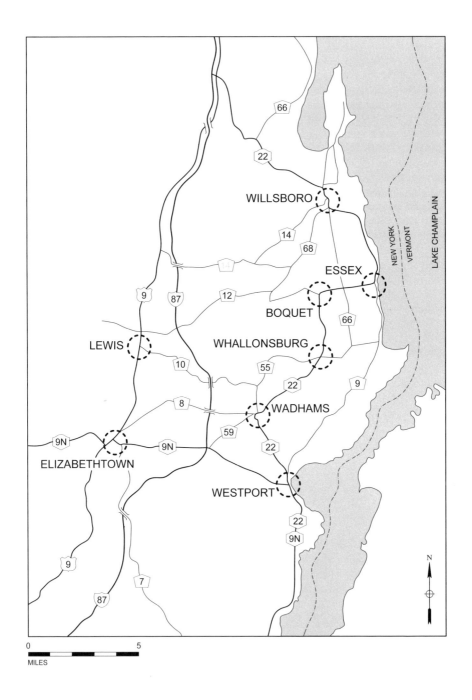

6

CENTRAL LAKE CHAMPLAIN VALLEY and INTERIOR

COMPARED TO MOST OTHER SECTIONS IN THIS GUIDE the area in Essex County that extends along Lake Champlain from just south of the hamlet of Westport to Willsboro Point and the interior lands near the Boquet River is small. Yet it arguably has the richest concentration of significant architecture, particularly from the 19th century. It ranks among the earliest parts of the Adirondacks to be permanently settled, as one of the earliest to spawn industrial development, and as having some of the best agricultural acreage. In eastern parts, the landscape is generally more open than wooded, with gently rolling terrain that renders it very different from the conventional view of an Adirondack setting; however, the economy of this area was closely tied to the natural resources of the interior throughout the 19th century, and the need for industrial and shipping centers along the lake was predicated on those resources. This pattern of growth stands in contrast to that along most of the Vermont side of the lake south of Burlington, where the economy was driven mostly by agriculture and concentrated settlement occurred to a lesser degree. That said, the populations of the three principal lakeside hamlets, Westport, Essex, and Willsboro, as well as the principal interior center, the county seat, Elizabethtown, seldom grew beyond 750, although Essex briefly had as many as 2,500 people during the mid-19th century. These hamlets remain small today because the shift from industry to tourism, which began in the 1870s and was more or less consummated by 1900, led only to modest new population increases.

THE FIRST PERMANENT SETTLEMENT IN THE TOWN OF WESTPORT occurred in 1785; however, until 1815 the territory lay within the Town of Elizabethtown, which was formed in 1798. Westport hamlet was surveyed in 1800, with thirty-four building lots. Eight years later Raymond Coll came from Ticonderoga [Section 5] to build a sawmill, gristmill, blacksmith shop, and lime kilns, as well as a brickyard. Westport Bay, one of the lake's largest, was conducive to shipping, and the opening of the Champlain Canal in 1823 provided a major impetus for trade. By the mid-19th century, the number of canal boats frequenting the bay was said to form a village in its own right, and with the boats came itinerant merchants purveying many goods that were otherwise unavailable.

Lumbering fueled the economy initially, peaking in the early 1830s, by which time it had spawned a substantial amount of building activity. Thereafter the iron industry emerged as the major engine for growth. Westport became a key link between mines in the Town of Moriah [Section 5] and the forges in the Boquet Valley. Merriam's forge was built on the Boquet River in 1825 and others lay farther north. Construction of the Sisco blast furnace (1848) on the point defining the bay's northern edge greatly boosted trade. The boom was short-lived. The Sisco furnace closed a decade after it opened. Efforts for a resurgence occurred when the newly formed Lake Champlain Ore & Iron Company built a blast furnace in 1869 at the foot of

Liberty Street in Westport, but operations lasted only four years. The arrival of the Delaware & Hudson Railway in 1876 was offset by a devastating fire that destroyed a major portion of the hamlet that same year. The railroad did spawn development of the Westport Pulp Mill, which opened in 1880 and eventually included a sawmill, spool mill, lathe mill, and shingle factory.

Westport Inn, Westport, 1887 and later, demolished 1966. (early 20th-century postcard)

The railroad's major impact was in allowing vacationers ready access to the lakefront. Summer visitors had come to Westport by boat as early as the 1840s, but the trade remained small, with little in the way of accommodations. The primary establishment, Person's Hotel, was a victim of the 1876 fire. What became the biggest draw a dozen years later was the celebrated Westport Inn. The establishment actually originated as the hamlet's first frame building, erected as a tavern in 1800 by John Halstead, who also had the hamlet surveyed that same year. To support its business, the Lake Champlain Ore & Iron Company purchased and enlarged the tavern in 1868, renaming it Marvin House. After that venture failed, the hotel and adjacent properties were acquired in 1887 by Alice Lee, one of the hamlet's wealthy residents, who transformed it into a first-class summer resort. The hotel remained in operation well after World War II, but a dwindling trade led to its demolition in 1966.

The Westport Inn likely fostered a trend that had begun earlier, with a number of well-to-do seasonal residents erecting houses to the south along the Main Street. This development accelerated during the early 20th century and continued to the southeast, hugging the shoreline off Dudley Road, with sizable residences that were away from public view. Toward that road's southern end lies Camp Dudley, which moved from New Jersey to Lake Champlain in 1903 [WP 1]. Westport's other principal attraction was (and remains) the county fairgrounds, which moved from Elizabethtown to the Westport waterfront in 1865 and relocated to a site near the railroad station in 1885, where it continues to operate [WP 23].

Along the Boquet River three miles to the northwest, the small hamlet of Wadhams was closely linked to Westport's 19th-century industrial development. Here a substantial falls attracted settlers as early as 1802. Initial attempts at establishing grist- and sawmills as well as a forge came to naught; however, the economy was revived following the arrival of General Luman Wadhams from Connecticut via Lewis [LE 2] in 1823. He replaced the derelict mills and attracted others to build new support facilities, including a store, inn, and school. Lumbering for construction became the principal industry during the 1830s and 1840s. By that time, too, agriculture emerged as a major source of revenue owing to the extent of cleared land and hospitable soil conditions. After the Civil War, iron making took on a new importance, in large part due to Daniel Payne, who became the driving force in the community, as Wadhams had been earlier. While the iron industry declined dramatically after the mid-1880s, agriculture, milling, and the production of lumber continued to be staples into the 20th century.

North along the river, Whallonsburg, a small crossroads settlement dating to the 1820s, became home to a sawmill, iron forge, carding mill, and plaster mill over the decades that followed. Like Wadhams, it was also a service center for the farms that surrounded it, many of them quite prosperous by the mid-19th century. The tiny hamlet of Boquet harbored milling and iron-making plants as well.

Westport was not the only beneficiary of the industries straddling the Boquet River. Lumbering occurred into the mountains ever farther west, and agricultural production blossomed on much of the cleared land.

Two and a half miles east of Boquet hamlet lies Essex, which during the 1820s and 1830s was arguably the most important community in the area. First settled in the late 18th century, Essex grew to become a supplier of several hundred lake craft during the War of 1812. Ransom Noble, who came from New Milford, Connecticut, in 1799, established a tannery, which prospered to the point that he was able to acquire huge tracts of timberland to supply his operation. Within two decades Ransom Noble & Sons had also emerged as a major force in lake commerce, transporting timber, potash, and iron ore. The company diversified to include sawmills, a forge at Willsboro, and a mine in Lewis. Son Belden Noble made a fortune in his own right, augmenting the business through real estate speculation and financial services, operating throughout the area. By 1855 the firm also held some 3,000 acres for agriculture.

Daniel Ross and his offspring complemented the Nobles in their enterprises. After opening the hamlet's first commercial establishment in 1784, he erected a sawmill at Boquet and a gristmill and an iron forge in Willsboro. In Essex he built a distillery, an ashery, and a wharf. Son Henry Howard Ross served in the U.S. Congress from 1825 to 1827, developed one of the foremost law practices in the area, and became the first Essex County judge in 1848. His brother, William Daniel Ross, continued family mercantile operations and ran the Boquet Iron Works, as well as a shipping line. He also ranked among the county's largest landowners. The two families did not enjoy a complete monopoly on business. The firm of Lyon & Palmer, for example, built a sash-and-blind factory in the early 19th century that lasted until 1879, when it was taken over by the Essex Horse Nail Company, which continued operations until the plant burned some forty years later. By 1850 Essex ranked as the lake's biggest port on the New York side, exporting goods from an interior area of considerable radius.

While Essex controlled shipping from the hinterland, the community never embraced the railroad. The town did not cooperate with the Delaware & Hudson in floating bonds to support construction of its line to Plattsburgh. The tracks were located over a mile to the west of the hamlet, and a station was not built there until 1886, a decade after that at Westport [WP 23]. Several houses were adapted for tourist accommodations, but there was never a fashionable hotel erected comparable to the Westport Inn. The eventual focal point for summer residency was the Crater Club, along the lake south of the hamlet. Founded in 1899 by entrepreneur and sportsman John Bird Burnham and largely developed by him, the club attracted writers, lawyers, and conservationists among others who enjoyed an informal, camp-like atmosphere amid wooded grounds in rustic cottages of Burnham's design. North of the hamlet, land along the lake began to be developed with large country houses, most of them out of view, around the same time. During the post–World War II era, the abundance of early 19th-century architecture remaining in Essex became an attraction in itself. Many of these places have been purchased and renovated for seasonal use or as places of retirement. Newcomers and long-term residents were instrumental in founding ECHO (Essex Community Heritage Organization) in 1970, the first preservation group in the Adirondacks, whose members have worked vigorously to protect the hamlet and its environs in subsequent decades.

Willsboro's roots extend back earlier than its neighbors'. In 1765 William Gilliland, an enterprising New York merchant, came to the area with the intention of developing a manor, much as Sir William Johnson was trying to do farther south [Section 2]. His grand vision never materialized beyond the inceptive stage, and circumstances surrounding the Revolution ruined him. Nevertheless the town was established in 1788 as Willsborough in his honor. Reputedly the first ironworks in the Champlain Valley began there two years later. Several others followed, the most ambitious of which was the blast furnace and forge built for Belden Noble. Iron dominated the economy for several decades, but started to decline during the mid-1880s. By that time, the town had become well known for the bluestone (a variety of limestone) that was quarried on Willsboro Point. Used extensively for building construction in the area, this product was also employed along the Champlain Canal and later for the foundations of the New York State Capitol and the Brooklyn Bridge.

One of the town's most enduring businesses was a pulp mill. In 1885 Augustus G. Paine came to Willsboro to take over the three-year-old operation, which his father, a New York banker, had received as a result of foreclosure. Under Paine's direction, the enterprise was reorganized as the Champlain Fiber Company and became part of the New York & Pennsylvania Paper Company. The plant grew to be the hamlet's pre-eminent industry until its closure in 1965. A very different enterprise has come to enjoy the same longevity. In 1949 Payson Hatch and John Kiehl opened the Willsboro Mining Company for the extraction and refining of wollastonite. Koert Burnham (son of John Bird Burnham) had uncovered a large deposit of this calcium-based mineral, long known as a reinforcing agent, near Willsboro a dozen years previous. He was instrumental in spurring companies to find modern applications (porcelain fixtures, roof finishes, vinyl tile, paper, and paint among them) and also in developing the process for its refinement. When the company foundered, Burnham secured a long-term lease from the Cabot Corporation of Boston, which took over operations in 1951 and built a large new plant two years later, soon becoming one of the largest producers of wollastonite in the country. The business changed hands twice thereafter, being acquired by current owner NYCO in 1979.

Well before quarrying or any other industry, Willsboro Point was a focus of lumbering and then agriculture. By the turn of the 20th century, lakefront acreage was

Champlain Fiber Company plant, Willsboro, begun 1885. (early 20th-century postcard)

being developed for summer residences, of which Augustus Paine's camp at Flat Rock was among the earliest. To the south and southwest of the hamlet, agricultural development prevailed during the 19th and much of the 20th centuries. One of the most intact early 19th-century farmsteads in the region lay a few miles north of the hamlet until it burned in August 2016.

Farther afield, the Town of Lewis was formed when it broke from Willsboro in 1805. Settlement had begun a decade earlier, but the major impetus for growth came from an iron forge, established around 1837, and which remained in operation until the late 19th century. As the iron industry started to recede in the 1890s, no other substantial source of revenue replaced it. The town's population declined 62 percent between 1880 and 1930. Some automobile-oriented development took place along US 9, especially in the small hamlet of Lewis, as improvements to that road were made during the interwar decades. Construction of the Adirondack Northway in the 1960s, however, has left Lewis somewhat isolated. Since its early settlement farming has been important, primarily in eastern parts adjoining the Champlain Valley where soil conditions are most favorable. Here John E. Milholland created an expansive model farm in the early 20th century [LE 6]. A native son who had made a fortune in New York, Milholland developed his estate as a center for community events as well as a retreat. In 1944 it was purchased by Ivan Galamian for the Meadowmount School of Music, a nationally renowned summer training camp for young musicians of exceptional talent.

Lying a few miles to the south on US 9, Elizabethtown was formed from Crown Point in 1798, several years after settlement began along the Boquet River. Although its situation was remote, it became the county seat in 1805, perhaps because it lay apart from the developing industrial and shipping hubs on Lake Champlain and thus was ostensibly less susceptible to the competing interests among them. To facilitate access, the Essex Turnpike Company was established in 1807 to build a road from Lake George to Elizabethtown (roughly the path of US 9), and in 1845 a plank road was laid to Westport, giving the community better access to the lake. But if

Elizabethtown was geographically removed, its development was spurred virtually from the start by the two families who were so instrumental in the ascendancy of Essex. Daniel Ross and his brother, Theodore, constructed one of the hamlet's first gristmills, opened a store, and purchased much of the land along the Boquet. Daniel built the first sawmill and a distillery, as well as invested in the community's nascent iron industry. By the 1810s, Ransom Noble's sons, Charles and Henry R., moved to Elizabethtown to operate a tannery and later opened a store for their leather products [EL 22]. Charles also owned a few thousand acres of timberland and several iron mines.

Iron became Elizabethtown's economic mainstay into the mid-19th century, but, as elsewhere in the area, was on the wane by the 1880s. A decade earlier, tourism emerged as an important substitute. Situated in a large bowl known as Pleasant Valley and surrounded by some of the High Peaks, Elizabethtown had a dramatic setting that was also among the most accessible interior Adirondack locations. The arrival of the railroad at Westport, eight miles to the east, made for a relatively easy journey by stage. The three-story Mansion House (later the Deer's Head Inn [EL 12]) was constructed on the hamlet's main street opposite the courthouse in 1873–74. Soon thereafter, the Valley House, a modest hostelry on the Boquet, was moved and enlarged. By far the most ambitious establishment was the Windsor, begun in 1876 by expanding a residence and aggrandized by large additions ca. 1881–82 and 1889–90. Both the Deer's Head and Windsor enjoyed long runs as fashionable

Windsor Hotel, Elizabethtown, 1876, ca. 1881, 1889–90, demolished 1968. (early 20th-century postcard)

hotels, operating into the 1960s. At the same time, a number of people attracted to the location erected substantial summer houses near the hotels on the main street and further afield. With a nine-hole golf course developed on the lower slopes of Cobble Hill in 1896 Elizabethtown became foremost a resort community where places developed for leisure dominated a genteel landscape.

Court Street, Elizabethtown. (ca. 1930s postcard)

*   *   *   *   *

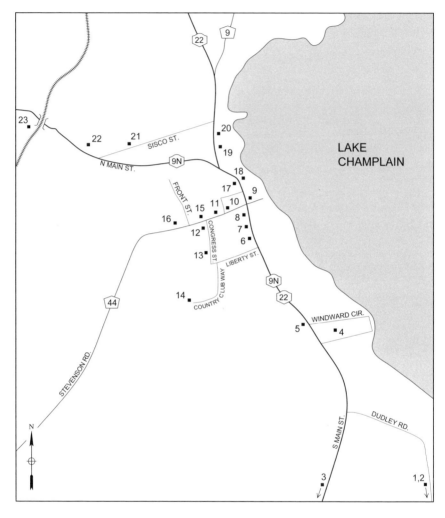

WESTPORT

Town of Westport, Essex County

Supporting a current population of around 500, the hamlet of Westport has experienced relatively little change over the past hundred years. Situated on sloping ground along the shore of Lake Champlain, the community continues to attract well-heeled seasonal residents and tourists. A large children's camp, the county fairgrounds, and a repertory theater fur-

ther boost the local economy. Westport is one of the few Adirondack communities on Lake Champlain to retain a consolidated school and an Amtrak station. The hamlet boasts a fine array of 19th-century houses in a mature landscape. The only major architectural loss has been that of the Westport Inn.

186

WP 1 CAMP DUDLEY

126 Dudley Road (accessible by prior arrangement)

Established in 1885, Dudley is the oldest children's camp in continuous operation in the United States. Begun under the auspices of the YMCA in northern New Jersey, the camp moved to Barbers Point on Lake Champlain in 1903, remaining there for five seasons. The current site, some 3.5 miles south of the hamlet, was acquired in 1908. Initially the complex was limited to tents pitched on the ground to form a large, horseshoe-shaped green where athletic and other activities occurred. Though the institution has grown substantially over the last hundred years, with a current camper population of around 350 and a staff of 150 occupying some 120 acres, the campus's original configuration remains quite evident.

Steps were soon taken to develop the site in a more permanent fashion. Platform tents were introduced in 1911. Two years later the **Lodge** (later renamed **Beckman Hall** to honor Herman Carl Beckman, who served as the camp's director from 1908 to 1947) was constructed at the northern end of the green to provide a commons and social hall. John F. Jackson, a New York–based architect who did extensive work for the YMCA, designed the building and may well have prepared plans for others. Though it burned in 1915, Beckman Hall was quickly rebuilt following the original plans. This sprawling shingled pile, sheltering an enormous space now used entirely for eating, was renovated in 1969 and 2004, but still retains much of its orig-

inal character. The **Witherbee Theater** of 1924–25, also designed by Jackson, defines the green's west side and echoes Beckman Hall's basic form. Funded by Mrs. Walter C. Witherbee of Port Henry in memory of her husband [Section 5], the facility includes a large performance space. A 2001 renovation added to the extensive porch.

At the green's southern end, **McLean Cottage** was erected in 1926 to house male visitors, mostly the fathers of campers. It, too, has been recently renovated to serve as off-season quarters for counselor training. A campaign to replace the tents

with **cabins** was launched in 1930, and all campers were so accommodated by mid-decade. Several cabins have been added since, bringing the total to forty-one. They stand in tight clusters along portions of the south and east sides of the green, many of them overlooking the lake. In contrast to most such quarters, these were designed more like miniature vacation residences, with slab log siding and masonry chimneys. Moreover, the cabins vary from one to another in their designs, while forming a unified ensemble. Each unit houses seven to eight campers, a counselor, and his assistant. Groups of parents and alumni raised the money to construct the cabins.

Below the cabins lies the **Avery Boathouse** of 1914, which originally included the camp library on its second level. Behind Beckman Hall, the **Post Manual Training Building**, known as the **Institute**, was constructed in 1913 from a donation by James H. Post. Adjacent is the camp **Office Building**, recently constructed, which forms a complementary addition to its earlier neighbors. Another recent addition is the **Middlebury Outdoor Pavilion** of 2013, a spirited interpretation of a lean-to and a bandshell that serves as a stage for performances on the green. Of note, too, is the **Roe house**, a former farm dwelling erected around 1835–40 on Dudley Road just north of the core.

WP 2 SCHOOLHOUSE
Dudley Road, .5 mile south of Main Street; 1816

This is probably the oldest schoolhouse to remain in the Adirondacks and reflects the importance accorded to education by at least some of the first generation of settlers. Although elementary in character, the building was nonetheless well constructed of limestone quarried nearby. It remained in operation for a century.

WP3 WESTPORT AIRPORT
6103 NY 9N; ca. 1930, hangar 1932

This small grass airstrip may be among the earliest in the Adirondacks. John de Blois Wack and his wife, Ethel Barksdale du Pont Wack, both licensed pilots, who had a large summer house nearby, spearheaded the project. During its early years, at least, the primary purpose of the airfield was to facilitate access to Westport for the Wacks (who had a main house in Santa Barbara and a ranch in Arizona) and other wealthy seasonal residents. The couple were also credited with initiatives

to remake the golf club [WP 14] and establish the Westport Yacht Club.

Of standardized steel-frame construction, the hangar represented a state-of-the-art facility of its kind when it was erected in 1932, and remains almost completely intact, a rare surviving example of its kind. Also noteworthy is a smaller hangar of somewhat later vintage, which serves the Planter Sky Ranch on Airport and Wheeler roads in Edinburg [Section 2].

WP 4 WINDWARD, COLONEL D. D. JOHNSTON HOUSE
5 Windward Drive, off Main Street (NY 9N); 1906; north wing 1907

A great shingled Colonial Revival residence of a kind found in resort communities in the Northeast, this house benefits from a hillside site that provides sweeping views of Westport Bay, the lake, and Vermont's Green Mountains. During much of the second half of the 20th century it served as an inn.

WP 5 BEECH HILL
6333 Main Street; 1836 (?); mid-19th century; later additions and alterations

A number of uncertainties surround the history of this house. It was ostensibly built in 1836 for the Reverend William W. Hickox, but this date is too early for its design, which appears to have been patterned after the Gothic cottages of Alexander Jackson Davis, probably as published in the plan books of Andrew Jackson Downing. More likely, the house was transformed or rebuilt for prominent local resident William Frisbie, who purchased the land in the mid-19th century. The north wing dates from later in the 19th century and seems quite pedestrian by comparison. The south wing came later still, commissioned by A. M. Sherwood from New York, who purchased the place in 1899 as a summer retreat. Reputedly his wife turned to her friend Stanford White for the design, but its appearance suggests otherwise. The front porch was replaced and other alterations occurred either under Sherwood's ownership or that of Mary McCarthy, who operated the Beech Hill Inn there between 1920 and 1935.

WP 6 SAWYER HOUSE
6447 Main Street; before 1858; additions ca. 1870s, ca. 1880s

Whatever the appearance of the original house, it was completely transformed around the 1870s by a lively front in the Second Empire mode. The porch was likely added not long thereafter. At least some of these changes may have occurred in refashioning the place as a seasonal residence. It is now the Victorian Lady Bed & Breakfast.

WP 7 BAPTIST CHURCH
6459 Main Street; 1877, W. S. Purdy, architect (New York)

During the 1870s the architect worked closely with the American Baptist Home Mission Society, and thus it is not surprising that he was commissioned to prepare plans for this church after its predecessor fell victim to the 1876 fire. Purdy also advertised the design for sale to other congregations. It has been preserved as a local history center.

WP 8 INN AT WESTPORT
1234 Stevenson Road (CR 44) at Main Street; ca. 1877; ground floor alterations 1928

Erected soon after the 1876 fire, this building was purchased by owners of the Marvin House (later the Westport Inn) as an annex. In 1928 its ground floor was remade for shops and was likely the work of New York architect and summer resident Russell F. Whitehead.

WP 9 COMMERCIAL BLOCK
6470–76 Main Street; ca. 1876–77

Like the hotel annex, this group of three stores was one of the hasty post-fire rebuilding projects. It is a good representative example of mid-19th-century commercial architecture on a relatively modest scale.

WP 10 WESTPORT LIBRARY ASSOCIATION
6 Harris Lane at Stevenson Road; 1887–88, Andrews & Jacques, architects (Boston); addition 1907–08; portions demolished 1959

Founded in 1884–85 by year-round residents, the association soon set about constructing a permanent home. Seasonal residents contributed significantly. Alice

Lee, who concurrently purchased the Marvin House (Westport Inn), was central to organizing the effort. The owners of what had been Person's Lake House, which had burned in the 1876 fire, deeded the adjacent land to the association with the provision that it always serve as a public park. As a result a rather diminutive shingled building has a strong civic presence. Designed by a prominent Boston architectural firm well known for its country houses, the library received a large addition, including its tower, in 1907–08, the result of another fundraising drive by Lee to honor John Tyler Cutting, a major donor before his death. The addition may well have been by the same architects. The portion housing a sizable community hall was demolished in 1959. What remained received historically sensitive renovations in 1991–92, designed by Crawford & Stearns, architects, of Syracuse.

WP 11 CHARLES EDDY HOUSE
1233 Stevenson Road; ca. 1833, Aaron Felt, builder

Westport's Federal and Greek Revival houses offer a vivid testament to the hamlet's growth and prosperity during the 1820s and 1830s. This chaste, gable-end residence was constructed for a prominent merchant and remained in the hands of descendants until 1962.

WP 12 SAMUEL FARNSWORTH HOUSE
7 Congress Street; ca. 1830s; ca. late 1880s

With a magisterial view, this Greek Revival house is among the most imposing in the hamlet. It was purchased in 1887 as a summer residence by James Howell, mayor of Brooklyn and an iron manufacturer. He added the rear section and it is likely his plant made the iron gates and fence along the street.

WP 13 WILLIAM CUTTING HOUSE
3 Liberty Street; 1836

A leading merchant, politician, and civic leader, Cutting outdid his contemporaries by erecting a massive, temple-front dwelling on a scale seldom seen in the Adirondacks during the early 19th century. The Lake Champlain Ore & Iron Company purchased the property in 1868 for executive use. Later, Alice Lee owned the house, using it to quarter guests.

WP 14 WESTPORT COUNTRY CLUB
49 Country Club Lane, off Liberty Street; 1927–28, Clark & Whitehead, architects (New York)

A six-hole course, created in the late 1890s as part of Westport Inn, was enlarged to nine holes around 1900; in 1928 it was completely redesigned as an eighteen-hole course by a New York golf architect, Thomas Winton, who worked extensively in New England, New York, and New Jersey. During this latter development campaign Whitehead's clubhouse was erected in a Colonial Revival vein somewhat suggestive of many 18th-century "Dutch" houses in the lower Hudson Valley.

WP 15 KIMBERLEA, RUSSELL F. WHITEHEAD HOUSE
1205 Stevenson Road; 1865; additions and alterations ca. 1920, Russell Whitehead, architect (New York)

After World War I, Whitehead purchased this house from Sarah Eddy and set about

remaking it inside and out in a whimsical, astylar vein as his family's summer residence. Later in the decade he became architect for the Westport Inn Realty Company. Aside from what may have been numerous small projects for the Westport Inn, he designed the yacht club (1927) and facilities for the Westport Country Club [WP 14].

WP 16 PLATT ROGERS HALSTEAD HOUSE
1193 Stevenson Road; ca. 1825 and later

A Revolutionary War veteran, Halstead came to Westport as a land surveyor, eventually accruing sufficient wealth to construct this substantial hilltop residence. He was later able to spend a major portion of each year in Florida, returning here for the summers. The fanciful porch was probably added around the 1880s.

WP 17 CHARLES HATCH HOUSE
Main and Merrihew streets; 1825 and later

Another early resident, Hatch built the hamlet's first store, was instrumental in establishing the town, and served as a judge. His large Federal house was subsequently occupied by a succession of prominent owners, including William Cutting's brother Franklin, and his son-in-law, Freeborn Page, who deeded the adjacent land to the library association. A grand stable and carriagehouse was built around the mid-19th century.

Next door to the north lies the **house** of **Aaron Mack** (1832), who served as town clerk, town commissioner, and trustee of the Essex County Academy. Hatch moved there in 1833. The dwelling itself was moved toward the rear of the property with the realignment of Main Street in 1970.

WP 18 METHODIST CHURCH
6486 Main Street; 1837; additions 1867; tower added later

The mid-19th-century front of this edifice is typical of the Methodists' penchant for plainness, with a slight nod to fashion in its use of lancet windows [see also ES 22]. The corner tower, by contrast, abandons all reserve, with a belfry more suggestive of an exposition building than a house of worship. In 1938–39 the congregation joined the Baptists to form what is now the Westport Federated Church.

WP 19 LAKE VIEW GRANGE NO. 970
22 Champlain Avenue (CR 22); 1921–28, Vernon Gough, builder

The National Grange of the Order of the Patrons of Husbandry was founded in 1867 to restore stability to agriculture in the South. Its agenda included agricultural education, cooperative buying and selling, and advocacy. Grange halls also became important social centers for rural populations. The movement grew to be a national one, taking root in Essex County in the 1870s. The Westport chapter was established in 1903 along with ones in Whallonsburg [WH 4], Crown Point, the Ausable Valley [JA 6, Section 7], and Willsboro. Twelve years after completion of this building the chapter moved to consolidate with that at Wadhams

[WD 4]. Thereafter, a roller rink occupied the premises until it was purchased by the American Legion in 1953. Eighteen years later the municipal government acquired it for use as a community and youth center. It now houses town offices.

WP 20 ALLEN GENERAL STORE
32 Champlain Avenue; 1878, W. W. Davis, builder (?)

Set well apart from businesses in the hamlet's small commercial center, this store block was built to serve the surrounding neighborhood. The second floor was likely used as a residence. Apart from the recent vinyl siding, the building's exterior has experienced little change.

WP 21 WESTPORT CENTRAL SCHOOL
25 Sisco Street; 1932–33; additions 1953–54, Sargent, Webster, Crenshaw & Foley, architects (Syracuse); gymnasium, Dodge Chamberlin Luzine Weber Architects (Rensselaer, N.Y.)

In its sparing, crisp development of detail, the original portion of this building bears affinity with one erected slightly later in Keeseville [KS 13] and may have been by the same architects, Alvin Inman of Plattsburgh and his associate Quentin F. Haig, who resided in Westport.

WP 22 ESSEX COUNTY FAIRGROUNDS
N. Main (NY 9N) and Sisco streets; 1885 and later

The unusually intact assemblage of late 19th- and early 20th-century structures lies on the fourth site of the fair. The event was initiated in 1848 near Keeseville and moved to Elizabethtown two years later. The fair relocated once again in 1865 to the Westport waterfront. Finally, the Essex County Agricultural Society purchased the current property in 1885 and erected **Floral Hall** as an exposition centerpiece that same year—the work of local builder David Clark. Adjacent at 3 Sisco Street the **Essex County Cooperative Extension Center** was built in 1923–24 as the Junior Achievement Building, where classes were held in manual arts and crafts until 1940. Subsequently it has housed Cornell University's extension services in agriculture and home economics.

WP 23 DELAWARE & HUDSON RAILWAY DEPOT
6705 N. Main Street; 1875–76; 1891; 1908

Except for North Creek [NC 7], this is the Delaware & Hudson's oldest station in the Adirondacks, although much of its appearance dates to additions and alterations made in 1891. The freight house was extended in 1908. The building was sold to the town in 1974, with Amtrak given a long-term lease. It has since been restored on the exterior, with the freight house imaginatively adapted as the Depot Theater. Like the station at Port Henry it also continues to serve train passengers. Though considerably altered, the nearby **Westport Hotel** at 6601 N. Main Street was built concurrently with the station to serve its trade (guest rooms did not open until 1879). Originally named the Gates House, it has been continuously operated ever since.

WADHAMS
Town of Westport, Essex County

While its industrial base has long since gone, leaving only the falls on the Boquet River to suggest that past, the small hamlet of Wadhams has otherwise experienced relatively little physical change since the 19th century and offers a good example of a rural center from that period. Surrounding the hamlet, an agricultural landscape on rolling terrain likewise gives some sense of what the area was like over a hundred years ago.

WD 1 TAYLOR HOUSE AND FARM
92 Taylor Road, off Youngs Road; ca. 1830s–40s

A remarkable surviving example of a farmstead developed around the second quarter of the 19th century, this complex is laid out in a traditional New England manner, with house and barn forming a linear progression extending back at a right angle to the road. But in contrast to many New England examples, the house is aligned with the barn instead of with the road. The front suggests a store of some kind, with living quarters and utility spaces behind. Here, too, the barns are connected to one another, but not to the house. The sequence of four barn sections indicates that the ensemble was erected in stages.

WD 2 AUTOMOBILE GARAGE
Westport Road (CR 22) at Elizabethtown-Wadhams Road (CR 8); ca. 1925

An early and now unusual remnant of the automobile's emergence as a transportation mainstay, especially in rural communities, this building likely contained sales as well as repair and maintenance facilities. It later served as offices for the nearby Anson Dairy.

WD 3 WADHAMS FREE LIBRARY
Elizabethtown-Wadhams Road at Westport Road and Boquet River; 1962–63, Curtis Lobdell, designer

Situated on a once prime industrial location, the hamlet's library manifests a relatively unconventional embrace of modernism in a small Adirondack community. The designer was the husband of the library association's president, and the labor to construct the edifice was in large part donated by residents.

WD 4 WADHAMS GRANGE NO. 1015
2 Church Street at CR 22; ca. 1845; 1874

The building's front section, erected as Luman Wadhams's store, was made into a larger emporium some thirty years later for H. C. Avery. The grange, formed in 1875 and the first in Essex County, moved into the building in 1911.

WD 5 WADHAMS AND WESTPORT POWER & LIGHT COMPANY HYDRO-ELECTRIC PLANT
8 Church Street; 1904; 1908

This rare vestige of a first-generation hydroelectric plant, one of the oldest in the state, was built for Daniel French Payne to supply power to Witherbee, Sherman & Company in Mineville [Section 5], eleven miles to the south. Soon the plant was also providing service to Wadhams and Westport, the generator for which was housed in the added northern section. From 1948 until it closed in 1969, the facility sold power to the Niagara-Mohawk Power Company. Seven years later Matthew Foley purchased the structure and resumed operations as an independent supplier. Some of the original machinery

remains; other vintage pieces of equipment have been taken from elsewhere.

WD 6 UNION CHURCH
33 Church Street; 1875; tower 1894

Constructed for a congregation that had been active since the 1830s, the building was partially financed by Daniel Payne. It was rededicated as a Methodist Episcopal Church in 1893, after which the ornate tower was added and the windows probably remodeled, transforming what had been a rather plain building. To the rear is probably the sole surviving example in the Adirondacks of a shed used to shelter congregants' horses and rigs in inclement weather. The church edifice is now a residence.

WD 7 CONGREGATIONAL CHURCH
2569 Lewis-Wadhams Road (CR 10) at CR 22; 1837, Jason Braman, builder; alterations 1898

What is now the hamlet's centerpiece was moved from the west side of the falls in 1866, a considerable feat for a small community at that time. The windows were installed in 1898. Three years later, a former stable and upstairs dance hall built around the 1840s as an annex to the adjacent Exchange Hotel (later Chappel House) was moved to the church's rear and converted to a **parish hall**. Occupying a key corner site, the hotel was demolished, the one major loss aside from mill buildings the town has suffered. The complex now serves the United Church of Christ.

WD 8 COMMERCIAL BUILDINGS

Opposite the church is a range of 19th-century store buildings of a kind once common to rural communities in many parts of the Northeast. The **J. R. Delano store and tavern (a)** (ca. 1829) at 2576 Lewis-Wadhams Road is the oldest. Its original selling space is more or less intact, now refurbished as a bakery and restaurant of area renown. While dating from some thirty years later, the **store building (b)** (ca. 1860) at No. 2572 retains the same basic characteristics. The **Union Store (c)** (ca. 1852) at No. 2570 was erected for William L. Wadhams as a cooperative venture run by some fifty to sixty farmers. Daniel Payne established a general store there in 1869, and under the auspices of later proprietors the premises continued to serve that function until 1985.

WD 9 WILLIAM L. WADHAMS HOUSE
*2565 Lewis-Wadhams Road; ca. 1852;
additions late 19th century*

Having taken over family interests, Luman Wadhams's son William built a simple, one-and-one-half-story house more or less concurrently with his store and across the street from it and his mother's residence. Not long after his death in 1865, the family's land and milling properties were purchased by Daniel Payne. It was likely that Payne built the rear additions as well as the front porch. For a number of decades in the 20th century it was run as a boardinghouse named Elmwood and is now offices for an insurance company.

WD 10 ELIZABETH MacDONALD AND DAVID BROWN HOUSE
224 Merriam Forge Road, mid- to late 19th century; additions 2003–05, Premises—Bryan Burke, architect

The original dwelling was built by a freedman who came to the area to work at Merriam's forge and was remodeled around the turn of the 20th century. The addition for MacDonald and Brown nearly doubled the house's size with a block containing an airy studio and, to one side, a sauna and children's loft above—all connected by a covered walkway that also serves as the primary entrance. Burke designed these components on a ten-by-five-foot module, with steel columns, each comprised of four angles (L-shaped bars) tied by welded spacers near the top and bottom—all resting on concrete footings. The walls are formed by steel-frame doors

with wooden slats as infill. Evocative of modernist design from half a century earlier and of traditional Japanese architecture without overt ties to either, the scheme is one of the most striking and original recent works of architecture in the Adirondacks.

WHALLONSBURG
Town of Essex, Essex County

Settled later than Wadhams, the hamlet of Whallonsburg is considerably smaller and less densely developed. It provides an interesting comparison as most of its buildings were erected during the late 19th and early 20th centuries. Nearby, on Walter and Leaning roads lie rich collections of farmhouses from the first half of the 19th century.

WH 1 ESSEX COUNTY HOME AND INFIRMARY
1447 NY 22; 1859–60 and later

Begun slightly before the rebuilding of the Warren County Home [WA 1], this complex is considerably more intact and conveys some sense of the isolation in which these refuges for the poor were situated. The institution itself was formed in 1832 on a forty-five-acre farm formerly belonging to shipbuilder John Winslow. An inspection in 1858 found the facility in deteriorated condition, and bolstered by the same legislation that led to the Warren County Home, construction began on the first of several new brick buildings: the **west wing** (behind the main block), which was the work of Keeseville builders Dowling & Prescott. The main section, or **east wing** facing the road, and the **milk house** were added in 1873–74 by the successor firm, Prescott & Weston. The **infirmary**, on the south side, dates to 1899. At various times, the complex sheltered orphans, wives of prisoners, paupers, physically handicapped persons, the elderly, and the mentally ill, averaging around 100 inhabitants at any given time. The county sold the complex in 1959, and much of it has sat vacant for decades.

WH 2 METHODIST EPISCOPAL CHURCH
1575 NY 22; 1888

Situated on the hamlet's edge, the former church is a variant on designs Philadelphia architect Benjamin D. Price prepared for the Methodists during the 1880s and 1890s. Others in the Adirondacks that were derived from this source include Methodist churches at Bolton Landing [BL 6, Section 1], Long Lake, Speculator, and Indian Lake, as well as the Presbyterian Church at Wanakena [WN 1, Section 10]. The church closed in 1994 and the building is now vacant.

WH 3 WHALLONSBURG SCHOOL
833 Walker Road (CR 55); 1932

Consolidating rural schools in a central district did not occur in every part of the Adirondacks during the interwar decades. Here the improvements entailed erecting a new, two-classroom building, decorous in its appearance and equipped with heating and plumbing systems. Similar projects were undertaken during the 1930s at Upper Jay [UJ 3, Section 7], Jay, Clintonville, and Hopkinton [HO 4, Section 8]. It is currently vacant.

WH 4 WHALLONSBURGH GRANGE NO. 354
1610 NY 22 at Whallons Bay Road (CR 55); 1915, Fred Nualla, builder (Port Henry)

When the Whallonsburgh Grange (formed in 1903) lost its quarters to fire, a new, purpose-built facility was constructed. Its form alludes to barns of the period. As was common to these facilities, the upstairs is a large, open space for meetings, dances, wedding receptions, dinners, and other collective activities that made the grange a multi-faceted community center. The building was moved a short distance in 1933 to allow for highway construction. After a period of declining use, ownership was transferred to the Town of Essex in 2006. Two years later the Whallonsburg Civic Association leased the premises for an event center, bringing back some of its historical role as a locus of community engagement.

WH 5 COMMERCIAL BUILDINGS

Most conspicuous among the hamlet's small cluster of commercial architecture is the **Whitcomb Garage (a)**, probably built in stages during the second quarter of the 20th century, at 1598 NY 22 where it intersects with Whallons Bay Road. As was typical in sparsely populated areas, such facilities normally included sales as well as service functions. Nearby at 870 Whallons Bay Road is the **J. H. Rice general store (b)**, dating to the late 19th or early 20th centuries and typical of the period. The **Ralph Lobdell feed and hardware store (c)** at No. 878 was built in 1925 and is another good example of a rural emporium of that time.

WH 6 REYNOLDS HOUSE
599 Walker Road; ca. 1815; porch mid-19th century

This one-and-one-half-story house may have been built for Abner Reynolds as his initial residence or for a relative. It received a porch and a few other embellishments during the mid-19th century. In recent years it has been carefully restored inside and out to its mid-19th-century appearance.

WH 7 ABNER REYNOLDS HOUSE
515 Walker Road; ca. 1830s

Reynolds's large brick house farther west is a more refined affair, with a well-detailed Greek Revival entryway. The exterior is somewhat unusual in its use of segmental arches over the entry and windows.

WH 8 HOUSE
Walker and Sayre roads; ca. 1850s

Little is known about this equally sizable wood-frame house of later vintage standing at the western end of Walker Road. Its size and configuration of dual entries suggest it may have been built for two generations or branches of a family. It may also have been built in two or more stages.

WH 9 BLACK KETTLE FARM
2 Leaning Road at Cook Road; early 19th century

What is now known as Black Kettle Farm has an unusual arrangement for the region, being built into the sloping ground and having a long, linear arrangement, with a porch extending across the main level. The dwelling was erected in at least three stages, its three-bay center section (door and two windows) appears to be the earliest. The two-bay (two windows) western section was then added. It was probably at this time or later that the rear ell (originally a barn) was constructed. Finally, the three-bay eastern section (window, door, window) completed the project. While the connected barn was a New England convention, other aspects suggest it may have been built as a memory image of 18th-century Dutch farmhouses in the lower Hudson Valley.

WH 10 STAFFORD HOUSES

Charles Stafford's house **(a)** of 1842 at 91 Leaning Road assumes a conventional form for large farm dwellings of its period, save for its abbreviation of a five-bay front to four. The **residence** constructed in 1824 for his father, **Richard Stafford (b)**, at 121 Leaning Road, has an elaborate Federal entryway surmounted by a Palladian window. A cooper from Rhode Island, Stafford purchased this tract above the Boquet River in 1809 and erected a dwelling on this site soon thereafter. The current house is a testament to his financial success and is reminiscent of ones in New England with which he would have been familiar prior to his move.

WH 11 H. T. HALE HOUSE
201 Leaning Road; ca. 1850

This dwelling occupies lower ground and is more modest—of a kind often found in the Champlain Valley, save for its use of uncut stone that was probably quarried nearby.

BOQUET
Town of Essex, Essex County

BO 1 BOQUET CHAPEL
2172 NY 22; 1855

Built as a mission of St. John's Episcopal Church in Essex [ES 21], the chapel was closely patterned after a design in Richard Upjohn's *Rural Architecture*, published three years earlier and a key work in disseminating the architect's approach to adapting "true" Gothic principles to small, inexpensive houses of worship. The effect is marred somewhat by the recent addition of an enclosed entry porch. It is now Foothills Baptist Church at the Boquet.

BO 2 OCTAGONAL STONE SCHOOLHOUSE
2214 NY 22; 1826, *Benjamin Gilbert, builder*

Planned to serve the community developing around Daniel Ross's large gristmill, then under construction, the school opened four years before a free public educational system was inaugurated by the state. The octagonal form was unusual in the region. Classes continued to be held in the building until 1952.

BO 3 CABOOSE HOUSE, ARLENE BIGELOW AND ANDREW RIETHEL HOUSE
982 Middle Road; mid-20th century; extensive alterations and additions 2005–06, Premises—Bryan Burke, architect

Here Burke transformed a modest, one-story prefabricated house situated on a long, shallow lot with linear additions designed on a low budget to accommodate three generations of a family. The result evokes similarly constrained modernist residential designs of the late 1930s and 1940s, especially those of San Francisco architect William Wurster.

ESSEX
Town of Essex, Essex County

The hamlet of Essex is an exceptional place, not only in the Adirondacks, but in the United States. Probably no better example can be found of what a prosperous, modest-sized port community was like around the mid-19th century. Essex has a rich array of residential, commercial, and institutional buildings erected between the 1820s and 1850s, and has lost very little of its architectural heritage. Moreover, little subsequent growth has occurred around the hamlet's perimeter, so that the historically abrupt transition from concentrated development to the open, agricultural landscape remains. Essex has served as a ferry landing for over two centuries, bringing an abundance of visitors from New England daily. In recent decades especially, residents have assiduously avoided making their community one focused on tourism, and the small commercial center caters as much to locals as to transients. Among Adirondack settlements, Essex is the most

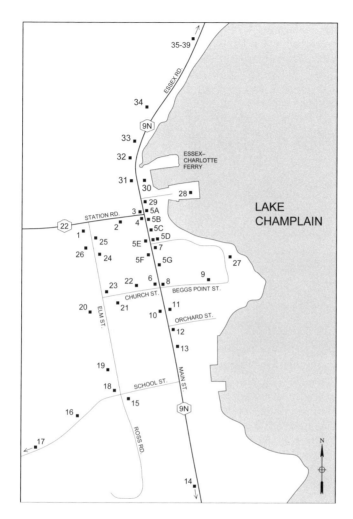

meticulously maintained, with numerous houses restored or sensitively rehabilitated by seasonal residents and retirees as well as long-term inhabitants.

ES 1 ESSEX UNION FREE SCHOOL
2722 Station Road (NY 22); 1867

A very rare surviving example from its period, the Union Free School was erected despite a town population decline of one-third during the previous decade. Perhaps anticipation of post–Civil War growth that never came lay behind the decision. A more concrete motivation was the number of prosperous families in the town, who may have pressed for better facilities for their offspring. Ransom Noble was a major donor, giving his house, which proved too small, but which may have been incorporated into the building that stands. During the 1990s it was restored by the Essex Community Heritage Organization (ECHO) and is now the Essex Heritage Center.

ES 2 CYRUS STAFFORD HOUSE
2736 Station Road; ca. 1847

The end-gable, three-bay form, popular for Greek Revival houses in New England during the second quarter of the 19th century, is fully developed in this house built for a prosperous merchant. The entryway appears to be derived from one in Minard Lafever's *Modern Builder's Guide* (1833), a widely circulated pattern book of the era.

ES 3 FIRST PRESBYTERIAN CHURCH
2743 Station Road; 1853–56, T. S. Whitby, architect (office location unknown)

The Presbyterian church was by far the most ornate and, with a construction cost of $10,000, one of the most expensive houses of worship in the county at that time. Ransom and Belden Noble gave the property and a substantial portion of the construction monies as well. The architect enlivened a conventional box-like form with rusticated quoins and door and window surrounds, all of them finely cut at the edges, framing rough-faced center sections. The bluestone, quarried at Willsboro Point, was also used for Belden Noble's Greystone [ES 32] nearby. The edifice now houses the Essex Community Church.

ES 4 WRIGHT'S INN
2313 Main Street (CR 9); ca. 1790; ca. 1800–20s and later

The southern five bays of this building define one of the town's oldest structures, which was erected as the Ferry House for

Daniel Ross. It was renamed Wright's Inn after its purchase by David Wright in 1799. By 1820 the northern section had been added. Having served as a hostelry well into the 20th century, it was purchased by summer resident Christian Heurich Jr. and given to the town in 1969. A gradual restoration and rehabilitation for town offices began in 1970 by ECHO as its first project. At that time the small entrance porch was added.

ES 5 STORE BUILDINGS

The commercial center of Essex is an unusually intact surviving example of its kind, the more remarkable because such districts were generally magnets for ongoing development into the early 20th century. **William D. Ross's store (a)**, built around 1810 at 2750 Essex Road, is the oldest of the group and an indicator of his family's leading position in mercantile enterprises. It functioned as both retail outlet and warehouse. The **commercial building (b)** next door at 2752 Essex Road was constructed around 1804 as a millinery and dry goods store, and in 1812 it was expanded for the law offices of William's brother, Henry Howard Ross. The two-tier porch was added around 1835. The edifice later served as the firehouse, and it may have been at that time that the sunburst motif was added to the pediment.

The wood-frame **commercial buildings (c, d)** at 2312 and 2310 Main Street were built during the 1840s and 1850s, respectively. The storefront of the former may well be original and certainly dates to an early period. Its neighbor housed a locally owned grocery store during a good portion of the 20th century. The 1840 **commercial building (e)** across the street at 2309 Main was once a tailor shop run by Henry Edwards. The modest wood-frame **commercial building (f)** at 2307 Main dates to the same decade and served as the post office during the early 20th century. The brick **commercial building (g)** at 2304 Main is also likely from the 1840s and contained two store units, the fronts of which appear to have been little changed. One of these is said to have served as a blacksmith shop. The second floor was probably always used for residential purposes.

ES 6 ESSEX INN
2297 Main Street; before 1810; addition 1810s; two-story porch added 1835

Complementing the store buildings is this equally rare surviving example of an early 19th-century inn in a hamlet setting. The southern portion was constructed by 1810 as a residence; the addition of similar arrangement to the north was constructed not long thereafter, presumably as the place was being transformed into a commercial enterprise. At this stage its appearance was similar to Wright's Inn [ES 4]. The two-tiered, colonnaded porch transformed its character to one more closely associated with a hostelry by later generations.

ES 7 THE MANSE
2306 Main Street; ca. 1830 and later

So named because of its long tenure as rectory for the First Presbyterian Church [ES 3], the Manse has a three-bay, gable-end configuration characteristic of many Greek Revival houses in the state. Similarly, too, it carries little ornamental embellishment. The entry porch and its side extension are later additions.

ES 8 RALPH HASCALL HOUSE
2302 Main Street; ca. 1810

Restored under the auspices of ECHO in 1985, the Hascall house employs patterns common to many New England dwellings during the second half of the 18th century. The wood-frame building experienced a series of alterations in the 19th century, all of which were removed in the restoration, a cause for some controversy among preservationists.

ES 9 HOUSE
9 Beggs Point Street; ca. 1830s

This wood-frame dwelling is an updated version of the Hascall house [ES 8], its main block articulated with Greek Revival details that are more prominent on the side elevations than on the façade.

ES 10 JOHN GOULD HOUSE
2285 Main Street; ca. 1833 and later

The house of John Gould, a well-to-do merchant, ranks among the largest in the hamlet. Its position, set back from the street, its dressed bluestone façade, and dearth of exterior ornament contribute to the imposing effect. By the time his residence was erected Gould owned most of the block. What remains of this property still has the imprint of a once-elaborate garden, with a gazebo, developed by the subsequent owner, Palmer Havens.

ES 11 HENRY GOULD HOUSE
2286 Main Street; 1846

Across Main Street lies the later residence of John Gould's brother, Henry, who also achieved prosperity as a merchant. It is a chaste version of the then-stylish Italianate mode and came toward the end of the hamlet's 19th-century boom years.

ES 12 CUPOLA HOUSE
2278 Main Street; ca. 1840s and later

This unusual dwelling appears to have been doubled in size at a reasonably early date, at which time the front and two-tier rear porches were added and the cupola placed atop what was likely a new hip roof. So expanding the residence suggests that it may have become a place catering to summer visitors, a function it (re)assumed in the 1990s.

ES 13 ESSEX GARAGE
2276 Main Street; 1938

One of the relatively few 20th-century buildings in the hamlet, it, too, has become a rare survivor, in this case of an early automobile service garage.

ES 14 SOUTH SIDE FARMS

The richness of agricultural land in this part of Essex County is indicated by its array of sizable farmsteads. Land began to be assembled as early as 1836 for what is now called **South Farm (a)** on Lake Shore Road (CR 9) south of the hamlet. Through the 19th century it served as a tenant farm for the Noble family. The early 20th-century barn is among the most notable buildings on the property today. The **Phillip Baldwin house (b)** at 1751 Lake Shore Road (ca. 1840) still commands a relatively open landscape, but would probably have enjoyed sweeping views all around in the 19th century, when the farm encompassed 240 acres. The porch appears to have been original, its southeast corner filled in for an additional room at an early date. The carriagehouse was erected in the mid-19th century. Farther south at No. 1440, the **Harris Stafford house (c)**, built about ten years earlier, is less grand, its reserve typical of many of the area's farm dwellings. The wood-frame wing was likely added at an early stage.

ES 15 JOHN MESICK HOUSES
294 School Road; ca. 1820s and later

For his retreat, Albany-based architect John Mesick, senior partner in one of the East Coast's leading firms specializing in the restoration and rehabilitation of historic buildings, created an unusual coupling. The eastern, one-story component of this pair was built around the 1820s as a tenant house for Henry Howard Ross. In 2004–05 it was doubled in size and otherwise transformed into a dwelling that seems more contemporary than a vestige of the early 19th century. Mesick was informed by regional vernacular sources, but also by the work of Thomas Jefferson, drawing from his firm's restoration projects at the University of Virginia. The adjacent building to the west was built in 1828 as a tenant house for Ransom Noble by P. P. Billings. Here, the exterior has been carefully restored.

ES 16 ESSEX GRADE AND HIGH SCHOOL
269 School Road; 1907–08

The Union Free School [ES 1] was replaced some forty years after it opened by this building, which reflected the modest size of the population. It closed in 1952 when the Essex school district was consolidated with that of Willsboro. The building is now a seasonal residence.

ES 17 RICHARD EGGLESTON HOUSE
7 School Road at Middle Road; ca. 1830; 1850s

This chaste Federal farmhouse was erected for the principal boat builder in Essex. The wood-frame wing was added some two decades later.

ES 18 NOBLE CLEMONS HOUSE
7 Elm Street; ca. 1850

Built for the owner of the Essex Inn, this imposing Italianate house was clearly meant to rival the community's finest examples from earlier decades. The front yard is defined by an ornate iron fence that was probably installed when the house was new.

ES 19 CHARLES FANCHER HOUSE
9 Elm Street; ca. 1824

The configuration of this three-bay, wood-frame house suggests it may have been planned to receive a two-bay addition at some later date, rendering the front symmetrical. Like the Hascall house [ES 8]

it is of a conservative Federal design. Here, however, the entryway is more stylish, with the door flanked by sidelights—all tied to an entablature. Fancher owned Wright's Inn and also served as postmaster.

ES 20 HICKORY HILL, HENRY HOWARD ROSS HOUSE
23 Elm Street; 1822; 1845

Ross's prominence as an attorney, judge, congressman, officer in the state militia, and town supervisor is well evident in this grand Federal house. The north wing was added to accommodate his law office. It may have been at this time, too, that the windows were changed from sash to casement and those on the ground level elongated.

ES 21 ST. JOHN'S EPISCOPAL CHURCH
4 Church Street; ca. 1835; altered 1880, Rev. John Henry Hopkins, designer; addition 1984

St. John's was built as a schoolhouse financed by the Rosses, with the intention that it would be converted to a church once

an adequate school building was erected. By 1853 the small Episcopal congregation was sharing the facility, taking it over twenty-four years later. Its present appearance owes much to an 1880 remodeling, which included a bellcote and ersatz buttresses. The west wing was added in 1984.

ES 22 METHODIST EPISCOPAL CHURCH
11 Church Street; 1835

Down the street, the Methodist Episcopal Church exhibits a plainness often preferred by members of that denomination. Originally it did boast a tower. From 1922 to 1930 it served as the Masonic lodge, and from 1932 to 2007 as the American Legion's quarters. It has since been owned by the town.

ES 23 SAMUEL SHUMWAY HOUSE
3 Church Street; ca. 1832

A larger version of the Charles Eddy house in Westport [WP 11], this substantial limestone residence shows that size was not always a determinant of whether the gable-end configuration warranted two or three window bays. Here three bays would fit easily had the owner so wished.

Shumway was a prominent local physician who practiced for several decades.

ES 24 HOUSE
32 Elm Street; ca. 1818; 1836

This building was constructed as a school, serving that purpose for nearly half a century. It closed when the Union Free School [ES 1] opened, but was not converted to residential use until the 1970s, when its exterior became one of the first restoration projects in the community.

ES 25 HOUSE
36 Elm Street; ca. 1830s

A diminutive gable-end house that bears comparison with some of its larger neighbors that employ the same basic form [ES 2, ES 23]. A good example of an early automobile garage, probably from the 1920s, lies adjacent.

ES 26 HOUSE
39 Elm Street; early 19th century

The elementary nature of this dwelling suggests it may be among the earliest to survive in the hamlet.

ES 27 ALAN WARDLE HOUSE
Beggs Point Street; 2001–04, Steven Holl, architect (New York)

On the edge of the waterfront lies a house of arresting design by one of the country's most celebrated contemporary

Daniel Ross had the wharf constructed at the beginning of the 19th century and the two-and-a-half-story building erected around 1812, more or less concurrently with his store [ES 5a]. The east section dates to around 1890. The low-slung appendage to the west was added around the 1970s to accommodate the Old Dock Restaurant.

ES 29 HOUSE
2754 Essex Road; 1904

Little is known about this relative latecomer to the hamlet, a lively if somewhat awkward rendition of late 19th-century Queen Anne and Colonial Revival motifs.

ES 30 RANSOM NOBLE & SONS WAREHOUSE
2756 Essex Road; ca. 1810; alterations ca. 1920s

The Noble company painstakingly constructed a waterfront warehouse that would protect its contents but, with ashlar (cut-stone block) walls, the building also stood as an emblem of their enterprise. Later it was used as a general store, with a shirt factory on the second level. Around the 1920s Ransom Noble's granddaughter, Maud Noble Harlan, converted the building into a concert hall, and it was probably at this time the appendages were constructed and the Palladian window inserted above the entrance. Around the mid-20th century it was donated by a descendant to the Masons and now hosts the Essex Theater Company.

architects. So radical a departure from local patterns generated controversy at the time its design was made public, but the house stands apart from its vintage neighbors and indeed is difficult to see save from the water. The design exemplifies Holl's approach, balancing a sense of solidity and permanence on one hand, and ephemerality and transience on the other. Here the mass vaguely suggests a remnant of a fort's bastion and also, with its copper-laminate skin, a nod to the Essex Horse Nail Company's plant that once occupied the site. The small windows that seem randomly scattered across wall surfaces convey an illusion of tattered fabric and give no hint of the lofty space that lies within.

ES 28 ROSS WHARF AND DOCK HOUSE
Off Essex Road on waterfront; early 19th century and later

The most conspicuous remnant of Essex's maritime heritage, this complex retains much of its early fabric despite longstanding changes in function. William

ES 31 BELDEN NOBLE MEMORIAL LIBRARY
2759 Essex Road; ca. 1840s; alterations 1899

More or less concurrently with the warehouse, the Nobles erected their store, purveying leather products from their **tannery**, located to the rear. Remarkably,

that wood-frame building, later modified to serve as a carriagehouse, still stands, albeit in semi-ruinous condition. The store building was itself modified to serve as a private library during the mid-19th century. In 1899 it was chartered by the state as the Essex Library after Adeline Noble left the building as a bequest to the town and as a memorial to her husband, Belden.

ES 32 GREYSTONE, BELDEN NOBLE HOUSE
2765 Essex Road; 1853–56, probably T. S. Whitby, architect; ca. 1890s; 1920s

Ransom Noble's fourth and youngest son, Belden, commissioned the most monumental residence in Essex, forming the southern end of what became known as Merchant Row. It was likely the work of architect T. S. Whitby, who concurrently prepared plans for the Presbyterian church [ES 3] using the same bluestone quarried at Willsboro Point, as well as the same stonemasons, carpenters, and painters. Some details were probably from Peter Nicholson's *New Practical Builder and Workman's Companion*, published in London in 1823. The elaborate iron fence is of the same period and may have been the work of a New York foundry. In 1880, the Nobles made Washington, D.C., their primary residence, spending summer months at Greystone. Seventeen years later their daughter, Maud, married James S. Harlan, a prominent attorney and son of a U.S. Supreme Court justice. It was probably the Harlans who added an ornate

secondary entrance and other append-ages to the west face. James Harlan also focused on developing Gladwater Farms (now Essex Farms), which he intended as a model of progressive agricultural practices, with a huge round barn (burned 1947) as its principal landmark. The south wing of Greystone, carefully designed to relate to the main block, dates to the 1920s and masks an automobile garage at its lower level. Greystone remained in the hands of descendants until 1975. Many of the Noble family furnishings remain in the house.

ES 33 SUNNYSIDE, HARMON NOBLE HOUSE
2775 Essex Road; ca. 1835

Two decades earlier than Greystone, Belden Noble's older brother Harmon commissioned this only slightly less imposing brick dwelling. Following Greystone, it received an iron fence in the 1860s. Around the same time Noble had an ebullient octagonal **pavilion** erected, which he may have used as an office.

ES 34 ROSSLYN, WILLIAM D. ROSS HOUSE
2783 Essex Road; early 19th century; additions ca. 1826–28

Built as wedding present for Ross's bride, Mary Ann Gould, the house was substantially expanded, with two bays added to the front, in the 1820s. It was probably at this time that the elegant Federal doorway was constructed. The Ionic entry porch could easily have been added in the following decade, but it dates to the early 20th century. Across the road lies a fanciful **boathouse** of 1898.

ES 35 CRYSTAL SPRING FARM
2847 Essex Road; late 18th–early 19th centuries; ca. 1850s

The original portion of this farmhouse may have been built as early as the 1780s. It was expanded and otherwise completely remade during the mid-19th century and is a good example of a large wooden dwelling of that period. One idiosyncratic aspect of the scheme is that the end windows on the second floor have always been blind. The front porch is of later vintage. The house was meticulously restored in 2014–16.

ES 36 REV. C. N. WILDER HOUSE
2852 Essex Road; late 1870s

What appears to have been built as an elegant summer house was actually commissioned by Laura Anne Noble for the pastor of the Presbyterian church [ES 3] in an expansive exercise of family largess. The south porch was added, probably in the early 20th century, when the building housed the Agawam Inn.

ES 37 ST. JOSEPH'S CATHOLIC CHURCH

2891 Essex Road; 1872–73

The remote location of this house of worship was a result of its having to serve congregants from Willsboro as well as Essex. The design seems more related to contemporary Roman Catholic churches in Québec Province than counterparts in the United States, a characteristic found in a number of northern Adirondack communities. The entry porch was probably added around the 1890s. As with many 19th- and early 20th-century Catholic churches, much of the construction was performed by parishioners.

ES 38 BLOCKHOUSE FARM, EZRA PARKHILL HOUSE

2916 Essex Road; ca. 1836

A one-and-one-half-story Greek Revival farmhouse of relatively modest size is given considerable prominence by its temple front, an unusual feature for antebellum houses in the region. The dormer windows were added later.

ES 39 BRAIDLEA FARM, D. CRAWFORD CLARK HOUSE

Essex Road; late 19th century

While most of the large summer houses built along Lake Champlain in the late 19th and early 20th centuries were sited away from public view, this complex presents an impressive face to the road. The estate contains two sizable houses. That furthest from the road, facing south, was probably built around the 1880s. Its ca. 1895 neighbor is

a vigorous exercise in the Shingle Style, a mode especially popular in resort areas during the late 19th and early 20th centuries. Much of the dwelling is contained by a great two-story gable roof, which seems to float above the deeply recessed ground floor. Massive piers and chimneys faced in cobblestone enhance the rustic effect. Between 1934 and 1974, the Oblate Fathers of Mary Immaculate ran the compound as the Shrine of Our Lady of Hope. Thereafter it returned to use as a seasonal residence.

WILLSBORO

Town of Willsboro, Essex County

Abundant evidence of early settlement in the town of Willsboro exists, but it lies in the rural landscapes bordering the lake and along roads extending to the interior. The hamlet mostly dates to a later period when the Champlain Fiber Company's pulp mill was in operation. The absence of that industry has taken its toll on the appearance of this community even though some industrial operations continue. Recent revitalization efforts, most notably with a long-vacant school building [WI 7], have proven successful. Much of the lakefront is lined with seasonal residences of varying size, while little change has occurred to the farmland to the south and southwest.

WI 1 ABRAHAM AIKEN HOUSE

3269 Essex Road (NY 22); ca. 1807

Arriving from Dutchess County, New York, in 1783, Aiken purchased some 300 acres, on which he erected a small log

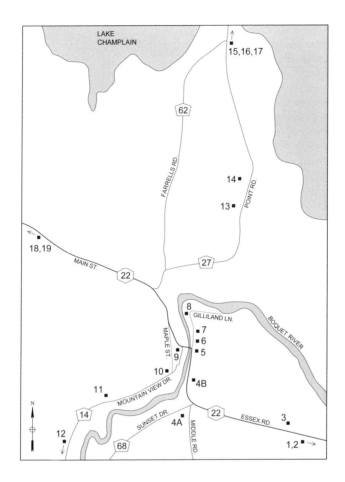

house the following year. Five years later he built a sizable barn, which remains on the property. After about two decades his farming yielded sufficient gain for him to erect the current dwelling, the earliest of the great farmhouses in the town.

WI 2 SHELDON-OWENS FARM
295 Essex Road; 1789 and later

Aiken's brother-in-law, Joseph Sheldon, came concurrently and acquired an adjacent tract that was nearly as large, to which he added 155 acres in 1797. The first barn dates to around 1789 and still stands. By the 1850s, two additional barns, a small granary, smokehouse, and sugarhouse were part of the compound. The family sold the farm in 1853 after their ca. 1800 house burned. The new owner, Edmund Hoffnagle, constructed a dwelling on the foundations of the old one. After two additional owners, a Canadian, John T. Owens, acquired the land in 1903. Between 1905 and 1925 he expanded farming operations, added acreage, remodeled the house (with a large new wing and porch), constructed new farm buildings, and made improvements to old ones. The farm remained in family hands until 1985. It now serves as a bed-and-breakfast, the many layers of its development well maintained.

WI 3 HOUSE
3414 Essex Road; probably after 1860

Serving a smaller, 130-acre farm, this dwelling illustrates the persistence of tradition that was not unusual in rural areas—its plainness derived from work of several previous decades.

WI 4 BARTON HOUSES

Arriving at Willsboro in 1839, Lyman Barton rose to prominence as a physician. The **house (a)** he purchased at 1283 Middle Road (CR 66), situated on open land above the Boquet Valley, was built around the 1820s. In 1849 he expanded and remade the dwelling with a two-story central block and one-story wings, all fronted by a long porch. Thirty-one years later he acquired a lot in the hamlet center at 3477 Main Street (SR 9N) and erected his second **house (b)** not long thereafter. His son, Guy Barton, took over the practice and in 1904 erected a sizable wing for his office and enlarged living quarters.

WI 5 PAINE MEMORIAL LIBRARY
2 Gilliland Lane; 1930, C. P. H. Gilbert, architect (New York)

A trio of buildings—library, bank, and school—all facing the Boquet River on the opposite side of where the pulp mill once

stood, were tied to the mill's chief executive officer, Augustus G. Paine. He gave the library in his mother's memory. The plan eschewed conventional configurations of the period, opting instead for a grand two-story hall that is more suggestive of an elaborate private library.

WI 6 CHAMPLAIN NATIONAL BANK
6 Gilliland Lane; 1921, C. P. H. Gilbert, architect

While a commercial enterprise, Paine's Champlain Bank carries civic qualities, particularly with its over-scaled entry portal. Appropriately, it now serves as the Willsboro Heritage Center.

WI 7 WILLSBORO HIGH SCHOOL
10 Gilliland Lane; 1927–28, Pember & Demers, architects (Albany); Ralph Signor, supervising architect (Plattsburgh, N.Y.); addition 1952, Benedict, Ryan & Sayer, architects (Plattsburgh); addition replaced by new addition 2011–13, Harris A. Sanders Architects (Albany)

Paine donated the land for the high

school, similar to one now demolished in Port Henry [Section 5]. This building, too, posed a preservation challenge after its closure in 2001. The internal configuration—with a gymnasium-auditorium capacity of 400 people, band room, locker rooms, and other spaces in addition to twenty-one classrooms—was seen as detrimental by prospective buyers. Eventually developer Eli Schwartzberg and his architects came up with a viable plan for conversion to the Champlain Valley Senior Community Center. To achieve needed living space a large addition was placed at the rear. While a straightforward and conservative design solution, this new component is both compatible with the original building and helps tie it visually to the larger ensemble.

WI 8 PHOENIX MILL
Gilliland Lane; 1810; rebuilt 1843

A unique survivor of its type in the Adirondacks, this gristmill was built for Essex entrepreneur William D. Ross. After the original structure burned, its shell was retained for the new facility, which operated into the 1930s. In recent years, the interior was again the victim of fire. Efforts are under way to stabilize what is one of the region's most important surviving industrial structures.

WI 9 WILLSBORO CONGREGATIONAL CHURCH
Main Street at Mountain View Road (CR 14); 1833–34, possibly Paul Boynton, builder

Constructed soon after the congregation

was established in 1833, this building retains a basic form that had been characteristic of the denomination's churches since the late colonial period. At the same time, without a gallery the mass is squatter and details make a gesture to current fashion: lancet windows on one hand and a neoclassical belfry on the other. With walls of locally quarried limestone, the effect is as robust as it is slightly awkward and naïve—a testament to the vigor of provincial design.

WI 10 WALLIS B. HOWELL HOUSE
5 Maple Street; ca. 1901–04; possibly C. P. H. Gilbert, architect (New York)

Built by the Champlain Fiber Company for its superintendent, this house draws vaguely from English arts-and-crafts work in an unpretentious manner. The architect may have been C. P. H. Gilbert, who Paine commissioned for his bank, library [WI 6, WI 5], and Lake Champlain camp, Flat Rock.

WI 11 NYCO MINERALS PLANTS
803, 819 Mountain View Road, 1953 and later

The Cabot Company's 1951 acquisition of the Willsboro Mining Company's wollastonite operation led to the construction of a new processing plant (**Plant 1**) in 1953, which replaced a much smaller one located near the now-demolished railroad station. **Plant 2** was erected in 1987–88 for making wollastoncoat, a surface coating for plastics. Both plants have experienced modifications to improve production. Large deposits of the mineral were discovered in the town of Lewis in 1960, and the open-pit mines there have since become the operation's major source. Cabot sold the business in 1969; a decade later it was purchased by NYCO, a subsidiary of Canadian Pacific Enterprises. Four-fifths of the world's supply of wollastonite comes from the United States, and the majority of that supply is from this facility.

WI 12 MID-19TH-CENTURY FARMHOUSES

Both the **Henry Hinckley (a)** and **Joseph Adams (b)** houses at 348 and 213 Mountain View Road (CR 14), respectively, date from the 1830s–40s and are adaptations

of the 18th-century New England pattern of having service outbuildings extend from the rear of the farmhouse. Here the wings project from the sides of three-bay, gable-end Greek Revival dwellings. The **Daniel Hayward house (c)** at 513 Sunset Road (CR 68) is of the same vintage and likewise based on New England building patterns, in this case a modest rendition of the so-called Cape Cod type, here with a relatively large and elaborate Greek Revival doorway. The **Van Orem farm (d)** at 1535 Jersey Road (CR 12) is a more polished rendition of the same form, probably dating to the 1850s or later. The property still has several barns and outbuildings; the **store**,

set along the road, is an especially unusual survivor.

WI 13 EDWARD FRANKLIN SMITH HOUSE
249 Point Road (CR 27); 1875

Seldom does one rural road anchor the spectrum of dwellings found here—from a pioneer cabin to a Gilded Age extravagance. Smith's house certainly falls into the latter category and is highly unusual in the Adirondacks. The owner was a descendant of Caleb Smith, an early settler, and became a very prosperous farmer. His ornate house bears comparison with Windridge in Harrisena [HS 1]. Later it served as a clinic, but has long stood vacant in deteriorating condition.

WI 14 FESTUS JONES HOUSE
401 Point Road; ca. 1830s

This house is similar to that at 3414 Essex Road [WI 3] save for its use of locally quarried bluestone—one of three built for the Jones family in the vicinity.

WI 15 EDGEWATER FARM, DANIEL ROWLEY JR. HOUSE
553 Point Road; 1796; ca. 1820 addition; main house ca. 1850s

Most of what can now be seen of Edgewater Farm was probably done around the 1850s for Daniel Rowley Jr., son of a farmer who came from Vermont and settled here in the late 18th century. The younger Rowley was not only a successful dairy farmer, but developed orchards and a lumbering business. The house remains in the hands of descendants.

WI 16 OLD ELM, ORRIN CLARK HOUSE
767 Point Road; 1841–42, William Gibbs, builder (Westport), and later

While Old Elm grew by accretions, its main block of locally quarried, dressed bluestone has changed very little. A kitchen wing was added in the mid-19th century; an attached shop to the rear dates from the same time or somewhat later. The porch was appended in the late 19th century. The property also has an unusually broad array of outbuildings, including an icehouse, smokehouse, and blacksmith

shop. Orrin Clark's farm was a particularly diverse operation that encompassed lumbering, burning charcoal, tending fruit orchards, and quarrying bluestone. Son Solomon focused on the last of these operations, extending his market as far south as New York City and earning a national reputation.

WI 17 SAMUEL ADSIT HOUSE
852 Point Road; 1778

Solomon Clark and brother Lewis married Rhoda and Elizabeth Adsit, respectively, both of whom grew up in a house that started as a single-room log cabin during the 1770s. Samuel Adsit and his wife arrived

from Dutchess County and squatted on the property, taking advantage of the confusion over land patents following the Revolutionary War. After Solomon's death in 1798, son Jacob took over, acquiring title to the property in 1818 and purchasing additional acreage. A number of appendages to the cabin were in place by 1830, and subsequent additions nearby doubled its size and completely changed its appearance. Earl E. van der Werker, who purchased the property in 1927, planned to demolish the house. When he discovered the log structure at its core, he attempted what seems to have been a relatively conscientious restoration. If not entirely accurate in some details, the structure is nonetheless a very scarce survivor of first settlement in the Adirondacks.

WI 18 CAMP POK-O-MOONSHINE
1391 Reber Road; 1905 and later (accessible by prior arrangement)

Among the oldest children's camps in the Adirondacks operated by the same family, Pok-O-Moonshine, named for a nearby mountain, has a rich collection of architecture. Charles Robinson, principal at Peekskill Military Academy, founded the institution in 1905 as combination school and camp, with lessons in mornings, outdoor activities thereafter. Following his death in 1946 the camp was taken over by daughter Sarah Robinson Swan, then her son Jack Swan in 1963. Four years later

Camp MacCready for girls was started on the adjacent Ryan farm, which had long supplied Pok-O-Moonshine with food.

The oldest sector has an unusually rich variety of rustic buildings, including **Robinson's own cottage**; **Master's Lodge**; a two-story **staff cottage**; **Point House**, which was on the property when it was purchased; **Indian Lore cottage**; **Monotonna Lodge**; and the **Trading Post**. When the 1911 dining hall burned, it was replaced by

a large A-frame structure, **Robinson Hall** (1960), designed by architect David Hammerstron of Roscoe, New York.

LEWIS

Town of Lewis, Essex County

On either side of the US 9 corridor, much of the land within the Town of Lewis has been reforested. Only a few scattered farmhouses indicate earlier uses. The small hamlet of Lewis, extending along the highway for over a mile, is thinly developed and offers few basic services. Farther east the landscape is more open and evidence of its agricultural past more evident.

LE 1 LEWIS CONGREGATIONAL CHURCH
8557 US 9; 1823–34; alterations 1875–76, George O. Roberts, builder

A small group began to establish a church in 1812 under the direction of Rev. Cyrus Comstock, who founded or aided in creating twelve Congregational churches in Essex County between 1812 and 1853. The exterior of this, Essex County's first church of that denomination, was completed in 1823, but a dozen years elapsed before the interior was finished. The 1870s alterations probably include removal of the gallery and installation of tall windows on side elevations. In 1921 the stamped metal walls and ceiling were installed and the rather ungainly porte-cochere was added. The adjacent hamlet cemetery opened in the early 1820s as well.

LE 2 GENERAL STORE
8549 US 9; mid- to late 19th century and later

A general store was on this site as early as 1816. The present building appears to date from the mid-19th century or somewhat later, and was operated by Ben Surprise. Between 1946 and 1967 it was run as an IGA grocery store. But for most of its life it has purveyed general, along with sometimes specialized, merchandise.

LE 3 L. RICE HOUSE
8527 US 9; ca. 1820s

Little is known about this decorous Federal-period house. With its three-part entry and Palladian window above, it bears affinity to the 1824 Richard Stafford house [WH 10b] and may have been the work of the same builder.

LE 4 WADHAMS-BARBER HOUSE
8001 US 9; ca. 1800 and later

Originally built as a tavern and soon used as a place to exchange horses on the road between Albany and Montreal, the establishment was run by George Phelps. Before he settled in the nascent hamlet that would bear his name, Luman Wadhams purchased the property in 1809. One of his sons, Edgar, was born here and later became the first Bishop of Ogdensburg. When Wadhams moved in 1823, the house was acquired by Major Jonathan Breckenridge, who built the first sawmill in Lewis. Orlando Kellogg, proprietor of the Windsor Hotel in Elizabethtown, resided here around 1900. In 1922 it was bought by Fenton Barber and named Clearwater Farm. Barber established the town's first hydroelectric plant on the premises. Behind the house stands an unusually large stable of early vintage.

LE 5 LEWIS SCHOOL DISTRICT SCHOOL NO. 3
5 Hyde Road at Lewis-Wadhams Road (CR 10); probably mid-19th century

A schoolhouse has stood on this property since 1814. The current building closed in 1945. It has been sensitively rehabilitated as a residence.

LE 6 MEADOWMOUNT, JOHN E. MILHOLLAND HOUSE AND FARM
1424 Lewis-Wadhams Road; 1900s–early 1910s, Alfred Bossom, architect (New York)

This expansive country place, developed on a scale that makes it unusual in the Adirondacks, was a sanctuary for its owner. Milholland made frequent trips to his "ranch" of 1,000 acres, likening them to Christ's pilgrimage to the wilderness. His father came to Lewis from Northern Ireland in 1841 and was able to secure his own land thirteen years later. Raised in a hardscrabble environment, John Milholland found a mentor in Congressman William Walter Phelps, who underwrote his attending New York University and supported his subsequent purchase of the *Ticonderoga Sentinel*. Milholland's editorials revealed a strong individualism. He called for preserving the Adirondack wilderness and restoring Fort Ticonderoga. After Milholland married in 1885, he sold the paper and went to work as a political writer for the *New York Tribune*,

where he became known as the newspaper's "great moral organ." Soon he was involved in national Republican politics, as a lieutenant to the newspaper's owner, Whitelaw Reid. Milholland's outspoken calls for reform, including civil rights for African-Americans and federal aid to education, brought an early end to his political activities. Undaunted, he launched a business developing pneumatic tubes for the U.S. Post Office Department, from which he made a fortune.

In 1898 Milholland bought what had been the family farm, with the intent of developing the property to aid the poor. Within a few years, however, he decided to create a refuge for himself and his family. How he came to know Bossom is unclear, but well before 1907 he engaged the architect in preparing plans for his estate and also had gotten him interested in reconstructing Fort Ticonderoga [TI 1, Section 5]. Milholland lived in the **first**, then the **second farmhouse** that he had acquired. Eventually construction began on the thirty-six-room "**big house**." Bossom's blueprints, dated September 1912, show a residence with more or less the same floor plan, but two-and-one-half stories tall, its exterior rendered in a vaguely Tudor mode. Whether these drawings were to enlarge the existing, recently built dwelling or whether Milholland insisted the scheme be scaled down to its present size before construction began is unclear. Whatever the circumstances, the current building has an unorthodox design, configured as if a relatively modest dwelling had been extended linearly to assume institutional proportions, with an immense, almost primordial chimney rising near the middle.

Supplementing the existing **farm complexes** that flank the big house, an expansive **model farm** was erected across the road. Most of the latter has been abandoned and is in an advanced state of decay. The main part of the estate has fared better. After lying vacant for a decade, it

was purchased in 1944 by Ivan Galamian, a celebrated violinist and teacher, who came to the United States in 1937 and taught at the Curtis Institute of Music in Philadelphia. Milholland's retreat was adapted as a summer camp for exceptionally talented young musicians (ages nine to thirty). Two years after founding the Meadowmount School of Music, Galamian became head of the violin department at the Juilliard School. His Adirondack institution continues to operate, with evening concerts held on the premises.

LE 7 HOUSE
407 Brainards Forge Road; ca. 1830s and later
A masonry version of the extended house in its "L" form, as seen in the wood-frame farmhouses outside Willsboro [WI 12a and b], this dwelling was embellished by an extensive porch added during the late 19th century. Nearby at 430 Brainards Forge Road lies a simple one-room **schoolhouse** from around 1850 that is now a residence.

ELIZABETHTOWN
Town of Elizabethtown, Essex County

Sadly, Elizabethtown gives little overt sense of its past as a fashionable summer resort. Without a lake or other major natural attraction, it was losing its luster among well-heeled vacationers by the 1940s. The big hotels—the Windsor and Deer's Head—were demolished in the 1960s, as were some of the finest summer houses. In their place came motorist-oriented businesses. The elm trees that lined

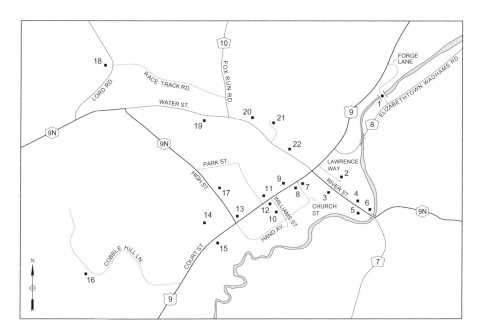

Court Street succumbed to disease. Besides county offices, Elizabethtown has a hospital, a senior citizens' home, and a large school, but the overall appearance lacks visual coherence. Despite such changes, the hamlet and its environs, with a population of 754 in 2010, still harbors significant traces of its heritage as an industrial center, as the county seat, and as a place of leisure for the well-to-do.

EL 1 FORGE BRIDGE
Forge Road at Elizabethtown-Wadhams Road (CR 8); ca. early 20th century

Located at a once major intersection of roads connecting Elizabethtown to Wadhams and Lewis, and where a forge had been erected in the early 19th century, this small Pratt truss bridge is of a kind that was widespread in the Adirondacks and elsewhere as improvements were gradually made to the road system. They are now scarce within the Blue Line; this one remains standing only because it is no longer used.

EL 2 ROBERT SAFFORD HALE HOUSE
8255 River Street, entered on Lawrence Way, off Maple Street (US 9) northeast of River Street (NY 9N); 1814, alterations and additions ca. 1850 and later

A protégé of Augustus Hand [EL 3], Hale was admitted to the bar in 1847 and acquired this early 19th-century house not long thereafter. Later he served as county judge and was a member of Congress from 1876 to 1881. Hale made extensive modifications to his dwelling over several decades to form an unassuming, accretive assemblage. Like Hand, he built his **law office** in separate quarters on the premises. During the post–World War II era, the property was acquired by the town for use as a social center. The construction in 1987 of a new facility for that purpose on the grounds has left Hale's buildings vacant.

EL 3 AUGUSTUS CINCINNATUS HAND HOUSE
8273 River Street; 1848–49; alterations ca. 1870s–80s and 1924–27

Hand moved to Elizabethtown from

Vermont in 1831, establishing a law practice that rivaled that of Henry Howard Ross [ES 20] in its regional prominence. He was elected to Congress in 1839, became a state senator in 1845, and served as justice in the New York Supreme Court in 1848. For his second house on this site, Hand built a grand brick Greek Revival residence unrivaled throughout the county except by the most ambitious residences of the Ross and Noble families in Essex. Some of the later additions that Victorianized the exterior were removed in the mid-1920s when the entrance porch was rebuilt in approximation of the original. Hand's descendants, including grandsons Augustus Noble and Learned Hand, both noted jurists, continued to occupy the house, now as a summer residence. It remained in the family into the mid-20th century, and now houses the offices of the Bruce L. Crary Foundation, providing college scholarships to Adirondack youth. **Hand's law office**, still standing, was erected on the premises around 1831 and received an addition around 1865.

EL 4 EDWARD TUDOR STRONG HOUSE
8222 River Street; ca. mid-1880s, William Ferrin, builder

During the second half of the 19th century River Street became a place of preference for the hamlet's professionals, including the physician who commissioned this commodious Victorian house.

EL 5 AUGUSTUS F. WOODRUFF HOUSE
8129 River Street; 1868, Augustus Woodruff, builder

Near the Boquet River, builder Augustus Woodruff erected his own house in the Italianate mode as a demonstration of his skills. He used the barn at the rear to supplement his income by making coffins. The dwelling has been sensitively rehabilitated as the Woodruff House Bed & Breakfast.

EL 6 OLD MILL ART SCHOOL
8214 River Street; early to mid-19th century; alterations and additions 1930s

What served as both a grist- and sawmill during the 19th century was transformed by Wayman Adams, a prominent portrait painter from New York, who founded a summer art school here in 1932. It operated for thirty-four consecutive summers. It is now the Old Mill Bed & Breakfast.

EL 7 ELIZABETHTOWN HIGH SCHOOL
7590 Court Street (US 9); 1915, Demers, Mosley & Champaigne, architects (Troy, N.Y.)

Now a rare surviving example of a first-generation, purpose-built high school in the Adirondacks, this facility came to serve both Elizabethtown and Lewis when their school districts joined in 1938. Four years later the high school moved to the remodeled Sunny Lawn, one of the hamlet's grandest summer houses on Court Street next to the Deer's Head Inn, leaving this building for the lower grades. A sprawling new school complex was erected in 1950–52 on Sunny Lawn's grounds and the elegant former residence was demolished. The old high school faced a similar fate, but was saved by the Essex County Historical Society, which formed in 1954 and bought the building for its Adirondack History Center Museum. Tangent to the building is a fire tower, assembled on the site from portions of those on Kempshall and West mountains, in Long Lake and Raquette Lake, respectively.

EL 8 ELIZABETHTOWN CONGREGATIONAL CHURCH
7984 Court Street; 1888–89, Robert W. Gibson, architect (Albany)

The finely crafted design of this building, done by one of Albany's leading architects of the late 19th century, reflects the prominence of Elizabethtown as a place of summer residence. Although the building is of modest dimensions its cost was about $10,000, a substantial sum at that time. It now is home to the United Church of Christ.

EL 9 BAPTIST CHURCH
7563 Court Street; 1837–38, alterations 1896

The boxy mass of this church was dressed up somewhat by the Colonial Revival motifs and stained-glass windows added to the façade some sixty years after its construction. In 1957, when the Baptists joined the Congregationalists across the street, the building was purchased by Edward and Jean Lee Campe, well-to-do summer residents, who gave it to replace the recently burned town hall. It continues to serve that purpose.

EL 10 EPISCOPAL CHURCH OF THE GOOD SHEPHERD
10 Williams Street; 1881–82, J. W. Pierson, architect (New York); ca. 1900; 1927, Pember & Demers, architects (Albany)

Though it does not appear so, the hamlet's Episcopal church is the product of numerous changes. Originally on Hand Avenue and High Street, two blocks away, the building was moved in 1899. It was probably at that time the exterior received its side tower and grouped lancet windows, as well as, perhaps, its apse. Stained glass was introduced in 1905. After a fire gutted the interior, the building was further remodeled in 1927.

EL 11 ESSEX COUNTY COURTHOUSE
7551–59 Court Street; 1823–24; 1843; 1880, Mr. Hughes, builder (Keeseville); 1882; 1910–11, Coulter & Westhoff, architects; 1927–29, William G. Distin, architect, Arthur G. Wilson, associate; 1965–66, Distin & Wareham, architects; 1995–96, Einhorn Yaffe Prescott, architects (Albany)

With components constructed over nearly two centuries, what is now known as the Essex County Center is an extraordinary example of accretive architecture, where, in most cases, additions were designed to be compatible with earlier parts. The initial parcel of land for this complex was acquired in 1809. After the first two courthouses burned, a one-story brick building was erected in 1823–24, to which a second story was added twenty years later. Still, the facility suffered from neglect, with county supervisors unwilling to allocate needed funds. Elizabethtown

residents decided to make up the difference. As a result, a large wing was added to the south in 1880 and the courtroom remade as a two-story space. Then in 1882 the portico and tower were added, using what was by then a retardataire neoclassical vocabulary and giving the core component of this complex its present appearance some sixty years after it was begun. Other additions, now gone, were made in 1885.

By the 1900s the building was again in a state of neglect. Residents of Port Henry launched a concerted campaign to have the county seat moved to their community and in 1907 commissioned Saranac Lake architect Max Westhoff to prepare plans for a new building. After the initiative to move the county seat was repulsed, efforts to improve the existing plant soon followed with a new county clerk's office, sheriff's house, and jail, also designed by Westhoff. Yet further additions were made by his successor, William G. Distin—on the northern end in the late 1920s and with a large southern block in the mid-1960s, the latter bolstered by federal money to have it also serve as a civil defense command center. Finally, in the 1990s, a large new courts building was erected at the northern end.

EL 12 DEER'S HEAD INN
7552 Court Street; 1808 and later

Constructed as a house, this building

was moved sometime after 1830 and became the annex to the Mansion House around 1872. The name was changed to Deer's Head Inn in 1901. The main building, adjacent to the south, was demolished in 1968, replaced by a supermarket. The former annex has survived as a restaurant.

EL 13 W. M. MARVIN'S SONS ELIZABETHTOWN GARAGE
7510 Court Street; 1908–09 and later

Elizabethtown's importance as a crossroads, with routes connecting Lake Champlain to the interior—as well as Albany to Montreal, in addition to its distinction as an elite resort—led to the development of several substantial garages during the inceptive period of automobile travel. In 1908, Fred and Edgar Marvin, whose great-great-grandfather had operated a cabinet and coffin shop locally as early as 1840, announced plans for the largest garage in the county. Accounts describe a wood-frame facility. The Marvins may have decided to erect the present concrete-block structure instead, or may have replaced their initial venture with this more fire-resistant building within a few years. Besides servicing cars, the business included a rental fleet and a sales facility that at various times included Maxwell and Paige automobiles. The family furniture store stood nearby until it burned in 1952.

EL 14 COBBLE HILL GOLF COURSE
Court and High (NY 9N) streets; 1896 and later

Golf courses began to be established in the Adirondacks at a relatively early date. Both the Lake Placid Club [Section 9] and the Loon Lake House [LN 2, Section 8] boasted nine-hole courses in 1895. At Paul Smith's hotel [Section 9] and here at Cobble Hill, courses were laid out the following year. The result of a golf club formed by regular guests at the Windsor Hotel, Cobble Hill began as a five-hole course, which was expanded during the early 20th century. An ornate clubhouse was erected in 1897 and lasted until it was demolished in 1962. The land was owned by the Hand family as late as 1945, when it was purchased by Mr. and Mrs. James Rosenberg, who deeded it to the town the following year as a memorial to World War II veterans. Set on gently rolling terrain, framed by the landform that gave the course its name and dotted by an array of mature evergreen and deciduous trees, the course forms one of the most picturesque landscapes of its kind in the park.

EL 15 ST. ELIZABETH'S CATHOLIC CHURCH
8434 Court Street; 1881; additions ca. 1916; additions and alterations 1922, Paul Jacquet, architect

St. Elizabeth's is the product of several building campaigns. In this case, a rather simple exterior was made more prominent with the addition of a corner bell tower. The expansion and remodeling of 1922 transformed the edifice with a lively faux half-timber sheathing and a porte-cochere at the new main entrance.

EL 16 SETH SPRAGUE TERRY HOUSE
127 Cobble Hill Road; 1905–06, Charles C. Oldruff, builder (accessible by prior arrangement)

Perched high above the hamlet, this rustic fantasy is one of two adjacent dwellings, served by a single barn, erected for a prominent New York attorney. The

principal elevation, facing northeast, has an enormous loggia, which functions as the principal entrance as well as an expansive outdoor living space. The main block of the house supports second-story projections—sleeping porches and an enclosed polygonal bay—on three sides, enhancing a sense of collage. The grounds contain two log cabins, one perhaps used as a study, the other perhaps as a playhouse. In the early 1960s the property was purchased by Norris and Mary Dolly, who winterized the house without significantly changing the character of its interior spaces. It is now run as the Dolly Family Lodge for seasonal rentals.

EL 17 THE BUNGALOW, JOHN JOHNSON HOUSE
8434 High Street (SR 9N); 1889–99, John K. Brown, builder; later additions

Fronted by a long porch, this low-slung summer house was sited for views of the golf course and the mountains beyond. Its configuration gives little hint of the rustic central hall, rising to the ridge of the roof inside. Second-floor bedrooms and the tower-like dormers fronting them were among the early 20th-century additions. The house now serves as the rectory for St. Elizabeth's Church [EL 15].

EL 18 PAULINE LORD HOUSE
55 Lord Road; ca. 1860s; alterations and additions ca. 1920s

Little is known about what was apparently first built as a farmhouse and later doubled as a summer boardinghouse named Pleasant Valley Farm. Probably after

World War I, actress Pauline Lord, who had a successful Broadway career during the 1920s, purchased the house and had it extensively remade as Silfred Farm.

EL 19 GREYSTONES, THOMAS W. LAMB HOUSE

76 Water Street; ca. 1919–20 and later, Thomas W. Lamb, architect (New York)

His career ascending as one of the nation's leading architects of theaters and father of what would become known as the movie palace, Lamb bought the property for his summer residence in 1919. He may have incorporated portions of the existing Pine Grove Cottage, built in the late 1870s, into his scheme, but any traces are difficult to decipher in the individualistic design he executed. The main block opens to a terrace (and the street) as if it were a garden elevation, bracketed by dressed stone portals and, immediately adjacent, enclosed side porches with cobblestone piers and base. This treatment continues on the east side of the low-slung rear wing, with an open porch above and a cobblestone turret at the southern end. Whimsy is taken to the level of minor details, where the soffits are sheathed in branches cut as if they were miniature logs projecting from the walls. The house was sold by the family in 1942; seven years later it reopened as an inn, Cobble Mountain Lodge, which closed in 1958 as Elizabethtown's appeal as a resort dwindled. For many years thereafter it provided housing for Meadowmount students [LE 6], but has lain vacant for over a decade.

EL 20 DURAND-BREWSTER HOUSE

139 Water Street; ca. 1895; additions and alterations 1931, Rockwell Kent, designer, William G. Distin, architect; later alterations

The capacious Victorian house built for Frank Durand was extensively remade for O. Byron Brewster, who was appointed county district attorney in 1915 and elected to the state supreme court in 1927—a post he held for twenty-eight years. His friend Rockwell Kent was responsible for the basic design, which transformed the house into one in a low-key Colonial Revival mode the artist favored; Distin was the architect of record.

EL 21 STONELEIGH, JUDGE FRANCIS A. SMITH HOUSE

18 Stoneleigh Way, off Water Street; 1887–88, Hartwell & Richardson, architects (Boston)

Set well back from the road, this rustic

wanted a summer residence that would evoke architecture they had seen in northern Germany. Inside lies a two-and-a-half-story stair hall, for which one is scarcely prepared given the house's compact form. With few changes inside or out, it is now the Stoneleigh Bed & Breakfast.

EL 22 CHARLES HENRY NOBLE HOUSE
195 Water Street; 1825

The Noble family's importance to Elizabethtown's early development is fully manifested by what was perhaps the most imposing building in the hamlet at the time of its construction. The entry porch is a somewhat later addition. Nearby at 213 Water Street is the **Noble store** of the same vintage, where harnesses, boots, shoes, and other products of the tannery that lay behind were sold.

stone residence exudes some of the massiveness found in the work of Henry Hobson Richardson, which Hartwell & Richardson (no relation) admired. They headed a firm much celebrated at that time for its country houses. Here, reputedly, the clients

NEW RUSSIA
Town of Elizabethtown, Essex County

NA 1 THE CRAGS, GEORGE B. SCHADMANN HOUSE
6007 US 9; early 19th century and later; major additions ca. 1925–26

Along the Boquet River south of the tiny hamlet of New Russia lies this idealized "Colonial" farm, the product of an extensive building campaign for the head of the Columbia Preparatory School in Washington, D.C. A portion of the house's rear wing is of a much earlier vintage and may have been built by Revolutionary War veteran Elisha Holcomb or one of his descendants.

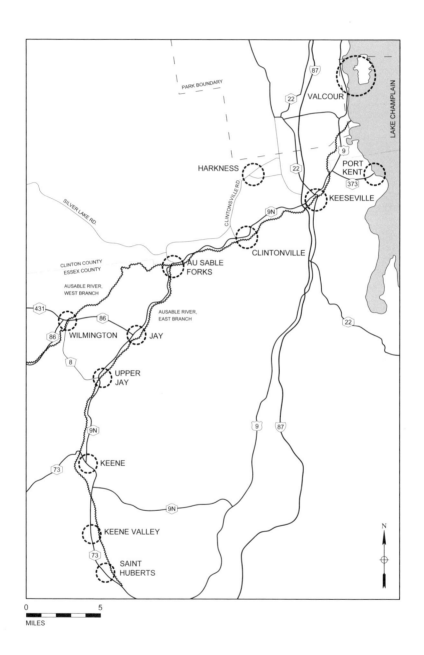

7
AUSABLE RIVER VALLEY

IN CONTRAST TO THE CHAMPLAIN VALLEY, where many settlements developed in competition with one another, those along the Ausable River, including the river's East Branch south of Au Sable Forks, established complementary and/or supportive relationships at an early date. Because the river valley afforded the easiest access to the timberland and mineral deposits lying well into the Adirondacks, settlement also commenced in many parts of the area by the first decade of the 19th century. Soon Keeseville began to emerge as a manufacturing center. Nearby iron mines supplied forges and bloomeries that were established in Clintonville, Au Sable Forks, and Jay. During the mid-19th century most of these operations were taken over by one based in Au Sable Forks, which became the dominant center. Farther south, the valley of the East Branch widens to encompass land developed for agriculture to sustain the burgeoning populations of the iron communities. At the southern end, the valley rapidly diminishes in breadth toward the river's headwaters in the Ausable lakes. Surrounded by the High Peaks, this landscape is among the most dramatic in the Adirondacks and became a destination for artists, tourists, and seasonal residents as early as the 1860s.

SITUATED WITHIN TWO TOWNS AND TWO COUNTIES—and until 2015 incorporated as a village—Keeseville's rise as a manufacturing center was predicated on water power from a series of rapids and falls near the northern end of the Ausable River. (Like other Adirondack rivers that drain into Lake Champlain or the St. Lawrence, the Ausable flows northward.) The hamlet grew around rapids named Anderson Falls. Ausable Chasm (a satellite community known in the 19th century as Birmingham) emerged less than two miles to the north and was likewise tied to Alice Falls, Rainbow Falls (really a rapids), and Horseshoe Falls. Beyond the second falls lies the chasm itself, where the river has carved a deep gorge through Potsdam sandstone in an irregular path for about two miles, and some two miles farther opens into the marshy flats that form its mouth. As a result, several tiny settlements developed to the south along the lake as shipping points for the Ausable Valley's products. Port Kent, about three and a half miles east of Keeseville, was the most important. Construction of the Port Kent–Hopkinton Turnpike (1828–34), which linked Keeseville to Au Sable Forks and continued across the northern Adirondacks, helped cement Keeseville's role as a transportation hub.

Keeseville's settlement began in 1808 when Jonathan Bigelow erected a dam and a sawmill at the rapids. Others, including John and Richard Keese, purchased the business. Their firm of Keese, Anderson & Keese, which in turn was expanded as the Keeseville Rolling and Slitting Mills Company to manufacture nails and boilerplates, was the first of its kind in the state when it began operations in 1816. Other plants for iron products followed, including the Keeseville Manufacturing Company (ca. 1820), Goulding & Peabody's foundry (1829), Eagle Horse Nail Company (1832), and E. & J. D. Kingsland & Company (1847). Founded in 1863 by Edmund Kingsland, the Ausable Horse Nail Company [KS 11a–11c] secured the rights to use a machine capable of making cut nails with heads that speeded their manufacture twenty-fold.

Eagle Iron Works, Keeseville, 1832. (ca. 1830s–40s print)

Selling both nails and the device that fabricated them led the company to local dominance during the second half of the 19th century. Though iron products drove Keeseville's economy, other industries flourished as well. Textile manufacturing began as early as 1819, and a huge woolen mill was erected in 1836 on the Ausable's east bank. (The structure remained until it burned in the 1960s.) Arriving from New Hampshire with his family before 1830, Charles Prescott set up shop as a carpenter and cabinetmaker. Son Rufus expanded the operation, purchasing the Potter & Richardson furniture manufacturing company around 1856. After its plant was destroyed by fire, the company acquired the former woolen mill in 1878. Reorganized ten years later as Rufus Prescott & Sons, the company not only made furniture, but sash, doors, blinds, and architectural elements. The operation also did a substantial business in building construction and even had an in-house architect, J. F. Caswell.

Rufus Prescott & Sons furniture mill, Keeseville, mid-19th century, burned 1969. (1950s–60s postcard)

It was considered the largest operation of its kind north of Troy. Several tanneries and lumber mills, a paper mill, a printing plant, and a brewery were among the other early enterprises. By the mid-1880s the village's population was nearly 3,000, almost twice that of 2010.

The iron industry declined during the 1880s and was gone by 1900. Still, a diversified economic base enabled Keeseville to remain a center for making furniture and other wood products as well as textiles well into the 20th century. The Prescott company took over the Ausable Horse Nail Company's factory after World War I. By the late 1960s, however, the industrial base had vanished. Without other sources of employment filling the gap, Keeseville became a bedroom community for the small city of Plattsburgh fourteen miles north.

Development around the falls near Ausable Chasm began even earlier than in Keeseville. By the 1820s there were a forge and rolling mill. Edmund and Jacob Kingsland built larger plants there in 1840 and 1852. The AuSable Chasm Horse Nail Works was founded in 1876 and operated until the turn of the 20th century. But as industry started to decline, tourism emerged as a significant force. Capitalizing on the spectacular topography of the chasm, the AuSable Company was formed in 1873 and erected the Lake View House. After that hostelry burned, the AuSable Chasm Company was created in 1896 to rebuild the hotel, which lasted until 1950. Several motels were built along US 9 between Keeseville and the falls, but they started to lose business after the Adirondack Northway, completed in 1967, bypassed the route [KS 22]. Still in private hands, the chasm remains a tourist attraction.

Hotel Ausable Chasm, Ausable Chasm, 1896–97, burned 1950. (early 20th-century postcard)

Northwest and east of Keeseville the land is relatively flat and conducive to agriculture. Farms flourished there during the 19th and early 20th centuries, serving Keeseville's substantial population and markets farther afield. In recent years marginalized farmland has been revived for organically grown produce, meats, and poultry as well as the making of beer and cheese.

Up the Ausable River, five miles southwest of Keeseville, the tiny hamlet of Clintonville was once a major supplier of iron. George Griswold built a dam and a forge there in 1810, but production was soon dominated by the Peru Iron Company, which between 1825 and 1829 developed two blast furnaces, a chain-cable factory, an anchor forge, and a nail factory, employing 400 to 500 people. Production peaked during the 1860s and 1870s, but most operations closed soon thereafter, unable to compete with those in Au Sable Forks.

Iron deposits were discovered at Arnold Hill, near Au Sable Forks, as early as 1806, and a forge was built in 1828—an enterprise that became the Sable Iron Company six years later. But the primary engine of growth was driven by brothers James and John Rogers, who had set up a small mercantile business in Keeseville during the mid-1820s. Completion in 1832 of the Port Kent–Hopkinton Turnpike as far as Black Brook, where significant deposits of ore lay, led the Rogers to purchase stock in the Sable Iron Company and soon gain complete control of the operation. In 1838 James moved to Au Sable Forks and John to Black Brook, some four miles to the west, to manage their new business. They began to acquire additional land for timber to make charcoal, and to buy other iron plants as well. By 1860 they owned bloomeries, rolling mills, and a large nail works in Au Sable Forks, mines nearby, and a host of support facilities—including woodworking mills for wagons and nail kegs, blacksmith and machine shops, farms, and boardinghouses. Their 75,000 acres allowed the harvesting of 1,000 acres annually to meet their charcoal needs. The operation was large enough to warrant an extension of the Whitehall & Plattsburgh (later Delaware & Hudson) Railroad to Au Sable Forks in 1868. Three years later the brothers reorganized their business as the J. & J. Rogers Iron Company, which by then counted upwards of 2,000 employees.

Rolling mill, J. & J. Rogers Iron Company, Au Sable Forks, mid-19th century. (ca.1870s–80s print)

Besides their extensive industrial plants and support facilities, the Rogerses kept tight hold on the development of Au Sable Forks. Workers were paid in scrip redeemable only at company stores. The largest of these, a three-story masonry building in the middle of the hamlet, was constructed in 1864 after a fire had ravaged the community. The Rogerses' paternalistic approach encompassed housing, which was generally of a higher caliber than that found during the 19th century in Mineville [Section 5] or Lyon Mountain [Section 8]—the two other large-scale mining communities in the northeastern Adirondacks. Unlike those places, Au Sable Forks never looked like a company town. Support also came for building churches and schools. The Rogerses strove to set a high moral tone for Au Sable Forks and Black Brook. They thoroughly immersed themselves in community life, sponsoring lectures, concerts, plays, patriotic celebrations, suppers, and other events. Their children attended local schools, and their houses lay in proximity to those of the workforce. On-the-job injuries were relatively few, and little strife existed between labor and management, in contrast to conditions at Mineville and especially Lyon Mountain. Most of the tension arose between the workers themselves—those of Irish origin, who comprised most of the miners and ironworkers, and the French-Canadians, who did most of the logging. As a result their residential enclaves were segregated.

Paper mill, J. & J. Rogers Company, Au Sable Forks, 1890s. (early 20th-century postcard)

It was not long, however, before readily available ore was depleted and a decline in the iron industry nationally led to substantial reduction in the Rogers Company's operations. During the 1880s employment diminished by half, and iron operations closed between 1890 and 1892. The company was reorganized, with James and son Henry in total control. They dismantled the ironworks at Au Sable Forks and built a pulp mill in its stead, retraining their workforce in the process. The new plant was complemented by a paper mill, begun in 1902, and the purchase of the Alice Falls Pulp Company near Ausable Chasm three years later. At the latter location the Rogerses formed the Au Sable Electric Power & Light Company, which eventually supplied electric power to Wilmington, Jay, Au Sable Forks, Keeseville, Port Kent,

Peru, Keene, and Keene Valley. Logging operations expanded southward to White-face Mountain and the High Peaks near Keene Valley. Only an attempt to transform Black Brook into a resort failed in this sweeping reinvention.

Despite the pronounced shift in its nature the Rogers Company induced little growth after 1920, save for a brief period during World War II, when major additions were made to the Au Sable Forks mill. Having depleted the local timber supply, the company imported pulpwood from Canada after the mid-1920s, and it began to sell parcels of its vast landholdings. The plant was purchased by New Jersey Industries in 1954 and closed four years later. No retransformation was forthcoming. Quarry-ing high-quality granite had been a secondary staple for Au Sable Forks since the early 20th century, but it could not compensate for the demise of the paper mill.

Farther south along the Ausable River, the hamlet of Jay's development was close-ly linked to Au Sable Forks. Settlement in Jay began in the 1790s. By that decade's end William Mallory had erected a sawmill and John Purmont an iron forge—one of the first in the Adirondacks. The J. & G. Purmont Company took over Mallory's expanding operation in 1809 and continued to grow in subsequent decades. J. & J. Rogers ac-quired the company in 1864 and located its new plant across the Ausable on the east side. By that time the entire working population of the hamlet was engaged directly or otherwise in the industry. Gently rolling terrain extending some distance from either side of the river was developed for agriculture to sustain workers in both Jay and Au Sable Forks. When the Rogerses closed their plant in the latter community they did so in Jay as well, but here nothing comparable to the paper mill took its place. In 1890, however, Harvey M. Ward founded the Ward Lumber Company, which became, and remains, the largest business of its kind in the valley and the only place where white pine is now milled in the park.

But if industry was to be no more, this part of the greater Ausable River Valley did emerge as an important place for various forms of leisure. Whiteface Mountain, one of the grandest in the Adirondacks, spurred tourism around its eastern face. On the West Branch of the Ausable, the hamlet of Wilmington, around which farm-ing had developed since the early 19th century, became a tourist destination with the construction of several hostelries, most notably the Whiteface Mountain House, which opened around 1900. Longstanding efforts to construct a scenic highway to the summit of Whiteface, opposed by some for its intrusion on the Forest Preserve, began to take shape by the late 1920s and were consummated with the opening of the Whiteface Veterans Memorial Highway in 1935 [WM 2]. Ski trails—known as Marble Mountain—were created on the east face in 1949. Under state auspices, the Whiteface Ski Center opened in 1958 and expanded over the next decade, luring summer visitors as well as skiers. By the 1950s fly fishing in both branches of the Ausable River became popular. Between Wilmington and the Whiteface highway's tollbooths, businessman Julian Reiss erected Santa's Workshop in 1948–49, a pio-neering theme park [WM 1]. The designer of that attraction, Arto Monaco, developed his own children's playground, the Land of Makebelieve, near his home in Upper Jay. Between the time it opened in 1954 and 1979, the latter theme park was flooded eleven times, prompting Monaco's decision to close. What was left was ravaged in one of the Ausable River's most severe floods, which occurred as a result of Tropical Storm Irene in 2011. Skiing and other recreation opportunities provided some of the impetus for developing AuSable Acres [JA 9]. Located on high ground between Au Sable Forks, Jay, and Wilmington, the tract was launched in 1963 as a planned

Whiteface Mountain House, Wilmington. (ca. 1930s postcard)

Upper Ausable Lake, Adirondack Mountain Reserve, Keene Valley. (late 19th-century photograph)

231

seasonal community for persons of middle income, one of the few to materialize in the region.

Timber and farm goods to help fuel the iron industry did much to sustain the hamlet of Keene into the mid-19th century. Thereafter, Keene and its southern neighbor, Keene Flats (renamed Keene Valley in 1883), began to attract visitors. Artists, ministers, writers, and others found the landscape a sublime embodiment of the picturesque ideal. At first, seasonal accommodations were mostly in farm dwellings adapted as boardinghouses, but some affluent summer visitors were building cottages by the late 1870s. Two sizable hotels, the Tahawus House (1872–74) and Adirondack House (1882), were erected in stages in the hamlet center. Two miles farther south, where the Ausable Valley meets the High Peaks, the Beede House was built in 1876. Unlike many other resorts in the Adirondacks, seasonal residents of Keene Valley were more focused on vigorous outdoor activities, along with pursuing creative ventures and intellectual exchange than on the indulgent routines of a hotel. Probably for that reason, hotels maintained relatively brief currency. Keene Valley became a resort of cottages, many of them situated to take advantage of mountain views. A rebuilt Beede House did survive by virtue of its conversion to a clubhouse for the Adirondack Mountain Reserve less than two decades after it was constructed. The continued increase in seasonal residents in the valley as far north as Au Sable Forks and the soaring rise in visitors engaged in mountain climbing, rock climbing, and skiing have had a major impact on the complexion and the economy of the area.

*   *   *   *   *

VALCOUR
Town of Peru, Clinton County

VA 1 BLUFF POINT LIGHTHOUSE
Bluff Point, Valcour Island; 1871–74
(accessible only by boat)

Lighthouses began to be constructed along Lake Champlain in 1826 in response to the increase of commercial traffic after the opening of the Champlain Canal in 1823. Completion of the Chambly Canal in Canada twenty years later, the removal of customs duties with Canada in the mid-19th century, and the need to ship ever larger amounts of iron ore and iron products all contributed to the demand for navigational aids. Thirteen lighthouses lined the lake's shores by 1891.

Overlooking an area where Benedict Arnold's fleet stalled larger British naval forces in 1776—one of the first water engagements of the Revolutionary War—the Valcour lighthouse is a good example of those erected a century later. Among the objectives of the federal Light-House Board, created in the 1850s, was to centralize control of design to ensure basic standards were met. With its light tower an integral part of the larger building, Valcour is similar to counterparts at Kings Point, New York (1877); the Penfield lighthouse in Connecticut (1874); and the Colchester Reef lighthouse in Vermont, among others in the Northeast.

The Bluff Point Lighthouse's function was superseded by a steel-frame tower (a short distance to the southwest) in 1929, and it was decommissioned three years later. The last in a succession of individual owners granted the Clinton County Historical Association a conservation easement prior to selling the property to the state in 1972. The entire island, one of the largest in Lake Champlain, is now part of the Forest Preserve, with the lighthouse protected as a historic site.

VA 2 HENRY SETON CAMP
Valcour Island; 1929, Charles Hoyt, builder
(Au Sable Forks) (accessible by boat)

The western side of Valcour Island became home to several dozen camps during the early 20th century, of which only that erected for Massachusetts financier Henry Seton remains. Faced in stone, the dwelling was constructed out of reinforced concrete, no doubt as a precaution against fire. The design is essentially ahistorical, but contains some vague allusions to early Dutch houses in the lower Hudson Valley and to postmedieval English cottages. Seton's 130-acre property is now part of the Forest Preserve, and the state has thus far resisted any plans to use the camp for a needed interpretive center.

VA 3 JOSEPH CROCKER SIBLEY – CELIA SIBLEY WILSON HOUSE
3712 US 9; ca. 1904–05; 1925; later alterations

After making his fortune in oil refining and serving as a member of the U.S. Congress from Pennsylvania, Sibley erected one of the most elaborate summer houses along the shores of Lake Champlain during the early 20th century. A decorous boathouse that also accommodated guests and an equally embellished stable remain from this first building campaign. The main house burned several years after Sibley's daughter received the property. She commissioned a dwelling of a very different sort. Taking advantage of sweeping views of the lake, the east (principal) face of the house has two tiers of porches, bracketed by stone walls, a design that may well have been inspired by what is now known as the Old Stone Barracks (1839) at the former U.S. Army post in Plattsburgh. The accomplished Colonial Revival design suggests the hand of Alvin W. Inman, who had recently established his practice in Plattsburgh, his hometown, after gaining experience in New York. In 1963 the property was sold to what is now State University of New York–Plattsburgh, for which it serves as a conference center.

VA 4 PLATT HOUSES
3633 and 3595 US 9

Following the Revolutionary War, state authorities granted Zephaniah Platt a huge tract to consolidate American interests in the upper Champlain and St. Lawrence valleys, an area where French-Canadian and Iroquois occupation had predominated. Platt established a new settlement, Plattsburgh, in 1785. Later he gave his eldest son, Robert, 700 acres of fertile land to the south. With its low-slung form and gambrel roof, **Robert Platt's house (a)** (1809 and later) at 3633 US 9 is reminiscent of "Dutch" farm dwellings in the lower Hudson Valley and was reputedly patterned after the elder Platt's residence in Dutchess County. The main porch and entryway appear to date from the 1830s or 1840s, and the side wing and its rear extension also are from a later period.

Robert's younger brother, **Jonas**, erected a **house (b)** nearby at 3595 US 9 around 1820. It shares the same basic form and likewise has had a number of modifications, including sizable two-story masonry extensions behind the main block. Prior to constructing his manse Jonas Platt served in the state assembly (1796) and senate (1810–13).

PORT KENT
Town of Ausable, Clinton County

PK 1 ELKANAH WATSON HOUSE
21 Lake Street; 1828; later alterations

What appears to be an eccentric variation on a Palladian composition, with a central two-tiered portico, this house may have been the product of numerous changes over time. It also may have been, according to local lore, the work of a "French" architect—perhaps one of several who came to the new republic in search of opportunities. Whatever the case, it is a prime candidate for detailed investigation.

A native of Plymouth, Massachusetts, Watson was apprenticed to celebrated Providence merchant John Brown in 1773. He made a fortune after settling in Albany, and in 1807 turned to farming in Pittsfield, Massachusetts. There he began a campaign to reform agricultural practices, organizing the Berkshire Agricultural Society and developing the concept of the agricultural fair. In 1828 he came to the Adirondacks, where he was instrumental in creating Port Kent for shipping iron and other products from the Ausable Valley. His vision of the region's development was broad. Watson played an important role in advancing the Port Kent and Hopkinton Turnpike and called for a counterpart connecting Boston to Lake Champlain. He developed his Port Kent estate for agricultural production and as a horticultural exhibition. Fourteen years after his arrival, he died there at age eighty-five.

234

PK 2 PORT KENT–BURLINGTON FERRIES
Dock at eastern end of NY 373

Two ferries carrying pedestrians and motor vehicles to Vermont are of a remarkably old age for commercial watercraft. The **Adirondack** was built in 1913 as the *South Jacksonville* at the Merrill-Stevens shipyard for the Jacksonville Ferry and Land Company, which served Florida's St. Johns River. Fourteen years later it was

sold to the Tacony-Palmyra Ferry Company in Philadelphia and renamed *Mount Holly*. Soon thereafter it was transferred to New York's East River. An extensive remaking occurred in 1938 for the Chesapeake Bay Ferry Company. Finally, it was purchased by the Lake Champlain Transportation Company in 1954 and has remained in seasonal service for over sixty years. The *Adirondack* is in fact the oldest double-ended American ferryboat still in operation. The somewhat larger **Champlain** dates to 1930, when it was built in Baltimore as the *City of Hampton* to connect Old Point Comfort to Norfolk, Virginia. It was acquired for Lake Champlain use in 1957, and it was probably at that time when the craft experienced some remodeling.

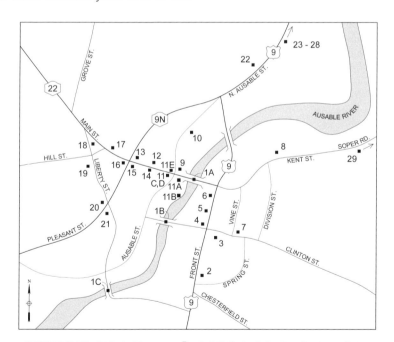

KEESEVILLE and AUSABLE CHASM

Town of Ausable, Clinton County, and Town of Chesterfield, Essex County

Some of Keeseville's industries continued into the mid-20th century; however, no major enterprise has replaced them. Many of those structures have been demolished or burned, and the hamlet's principal business artery, Front Street, has been marred by several new commercial facilities that are out of character with its compact structure. Still the hamlet retains one of the richest collections of 19th-century commercial, institutional, and residential architecture and engineering in the Adirondacks—work that affords vivid evidence of the wealth that once existed there.

KS 1 BRIDGES

Spanning the Ausable River was, of course, essential to Keeseville's development, but unlike other Adirondack communities, where few bridges of any vintage survive, the hamlet boasts three notable 19th-century examples that remain because one is of unusual structural strength, the second is strictly for pedestrians, and the third is no longer used.

Situated at a critical juncture just below the rapids, what is now known as the **Stone Arch Bridge (a)**, on Main Street

(NY 22) at the Ausable River, was built massively by Solon Townsend in 1843 to withstand the strong pressures of rushing waters intensified by Anderson Falls. Probably no other bridge in the Adirondacks ever approached its strength. With a span of 110 feet it remains as a striking testament to the importance of the community as a manufacturing center during the mid-19th century.

Replacing two suspension bridges before it, the **Swing Bridge (b)** (1888) was

built to facilitate the routine circulation of the workforce. A product of the Berlin Iron Bridge Company of East Berlin, Connecticut, the structure is now a rare example of its kind in the United States. The **Upper Bridge (c)** (1888), connecting Lower Liberty Street and Mill Hill Road, is likewise the third on its site. It is of a type once common, but is a rare surviving example of the work of its manufacturer, Murray, Dougal & Company of Milton, Pennsylvania. It is also the oldest wrought-iron truss bridge in the Adirondacks and the earliest known example of two-span, pin-connected Pratt through-truss bridge in the state.

KS 2 CATHOLIC CHURCH OF THE IMMACULATE CONCEPTION
Front and Spring streets; 1835; early 1850s; ca. 1881

Scattered throughout Keeseville are five churches that span a century to embody the varied nature of the hamlet's population. The oldest, Immaculate Conception, was built to house the swelling contingent of Irish and French-Canadian immigrants

and is one of the earliest Catholic churches in the Adirondacks. Even though the
French-speaking congregants formed their
own church in 1853 [KS 15], the Anglo-Irish
population continued to grow, leading to a
two-bay extension. The visual prominence
of its site was enhanced by the addition of
the tower three decades later.

KS 3 ST. PAUL'S EPISCOPAL CHURCH
107 Clinton Street; 1853; 1877

Unlike many Episcopal churches, St.
Paul's was initially a rather plain building,
lacking the Anglican associations found
with counterparts in Lake George [LG 9b,
Section 1] or Warrensburg [WA 3, Section
4]. More than two decades after its construction, however, the building was given
greater prominence with a stylish corner
tower in 1877.

KS 4 UNITED METHODIST CHURCH
*1699 Front Street (US 9) at Clinton Street
(CR 16); 1878*

When it was constructed, the Methodist church stood apart in its vigorous interpretation of Gothic precedent and its
tall, angled corner tower. The scheme was
actually based on an 1871 design by Iowa
architect W. W. Sanborn that was published in the annual report of the Methodist Board of Church Extension.

KS 5 COMMERCIAL BUILDINGS
1701-19, 1725-31 Front Street

Despite the encroachments made on
the hamlet's business center since the
1950s, a number of noteworthy buildings
remain. Most of them are attached. The
stone end walls of **1701 Front (a)** suggest
they were part of an earlier structure incorporated into the present two-story
building. The **Kingsland Block (b)**, extending from 1703 to 1709 Front, was erected
in two stages—1868 and 1885—that are of
matching design. The latter two units retain their original storefronts. The two
commercial buildings (c) at 1711-13 and

1715-19 Front are variations of the Kingsland Block and probably date to the same
period. The latter building also boasts its
original storefronts. Both Edmund and
Robert Kingsland owned stores on Front
Street, which they used to sell company
products and other goods. Farther down at
1725-31 Front is the **Mould Block (d)** of
1868. No. 1731 was originally the centerpiece; the three units to its north were demolished for a convenience store.

KS 6 KEESEVILLE PUBLIC LIBRARY
*1721 Front Street; ca. 1934-35, Alvin W.
Inman, architect (Plattsburgh, N.Y.)*

On the site formerly occupied by a
bandstand, the character and scale of the
library is more one associated with a genteel suburb of the interwar decades than a
19th-century industrial center. The dispar-
ity between it and its commercial neighbors was no doubt intentional. To quickly
replace a facility that had burned in late
November 1933, Inman more or less replicated his design for the Baker Memorial
Library in nearby Peru, New York (1926-27).

KS 7 JAMES MILLS HOUSE
*96 Clinton Street; 1836, Seneca and Isaac
Perry, builders; porch ca. 1900s-10s*

A three-bay gable-end Greek Revival
house found in many hamlets of the eastern Adirondacks was given a commodious
side porch in the early 20th century, with
a cobblestone base somewhat incongru-
ously supporting squat Tuscan columns.
The latter were probably used to relate to

the original design. The building has been preserved as the Anderson Falls Heritage Museum.

KS 8 THOMAS A. TOMLINSON HOUSE
72 Kent Street (CR 17); 1846 and later

Overlooking the hamlet lies a temple-front house, ostensibly in the Greek Revival mode, but with Tuscan columns, erected for Keeseville's first lawyer, who also owned property in the commercial center and served in the U. S. Congress. Along with Oliver Keese, Tomlinson developed a sawmill and lumber business in Franklin County near Upper St. Regis Lake in 1851. The side porch appears to be an addition, as are the sections to the rear.

KS 9 FIRST CONGREGATIONAL CHURCH
1746 Main Street; 1851–52, Solomon
Townsend, builder

Not surprisingly, the Congregationalists built one of the largest, most structurally solid and centrally located houses of worship in the community. It is also one of the plainest, running counter to the mounting taste for embellishment during the mid-19th century, and inherently conservative in its form as well as its details. The edifice later became home to the Presbyterians. Thereafter it was used for high school graduations until it was sold to the Masons in 1937 and served as the Ausable River Lodge No. 149. Much of the interior, as redecorated in 1874, survives due to the Masons inserting a small structure for their use within the worship space.

KS 10 RESIDENTIAL ROW
162–66 Ausable Road; ca. mid-19th century;
later alterations

Local tradition holds that this long, narrow limestone building was constructed as a brewery. The masonry reveals changes were made to the walls, plausibly to adapt the building into a residential row at an early date. Certainly using stone for such modest dwelling units would have been an unusual practice in the region at that time. If the original use was industrial, it is a one-of-a-kind survivor in the park.

KS 11 MAIN STREET COMMERCIAL BUILDINGS

While commercial development along Front Street was primarily retail oriented, that along Main represented the community's industrial operations. One of Keeseville's most important businesses during the second half of the 19th century, the **Ausable Horse Nail Company** came to enjoy an international trade and employ some 200 people. Founded by Edmund Kingsland in 1863, it acquired the compound built by the **Eagle Horse Nail Company**. The **office building (a)** (1852) at 1745

Main Street also included storage facilities and, upstairs, quarters for Daniel Dodge, a local inventor. Apprenticed to a blacksmith in his youth, Dodge spent eight years attempting to develop a machine that would make high-quality nails for horseshoes. An unsuccessful machine patented in 1852 was followed by one that effectively emulated the blacksmith's work by forging nails (patented 1856, 1859, and 1864). The two companies that procured the rights to this innovation were Edmund Kingsland's and the Chicago-based Northwestern Horse-Nail Company run by his brother Jacob D. Kingsland. The building's interior has been sensitively rehabilitated as offices for Adirondack Architectural Heritage, which bought the property in 2008.

Behind at 126 Ausable Street lies the **Eagle Horse Nail Company's** original **mill (b)** (1849), also taken over by Kingsland. This linear structure is comprised primarily of sandstone walls supporting a timber roof, the northern section of which was raised around the 1860s–70, supported by queenpost trusses. The mill was one of several adjacent plants used by the business during its heyday. Most other components of the complex have burned or been demolished, but several masonry buildings that were once a part of the plant can be seen farther south on Ausable Street. The original mill building is the only intact industrial structure from the mid-19th century and only one of three such buildings dating before 1900 remaining in the park. AARCH has repaired and stabilized the building fabric and implemented covenants to ensure its preservation by future owners.

Next door, at 1749 Main Street, lies a somewhat smaller sandstone building that was constructed around 1856 as the company's **shipping office (c)**. It was taken

over by the **Ausable Valley Grange No. 973** in 1903 and has experienced little change inside or out. The extraordinary weathervane atop its roof was once rivaled by a large wooden eagle atop the company's office building.

Farther west at 1753 Main lies a commercial block constructed around 1825 as the

Keese & Hurlberty general store (d), one of the oldest of its kind in the region. It was later used as a doctor's office, then a law office, before being converted to a residence in the early 20th century. Around that time the side porch was added. Across the street at 1758 Main is the diminutive brick **office building of Richard Keese II (e)**, erected in 1825, from which he ran some of his many businesses.

KS 12 RICHARD KEESE II HOUSE
1760 Main Street; ca. 1823

Paralleling Merchant Row in Essex [ES 32–34], several of Keeseville's richest inhabitants clustered their houses to form a distinctive enclave between the 1820s and early 1850s. Richard Keese II, son of one of the key figures in establishing the hamlet as a center for iron products, commissioned an unorthodox residence that is set well back from the property line. It has a massive sandstone façade, unrelieved save for an elaborate Federal doorway and large attic fanlight. The planarity of this front is accentuated by the stepped gable end that may have been intended to allude to 17th-century Dutch colonial precedent in New York, but has the scale more associated with early 19th-century industrial plants.

KS 13 SILAS ARNOLD HOUSE

1764 Main Street; ca. 1820; 1840, Seneca Perry, builder

Next door, the Arnold house was effectively transformed into a gable-end Greek Revival design in 1840 by the prominent local builder Seneca Perry. The owner began to amass his wealth from the iron mine at Arnold Hill near Au Sable Forks. Once established in Keeseville, Arnold augmented his coffers through banking and insurance services. His daughter married Richard Keese II, uniting two family fortunes.

KS 14 EDMUND KINGSLAND ROMEY HOUSE

1759 Main Street; 1885; 1903

Following the destruction of the Ausable House hotel by fire, Romey, president of the Keeseville National Bank, seized the opportunity to erect an expansive dwelling in the vicinity of his forebears. Rendered in a reserved interpretation of the Queen Anne mode, the house was made more severe by the porch and porte-cochere additions nearly two decades later.

KS 15 NELSON KINGSLAND HOUSE

1765 Main Street; ca. 1850, Seneca and Isaac Perry, builders

One of three brothers who came to Keeseville from Vermont, Nelson and his older brother, Edmund, arrived in 1826. They soon established a factory for wagons and sleighs. After spending five years as a merchant in Titusville, Pennsylvania, Nelson returned to Keeseville in 1865, purchasing the foundry and machine shop of Goulding & Peabody. He secured the right to manufacture Daniel Dodge's horse-nail machine for European export, but also did a substantial business producing agricultural implements. Nelson Kingsland also became the first president of the Keeseville National Bank and vice-president of the Ausable Horse Nail Company; additionally, he speculated in local real estate.

With proportions characteristic to a large dwelling of the mid-19th century, his residence is otherwise rather conservative—a reiteration of that built by brother Edmund [KS 16] two decades earlier. It has lain vacant for some years.

KS 16 EDMUND KINGSLAND HOUSE

1769 Main Street; ca. 1832, Seneca Perry, builder

Edmund Kingsland was arguably the central figure in Keeseville's rise to industrial prominence. In 1826 he sold his ironworks at Fair Haven, Vermont, and moved to Keeseville, commissioning this grand Greek Revival house several years thereafter. Besides his business of making wagons and sleighs he leased the Boquet Iron Company in Willsboro from William D. Ross [Section 6] from 1839 to 1847. Subsequently he joined his other brother, Jacob, to form the E. & J. D. Kingsland Company. The firm built a substantial forge near Ausable Chasm and purchased the Keeseville Manufacturing Company's ironworks. Five years later the firm built a rolling mill at Ausable Chasm, and, prior to 1860, purchased the former woolen mill for the manufacture of knives, axes, and other edge tools. All these operations were sold shortly before he formed the Ausable Horse Nail Company in 1863.

KS 17 KEESEVILLE CENTRAL SCHOOL

1790 Main Street; 1936–39, Alvin W. Inman, architect (Plattsburgh, N.Y.), Quentin F. Haig, associate (Westport)

When a new school was constructed for the hamlet in 1915, it seemed a major advance from the 1845 facility it replaced. After another twenty years, however, the building proved inadequate for a consolidated program and was replaced through phased construction on the same site. The new building became redundant with the creation of the Ausable Valley Central School District in 1972 and now serves as town offices.

esque and Baroque elements in a manner then fashionable in Québec, the home base of both architect and builder (Walter Brothers). After a major fire in 1926, most of the granite exterior walls were retained, but the clerestory on the side elevations had collapsed and was not replaced; the new roof ran uninterrupted from the ridge line to the outer walls. The towers were lowered, and the interior was redone, but along lines reminiscent of the original. The reconstruction was conducted by a local builder, Moses Rabideau, who had worked for Rufus Prescott & Sons since the 1870s.

KS 18 ST. JOHN THE BAPTIST CATHOLIC CHURCH

1803 Main Street; 1901–02, J. O. Turgeon, architect (Montreal); alterations 1926–27

By far the most elaborate house of worship in Keeseville (and elsewhere in the Adirondacks) was erected by the Catholic congregation dominated by persons of French-Canadian origin, on orders from Bishop Henri Gabriels, head of the Diocese of Ogdensburg during the early 20th century, who considered their existing quarters [KS 19] unworthy. The result was a conspicuous assertion of French-Canadian identity, using a mélange of Roman-

KS 19 FIRST BAPTIST CHURCH

61 Liberty Street; 1826; additions and alterations 1853

Built a quarter century earlier, the Baptist church was originally a wooden version of that of the Congregationalists. After purchase by the French-Canadian Roman Catholic congregation in 1853, it was embellished with a spire (now lost), round-arched windows, and classical details. It was moved in 1901 when the congregation decided to erect a new St. John the Baptist Church [KS 18] on the property. Long vacant, the older building is in the process of being rehabilitated.

KS 20 J. WILLARD HOUSE

37–41 Liberty Street; ca.1850

Constructed for a daughter of Nelson Kingsland and her husband, this house has an unusual configuration, with a central wing projecting in front. The variety presented by this arrangement, enhanced by flanking porches, manifests the rise in a taste for the picturesque by 1850, while many of the details are drawn from earlier, Greek Revival motifs.

KS 21 DOWLING HOUSE
100 Pleasant Street; ca. 1850s

A near contemporary of the Willard house, this dwelling was at once more current in its use of the then fashionable Italianate mode and more conservative in its simple, rectangular form and sparing use of detail. The one-story extension appears to be original and may have served as an office.

KS 22 MOTELS

As a group, these three motels along US 9 between Keeseville's center and Ausable Chasm comprise an increasingly rare cluster of tourist facilities from the post–World War II era. They illustrate common variations found at independently owned and operated establishments that then characterized highway-oriented accommodations. Unfortunately the future of at least two of them is problematic.

All three appear to have been constructed during the 1950s. The **Blue Spruce Motel (a)** at 1810 US 9 is arranged around an open landscaped area. Like many such establishments, it may have been erected in several stages. The **Grand Prix Motor Lodge (b)** at 1867 US 9 has a simple elongated "L" configuration, the rear portion of which was later truncated. The **Villa Motel (c)** at 1875

US 9 is the largest and is set in a linear form parallel to the road. It began as the Village Motel in the 1940s or earlier, with a group of cabins arcing around what may have been a farmhouse converted into a filling station, restaurant, and proprietor's quarters. To this assemblage, parts of the current facility were added over time.

KS 23 SCHOOL
14 Old State Road; ca. 1920s

Little is known about this anomalous one-room school building. Its elegant stonework and elevated floor, as well as the quality of its composition and detailing, make it seem as if it is a fragment from one of the suave, medievalizing dormitories built (at great cost) for Princeton University during the early 20th century. Who funded this small building, which also reputedly had a hefty price tag, and why such monies were channeled into this project are questions that remain.

KS 24 AUSABLE CHASM BRIDGE
US 9 at Ausable River; 1932–34, New York State Department of Public Works, designer and builder

Few bridges in the Adirondacks have comparably dramatic settings, with Ausable Chasm on one side and Rainbow and Horseshoe Falls on the other. A bridge has existed at this section of the river since 1810, when one was built as part of the Great Northern Turnpike linking Albany with Montreal. The current structure was likewise part of the development of US 9 into a major highway. Instead of following the winding path of its early 20th-century predecessor, the bridge follows a more direct one that was occupied by a railroad bridge until it was demolished in 1927. The new structure was specially designed in response to the setting, with a riveted steel arch, 222 feet long, spanning the gorge, anchored by massive concrete piers sheathed in rough-faced sandstone and two short concrete-arch spans on the north side.

The structure's predecessor, known as the **Old State Road Bridge** (ca. 1910) at Old State and Mace Chasm (CR 71) roads, is a good example of a Pratt, pony-tail truss configuration, widely used at the turn of the 20th century.

KS 25 RAINBOW FALLS HYDROELECTRIC PLANT AND DAM

Off Old State Road at Ausable River; 1925–26

Built under the auspices of the J. & J. Rogers Iron Company of Au Sable Forks to supply its industrial enterprises and a host of area communities, this plant supplemented one built upriver at Alice Falls. While most such facilities were utilitarian in nature [WD 5, Section 6], the two buildings here were more decorous, perhaps a response to the well-heeled tourists who then frequented the environs. The plant was acquired by New York State Electric & Gas Corporation in 1930.

KS 26 HERBERT ESTES HOUSE

1131 Mace Chasm Road, off US 9; ca. early 1880s

In 1877 Estes was sent by his Montreal employer, W. H. Mooney & Company, to head the mechanical department of the firm's horse-nail factory at Ausable Chasm. Within a few years he became plant superintendent, and this capacious stone dwelling was erected directly above the works as his residence. The house's T-shaped form suggests it was derived from pattern-book designs popular during the mid-19th century. In 2011 it received a new lease on life as the North Star Underground Railroad Museum.

KS 27 AUSABLE CHASM CAMPGROUND LODGE

NY 373, off US 9 at Mace Chasm Road; ca. 1970

Along with state-owned campgrounds, commercial ventures of this sort have abounded in the Adirondacks since World War II. This example, developed by the company that operates Ausable Chasm as a tourist destination, is typical in its systematic subdivision of wooded land primarily for recreational vehicles and trailers, but also for tents. The lodge, containing a lobby and office, is more prominent—in its location and form—than at most campgrounds, here capitalizing on the mid-20th-century popularity of the A-frame to give the place a distinct image.

KS 28 CARPENTER FLATS BRIDGE

US 9 at Ausable River; 1941; American Bridge Company, manufacturer and builder (Coraopolis, Pa.)

Some three miles north of Ausable Chasm is the largest of a number of steel camelback-truss bridges erected throughout the Adirondacks prior to World War II as part of an ongoing campaign to upgrade major highways. Other sizable examples, using cross-trusses as bracing, can be found on NY 8, crossing the Schroon River west of Brant Lake, and on SR 30 crossing Long Lake. Most smaller renditions of this type have been replaced in recent years, but two remain on NY 74, crossing the Schroon River at Severance and on NY 9N, crossing the West Branch of the Ausable River at Au Sable Forks. The Carpenter Flats Bridge is both longer and wider than others in the Adirondacks and may have been designed to accommodate an eventual three or four lanes.

Founded in 1900, American Bridge was a consolidation of twenty-eight large-scale steel fabricators; two years later it became a subsidiary of U.S. Steel. The company was involved in the construction of numerous major bridges and skyscrapers.

KS 29 ASA MOON HOUSE

810 Mace Chasm Road (CR 71); ca. 1835–40

Much like the nearby Champlain Valley, the rolling land east-southeast as well as north of Keeseville proved conducive to agriculture. The burgeoning population of the nearby industrial center during the 19th century made for a lucrative market, enabling farmers such as Moon to prosper. The **farmhouse** adjacent to the south at 764 Mace Chasm Road was constructed at least a decade later using the same basic form. Also of note is the Greek Revival **farmhouse** at 481 Mace Chasm Road, which couples a two-story gable-end central section with a recessed entry, along with one-story wings—a configuration only occasionally used in the region [see HS 3, Section 1].

HARKNESS
Town of Ausable, Clinton County

HK 1 PETER KEESE HOUSE
279 Union Road, 1832 and later

Northwest of Keeseville, the rural community of Harkness once supported a small enclave of farmers, including a number of Quakers, beginning in the late 18th century. While most of the evidence of that settlement no longer exists, the sandstone house of Peter Keese, a son of the elder Richard Keese, was probably the grandest residence. Along with several outbuildings it has sustained little modification since the 19th century.

HK 2 THOMAS MILLER HOUSE
664 Hallock Hill Road; 1822

More modest, and typical, of dwellings in the settlement is the one-and-one-half-story sandstone house built for millwright Thomas Miller a decade earlier. It has recently benefited from a careful rehabilitation. Most other evidence of the Quaker settlement is gone or has been extensively altered.

CLINTONVILLE
Town of Black Brook, Clinton County

CT 1 METHODIST EPISCOPAL CHURCH
1268 NY 9N; ca. 1833–34; additions 1869–70

The most prominent building in this former industrial hamlet was originally erected behind its current site. The move of 1869–70 transformed the edifice by placing it on a new ground story (enabling the worship space to be on the upper level) and adding an embellished projecting entrance, bell tower, and new windows.

AU SABLE FORKS
Town of Jay, Essex County, and Town of Black Brook, Clinton County

Wedged between hills where the Ausable River joins to combine its East and West branches, Au Sable Forks has an agreeable setting that is also prone to floods. The hamlet and environs had a population of only 559 in 2010, a third of that in Keeseville. But like Keeseville it straddles two towns and two counties. It has been bereft of a major employment base for decades; commuting is a necessity for many workers. Still, the hamlet has been able to maintain much of the neat and respectable character the Rogers family sought to implant over a century ago. As in most other parts of the Adirondacks, the industrial plants have long gone, and the principal streets are no longer lined with trees. Nevertheless, much of its 19th- and early 20th-century building stock remains.

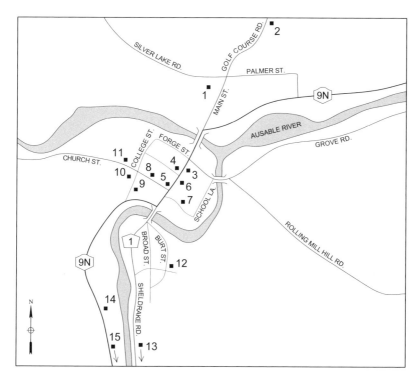

AF 1 D'AVIGNON-ROGERS HOUSE
25 N. Main Street; ca. mid-19th century;
additions ca. 1870s

Francis d'Avignon II was a well-established physician in Québec, who participated in the Canadian Rebellions of 1837 and was sentenced to death. He managed to escape from prison and fled to Au Sable Forks, where he established his professional practice anew. He served as a surgeon during the Civil War and was incarcerated at Virginia's notorious Libby Prison. D'Avignon survived that ordeal only to die at age fifty-nine in 1866. Following his marriage in 1874, James Rogers Jr. bought the house, adding the front section.

Despite their wealth, the Rogers family, unlike the Witherbees in Port Henry [Section 5], never built grand residences. This pattern is further evidenced in the house next door at 17 N. Main Street (1890), which was acquired by Rogers's son, Henry Geer Rogers, in 1901 from a Dr. Spaulding. It appears to have been built around the 1870s and was perhaps enlarged after Rogers's purchase.

AF 2 FAIRVIEW CEMETERY
Golf Course Road, opposite Ausable Valley
Golf Course; mid-19th century and later

Above the hamlet lies the community cemetery, which the Rogers family probably did much to develop and maintain. Though laid out on a grid, the plantings on the grounds and bordering woods give it some of the qualities of a picturesque design.

AF 3 BANK OF AU SABLE FORKS
14230 NY 9N; 1925, William G. Distin, architect

Organized in 1910, the bank represented a significant step from the company scrip payments that characterized transactions in the hamlet during the 19th century. Erected after a major fire destroyed much of the community, this building of relatively modest size has a classical façade set at a grand scale that conveys an appropriate sense of solidity and permanence. It has passed through a series of owners and is now a unit of Community Bank.

AF 4 UNITED METHODIST CHURCH
NY 9N at Pleasant Street; 1925–26, William G. Distin, architect

Replacing the 1848 building that had recently been renovated only to be consumed in the 1925 fire, this edifice was constructed of sandstone donated by the Rogers Company from several of its vacant Clintonville structures. Sporting a few Colonial Revival details, the building also harkens back to early and mid-19th-century Methodist churches in its basic form and simplicity.

AF 5 HOLY NAME CATHOLIC CHURCH
NY 9N and Church Lane; 1929–30, D. D. Kieff, architect (Watertown, N.Y.)

The Catholics took longer to rebuild, commissioning an ambitious design from an architect who had done a number of projects for the Diocese of Ogdensburg. Drawing on the trend toward abstracting English Gothic precedent, Kieff's scheme is more robust with its use of rough-face random ashlar, using granite quarried nearby. As with the Methodist church, the Rogers Company contributed to its construction.

AF 6 ST. JAMES EPISCOPAL CHURCH
14246 SR 9N; 1876, E. C. Ryer, architect (Burlington, Vt.); rebuilt 1925–26

As originally constructed, St. James continued the tradition of Anglican-inspired Gothic churches from the mid-19th century [LG 6b, Section 1; WA 3, Section 4], updated with a tall wooden spire and other details. James Rogers—both father and son—and Henry Graves (the senior Rogers's brother-in-law) comprised the building committee. The reconstruction, directed by senior warden Henry Rogers, retained the masonry walls, but modified the tower and other appendages.

AF 7 SCHOOLS

Now used for town offices and service facilities, these two former school buildings speak to the rapidly changing agenda of public education during the early to mid-20th century. A Union Free School was established in Au Sable Forks in 1883. Four years elapsed between the time it burned in 1908 and the completion of the **Town of Jay School (a)** in 1912 at 15 School Lane. It was designed to accommodate all grades and contained modern amenities, but encompassed little aside from classroom and basic support spaces. The drive for consolidation was under way locally by 1929 when Plattsburgh architect Alvin W. Inman prepared plans for a building to serve students from the towns of Jay and Wilmington. Federal aid resulting from the Depression enabled the program to go forward on a somewhat reduced scale. His **Jay Central School (b)** (1933–35) at 11 School Lane

includes a large space that doubled as auditorium and gymnasium and also had rooms dedicated to specialized instruction. To compensate for the scaled-back program, the older building became the high school. Both facilities were redundant when a new consolidated plant was built in Clintonville to serve the towns of Jay, Wilmington, Black Brook, and Ausable in 1972.

AF 8 JOHN AGNEW HOUSE
14 Church Lane; ca. 1870s and later

Nothing is known about the circumstances leading to the array of unorthodoxies on this wood-frame house. Using round-arched windows was by no means uncommon in the mid-19th century, but capping them with ogee moldings was a pronounced departure, at least in the Adirondacks. Probably during the late 1880s or early 1890s the porch was reworked with a chamfered projection, above which was added an angled porch to serve the second floor.

AF 9 FRANK L. KEMP HOUSE
12 College Street; ca. 1900

Built for a businessman and theater owner, this house is a spirited rendition of the popularized Queen Anne mode, while making use of architectural details that seem to span several decades.

AF 10 HENRY DUNCAN GRAVES HOUSE
13 College Street; ca. 1879–81, F. L. Perkins, architect (office location unknown)

After clerking in Plattsburgh, Graves came to Au Sable Forks in 1845, where he held a similar post at what would become the J. & J. Rogers Company. His ascendancy was swift: He married Katherine, the second daughter of James Rogers the elder, in 1861, and then became chief financial officer. He was named to the board in 1871, became vice president six years later, and assumed the presidency two years after that. Concurrently, he began work on a house that would have seemed extravagant ($75,000) in almost any city and far surpassed the Rogers family's residences. While the home base of its architect is unknown, the builder was Rufus Prescott & Sons from Keeseville.

Less than ten years after the house's completion, it was discovered that Graves had siphoned money from the company to construct his thirty-room manse. Because Katherine Graves was a member of the Rogers family, the couple was allowed to live in the service area, but forbidden to use other portions. In recent years, several parties have schemed to rehabilitate Graves's grand residence; however, it remains vacant.

AF 11 AU SABLE FORKS ELEMENTARY SCHOOL
Church Street, east of College; ca. 1970s; additions 2012–13, SEI Design Group, architects (Albany)

Even with consolidation in the 1970s, an elementary school was built for children of Au Sable Forks. What began as a modest facility has recently been enlarged, with a new front section that again gives public education a lively civic presence.

AF 12 FEATHERSTON HOUSES

Broad & Burt lanes; 1900s, George and Emerson Featherston, developers

Built from standardized plans, these wood-frame dwellings were targeted to white-collar employees of the Rogers Company. Decorous without pretense, they exemplify the neat and orderly character cultivated throughout the hamlet during the early 20th century.

AF 13 ASGAARD FARM

Asgaard Way, off Sheldrake Road (CR 65); ca. 1927–28 and later, Rockwell Kent, designer

Rockwell Kent was the first artist of note to make the Adirondacks his home base, moving from New York in 1927. A protracted search in Essex County led to his finding this spectacular site along the Ausable River south of the hamlet. He created a place where he could work in seclusion, but also entertain his many city friends. The dairy farm was an important source of income. Trained as an architect, but never having practiced, he now put his talents to work, designing the family house, his studio, barns, and other buildings, modifying them on occasions where shifting needs warranted. The ensemble was in part a manifesto against modernism, evoking instead values then associated with the early American past that Kent held dear. The main house burned in 1969 and was replaced by a smaller, less distinguished one, also of his design. In recent years farming operations have been revived. The group is best seen from Sheldrake Road; part of the grounds are accessible at times when the farm store is open.

AF 14. WORKERS' HOUSING

14050–56 NY 9N; probably late 19th century

This multi-unit structure was one of several built to serve the Rogers Company workforce. Whether it was originally a boardinghouse or a group of apartment units is unclear.

AF 15 CARNES GRANITE COMPANY

14026 NY 9N; ca. 1924

An important embodiment of Au Sable Forks' granite industry, this structure was built for W. R. Carnes, who came from Vermont to West Chazy, New York, in the early 20th century. After establishing the West Chazy Granite Company, Carnes formed the Au Sable Forks Granite Company in 1908. He had three partners in the latter venture, including Edward Featherston, on whose land the deposit was located. The two businesses consolidated in 1938, with Au Sable Forks the base of operation. The quarries were later closed, but the company continued to be run as a retail outlet for monuments, operated by Carnes's son and later his grandson. Ravaged by floodwaters in 2011, the structure may yet be renovated.

WILMINGTON

Town of Wilmington, Essex County

Situated at the foot of Whiteface Mountain along the West Branch of the Ausable River, the hamlet of Wilmington is topographically dramatic, but the landscape's impact is diminished by the extent of tourist-oriented commercial development that relates little to its surroundings. Other such features, however, are of considerable interest and have become important contributors to the community's heritage.

WM 1 SANTA'S WORKSHOP AT NORTH POLE, NY

324 Whiteface Memorial Highway (CR 431); 1948–49 and later; Arto Monaco, designer (Upper Jay), Harold G. Fortune, builder (Lake Placid) of original components

Thought to be the first theme park targeted to young children in the United States, Santa's Workshop was certainly a pioneer and unique in the state when it opened in 1949. In contrast to other Adirondack tourist attractions, which focused on natural features or historic sites, this place was entirely new and manmade. Situated on a fifteen-acre mountainside tract roughly halfway between the hamlet of Wilmington and the entrance to the scenic highway on Whiteface Mountain, this complex was conceived by Julian Reiss, who owned a car dealership on Long Island. A devotee of the Adirondacks, Reiss took his family on a vacation there right after gasoline rationing ended in 1945. During that visit his young daughter asked if she could see Santa Claus. He could only answer no; however, the idea of building a North Pole village caught his imagination.

Reiss met Arto Monaco, a toy and set designer who had worked for Disney Studios but had returned to his home in Upper Jay. Monaco expressed serious interest in creating a fantasy village, and Reiss persuaded his father, a banker and shipping magnate, to fund the venture. Howard G. Fortune, a Lake Placid builder who specialized in log cabins and owned considerable acreage in the vicinity, convinced Reiss on the location due to its forested setting, the scenic highway, and nearby ski facilities.

The three men became partners. Monaco made sketches and closely supervised Fortune's construction crew, who began working in the spring of 1948. When it opened the following year Santa's Workshop drew visitors far beyond anticipation, and by the season's end 2,000 to 3,000 people came daily. In addition to meeting fabled characters, children could interact with animals—this was among the first petting zoos in the country—and watch live entertainment. Santa's Workshop received national attention. The *Saturday Evening Post* deemed it one of the most novel attractions in the East. Disney sent a team to examine the premises.

The complex was gradually expanded, and in 1953 an official North Pole post office was opened. Amusement rides, including a reindeer carousel, were introduced in the early 1960s. Operating the year-round enterprise became Reiss's primary occupation. He died in 1959, but the enterprise continued to be run by members of the family until 2002. The original section remains intact and is now the major extant example of Monaco's fanciful theme park designs.

WM 2 WHITEFACE MEMORIAL HIGHWAY
Entrance 3 miles west of NY 86; 1929–38, New York State Department of Public Works, architects and engineers

Ascending almost to the summit of Whiteface Mountain (elevation 4,867 feet), this scenic road was born out of controversy. Creating such a route was proposed around 1900 by the proprietors of the Stevens House in Lake Placid [Section 9] to further that community's draw. Constructing a road up Pike's Peak in 1915 gave added impetus to the idea, and a group of Lake Placid and Saranac Lake businessmen formed the Adirondack Civic League for that purpose. Attempts to pass legislation allowing the road within the Forest Preserve began during the early 1920s. Though opponents considered it a breach of the state's conservation policy, popular opinion was strongly in favor, and the authorizing bill was passed in 1927. A state Whiteface Memorial Highway Commission was established to implement the plan—a process that extended from 1929 to 1938. Road construction began in 1931; the following year the Department of Public Works staff held an in-house competition for the design of the buildings. The road was dedicated in 1935, but the last building was not completed until three years later.

At the entrance, the **tollgate and toll collector's residence** (1932–33) were the work of DPW architects Alexander Richter, Angelo De Sousa, and Mario Bianculli, whose plans for the former were probably inspired by ongoing rustic work in national parks. The latter is a studied iteration of a Swiss chalet, enunciating associations between the Adirondacks and the Alps that gained new currency with the 1932 Winter Olympics. Like work in the national parks, the road itself takes a winding route in response to topography and to provide a range of views. Instead of a guardrail, jagged pieces of granite that had been blasted to form the road are laid in low barrier walls and in some places rise as a freestanding range. At the road's terminus lies the **Castle** (1935–36), a rest house and restaurant designed by Frederick Stuart Greene, who set aside his earlier chalet design after a trip to England. His medievalizing block, extending from the mountain face, suggests a fragment of some ancient fortification. At the same time the twin portals allow motorists to drive through the building twice, making a U-turn before proceeding to the narrow parking area. From there a long, winding stone path ascends to **Summit House** (1932, 1936–38), which can also be reached via a tunnel and elevator. The work of architects Gustav Mortensen and Carleton Craig, this low-slung domical structure of thick granite walls was designed to relate to the rugged, treeless landscape.

WM 3 WHITEBROOK DAIRY BAR
5660 NY 86; 1968, Michael Sibalski, designer and builder

Of a kind once common to American highways, this frozen custard stand is now a rare survivor.

WM 4 WILDERNESS INN
5481 NY 86; 1940s and later

Built as Camp Romang, this classic roadside establishment includes a restaurant and bar in the main building, with cabins at the rear. It was constructed for Glenn and Helen Bacon and named after her father, George Romang, who moved to Wilmington in 1935. Inside and out, the design has vaguely Alpine overtones that are most effectively seen when, at dusk, the premises are illuminated by a forest of Christmas lights.

WM 5 WHITEFACE CHALET
788 Springfield Road (CR 12); 1961
Of the many commercial enterprises in the area that are draped in Alpine garb, this twenty-two-room motel is among the most forthright in its pairing of historical fantasy with the pragmatic concerns of transient accommodations for a middle-class clientele. While most motels in the Wilmington area were located along the major highway (NY 86), this one faces a secondary road and is set well back in a verdant landscape.

WM 6 JOHN SWEENEY–LAUREN McGOVERN HOUSE
589 Hardy Road; barn ca. 1910s; conversion to house ca. 1980–81; full conversion begun 1994, John Sweeney and Lauren McGovern, designers and builders

Bucking the stereotypes of rusticity in the Adirondacks, this design transformed a barn in a thoroughly contemporary way, while using readily available materials in a straightforward manner that eschews rustic pretense. The barn, along with the farmhouse across the road at No. 591, were built from stock Sears, Roebuck & Company plans for Barton Storrs, probably in the 1910s. Around 1980 the barn and adjacent land were purchased by Robert and Laura Devinney, who began the conversion to a bed-and-breakfast, adding cross gables and other features. This project was soon terminated, however. Additional changes to the exterior and a complete remaking of the interior were undertaken in 1994 by Sweeney and McGovern for themselves. Most work was completed by the decade's end.

WM 7 WILMINGTON INTERDENOMINA-TIONAL CAMP MEETING
704 Hardy Road; 1905 and later (accessible by prior arrangement)
Unlike Methodist camp meetings of the 19th century, this compound not only was ecumenical in its outreach, but also more loosely configured. The organization was created by Dan Haselton, who had recently inaugurated what would become one of the area's major lumber supply companies, his brother Halsey, and Dean Hardy, also a year-round resident. A birch-bark cabin is the only original remnant. Most cabins and other buildings date from the 1920s and later. The tabernacle burned around 1940 and was replaced soon thereafter. Sessions originally lasted two to three weeks, but are now shorter.

WM 8 HASELTON SCHOOL
1804 Haselton Road (CR 12); early 20th century
This simple one-room school replaced an earlier one on the same site. Directly across the road is a farmhouse built for Nathan M. Markham in the 1850s, to which a number of additions have been made. Along

with the early 20th-century barn nearby the buildings are reminders of a rural landscape that is becoming increasingly scarce.

JAY

Town of Jay, Essex County

Like so many other communities in the eastern Adirondacks, the small hamlet of Jay suggests a rural agricultural center of long standing, but bears scant evidence of its industrial heritage. The hamlet grew in a linear fashion. A green dating from 1798 lies at the intersection of the crossroad leading east across the Ausable River and west to Wilmington. Of all the areas along the Ausable, that around Jay hamlet was the most intensely developed for agriculture during the 19th century. Farmhouses and sometimes barns and other remnants of that past are still important contributors to the landscape.

JA 1 JAY COVERED BRIDGE
Covered Bridge Road at Ausable River; 1857–58, George M. Burt, builder; numerous later modifications; reconstructed 2003–04,

Alpine Construction, builder (Schuylerville, N.Y.)

Spanning the river at this juncture became increasingly important to connect Jay to Keeseville and later to the burgeoning iron industry at Au Sable Forks, which spurred a revival of manufacture in Jay. A bridge appears to have existed here well before the first recorded one was constructed in 1847–48. A flood destroyed that structure less than ten years later, an event that also heavily damaged the adjacent Purmont ironworks and contributed to that operation's demise. When James and John Rogers purchased what remained of the enterprise in 1864, they constructed a new plant on higher ground across the river, making the replacement bridge even more important to the local economy.

George Burt, a prominent lumber dealer and building contractor, erected the new bridge using some of the timbers of the earlier one, going as far as Clintonville to retrieve them. He employed a Howe truss, then standard for wooden bridges of any length. The structure remained unaltered until 1953, when an accident led to adding three piers of reinforced concrete and steel

I-beams to bolster its 160-foot-long span. A new, earth-filled concrete abutment at the north end was built. I-beams supporting the bridge deck were inserted in 1969. Twenty-three years later the state Department of Transportation determined the need to construct a new bridge upstream. Jay residents launched a campaign to save the covered bridge. The bridge was closed, dismantled in four sections, and moved close by in 1997 under the provision that it would be reconstructed once the upstream replacement was completed. The reconstruction process entailed new exterior materials and some replacement of the structure as well. Considered an icon by the community, the bridge is one of the oldest of its kind remaining in the state and only one of two left in the Adirondacks [see ED 2c, Section 2].

JA 2 JESSE TOBEY HOUSE
13001 NY 9N; ca. 1819; additions 1928

The sizable house was built as part of a 250-acre farm, whose owner was also involved in the iron industry. Following Tobey's death, his daughter, Harriet, and her husband, Jerome Stickney, a dentist from Au Sable Forks, operated a tourist home on the premises, adding a large, connected building at the rear in 1896. Their daughter, Anna Laurie Stickney, in turn demolished that appendage for a new one of more modest dimensions and added the entry and side porches in 1928. By this time the establishment was known as the Tobey Homestead. It is now, again, a residence.

JA 3 FIRST BAPTIST CHURCH
12987 NY 9N; 1829–30, John Purmont, builder

While the church was formed in 1798, the congregation had to wait over thirty years for a permanent home. The consummation of that effort was likely bolstered by Jay's rise as a manufacturing center. The design was conservative for its date, reminiscent of Protestant meeting houses

in New England from the turn of the 19th century. Purmont was responsible for numerous buildings in the area and also established the hamlet's first iron forge.

JA 4 SHADYSIDE, HALL-DAY-D'AVIGNON HOUSE
6760 NY 86 at NY 9N; 1814, John Purmont, builder; additions ca. 1849 and later

Built for the Hall family, the house received a large new front section following its purchase in 1849 by David K. Day, who managed farms and a general store. Despite its date, the added section is rendered in a manner common to Federal houses of some twenty to thirty years previous. The porch is a later addition. During the Depression the building was operated as an inn by Day's daughter-in-law, Nellie. Following her death in 1943, the place was taken over by daughter Helen and her husband, Francis Joseph d'Avignon, grandson of the Au Sable Forks surgeon [AF 1]. It remains in the family as a summer residence.

JA 5 METHODIST EPISCOPAL CHURCH
12961 NY 9N; 1838–39

In predictable Methodist fashion, the edifice is rendered as a plain box, with only the use of lancet windows as a nod to contemporary fashion. Though its exterior suggests masonry construction, the building actually employs a heavy timber frame, with brick as a veneer. It now houses the offices of *Adirondack Life* magazine.

JA 6 AUSABLE VALLEY GRANGE
12953 NY 9N; 1909

The importance of farming in the area is reflected in the size of this purpose-built grange hall, erected not long after the Ausable Valley chapter was formed. The building later served as a general store. It has been well preserved as the Jay Craft Center.

JA 7 NATHAN AND WILLIAM SOUTH-MAYD HOUSES
NY 9N and Stonehouse Road; 1829; ca. 1830, John Purmont, builder

Commodore John W. Southmayd received a large land grant as recompense for donating his fleet of boats on Lake Champlain to the U.S. Navy during the War of 1812. The prospects of both agriculture and the iron industry attracted him to the area, where he built what may have been the grandest house in the town for his eldest son, **Nathan (a)**, around 1829. Constructed of roughly coursed granite, quarried from the property, it retains its commanding presence. The house remained

in the hands of descendants until 1954. Adjacent to the north, facing Stonehouse Road, Southmayd had a similar residence constructed for his younger son, **William (b)**, approximately one year after the first. Both were the work of Jay builder and entrepreneur John Purmont.

JA 8 NEWELL-BOYNTON FARM
687 Stickney Bridge Road; house ca. 1835 and later

This compound is an unusually complete surviving example of a 19th-century farmstead in the area. Besides barns for cows, horses, and hay, the yard includes a bunkhouse, stable and woodshed, granary, and pump house.

JA 9 AUSABLE ACRES
Ausable Drive approx. 3.5 miles north of NY 86; begun 1963, John Eaton, developer (Rochester, Vermont); Dick Shampeny, planner, designer, builder

When Vermont lumberman John Eaton purchased 6,000 acres of hilly land between Au Sable Forks, Wilmington, and Jay, it was for the abundant timber it offered. He soon changed his plans, deciding to create a seasonal residential community

ment regulations were enacted under the Adirondack Park Act of 1973. Eaton died before many of the lots were sold, and for a number of years the project languished. Some new construction, however, has occurred recently, and a property-owners association has taken an active role in maintaining the qualities Eaton promoted. What was built early on provides a good sampling of the A-frame and "chalet" lodges that were popular during the post–World War II era. Examples include **dwellings** at **607** and **612 Ausable Drive**, **8** and **28 Beech Street**, **23 Lakeside Drive**, and **95**, **153**, and **310 Sawmill Drive**, as well as at **Forest** and **Traum roads** in **Kitzbuhel**.

with 500 one-acre lots for middle-income families. The site planning was done to minimize intrusion on the "forest feeling" of this "wilderness tract." The scheme entailed over twenty-seven miles of graded roads, an eighteen-acre lake and recreation area, ski and riding trails, and tennis courts. A landing strip was created nearby. Eaton's company provided stock plans for houses or would build to order. Either way, dwellings were designed and built by Shampeny, a relation through marriage, in a manner he and Eaton considered appropriate to a northern, mountainous setting. The company provided financial services for both lot purchase and house construction. It also supplied water and electricity, maintained the roads, and opened and closed houses upon request. Deed restrictions governed land use. A much smaller contiguous tract, **Kitzbuhel**, was similarly developed for year-round occupation.

Eaton's project was unusually ambitious in both size and its comprehensiveness in the Adirondacks, and probably no comparable scheme has been realized within the Blue Line. AuSable Acres does not appear to have generated the controversy that other, unrealized large-scale developments would later ignite in northwestern parts of the park, especially after develop-

JA 10 ROBERT FARKAS AND ANNIE SCAVO HOUSE
214 River Road, AuSable Acres; 2011–12, Premises–Bryan Burke and Beverly Eichenlaub, architects

Responding to a shallow site, with mandated setbacks from both road and the West Branch of the Ausable River, this wood-frame dwelling sheathed in cedar siding is given a seemingly casual, linear arrangement. A dramatic sequence of high-ceilinged rooms, spanned by lightweight steel trusses, open onto the wooded, steep-sloping site that extends to the river.

UPPER JAY
Town of Jay, Essex County

UJ 1 STONE HOUSE FARM
12277 NY 9N; ca. 1810 and later

Long owned by members of the Wells family, this modest farmhouse lay abandoned as a shell for over a half century before its purchase in 1957 by Clyde Ward, a New Jersey–based builder. He renovated the residence and added a rear wing that was completed in 1966.

AF 5b], this two-room elementary school was constructed for a considerable sum at the height of the Depression, creating the most architecturally impressive rural school in the Adirondacks. Under the circumstances, might the Smiths [UJ 3] have contributed anonymously to the building budget, even though they suffered substantial losses after the stock-market crash in 1929?

UJ 2 UPPER JAY SCHOOL
12258 NY 9N; 1932–33, Alvin W. Inman, architect (Plattsburgh, N.Y.)

While plans for a consolidated school system for the Town of Jay foundered [see

UJ 4 UNITED METHODIST CHURCH
11209 NY 9N; 1895–96

From 1856 until 1894 the Methodists shared quarters on this site with Congre-

UJ 3 WELLS MEMORIAL LIBRARY
11234 NY 9N; 1906–07; addition 2000–01, Argus Architecture and Preservation (Troy, N.Y.)

This modest, but artfully designed, library was the gift of Jean Wells Smith and her husband, Wallis Craig Smith, in memory of her parents. A descendant of some of the area's earliest settlers, she was born and raised in the Midwest, where her father prospered in retail, lumbering, and railroad enterprises. In 1901, two years after inheriting considerable acreage in Upper Jay, Jean Wells married Smith, a prominent lawyer and civic leader in Saginaw, Michigan. The newlyweds soon erected Wellscroft, a great Tudorish manse of some 15,000 square feet, which is maintained as a residence nearby.

The library's design echoes motifs found at Wellscroft and was probably by the same unknown architect. The recent addition deftly responds to the original building in its massing, materials, and motifs. Exemplifying its role as community center, the building included a meeting room for local groups. Lawn tennis, volleyball, ice-skating, and plays occurred on the grounds.

gationalists. After acquiring the building, the Methodists had it moved and erected the current edifice, which was based on a design by Philadelphia architect Benjamin D. Price for his 1890 book, *Small Catalogue of Churches*. It has lain mostly idle for some years, but is well maintained and used for special events.

UJ 5 KEITH & BRANCH FORD MOTOR COMPANY ASSEMBLY PLANT AND SHOWROOM
12198 NY 9N at Springfield Road (CR 12); ca. 1920

In 1910 Earl Keith and Robert Branch formed a partnership, purchasing a large general store built soon after the Civil War by Ashley Prime, an establishment where Branch had previously worked. They secured a Ford franchise four years later and in 1915 opened the Central Garage for automobile service. After World War I they erected this three-story building across the street for the final assembly and sale of Fords. Car frames were shipped by rail to Au Sable Forks, where youths were hired to drive the vehicles, still without their bodies, to Upper Jay. The practice of completing assembly off-site was apparently a common cost-saving measure for Ford. The substantial farming population nearby made the hamlet a strategic location for the enterprise, in spite of its lack of a direct rail connection. The business continued at least until the mid-1940s. From a technical perspective the building

was crude for the functions it contained, with heavy timber framing and a non-motorized freight elevator. A very rare survivor of its kind, it is now the Upper Jay Art Center and Recovery Lounge. Though closed in the late 1960s, the general store survived until it burned in 1994.

UJ 6 NAVAJO LODGE
12134 NY 9N; ca. 1890s and later

Little is known about the history of this small hotel, the fabric of which suggests it was built in the late 19th century. In its size and quasi-domestic character, Navajo Lodge is similar to a number of modest hospitality establishments that once operated in the Ausable Valley.

UJ 7 HIGHLANDS FARM
402 Styles Brook Road (CR 52); ca. late 1920s, George Senecal, builder

Originally called Upland Meadow Farm, this sizable dairying operation was commissioned by Samuel Thorne, a prominent New York attorney, who in 1925 purchased (and added to) a large summer house in Keene Valley.

KEENE
Town of Keene, Essex County

Long a crossroads, connecting routes down the Ausable River and to Lake Placid with others leading south and east, the hamlet of Keene retains an array of commercial, institutional, and residential buildings from the 19th century. Recently some of these have been rehabilitated to serve a local market, including a sizable contingent of seasonal residents, but also people driving through on NY 73, one of the most scenic and heavily traveled roads in the Adirondacks.

KN 1 NEWELL REYNOLDS HOUSE
11128 NY 9N; 1825; additions 2007–8, Nils Luderowski, architect

Like Southmayd [JA 7], Reynolds was a general in the War of 1812 and received a large land grant (714 acres) as a payment for his services. Erected eight years after he acquired the land, this capacious Federal house attests to his success in the area. Reynolds occupied the premises for over forty years. During the 20th century it served a variety of functions, including quarters for a church and a restaurant. NY 9N was realigned well to the rear of the dwelling in the mid-20th century. Since its purchase in 1995 by Nils and Muriel Luderowski, the house has been sensitively rehabilitated and a sizable wing added to the west. Here, the architect created a juxtaposition of opposites. The low-slung addition differs from the older building in almost every respect, yet in a complementary relationship. (The old road is now a driveway; the house can be seen from NY 9N.)

KN 2 ELM TREE INN
NY 73 and NY 9N, northwest corner of intersection; 1823–24 and later

One of the oldest places for overnight accommodation still standing in the Adirondacks, the original portion was constructed for David Graves, who also owned a forge nearby and built a hotel, the Keene Center House, shortly after the inn. In 1866 it was converted to a store and post office, but reverted to its initial function in 1905. Reopened as the Elm Tree Inn by Monty Purdy in 1947, the establishment thrived as an informal watering hole during the second half of the 20th century. Though additions and numerous alterations were made over many years, the original building is still quite evident. Regrettably it has been vacant for over a decade.

KN 3 KEENE GENERAL STORE
10923 NY 73; 1905; 1922

The recent "rustic" embellishments notwithstanding, most of the early 20th-century fabric of this building remains intact. Within the park, it is a relatively large surviving example of its type. After a long vacancy, it has been revived as an emporium for household furnishings, Dartbrook Rustic Goods.

KN 4 GOFF-HEALD HOUSE
10917 NY 73; between 1852 and 1869; later alterations and additions

Originally constructed as a residence for George Goff, this building was converted in 1882 to a store, probably with a dwelling unit on the second floor. The fanciful two-story porch appears to have been added later, perhaps in the early 20th century.

KN 5 FRANKLIN MONROE HEALD HOUSE
10918 NY 73; 1889–ca. 1908, Franklin Monroe Heald, designer and builder

Heald, who had owned the Goff house from 1871 to 1882, erected this eccentric concoction as an addition to a log cabin (demolished 1923), ostensibly to enjoy some spatial separation from his wife. He also claimed to be the grandson of a European aristocrat, whose great stone house he wished to emulate.

KN 6 KEENE TOWN HALL
10892 NY 73; 1882; 1894

A slightly earlier version of Lake Pleasant's town hall [SP 7, Section 3], Keene's governmental center has always served that purpose.

KN 7 UNITED METHODIST CHURCH
10881 NY 73; ca. 1836; 1875

While the form of this edifice suggests it could have been constructed soon after the land for it was acquired in 1836, details inside and out indicate it was extensively remodeled, if not rebuilt, some four decades later. The building has recently been converted to an art gallery, with minimal changes to its fabric.

KN 8 NORMAN DIBBLE HOUSE
141 Hulls Falls Road; ca. 1890–91 and later

Arriving from Vermont in 1844, Dibble became a prosperous farmer and a key figure in shaping Keene Valley during the post–Civil War era. When he acquired Bruce Farm in 1865 he ran a boardinghouse on the premises, catering to the growing numbers of visitors attracted to the valley's scenic attributes. He expanded his business dramatically when he erected the Tahawus House (1872–74), the first major hostelry in Keene Valley. In 1883, seven years after he enlarged the establishment,

he sold it to George Egglefield and erected a house for himself next door. Ever restless, he undertook building the Hulls Falls Road house less than a decade later. In his pursuit of having the finest house in the town, he commissioned one of the community's largest dwellings that also afforded a contrast in its array of fashionable Queen Anne details. Here he returned to farming, but also kept the front portion of the house for paying summer guests. Two barns remain part of the complex.

KEENE VALLEY and ST. HUBERTS
Town of Keene, Essex County

With a scattering of commercial buildings amid houses and various institutions, spanning a century and a half of development, the hamlet of Keene Valley testifies to change as much as to continuity. The settlement lies toward the southern end of the Ausable River Valley, which diminishes noticeably as one approaches from Keene. Below the hamlet, the valley becomes even narrower, defined more by mountainsides than by flat land, ending at St. Huberts, a settlement consisting of only a few houses and a chapel.

KV 1 HIRAM HOLT HOUSE
47 Holt Road, off NY 73; ca. 1860

A mid-19th-century farmhouse in early 19th-century form, this dwelling has long served as a summer residence. The porch likely dates to around 1900 and was reconstructed in 2013–14 when the building was set on a new foundation. Otherwise the exterior fabric is little altered.

KV 2 KEENE VALLEY LIBRARY
1796 Main Street (NY 73); 1896, Arthur Trumbull, builder; Rev. William Hodge, designer (Philadelphia); fireproof room 1931; new children's room and stack area 1962, Gilbert Switzer and Sidney T. Miller, associate,

architects (New Haven); archives room, children's area, and renovated librarian's area, 1985, Wareham, De Lair, architects

Since 1891 the library has been operated for the public by a private association. Its first (and only) purpose-built quarters were designed by a Presbyterian minister from Philadelphia and long-time summer resident. Whether it was he who conceived the pyramidal roof capped by a monitor that helps to anchor the structure, allowing for a lofty, clear-span space inside, is unknown. The addition by Miller, another summer resident, is an admirable coupling of modernist design with a markedly older building.

KV 3 CARLOS WHITE HOUSE
1794 Main Street; 1882, Carlos White, builder; later additions

Soon after arriving from the town of North Elba [Section 9] with his wife, White built their commodious house in part, no doubt, to demonstrate his skills. It also served as the initial home of the library. After purchase by Lydia Lyon in 1895 it was run as a boardinghouse for a number of years. More recently it has served as a seasonal residence.

KV 4 KEENE CENTRAL SCHOOL
33 Market Street; 1935–36, Alvin W. Inman, architect (Plattsburgh, N.Y.); addition 1998–2000, Collins & Scoville, architects (now CS ARCH) (Albany)

Plans for a consolidated school were initiated as early as 1929, but like Au Sable Forks, it was the availability of federal aid that enabled the project to go forward. Perhaps to minimize costs, Inman slightly

modified plans for that other community's building [AF 5b] here.

KV 5 BIRCH STORE
1778 Main Street; ca. 1890; before 1910; later additions

Since its second story was added in the early 20th century, this retail facility has seen remarkably little change save in the goods it purveys—an unusual example of continuity for buildings of its kind.

KV 6 WILTON MERLE SMITH HOUSE
Trail's End Road, .3 mile west of NY 73; 1902, probably Arthur Trumbull, builder; later additions

Constructed as a summer cottage, this wood-frame dwelling, like the now altered house remade at about the same time for George Notman at 1798 Main Street, has a deeply recessed front porch under an expansive gambrel roof, with an economic play of Colonial Revival motifs. Merle Smith, a minister and a man of considerable means, owned a substantial amount of land, which he developed for summer cottages. His house was converted to year-round use in 1940 and has functioned as a small hostelry (Trail's End Inn) since 1962.

KV 7 AUSABLE CLUB
Ausable Road, off NY 73, St. Huberts; 1890, Wilson Brothers & Company, architects, H. A. Macomb, principal-in-charge (Philadelphia)

(note: all drives and other property adjacent to Ausable Road are private; public parking for those embarking on High Peaks trails is at the road's southern end adjacent to NY 73)

This remarkable clubhouse for the Adirondack Mountain Reserve (Ausable Club) has a complex past. Its spectacular site, with a panoramic view of Giant Mountain and other High Peaks, was first developed for the Beede House in 1876. The remoteness of the location, its scenic attributes, and ready access to vigorous climbs as well as fishing in the Lower and Upper Ausable lakes several miles to the west drew a well-heeled crowd from New York, Philadelphia, and other major East Coast cities. The Adirondack Mountain Reserve (AMR) was formed in 1887 by a contingent of the hotel's stalwarts, led by Philadelphia mining engineer William G. Neilson, to purchase some 25,000 acres so that the pervasive wild lands could be maintained in perpetuity. But in contrast to other private stockholder preserves such as the Tahawus Club (formed 1877) [TA 1, Section 11] or Adirondack League Club (1890), the mountain trails on AMR land have always been accessible to the public. The lakes, on the other hand, were strictly for use by members and their guests.

Two years after creation of the AMR, the hotel's proprietors announced their intention to sell. To protect the substantial investment just made, Neilson again mustered a group, forming the Keene Heights Hotel Company to acquire the building and its extensive grounds, which included a number of cottages. Part of their plan, too, was to improve the physical plant. As negotiations were nearing conclusion, the hotel was ravaged by fire in March 1890. Undaunted, Neilson commissioned his architect to design a new building. Plans were quickly drawn, a large construction crew assembled, and the edifice was erected in a matter of four months—a remarkable feat given the site's isolation from railheads and even from regional suppliers.

Despite the harried conditions, Macomb produced an exceptional design. While most resort hotels of the period were boxy affairs, here the mass is relieved by angled window bays connected by mock balconies. To capture a variety of views, one section of the building is set at an oblique angle, joined to the main block by a three-tiered porch configured as if it were a turret—a singular solution at that time. (A saucer dome and flared "baffles" were added to the turret roof at some point during the interwar decades.) Macomb was a member of a pioneering firm that specialized in both architecture and engineering. Its staff was experienced in resort hotel design. Wilson Brothers had prepared plans for the Sagamore Hotel in Bolton Landing (1882–83; see Section 1) and for hotels to bolster the business of the railroad companies that ranked among their primary clients. Macomb could likely draw on his firm's extensive ties with building trades to gather a group of people seasoned in many aspects of construction on such short notice.

The newly christened St. Hubert's Inn did not last long. The depression of the mid-1890s and a series of devastating forest fires in the Adirondacks took their toll. The hotel closed in 1904, but was reopened two years later as the AMR's clubhouse. For over a century it has survived with very few modifications inside or out. Absent the economic pressure of keeping a commercial hotel viable, both the building and the informal routines it enables have resisted change. Now it ranks among the most fully preserved late 19th-century resort hotels in the United States.

The adjacent **golf course** was opened around 1900 with six holes; their number was expanded to nine in 1938. To serve the club's population and others in Keene Valley, **All Souls Chapel** was constructed nearby on St. Huberts Road in 1917, from a design by Rev. Hobart B. Whitman, rector of Trinity Episcopal Church in Athens, New York.

8

SARANAC, CHATEAUGAY, and ST. REGIS RIVERS

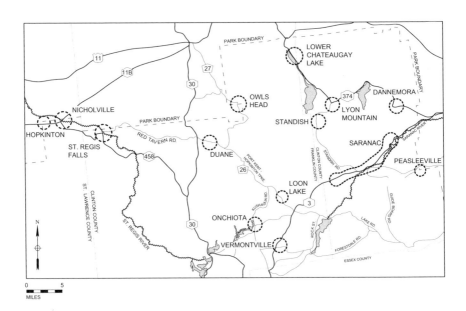

ENCOMPASSING PORTIONS OF EIGHT TOWNS IN CLINTON, Franklin, and St. Lawrence counties, this section comprises an assortment of places in the sparsely settled northern Adirondacks. Several communities are tied to the Saranac River, which was first occupied and began to support industries during the early 19th century. Farther north, the Chateaugay River is fed by two lakes within the Blue Line: Lower Chateaugay Lake became important for the iron industry as a result of ore extraction at Lyon Mountain beginning in the 1870s, while Upper Chateaugay Lake long served as a center for sportsmen and later for tourists. Loon Lake, feeding into the North Branch of the Saranac River, emerged as a major resort by the late 1880s. The St. Regis River spawned industry during the latter decades of the 19th century and anchored agricultural settlement. Vast portions of the area are still uninhabited. Some roads, most notably portions of the Port Kent–Hopkinton Turnpike between Loon Lake and St. Regis Falls, pass primarily through wild land. Although industry played a major role in developing the economies of many communities throughout this section, in some cases as late as the mid-20th century, the overall sense today is one of remoteness where untended natural landscapes dominate.

SOUTHWEST OF PLATTSBURGH, EASTERN PARTS of the Saranac River Valley within the Blue Line were among the first to be permanently settled. The hamlet of Saranac (originally Saranac Hollow) had occupants as early as 1802, and an ironworks was established there in 1826. Rebuilt twice, after a disastrous flood in 1830 and again fifteen years later, the forge was acquired by Bowen & Signor in 1873, when it was rebuilt once more as part of a multifaceted enterprise. The company had a large store in the hamlet and added a rolling mill to its inventory in 1878—the only plant of its kind in the county. About a mile to the west, Moffitsville (originally Russia) had three forges by the close of 1845. Two of these were acquired by Shepard Bowen in 1862 and were replaced by larger facilities a decade later after Bowen partnered with P. W. Signor. Bowen's previous partner, Andrew Williams, joined forces with Smith Weed, one of the area's most aggressive entrepreneurs, and, briefly, with lumber baron C. F. Norton to form the Chateaugay Ore & Iron Company at Lyon Mountain.

Williams, Bowen, and Signor rode the crest of the valley's iron boom. Saranac's population increased from 1,695 in 1845 to 4,552 in 1880. The decline was swift thereafter due to ore depletion and a market downturn. Bowen & Signor, Saranac's foremost company, closed in 1887. The valley's only other significant business endeavor had been a glassworks in the hamlet of Redford, two miles southwest of Moffitsville, an enterprise that began under the auspices of Corning & Cook in 1831 and ceased operation twenty years later. In the wake of industrial decline dairy farming became widespread, sustaining a much smaller population.

Clinton County Correctional Facility, Dannemora. (early 20th-century postcard)

Iron also provided an impetus for the early development of Dannemora, a hamlet north of Saranac that was settled in 1836. The circumstances under which the community developed, however, could not have been more different, rendering Dannemora an anomaly within the Adirondacks. Two years after iron deposits were discovered in 1842, legislators in Albany appropriated funds to build a prison, the state's third, where the costs of incarceration would ostensibly be offset by manufacture. Besides the mines, the prison included charcoal kilns, a nail factory, rolling mill, machine shops, and a foundry. A workforce, largely comprised of convicts, constructed the prison and its ironworks in 1845. The operation was never cost-effective, and iron operations ceased in 1877. The prison nevertheless continued to expand. Following a large riot in 1929, most of the facility was rebuilt incrementally over a number of years.

In 1803 Daniel Lyon came from Vermont to develop a farm at the base of the mountain that would later bear his name. Ore was discovered nearby twenty years later. Yet Lyon Mountain did not emerge as a major industrial area for another half century. Access to markets from this remote location was the major stumbling block. Soon after mining operations started in earnest during the early 1870s a plank road was built to the forges at Saranac, which never had rail access. In 1875 the Belmont Iron Works, one of the largest bloomeries in the United States, was constructed at the mouth of Lower Chateaugay Lake, about halfway between the mine and the nearest station, that of the Ogdensburg & Lake Champlain Railroad Company in the village of Chateaugay (beyond the Blue Line). But a more direct, if somewhat longer and more topographically challenging, route was due east to Plattsburgh. In 1878 the Delaware & Hudson had organized the Plattsburgh & Dannemora Railroad to improve access to the prison. The following year the Chateaugay Railroad was formed as another D&H subsidiary, taking over the Dannemora line and extending it to Lyon Mountain.

The mastermind behind overcoming Lyon Mountain's remoteness was Smith Weed, the Plattsburgh entrepreneur who, with Andrew Williams, formed the Chateaugay Ore & Iron Company in 1873. Between 1865 and 1874, Weed played a prominent role in the state assembly. It was probably when he was a member of that body's railroad committee that he was instrumental in convincing D&H executives to build the line from Whitehall to Plattsburgh, a project that was well under way when the Chateaugay company was formed. The railroad was not only a boon to businesses in Ticonderoga, Port Henry, and Willsboro, but also laid the groundwork for Plattsburgh's emergence as a major commercial center. Extending the Dannemora line to Lyon Mountain would not only enable shipment of a seemingly limitless supply of high-grade iron, but also allow the railroad reasonable access to the central Adirondacks. Following its completion as far as the Lyon Mountain mines, the railroad was further extended to Loon Lake in 1886 and to Saranac Lake the following year.

The railroad transformed Lyon Mountain. Few people lived there in 1875; four years later the hamlet harbored around 700 people, most of them miners. The population grew to 3,000 by 1883, at which time iron operations included a blast furnace in Plattsburgh and another in Standish, a satellite community of Lyon Mountain lying some three miles southwest. Mining operations supplied over sixty other forges as well. Drilling began as a means of securing ore deposits more efficiently. A new surge in demand for the exceptionally high-grade ore began in 1899. Strapped for adequate capital, the company leased its mines, furnaces, and vast landholdings (some 100,000 acres) to the D&H, which in turn floated a $1.5 million bond to embark on an ambitious expansion program. Tunnels replaced open-pit mines, a major investment was made in new equipment, and the community was thoroughly remade.

During the late 19th century the hamlet of Lyon Mountain embodied all the negative associations of a company town. Habitation was crude; most dwellings were log cabins, and the housing shortage was chronic. Many of the early accommodations were boardinghouses. As more houses were constructed for families, taking in at least one extra boarder was a common practice. Amenities were few. Wages were low.

Shaft Head Frame, Change House and Mill.   C. O. & I. Co. Mines, Lyon Mountain, N. Y.

Head frame, change house, and mill, Chateaugay Ore & Iron Company mine, Lyon Mountain.
(early 20th-century postcard)

Dangers were plentiful: over 165 people died in the mines and debilitating injuries were far greater. Training was poor. Miners were treated as an expendable resource. Friction existed between ethnic groups as well. Into the early 20th century, Lyon Mountain was considered to be verging on lawlessness. Profits also suffered as a result of poor management. The D&H sought to improve matters with the appointment of James Linney as superintendent in 1919. Linney ran the community like a dictator, but he did manage to introduce a greater sense of order. He also built a sizable number of new dwellings, a school, athletic field, swimming pool, and tennis courts, and introduced plumbing and electricity to the homes of the rank-and-file.

Lyon Mountain suffered greatly from the Depression, and mining ceased for much of the decade. In 1939, concurrent with its acquisition of the Witherbee, Sherman plant [Section 5], Republic Steel purchased Lyon Mountain. The demands of World War II and the Korean War led to a swift renewal, yet thereafter the operation experienced a steady decline. Republic abandoned its operations there in 1966. Company housing was sold; the mining area turned over to the Town of Dannemora.

Farther north, the first permanent settlers arrived at Lower Chateaugay Lake in the 1810s with the intention of farming. A more lucrative pursuit soon became accommodating those who came to hunt around the Lower and Upper lakes. Completion of the Ogdensburg & Champlain Railroad in 1852 helped advance the area for development, and after the Civil War the tourist clientele began to expand beyond sportsmen. The Merrill House (ca. 1867) was the first hotel, and its location on Upper Chateaugay Lake did much to advance that setting for vacationers. Four hotels and some camps stood along its shores by the 1880s. Comparable development on Lower Chateaugay Lake was arrested with the building of the Belmont Iron Works in 1875. During most of the 20th century both lakes have benefited as recreation areas, their shores lined with increasing numbers of seasonal houses.

Some seventeen miles south of Upper Chateaugay Lake, across land that remains almost entirely wild, is Loon Lake (not to be confused with the Warren County lake and settlement of the same name in Section 4). Lying on the Port Kent–Hopkinton Turnpike, this area experienced little settlement save for an occasional inn catering to travelers through the wilderness until 1848, when Willis Hodges attempted to establish a community for free blacks on a 200-acre tract by the lake's shore. Only about ten families came, and the initiative was abandoned after two winters owing to both the harsh climate and a terrain inhospitable to agriculture. A far more successful venture was undertaken thirty years later by Ferdinand and Mary Chase, who had taken vacations there and saw the lake's potential as a haven for outdoor enthusiasts. Their Loon Lake House, opened in 1879, grew into a 4,000-acre resort, with numerous cottages, one of the fanciest boathouses in the Adirondacks, a golf course, and other amenities. The enterprise prospered through the 1920s and continued for another three decades. Many of the remaining buildings have been maintained or revamped for continued seasonal use.

Loon Lake House, Loon Lake, 1878–79, demolished 1968–69. (early 20th-century postcard)

Along the next twenty-five miles of the turnpike little development occurred. Midway lies the tiny crossroads hamlet of Duane. Its namesake, Schenectady lawyer James Duane, married Harriet Constable, who inherited a tract of over 44,000 acres in the area in 1821. Duane had the land surveyed and established a 300-acre farm where he and his bride settled in 1825. His efforts to spur growth, including the construction of an iron forge in 1828, had little impact, however, and Duane joined the ranks of early settlers who failed to create a great estate in the Adirondacks. That effort was revived during the 1880s when Robert Schroeder acquired more than 2,100 acres around nearby Debar Pond, some of which he cultivated for hops. His plantation became an unusually large one; most hop fields in the state were less than ten acres. As an emblem of his ambition Schroeder erected a sixty-room house by the lakeshore, but the business ended following his death in 1913, and the house was later demolished.

Strategically located along the St. Regis River, the hamlet of St. Regis Falls began to emerge during the 1860s after Charles and John Hammond from Crown Point [Section 5] built a sawmill there. Little growth occurred for two decades, however. The situation changed markedly when John Hurd, a Bridgeport, Connecticut, industrialist (and P. T. Barnum's son-in-law), along with two partners, purchased the mill and some 60,000 acres to the south, establishing the St. Regis Lumber Company in 1882. To access their vast timber holdings, Hurd and his associates built the Northern Adirondack Railroad, the first in the region primarily developed for logging purposes. By the decade's end the line extended to Tupper Lake, where Hurd constructed the largest sawmill in the state [Section 10]. St. Regis Falls boomed as a center for producing paper and other wood products into the early 20th century. Thereafter, resource depletion led to a decline; most mills had closed by 1930. No new businesses came in to fill the large void.

Northwest down the river, the small agricultural communities of Nicholville and Hopkinton in St. Lawrence County were settled much earlier, at the turn of the 19th century, and have had less mercurial histories. They lie on the edge of the Blue Line in what is really a part of the St. Lawrence River Valley, where the climate is somewhat less challenging and the soil far more conducive to farming. Although agriculture no longer thrives in the area to the degree it once did, ample evidence of an underlying continuity prevails in the landscape.

*   *   *   *   *

TOWN OF SARANAC

Clinton County

Lying within a few miles of one another along the Saranac River, the small hamlets of Picketts Corners, Saranac, Moffitsville, and Redford have experienced little in the way of significant physical change over the last century, save for improvements to NY 3 as the principal link between Plattsburgh, the village of Saranac Lake [Section 9], and the interior Adirondacks. Agriculture has long served as the economic base and concentrated settlement is scarce, most of it emanating from the iron industry that dominated the area up to the 1880s. Large portions of the surrounding farmland remain open, if not always in active use, and still possess numerous examples of rural architecture from the late 19th and early 20th centuries.

SA 1 EDMUND J. PICKETT HOUSE

51 Ganong Drive at Chazy Lake Road, Picketts Corners, 1893

This sizable dwelling attests to the prosperity of its owner, who operated a store across the intersection, was the town supervisor, and served in the state assembly.

SA 2 FARMS

Among the many farmsteads that remain here, several near the hamlet of Saranac afford good illustration of three-quarters of a century of agricultural settlement. The two-and-a-half-story stone **Wales Parsons house (a)** at 87 Soper Road, which dates from the mid-1880s, has a traditional form, symmetrically composed, with a central entrance, but also a cross-gable roof, bracketed eaves, and other nods to current fashion. Larger than most dwellings in the area, it embodies Parsons's success not just as a farmer, but also as a merchant dealing in dry goods, clothing, and groceries. The **farm (b)** at 317 Picketts Corners Road was probably developed several decades later and is a good example of many such places from the late 19th century. The house appears to be the product of several building campaigns. A small barn and other outbuildings remain. Farther north, at 403 Picketts Corners Road, is a **farm (c)** still in operation, with a fleet of barns and silos from the early to mid-20th century. The small **farm (d)** at 659 Nashville Road appears to date from the late 19th century and has an unusually intact assemblage of barns and other outbuildings from that period.

SA 3 SARANAC RIVER BRIDGE
Soper Road at NY 3, Moffitsville; 1910

A Pratt-truss steel bridge of a kind once ubiquitous in the Adirondacks and many other parts of the country, it was built as part of early efforts to improve rural roads. The structure survives only because it is no longer used.

SA 4 STORES
NY 3 and Charles Street, Redford; ca. early 20th century and later

Well before it became a designated state highway, NY 3 served as Redford's commercial corridor and the anchor for its industrial activities. Two vestiges are good examples of the simple wood-frame emporia that were common to many Adirondack communities. At the northeast corner of NY 3 and Charles Street lies a former **general store**, once operated by **Oliver Gosselin (a)**, which in later years served as a restaurant and nightclub. The two-tier porch across its narrow front may well have been added. A short distance to the west of Charles is another former **general store**, once operated by **Eli Russell (b)**, with its long face oriented to the street and sizable living quarters for the proprietor above. The garage to one side was likely added in the 1920s.

SA 5 CATHOLIC CHURCH OF THE ASSUMPTION OF MARY
78 Clinton Street at Maple, Redford; 1854– 55; later alterations and additions

Replacing a log structure built in 1838, the new church was erected to serve the growing French-Canadian population attracted by the iron and glass industries. It was constructed under the auspices of the Missionary Oblate of Mary Immaculate, members of which had come from Montreal in 1853 to oversee building St. Peter's Church in Plattsburgh. They soon determined Redford warranted its own house of worship. The plans of St. Peter's, designed by Montreal architect Victor Bourgeau, may have provided the basis for the markedly smaller Redford edifice. Certainly the original Gothic interior (now altered) and tall bell tower (later replaced) were consonant with Bourgeau's work. The log church was moved rather than demolished, and in 1924 it was moved again to the rear of its replacement structure, encased in stone, and incorporated as the sacristy.

SA 6 HOUSE
5662 NY 3, Riverview (Town of Black Brook); 1854

A very rare vestige of a pioneer homestead, this log house appears to have experienced little change on its exterior. At the time of construction it was unusually large

for the area and was reputedly used as an informal social center for this tiny Saranac River community. It now lies vacant.

PEASLEEVILLE
Town of Peru, Clinton County

PE 1 ST. PATRICK'S CATHOLIC CHURCH
Patent Road, approximately 3 miles south of

Peasleeville Road; ca. 1840–41 and later

One of the earliest extant Catholic churches in the Adirondacks, St. Patrick's was formed to serve subsistence farmers of Irish origin in the vicinity. Though it appears to have been altered on several occasions and the tower was probably an addition, the basic form remains intact. The church and adjacent burial ground command a sweeping view of the Champlain Valley.

DANNEMORA
*Towns of Dannemora and Saranac,
Clinton County*

Counting its sizable incarcerated population, the village of Dannemora is the second largest (3,936 people in 2010) community in the Adirondacks. The high walls of the prison itself, constructed after a riot in 1929, loom over the otherwise modest settlement. The contrast is the more dramatic by virtue of Dannemora's sloping site, from which portions of the Saranac and Champlain valleys are readily seen.

DN 1 CLINTON CORRECTIONAL FACILITY
Cook Street (NY 374) between Emmons and Clark streets; late 19th and 20th centuries (note: photography anywhere on the premises is forbidden)

The site of the state's third prison was selected by Ransom Cook (who became the first warden) in part for its iron deposit and also for its isolation, which was seen as a deterrent to escape attempts. A bill authorizing construction of the compound was passed by the legislature in 1844. Patterned after the state prison at Auburn, with cells opening onto multi-tier galleries that faced the outer walls, the high-security complex opened in 1845 and contained some 500 inmates. An addition to the existing building (East Hall), and two new cellblocks (South and West halls), and a large warden's quarters were all erected in

1880. Four years later the perimeter stockade was replaced by stone walls. An administration building, a bathhouse, and an electric chair were added around 1892. A tuberculosis ward was established in 1901, expanded six years later, and replaced by a separate hospital in 1918. As a result of the 1929 riot, the facility was extensively rebuilt over the next thirteen years. The perimeter wall was extended to its current formidable height and a new power plant built in 1930–32 several blocks to the south. Prisoners constructed the medievalizing Church of the Good Thief within the compound in 1939–41.

Adjacent to the south and readily seen from Cook Street, the former **State Hospital** of 1899–1900 was the first in New York built to house "such male prisoners as are declared insane while confined to a state prison or reformatory," and was in large part constructed by prisoners. Its Richardsonian vocabulary was a hallmark of the first state architect (and Keeseville native), Isaac Perry. It ceased to operate as a mental facility in 1972 and eventually became a medium-security prison.

DN 2 ST. JOSEPH'S CATHOLIC CHURCH
179 Smith Street at Emmons; ca. 1883–84 and later

Replacing a wood-frame structure of 1859, the current masonry building appears to have been a very plain design original-ly. It was exuberantly embellished with a tower and flanking pinnacles in 1896. The transept was added around 1915–16. Parishioners constructed substantial portions of the assemblage and may have contributed to the fanciful design as well.

DN 3 TOWN OF DANNEMORA HIGHWAY DEPARTMENT BUILDING
End of Higby Road, off NY 374, 6.8 miles west of hamlet; 2010–13, Premises–Bryan Burke, architect

While most public buildings designed for utilitarian purposes in recent decades are pedestrian in character, this facility demonstrates that attention to massing, proportion, and detail can lead to more visually appealing results even when, as here, the architect was commissioned to modify a standard kit plan. Adjacent lies a large Quonset hut, one of two transported to and reassembled on the site to service a now defunct Atlas-F missile silo. Operated between 1961 and 1965 by the 556th Strategic Missile Squadron at the Plattsburgh Air Force Base, the silo was one of six erected within the Blue Line. Others were at Willsboro, Lewis, Au Sable Forks, Redford, and Riverview.

DN 4 FARMHOUSE CONVERTED TO ROADSIDE SERVICE FACILITY
2914 NY 374; late 19th and 20th centuries

Though it no longer caters to motorists, this property is a rare surviving example of the once common practice of rural families augmenting their incomes during the interwar decades by adding facilities to sell gasoline, food, and other products.

The farmstead probably dates to the late 19th century.

LYON MOUNTAIN
Town of Dannemora, Clinton County

Along with Mineville and Witherbee [Section 5], Lyon Mountain was the most ambitious company town developed within the Blue Line. Similarly, too, the community retains a rich array of employee housing from the early 20th century. Here accommodations for miners and their families were clustered in a single enclave on the mountainside, just to the west of the mines, while managers' dwellings occupy lower ground convenient to what were once commercial and institutional facilities. Though most houses have experienced at least some alteration, the hamlet's landscape as a whole still offers a vivid sense of its industrial past.

LM 1 ST. BERNARD'S CATHOLIC CHURCH
10 Church Point Road, off NY 374; 1901–02

With Lyon Mountain's large Catholic population, including people of Italian, Polish, Irish, and Mexican origin, as well as a number of French-Canadians, St. Bernard's was the dominant house of worship. The current building replaced a wooden one of the 1880s that burned. Originally faced in brick, the edifice was resurfaced in Permastone in 1950. Prominently placed at the northern edge of the community, the church site also affords a good vantage point to view the mountain and the abandoned mill building that is among the last surviving structures of the mine.

LM 2 LYON MOUNTAIN HIGH SCHOOL
East side of NY 374 in hamlet center; 1929, 1931–32, Peter S. McMenamin, chief engineer for the Chateaugay Ore & Iron Company, designer

Even with its windows covered, this school's strong abstract qualities retain much of their visual impact. One of the last projects the company undertook to improve conditions for workers and their families, the building was erected in two stages: the auditorium in 1929, the classrooms in 1931–32. After the school closed, the building was used as the Lyon Mountain Correctional Facility from 1984 until 2011. The playing fields lie across NY 374, behind the range of managers' houses. The large wooden **grandstand**, erected by the company in 1933, attests to the importance of baseball in community life (and its role in channeling youthful energy away from illicit activities).

LM 3 COMPANY HOUSES

Situated at 3863–3903 NY 374, farthest from the mine and closest to the school and other community facilities, a range

been intended for railroad employees. Adjacent to the west lies the sole remaining example of a former railroad car, deaccessioned by the D&H and incorporated as part of a dwelling. Several cases of this ad hoc augmentation of domestic shelter occurred in the community.

Situated on both sides of Standish Road (2899–75, 2890–76), a cluster of log **houses** (c) probably date to the late 19th century and are the oldest dwellings extant in the community. While they have been resur-

of semi-detached **managers' dwellings (a)** erected around the early 1920s provided a respectable face for those passing through the area. Like many of the miners' houses up the hill, these probably were built of poured concrete. Along the service alley at the rear is a striking range of prefabricated, sheet-metal **garages** that were assembled concurrently with the dwellings or soon thereafter. Facing the Delaware & Hudson Railway station at 2925–31 Standish Road is a row of wood-frame **houses (b)**, probably erected in the 1920s, which may have

faced, enlarged, and otherwise modified, their original form is readily discernible. To the south on Standish Road lie a number of two-story (2841–49, 2848–70) and one-and-one-half-story (1811–37, 2012–36) semi-detached **houses (d** and **e)**, all constructed of poured concrete. These, like the managers' houses **(a)**, were in all likelihood part of the reform efforts instigated by mine superintendent James Linney during the 1920s. As a result, depending upon family size and probably seniority, miners could be housed in quarters that were spacious and contained both indoor plumbing and heating, in marked contrast to most of the company's earlier housing. Similar dwellings also stand along Second and Third streets. What appears to have been built as a **boardinghouse (f)** on Power House Road probably dates to the late 19th century. Later its exterior was stuccoed to blend with the new dwellings nearby.

LM 4 DELAWARE & HUDSON RAILWAY STATION
2914 Standish Road; 1913–14

Replacing an 1880 facility, the D&H employed a dignified, if unassuming, design for a station that catered to people destined for the hotels and camps on Upper Chateaugay Lake as well as those doing business in the mining community. The railroad ceased operations there in 1949–50, and the station was subsequently used as a post office and a tavern. Badly deteriorated, it was acquired by Friends of Lyon Mountain in 2000 and has been restored as a local history center.

STANDISH

Town of Saranac, Clinton County

SD 1 COMPANY HOUSES
2061–67 Standish Road, early 20th century

The tiny hamlet of Standish (named for Smith Weed's mother's family) was developed by the Chateaugay Ore & Iron Company in the early 1880s in conjunction with constructing a blast furnace. Located about three miles southwest of Lyon Mountain, the site may have been chosen for its relatively level ground. In the community's heart along Standish Road lies a range of modest single-family houses, built by the company in the early 20th century using concrete blocks, perhaps following the example of Witherbee, Sherman in Mineville [Section 5].

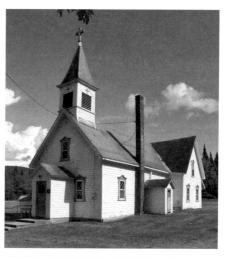

SD 2 ST. MICHAEL'S CATHOLIC CHURCH
Standish Road south of hamlet center; 1888–90

This modest wood-frame house of worship offers a vague memory of the rural Catholic churches its eastern European parishioners had left behind.

LOWER CHATEAUGAY LAKE

Town of Belmont, Franklin County

LW 1 BANNER HOUSE
5880 NY 374; 19th and early 20th centuries

Located near the northern end of Lower Chateaugay Lake, the Banner House is one of the earliest extant resort hotels remaining in the Adirondacks, persisting in spite of nearby industrial development during the last quarter of the 19th century.

In the 1830s Jonathan Bellows began to open his six-room house to lodgers. This structure was likely the one-and-one-half-story dwelling that appears in the center section of the complex in late 19th-century images. Between 1838 and 1843 he erected a purpose-built facility, which is probably the one-story annex that remains at the northern end. At this point, if not earlier, Bellows called his establishment the Chateaugay Lake House. Later, porches were added to both sections. Until the arrival of the railroad in the 1850s most visitors were men on fishing and hunting expeditions.

The facility was expanded after the Civil War, probably with the seven-bay, two-story south section, which helped transform it into a full-fledged resort hotel. In 1891 Bellows's grandson sold the establishment, which was renamed Banner House. Around the 1910s fire destroyed the center section; it was replaced by a two-story addition to the southern section, the two-tier porch of which was replaced by a single-story one across the entire front. It may have been at this time, too, that the large service wing was added at the rear. Although it remained in operation until recently, the hotel now lies vacant, awaiting an uncertain fate.

VERMONTVILLE
Town of Franklin, Franklin County

VT 1 FRANKLIN TOWN HALL
7 Cold Brook Road at NY 3; 1912

After much of the area had been logged during the first half of the 19th century, raising sheep became the primary source of income. The original (1878) school on this site was the first in the town. The current building is a good example of an early 20th-century rural schoolhouse. It remained in that capacity only for a decade when the town purchased it for offices. Functioning as the town hall for over ninety years, the building has had few exterior changes save for the recent access ramp.

VT 2 PILGRIM HOLINESS CAMP
246 Swinyer Road; 1910 and later
When established in 1910, an offshoot of the Pilgrim Holiness Methodist Church in Lake Placid, the camp-meeting site consisted of tents, some perhaps set on platforms, others pitched on the ground. The cabins were added on a more or less individual basis, most of them probably before 1940. The tabernacle was rebuilt after the original collapsed under a heavy snow load in 1959. A 1972 addition to the dining hall doubled its size. A four-unit "motel" was erected in 1973–75 and the Prayer Chapel in 1979. Despite the many changes, a sense of continuity has been maintained in this very simple iteration of the Methodist camp-meeting idea.

**VT 3 FRANKLIN AND UNION FALLS DAMS
AND HYDROELECTRIC PLANTS**
*Franklin Falls Road (CR 48) at Franklin Falls
Pond, town of Franklin; and Alder Brook
and Union Falls roads at Saranac River
and Union Falls Pond, Town of Black Brook,
respectively; both 1904–08, Lem Merrill,
engineer, P. B. McKay, builder*

The advent of electricity in the late 19th
century posed particular challenges for
small, remote Adirondack settlements. At
an early date (1890) Paul Smith, hotelman
extraordinary, constructed a hydroelectric
plant at Keese Mills to serve his establishment [Section 9]. The venture proved so
successful that he embarked on a much
more ambitious plan that would supply
communities in the surrounding area.

Franklin Falls was the first place within
the Blue Line to be permanently settled in
the county. A dam and sawmill were built
there in 1827, but the location proved too
remote for a successful operation. Nearly
twenty years later a new owner constructed both a mill and a substantial hotel, the
Franklin House. Although it burned in 1852,
the hotel was quickly rebuilt (Smith was
married there in 1859) and lasted until
1937. Smith purchased the property for his
plant in 1892. The Paul Smith Electric Light,
Power & Railroad Company was established
in 1906, as the new facilities there and at
Union Falls were nearing completion.

A by-product of Smith's damming of
the Saranac River at two points was the
creation of Union Falls Pond, flooding 270
acres in the process. The state and subsequently the Association for the Protection

of the Adirondacks sued him for encroach-
ing on state land, but the matter was settled by 1912. The company expanded its
services beyond the hamlets of Gabriels,
Bloomingdale, and Saranac Lake to Lake
Placid in 1915 and Tupper Lake ten years
later, encompassing much of the northern
interior Adirondacks in the process. Niagara-Mohawk Power Company purchased
the operation in 1965, and it continues to
generate power.

Both plants remain intact on their exteriors. On Plank Road 2.5 miles east of
Franklin Falls lies the **Ike Arnold School**,
dating to the early 20th century and in
operation until 1968, when the school districts around Saranac Lake finally consolidated. It has been sensitively rehabilitated
as a residence.

ONCHIOTA
Town of Franklin, Franklin County

**ON 1 TOMEY GENERAL STORE AND
GASOLINE STATION**
*Gabriels-Onchiota (CR 30) and Kushaqua
roads*

Situated between Rainbow Lake and
Buck Pond, the tiny hamlet of Onchiota
functioned primarily as a service center. The major establishment was run by
Hayden Tomey, who had come as a child
and eventually acquired extensive acreage
in the area. Dating to the early 1920s, with
later additions, his store also served as the

post office. The storybook imagery used for the gasoline station across the road has rendered it a community landmark since its construction around 1930.

chitects were probably responsible for the somewhat later chapel, rendered in a spirited medievalizing mode that draws from Bavarian and English sources. Other facilities were added as well, housing 150 pa-

ON 2 STONY WOLD HALL
Kushaqua–Mud Pond Road, 2.4 miles north of Onchiota, 5.3 miles southwest of Port Kent–Hopkinton Turnpike via Thatcherville Road; 1909, probably Renwick, Aspinwall & Owen, architects (New York)

In complete isolation along a dirt road that can be difficult to navigate, this well-maintained building stands in striking contrast to its environs. It was constructed as a combination chapel and recreational center for the Stony Wold Sanitorium. Founded in 1901 by Elizabeth Newcomb, wife of a prominent New York physician, the establishment focused on young women suffering from tuberculosis who could not afford proper care. Designed by the distinguished New York–based firm of Renwick, Aspinwall & Owen, who had already done work at the Adirondack Cottage Sanitarium in Saranac Lake [SL 38, Section 9], the main building was configured to suggest a grand country house. The same ar-

tients in fourteen buildings on 18,000 acres at the institution's peak in the 1930s. Stony Wold closed in 1955. Three years later it was sold to the White Fathers, a Catholic order conducting missionary work in Africa, and re-opened as St. Joseph's Seminary. The site's remoteness, however, led to closure once more in 1966. Most of the land was purchased by the state for inclusion in the Forest Preserve in 1974 and the complex was demolished. The chapel, however, remains in private hands as a residence.

ON 3 BRIDGE
Mud Pond and Sand Piper roads at North Branch of Saranac River, 2.2 miles northeast of Stony Wold; ca. early 20th century

Similar to that crossing the Saranac at Moffitsville (SA 3), this Pratt-truss bridge is likewise closed to traffic.

LOON LAKE

Town of Franklin, Franklin County

LN 1 MERRILL INN
3801 Port Kent–Hopkinton Turnpike (CR 26); 1831 and later

Built after the turnpike's opening to provide accommodations for travelers through a wilderness setting, the inn also functioned as the first post office in the town and provided space for town meetings. A remarkable surviving example of its kind, the inn was constructed for Robertson Merrill and operated by him until 1860. Over the next half century it was run as the Littlejohn Tavern. The building is now a residence.

LN 2 LOON LAKE HOUSE CAMPUS
Port Kent–Hopkinton Turnpike and tangent roads; 1882 and later

Ferdinand and Mary Chase's gamble on developing Loon Lake as a resort met with success from the start. He had some experience in the business as a clerk at a hotel in Essex Junction, Vermont. They were also familiar with the territory, having spent several vacations camping there. Despite, or perhaps because of, its remoteness (guests had to travel by stage on the turnpike from Lake Champlain, over thirty-five miles) their Loon Lake House prospered. A hulking two-and-a-half-story log structure opened in 1879. Only three years later they erected a grand four-story wood-frame pile sporting an ornate two-story porch. Two sizable annexes were erected, the first—the largest and most elaborate in the complex—in 1893, the second a dozen years later. Guests could lease land and build cottages. A nine-hole golf course was laid out in 1895—one of the first in the Adirondacks—to which another nine holes were added in 1926. Accommodating up to a thousand visitors, the complex had its own water and gas systems as well as a farm, making the operation for the most

part self-sufficient. Three presidents were among the guests. Growth was fueled by the arrival of the D&H's Chateaugay Railroad at the lake's northern end in 1886 and the New York Central's Adirondack & St. Lawrence Railroad six years later.

The Loon Lake House flourished through the 1920s but went into receivership in the Depression. It closed during World War II, reopening without great success thereafter. The main building burned in 1956, and subsequently many remnants were sold at auction. The first annex was demolished in 1968–69. Beginning in the 1980s, however, the sense of isolation amid a rugged natural landscape again attracted investment. Outside of the grounds of the Ausable Club [KV 7], Loon Lake is the most intact example of a hotel-based 19th-century resort community in the Adirondacks.

What is now known as **Irish House (a)** was constructed around 1905 as the second of the two annexes to the Loon Lake

House and lay behind (to the south of) the larger first annex. The main hotel building was near the lake a short distance to the northwest of the first annex. Located at 3390 Port Kent–Hopkinton Turnpike, this is the only surviving remnant of the hotel complex. It has continued as an inn since the tract was sold in 1958. To the south (No. 3400) lies the small, slightly Japanesque building constructed in 1895 as the **golf house (b)**. Across the road and probably dating to the early 20th century, **Fairchild (c)** is unusual among the cottages at Loon Lake in its log construction. The Chases leased a strategic lot to Fremont Smith for construction of his **general store (d)** (No. 3401) around 1905. In the 1970s it served as a restaurant and art gallery, but is now vacant. Some two decades earlier, on a contiguous leased lot (No. 3389) Smith commissioned a sizable two-story **cottage (e)** for his family—one of the largest and most fanciful in the compound.

Across the road on Loon Lake Terrace are three late 19th-century cottages—**Friends, Echoes,** and **Shady Lawn (f)**. Behind them,

at 23 Garden Lane, is **President (g)**, dating to 1885 and originally called Sunset. The renaming occurred after it had, at various times, been occupied by presidents Harrison, Cleveland, and McKinley. Across Garden Lane and now much altered is **Wayside**, originally owned by Prentiss Lovering and operated as a tavern; this was where the Chases stayed when they bought the initial ten acres for their hotel. At 3385 and 3374 Port Kent–Hopkinton Turnpike are **Ridgewood (h)** and **Fairview (i)**, respectively, which appear to be from the early 20th century. A number of other cottages, not easily seen from a public road, have lakefront orientations. Yet the overall arrangement of dwellings, mostly to the east of the hotel grounds, suggests an informal, intimate, and somewhat inward-oriented community for which the lake itself was only one of the attractions.

Farther north, where Bass Lake Road intersects Port Kent–Hopkinton Turnpike, lies an A-frame **house** that appears to date from the 1960s and is a good example of a type used for many modest vacation dwellings. Its prominent location suggests the house

may have been used as a model home and real estate office for the small residential subdivision along Bass Lake Road.

LN 3 STABLE
2756 Port Kent–Hopkinton Turnpike, 2.7 miles north of Loon Lake; ca. mid-1880s

This log structure was built to accommodate horses used for stages running from the Loon Lake depot of the Chateaugay Railroad, which lay directly across the road, to the Loon Lake House. Quarters for the stable keeper are in the front section. Unaltered, this one-of-a-kind survivor of the railroad era in the Adirondacks is now used as a hunting camp.

DUANE
Town of Duane, Franklin County

DU 1 DEBAR POND LODGE
Port Kent–Hopkinton Turnpike (CR 26), .2 mile south of Pond Road (CR 27) intersection; drive to parking area .7 mile; 1939–40, William G. Distin, architect

Robert Schroeder's enormous house lay vacant after his death in 1913. When Arthur Wheeler of Palm Beach bought the property twenty-six years later the derelict building was demolished and in its stead rose what is arguably the last of the great private camps in the Adirondacks—a type that Distin and his firm, founded by William L. Coulter in 1897, had a major role in developing. Constructed of cedar logs, the expansive dwelling contains seventeen rooms, including a two-story central hall. As was characteristic of at least several of Distin's camps, the mass is broken down with a series of horizontal extensions that make the building seem less imposing and more harmonious with its wooded environs than those built a generation earlier. Debar Pond Lodge is masterfully sited partway up a gentle rise from the body of water that is its namesake. Set amid a scattering of pine trees, the camp seems barely to emerge from the ground from its main approach. Viewed from the water, on the other hand, the slope of the terrain and symmetrical composition of its main block on this south side enhance the building's prominence. The 1,200-acre property changed owners once, in 1959, before it was acquired by the state twenty years later. At that time the owners secured a leasehold to the camp and its adjacent acreage. Since the expiration of that agreement in 2004 the future of this distinguished example of camp architecture has remained in limbo.

DU 2 METHODIST EPISCOPAL CHURCH
1146 Port Kent–Hopkinton Turnpike; 1883–85
This simple house of worship, combining a traditional form with some reserved yet stylish details of a more contemporary vein, is the most conspicuous legacy of Robert Schroeder's attempt to develop the area. It has long since ceased to serve its original purpose, but is preserved as a community shrine. Across the road lies a recently rehabilitated one-room **schoolhouse**, probably also dating to the late 19th century.

OWLS HEAD

Town of Belmont, Franklin County

OW 1 STORE
28 Ragged Lake Road; ca. early 20th century
Amid this small hamlet near the fringe of the Adirondacks is a good example of an early 20th-century store, with owner's quarters above. It likely had a porch on its front; otherwise it is little changed on the exterior.

TOWN OF SANTA CLARA

Franklin County

SR 1 RED TAVERN HOTEL
Red Tavern Road, 6.2 miles west of NY 30; 9 miles east of St. Regis Falls; ca. 1879–80 and later

Along the Port Kent–Hopkinton Turnpike (this portion has been renamed Red Tavern Road), this isolated hostelry of long standing was built for Dan McNeil to accommodate travelers amid a large wilderness area. It replaced the original inn of the 1830s. For many decades the establishment has catered to hunters and anglers (the St. Regis River is close by), and, while altered on a number of occasions, it still retains much of its early character as well as its function.

Although it might be mistaken for a century-old facility that has been renovated, this diminutive power plant was constructed in recent decades by Matthew Foley, who earlier rescued the Wadhams and Westport Power & Light Company hydroelectric plant in Essex County [WD 5, Section 6], and his brother-in-law. This site was probably that of Charles and John Hammonds' sawmill and later was occupied by the boiler house of the St. Regis Lumber Company. No vestige of the dense industrial landscape along the river remains.

ST. REGIS FALLS

Town of Waverly, Franklin County

NICHOLVILLE

Town of Lawrence, St. Lawrence County

SI 1 RIVERSIDE RESTAURANT
South Main Street (CR 458) at St. Regis River; ca. 1880s–early 1890s and later
St. Regis Falls has unfortunately lost much of its architecture as well as its economic base. Among the most significant remnants of its industrial heyday is this commercial establishment, which offered food, drink, and overnight accommodations beginning in the late 19th century. By 1906 it was known as the Albion Hotel and was later renamed the Riverside Restaurant. Considering its age and use, the building remains relatively intact.

SI 2 AZURE MOUNTAIN POWER COMPANY HYDROELECTRIC PLANT
South Main Street and South Prior Road, 1992–93; Matthew Foley and Everett Smith, builders

NI 1 MERRILL & FISK BLOCK
6 Port Kent Road; 1866 and possibly later
Although the 19th-century character of this small hamlet has been substantially altered, Nicholville retains some consequential buildings from its early decades of development. Foremost among them is this commercial building, which was constructed to house the furniture store of D. L. Merrill and the hardware store of B. F. Kellogg. The two-story section may have been added at an early date and now accommodates the community's post office.

NI 2 HOUSES
Adjacent to the east lies a range of modest residences that collectively form an instructive sample of basic design patterns during the mid-19th century. The one-and-one-half-story Greek Revival **house (a)**

at 10 Port Kent Road probably dates from the 1840s or 1850s, with a heavily scaled porch and an entryway embellished with engaged columns, pilasters, sidelights, and fanlight—all indicating that limited size did not always preclude public presentation. The **house (b)** at 20 Port Kent Road is a good example of a two-bay gable-end dwelling likely dating from the 1870s or even later. The **house (c)** next door (No. 24) has the same configuration but appears to have been erected prior to the Civil War. Its unadorned brick walls are offset by simple Gothic Revival details on the entry porch and bargeboard. Behind lies a stable with board-and-batten sheathing, probably created during the same period. Finally the **house (d)** at No. 28 is another variation, with a somewhat fancier entry porch and a more complicated form, with a recessed section set at right angles to the front.

small industries established themselves nearby. Revealing his Vermont origins, Hopkins laid out a green around which key community functions could be located, most notably this church, which was organized in 1808. The congregation had several quarters on this site before the stylishly Queen Anne edifice was erected.

HOPKINTON
Town of Hopkinton, St. Lawrence County

HO 1 JASON BRUSH HOUSE
3107 NY 11B; ca. 1870

The level of prosperity that farmers could attain in the area is exemplified by this grand Italianate house built for the son of Eliphalet Brush, who, along with Roswell Hopkins, was key to initial development of the town. Jason Brush's son, John T. Brush, owned the New York Giants from 1890 until his death in 1912. Directly across the road lies another ambitious farm dwelling, erected for Joel Goodale around 1870, which has been subject to a number of disfiguring changes.

HO 2 FIRST CONGREGATIONAL CHURCH
9 Church Street; 1892

One year after the town was formed, Roswell Hopkins began to develop the hamlet with a gristmill along Lyd Brook, a tributary to the St. Regis. Several other

HO 3 TOWN HALL
15 Church Street; 1870, later alterations

Replacing the 1815 schoolhouse, the Hopkinton Town Hall is the earliest surviving example of its type within the park. It is also substantially larger than other 19th-century Adirondack examples, reflecting the more advanced agrarian economy that existed in this extension of the St. Lawrence River Valley.

HO 4 FRENCH HILL SCHOOL, HOPKINTON DISTRICT 14
Wilson Road, .1 mile east of Lake Ozonia Road and 1.9 miles west of CR 458; 1932

While not as large or embellished as examples in Whallonsburg [WH 3, Section 6] or Jay [UJ 2, Section 7], this schoolhouse is another telling example of the persistence in developing rural facilities well into the 20th century. It remained in operation until 1952.

9

NORTH-CENTRAL LAKES

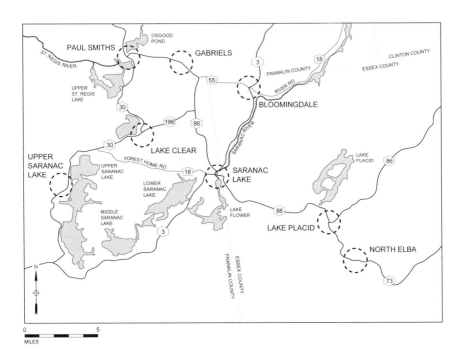

EXTENDING EAST TO WEST, FROM UPPER CASCADE LAKE in the High Peaks to Upper Saranac Lake, this section encompasses some of the most prolific resort development in the Adirondacks. Recreational pursuits began there during the mid-19th century, and the area remains heavily populated by seasonal residents and short-term visitors. They are accommodated at campgrounds, children's camps, institutional retreats, small cabins and motels, posh resorts, modest summer cottages, and grand, multi-building camps. The land is used for almost every conceivable form of outdoor activity—hiking, climbing, long-distance running, swimming, boating, golf, and tennis among them. It is also the area where winter sports, from snowshoeing to bobsledding, began in earnest within the Adirondacks and where many of these activities are the most intensely conducted.

After the initial clearing of farmland, logging played only a minor role in the economy, and almost none of the extractive industries so important to the region farther east figured to a significant degree. Relatively flat land southeast of the village of Lake Placid and north of the village of Saranac Lake supported agriculture well into the 20th century. The latter community attained a unique economic base during the late 19th and early 20th centuries as a pioneering center for the treatment of tuberculosis in the United States.

This section of the book includes portions or all of five towns—North Elba, St. Armand, Harrietstown, Brighton, and Santa Clara—in Essex and Franklin counties. The great majority of land is part of the Forest Preserve, most of it designated as wilderness or for wild forest and primitive use. At the same time, the area includes the largest village within the Blue Line—Saranac Lake (population 5,406 in 2010)—and the largest town—North Elba (8,957), of which Lake Placid is the center. The architectural resources within this area, dating from the mid-19th century to the present, are among the richest in the park.

ASIDE FROM LAKE PLACID, THE TOWN OF NORTH ELBA has never had much in the way of concentrated settlement; however, the area along NY 73 southeast of the village, still sometimes referred to as North Elba, was among the first settled and forms a coherent landscape. In 1811 Archibald McIntyre started the Elba Iron Works on land near present-day Adirondak Loj Road, mining ore near the Cascade lakes. The yield was of insufficient grade and transporting it too difficult to compete with operations along the Ausable Valley, and the operation closed after six years. Most settlers attracted by the ironworks left, and, although a few families did come to farm in the 1820s and 1830s, North Elba had a very small stable population. The situation began to change a decade later due to the initiative of a rich abolitionist from central New York, Gerrit Smith. Having inherited a large tract of land in North Elba, Smith pledged a portion of it—some 16,000 acres—to be divided into 400 forty-acre parcels for African-American homesteaders. Settlers began to arrive at an area still known as the Plains of Abraham in 1847, but no more than sixty people at the very most had come by the close of 1850. The highly publicized venture did attract abolitionist John Brown, who moved there with his family in 1849 [NL 8]. The attention given to what proved to be a short-lived settlement unintentionally attracted others to the area. A post office was established and the town was formed in 1849. Farming became the predominant occupation through the remainder of the century and into the next as well.

Lake Placid from Mirror Lake, showing Stevens House, 1886–87, 1899–1902, demolished 1947. (early 20th-century photograph)

The rugged landscape of the High Peaks spawned two small resorts in 1878. Located between the Cascade lakes, the Cascade House was set in a dramatic pass connecting to the Ausable Valley, with about a 1,000-foot drop in elevation. Even though this topographical configuration generates some of the worst weather conditions in the Adirondacks, the hotel survived nearly fifty years, the last few of which were as part of the Lake Placid Club. South of the Plains of Abraham at Heart Lake inventor Henry Van Hoevenberg built Adirondack Lodge, a remarkable two-and-a-half-story log structure—one of the few hostelries of its size in the region to manifest an aggressively rustic character. The Lake Placid Club acquired it too in 1903, only to have it burn three years later. In the late 1920s the club commissioned a more modest building for what was called its Forest Branch [NL 4]. It now serves as quarters for the Adirondack Mountain Club, a popular hikers' organization.

By far the most significant recreational developments in North Elba have been for the 1932 and 1980 Winter Olympics. The bobsled run envisioned for the 1932 games was the first in the United States. Using the site initially chosen, which lay in the Forest Preserve, was ruled unconstitutional by the courts as a result of a lawsuit by the Association for the Protection of the Adirondacks. A new location on Mount Van Hoevenberg was selected after the acreage was transferred from the Lake Placid Club. The facility [NL 3] was not only a centerpiece of the 1932 event, but a catalyst for the ongoing pursuit of sliding sports in this country. The Intervale Olympic Ski Jump Center [NL 7] was constructed for the 1980 games on the same site developed for the preceding event half a century earlier. This project generated controversy due to the height of its towers. Both sites remain in use and are also tourist attractions.

Whiteface Inn, Lake Placid, 1914–15, demolished 1985. (ca. 1930s postcard)

The area that would become the village of Lake Placid began to be settled by a few farmers; however, the location emerged as a magnet for visitors almost at once. Joseph V. Nash was the earliest to move there, arriving in 1850 and expanding his farmhouse to accommodate guests five years later. Known as the Red House, the establishment enjoyed considerable popularity. In 1871 Benjamin Brewster, who had come a year after Nash, opened the first purpose-built hostelry, the Lake Placid House, which looked like an oversized inn or boardinghouse. Not to be outdone,

Nash erected the larger, more hotel-like Excelsior House in 1876–77. Both had spectacular sites on the ridge between Mirror and Placid lakes, with sweeping views of Whiteface Mountain to the northeast and the High Peaks to the south. John Stevens acquired the Excelsior two years after it opened, rechristening it the Stevens House. After a devastating fire in 1885, he erected a much larger facility, aggrandizing it in 1899–1900. Accommodating around 500 patrons, more than six times the capacity of the Excelsior, the Stevens House at the turn of the 20th century ranked among the finest resort hotels in the Adirondacks.

The Stevens House also had competition. A major rival was the Grand View House, built on a north-south ridge paralleling the main street in 1878 and substantially enlarged three times to accommodate over 300 guests by 1893. Nearby, the Allen House was the largest in the village when it opened in 1880 (only to burn in 1886). The adjacent Mirror Lake House (not to be confused with the more recent Mirror Lake Inn [LP 16]) opened in 1882 and was completely transformed by the decade's end to accommodate 300 guests. Farther afield, the Ruisseaumont Hotel (1891–92), catering to a Jewish clientele, lay along the south shore of Placid Lake—a remarkable pile with three tiers of porches and an adjacent compound of tents. On the lake's north shore the Whiteface Inn was built as the Westside Hotel in 1882 on a 400-acre tract. A new building was erected in 1901, with a huge, very stylish addition of 1906–07. After it burned only two years later it was replaced in 1914–15 by a sprawling pile more akin to counterparts in the national parks of the West than other Adirondack establishments. At that time an 1898 golf course was replaced by one of nine holes closer to the hotel.

Lakeside Club House, Lake Placid Club, 1895 and later, burned 1992. (early 20th-century photograph)

The village also was home to a number of smaller, less expensive hostelries erected during the late 19th and early 20th centuries, but even without these Lake Placid had the highest concentration of resort hotels within the Blue Line. And it was the grand hotels that set the standard for the community becoming a premier resort in the eastern United States. That stature was furthered by the construction of lavish camps around Placid Lake beginning in the 1870s. While many of these exuded the rustic qualities that became associated with architecture in the Adirondacks, many others, especially from the early 20th century, appeared more like large suburban or country houses. All these developments were furthered by the arrival of the railroad service, extended from Saranac Lake in 1893. There was a third component, which, in combination with the density of grand hotels and grand camps, made Lake Placid unique among resorts within the Blue Line. That component was the Lake Placid Club, which by 1920 had become one of the biggest and most unusual institutions of its kind anywhere in the country.

Unlike most social organizations, which, irrespective of location, demographics, or stated purpose, are formed by kindred spirits, the Lake Placid Club was established in 1895 by Melvil Dewey, who then served as librarian for New York State's university system. Dewey already had accomplished much, creating in 1876 the library classification system that bears his name and is still widely used. Soon thereafter he was instrumental in founding the American Library Association, the *Library Journal*, and the American Metric Bureau. In 1883 he was appointed librarian at Columbia University and founded the nation's first library school there four years later. In the early 1890s he began a three-year search for a place to which he and his family could retreat in the summers. Mirror Lake was chosen as the site, not just for a cottage, but for a colony that he would operate for teachers and librarians. Within a few years the concept evolved into one of a club for the affluent, irrespective of occupation. Dewey conspicuously promoted his agenda, enumerating the characteristics desired for membership and overtly excluding Jews. (In the early 20th century several prominent New York Jews who had grand camps on Lower and Upper Saranac lakes successfully secured his dismissal as a state employee due to this policy.)

Dewey remained unapologetic and unrelenting in his now full-time focus on advancing the club. Attracting wealthy white Protestant families from many parts of the country, the institution grew at a furious pace during the first three decades of the new century. From an initial five acres, club property grew to encompass over

Toboggan slide, Lake Placid Club. (ca. 1920s postcard)

2,000 acres in 1902 and some 10,000 acres by 1925. The grounds boasted five club-houses, a huge concert hall, an amphitheater, dozens of cottages, three golf cours-es (the first of which was the earliest in the Adirondacks), and forty-four courts for tennis and other games. Thirty-eight farms supplied fresh produce, meats, and poultry. Dewey kept the club open during the winter, beginning in 1904–05, to pro-mote skating, skiing, hockey, dogsled races, and other outdoor activities. Soon the club had its own ski jump and toboggan run. Besides acquiring the hotels at Heart and the Cascade lakes, the club purchased land for hiking trails and cross-country skiing. The club also sponsored the founding of a boys' boarding school, Northwood [LP 19], adjacent to its grounds, and in 1925 created the Lake Placid Club Education Foundation to hold its vast stable of assets. The main campus alone was enormous, occupying much of the acreage east of Mirror Lake. Overwhelming even the finest hotels in the sheer volume as well as the caliber of its amenities, the club became the village's primary economic engine.

The Lake Placid Club was instrumental in developing the village as a leading winter resort not just through the diversions it offered to its membership. In 1929 Godfrey Dewey, who was assuming his father's role as the driving force behind the organization, pursued securing the village as host to the newly formed Winter Olympics. After touring the two previous sites, Chamonix and St. Moritz, he lobbied Olympic officials, Governor Franklin D. Roosevelt, and state legislators, securing of-ficial designation in 1929 and becoming president of the III Winter Games Commit-tee. Most of the $1.5 million price tag came from the state, but Dewey also pushed through a sizable bond issue for the town, with club members the major purchas-ers. (Still, the town's debt of over $52,000 was not fully paid until 1973.) The most expensive projects were an enormous indoor arena [LP 6] and the bobsled run [NL 3]. As a result of these facilities, as well as ski jumps at Intervale [NL 7], Lake Placid had unrivaled facilities for training and competitions in a variety of winter sports.

A new committee succeeded in having the village host the 1980 Winter Olympics as well, insisting it would bolster a sagging tourist business. Equally important, it would give the village long-term facilities for Olympic and competitive sports train-ing, expanding upon and improving those created for the 1932 event. No financial burden would be placed on local (or seasonal) residents; federal funding would cov-er the majority of the cost, supplemented by the state and the Olympic organizing committee. Still, the price tag rose from an anticipated $50 million (more than sixty times that of the 1932 games, not adjusted for inflation) to around $200 million. A large new arena, ski jumps, and other components of the project contributed to the high price. Accommodating the public also became a formidable challenge. Daily visitation was estimated to be around seven times greater than in 1932—far more than the village could accommodate—necessitating a cumbersome transportation system from communities miles away to multiple sites. (Private cars were banned from the village and satellite facilities.) While the games enhanced the village's position as a winter sports center, they also led to Olympic officials determining that future events would have to be held in communities that could sustain the for-midable demands placed upon them. The Lake Placid Club committed substantial resources to the event, overextending itself financially and hastening its demise.

The 1980 Olympics were emblematic of the transformation of Lake Placid from a resort primarily catering to the rich to one that depended upon a mass audience. As in many other places, the Depression and changing vacation patterns were the death knell for the grand hotels. After sitting vacant for some years, the Stevens House was demolished in 1947. The Grand View lasted a little longer, but it too met its destruction in 1961. The Lake Placid Club increasingly struggled to maintain its enormous physical plant at a time when much of its membership was no longer content to spend a month or more at a single place. Moreover, its precinct became far more exposed to general view with widespread automobile use since the main campus was traversed by a number of public roads. In a last-ditch effort to augment revenue, the club opened its facilities to anyone who could pay the fee, driving away some members in the process. The organization closed its doors for good the same year as the Winter Olympics; its many buildings were gradually demolished or burned over the next two decades. Well before then Lake Placid had become much more accessible to a broad public with the opening of the Northway in 1967. Motels were constructed in considerable number between the late 1950s and 1970s. The fancy shops that once lined Main Street were replaced by ones purveying souvenirs and outlet goods. No place in the Adirondacks has a higher visitation level, attracting small conventions as well as youth hockey tournaments.

Hotel Ampersand, Lower Saranac Lake, 1888, 1891, burned 1907. (early 20th-century postcard)

Despite the village's changing complexion, the many camps on Placid Lake remain for the most part intact and in demand among those who can afford the hefty price of owning or renting them. A number of sizable new dwellings for seasonal residents have been constructed in the area as well. The most conspicuous initiatives to retrieve Lake Placid's once pervasive aura of elegance are two elaborate resort hotels, the Whiteface Lodge and the Lake Placid Lodge [LP 23 and 24] constructed in the first decade of the 21st century.

Lying about seven miles to the northwest, Saranac Lake also had an early history of catering to leisure-minded visitors, but the main thrust of its development occurred for entirely different reasons. Remoteness hampered settlement through the first half of the 19th century. Only about fifteen families occupied the community in 1856, sustained by supplying goods to loggers and sportsmen. William Martin, who came to the village in 1849, opened one of the first purpose-built hotels in the Adirondack interior in 1852. Officially called the Saranac Lake House but widely known as Martin's, it was located well beyond the village's western edge at the northern end of Lower Saranac Lake. Several expansions were made to the establishment over the next twenty years as its clientele broadened to families seeking an isolated quasi-wilderness environment. In 1888 the hotel experienced its most extensive transformation into an elegant resort, only to burn six years later. Nearby to the southwest, the Alexander House (renamed the Algonquin in 1890) was erected in 1884, its amenities steadily increasing into the early 20th century. Not long thereafter the Del Monte Hotel (Hotel Van Dorrien by 1905) was erected nearby, but burned less than three decades later. All these establishments were overshadowed by the Hotel Ampersand (1888, 1891), which from the start was a sumptuous resort that, unlike most of its kind, operated year round. It, too, met an early end, consumed by fire in 1907.

Building the Algonquin, Del Monte, and Ampersand as well as aggrandizing Martin's were all perpetrated by the rise of the village as a center for the treatment of pulmonary tuberculosis. The disease was so pervasive during late 19th-century America that, in 1873 alone, it killed one out of seven in the general population. Thirty-five years later, TB claimed around 400 people in the United States each day. Saranac Lake's transformation as a treatment center was in large part due to Edward Livingston Trudeau, a New York physician and outdoor enthusiast, who was diagnosed with TB when he was twenty-five. A prolonged stay at Paul Smith's hotel, some twelve miles to the northwest of Saranac Lake, led to his apparent recovery, only to suffer a relapse after his return to New York. Trudeau retreated to Paul Smith's in the spring of 1874 and stayed through the following year. From 1875 to 1883 he boarded at a Saranac Lake house, and then built a dwelling for himself and his family. By that point people suffering from the disease were migrating to the village for the cold, fresh air (some had come to Martin's for that reason as early as the 1860s). Recovering his health, Trudeau opened the Adirondack Cottage Sanitarium in 1884 [SL 38], the first successful venture of its kind in the country. Although TB was the leading cause of death, American medical authorities, incredibly, did not consider it a public health problem. Trudeau's maverick venture was modeled after Herman Brehmer's Goebersdorf in Germany, with a focus on providing fresh air, exercise, good food, and ample rest. Concurrently, Trudeau conducted experiments, building upon recent research on the disease's origins by another German, Robert Koch, and adding significantly to the scientific knowledge [SL 25].

Robert Louis Stevenson's stay in Saranac Lake during the winter of 1887–88 helped give the village national recognition as a treatment center [SL 31]. The concurrent opening of the Chateaugay Railroad greatly facilitated access. (Before, most people took an arduous trip by stage from Au Sable Forks [Section 7] some twenty-eight miles to the east.) At a time when many resort hotels and even communities in the Adirondacks refused to take in TB patients, Saranac Lake opened its doors. The result was a veritable boom. A number of houses were adapted to function as small commercial sanitaria, known as cure cottages, and others that were purpose-built began to appear in the early 20th century. An 1893 subdivision, Helen Hill [SL 27] had an especially large concentration of these establishments, most of them operated by nurses and holding around a dozen patients. The Highland Park subdivision of 1898 [SL 37] was developed as a grand avenue adjacent to Trudeau's sanitarium for patients who could afford treatment at home, staying with their families. Nearby Cottage Row was an enclave of small purpose-built commercial sanitaria [SL 36].

Saranac Lake's rise as a TB center spawned other large sanitaria in nearby rural areas. About eight miles north the Sisters of Mercy established the Sanatorium Gabriels (1894–97) for persons of modest means [GA 4]. Farther north, a prominent New Yorker established Stony Wold Sanatorium in 1901 for the care of poor women [ON 2; Section 8]. Less than four miles to the southwest of Saranac Lake at Ray Brook, the New York State Hospital for Incipient Pulmonary Tuberculosis opened in 1904, the second state-sponsored facility of its kind in the United States. Not far from Gabriels the Independent Order of Foresters created the Rainbow Sanatorium in 1910. Finally, the National Vaudeville Artists built a facility (renamed Will Rogers Memorial Hospital in 1936), which opened just east of Saranac Lake in 1929 [SL 1].

The great influx of patients, families, and friends led to a proliferation of hotels concentrated in an emerging commercial core. Around a dozen were constructed or enlarged between the 1890s and the 1920s. By the latter decade the village boasted the greatest variety of emporia in the Adirondacks and also the region's largest movie theater, the Pontiac (1917). Saranac Lake incorporated as a village in 1892, the first community to do so within the Blue Line. It was also the first community to commission a plan to help shape development, prepared by the renowned Olmsted Brothers firm in 1907–08. The village board rejected the plan as being too expensive; however, the Village Improvement Society was formed in 1910 to implement some of its recommendations, including the creation of a park contiguous to the business district on Lake Flower.

As a cure center, Saranac Lake attracted a considerable number of accomplished persons—bankers, real estate brokers, writers, lawyers, and doctors among them—who were suffering from tuberculosis. Many of them stayed, endowing the community with a substantial professional class. For example, Saranac Lake was the first, and for a long time the only, Adirondack community to sustain an architectural practice for any duration. The firm founded by TB patient William L. Coulter in 1897 became well known for its houses and grand camps, and grew to encompass a wide range of buildings in many parts of the region through a succession of partners, finally closing its doors after a century. A second firm, Scopes & Feustmann, was active from 1903 until 1931, specializing in hospitals and civic buildings in the region and beyond. By the early 20th century Branch & Callanan emerged as a major contracting company and supplier of building materials [SL 33]. Saranac Lake also became the largest early provider of electricity based within the Adirondacks with the company founded by Paul Smith in 1907.

Well before Melvil Dewey introduced winter sports at the Lake Placid Club, Trudeau helped create the Pontiac Club in 1896. That organization inaugurated the Winter Carnival, which included toboggan racing, ski jumping, hockey games, and speed skating. Two years later the carnival sponsored building the first Ice Palace (designed by Coulter) as its symbol, starting a tradition that lasted until 1918 and was revived after World War II. From Trudeau's perspective the carnival was an important means of furthering the activities of TB patients able to participate and of entertaining others too weak to do so.

Ice Palace, 1909 Winter Carnival, Saranac Lake. (1909 photograph)

After World War II the discovery of antibiotics as a cure for tuberculosis led to a significant challenge to the local economy. While many businesses ended, Saranac Lake's revenue base eventually became more diversified. Trudeau's sprawling campus of over forty buildings closed in 1954, but the sanatorium was reorganized as the Trudeau Foundation Research Laboratories (now Trudeau Institute), with new quarters on the site formerly occupied by the Algonquin Hotel, opening in 1964 [SL 41]. The sanatorium grounds were taken over by the American Management Association in 1957. The Will Rogers Hospital lasted until 1974, and after lying vacant for six years it found new life as a retirement home. A large general hospital, serving much of the region, opened in 1967, replacing one built over fifty years earlier [SL 4], which in turn became part of the campus of North Country Community College. The grounds of Paul Smith's hotel were reincarnated as Paul Smith's College [PS 5] after World War II. About midway between Paul Smiths and Saranac Lake, the only commercial airport [LC 3] in the Adirondacks was established in 1946. At Ray Brook, the state sanitarium closed in 1971 and became a short-term drug rehabilitation center, then Camp Adirondack (prisoners there were employed at improving state campsites, cross-country ski trails, and other work in the Forest Preserve), and finally the medium-security Adirondack Correctional Facility. Nearby, buildings constructed as the athletes' Olympic Village for the 1980 games became a federal correctional institution. Well before then Ray Brook became home to the Adirondack Park Agency and regional offices of the state's Department of Environmental Conservation and also the State Police. In recent years boosters have endeavored to have Saranac Lake become a mecca for visitors drawn to the area's extensive outdoor recreation opportunities, reviving the commercial core as a somewhat more decorous and tradition-based alternative to Lake Placid's Main Street.

The rich history of the rural community known as Paul Smiths is in inverse proportion to its size. In 1852, concurrent with the building of William Martin's wilderness hotel on Lower Saranac Lake, Paul Smith opened the modest Hunter's Home, with a capacity for only ten people, near Loon Lake [Section 8]. Six years later, with

Paul Smith's hotel, Lower St. Regis Lake, 1885–86 and later, burned 1931. (early 20th-century photograph)

the encouragement of one of his clients, Smith began work on a large but still elementary and isolated establishment, which he called the St. Regis Lake House. When it opened, what became universally referred to as Paul Smith's had a mere seventeen guest rooms. Between 1875 and 1898 the building was substantially enlarged at least four times to accommodate 500 patrons. Paul Smith's grew to be not only one of the largest hotels in the Adirondacks but one of the most celebrated, a favorite resort for rich families from major East Coast centers. Near the hotel proper a casino was built on the lakefront, containing a stock-exchange room, grill room, smoking den, and other male haunts above the boat slips. At nearby Osgood Pond, he developed a golf course and clubhouse on a portion of "Paul Smith's Adirondack Park," a 40,000-acre tract maintained for outdoor activities. The arrival of the Chateaugay Railroad in 1887 and the New York Central five years later at Lake Clear Junction, seven miles to the south, greatly facilitated access. In 1907 Smith developed an electric railroad line between the station and his hotel, where side tracks were available for private cars. Cottages were erected on the hotel grounds during the 1880s and 1890s [PS 5], but far more important in sealing the hotel's reputation as a haven for the upper crust was the sale of land for camps around Spitfire and Upper St. Regis lakes (both connected to Lower St. Regis Lake) and, later, on Osgood Pond. Between the 1870s and the early 20th century a stunning array of lakeside compounds, many of them encompassing a dozen or more buildings, were constructed in varied and often highly individualistic rustic modes [PS 2].

For a quarter century Smith relied heavily on the managerial skills of his wife, Lydia, for both the operation and enlargement of the hotel. After her death in 1891, son Phelps Smith took over many of these responsibilities; following his father's death in 1912, he and his brother, Paul Jr., ran the establishment. But even legendary status could not arrest declining patronage by the late 1920s as a result of the trend away from long stays at a single hotel. In 1930 the great wooden pile burned, and the Depression precluded rebuilding despite Phelps Smith's wish to do so. He died in 1937, and his will stipulated that his $2 million estate be used to establish a college specializing in subjects pertinent to his family's legacy and to regional needs: hotel management and forestry. The new institution, appropriately named Paul Smith's College, opened ten years later, occupying the many buildings that had long lain vacant after the hotel was destroyed.

Settlement began along the shores of Upper Saranac Lake much as it did at Lower Saranac, with wilderness hotels. Jesse Corey built Rustic Lodge in 1850 at the lake's lower end. Nearby Virgil Bartlett, who had run Martin's for two years, erected another simple lodge for fifty patrons in 1854. Both establishments operated until near the century's end. A similar hostelry, the Prospect House, was constructed for Daniel Hough at the lake's northern end around 1864 and was modeled after Paul Smith's in its inceptive stage. Within a decade Hough enlarged the building several fold. Under new management it was named Saranac Inn and expanded again in 1888-89. Further additions were made thereafter, followed by an extensive rebuilding in 1916-17.

Saranac Inn, Upper Saranac Lake, ca. 1864, 1870s, 1889-89, and later, demolished 1978. (early 20th-century photograph)

More aggrandizement during the 1920s ballooned its capacity to about 1,000 guests. Well before that time the Saranac Inn rivaled Paul Smith's as a low-key, albeit sumptuous, retreat for a genteel (and gentile) elite. It enjoyed unusual longevity, operating until 1961. The other grand hotel on the lake was near the southwestern end. Opened in 1889, the Wawbeek was an elaborate, turreted pile, which attracted widespread attention, but survived only until the early 1920s.

Hotels were but a part of the equation. By the early 20th century Upper Saranac was known foremost as a setting for grand camps. In contrast to the relatively intimate scale of Spitfire and Upper St. Regis lakes, Upper Saranac is the sixth largest lake in the Adirondack Park, with thirty-seven miles of shoreline. Boasting numerous coves and some islands, the lake was ideally suited for building ambitiously while maintaining a sense of privacy. Clients wishing a camp on the lake became a basic staple for William L. Coulter's architectural firm, and his work there is among his most creative. Together with Spitfire, Upper St. Regis, Raquette, and Big Moose lakes, Upper Saranac has one of the richest assemblages of camp architecture. Most of these compounds remain, all but a few in residential use, sequestered from public view.

*   *   *   *   *

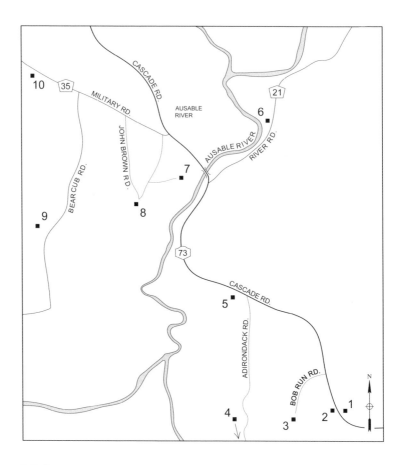

NORTH ELBA

Town of North Elba, Essex County

NL 1 NORTH COUNTRY SCHOOL AND CAMP TREETOPS
4382 Cascade Road (NY 73) (accessible by prior arrangement)

The understated grounds of this co-educational boarding school and children's camp might at first seem the product of rather haphazard development over time when in fact they were carefully orchestrated by one of its owners, Douglas Haskell, between the 1930s and 1960s. Among the most distinguished architectural journalists of the 20th century, Haskell designed or added to many of the buildings, undertook

the site planning, and in other ways manipulated the landscape. The result is an unorthodox synthesis—a celebration of a traditional rural environment, where physical change was predicated on incremental, pragmatic decisions; a manifestation of its designer's high-style modernist ideals; and a freewheeling, even idiosyncratic, exercise in individualism that characterized much of the region's rustic architecture.

Camp Treetops was established in 1920 by Columbia University philosophy professor Donald Slesinger and his wife, Dorothy, as an experimental adaptation

of the progressive educational approach advanced by John Dewey and William Kilpatrick. To supplement his income, Haskell joined the staff in 1925. When the Slesingers left for Chicago three years later, they entrusted the camp's directorship to Haskell and his wife, Helen, a specialist in physical education and advocate of the progressive approach to schooling more broadly. In 1933 the Haskells purchased the enterprise. Among the counselors were Helen's sister, Leonora Clark, and her husband, Walter, both of whom taught in a model progressive school in Westchester County. When the Clarks contemplated starting a school of their own, the Haskells offered part of their 160-acre property. A school building could prove an asset to the camp in summertime. The venture also gave Haskell, who had been architecture critic for the *Nation* since 1931, but who had neither formal training nor experience in architecture, the opportunity to gain new insights on the processes of design and construction, as well as to put some of his ideas into concrete form.

The resulting **main building** of North Country School (1937–38), which Haskell created with practical assistance from his New York architect friend Henry S. Churchill, was unassuming in character, but meticulously tailored to the climate, oriented for maximum solar gain and configured to accommodate all functions in an atmosphere that carried both domestic and communal associations. Enrollment grew quickly, prompting a much larger **addition** designed in 1942 and built in 1946–47. Anchored by a turret (or a silo?) and with a Quonset hut incorporated at one end, this appendage was a more whimsical exercise in what might be taken for ad-hocism, but in fact was developed almost entirely on a functional basis. During World War II Haskell had three dwellings built for camp counselors—**Corn Crib**, **Hanging House**, and **Wing House**, each crafted as an experimental prototype for mass-produced housing—a subject of enduring interest to him. Haskell also added to the **main building** at **Treetops** and to the 19th-century **farmhouse** where he and

Helen lived. Prior to the school's construction, Haskell introduced 10,000 non-native pine, cedar, and spruce trees to differentiate areas used foremost by the camp from those of the new institution. This plantation included several clearings, varied in size and shape, where camping could occur and later where additional school buildings were erected. Other trees formed a second grouping that shielded the grounds from the highway, helped frame some of the farm buildings (actively used by school and camp), and provided a portal to open fields beyond. Walter Clark later recounted that nothing was added or taken away from the campus that was not the result of Haskell's focused study.

Haskell secured the services of his friend, the distinguished architect Harwell Hamilton Harris, to design the headmaster's residence (**Glass House**, now the admissions office) in 1944 and, much later, four dormitories in one of the wooded glades—**Algonquin, Bramwell, Cascade,** and **Mountain houses** (1967–68). Paul Nowicki, a potter who long served as a Treetops counselor, designed the elegantly intricate **pottery shed** ca. 1972. The Clarks' son, Allan, one of several alumni who became architects, prepared plans for the **camp director's residence** in 1985. The most recent addition is **Clark House** (2008–11), a zero-energy-use dormitory housing ten to twelve students, with two faculty apartments designed by architect Steve Tilly of Dobbs Ferry, New York.

NL 2 ROUND LAKE FARM
4379 Cascade Road; ca. late 19th century

An all-too-rare surviving example of the farms once numerous in parts of the Adirondacks, this complex has been preserved as a seasonal residence for at least eight decades.

NL 3 MOUNT VAN HOEVENBERG
OLYMPIC BOBSLED RUN
End of Bob Run Lane, off Cascade Road (NY 73); 1930, Stanislaus Zentzytsky (Germany), designer; lower mile of course modified 1978–79, Sargent, Webster, Crenshaw & Foley, architects and engineers (Syracuse); later additions

Constructed at great cost for the 1932 Winter Olympics, this was the first bobsled run constructed in the United States,

where the sport was scarcely known. Famous for his runs in Europe, Zentzytsky departed from precedent in creating a course that was longer by a third (one and a half rather than the usual one mile), steeper, and with more pronounced curves. The run was built of earth for straightaways and stone for the twenty-two curves—all surfaced in ice, using a spray mixture of snow and water. Completed well before the games, the run allowed the American team time to practice on what was considered the world's most challenging course. The team also needed to adjust to their invention of sleds steered by wheels instead of ropes. At the games, the U.S. contingent won two gold medals and a silver as well. Americans came to dominate their newly adopted sport internationally for over two decades.

Although they initially applauded the run, Europeans criticized it after the games as being too dangerous, persuading the International Olympic Committee to declare one mile as the official standard. As a result the upper third of the Mount Van Hoevenberg course was abandoned (it still exists, however). As the only bobsled run in the United States, the facility continued to be the essential training ground after World War II, and it hosted four World Bobsled Championships between 1961 and 1978. Subsequently it was reconditioned for the 1980 games. Refrigeration pipes were embedded in the concrete that now covered the track surface, allowing practice to occur beyond the coldest months. A luge track was constructed on adjacent land. Besides a new start house, the run was punctuated at its end by the **Mount Van Hoevenberg Bobsled Finish Building** of 1967–69, with an extensive viewing platform indoors and out. Designed by Barker & Henry, a Glens Falls architectural and engineering firm, it was renamed **Lamy Lodge** after a prominent bobsledder in 1993.

These changes were minor compared to those made for a new combination bobsled and luge track in 1990. The old trail seems like a narrow road through the forest, but its successor is akin to an elevated superhighway. Part of the old run has since been used as a tourist ride.

NL 4 ADIRONDAK LOJ
End of Adirondak Loj Road, 4.8 miles south of Cascade Road; 1927, William G. Distin, architect

When the Lake Placid Club acquired Henry Van Hoevenberg's Adirondack Lodge (promptly applying Dewey's phoneticized spelling: Adirondak Loj) as a staging area for climbs in the High Peaks, it may not have been as popular an attraction as anticipated. Over twenty years elapsed before it was replaced by this modest facility, a project fostered by the newly formed Adirondack Mountain Club's assuming responsibility for maintaining trails and shelters in this part of the Forest Preserve. Appropriately it was purchased in 1958 by the Adirondack Mountain Club, which developed an extensive campground nearby. Since then it has been a major destination for outdoor enthusiasts.

NL 5 OWEN TORRANCE HOUSE
5184 Cascade Road; 1867 and later

Owen Torrance was among the early settlers in North Elba, arriving from Jay [Section 7] to farm in 1865. Built two years later, the farmhouse remains intact. The porch was probably added in the late 19th century; the west wing somewhat later. It

remains in the hands of descendants. The current owner, Peter Torrance, is a noted designer and builder of rustic houses.

NL 6 RED BARN, WOODLEA FARMS
118 River Road (CR 21); ca. 1914

This enormous barn, constructed for the Lake Placid Club to accommodate a herd of Holsteins, is on one of many settlement-period farms the club acquired to support its burgeoning membership and staff. The land was initially cultivated around 1855 by the Thompson family, who, like the Torrances, were pioneers in the area.

NL 7 INTERVALE OLYMPIC SKI JUMP CENTER
Ski Jump Lane, off John Brown Road; 1976–79, Stone & Webster, architects (Toronto), Karl Martitsch, principal-in-charge

One of the most conspicuous remnants of the 1980 Winter Olympics was intended to help set a new standard in such facilities. Martitsch, who was a seasoned veteran of the sport and had become a specialist in a rarefied field, enjoyed an international reputation for the more than thirty jumps he had designed. The ninety-meter jump was equipped with a starting platform that could be adjusted according to wind velocity and weather conditions. The slopes of both the ninety- and 120-meter jumps were refrigerated to ensure even surfaces. The hill slope was refashioned so that jumpers would never be high off the ground. Considerable attention was given to configuring the grounds to optimize sightlines for viewers as well as officials and the press. The starting platform was also designed to accommodate visitors when not in active use.

Supporters of the games were enthusiastic, one member of the local committee declaring, "It will be almost an art object." But many environmentalists considered it a travesty, fouling the majestic landscape of the High Peaks—a sentiment that prompted one hotelier to quip, "When they put up the Eiffel Tower people thought it was an eyesore." Despite the protests, the APA approved the project. Whatever one's individual opinion, the towers were as carefully thought out in terms of appearance as they were for functional performance.

NL 8 JOHN BROWN FARM
End of John Brown Road; 1855, Henry Thompson, builder

While it has long served as a shrine to the notorious abolitionist John Brown, this farmstead was only marginally a part of his chaotic life. In 1849 Brown acquired the land from Gerrit Smith with the intention of moving there and creating a farm that would serve as a model for the struggling enclave of free blacks that Smith's gifts of land had enabled to settle there. Leaving his collapsing wool brokerage business in Springfield, Massachusetts, Brown and his family rented a nearby farm from 1849 to 1851. Financial difficulties led Brown, his

wife, and younger children to move to Akron, Ohio, while a daughter and her new husband, carpenter Henry Thompson, remained. When the Browns returned four years later, his son-in-law built their new quarters. But Brown soon left again, this time to advance his cause of insurrection in Kansas. He returned for only six brief visits before his demise at Harpers Ferry. According to Brown's wish he was buried here in 1859, but the family left for California four years later.

Soon efforts were under way to make the site a memorial. Journalist Kate Field purchased the farm in 1870 and formed the John Brown Association to care for the property and keep it accessible to visitors. Following her death it was deeded to the state in 1896. Under the auspices of the state's Forest, Fish & Game Commission, a fence was erected around the graves of Brown, as well as two of his sons, and nine of his followers, who had been reinterred there in the late 19th century. In 1921 the barn was relocated to give the house more prominence. The John Brown Memorial Association was formed the following year, raising funds for a statue, which was dedicated in 1935. The state Department of Education undertook a renovation in 1957–59 with the aim of bringing the house back to something that approximated its appearance a hundred years earlier. Since 1972 it has been operated by the New York Office of Parks, Recreation, and Historic Preservation.

NL 9 HEAVEN HILL FARM, HENRY UIHLEIN II HOUSE
302 Bear Cub Road (CR 26); ca. 1941–42; addition 1954–55, J. Bradley Delehanty, architect (New York)

When he was in his forties, Henry Uihlein, grandson of the president of the Joseph Schlitz Brewing Company, purchased 600 acres from the Lake Placid Club to build a year-round residence with a panoramic view of the High Peaks. The land had been farmed for a century, and

the center section of the house Uihlein commissioned lay on the foundations of one built for Horatio Hinckley around 1840. As with a number of country houses from the interwar decades, this one has a telescoping configuration, breaking down its mass in a manner compatible with its stylized Colonial Revival imagery.

Uihlein was introduced to Lake Placid after contracting tuberculosis while in college. Following recuperation and marriage, he engaged in real estate development, returning to Lake Placid for the summers. When he established Heaven Hill, Uihlein focused on breeding prize-winning Jersey cattle and had a celebrated maple-syrup operation. He also devoted much of his time, and money, to philanthropic causes. After he died in 1997 (at the age of 101), 200 acres of the farm were donated to Cornell University for agricultural research facilities. The house is used as the quarters for the Adirondack Foundation, which focuses on grants for education, the arts, and human services.

NL 10 STAGECOACH INN

Stagecoach Road, off Old Military Road (CR 35), east of Station Street; ca. 1865 and later

Situated along one of the area's oldest roads, this stage stop was built by Martin Lyons shortly after he purchased the property and was called Lyon's Inn. A previous lodging house on the site dated to the early 1830s. Despite many changes and some rebuilding after a fire in 2002, the inn still evokes a distant past.

LAKE PLACID

Town of North Elba, Essex County

Though the Lake Placid Club, the grand hotels, and other landmarks of the village's heyday as an elite resort have gone, ample physical evidence of that era remains. A careful reading also indicates that during the 19th and early 20th centuries development grew around two sectors, the "lower" one in the vicinity of the railroad terminus and the "upper" one on Signal Hill and the ridge extending south along the west side of Mirror Lake. The Lake Placid Club carved out its own sector along Mirror Lake's east side. Upper and lower sections were joined by civic facilities: the Town Hall (1916, altered), the High School (1915–16) [LP 5], the Post Office (1935) [LP 8], and the Olympic Arena (1931–32) [LP 6]. Some commercial activities developed in this mid-ground as well, but the retail core emerged to the north along Main Street where it still flourishes. Some business buildings were of masonry construction with fronts befitting a stylish resort community, but many others were (and still are) less decorous wood-frame blocks. Main Street was never an elegant affair. Along with Saranac Avenue to the west and Cascade Road to the south, Main Street also anchors most of the post–World War II tourist accommodations. Residential areas generally do not possess the architectural richness found in Saranac Lake counterparts save for the small concentration of once-seasonal dwellings on Signal Hill built during the early 20th

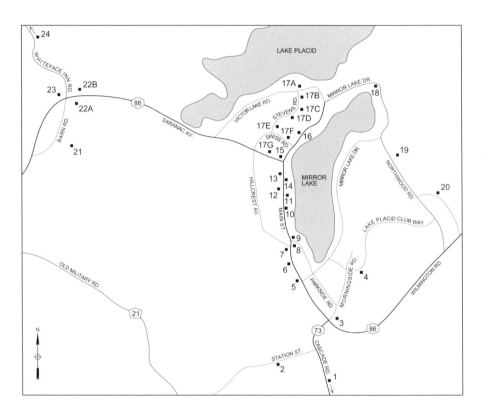

century [LP 17]. Besides the camps on Placid Lake, grand seasonal (and, increasingly, year-round) dwellings are scattered through the environs.

LP 1 SCHULTE FAMILY LODGE
3866 Cascade Road (NY 73); 1948; additions 1978, 1980, Rolf Schulte and Hein Gebensleben, designers and builders

During the second half of the 20th century numerous tourist facilities carried Alpine imagery to foster associations between that region and the High Peaks. In many cases the entrepreneurs who undertook these projects were of Germanic lineage. Such was the case with Rolf and Brigit Schulte, who in 1971 purchased a cluster of wooden cabins, still standing toward the rear of the property, built for Robert Taylor shortly after World War II. In 1958 Paul and Eva Hurley had acquired the enterprise and added a swimming pool. Thirteen years later the Schultes took over the operation. Anticipating the 1980 Winter Olympics, they added the two front buildings. Rolf Schulte worked with Gebensleben, a builder of East German origins, on the pair.

LP 2 SARANAC & LAKE PLACID RAILROAD STATION
242 Station Street; 1904

Extending the Chateaugay Railroad's line, the Saranac & Lake Placid Railroad's

tracks connected Lake Placid in 1893. Erected eleven years later, the new station was given a decorous design befitting an affluent resort. It was undertaken by the Delaware & Hudson to serve the consolidated line of the Chateaugay and the New York Central, which met at Saranac Lake. Passenger service ended in 1965, but a tourist train operated by the Adirondack Scenic Railroad between the station and that at Saranac Lake began operations in 2000. Since 1967 the depot has housed the Lake Placid–North Elba Historical Society. Nearby is the **Hurley Brothers store**, built in 1909 by Carter Pierce to purvey grain, hay, lumber, and coal. It remained in continuous ownership at least into the 1990s, but is now vacant.

LP 3 LAKE PLACID CLUB RESORT CONDOMINIUMS

Off Morningside Road, 1980–81, Massanutten Village, Inc., developer; Wallace, McHarg, Roberts & Todd, architects (Philadelphia)

Soon after the Lake Placid Club filed for bankruptcy Massanutten Village, a Virginia-based resort developer, purchased the property for $10.8 million and announced plans for an investment of as much as $160 million over fifteen years. Work started with constructing these time-share units to build business for the hotel that would occupy the renovated clubhouse. Each of the new dwelling units was divided into fifty-two shares (one week). After this complex was completed a halt was called by a state court due to numerous complaints, and not long thereafter Massanutten's CEO, John Swaim, was arrested for grand theft stemming from unpaid loans from several banks. Swaim struggled to keep his Lake Placid development, but the Federal Savings & Loan Insurance Corporation took over ownership in 1985, by which time Swaim had been convicted. No bidders emerged when the complex was again put up for sale. Two years later, however, Guinness PLC (with first a Toronto, then a Baltimore partner) proposed the Gleneagles Resort, a $200-million project that would be realized over ten years. In the face of environmentalist opposition, the developers scaled down their plans, only to withdraw in 1990. A major portion of the former clubhouse burned in 1992 and another section was demolished that same year. The remainder of the complex met the same fate in 2001–02.

Facing one of the former club's upper golf courses, Swaim's condominiums were among the first of their kind in the Adirondacks. Designed by a nationally prominent architecture, landscape, and planning firm, they were intended to respect topography and possess a relatively intimate scale while containing spacious quarters. Later owners have added a number of other clustered units to adjacent land.

LP 4 HOUSE

76 Lake Placid Club Way; ca. early 1950s, Robert Allwork, architect

Allwork's style embodied a mix of tradition and modernity that made it very appealing to some Lake Placid Club members seeking to build a residence during the post–World War II years. Facing what was a club golf course, this house sat amid a cluster of some of the largest member cottages dating from the early 20th century, most of which are now gone. The nearby golf house, also of his design, has been extensively altered.

LP 5 LAKE PLACID HIGH SCHOOL
34 School Street, off Main; south wing designed 1915–16, built 1921–22, Demers, Mosley & Campaigne, architects (Troy); center and north wing, 1934–35, H. O. Fullerton, architect (Albany); later additions

In 1916 Lake Placid residents approved a bond issue for the "finest School in the Adirondacks," one befitting the stature of their community and one that was indeed more ambitious than any other within the Blue Line. Constructed after World War I, the south section was probably conceived to be part of a larger complex. As realized with Public Works Administration funding over a decade later the central section looks as if it had been designed in the 1910s, not the 1930s. Whether Fullerton developed his own scheme to be compatible or simply used drawings prepared some twenty years earlier is unknown. The original section was modified—its entrances removed and its blank, recessed end walls brought out and treated as extensions of the existing window bays. The north section replicates this treatment. The ensemble is more metropolitan in character than what was commonly found in a somewhat remote, predominantly rural area. The track laid out in front of the building as a speed-skating venue for the 1932 Winter Olympics enhances its impressiveness. During that event, the school harbored changing rooms for skaters, as well as spaces for officials and the press.

LP 6 LAKE PLACID OLYMPIC CENTER
2634 Main Street (NY 86); 1931–32, William G. Distin, architect, Arthur G. Wilson, associate; altered 1962–63; 1978–79, Hellmuth, Obata & Kassbaum, architects (St. Louis)

Originally known simply as the **Olympic Arena**, the 1931–32 facility, now named in honor of champion skater and Lake Placid native **Jack Shea (a)**, permitted Olympic

figure skating, hockey, and curling to occur indoors for the first time in the United States. Only arenas located in large urban centers, few of which were constructed solely for athletic purposes, rivaled its size and equipment. Steel arches allowed clearspanning a space measuring 143 by 238 feet and capable of holding over 3,300 people (over 5,000 when the ice sheet was not it use). The arena helped pay for itself after the games, hosting conventions, training sessions, and public skating. Though somewhat disfigured by alterations of 1962–63 and 1978–79, the salient attributes of the structure remain evident.

Designed by the nation's premier specialists in large-scale sports facilities, the tangent **Herb Brooks Arena (b)** (1978–79) exposes its eleven steel trusses, visually interwoven with the projecting glass-enclosed stairways, to give the building a commanding presence. With twice the seating capacity of its predecessor, the building significantly expanded the scope of indoor activities that could occur at a given time during the games and on other occasions. Combined, these two structures comprised the largest and best-equipped indoor skating facility in the United States and have made Lake Placid a major training and exhibition ground for indoor winter sports.

LP 7 LAKE PLACID CONFERENCE CENTER AND VISITORS BUREAU
2608 Main Street; 2009–11, Edgecomb

Design, architects (Warren, Vt.)

The new conference center was erected to augment the arenas, providing space for smaller gatherings and trade shows as part of an ongoing effort to expand Lake Placid's draw as a business destination. The aggressively modernist design abandons rustic clichés while using materials and some forms that allude to regional traditions.

LP 8 UNITED STATES POST OFFICE
2591 Main Street; 1935–36, Louis A. Simon, Supervising Architect of the Treasury (Washington, D.C.)

Abstracting classical motifs with economy and reserve, the staid exterior of this building imparts its civic function. Inside are five murals depicting winter sports painted in 1936–37 by Henry Billings. The artist worked on at least three other New Deal–era post offices.

LP 9 ADIRONDACK COMMUNITY CHURCH
2583 Main Street; 1922–27, Joseph Hudnut, architect (New York); William G. Distin, supervising architect; parish hall (Edmund Hall) 1958

This workmanlike interpretation of English Gothic sources was designed by a professor at Columbia and specialist in church architecture. The tower is clearly an addition, probably erected toward the end of the long construction period. Hudnut went on to head Columbia's School of Architecture in 1933–35, but he is best remembered as the first dean of Harvard's Graduate School of Design, hiring Walter Gropius as its principal instructor and catapulting the program into the limelight of Modern architectural instruction.

LP 10 F. B. GUILD MEN'S STORE
2493 Main Street; 1915–16, Grand Rapids Show Case Company, interior designer (Grand Rapids, Mich.)

One of the most interesting and certainly the most intact of Main Street's early 20th-century commercial buildings is that

built for Forest B. Guild, a well-known merchant dealing in men's clothing, shoes, and sporting goods. Guild contracted with the Grand Rapids Show Case Company, a firm nationally known for its store fixtures, but also one that was beginning to focus on laying out store interiors to maximize convenience, efficiency, and impulse buying—a pioneering pursuit at that time and one that seems to have been a novelty in the Adirondacks. Drawings prepared by the Grand Rapids company were given to an unidentified Saranac Lake architect to design a suitable enclosure. At least some of the second floor was allocated for apartments; Guild's own house lay at the rear bordering Mirror Lake. Little alteration has occurred inside or out. The building will soon be demolished by the new owner, Northwood School [LP 19].

LP 11 BANK OF LAKE PLACID
2483 Main Street; 1915–16, Floyd Brewster, architect; additions 1930; later alterations

One of several buildings of its type in the Adirondacks with monumental overtones, the Bank of Lake Placid exterior was sorely compromised when its cornices were removed in 1956. New ones were added in 2014, but they err from the originals (and violate the classical sense of hierarchy) by having the principal cornice extend above the attic story rather than below it. Little is known about the architect, who had a local practice briefly during the 1910s. Another major example of his work, the **Masonic Building** (1915–16) at 2511 Main, is worth noting even though it, too, has been compromised by the removal of its cornice, in 1946.

LP 12 ST. EUSTACE EPISCOPAL CHURCH
2450 Main Street; 1898–1900, William L. Coulter, architect; moved and enlarged 1926–27, William G. Distin, architect, Arthur G. Wilson, associate

A modest, shingled edifice built to serve the summer colony was moved a quarter century later from its original location near the Stevens House to its current and far more prominent site overlooking Main Street and Mirror Lake, land previously occupied by the parish rectory. Distin heightened the old church, inserting a raised basement, and replaced its diminutive tower with a massive stone one. Otherwise the exterior of the building designed by the founder of his firm was little altered.

LP 13 PALACE THEATER
2432 Main Street; 1925–26, John N. Linn, architect (Brooklyn)

The Palace Theater has been meticulously maintained for nearly ninety years. Built for the Adirondack Theater Corpora-

tion, it was the second largest in the region, seating 1,000 people, surpassed only by the Pontiac in Saranac Lake. Reginald Clark, its owner since 1960, deftly kept the main part of the auditorium intact, while converting the balcony into smaller venues for screening films. The organ is still used, reportedly the last Robert Morgan Orchestral Organ that remains operating in its original place.

LP 14 MALONE BLOCK
2455 Main Street; 1929; storefront remodeled ca. 1980s

The commercial building erected for Leo Malone was for many years the home of Razook's, a high-style women's apparel store that catered to affluent seasonal residents. While the display windows at street level have been modified, the decorous classical enframement remains. Above is a pair of additional display windows, slightly projecting and articulated with lacy ironwork—a treatment befitting the elegant wares once available there.

LP 15 LAKEVIEW MOTOR INN
1 Mirror Lake Road at Saranac Avenue; 1961–62

Originally called the Lakeside Motor Inn, this was among the first of a new generation of hostelries in Lake Placid. Set back from the street, each room opening to a private outdoor sitting area overlooking a broad lawn and Mirror Lake, the Lakeview combined some of the amenities associated with a resort hotel with the conveniences of a contemporary motel. The complex significantly expanded the operations of Peter Roland, whose Homestead Inn, a modest but highly popular establishment, stood just across Saranac Avenue since the early 20th century. That building was replaced by a Hilton Hotel (now High Peaks Resort) in anticipation of the 1980 Winter Olympics.

LP 16 MIRROR LAKE INN
77 Main Street; 1988, CI Design, architects (Boston), Richard Rankin, principal-in-charge

Though of recent construction, this locally renowned hostelry has an unusual and rich past. The core of the original building was erected in 1871 as a house by an early settler, Benjamin Brush, who sold most of his remaining acreage to hoteliers John A. and George A. Stevens. Using her mother's money, Clemina Alford purchased the building around 1925 and converted it to a hotel. An enterprising and determined businesswoman, Alford started hotel-keeping in her parents' Lake Placid house when she was seventeen. She later moved to Massachusetts where she married William Rufus Wyckoff, who had become financially well-off for his role in setting up the Fuller Brush Company's system of door-to-door sales.

Soon the couple relocated in Lake Placid. While he became active in the Chamber of Commerce, she developed her business. Soon the Mirror Lake Inn (originally using Melvil Dewey's spelling Mir-a-Lak) became a celebrated place for eating and gathering among locals as well as tourists. Numerous additions and alterations were made prior to World War II, with the mansarded house given an accretive, vaguely colonial, aura. During the Depression and postwar years, when most Lake Placid hotels were experiencing hard times, the Mirror Lake Inn continued to flourish, becoming the community's premier place for dining and overnight accommodation.

Eventually Clemina's son Robert was given ownership of the operation. To his mother's dismay (she sued him) he sold it to Edward Weibrecht in 1976. After the main building burned to the ground in 1988, it was reconstructed using a steel frame and other fire-resistant materials, but fashioned along the lines of its predecessor inside and out to evoke a sense of continuity of the place.

One of the hotel's annexes, **Lake House** (directly across the street), survived the fire. Its date of construction is unknown, but it may have been part of the inn's early expansion program in the 1920s.

LP 17 SIGNAL HILL HOUSES

Aside from the camps facing Placid Lake, a number of stylish cottages were erected on Signal Hill, many of them on land purchased from the Stevens House. Built for a Philadelphian, **John W. Naylor, Bide-a-Wee (a)** (1899–1900) at 213 Victor Herbert Drive is one of architect William L. Coulter's early designs, using Tudor imagery, of which he seems to have been especially fond. Later, it was occupied by Metropolitan Opera diva Alma Gluck and her husband, violinist Efram Zimbalist. Across the street at 190 Stevens Road, **Malcolm MacDonald's Awassnook (b)** (1895) was among the first cottages in the precinct. The owners were habitués of the Mirror Lake House until it burned and purchased the land for their cottage soon thereafter. Little is known about the **Silo House (c)** (ca. 1899) at 174 Stevens Road, so named because of its miniature turret. It may have been constructed as an elaborate stable that was later converted to residential use. Coulter designed **Hetscamp** (1902–03) at 154 Stevens Road for **George S. Daniels (d)**, the general passenger agent of the New York Central Railroad, orienting the house to the sweeping southern views. On

the other hand the **house (e)** at 92 Stevens Road was not well situated for vistas and has a standard frontal orientation. **George Hamlin (f)**, a nationally prominent tenor, commissioned Max Westhoff to design the

chalet-inspired residence at 26 Swiss Road in 1916. As this enclave was taking shape, around 1906, **George A. Stevens** himself used a more visible lot at 2357 Saranac Avenue for his own elaborate year-round **house (g)**, which is a spirited interpretation of the Colonial Revival.

LP 18 CAMP ALTAI
312 Mirror Lake Road; 2012–13, Nils Luderowski, architect
An imaginative design inspired by Shingle Style and Arts and Crafts precedents, this dwelling fits well within the realm of early 20th-century resort architecture in the region.

LP 19 NORTHWOOD SCHOOL
92 Northwood Road; 1911–12, Max Westhoff, architect; gymnasium 1913–14, Westhoff; west and south wings 1928–29, William G. Distin, architect, Arthur G. Wilson, associate; science wing 1948, Distin; later alterations and additions

Northwood began at the Lake Placid Club in 1905 as a program for sons of members and others sponsored by members. Originally housed in club cottages, the school expanded quickly, prompting it to erect permanent quarters, where students could board, on land owned by the club just north of its campus. Architect Max Westhoff, who had worked on other projects for the club, developed a design that was compatible with the main lodge, while also distinct in its appropriation of references to German postmedieval vernacular sources. When the school's head, John M. Hopkins, retired in 1921, the plant was taken over by a newly formed girl's school, Montemare, which was also created under the club's auspices. The Lake Placid Club Educational Foundation purchased the property in 1926, at which time it was given the name Northwood School.

Though the overall effect is accretive, each addition to the building deviated little from earlier portions in its elements and details—a tribute to school tradition, perhaps, but also to an architectural firm's pursuit of continuity over several decades.

LP 20 PIERCE HOUSE

32 Cobble Hill Road; ca. 1915

Much information remains to be found about this house, reputedly designed for an owner of S. S. Pierce & Company of Boston by an artist friend. What appears to be an extensive use of logs for rafters, purlins, posts, and brackets may in fact be more decorative than structural, but nonetheless gives the house a spirited and somewhat unorthodox character.

LP 21 W. ALTON JONES CELL SCIENCE CENTER

48 Barn Road; 1968–71, James L. Coquillard, architect (office base unknown)

A longstanding national need for a permanent laboratory devoted to cell science research was met by Nettie Marie Jones as a memorial to her late husband, W. Alton Jones, former chairman of the board of Cities Service oil company (Citco) and prominent Lake Placid summer resident. Encompassing 44,000 square feet the facility included spaces for small conferences and for experiments in genetics, immunology, virology, and insect physiology. The W. Alton Jones Foundation contributed both

to the building's construction and to operations through 1979. Subsequently it was taken over by the newly formed W. Alton Jones Cell Science Center, which increased staffing tenfold and acquired an international reputation for its work. The center was dissolved in 1996 and the plant was taken over by another new organization, the Adirondack Biomedical Research Institute. It too dissolved, in 2000, leaving the building vacant and perhaps underscoring the challenges of maintaining major research facilities in so remote a location.

LP 22 MINIATURE GOLF COURSES

Facing one another, two miniature golf courses built more or less concurrently exhibit the highly scenographic approach to designing such facilities in recent decades. **Pirate's Cove Adventure Golf (a)** at 1980 Saranac Avenue is part of a Michigan-based chain that earlier built a course at Lake George [LG 2]. Opening in 2003, this unit replaced Around the World, a miniature golf course developed in the mid-1970s. **Boots and Birdies Miniature Golf (b)** (ca. 2002) at 1991 Saranac Avenue was designed as Edge of the Forest by Brian Marshall. The project was taken over and completed by Lake Placid entrepreneur Steve Wilson. The Marshall family regained ownership around 2011.

LP 23 WHITEFACE LODGE

2231 Saranac Avenue at Whiteface Inn Road; 2002–05, Resort Contracting, designer-builder

Since 2000 Lake Placid has again become a place of grand resort hotels, although they are neither as numerous nor as conspicuously situated as their 19th-century predecessors. Whiteface Lodge is a striking example of how an ordinary location can be transformed into a spectacular, somewhat inward-looking environment. The hotel was conceived by Joseph Barile, a local entrepreneur, for whom it became a work of passion. In developing the design,

Barile made a study of both Adirondack camps and hotels in the western national parks. Beyond effect, he and his wife, Priscilla, who designed much of the interior work, paid unusual attention to detail and craftsmanship in what was a very ambitious design-build project. Inside and out the building has much of the feel of a great early 20th-century rustic hotel, including a sumptuous use of materials and execution seldom found today. At the same time, the design is quite original in its motifs, spatial development, and layout.

LP 24 LAKE PLACID LODGE
Near end of Lodge Way, off Whiteface Inn Road; 2006–08, Truex Cullens, architects (Burlington, Vt.)
Lake Placid Lodge is an equally spirited reinterpretation of rustic architecture from the turn of the 20th century, although the vocabulary is quite different and the main

building alludes to large country houses more than hotels. The establishment lies on the shore of Placid Lake (compensating somewhat for the loss of the nearby Whiteface Inn), where a private camp was built in 1882. After World War II that camp became an inn called Placid Manor. In the mid-1980s it was purchased by David and Christie Garrett, who had turned Wonundra, the Rockefeller camp on Upper Saranac Lake, into a posh hotel. The Garretts developed their new acquisition as a five-star restaurant and hotel, renaming it Lake Placid Lodge. The building burned in 2005. Its much more ambitious successor manifests their goal to bring a new affluent clientele to the area.

RAY BROOK
Town of North Elba, Essex County

RB 1 TOURIST FACILITIES
The enormous state hospital at Ray Brook drew many family members and friends of patients, creating a market for inexpensive overnight accommodations. The location was also attractive for vacationers in search of less costly rooms than those available in Lake Placid and Saranac Lake. Among the several cabin clusters developed there during the interwar decades, two have survived as especially good examples. The **Tail o' the Pup restaurant and Evergreen Camps (a)** (1927 and later) at 1152 NY 86 was preceded by a tearoom built around 1919. The small, drive-up eatery that replaced it is an unusually intact example of a type once common

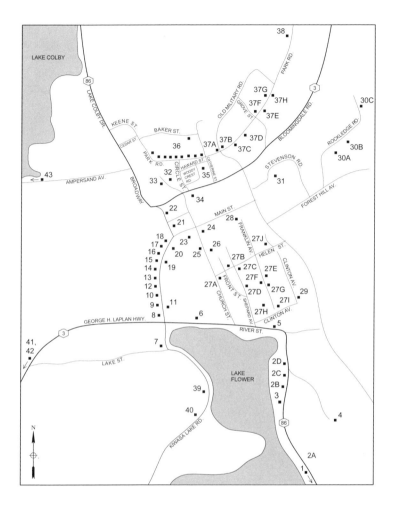

along American highways. The adjacent cabins were probably erected in the 1930s.

A short distance to the west lie **Moreno's Cottages (b)** (1926 and later) at 322 Ray Brook Road, just off NY 86. Anthony Moreno came to the area after World War I, afflicted with tuberculosis. Upon recuperating, he erected a small house and developed a chicken farm in 1926–27. After marrying a nurse from the Ray Brook hospital, he constructed a larger house in 1930 and converted the original one into a rental cabin to supplement a meager income. This modest enterprise proved sufficiently profitable to build a range of nine

additional cabins by 1934—all constructed by Moreno himself. Within a decade, the exteriors received "brainstorm" (live edge) siding to give them a more rustic appearance. The complex remains little changed, now maintained by Moreno's niece and her husband.

SARANAC LAKE

Towns of Harrietstown and St. Armand, Franklin County, and Town of North Elba, Essex County

Framed by hills on all four sides, Saranac

309

Lake has a relatively high density of development, with a street configuration that is more irregular than in most Adirondack communities. Although it has lost all but one of its in-town hotels and some other key landmarks, the village has among the richest arrays of late 19th- and, especially, of early 20th-century architecture in the region. The commercial center, extending primarily along a two-block stretch of Main Street, thence Broadway, is the most urban in character within the Blue Line. The care of TB patients brought more than the usual amount of revenue to many residents and did so on a year-round rather than seasonal basis. Thus, in contrast to communities such as Ticonderoga or Keeseville, where a relatively small number of industrialists commanded much of the wealth, Saranac Lake had a relatively stable middle class. This general prosperity is evident in many parts of the residential tracts that occupy the slopes surrounding the core. Most of the largest dwellings were constructed for the affluent who suffered from tuberculosis or their physicians. While evidence can be found of the economic decline that persisted after the village lost its primary economic base, efforts to introduce new sources of revenue have spawned gains in recent years.

After World War I playwright Edward F. Albee and a small group of prominent vaudevillians organized National Vaudeville Artists to provide care for ailing performers, acquiring forty acres of then rural land south of the village in 1925. Two years later a subsidiary was created to erect a hospital for tubercular victims. Funds were sufficient for Scopes to design a rambling Tudorish pile that looked more like a high-end apartment building of the period than a hospital. Residents had private rooms and could partake in embellished public spaces. Six years after it opened the institution was transferred to the Will Rogers Memorial Commission to accommodate all those who worked in the entertainment industry. Following its closure in 1974, the building remained vacant, save for a brief occupation by the press corps during the 1980 Winter Olympics and an unsuccessful attempt to convert it to time-share apartments, until it was purchased in 1996 and rehabilitated as a retirement community.

SL 2 MOTELS

The village's emergence as a tourist destination is chronicled through the construction of these motels sited on Lake Flower. The **Sara-Placid Motor Inn (a)** (ca.

1959; originally Riebel's Lake Flower Motel) at 445 Lake Flower Avenue (NY 86) is a classic example of modest-sized facilities that proliferated during the mid-20th century, here oriented to one of the lake's coves. Farther north the **Lakeside Motel (b)** (1958) at No. 258 was designed by Distin & Wareham with two ranges of rooms (the owner's residence above one of them) facing one an-

SL 1 WILL ROGERS MEMORIAL HOSPITAL
78 Will Rogers Drive, off NY 86; 1928–29,
William H. Scopes, architect

other. Additional units were added about four years later. Next door, the **Adirondack Motel (c)** (before 1958) at No. 248 had a similar arrangement with extensive alterations and additions made around 1963. Finally the **Lake Flower Inn (d)** (ca. 1955) at No. 234 has capacious owner's quarters and a swimming pool by the lake. As a group they afford good illustration of the scale, character, and variations found in independently developed motels of the era.

SL 3 MOUNTAIN MIST ICE CREAM STAND
260 Lake Flower Avenue; 1952

Amid the motels is probably the first example in the Adirondacks of a post–World War II phenomenon, stands dispensing frozen custard. With a canted, glazed serving space, Mountain Mist's configuration was a standard one for such drive-up establishments. Freeman Baker commissioned the structure to enhance his adjacent marina. Well maintained by the present owners, it is an all-too-rare vestige of the era.

SL 4 GENERAL HOSPITAL OF SARANAC LAKE
End of Winona Avenue; 1912–13, Harry Leslie Walker and Beverly King, architects (New York); additions 1923; later additions

At a time when hospitals were still primarily fixtures of sizable urban centers, Saranac Lake received what was probably the Adirondacks' first purpose-built facility of this kind through a gift from Redfield and Emily Dutton Proctor, who owned a camp on Placid Lake. The original building (central section and south wing) housed a mere twelve patients. The five-room north wing and a ten-room maternity wing were added in 1923.

When the facility was replaced by a much larger hospital in 1967, the building became the administrative center for the newly formed North Country Community College. Two years later Benjamin Thompson Associates, a distinguished architectural firm based in Cambridge,

Massachusetts, was commissioned to prepare a master plan for the 117-acre site. Thompson unveiled a proposal, which included designs for five buildings, in 1970, but nothing came of his scheme.

SL 5 NORTH ELBA TOWN HOUSE
193 River Street; 1927, Paul Jaquet, architect

The fact that a substantial portion of people residing in the town of North Elba also live within the village of Saranac Lake prompted the construction of this annex to the town hall in Lake Placid. Bringing greater efficiency to voting and judicial proceedings were among the objectives, but town leaders also likely wanted to establish a political presence as their Harrietstown counterparts were erecting a very impressive building nearby [SL 8]. Though modest in size, the building is indeed conspicuous with a Greek temple front inspired by early 19th-century examples in the northeastern states.

SL 6 ST. BERNARD'S SCHOOL
32 River Street; 1923–24, Paul Jaquet, architect

For his church, Jaquet designed a compact, yet impressive school building that weaves Tudor-inspired motifs into a forceful, quasi-abstract composition.

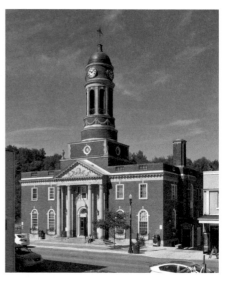

SL 7 PAUL SMITH'S ELECTRIC LIGHT, POWER & RAILROAD COMPANY BUILDING

3 Main Street; 1927, John Sweeney, designer

Two years after forming his own power company, Paul Smith acquired the Saranac Lake Electric Company as part of his campaign to develop the area's principal utilities operation. By the time this building was erected for son Phelps Smith, the company was providing services as far afield as Tupper Lake. The site, where the Saranac River is dammed to become Lake Flower, was first developed for a sawmill in 1827, when the area was still mostly wilderness. In 1894 the Saranac Lake Electric Company built a powerhouse on the site, to which Smith's building became the frontispiece. Although somewhat awkward and naïve in its design, the new steel-frame terra-cotta–clad building was a powerful manifestation of the Smith family's pivotal role in the area. The ground floor was devoted to a showroom for appliances; office space (mostly one large room) occupied the second floor, while the third was used for public meetings and appliance demonstrations—all served by an electric elevator (its equipment housed in a decorated tower). The adjacent bridge was probably done in conjunction with the project. The dam was rebuilt first with WPA funds in 1938 and again around the 1980s. The village has owned Smith's building since 1986.

SL 8 HARRIETSTOWN TOWN HALL

39 Main Street; 1926–28, Scopes & Feustmann, architects

Heralding the entry to Saranac Lake's commercial center, this grand building was constructed at the height of the village's prosperity, replacing the 1886 town hall on the same site that burned in 1926. The architects drew freely from an array of late 18th- and early 19th-century American classical sources, most conspicuously the work of Charles Bulfinch in eastern Massachusetts. Here, precedents were interpreted with a greater sense of grandeur to create an impressive public building. An auditorium that has been used for events of all kinds, including Big Band dances, occupies a good portion of the facility at the rear.

SL 9 TOUSLEY BUILDING

47–49 Main Street; 1924, A. L. McGill, architect (Rye, N.Y.)

A single block of Main Street encompasses an unusual variety of commercial buildings spanning nearly a century of development. The terra-cotta–faced Tousley Building was constructed as a sales and service facility for Dodge automobiles.

SL 10 MILO MILLER STORE
51–53 Main Street; 1867, later alterations

Next door, the small wood-frame building that was originally Milo Miller's store is the oldest of its kind to remain in Saranac Lake and was one of the few emporia operating when E. L. Trudeau arrived in the mid-1870s. Miller sold flour, groceries, sugar, tobacco, and medicines. He was the grandson of Pliny Miller, the second known settler in the community.

SL 11 COMMERCIAL BUILDING
50–52 Main Street; ca. 1880s–90s and later

Little is known about this three-story wood-frame building, which appears to have been built in two stages. The projecting storefronts and second-story porch suggest an addition from around the turn of the 20th century, the porches to accommodate TB patients.

SL 12 COMMERCIAL BUILDING
57–59 Main Street; 1879; 1900

To the north of Miller's store is a larger wood-frame structure capped by a mansard roof built for him about a decade later. It is mostly hidden from view by the front that was added in 1900. The new façade is a good example of the extensive glazing used on upper floors of many commercial buildings at the turn of the 20th century.

SL 13 DONALDSON BLOCK
63–65 Main Street; 1901

The Donaldson Block is more historicizing than its neighbor to the south, with an arched center section (originally with recessed porches) and a pronounced cornice. Owner Alfred L. Donaldson, a banker who later wrote the landmark *History of the Adirondacks* (1921), came to Saranac Lake to treat his tuberculosis. He intended the apartments on the upper two floors of this speculative commercial building to accommodate other patients. Among the early tenants was photographer William L. Distin, whose son became one of the region's leading architects.

SL 14 HAASE BLOCK

67 Main Street; 1907, Scopes & Feustmann, architects; ground floor altered 1987, Wareham, De Lair, architects

The steel-frame Haase Block is another business building with upper floors tailored to TB sufferers. A young Episcopal clergyman and heir to a food-distribution company in St. Louis, William Haase contracted tuberculosis and came to Saranac Lake accompanied by his wife and her mother in 1903. With his improving health, the couple decided to remain and immersed themselves in business and civic affairs. The ground floor originally housed the offices of the building's architects, as well as the Saranac Lake National Bank and a jewelry store.

SL 15 HUDSON RIVER TELEPHONE COMPANY EXCHANGE

69 Main Street; 1909, probably Max Westhoff, architect

This building was owned by Max Westhoff and is likely his design. Its cornice was removed in 1964 and replaced by a smaller one eighteen years later.

SL 16 MARINE MIDLAND BANK

75 Main Street; 1906–07, Coulter & Westhoff, architects; new front and other alterations 1962–63

Coulter & Westhoff designed this building for the Adirondack National Bank, which was founded by Donaldson and two other TB patients, in a vigorously rendered classical composition. It was arguably the most impressive bank building in the Adirondacks until its façade was demolished and interior extensively remade for the Marine Midland Bank in the early 1960s. Many preservationists still decry the loss. At the same time, the new design is a solid rendition of the modernist aesthetic from the mid-20th century and makes for a striking counterpoint in the urban landscape, underscoring Main Street's long history as a commercial hub.

SL 17 FOWLER BLOCK

77 Main Street; 1900, William H. Scopes, architect; rear addition 1926, William G. Distin, architect

Designed by Scopes before he established his own office, the Fowler Block gives special emphasis to the porches accommodating TB patients—an early indication of the focus the architect would devote to such problems in future years. W. Smith Fowler owned a livery service and speculated in real estate.

SL 18 ROBERTS BLOCK

79 Main Street; 1900; storefront altered 1923, Robert Voris, architect (New York)

The Roberts Block follows the same basic program as the Fowler, but has a more massive street face. William F. Roberts was one of the village's pioneer real estate brokers. In 1923 Thomas F. Finnegan leased the retail space at ground level, opening a clothing store that would enjoy prominence into the 21st century. The storefront created for Finnegan has a recessed entry, which was a new device intended to augment window displays and lure customers inside. The emporium has survived virtually unchanged.

SL 19 COULTER BLOCK

78–84 Main Street; 1899–1901, William L. Coulter, architect; ground floor of nos. 82–84 altered

The Coulter Block is actually two buildings that were erected in rapid succession, their spaces joined at the upper two levels. Owned by Coulter, they provided additional revenue as well as space for his firm's office. They also helped set a new standard for appearances and accommodations in the commercial district.

SL 20 W. C. LEONARD & COMPANY DEPARTMENT STORE

86 Main Street; ca. 1897–1900; addition ca. 1905–06; new front 1922–23, Paul Jaquet, architect; later alterations

When first built, Leonard's department

store looked more like a holdover from earlier decades than Coulter's building. Established by Marcellus and son William C. Leonard, the emporium emphasized affordability over fashion. The business prospered, prompting a four-bay addition to the southwest. It replicated aspects of its predecessor, but the streetfront was treated as a single composition at two levels, with a wide, recessed entry and display windows extending the length of the second floor. Later the first section was likewise modified and other details altered to unify and modernize the entire façade.

SL 21 LOOMIS BLOCK
14–16 Broadway; 1898–99 and later

What was originally a three-story brick building was erected for Frederick W. and Hattie G. Loomis to accommodate their store on the ground floor and apartments above. The emporium thrived as a major purveyor of hunting equipment and school supplies, subsequently expanding to encompass timepieces, jewelry, household appliances, and dry goods. In 1920 the property was sold to George and Annabell Downing, who had the ground floor modified into three store units, the fronts of which remain intact. Later in that decade the third floor was damaged by fire and not rebuilt. It was probably after the fire that the exterior was stuccoed.

SL 22 ADIRONDACK HARDWARE COMPANY
28 Broadway; ca. 1897–98

The largest store building in downtown and one of Saranac Lake's major businesses was developed by partners Michael J. Callanan, whose brother William headed the area's leading building supply firm [SL 33], and George L. Stark, a former schoolteacher who later married Callanan's sister. (A third partner sold out soon after the building's completion.) The emporium supplied furnishings for many of the houses William's firm constructed and

developed an international trade as manufacturer of the "Adirondack recliner"—a chair tailored to TB patients. Renamed George L. Starks & Company in the 1920s, the business continued until 1962. Subsequently it served as a furniture and later a hardware store.

SL 23 HOTEL SARANAC
100 Main Street; 1926–28, Scopes & Feustmann, architects

Scopes was the developer as well as the architect of this massive pile. Building a hotel of a kind that was emblematic of a substantial urban center was an audacious move even as the village was experiencing unprecedented prosperity. Scopes sold bonds to most businesspeople in the community and many others as well. With 100 rooms, an arcade, and a grand ballroom and roof garden on the second floor, the six-story hotel was a local sensation. But it was not a financial success and nearly ruined Scopes. Paul Smith's College purchased the building in 1961 for its hotel-management school, operating it for several decades. It is currently being rehabilitated as part of another ambitious plan to have the village become a major tourist destination.

SL 24 EPISCOPAL CHURCH OF ST. LUKE THE BELOVED PHYSICIAN

136 Main Street at Church Street (NY 86); 1878–79, Richard Michell Upjohn, architect (New York); later alterations; parish hall 1891 and rectory 1890s, both Renwick, Aspinwall & Renwick, architects (New York)

This accomplished High Victorian Gothic design was the work of a specialist [see also BL 6, Section 1], whose father had been the dean of Protestant church architecture before the Civil War. E. L. Trudeau chaired the building committee of this, the first church in the village, and served as warden and treasurer for thirty-eight years. The parish hall also housed Saranac Lake's library until 1907. The sanctuary was altered in 1938–39.

SL 25 SARANAC LABORATORY FOR THE STUDY OF TUBERCULOSIS

89 Church Street; 1894, Renwick, Aspinwall & Renwick, architects (New York); Joseph Baxter Black Memorial Laboratory (to south) added 1926, G. G. Symes and R. W. McLaughlin, architects (office base unknown); second levels of both buildings added 1934, Holden, McLaughlin & Associates, architects

Built for Trudeau with funds from philanthropist George C. Cooper, who was also a friend and patient, it was the first building designed for the study of tuberculosis in the United States. The facility contained pathology, bacteriology, and chemistry laboratories, which proved instrumental in research that further isolated the causes of the disease. J. Lawrence Aspinwall, the partner-in-charge of the design, was Trudeau's cousin. The facility closed in 1964; Paul Smith's College occupied the premises between 1966 and 1987. In 1998 it was donated to Historic Saranac Lake, which operates it as the Saranac Laboratory Museum.

SL 26 HUGH M. KINGHORN HOUSE

78 Church Street; ca. 1880; extensively remodeled 1917, Scopes & Feustmann, architects

The architects' remaking of this house for a prominent physician specializing in the treatment of tuberculosis gives little indication that an older building lies at its core. A number of physicians resided in the vicinity, clustered around Trudeau's dwelling at the southwest corner of Church and Main streets.

SL 27 HELEN HILL HOUSES

This speculative subdivision was spearheaded by Lake Placid attorney Frederick Isham, who also lobbied for Saranac Lake's incorporation. He had the land surveyed in 1892 and acquired additional acreage over the following two years. Work began grading streets in 1896. Over eighty houses were built on the tract by 1908; fewer than twenty between then and 1931. Helen Hill was an important proving ground for the design of cure cottages. Physician Lawrason Brown, medical director at Trudeau's sanitarium, began experiments with having patients sleep on porches around 1901–02, and this feature soon became a standard component of any building housing those so afflicted. Early on, upstairs porches were added to many dwellings, but they became an integral design feature in new construction. Sliding windows were often used to allow shelter from the elements.

Designed by Scopes & Feustmann and built around 1911–13 for a local merchant, the **Earl Lanier Gray house (a)** at 27 Helen Street also weaves sitting and sleeping porches into its compact mass, suggesting that a member of the family suffered from TB or that the owners may have planned to take in one or more patients. It became a cure cottage in 1925. Silas Blauvelt, the builder of the **Noyes boardinghouse (b)**

at 35 Helen Street (ca. 1898), constructed it as a speculative investment, leasing it as a boardinghouse. In 1908 it was sold to Mary and Catherine Noyes and continued its function. Over the years a number of porches were added to the second and third floors, effectively transforming it into a cure cottage. The **Kennedy cottage (c)** (1897) at 98 Shepard Avenue is a good example of a small private sanitarium, or cure cottage. The National Vaudeville Artists sent patients there before completion of its own facility [SL 1]. The **Morse cottage (d)** (before 1908) at 90 Shepard is similarly an instructive example of a purpose-built cure cottage where porches are an integral part of the building.

Little is known about the early 20th-century **house (e)** at 84 Franklin Street, with its spirited and economical interpretation of Alpine motifs, save that it was probably not built to accommodate patients. Across the street at No. 83, **Bide-A-Wee (f)** was erected in 1901 as a single-family residence and later modified to serve as a cure cottage, one of four on the block operated by Anna Fallon Burnett. The **Neil cottage (g)** (ca. 1910–11) at 76 Franklin was

artfully designed to accommodate TB patients, with four levels of porches at its rear. Built in 1908 for a physician, S. Lusgarten, the **Bogie cottage (h)** at 25 Franklin was designed by Coulter & Westhoff. It was transformed into a sanitarium during the 1920s, with an array of porches that are well integrated into the overall design. Far grander than other Helen Hill dwellings, the **Daniel W. Riddle house (i)** was built around 1898–1900 at 8 Franklin Street for a Civil War veteran who came to the

village afflicted with tuberculosis in 1878. After his health improved Riddle became manager of the fashionable Saranac Inn on Upper Saranac Lake in 1886. He was also well versed in building and directed the early construction at Trudeau's sanitarium. Riddle prospered sufficiently to erect (and perhaps design) this impressive, if somewhat disjointed, essay in the Colonial Revival. After his death the house was run by his widow as a cure cottage. The **D'Aigneau cottage annex (j)** (1923) at 103 Helen Street is a late example of the cure cottage. It may have been adapted from a pattern-book design.

Jacob Smith Moody, one of Saranac Lake's first settlers, who came in 1819. Initiated as a family cemetery during the mid-19th century (the oldest headstone dates to 1843), plots also were given freely to others. In 1894 one and one half acres were acquired by St. Bernard's Catholic Church. Pine Ridge was incorporated in 1916, purchasing what until then had been known as the Moody Cemetery or the Old Protestant Cemetery. The terracing and stone retaining walls appear to date from that period, as does the abundance of now mature trees, some planted in a row, others more informally. In 1919 the Hebrew Memorial Cemetery was dedicated on part of the tract.

SL 28 RECEPTION HOSPITAL
129 Franklin Street; 1903–05, Scopes & Feustmann, architects

Initiated at E. L. Trudeau's urging by Mary Prescott, this building was developed as a nursing facility for seriously ill tuberculosis patients—ten ambulatory, ten bedridden. Having "recovered" from the disease herself, Prescott raised the necessary funds and helped support its operation. The commission launched its architects' careers as hospital specialists. The institution closed in 1949 for lack of funds, after which it housed the educational activities of the TB patients' Study and Craft Guild. For a while it served as a girls' dormitory for North Country Community College, and it is now an apartment building.

SL 29 PINE RIDGE CEMETERY
Entered from Fawn Street, off Pine Street

Situated on a gently sloping site, Pine Ridge is the product of gradual evolution. The land was part of a farm developed by

SL 30 ROCKLEDGE

Rockledge was one of two planned subdivisions spurred by the success of Highland Park [SL 37], but with larger lots set in informal arrangements that responded to the irregular topography. The Rockledge Company was formed in 1909 under the auspices of Walter Cluett, president of Arrow Shirts, who was instrumental in securing the Olmsted Brothers to prepare the town improvement plan and commissioned them to design this seventy-three-acre subdivision as well. Joining Cluett in the venture were Arthur Chalmers, a manufacturer from New York; George Duryee, Highland Park's first resident [SL 37c]; and Eddy Whitby, a real estate broker from Montclair, New Jersey. The project failed to meet expectations; only six houses were constructed by 1940.

Sizable dwellings commissioned to accommodate an individual tuberculosis patient generally avoided any overt signs of their underlying purpose. Built in 1915 for **Peyton Clark**, a civil engineer whose wife suffered from the disease, **Woodthorpe (a)** at 36 Rockledge Lane is one of the few houses erected in the subdivision during its initial decade. Scopes & Feustmann created a suave rendition of contemporary Arts and Crafts design that discreetly weaves the porches into the mass at one side.

Well-developed examples of Modern residential architecture from the mid-20th century are few and far between in the Adirondacks. As with many such dwellings, **Arthur Wareham's** own **house (b)** (1958) at 46 Rockledge is oriented to the rear yard rather than the street. Like much of Wareham's work it was designed to be constructed quickly, easily, and economically.

Built around 1911–12 for **Arthur Stanley**, the founder of Stanley Tool Company, the **house (c)** at 66 Rockledge helped set a tone for development that surely pleased the subdivision's developers. Despite its size, this dwelling has an understated entrance, set below the main floor. The informality of the whole composition offers contrast to the nearby Clark house. It may also have been designed by Scopes & Feustmann.

SL 31 ANDREW BAKER HOUSE – ROBERT LOUIS STEVENSON COTTAGE
45 Stevenson Lane; 1865–66 and later

This small dwelling, one of the oldest in the village, was built for Andrew Baker, a successful local guide, who rented out space to sportsmen and later adapted it as a cure cottage. It gained celebrity when Stevenson spent the winter there in 1887–88. The house remained in the family until the Stevenson Society of America purchased it in the mid-1920s, preserving the property as a small museum.

SL 32 UNION DEPOT
Depot Street; 1904

The most impressive railroad depot in

the Adirondacks, this facility also likely had the most year-round traffic. The first train of the Chateaugay Railroad (D&H) arrived in 1887, the first of the New York Central five years later. Between the 1910s and 1930s eighteen to twenty trains came daily. The D&H terminated service in 1946, New York Central in 1965. After lying vacant in an advancing state of decay for three decades it was restored (without its massive stone porte-cochere) in 1997–98, reopening two years later to serve the Adirondack Scenic Railroad.

SL 33 BRANCH & CALLANAN OFFICES
33 Depot Street; 1930–31, Scopes & Feustmann, architects

One of the largest building supply and contracting firms in the Adirondacks, the company was formed with the partnership of Augustine Branch from Keene and William J. Callanan from Keeseville, where he had been superintendent of the furniture department of Rufus Prescott & Sons [Section 7]. By 1896 the operation was making doors, sash, and blinds. It began constructing houses by 1902; six years later it had some sixty buildings to its credit, with over 500 employees. Among the firm's major projects were the Hotel Saranac [SL 23], Sanatorium Gabriels [GA 4], many buildings for the Trudeau Sanatorium [SL 38], and the Will Rogers Memorial Hospital [SL 1].

Son Andrew Callanan took over the operation in 1941, but only three years later he was succeeded by Marie Jaquet, whose husband, architect Paul Jaquet, became vice-president. In 1950 William G. Distin Jr. joined the company. He became manager three years later and bought Branch & Callanan in 1960, continuing operations until

319

1993. Unlike his father, Distin never became an architect, but he did design some of the buildings his firm constructed.

A major fire ravaged the property in 1930, leaving only the office building, which was burned to the point it was rebuilt. Adjacent to the north lies a large **lumber shed**, which was probably constructed at the same time as the offices.

SL 34 DRURY COTTAGE
52 Bloomingdale Avenue; ca. 1912, probably Peter Tanzini, builder

Built for livery operator Merton Drury, this highly individualistic cure cottage, much of it faced in cobblestones, was likely the work of Peter Tanzini, who came from Italy to install the Italian-made altar at St. Bernard's Catholic Church (1910–11), and remained as a builder specializing in cobblestone work.

SL 35 ALBERT HENRY ALLEN HOUSE
11 Woodycrest Road; 1909, Scopes & Feustmann, architects

A compact residence with a complex composition and boldly scaled entrance porch and chimney that render the effect more impressive than the actual dimensions might suggest, this dwelling is another example of the architects' ability to downplay the cure cottage function.

SL 36 COTTAGE ROW

What has long been called Cottage Row is the best-known and densest concentration of purpose-built facilities for the care of tuberculosis patients in the village. Calvin Brown subdivided fifteen acres of his farm for this purpose in 1896, and the first cure cottage was erected there five years later. The remainder of this precinct was formerly on Ensine Miller's hop farm. The block in this latter tract bounded by Park Avenue and Catherine, Baker, and Circle streets was purchased by Scopes & Feustmann and developed by them during the early 1910s. The **Helen Scopes Turner cottage (a)** (ca. 1910) and **Feustmann cottage (b)** (1910) at 76 Catherine Street and 185 Park Avenue, respectively, are known to be their work. In all likelihood, the firm also designed the **Charles Wicker cottage (c)** (ca. 1910), **Clara Black cottage (d)** (ca. 1910), and another **cottage (e)** (ca. 1912) at 177, 169, and 172 Park Avenue, respectively, as well as the **cottage (f)** (before 1911) at 88 Baker Street. Despite the speculative, for-profit complexion of this venture the architects appear to have gone to great lengths to make the precinct look like a middle-class suburb, bereft of any institutional overtones, with each building given a distinct design.

In contrast, the **Coleman-Gonzalez sanitarium (g)** (ca. 1918) at 163 Park Avenue, designed by Edgar T. Coleman, head draftsman for Scopes & Feustmann and himself a victim of tuberculosis, is the village's largest surviving example of a single-building commercial sanitarium and clearly enunciates its purpose. With a capacity of twenty-five patients, the facility was extensively used by National Vaudeville Artists until its own sanitarium was built [SL 1]. Alfredo Gonzalez, who had come from Puerto Rico for the cure in the mid-1920s, acquired the building in 1935. He catered to Spanish-speaking people. His most famous patient was Manuel Quezon, president of the Philippines. After moving his government-in-exile to Washington during World War II, Quezon came to Gonzalez's sanitarium in 1944 and died later that year.

Though more domestic in character, the **Collins-Beattie (h)** (before 1910) and **Richards (j)** (ca. 1923) **cottages** at 153 and 145 Park Avenue, respectively, have extensive porches on two levels as integral components. Such may have been the case on all three levels of the **Arms cottage (i)** (ca. 1910) at 149 Park, with the upper two later enclosed. The **Louis Y. Clark house (k)** (ca. 1910) at 141 Park was one of two in the precinct built as single-family residences with a capacity of one or two persons afflicted with TB as boarders.

SL 37 HIGHLAND PARK
Park Avenue

The most fully realized and prestigious of the elite residential enclaves developed for those suffering from tuberculosis, Highland Park lies adjacent to Trudeau's sanitarium. Trudeau had purchased the land in 1891, but sold this acreage after determining that he did not need it. The buyer was another physician, Ezra S. McClellan, who began developing the tract by 1898. Deeds stipulated forty-foot setbacks and a minimal cost of $2,500 for the houses. No commercial sanitaria (cure cottages) were permitted as they were on Helen Hill [SL 27] or, later, at Cottage Row [SL 36]. The precinct is much like others developed along an avenue for the affluent at the turn of the 20th century, with the houses exhibiting considerable variety in design. As a setting Highland Park is mostly intact, with the majority of its residences retaining their single-family function.

The ca. 1905 **house (a)** at 247 Park Avenue appears to have been an anomaly in Highland Park as it was built as a rental property by **Walter H. Larom**, rector of St. Luke's Church. New York Giants legend **Christy Mathewson** was the first occupant of the **house (b)**, still known by his name, at 281 Park, between 1924 and his death from TB a year later. (His widow continued to live there into the early 1950s.) **Highland Manor (c)** (1903–04), at 286 Park Avenue, the second house erected in the tract,

was probably William L. Coulter's largest residential building aside from the camps he designed on the Saranac lakes. It was commissioned by **Agnes McIntosh**, who died within two years after its completion, and was subsequently purchased by physician **Joseph Nichols**, also afflicted with TB, who died in 1910. It was Nichols who had Coulter's firm prepare plans for the **carriagehouse** in 1907. His widow, however, remained for another fifty-four years, frequently entertaining neighbors and other area physicians.

Built around 1902 from plans by William H. Scopes, the **house (d)** at 308 Park Avenue was purchased by New York newspaper broker and owner **Charles M. Palmer** in 1927 when one of his sons became afflicted. Palmer commissioned William G. Distin to extensively remake the residence, which he dubbed the **Pink Palace**. The son regained his health, but the family remained as part-time residents until

Charles Palmer's death in 1949 at age ninety-three. It was later the home of William Steenken, director of the Trudeau Laboratory from 1947 to 1965. **George V. W. Duryee (e)** was a New York banker who came to Saranac Lake in 1892 for health reasons and subsequently established a successful local real estate practice. He was the first to purchase a lot in the subdivision at 334 Park Avenue, commissioning Coulter to design his house in 1898. Duryee was a business associate of **Frank Creesy**, for whom his friend Coulter prepared plans in 1900 of a very different **house (f)** across the street at 333 Park. Like McIntosh, he died not long after moving to his new residence, which was purchased by **Lawrason Brown**, the assistant resident and later resident physician at Trudeau's sanitarium and the key figure behind developing the porch as an essential curative fixture. Around 1904 **Ellwood Wilson**, engineer for the village, commissioned Maurice Feustmann to design a **house (g)** at 347 Park that would remind his wife of one she remembered from her two years' stay in Switzerland, although it bears greater affinity to contemporary Arts-and-Crafts work. **Thomas Bailey Aldrich** was a prolific novelist as well as editor of *Every Saturday* (1865–75) and *Atlantic Monthly* (1881–90), whose 1901 move to Saranac Lake was prompted by his son's contracting tuberculosis. Designed by Coulter in 1902, his rambling, shingled house, **The Porcupine (h)**, at 350 Park ranks among the largest on the street.

SL 38 ADIRONDACK COTTAGE SANITARIUM – TRUDEAU SANATORIUM
Park Avenue from west gates to Trudeau Road (note: only Park Avenue is a public right-of-way: all drives and the grounds are privately owned and are not accessible)

This first-of-its-kind institution in the United States was the product of ongoing experimentation and change. Trudeau began purchasing land in 1884 with a sixteen-acre parcel adjoining the principal entrance on what is now Trudeau Road. Other parcels were added as his capital permitted or through donations, resulting in a total of about sixty-six acres in 1908. Nothing remains on the grounds of the earliest buildings [see SL 41], but during the initial decade Trudeau and his associates developed the concept of creating an informal compound, with a cluster of small cottages, each housing two to four patients, to afford a sense of privacy and independence, eschewing institutional associations. Always adept at raising funds for his cause, Trudeau also found that potential donors were more likely to give the money needed for a modest building than contribute to the erection of a larger one.

After little more than a decade Trudeau engaged his cousin, J. Lawrence Aspinwall, a partner in the prominent New York architectural firm of Renwick, Aspinwall & Renwick, to design a new **Main Building (a)**

(1896), fashioned like a large country house of the period, with an enormous front porch (now glazed) and a smaller one on the second floor, both of which were used as outdoor resting places for patients. The

same year, with his assistant, William L. Coulter, Aspinwall designed **Baker Chapel (b)**, faced in rocks that appear simply to have been dropped into their places—an homage to Henry Hobson Richardson's boulder-encrusted Ames gate lodge in North Easton, Massachusetts. Now on his own, Coulter prepared plans for the **Ladd** and **Anderson cottages** (1899–1900, 1898, respectively) adjacent to the 1889 **Trudeau Cottage (c)**, forming a range between the chapel and headquarters building.

Following Trudeau's death in 1915, what had been established as the Adirondack Cottage Sanitarium became the Trudeau Sanatorium, which focused more on caring for patients who could not care for themselves, necessitating a sizable nursing staff. The change also entailed undertaking more scientific functions, which required specialized buildings. The **Trudeau Research and Clinical Laboratory (d)** (1924) by Scopes & Feustmann, lying to the west of the Main Building, is an early manifestation of the shift. Across the road the rather formal Georgian-inspired **James Memorial Staff Building (e)** of 1929 reflects the tendency to have many more patients under one roof, although the accommodations were still broken down into relatively intimate spaces. Scopes & Feustmann's **Blumenthal Cottage (f)** (1930) south of Anderson Cottage follows a similar program. North of the James Memorial, the **Ethel Saltus Luddington Memorial Infirmary (g)** (1926), also by Scopes & Feustmann, is among the largest on the campus and was devoted to caring for bedridden patients. Most notable among the staff houses is the **Lorna Valentine Mallinson Memorial (h)** (1930), designed by Scopes & Feustmann as a duplex for married laboratory workers, coyly disguised as a single-family house.

The sanatorium closed in 1953, and the property was sold four years later to the American Management Association for its international support-service center. Some of the buildings have since been demolished and several new ones added. The campus nevertheless retains much of its historic character.

SL 39 MILO MILLER HOUSE
126 Kiwassa Road; ca. 1890s

Facing Lake Flower on what was then the edge of settlement, the grand Queen Anne house was built for one of the village's leading merchants [see SL 10].

SL 40 WILLIAM L. DISTIN HOUSE
186 Kiwassa Road; ca. early 1920s, William G. Distin, architect

Architect Distin designed this modest house, with an expansive living porch above the garage for his photographer father.

SL 41 LITTLE RED
154 Algonquin Avenue, off NY 3; 1884–85

This, the second building in Trudeau's Adirondack Cottage Sanitarium and the only one from its initial development to survive, exemplifies the physician's concerns for creating an atmosphere of privacy and intimacy, while also being a decorous part of a larger community. Even with its ornamental woodwork, the cottage cost a mere $350. Relocated several times, it is now prominently positioned on the grounds of the **Trudeau Institute** (1962–64), designed by Distin & Wareham.

SL 42 SARANAC LAKE MARINA
4901 NY 3; 1924 and later

Originally called Crescent Bay Marina, this was a large facility of its kind, which eventually included cabins, a restaurant, and a filling station and garage. It was built for Harry Duso, and until recently remained operated by members of the family. It is now a rare example of its kind from the first half of the 20th century. Regrettably many of the covered boat slips are in an advanced state of deterioration.

SL 43 GUGGENHEIM CAMP
1468 Forest Home Road; ca. late 1920s
(accessible by prior arrangement)

Mining magnate and philanthropist Edmond Guggenheim purchased two camps, Rock Ledge and Idle Point, on Lower Saranac Lake in 1917 and demolished them within the next decade. His new compound, probably completed not long after the earlier ones were gone, avoids many of the rustic conceits common to large camps of earlier decades. Unassuming from the exterior, the main lodge contains a vast, two-story hall, fronted by a low, screened porch. The entry gateposts, an unusual appendage for Adirondack camps, were likely inspired by the ones William L. Coulter designed for Knollwood, a grand, four-family compound farther down the road. No evidence exists that Coulter's successor firm designed Guggenheim's camp; the architect remains unknown. In 1963 Guggenheim donated the property to the Diocese of Ogdensburg, and it is now used as a retreat.

BLOOMINGDALE
Town of St. Armand, Essex County

The small hamlet of Bloomingdale thrived during the second half of the 19th century as a center for logging. The Saint Armand Hotel was a major stage stop. Paul Smith was among its regular guests. Its position along the Saranac River and at the intersection of important overland routes, including that connecting Plattsburgh with the central Adirondacks, kept the community engaged in later years. But many residents moved to Saranac Lake once it became a center for tuberculosis treatment. Bloomingdale terminated its incorporation as a village in 1985.

BM 1 ST. ARMAND TOWN HALL
1702 Main Street (NY 3); 1903, William H. Scopes, architect

The evidence of the hamlet's once significant role in the area can be seen in some of the buildings that remain major landmarks. Most prominent is the town hall, the exterior configuration of which, especially with its original spire, is suggestive of the late 18th-century New England meeting house. (The ground floor windows have been shortened.) Like the Harrietstown Town Hall that Scopes's firm would design over two decades later [SL 8], this building is among the largest for housing a local government within the Blue Line.

BM 2 NORMAN'S GENERAL STORE
Main and State streets, 1902

Across the highway lies a landmark of a very different sort. Built for Matthew Norman, it was a primary source of consumable goods for many years and remained in the family until its recent closure. Around the late 1950s the exterior was modernized with a windowless front, a feature then fashionable among many merchants.

324

BM 3 EPISCOPAL CHURCH OF THE REDEEMER
State Street and Bloomingdale Road; 1882, Richard Michell Upjohn, architect (New York)

Trudeau's securing the services of Upjohn for St. Luke's in Saranac Lake [SL 24] may have encouraged the retaining of the architect for this mission of St. John's in the Wilderness at Paul Smiths [PS 3]. Prominently sited on a gore lot, the building is a testament to the inventiveness with which Upjohn could manipulate Gothic motifs. It has lain vacant for many years.

BM 4 HOUSE
320 River Road (CR 18); ca. late 1960s

East of the hamlet lies a polygonal house, the mass of which is determined by the geodesic dome that forms its structure. Developed by maverick architect and inventor Buckminster Fuller in the early 1950s, the geodesic dome was intended to provide a lightweight, portable frame that could be quickly assembled in remote locations and also to offer uninterrupted enclosure for large spaces. During the 1960s and 1970s it became a popular structure for alternative housing in many rural areas across the country.

GABRIELS
Town of Brighton, Franklin County

GA 1 DONNELLY'S DAIRY FARM
1556–64 NY 86; late 19th century and later

Much of the land south of the tiny hamlet of Gabriels was long used for agriculture. An important remnant is this farm, which dates to the late 19th century and was purchased by Martin Donnelly in 1920. Three years later he erected the enormous **dairy barn**, one of the best examples remaining in the Adirondacks, from timber cut the previous winter, milled in Bloomingdale, and brought to the site on horse-drawn sleds. The **dairy processing plant** in front dates to 1946, with an addition built in the 1960s by Clifford Donaldson. The **ice cream stand**, offering products that have acquired a local legendary aura, was erected in 1953, the work of builders David and John Martelle, who converted a warming hut from a former ski slope nearby.

GA 2 ASPLIN TREE FARM
1495 Bloomingdale Road; 1922, Ben A. Muncil, designer and builder

The barn complex that long served the Asplin Tree Farm was built as a model farm to serve Northbrook Lodge, an enormous camp on Osgood Pond owned by Wilfred L. McDougald, a member of the Canadian Parliament. Muncil organized the buildings in an irregular composition predicated on functional relationships, but also one that deftly addresses the gently rolling landscape. Sheathed in his trademark "brainstorm" siding, the buildings have been well maintained. Asplin purchased the property in 1960, developing what was reputedly the largest Christmas tree farm in the state. It is now Moody's Tree Farm and is accessible when the shop is open.

GA 3 CATHOLIC CHURCH OF THE ASSUMPTION
826 NY 86; 1922–23, Ben A. Muncil, designer and builder

Muncil's building was a variation on a 1910 design of the Catholic Church Extension Society. He did a similar scheme for St. John's in the Wilderness at Lake Clear (1917). Another version was built for St. Paul's in Bloomingdale (1930–31).

GA 4 SANATORIUM GABRIELS
NY 86 west of Gabriels-Onchiota Road (note: as of this writing the grounds are not accessible to the public. They are included in the hope that they will be preserved and can be publicly seen, serving a new, compatible function in the foreseeable future)

Established in 1894 by the Sisters of Mercy, this was the first sanitarium built in the region after Trudeau's at Saranac Lake [SL 38] and was created to serve persons of modest means. It was also the first in the region to accept African-Americans. William Seward Webb and Paul Smith donated the initial 100 acres; the state granted an additional 600, rendering the institution unusually well endowed in land. In contrast to Trudeau's sanitarium, the principal buildings at Gabriels, erected between 1895 and 1927, were quite large, the early ones inspired by resort hotels. State architect Isaac Perry volunteered his services for

the first three: the Administration Building, Rest-A-While Cottage, and **Kerin Cottage**, a much smaller edifice (all 1895–97). He may also have drawn plans for the **Church of the Blessed Virgin Mary**, which was apparently designed in the 1890s, but not executed until sometime between 1904 and 1910.

By 1903, the complex had about a dozen buildings and its own water and electrical systems. Two years later the state acquired a 200-acre farm on Hobart Road. The Administration Building burned in 1916, and most of the other early components are now gone as well. A major addition occurred after World War I when two buildings (**Units 3** and **4**), each housing forty-four patients, were donated by the Knights of Columbus and designed by the renowned New York architectural firm headed by John Russell Pope in 1926. Pope's office also prepared plans for the adjacent **Infirmary** the following year. All three buildings were components of a very grand design he developed for the entire complex around 1918, a plan that never seems to have gone beyond the schematic stage.

Paul Smith's College purchased the property in 1965 for its forestry program, but found the physical plant unwieldy. It was sold to the state in 1980 and reopened two years later as a minimum-security prison (Camp Gabriels). That institution closed in 2009 and the campus has since lain vacant. A proposal for a children's camp on the property has been stymied by an environmental group that is pressing for the land to become part of the Forest Preserve.

PAUL SMITHS
Town of Brighton, Franklin County

Paul Smiths is not a hamlet, but a scattering of two small, year-round residential enclaves (on NY 86 and on Keese Mill Road)—Paul Smith's College is between the two, and camps on Spitfire and Upper St. Regis lakes and Osgood Pond are nearby.

While long settled, the area still conveys a sense of remoteness.

PS 1 BRIGHTON TOWN HALL
NY 86 and Jones Pond Road; 1914, Ben A. Muncil, designer and builder

This carefully composed but unassuming building has long catered to a variety of functions, from official meetings to public events. Along NY 86, just to the south, is a group of houses built around the turn of the 20th century by guides in Paul Smith's employ. Smith paid them well and paid them year-round, leading to the popular appellation of this enclave as "Easy Street."

panies and became a nationally prominent dealer in railroad and other bonds. Six years later he married Olive Moore, who had pursued a career in comic opera. She clearly had a taste for the unconventional that is embodied in the singular character of this sprawling complex. The initial building campaign included main living hall (burned in 1966), dining room and kitchen, owner's cabin, three guest cabins, and some of the service quarters. Begun three years later, the second campaign included the "Hermit's Hut," bowling alley, lakeside teahouse, tennis courts and pavilion, and probably additions to the service quarters.

PS 2 WHITE PINE CAMP
End of White Pine Camp Road, off NY 86; 1907–08, William Massarene, architect (New York); additions 1911, Addison Mizner, architect (New York) (accessible by regularly scheduled tours)

Situated on a knoll overlooking Osgood Pond, White Pine Camp was commissioned by Archibald White, a Midwestern entrepreneur, who, after retirement in 1899 at age thirty-two, acquired gas com-

No clues have been found to suggest why White did not retain Massarene (about whom little is known) for the additions, hiring instead a young and relatively inexperienced Mizner. Whatever the circumstances, Massarene later recalled that some features were inspired by Tuscan vernacular buildings the Whites had seen while abroad during the time the project was under way, which may explain some of the ad hoc nature of the porch configurations.

Many interior details are eccentric as well. It was here, too, that builder Ben Muncil first applied his "brainstorm" siding, comprised of relatively wide clapboards with the bottom edge left rough, sometimes with the bark still on.

In 1920 Irwin Kirkwood, publisher of the *Kansas City Star*, and his wife, Laura, purchased the camp. Six years later they loaned it to President Calvin Coolidge and his family for use as the summer White House. Kirkwood sold White Pine in 1930 to Mrs. Edgar Stern and Mrs. David Levy, daughters of Julius Rosenwald, the great philanthropist, who had amassed a fortune as the driving force behind Sears, Roebuck & Company. They, in turn, donated White Pine Camp to Paul Smith's College in 1948. After years of deferred maintenance, the property was purchased in 1983 by Howard Kirschenbaum, who has meticulously restored its components and created a consortium of about fifty investors who occupy the buildings, rent units to others, and make the property accessible on a limited basis.

PS 3 ST. JOHN'S IN THE WILDERNESS EPISCOPAL CHURCH
NY 83, just east of NY 30; 1928–30, William G. Distin, architect, Arthur G. Wilson, associate
Before he took steps to build St. Luke's in Saranac Lake [SL 24], E. L. Trudeau conceived and raised the money for the first St. John's in 1876. Constructed of logs and on land donated by Paul Smith, the church was a welcome addition for guests at his hotel and for the growing number of nearby camp owners. After that building burned in 1928, Distin was commissioned to design the current one, which he developed in an adept rendition of "modern" Gothic as advocated by the great Boston architect Ralph Adams Cram.

PS 4 ST. GABRIEL THE ARCHANGEL CATHOLIC CHURCH
Just off NY 30 north of junction with NY 86; 1894–96, Ben A. Muncil, builder

Paul Smith also donated the land for this church serving his employees and their families. Given his interest in wood textures, Muncil may well have devised the fanciful patterns that sheathe this wood-frame building. Deconsecrated some years ago, the edifice has been reasonably well maintained, but awaits an uncertain fate.

by is **Overlook Hall** (2011), designed by buildings and grounds supervisor Steven McFarland and BBL Builders of Albany, with HCP Architects (also of Albany) as architect of record. Arcing along a ridge, this large dormitory is broken down into a series of parallel pavilions that abstractly allude to rustic lodges with economy and flair. The most important remnants of the hotel era are **Glover Cottage** (ca. 1890), named after prominent Washington, D.C., banker Charles Glover; and **Baker Cottage** (1893), one of the most elaborate—all fac-

PS 5 PAUL SMITH'S COLLEGE
Main entrance at junction of NY 30 and NY 86

Founded on the grounds of Paul Smith's hotel through the bequest of son Phelps Smith, the college opened in 1947 with 150 students. This private institution of higher learning has grown considerably in recent decades, adding programs in the culinary arts, fisheries and wildlife science, biology, natural resource management, and business. Gradually buildings that were part of the hotel's infrastructure have been replaced by new facilities. The centerpiece of the campus is the **Joan Weill Adirondack Library** (2000–02), designed by the prominent Boston architectural firm of Perry Dean Rogers Partners, in a manner consonant with the northern landscape without resorting to period clichés. Near-

ing Lower St. Regis Lake and somewhat removed from the hotel's site.

PS 6 ADIRONDACK PARK VISITOR INTERPRETIVE CENTER
NY 30, 1 mile north of the campus entrance; 1985–89, Architectural Bureau of the State Office of General Services (Albany)

This facility is the larger of two conceived to help inform visitors of the park's ecological importance as well as the appeal of its natural features. Among those targeted were people not planning hiking or canoe trips and schoolchildren. In this respect the building is a portal to the center's 3,000-acre tract of wild lands, which are accessed by twenty-five miles of trails. The building has moments of graceful elegance in its use of finely detailed wood and glass as responsive counterpoints to the environs. The center lies on land leased from Paul Smith's College, and when this state facility was threatened with closure for budgetary reasons, the college took over the operation in 2011, supplementing its own conservation programs and adding public events.

PS 7 ST. REGIS PRESBYTERIAN CHURCH
Keese Mills Road, 2.5 miles west of NY 30; 1899, William L. Coulter, architect
One of Coulter's most imaginative plays with English postmedieval sources, this chapel was funded in part by Helen Louisa (Mrs. Anson) Phelps Stokes, a camp owner on nearby Upper St. Regis Lake. Congregants included some who serviced the camps and lived in the small settlement on Keese Mills Road to the southeast as well as camp owners and their guests.

LAKE CLEAR

Town of Harrietstown, Franklin County

LC 1 NEW YORK CENTRAL RAILROAD STATION
Junction Road, off NY 30; 1893
South of Paul Smiths, the small hamlet of Lake Clear has played an important role as a transportation hub in the north-central Adirondacks for over a hundred years. Here William Seward Webb's Mohawk & Malone

(New York Central) Railroad met its Saranac Lake branch in 1892. The building's exterior has recently been restored. Here, too, lay the southern terminus of Paul Smith's electric rail line that connected to his hotel. Nearby is **Charlie's Inn** (a name acquired in the mid-20th century), built in 1891 and a central establishment in the little boom town that once served the railroad.

LC 2 LAKE CLEAR SCHOOL
NY 30, less than .5 mile north of NY 186; 1954–55, Distin & Wareham, architects
Wareham employed prefabricated window-wall units in what must have seemed a strikingly modernist composition to area residents. It is now a rare surviving example of a school from the postwar era that has not had its character changed through window replacement. With the school now closed, the building's fate is uncertain.

LC 3 ADIRONDACK REGIONAL AIRPORT
98 Airport Road, off NY 186; 1947–49, William G. Distin, architect
The first (and only) field with regularly scheduled commercial service within the park, this facility was conceived as early as 1940. The field opened in 1942 and direct service by two carriers began four years later. Major improvements were undertaken in 1947–49, financed by the Federal Airport Act and included a paved runway, hangar, and the **administration building–terminal**. The building makes a nod to regional imagery, but gives little indication of its purpose. The one-story wing that now serves as the principal waiting room is a later addition.

UPPER SARANAC LAKE
Town of Harrietstown, Franklin County

SN 1 CAMP CANARAS AND CAMP NE-PAH-WIN
5002 NY 30; ca. 1913 and later (accessible by prior arrangement)

Both camps were built for Robert Bentley, who purchased three separate parcels from the Upper Saranac Association between 1913 and 1916. Construction occurred incrementally, a process that was common in the development of camps with multiple buildings. The last edifice constructed was Pine Cottage at Ne-Pah-

Win (1930), designed by William G. Distin. With a total of twenty buildings, this pair of camps is a revealing example of the fact that, despite their size, many such compounds had neither large buildings nor assumed a cultivated rustic character. In both respects they stand in marked contrast to Adolph Lewisohn's Prospect Point [SN 2].

The Bentleys sold the complex to Laurance Rockefeller, who after a few years gave it to the Sloan-Kettering Institute for Cancer Research, which used the premises as a retreat for its specialists. Through an outside donor, St. Lawrence University purchased the camps in the mid-1960s. They remain, little altered, as a conference center.

SN 2 PROSPECT POINT CAMP – YOUNG LIFE SARANAC VILLAGE
4014 NY 30; 1902–04, William L. Coulter, architect; numerous alterations and additions (accessible by prior arrangement)

Copper magnate, financier, art collector, and philanthropist Adolph Lewisohn commissioned one of the grandest camps ever built in the Adirondacks. Perched high above the lake at the end of the peninsula for which it was named, the camp had around forty buildings on a tract of 4,000 acres. At the core, the main lodge is a spirited and rather inventive interpretation of a chalet, cruciform in plan, surrounded by an enormous porch with log posts and skirting wall. To the west is an equally lavish dining hall, and beyond on either side are large lodges for guests—all four buildings connected by covered walkways made of logs. Below the dining hall is a two-and-a-half-story boathouse, among the largest in the Adirondacks. Coulter used logs to great decorative effect as structure and, in slab form, as sheathing, encasing chimneys and railings. In the eaves he used split logs as vertical frames for birch-bark panels, enlivened by inverted chevrons at the base. (He reversed this pattern for many of the railings.)

Two years after Lewisohn's death in 1938, Prospect Point was sold to Mladek Willy, banquet manager at the Waldorf Astoria, who ran it as a lodge, Sekon-in-the-Pines, without great success. In 1951 it became a girls' camp. Since 1969, when the remaining 105 acres were purchased by Young Life Ministries, an interdenominational Christian youth organization based in Colorado Springs, the campus has been intensely used, now for week-long programs conducted during an extended season. While many alterations have occurred, much of the character of the principal buildings has been retained. The exteriors of several of the new facilities, most notably the Leaders' Lodge (1998, Cummings, Pash & Hadsell, architects, Binghamton, N.Y.), Prospect Point, and Loon Lodge (2002, Beckwith Group, architects, Pleasant Valley, N.Y.), make overt references to the original buildings in a deferential, but confident, way that avoids parody.

SN 3 EAGLE ISLAND CAMP

Eagle Island; 1902–03, William L. Coulter, architect (accessible by boat) (note: as of this writing the camp is not publicly accessible; however, plans are under way to give it a new recreational purpose so that the complex can again be seen through prior arrangement)

Set on its own thirty-one-acre parcel just below the narrows that define the lower half of the lake, Eagle Island Camp ranks not only among the most ambitious examples of its genre, but also one of the most imaginative. It is arguably Coulter's most original design.

The complex was commissioned by New York banker Levi P. Morton, who had served as vice-president of the United States under Benjamin Harrison and subsequently as governor of New York. After spending two summers in the Adirondacks, Morton, by then in his mid-seventies, purchased the island in 1898. In all likelihood he gave Coulter a free hand in developing what proved to be an unusually inventive design that is as theatrical as it is vigorously muscular. While rivaling the size of the more-or-less contemporary Prospect Point and configured in a similar fashion, with several large main buildings set in a gentle arc and connected by covered walkways, Eagle Island is markedly different in character.

Here the buildings partake of a water view screened by a carefully thinned cedar forest, a manipulation of the landscape that permits vistas while ensuring privacy. William West Durant had taken this approach at Pine Knot [RL 6, Section 12], and Massarene would later do so at White Pine Camp [PS 2]. Such unobtrusive integration with the site had in fact become a frequent practice for camps by the early 20th century. The effect is the more striking at Eagle Island given the nature of the progression from the boathouse, the principal means of access to the core of the complex. From its approach, the main lodge seems almost incidental, while from the water side it rises as if some great primeval hall, encased by an immense, bark-clad cedar-log porch, the upper portions of which are enlivened by a screen of cedar poles. The lodge is connected ceremoniously to the octagonal dining pavilion (which fronts a large service building), while the link to the family quarters to the east generates quite the opposite effect. As a group, these buildings seem more the result of additions and modifications over time, some performed on an ad hoc basis, than they do the product of a single conception.

Inside, Coulter intensified the manipulation of rustic elements to create a sense of theater. For the lodge's great hall, the actual wood-frame structure is disguised by what appears to be a support system of logs and poles, with a column-and-girder frame supporting hammer-beam trusses. The dining room is topped by log trusses fanning as spokes from a central suspended pole.

The main ensemble is framed to the west by a guest house that is somewhat

reminiscent of Durant's cabin at Pine Knot. On the other side, the ornate original boathouse stands relocated and modified to serve as additional quarters. To the north lies an array of service buildings as well as a second, larger boathouse.

Following Morton's death, the camp was sold to Henry Graves of South Orange, New Jersey. In 1937 it was donated to the Girl Scout Council of Greater Essex and Hudson Counties (New Jersey), which used it as a summer camp through the 2008 season. Remarkably, few changes were made to the original complex during its long period of active use. Since it became vacant, Eagle Island has continued to receive essential maintenance. In 2015 the Friends of Eagle Island undertook restoring the complex and revitalizing it as a retreat for children and their families.

SN 4 CHAPEL ISLAND PRESBYTERIAN CHAPEL

Chapel Island; 1957–58; Distin & Wareham, architects (accessible by boat)

The original chapel was built in 1889 to serve seasonal residents with camps on Upper Saranac Lake and was a miniature version of the more-or-less concurrent Saranac Lake Presbyterian Church (altered). Its design also bears affinity to that still intact at Childwold [CI 1, Section 10]. After the edifice burned in 1956, Distin prepared plans for a new one that would evoke tradition if not its actual predecessor. His design employs a wood frame, sheathed in brainstorm siding with five spruce logs serving as buttresses on each side. In its form, the building is somewhat reminiscent of its architect's remodeling of St. Eustace in Lake Placid [LP 12].

10
NORTHWEST LAKES

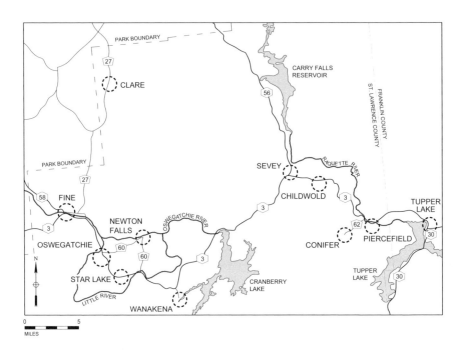

SECTION 10 ENCOMPASSES A SIZABLE PORTION of the northwestern Adirondacks, most of it in St. Lawrence County, but also a small part of western Franklin County. A great majority of this area is without human settlement; some of the land is part of the Forest Preserve, but more acreage remains in private hands. The area remained almost entirely wilderness until after the Civil War. Thereafter, development came slowly with the population concentrated in a few small hamlets. The three largest lakes, Tupper, Cranberry, and Star, emanate from two rivers, the Raquette and Oswegatchie, and they all figured importantly in development. Most of the communities included are along what is now NY 3, a winding east-west highway extending from the village of Saranac Lake to Watertown, well beyond the Blue Line. During the late 19th and early 20th centuries logging formed the primary economic base for the area, which also had the most intense network of narrow-gauge logging railroads. Mining was an important enterprise around Star Lake. But unlike some industrial centers in the eastern Adirondacks—Ticonderoga, Port Henry, Keeseville, and Au Sable Forks, most notably—operations in this section of the park were almost entirely financed by outside capital, reflecting a broad shift in the nation's economy. Whatever wealth was amassed through these industries was channeled to owners outside the Adirondacks.

Accommodations for vacationers were scattered throughout the area. A number of small establishments catered to fishermen and gamehunters. Several modest resort hotels were built during the late 19th century on the shores of Cranberry and Star lakes. Camps were developed at those two communities as well as Tupper and Mount Arab lakes, and Wolf Pond.

THE VILLAGE OF TUPPER LAKE WAS THE PRIMARY CENTER for industry, and it remains one of the largest communities in the Adirondacks (3,667 population in 2010). Some meager settlement occurred as early as the 1840s, but signs of permanency did not begin until the following decade with logging operations established by the Maine-based Pomeroy Lumber Company. After the arrival of the Northern Adirondack Railroad in 1889, substantial development took hold. Conceived by John Hurd, who had established the St. Regis Lumber Company in 1882 [Section 8], the line was extended southeast from St. Regis Falls to what became the hamlet of Santa Clara in 1886. Two years later Hurd entered a partnership with Titus B. Meigs to form the Santa Clara Lumber Company, which provided the capital necessary to continue the line to Tupper Lake. Hurd's railroad, coupled with the arrival of William Seward Webb's Mohawk & Malone (New York Central) Railroad soon thereafter, created a separate community, Tupper Lake Junction, one and one half miles to the west of the older settlement. (Both are part of the present-day village.) The residential blocks in this new section developed not only in response to sawmills, but also to service what became the major railroad yard in the Adirondacks.

Big Mill, Tupper Lake, 1890, closed 1926. (early 20th-century postcard)

His railroad completed, Hurd commissioned an enormous lumber manufactory, known as the Big Mill, which was the largest of its kind in the state and probably in the Northeast. His heavy investments and a quixotic attempt to double-deal Webb led Hurd to declare bankruptcy in 1895. No longer in his hands, the plant continued to operate until 1926. Hurd's project also spurred a number of other timber-related

335

operations. A small mill a few miles to the west developed in 1892 by the Piercefield Paper & Manufacturing Company was purchased by the newly formed International Paper Company a half-dozen years later and expanded into a major plant. The Brooklyn Cooperage Company opened for business in Tupper Lake in 1900. By that time the village boasted five large sawmills, rivaling Glens Falls in their combined output of lumber.

International Paper Company mill, Piercefield, ca. 1898. (early 20th-century postcard)

As a result, both east and west portions of the village boomed during the 1890s and 1900s, when the population rose to nearly 4,000. A major fire in 1899 destroyed around 160 buildings in the eastern sector, spurring reconstruction of a more substantial nature. This portion of the community now developed with the largest concentration of business, institutions, and residences. Tupper Lake never acquired the trappings of wealth, yet for at least several decades it was the biggest industrial center in the Adirondacks. Even as available timber supplies were depleted in the 1910s and some plants slowed down their operations or closed altogether, the village attracted new industry. Most important among these ventures was the Michigan-based Oval Wood Dish Corporation, which took over the property formerly occupied by the A. Sherman Lumber Company sawmill in 1915 and constructed a large plant immediately thereafter [TL 7].

Local leaders sought to augment the timber industry through other means. Land was donated for the immense Sunmount Veterans Hospital, a tuberculosis sanitarium, in 1922, and the facility was dedicated two years later. Closure as a federal institution came in 1965, but the state took it over as a mental-health center (now Sunmount Developmental Center) that same year. During the Depression the head of Oval Wood Dish warned of the need to attract vacationers, and his company donated the land for a golf course and the Sugar Loaf ski slope on Mount Morris south of the village. Unable to enlist state support, the town developed a new, larger ski area nearby in 1960, which was further expanded over the next two decades. By the early 1980s, the enterprise was laden with debt, a situation not resolved until it was sold to a private-sector operator in 1988. In recent years, an initiative to create a major year-round tourist attraction succeeded with the opening in 2006 of the Wild Center, a natural history museum devoted to the Adirondacks [TL 1]. Efforts are also under way to make the commercial district more attractive with the introduction of new businesses and the rehabilitation of buildings. Still, the cumulative effect of these campaigns has yet to overcome completely the loss of traditional industries. An ongoing attempt to create a large resort community nearby has been beleaguered by controversy, spurring not just opposition among environmentalists, but also skepticism by those who fear it would become a failed enterprise, incurring significant debts in the process. Ironically, several grand camps are sequestered in preserves not far from the village; however, these alone do not generate a trade comparable to that at Lake Placid or Saranac Lake. Giving the third-largest community in the Adirondacks a solid, diversified economy remains a challenge.

Just north of Tupper Lake, Ferris J. Meigs of the Santa Clara Lumber Company created Big Wolf Park, a private preserve, in 1916. Members of the family and friends added camps around what came to be known as Wolf Pond during the years that followed, and the enclave grew to include other parties as well. Similarly, a camp colony grew around Mount Arab and Eagle Crag lakes to the west during the early 20th century. By far the most ambitious resort plans were made by Addison Child, who came to the area from Boston in 1878, purchasing 15,000 acres northwest of Tupper Lake. He managed to sell some lots, creating the tiny hamlet of Childwold, but the area was ill-suited to anything save the most rudimentary subsistence farming. Undaunted, he erected a grand hotel (1888–89) near the shores

Childwold Park House, Childwold, 1888–89, demolished 1946. (ca.1890 photograph by Seneca Ray Stoddard)

of Lake Massawepie. A golf course, tennis courts, a bowling green, and a baseball diamond were among the amenities advertised. The Childwold Park House was enthusiastically received, and sufficiently popular to warrant a major addition in 1892–93, which, coupled with eighteen cottages built on the grounds, brought the total capacity to 350 guests. Success was not enduring, however. Poor management led to the hotel's closure in 1909. Lumber baron William L. Sykes purchased the property eight years later for use as a private preserve. The family sold most of their retreat in 1946, but kept the cottages for another five years until the remaining land

337

was sold to the Boy Scouts for a summer camp.

The Childwold Park House would not have grown as much as it did without the arrival of the Mohawk & Malone (New York Central) Railroad, which built a station there in 1891. Railroads were responsible for most developments farther west as well. Sykes's Pennsylvania-based Adirondack Lumber Company built a line (incorporated as the Grasse River Railroad two years later) from Childwold to its anticipated settlement at Conifer in 1913. The rails were then extended to Cranberry Lake, where Adirondack Lumber built a large mill in 1917. The new line was also conceived to stimulate tourism along the lakeshore, one of several instances where resort and industrial development went hand in hand in the western Adirondacks. Sykes's North Country venture was never as profitable as those in Pennsylvania, however. The Cranberry Lake mill operated only ten years; that at Conifer was purchased by others in 1949, but not rebuilt after a major fire eight years later.

Farther west the Adirondack & Carthage Railroad was instrumental in developing three other industrial communities—Wanakena, Newton Falls, and Star Lake. Chartered in 1883, the line was financed by Byron Benson, who had made a fortune with the Tidewater Pipeline Company, which serviced the oil fields of Pennsylvania. Benson undertook his Adirondack project to tap ore deposits at the mines that would bear his name near Star Lake [BE 1]. The A&C reached that destination in 1889 and five years later was extended to service a paper mill under construction at Newton Falls. A second extension was created in 1902 under the name of Cranberry Lake Railroad, which went from Benson's mine to the developing company town of Wanakena.

After their two large-scale ventures in northwestern Pennsylvania were nearing an end due to depleted resources, the Rich Lumber Company, formed by brothers Herbert and Horace Rich in 1885, set its sights on the western Adirondacks. In 1901 the company purchased over 15,000 acres and established Wanakena as its base of operations. The scale of this enterprise was substantial. Trainloads of lumber and other materials were transported to the site from one of the company's now abandoned Pennsylvania settlements for the construction of new buildings. Several sawmills were constructed by affiliated parties all under contract with Rich Lumber. The operation closed after eleven years, but a significant portion of the tract was dedicated to the formation of a New York State ranger school [WN 2], and many components of the hamlet remain in use, now primarily as a seasonal community [WN 1].

Newton Falls was developed by James L. Newton of Watertown, New York, capitalizing on the abundance of timber, waterpower, and railroad access, to feed the nation's seemingly insatiable appetite for pulp. In striking contrast to Wanakena, the plant at Newton Falls was unusually long-lived, operating for over a century when it closed in 2001. Unlike Wanakena, too, Newton Falls has had no alternative source of revenue. The loss of Benson Mines in 1978 has likewise cast a pall on the economy of nearby Star Lake. Here, however, a substantial resort trade emerged as a result of the Adirondack & Carthage Railroad's arrival in the late 19th century. At least half a dozen hotels were operating along the lakeshore in 1910, of which the Star Lake Inn was the largest and most prestigious. Even though the hotel business was waning by the late 1930s, activities would soon accelerate at Benson Mines, bolstered by the pressing need for steel during World War II. Like Cranberry Lake, Star Lake continues to attract seasonal residents and other vacationers, but has never developed into a major resort.

The tiny hamlet of Fine, on the western edge of the park, is part of a very different

Newton Falls Paper Company mill, Newton Falls, 1895–96 and later, closed 2001. (early 20th-century postcard)

Star Lake Inn, Star Lake, 1887, 1900s, demolished ca. 1962–63. (early 20th-century postcard)

landscape. This area was settled much earlier, beginning in the 1830s. Soil conditions were more conducive to farming, and much of the land was cleared for this purpose, but remoteness ensured that agriculture remained at a subsistence level. A tannery was built in the hamlet in 1869–72, and the St. Nicholas Hotel opened in that latter year, catering to hunting and fishing parties. The hamlet prospered as a small industrial center for several decades, but subsequently began a long decline from which it never recovered.

* * * * *

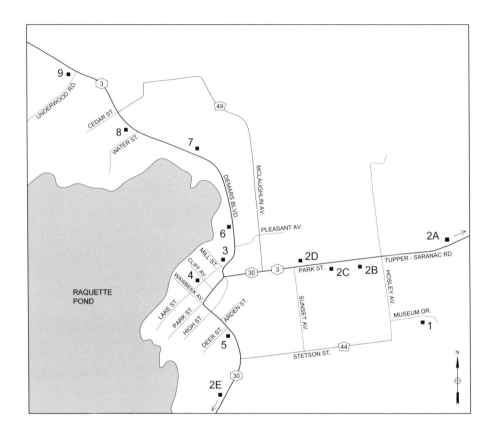

TUPPER LAKE

Town of Tupper Lake, Franklin County

The village of Tupper Lake is divided into two sections that wrap around the upper portion of Raquette Pond, the northern extension of the body of water that is also called Tupper Lake. The southern portion of this settlement contains the main commercial district, the school, the library, most houses of worship, motels, the Sunmount Developmental Center, and the Wild Center, in addition to well-developed residential areas. Just to the north the flatlands were once occupied by sawmills and other industrial operations, including the long-vacant plant of the Oval Wood Dish Corporation. Much of this acreage is now consumed by recent commercial development, though an expansive public park that was developed during the Depression lines the lakeshore. To the northwest lies the area that emerged as a result of the railroads, which is primarily residential, with a scattering of commercial and institutional buildings.

TL 1 THE WILD CENTER, NATURAL HISTORY MUSEUM OF THE ADIRONDACKS

Museum Drive, off Hosley Avenue; 1999–2006, Hellmuth, Obata & Kassbaum (HOK), architects (St. Louis); Wild Walk, 2013–15, Office of Charles P. Reay, architect (St. Louis); Linearscape, associate architects, Ting Chin principal-in-charge; Wayne Striker, project manager; Robert Sillman Associates, structural engineers (New York); William Palmer, landscape designer

Since its opening the Wild Center has become a major destination for tourists and residents, adults and children. It was conceived by Elizabeth (Betsy) Lowe, who, after working in public affairs at the Department of Environmental Conservation for nearly twenty years, left in 1998 to devote her full energies to creating a place that would advance a sense of respect for, and the need to take care of, the Adirondacks' natural environment. Part of her concern stemmed from her experience at the DEC, which, along with the Adirondack Park Agency, was viewed as an alien overlord by many people living within the Blue Line. Local support for this private-sector initiative was strong. Tupper Lake voters approved donating a thirty-one-acre site at the eastern edge of the village for a museum where the landscape would figure as importantly as the exhibits inside. Lowe and a seasonal resident, Donald (Obie) Clifford, proved adept at securing the monies needed from a broad spectrum of individual, corporate, and government sources and did so in short order. After nearly a year in development the master plan was completed in 1999. Site preparation began in 2002; groundbreaking occurred two years later.

The architects selected to design the project were well known for their National Air and Space Museum in Washington, D.C. (1971–75) and, closer to home, for their large arena built in conjunction with the 1980 Winter Olympics in Lake Placid [LP 6, Section 9]. Charles "Chip" Reay, the partner-in-charge, had worked on both. For the Wild Center he had the opportunity to plan the site, the building, and the nature of the exhibits. Having previously been a sand quarry, much of the land needed to be reclaimed and natural features introduced. A pond became the centerpiece, and Reay determined the museum's main floor would rest below the waterline to foster a sense of immediacy and interaction between indoors and out. Rather than being collections-based, the museum is a celebration of living things, focusing on aquatic life. This multi-dimensional presentation area wraps around a central space for temporary exhibits. Separating the exhibition area from an auditorium, shop, and other spaces, the rotunda (Great Hall) is articulated by white birch tree trunks. To underscore how the Adirondacks can show ways of living in harmony with the natural world, the building maximizes year-round use of natural light. It is also the first LEED-certified museum in the state.

Added several years later, but part of the initial concept, the Wild Walk is perhaps the most inventive aspect of the whole scheme. Extended through part of the adjacent wooded area, this "elevated journey" occurs on walkways linked by eight platforms. Half of those decks are suspended from a series of thirteen "tree towers"—each comprised of five corten steel poles joined at the top like a teepee—that provide visitors a new perspective on the forest landscape. Fantasy worlds comprise the four other viewing perches: a "twig treehouse," a "snag" (a giant tree trunk), a simulated bald eagle's nest, and an enormous "spider's web." Technical prowess and flights of the imagination are interwoven throughout. Predators and prey in the forest form the basis of interpretation, but like the great spiral ramp at the Guggenheim Museum or the Highline in New York, the experience of moving through elevated space is an attraction in itself.

TL 2 MOTELS

Five motels afford an encapsulated history of the type's evolution from the 1930s through the 1960s. They were all developed to capture some of the many motorists using two of the major routes traversing the Adirondacks. Unlike counterparts in Lake George or Lake Placid, they served people traveling through as much as those vacationing in the area. Most of them also catered to family members of Sunmount patients. As a crossroads and as one of the largest communities in the region, Tupper Lake was a logical place to concentrate lodging once the car became the pervasive means of travel.

Not long after the first units of **Northwood Cabins (a)** were built around 1935 east of the village at 2775 NY 3 and 30, this unusually well-preserved complex was moved a short distance to accommodate highway improvements made in 1937. Like many such places it grew incrementally. A year after its purchase by the Sears and LaPorte families in 1939, the house was erected from a kit manufactured by Sears, Roebuck. Additions to that residence and more cabins were built in 1947.

The business did not change hands until 1972 and continues to be well maintained.

The **Park Motel (b)** at 336 Park Street was initially developed in the late 1940s along the same lines, but in this case two groups of cabins are of conspicuously different design. Most existing units were moved toward the property's rear to make way for newer, joined units that were added around 1962 and rendered in a modernist idiom then popular. Built for Auype Shaheen and others in his family, **Shaheen's Motel (c)** at 314 Park Street was designed

around 1968 by an unidentified Syracuse architect. His scheme exemplifies the tendency, even among independent owners, to build larger, two-story facilities at that time. Another classic example of its period, the **Tupper Lake Motel (d)** at 255 Park Street was laid out around 1957 in a "U" configuration to maximize use of a relatively compact lot. Swimming pools were not uncommon amenities at motels by the late 1950s. This one could be part of the original scheme.

The "English Colonial Cabins" with "De Luxe Rooms" at **Shore Acres (e)** at 1976 NY 30, while no longer in use, would have been considered more commodious than many motorists expected at the time they were built in the 1930s. Both the buildings and their layout convey a greater concern for presentation than either the Northwood or the Park. The still-operating Skyline Ice Cream stand in front probably dates to the late 1950s.

Rendered in a modernist vocabulary, with a bold composition, soaring interior space, and pervasive use of natural materials, the design recalls some of the visitor centers constructed in national parks, especially those in the West, during the Mission 66 program (1957–66).

TL 3 BETH JOSEPH SYNAGOGUE
55 Lake Street (NY 3); 1905–06

Now preserved as a museum and meeting center, as well as for occasional religious services, Beth Joseph was the first purpose-built synagogue constructed in the Adirondacks. Both Jewish and Christian residents of Tupper Lake donated funds for its construction. Some of the wealthy Jewish camp owners on the Saranacs and other lakes contributed as well. The design includes an elementary iteration of Romanesque elements common to urban synagogues a half century earlier, here updated with a few classical details. As a wooden building (with the interior sheathed in tongue-and-groove siding then popular in the Adirondacks), the synagogue is an unusual surviving example of its type in a predominantly rural area.

TL 4 GOFF-NELSON MEMORIAL LIBRARY
41 Lake Street; 1970–72, William A. Prescott Associates, architects (Plattsburgh, N.Y.)

For over half a century after its founding in 1914, Tupper Lake's public library existed in makeshift quarters—house, hotel, town hall, and school. The bequest of a life long resident, Charity Goff Nelson, enabled the construction of a new facility that outpaced most others in the Adirondacks.

TL 5 ST. ALPHONSUS CATHOLIC CHURCH
48 Wawbeek Avenue (NY 30); 1941–42, James J. O'Shaughnessy, architect (Boston)

The tendency during the interwar decades to design churches based on medieval precedents in increasingly abstract ways is well evident here, weaving Romanesque-inspired elements into a strong composition that testifies to the importance of the village's Catholic population.

TL 6 TUPPER LAKE MUNICIPAL PARK GRANDSTAND
Demars Boulevard (NY 3), opposite Pleasant Avenue; 1938

Tupper Lake's Municipal Park was one of several projects implemented as part of

New Deal relief. Voters approved purchasing the lakefront acreage from the Oval Wood Dish Corporation in 1932, enabling industrial wasteland to be reclaimed as a public amenity. Plans originally called for two campgrounds accommodating trailers, a playground, paved parking lots, toboggan slide, grandstand, two putting greens, and handball, volleyball, and tennis courts. Of those components realized, the grandstand, with a seating capacity of 600 people, is the most conspicuous and has remained virtually unchanged over nearly eight decades.

TL 7 OVAL WOOD DISH CORPORATION PLANT
104 Demars Boulevard (NY 3); 1916–17 and later, John L. Graham, designer and engineer (Reynoldsville, Pa.)

Based in Traverse City, Michigan, the Oval Wood Dish Corporation (OWD) planned to relocate in that state's Upper Peninsula, but a vacation trip to the Adirondacks in 1913 by two company executives convinced them to move to the North Country instead. They anticipated building their new plant in Utica, but were persuaded by the New York Central to locate in Tupper Lake, a move that gave a great boost to the carrier's Adirondack Division as well as to the local economy. What became the county's largest single industry made disposable wood-veneer dishes, ice cream sticks, wooden spoons and forks, and hardwood flooring as well as lumber. To fuel production, the company bought some 75,000 acres of timberland in Franklin and St. Lawrence counties and, to access them, built railroad lines that extended nearly as far as the Carry Falls Reservoir. Construct-

ed of reinforced concrete, the sprawling plant encompassed some 350,000 square feet. The designer was a mechanical engineer, specializing in sawmill machinery. He had already worked for the Santa Clara Lumber Company on the Big Mill.

After nearly fifty years of operation, OWD closed its plant in 1964. The Adirondack Plywood Corporation purchased the property that same year, and optimism mounted further when that business was sold to the U.S. Plywood Corporation in 1965. The new owners invested heavily in improvements, but decreasing rail service led them to cease operations five years later. While some portions of the complex have been used since and the town government occupies the former **office building** at 120 Demars Boulevard, efforts to rejuvenate this major monument to the region's industrial heritage have thus far been unsuccessful.

TL 8 PRESBYTERIAN CHURCH
178 Main Street (NY 3); 1901

Now used as the Adirondack Adult Center, the exterior of this edifice is well preserved as an example of the freewheeling manipulation of medieval sources commonly found in churches serving suburban and resort areas during the latter decades of the 19th century.

TL 9 HOLY NAME CATHOLIC CHURCH
114 Main Street; 1922–24, Paul Jaquet, architect

A second Catholic parish was formed in 1904 to obviate the long trek from this northern part of the village to St. Alphonsus [TL 5]. A frame building was finally completed in 1910, only to burn a dozen years later. The replacement employs a twin-towered façade and Romanesque motifs in a way no doubt calculated to make this Tupper Lake Junction's dominant landmark.

PIERCEFIELD
Town of Piercefield, St. Lawrence County

PI 1 HAMLET

After the International Paper Company purchased the small Piercefield Paper Company in 1898, it not only greatly expanded the operation, but also constructed some sixty houses, a hotel, store, school, community building, and hospital to create an environment attractive to the workforce. By 1920 the community had nearly 1,500 inhabitants, roughly three times its population in 2000. Despite the mill's closure in 1933, at the height of the Depression, Piercefield has managed to survive as a satellite of Tupper Lake. The mill and other key buildings have been demolished, but much remains to convey a sense of what this company town looked like a century ago.

To the west, at the end of Conifer Road, lies another industrial hamlet, **Conifer**, the last company town initiated in the Adirondacks. William Sykes's Adirondack

Lumber Company developed the small community with a modest hotel on land purchased in 1910. The plant, built to make hardwood flooring, was purchased by another party in 1949, but was not rebuilt after a major fire eight years later. Some remnants of the community still exist.

CHILDWOLD
Town of Piercefield, St. Lawrence County

CI 1 CHILDWOLD PRESBYTERIAN CHURCH
104 Bancroft Road, off NY 3; 1892–93

Though most of Addison Child's extensive development projects have long since gone, the church is still in use. One of seventeen houses of worship in Franklin and St. Lawrence counties founded between 1889 and 1904 by the Reverend Richard G. McCarthy, this edifice is a condensed version of the one he initiated at Saranac Lake (1889; altered). Both share individualistic juxtapositions of domestic and churchly features—a front porch surmounted by a rose window and tower. Here, the large window bays topped by jerkin-head (clipped gable) roofs on the side elevations are no less unorthodox, contributing to a character well suited to a resort community. The original paint scheme, highlighting trim, enhanced the whimsical effect that was no doubt appreciated in a resort setting.

CI 2 ADDISON CHILD HOUSE
46 Bancroft Road; ca. 1878 and later

An even more unusual survivor is Child's own residence, a rare example of a settlement-period log structure still standing in the Adirondacks. When log buildings were retained in later years, they were commonly sheathed in clapboards to reduce their "primitive" appearance. Here, however, early 20th-century and later additions left the core readily visible.

SEVEY
Town of Colton, St. Lawrence County

SV 1 WINDFALL HOUSE
94 NY 56, just north of NY 3; ca. 1867–68 and later

Built primarily for hunters from the St. Lawrence Valley, this is one of the oldest surviving wilderness hotels in the Adirondacks. The tiny crossroads settlement was named for the first proprietor, Johnston Sevey. The establishment remained in family hands until 1960. Long vacant, the building's exterior stands little altered save for the collapse of its front porch. Regrettably, the ruinous state into which it has been allowed to lapse, combined with its still remote location, makes preservation an unlikely outcome.

WANAKENA
Town of Fine, St. Lawrence County

WN 1 HAMLET
If practical considerations drove Leon-
ard Wilson, the Rich Lumber Company's advance man, in the selection of a site for Wanakena as the company's new base of operations, other factors may have entered the equation as well. Located along the Oswegatchie River where it begins to widen into Cranberry Lake, the setting certainly would have had some picturesque appeal. The hamlet was segregated by the river from the several mills, and they in turn were oriented in the opposite direction, toward a dammed mill pond to the south. To reach the mills, the company constructed a wooden **suspension footbridge** (ca. 1902) at the end of Second Street, a structure more suggestive of a pleasure ground than an industrial community. This local icon was destroyed in a 2014 flood, but has been reconstructed. The remaining **houses** are sufficiently commodious to suggest they were designed for families. Most of them line Second and Third streets for a block north of the river. In between lay a spectrum of community facilities, of which the **Western Presbyterian Church** at 24 Second Street is the most conspicuous remnant. Built in 1903 from a design by Philadelphia architect Benjamin D. Price in his *Catalogue of Architectural Plans* (1899) [see also BL 6], the edifice has been preserved as a museum. There was also a large general store, a clubhouse with library and bowling alley, and a restaurant. As the hamlet quickly grew to accommodate some 500 inhabitants it also became a staging ground for tourists headed for Cranberry Lake. As one of the first buildings in the hamlet, the Hotel Wanakena was erected to house people on company business, but, especially with a large addition made in 1906, its size and appearance suggested it was also conceived as a place for tourists or sportsmen.

WN 2 ADMINISTRATION BUILDING, RANGER SCHOOL, SUNY COLLEGE OF ENVIRONMENTAL SCIENCE & FORESTRY
End of Ranger School Road, 1.2 miles east of Second Street; 1927–28, Office of the State

Architect (Albany); later additions

With thirty miles of logging railroad lines and twelve logging camps, Rich Lumber soon depleted its holdings. Operations ceased in 1912 when the company relocated to Vermont. Much of the hamlet survived, however, because the topography and the amenities the company provided made it an ideal setting for a low-key enclave of seasonal and retirement houses. Even the hotel lasted for another half century. But probably nothing would have been saved were it not for the Ranger School. J. Otto Hamele, who was charged with disposing of the houses and other assets the company left behind, devised a means by which the town would not be deserted. With the Riches' approval, he offered 1,800 acres of land to the newly created state College of Forestry that was affiliated with Syracuse University. In turn, the school's dean, Hugh Baker, persuaded

the donors that a ranger school was needed more than their initial idea of an experimental station. Baker moved quickly, and by the close of 1912 his project was under way.

Forestry schools were then in their infancy; Baker's program at Wanakena was the first in the U.S. to adopt the European practice of having instruction outside the academy on land that itself could serve as a classroom. It was also the first such school to survive for more than a short time. As the program matured, plans were made to replace the initial temporary buildings with a more suitable facility. After a number of delays construction began in 1927 on what is now called the Administration Building (which has always contained a variety of functions). The school has continued to grow, with a west wing constructed in 1961–62 and a larger, more compatible addition of 2001–02.

WN 3 KNOLLWOOD BRIDGE
Near end of Sunny Lake Road, 3 miles south of NY 3, at Oswegatchie River, Star Lake; 1918–23, Frederic R. Calkins, designer (note: the structure can be readily seen from the road, but it and the grounds to which it leads remain in private hands and are not accessible to the public)

To the west, well beyond the hamlet, lies this fanciful, arched suspension bridge for pedestrians. Calkins, a Watertown surgeon, designed the structure to serve as the portal to his rustic camp.

NEWTON FALLS

Town of Clifton, St. Lawrence County

NF 1 HAMLET
CR 60, north of NY 3

James L. Newton purchased over 15,000 acres in 1887, conveying them to his Newton Falls Paper Company a year after its incorporation in 1894. Besides a **dam** and **hydroelectric plant** the company built two churches, a schoolhouse, the **Newton Falls Hotel** (the primary function of which was as a men's boardinghouse), and a number of **employees' residences**, as well as its own **pulp mill** in the course of two years, beginning operations in 1896. Most of the mill's early components, save for the landmark 200-foot-tall **smokestack** built in 1916 by James A. Outerman, were destroyed to make way for new facilities after World War II. A major structure was added in 1969, and the **boiler plant** was constructed eleven years later from plans by Wareham, De Lair, with Roger G. Bloomfield as consulting engineer. Much of the early employee housing remains along the principal (Grove) street as well as along Front and Elm streets. Some Sears, Roebuck kit houses were added to the community around 1915. A separate enclave for higher-level employees was constructed in 1947 along **Wilsey Circle**, approximately one mile to the south on CR 60.

McGraw-Hill purchased the plant (and the hamlet) in 1920, operating it for sixty-four years. The plant was sold to a venerable Swedish conglomerate, which invested as much as $100 million in new equipment and other improvements during the 1980s. Strained labor relations prompted a new sale only eleven years later to the Wisconsin-based Appleton Paper Company, but operations ceased in 2001. A subsequent attempt to revive the facility did not last long. The future of one of the most intact industrial communities in the Adirondacks remains uncertain.

BE 1 BENSON MINE COMPANY – JONES & LAUGHLIN STEEL COMPANY IRON MINE AND PLANT

BENSON MINES and STAR LAKE

Town of Fine, St. Lawrence County

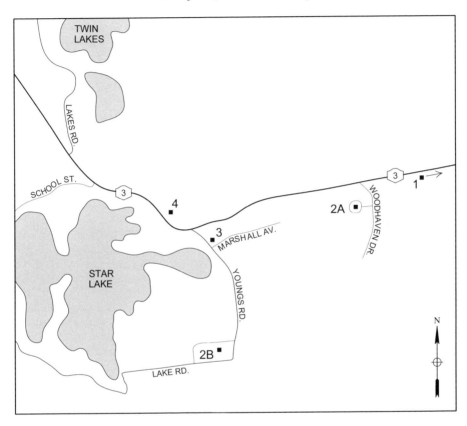

NY 3 and CR 60; 1940s and later

While operations began at Benson Mines in 1889, immediately following the arrival of the Adirondack & Carthage Railroad, the most intense activity occurred during World War II, when the federal government built a plant to extract low-grade magnetite ore from an open-pit mine. The plant was run by Jones & Laughlin Steel Company, which purchased the property after the return of peace. Benson Mines remained a sizable enterprise for some three decades, but was closed in 1978 when the company secured a cheaper source of ore elsewhere. Much of the plant remains in derelict condition. Most prominent from public rights of way are the streamlined **entrance gates** and two **bridges** connecting fields on either side of CR 60.

BE 2 COMPANY HOUSING

While most mine employees lived close to the operation, those in the upper ranks lived over a mile away in the hamlet of Star Lake. A cul-de-sac **residential development (a)**, probably a company project from the 1920s, at Woodhaven Drive and Bach Circle, off NY 3, has standardized designs of an elementary sort, but also generously sized lots in a sequestered location.

Around 1950 Jones & Laughlin contracted with National Homes Corporation of Lafayette, Indiana, a major manufacturer of prefabricated houses, to develop **Sunnyview (b)**, two blocks of modest ranch houses, in an effort to attract and retain employees. They are located at 399–425 Lake Street and 20–35 Griffin Avenue, off Youngs Road, at what was then the southern edge of Star Lake.

BE 3 WESTERN ADIRONDACK PRESBYTERIAN CHURCH
11 Youngs Road; 1943; additions and alterations 1964–65

What appears to be a mid-20th-century A-frame structure is in fact the result of a major remaking of an earlier church, which in turn replaced an 1893 edifice that burned in 1938. The transformation occurred when the Presbyterian churches here and at Newton Falls consolidated. By 1974, the parishes at Wanakena and Cranberry Lake had also joined. Funding for the work likely came at least in part from Jones & Laughlin.

BE 4 STAR LAKE SCHOOL DISTRICT SCHOOL NO. 9
4195 NY 3; 1882; 1892

This rare surviving example of an early schoolhouse in the western Adirondacks was doubled in size (and simplified in design) after the railroad's arrival and the opening of Benson Mines. Beginning in 1952 the building housed some town services. A successful preservation campaign in 2010–12 led to its rehabilitation as the Adirondack Exhibit Center, devoted to local history and culture.

OSWEGATCHIE
Town of Fine, St. Lawrence County

OS 1 FIRST BAPTIST CHURCH
474 Oswegatchie Road; 1890

Situated along the river that is its namesake, Oswegatchie briefly became a boomtown in anticipation of and following the Adirondack & Carthage Railroad's arrival in 1888. Sawmills, store blocks, and hotels were all undertaken. Little evidence of the short-lived prosperity remains save for this house of worship, which originally was home to both Baptists and Methodists in union. It is now a residence.

FINE
Town of Fine, St. Lawrence County

FI 1 CONCRETE-ARCH BRIDGE
CR 27A at Oswegatchie River; ca. 1924,

The development of a statewide highway system during the interwar decades was especially important in linking the re-

350

mote communities of the western Adirondacks. This bridge is a rare survivor of that era, situated about 2.5 miles west of the hamlet of Fine, along a concrete highway that was begun in 1924 to tie that community with Star Lake. Now servicing a tertiary road, the bridge has had its deck widened, but is nonetheless probably the best surviving example of its kind in the park.

FI 2 FINE TOWN HALL
91 NY 58; ca. 1884

The tiny hamlet of Fine retains a sense of the remoteness characteristic to many western Adirondack settlements, giving no evidence of an industrial base that ended over a century ago. The wood-frame town hall is configured much like store blocks found in fledgling Adirondack communities. Here the second floor served as a community auditorium, while town offices occupied the ground level.

FI 3 FIRST METHODIST CHURCH
NY 58; 1883–84, J. Irving, builder

To the west on the opposite side of the highway is another survivor of Fine's early development, the first house of worship erected anywhere in the town, and a good example of late 19th-century rural church design. It has experienced few changes, but has long stood vacant.

TOWN OF CLARE
St. Lawrence County

CR 1 CLARE TOWN HALL
CR 27; 1897, John Bird, builder

The second smallest town in the Adirondacks, with a population of 105 in 2010, Clare was also one of the last to be formed (1880). After early lumbering activity, the land was primarily used for farming. Most of the few businesses it supported have long gone. However, the former town hall, built by the highway commissioner, John Bird, remains intact. The interior space is devoted to an auditorium for town meetings and events. Although official functions moved elsewhere in 1968, the building is maintained as a community center.

11
CENTRAL LAKES

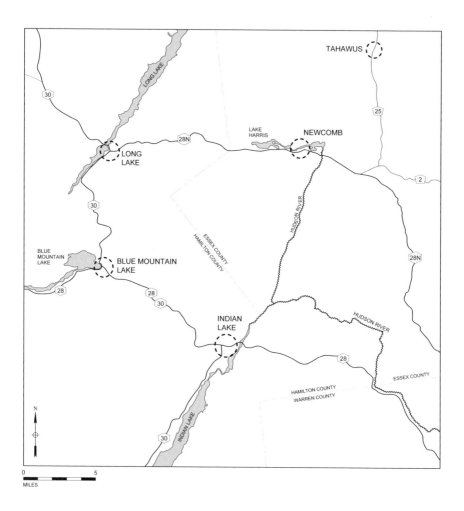

IF THERE IS AN OVERARCHING HISTORICAL FACTOR characteristic to this area—encompassing Lake Henderson at Tahawus; Harris, Newcomb and Rich lakes in Newcomb; Long Lake; Little Tupper Lake; Blue Mountain Lake; and Indian Lake—it is remoteness. With few exceptions, what scarce concentrated settlement there was occurred late, was shaped by the challenges of transporting people and goods over long distances, and for a considerable time remained in a primitive state. Unlike most parts of the Adirondacks, the railroad never entered this area until a restricted route was constructed to serve the titanium mine at Tahawus in the 1940s. Thomas C. Durant's Adirondack line, which terminated at North Creek [Section 4], over thirty miles from Blue Mountain Lake, did have an impact on resort development there and at Long Lake. William Seward Webb's Mohawk & Malone (New York Central) Railroad passed along the northwestern rim of the area. Its stations there served a few large preserves, facilitating the construction of camps and the extraction of timber. William West Durant's extension of the line from Old Forge to Blue Mountain Lake in 1899 had a consequential impact on the resort development of Blue Mountain Lake. Still, the railroad's overall effect on the area was never as great as it was in most of the other portions of the park. As a result, industrial growth was negligible after early logging ventures and, decades later, some additional tree harvesting on preserves. The major exceptions were mid-19th-century ironworks and the mid-20th-century titanium mine at Tahawus. Remoteness did, however, attract hunting and fishing parties, vacationers who wished to enjoy hotel luxuries in a wild setting, and others who yearned to build a camp in splendid isolation.

THE RURAL AREA LONG KNOWN AS TAHAWUS WAS OCCUPIED far earlier than other parts of this section. After closing his Elba Iron Works [Section 9] in 1817, Archibald McIntyre and several associates established a new operation on a 106,000-acre tract just south of what is now called Lake Henderson. In 1832–33, after discovering a large deposit of unusually high-grade ore, McIntyre built a forge. The enterprise failed because, with a high concentration of titanium dioxide, the iron proved hard to smelt. A renewed effort six years later, now under the auspices of the Adirondack Iron & Steel Company, ended with similar results. The logistical challenges also were formidable. To secure supplies and ship its ore, the company had to construct a road over rugged terrain to the Schroon River, itself a remote location, some twenty miles to the east.

Undaunted, McIntyre's son-in-law and works manager, David Henderson, spearheaded the building of a state-of-the-art blast furnace in 1843–44. This venture likewise fell below expectations. Henderson died accidentally the following year. Still the company's leadership embarked on further improvements in preparation for developing a steelworks. While they failed to secure the investment necessary to consummate the project, McIntyre and his partners contracted with Joseph Dixon in 1848 to build a plant for the manufacture of steel in Jersey City. Dixon's pioneering works soon produced steel of exceptionally high grade. A year later the Adirondack Steel Company was incorporated to manage production on a commercial scale, but problems arose meeting the demand and making steel of consistent quality. The Jersey City plant closed in 1853 and an enormous new blast furnace constructed at Tahawus for this enterprise shut down the following year after only two cycles of operation [TA 2a].

To make matters worse, a flood ravaged a sizable portion of the plant in 1856. McIntyre's death two years later led the remaining partners to relinquish hope for any swift revival. Still, they refused to abandon the enterprise, hiring a succession of caretakers to protect their investment. Besides the plant, the company owned the community that served it (renamed Adirondac in 1848), which contained around twenty-five houses, a large boardinghouse, carpenter and blacksmith shops, saw- and gristmills, a powerhouse, and a building used both as the church and school. The little hamlet and the land itself proved to be the company's greatest asset. A

Adirondack (later Tahawus) Club, Tahawus, adapted from boardinghouse at Upper Works of Adirondack Iron & Steel Company, ca. 1830s–40s. (ca. 1880s print)

portion of the tract was leased in 1876 to the Preston Ponds Club (renamed the Adirondack Club a year later), one of the first property-owning organizations devoted to hunting and fishing in the park. Comprised mostly of well-heeled New Yorkers, the club adapted the big boardinghouse to its needs, and over the years it retrofitted some of the other buildings in the compound, while in other cases building anew on old foundations. Reorganized as the Tahawus Club in 1898, the group continued to occupy the premises until 1947.

At the outset of World War II, the National Lead Company, through the federal Defense Plant Corporation, acquired a large portion of the tract and received monies to develop an enormous open-pit mine for titanium dioxide—the very substance that had thwarted McIntyre's iron production. The project entailed a plant to create a by-product, iron sinter, for the making of steel; a community for workers and their families (the only place ever officially called Tahawus); and a railroad that connected to the existing line at North Creek. National Lead's holdings encompassed around 7,000 acres, including those occupied by the Tahawus Club. The plant operated until 1989, but the company divested itself of the village twenty-six years earlier when most of the buildings were moved to form the Winebrook Hills section of Newcomb [NE 1]. In 2003 the Open Space Institute purchased the now 10,000-acre Tahawus Tract, setting most of it aside for conservation.

Some settlement occurred in the area that would become Newcomb hamlet as early as the 1820s, but it was not until the century's third quarter that the place emerged as a lumbering center. By 1900 its major draw was as a hunting and fishing destination. An abundance of lakes, ponds, and brooks, as well as the headwaters of the Hudson, combined with a relatively gentle terrain made the territory ideal for such activities. The Wayside Inn was one of several hotels constructed around the turn of the 20th century. The most ambitious enterprise was the Lake Harris House (1903), which was part of a 6,000-acre tract. Two large preserves, Santanoni

Lake Harris Hotel, Newcomb, 1903, ca. 1912, burned 1944. (early 20th-century postcard)

[NE 2] and Arbutus [NE 3], were created in the vicinity by Robert Pruyn and Archer Huntington, respectively.

Long Lake's history is in many respects similar. Situated some twenty-five miles to the west of Newcomb, the area was even more isolated. The town was formed in 1837, nine years after Newcomb, and settlement was likewise slow to occur. By the 1850s some subsistence farms existed on the shores of the lake—really a fourteen-mile-

Hotel Sagamore, Long Lake, 1891–92, demolished early 1960s. (ca. 1920s postcard)

long widening of the Raquette River—and lumbering abounded during the mid-19th century as well. But even before Newcomb, Long Lake attracted visitors entranced by its wild lands. This popularity received a great boost in 1869 with the publication of William H. H. Murray's *Adventures in the Wilderness*, which featured Long Lake as one of its principal settings. The following year, the well-known artist Arthur F. Tait established a camp nearby on South Pond. His paintings and, especially, his prints published by Currier & Ives, became a primary means by which the public first gained a sense of the region's natural landscape. Hotels began to be built on Long Lake in the 1870s. Among these the four-story Sagamore (1882–85) was the grandest. When it burned a mere four years after its opening, the pile was rebuilt along even more ambitious lines, with a capacity of up to 250 guests. The Sagamore enjoyed a long life, operating until 1946. Another seventeen years elapsed before it was demolished.

Beginning around the turn of the 20th century a number of sizable camps were constructed along the lake's northern shores. Some of the largest private preserves in the Adirondacks lay farther to the northwest and west. William C. Whitney's park (1898) around Little Tupper Lake entailed over 71,000 acres by 1901 and became a showcase for forestry practices. William Seward Webb started the conservation trend in the region, commissioning Gifford Pinchot, later the first chief of the U.S. Forest Service, to survey his adjacent Ne-Ha-Sa-Ne Park (1890) of 112,000 acres, a study that became a model for American foresters. To the south lies Brandreth Park (1851) of 27,298 acres. Amid these preserves, Charles Daniels's great lodge, Tarnedge (1912–13) [LO 8], sat on a "minor" holding at 5,568 acres.

Some lumbering was done at Blue Mountain Lake in the early 19th century, but soon after the first settlers arrived in the 1840s, accommodating visitors became a primary source of employment. Lodgings, not surprisingly, were rudimentary, beginning when John G. Holland came from North Creek to erect the Blue Mountain Lake Hotel, a two-and-one-half-story log structure situated in what would become the hamlet's center. On a bluff one mile to the north Tyler Merwin added a log structure to his farm, opening it as the Blue Mountain House in 1874. The annex [BK 1], built two years later, survives on the grounds of the Adirondack Museum. When his first building burned in 1880, Mervin constructed a frame one that was still elementary in character. On the other hand, Holland added a sizable, embellished three-story building to his establishment in 1877–78, the first to attempt any pretense at luxury. When this burned in 1886, he rebuilt again in an even more lavish manner, creating a hotel that necessitated more financial outlay than the summer season warranted. When that building burned in 1904 no successor rose in its place.

Even at its height, Holland's hotel was dwarfed by the Prospect House, situated on the lake on a point not far to the west. Built for Thomas C. Durant's nephew, Frederick C. Durant, in 1880–82, the hostelry was four and a half stories high; its main porch rose three tiers, extending 255 feet end to end. Durant conceived his operation as one rivaling the Fort William Henry Hotel, in Lake George [Section 1] or the grandest hotels in Saratoga. The Prospect House boasted a hydraulic elevator, and its management asserted that it was the first hotel in the world to have electric lighting throughout its interior. The Prospect House, too, proved unjustifiably expensive to operate. After changing hands twice before closing in 1903, the hotel stood vacant for another dozen years before it was demolished.

The rise of Blue Mountain Lake as one of the Adirondacks' most stylish resorts was fostered by improvements made by Thomas C. Durant in the road and stage

Prospect House, Blue Mountain Lake, 1880–82, demolished 1915–16. (early 20th-century postcard)

service from North Creek. Webb's railroad, which reached the hamlet of Fulton Chain (now Thendara) in 1892, also opened access from the west by steamboat via the Fulton Chain of lakes [Section 12]. Durant's son, William West Durant, came to the area in 1876 to stimulate resort development. With the help of Collis Huntington and others he succeeded in shortening the trip to Blue Mountain Lake by extending Webb's railroad to Raquette Lake in 1899. The following year he opened a three-quarter-mile railroad on Marion River Carry, connecting steamboat service from Raquette Lake to the Eckford Chain (Utowana, Eagle, and Blue Mountain lakes). Durant focused his projects on Raquette Lake, but near the end of his episodic career in real estate development, he created the Eagle's Nest Country Club in 1900 with the hope that it would stimulate camp building on Blue Mountain Lake. When he was forced into bankruptcy four years later, the Blue Mountain Lake Land Company took over Durant's holdings. One of the company's principals, New York copper magnate Berthold Hochschild, purchased Durant's stillborn country club in 1904 and built a sizable camp there. Others were erected nearby as well as elsewhere on Blue Mountain Lake. With the hotel era largely past by 1905, the community endured as a place of substantial, but generally not lavish, summer residences.

Berthold Hochschild's son, Harold K. Hochschild, developed a keen interest in the region and began to meet with Durant in 1928. Hochschild also collected a great array of historical material related to the Adirondacks. The first manifestation of his pursuits was the 600-page *Township 34*, privately published in 1952 (and long available in multi-volume reprint editions). The next year he assumed the presidency of the Adirondack Historical Association, formed five years earlier with the aim of creating a regional museum. Hochschild had the drive, the intelligence, the knowledge, and the money to make what would become the Adirondack Museum [BK 1] a reality. He chose the site (formerly occupied by the Blue Mountain House), set the tone for exhibitions, and donated his formidable collection. Since its opening in 1957, the museum has become a favorite destination for tourists, an indispensable resource for study, and a repository for small structures of many kinds that otherwise would have been lost.

Like Long and Blue Mountain lakes, the hamlet of Indian Lake began to experience permanent settlement on a small scale by around 1840. Lumbering was the mainstay, but sportsmen started to arrive as early as 1853. The town was formed five years later. Growth was facilitated by Thomas C. Durant's railroad, but the major impetus for recreational development occurred over a quarter century later when one of the

Cedar River House, Indian Lake, ca. 1863, demolished ca. 1950s. (early 20th-century postcard)

largest dams in the park was constructed in 1898, greatly enlarging the lake and, as a result, the opportunities for leisure. Several modest hotels were constructed near the lake's western shore, but the area never approached Blue Mountain or Long lakes as a prominent resort.

*　*　*　*

358

TAHAWUS

Town of Newcomb, Essex County

TA 1 TAHAWUS CLUB

Lower Works Road, off Tahawus Road; mid-19th century; 1877; 1894 (note: while Upper Works Road is a public right-of-way, all property around it remains in private hands and is not publicly accessible)

The same year it was formed (1877) the Adirondack Club also established a clubhouse at the site of the Adirondack Iron & Steel Company's Lower Works, some six miles south of its main compound at the Upper Works. At that time, one of the iron company's buildings was enlarged to suit its new purpose. Additional work in the 1890s brought the clubhouse to more or less its present appearance. In 1929 the club purchased some 6,000 acres around the Lower Works from the Adirondack Iron & Steel's successor, the McIntyre Iron Company. This acquisition was sold to National Lead in 1941, at which time the Tahawus Club became the Upper Works Club. The old Lower Works clubhouse had lain vacant for some years when, in 1947, National Lead took over all the Upper Works property and sold the Lower Works acreage to a reorganized Tahawus Club. The building itself is not only one of the few survivors from the ironworks, but also an important example in the Adirondacks of a sporting club from the 19th century.

TA 2 ADIRONDACK IRON & STEEL COMPANY UPPER WORKS

Upper Works Road, 3.2 miles north of

Tahawus Road and 6.8 miles north of Blue Ridge Road (CR 2)

Completed in 1854, the **blast furnace (a)** proved to be the company's last hurrah. But it was also an audacious enterprise that reflected the latest developments in the manufacture of iron. The Tahawus stack rises forty-five feet from its base, above the average for new furnaces at that time and at least ten feet higher than the company's 1844 blast furnace. This greater height allowed for a substantial increase in output. Higher stacks had been introduced in Pennsylvania earlier with the use of anthracite coal instead of charcoal as fuel. Here the company still used charcoal, but took advantage of new developments that yielded a stronger product and worked effectively in the taller furnace. Because this new generation of furnaces were both larger and required higher temperatures, an intricate framework of rods and wrought-iron bands were woven into the masonry structure to counteract greater forces of expansion. The furnace was state of the art and the more impressive for being built in so isolated an area.

The combination of a very short period

of use and the fact that the site was left alone for so many years has contributed to its unusually good condition, and its fabric has been conserved in recent years by the Open Space Institute. The furnace is one of a very few, and arguably the most important, manufacturing structures associated with the iron industry remaining in the Adirondacks and is also likely among the most ambitious surviving examples of its type anywhere from the pre–Civil War period.

The only remaining building from the hamlet of McIntyre (later Adirondac), the semi-detached house known as the **McNaughton cottage (b)** (ca. 1834) was one of several that were adapted by Adirondack (Tahawus) Club members for their use. By the late 19th century, it was the cottage of James McNaughton, McIntyre's grandson, who played host to Vice-President Theodore Roosevelt in 1901. The trip was cut short by William McKinley's assassination. Since its acquisition by the Open Space Institute in 2003, the exterior has been brought back to its mid-19th-century appearance. Just to the north lie ruins of later Tahawus Club buildings.

TA 3 AIDEN LAIR
NY 28N, about 7 miles southeast of Blue Ridge Road; 1914

Around the 1840s Sheldon Hewitt and son-in-law Daniel Gates erected an elementary log structure catering to travelers on this route connecting North Creek and the Upper Hudson with Long Lake. By the 1860s, it became a lodging place for the increasing numbers of hunters and fishermen. Thomas Murphy replaced it with a new lodge after purchasing the property in 1880. That, in turn, was replaced by a sizable frame hotel constructed for Michael Cronin after his purchase in 1893— the building where Theodore Roosevelt stopped during his breakneck carriage ride from Tahawus to North Creek as McKinley lay dying in Buffalo. Cronin's lodge burned in 1914 and was quickly rebuilt on the op-

posite side of the road. He died that same year, but his widow maintained the establishment for another forty years. Situated in an area that is nearly as isolated as it was a century ago, Aiden Lair has stood vacant for many years and is now in a state of conspicuous deterioration.

NEWCOMB
Town of Newcomb, Essex County

The hamlet of Newcomb has long assumed a linear form stretching along NY 28N for several miles, all at a low density. A few public and commercial services are scattered along this path. Although it has lost the industrial base that was its lifeblood when National Lead ceased operations, the community has been resourceful in capitalizing on its historic assets and its topography to foster tourism. While many similar hamlets have decayed, even disappeared, Newcomb offers welcome signs of stability.

NE 1 WINEBROOK HILLS
Adams Lane and tangent streets off NY 28N

During the 19th century, mining town buildings were sometimes moved from a site that had been depleted to a new place endowed with a rich potential yield, especially in the West. However, the National Lead Company's decision to relocate most of its Tahawus buildings to the hamlet of Newcomb in 1963 was an unusual one for its time and place. The project was prompted by the discovery that the existing settlement stood above a major titanium deposit. Workers were given the option of purchasing the house they currently rented on favorable terms. They would have to drive instead of walk to work, but they could enjoy cleaner air, less industrial traffic, sweeping views, and proximity to more services and people. **St. Barbara's Episcopal Church (a)** (1957–59) at 4 Adams Lane serves as a portal to the subdivision where it intersects NY 28N. The building's core was actually constructed as a camp at the Tahawus Club's Upper Works that was first moved to the community of Tahawus in the mid-1950s and substantially modified there to serve as a church. A small store (ca. 1940s) was moved to 8 Adams Lane, where it served the same basic function until it burned around 2014. Before then, **St. Therese Catholic Church (b)** (1948–50) at 14 Adams Lane completed the trio of non-residential buildings at Winebrook Hills's entrance. Beyond on Sanford Lane and adjacent streets are the **houses (c)**, most of them constructed in three campaigns: 1941, 1944, and 1947. Those dwellings erected in 1944 were built by Duplex Construction Company of Glens Falls.

NE 2 CAMP SANTANONI
Santanoni Lake Road, entrance .2 mile off NY 28N (note: motor vehicle access beyond the entrance parking lot is prohibited. Visitors to the farm and main lodge, a round trip of ten miles, must walk, bicycle, ski, snowshoe, ride horses, or contract a ride on a horse-drawn wagon)

Camp Santanoni was, and remains, one of the grandest camps in the Adirondacks and one that had little precedent in its combination of epochal scale and isolated location. Situated in a 12,663-acre preserve that took over a decade to assemble, beginning in 1890, the camp consists of three complexes: one at the entrance, a second developed as a model farm, and the third consisting of the main lodge and outbuildings—all connected by a five-mile-long drive. The preserve includes several bodies of water—Duck Hole, Newcomb Lake, and Ward, Shaw, and Moose ponds. It borders Lake Harris, Rich Lake, and Wolf Lake and also includes three mountains, Baldwin, Moose, and Wolf Pond.

A patrician Albany banker, Robert Clarence Pruyn, and his wife, Anna Martha Williams Pruyn, conceived this vast estate. She had a special fondness for wild landscapes and relished the remoteness of residing at the lodge on the shores of Newcomb Lake. Robert Pruyn was more enamored with pastoral landscapes and made the farm, which eventually had some 200 cleared acres, the focus of his attention. Robert Pruyn was introduced to the area as early as the 1870s by his friend, New York architect Robert H. Robertson, who was a member of the Adirondack (Tahawus) Club [TA 1].

The principal building at the entrance is an expansive **gatehouse**, which also included the manager's residence. Designed by the young New York architectural firm of Delano & Aldrich in 1905, its relatively low-key shingled mass is punctuated by a ceremonious arcuated stone portal, positioned to necessitate a devious, semi-circular path in an otherwise direct route into the preserve. Beyond lies the **West Cottage**, a farmhouse that existed when Pruyn purchased this parcel in 1903 and one that was renovated for staff quarters.

About a mile beyond the gate lodge lies the **farm complex**, begun when a barn was erected around 1895. The compound grew substantially between 1902 and 1908 according to plans Pruyn commissioned from Edward Burnett, who had developed one of the earliest "model" farms (i.e., based on scientific management) at Biltmore, George Washington Vanderbilt's estate near Asheville, North Carolina. Around 1900 Burnett established an architectural practice in New York, specializing in such work. Here the barn received a large addition, and a piggery, chicken house, blacksmith shop and garage, and an icehouse as well as other farm buildings were constructed. On the opposite side of the drive lies the **herdsman's cottage**, an extensive remaking of a mid-19th-century farmhouse; **gardener's cottage**; and **creamery**—the latter designed by Delano & Aldrich. The **farm manager's house** was built around 1919 from plans by Harris Homes of Chicago.

The drive terminates at the **main lodge**, an enormous building designed by Robertson in 1893 and the focus of camp life. Robertson's plan was unorthodox. While sizable Adirondack camps up to that point generally entailed multiple buildings divided by function, a practice fostered by William West Durant at Camp Pine Knot, on Raquette Lake [RL 6, Section 12], and continued into the early 20th century, the lodge here consists of five log pavilions all connected by a porch of some 5,000 square

feet and covered by a roof more than three times that size, to which a substantial service wing is appended at the rear. At the center is a grand two-story living hall at the front and a one-story dining and library area at the rear, all of which form a continuous space, punctuated only by a massive freestanding central stone chimney with fireplaces set back-to-back. Above split-log wainscoting, the walls are sheathed in birch bark in the front, Japanese tatami mats in the rear. Two pavilions containing bedrooms and ancillary spaces are set progressively back on each side of the central pavilion.

This singular configuration allowed for numerous informal sheltered outdoor sitting areas, helping to give a sprawling compound a fairly intimate scale, and it allowed family and guests to move from one part to another without exposure to rain. The idea may well have emanated from Robert Pruyn's experience as a youth staying with his father, the first U.S. minister to Japan, in quarters adapted from an old temple. The concept could have been reinforced by an ongoing interest in Japanese art and culture. The spirited rusticity, on the other hand, may well have been encouraged by Anna Pruyn. It is unrelated to Robertson's other work. (Forest Lodge, which he designed for William Seward Webb at Ne-Ha-Sa-Ne Park the year before—the one camp that rivaled Santanoni at that time—was entirely different in its character.) And buildings at the Adirondack (Tahawus) Club were of a much plainer sort.

The other two key buildings at the main compound are a **boathouse** (ca. 1895) and **artist's studio**, the latter designed around 1905 for son Edward Pruyn by Delano & Aldrich.

Camp Santanoni remained in the family until 1953, when it was purchased by brothers Myron and Crandall Melvin of Syracuse. The new owners did much to revive an estate that had suffered from two decades of deferred maintenance, but the scale of work required even for basic tasks led to efforts to sell the land to the state for incorporation into the Forest Preserve.

When the transaction was consummated in 1972 (facilitated by the new Adirondack chapter of the Nature Conservancy), many people assumed that, left to the elements, the buildings would collapse and the acreage would become wild again. A preservation campaign was launched in 1990, spearheaded by Adirondack Architectural Heritage, newly formed for that purpose, and joined by the Town of Newcomb. The initiative eventually led to the state's declaration of the building compounds as a historic district within the Forest Preserve. Through AARCH's own work most of the buildings have had their fabric restored. (Sadly, the barn burned from an undetermined cause in 2004.) The successful campaign should be seen as a model for reconciling the concerns of land conservation and historic preservation. The results allow the public an unparalleled opportunity to experience one of the region's epic undertakings from over a century ago.

NE 3 CAMP ARBUTUS

Arbutus Lane, off NY 28N, 3.5 miles west of Santanoni Lake Road (accessible by prior arrangement)

During the late 1890s William West Durant began developing four of the properties his company held in Newcomb. Arbutus Preserve was the largest of these, encompassing 1,536 acres. There, on the shores of Arbutus Pond, he built Mossy Camp around 1898. (How much of a direct hand, if any, he had in the design is unknown.) Archer Huntington, the adopted son of railroad magnate Collis P. Huntington (Durant's patron and financial mainstay), acquired the Arbutus and also Goodnow Mountain preserves from Durant in 1899. An avid outdoorsman, the younger Huntington shunned ostentation. He had inherited Camp Pine Knot [RA 6, Section 12], but would not use it. In contrast, Mossy Camp, which he renamed Camp Arbutus, consisted of three main buildings of modest size and ancillary structures. Around 1908

Huntington added an impressive stone **carriagehouse and stable**, heralding the approach to the main portion of the camp. After his marriage to sculptor Anna Hyatt in 1923 a large studio and other buildings were erected. Earlier Huntington had significantly added to his landholdings, which totaled some 15,000 acres by 1911.

In 1932, a major share of the preserve was given to the College of Environmental Science and Forestry, part of the State University of New York system, as a laboratory for forest and wildlife management, with the remainder donated seven years later. While some of buildings have been demolished, a number, including the original **main lodge** of Mossy Camp, remain.

LONG LAKE

Town of Long Lake, Hamilton County

Straddling the narrows of a lake of the same name, the hamlet of Long Lake is the primary service area for town residents, owners of camps extending over a considerable radius, and the many tourists who pass through this crossroads community. The hamlet's commercial corridor, NY 30, is among the most heavily traveled roads in the region.

LO 1 HOSS'S COUNTRY CORNER

1133 Deerland Road (NY 28N) at Main Street (NY 30); ca. 1905 and later

The Long Lake Hotel, a pioneering establishment that was operating by 1867, occupied this site. Enlarged and remodeled in 1875, the hostelry lasted another thirty years until it burned. A grocery store, the core of the present building, was erected in its stead. John and Lorrie Hosley acquired the property in 1972, gradually expanding the scope of merchandise and embellishing the building with rustic conceits. They also acquired Stewart's Cabins to the rear and converted the units into shops, creating a classic tourist enclave.

LO 2 CUSTARD'S LAST STAND
1 Lake Street (NY 28N and 30); 1958

Robert and Barbara Jennings built this structure adjacent to their residence to supply summer employment for their teenage children. The design was inspired by the Mountain Mist Ice Cream stand in Saranac Lake [SL 3, Section 9], but it is simpler in detail and bolder in appearance. Barbara Jennings was actually the first to benefit from the proceeds, using them to attend Paul Smith's College [PS 5, Section 9]. With few changes made to either the building's fabric or the equipment inside, it is an extraordinary remnant of post–World War II roadside concessions, and one that still does a respectable summer business.

LO 3 PLUMLEY'S LONG LAKE GARAGE AND TAXI SERVICE
1179 Main Street (NY 30), ca. 1900s–10s

This early automobile service center was a Sacony (Standard Oil of New York) outlet, offering gas and oil, as well storage, auto livery, towing, tires and tubes, and accessories. Earl Plumley's business started in 1903, and it is likely that the substantial quarters that survive were constructed, perhaps in stages, not long thereafter. The building now serves as a town garage.

LO 4 FORESTER'S HALL
1222 Main Street; 1897

A building that has long housed retail enterprises was constructed by the Independent Order of Foresters, which was formed in 1897 by thirty Long Lake residents. Their

edifice was erected primarily to rent "for all public purposes and entertainments." Meetings, dances, graduation ceremonies, and basketball games were among the events held there until the group filed for bankruptcy in 1921. Thereafter, it was used for mercantile purposes, most notably as Joseph and Christine Becker's general store from 1928 to 1981. Movies were shown upstairs. It subsequently became Adirondack Outfitters of Long Lake and, in 1996, Adirondack Hardware. The building has experienced relatively little physical change.

LO 5 ADIRONDACK HOTEL
1245 Main Street; 1903–04; 1914

Like so many Adirondack hotels, this one replaced the earlier Lake House (1878–79), built by Cyrus Kellogg after selling the Long Lake Hotel. Following the loss of the Lake House to fire in 1901, Patrick C. Moynehan, a Glens Falls lumberman and business partner with William C. Whitney, commissioned the present building. The brainstorm siding is relatively recent. This establishment and the Long View Lodge [LO 11] are good examples of medium-sized tourist hotels once numerous in the Adirondacks.

LO 6 CEDARLANDS GATEHOUSE
End of Kickerville Road, 2.9 miles northeast of NY 30; ca. 1911, Beecher Wilson, builder

After spending several summers at the Sagamore Hotel, Brooklyn real estate mogul Thomas Walker developed Cedarlands as a camp of 35,000 acres. Merlin Austin, a local guideboat builder, apparently designed the original lodge. The boathouse and caretaker's house were built by G. H. Rogers of North River. The Upper Mohawk Council of the Boy Scouts acquired much of the tract in 1963. This fanciful stone gatehouse is now a residence.

LO 7 LITTLE TUPPER LAKE HEADQUAR-TERS, WHITNEY INDUSTRIES
901 Sabattis Road, 4.6 miles from NY 30

In 1897 William C. Whitney, New York attorney and businessman, retired Secretary of the Navy, and grandson of Cornelius Vanderbilt, teamed up with Patrick C. Moynehan, a Glens Falls lumberman, to purchase some 68,000 acres of central Adirondack land. They hired Henry S. Graves, a disciple of Gifford Pinchot, to prepare a forestry plan, one of the first on a large scale. The initial run of logging began according to this scheme in 1898 and lasted until 1909. Three years later son Harry Payne Whitney established the Whitney Realty Company (later Whitney Industries) to oversee the operation. His grandson Cornelius Vanderbilt Whitney took the helm in 1931. By the eve of World War II, Whitney Industries held some 96,000 acres, employed around forty families, owned 150 buildings, and had about 200 miles of fire trails. Fishery management became as important a goal as forest conservation and replenishment.

The Whitneys never built a grand camp, and indeed did not use the Adirondacks as their principal place of resort during the summer. While most of the tract remains in family hands, 14,700 acres, including most of Little Tupper Lake, were acquired by the state in 1998 to stave off a subdivision plan. The Little Tupper Lake Headquarters complex, service center for six family camps as well as the forestry enterprises, was part of the extensive infrastructure developed by Whitney Industries long before that purchase. The sizable **manager's office and staff quarters**, dating from the early 20th century, is prominently sited on a crest overlooking the lake.

The small cluster of **staff houses**, erected around 1947–48 for lumber camp managers, was planned as the beginning of a complex of 150 dwellings. They were designed by a long-forgotten but talented New York architect, Henry Hebbeln, with William Hunt Dietrich as an associate, in a refined modernist idiom. After graduating from Cranbrook Academy, in Michigan, Hebbeln worked for several leading figures in Modern architecture: Alvar Alto, Antonin Raymond, and William Lescaze. His work here also seems inspired by the recent houses of Marcel Breuer. Each dwelling was sited to capture winter sun and allow some degree of privacy. The built-up copper roofs were set at a slight slope to facilitate water run-off while retaining snow as an insulator. Had the whole enclave been realized, it would have been an important example of Modern community design of the period.

The Department of Environmental Conservation now uses the compound to oversee management of the Whitney Wilderness Area of the Forest Preserve.

LO 8 TARNEDGE
1745 Sabattis Road; 1912–13 and later
(accessible by prior arrangement)

In 1912 Charles and Florence Goodyear Daniels commissioned an immense half-timbered lodge on Bear Pond, to the west of Little Tupper Lake amid a 5,000-acre tract. While a challenge to access by automobile, it was located close to the Sabattis station (Long Lake West) of the New York Central Railroad. The brooding design by architect Neil Smith gave little indication of its isolated circumstances. Called Tarnedge (beside the lake), the estate included an adult-size **playhouse**, a **barn**, and **staff quarters**, as well as a nine-

hole golf course. After its purchase in 1957 by the Watchung (New Jersey) Area Council of the Boy Scouts of America, the main lodge was demolished, but other buildings were retained to serve as the Sabattis Adventure Camp. The playhouse is undergoing a major repair program.

LO 9 BOG RIVER FALLS BRIDGE
CR 421, .6 mile west of NY 30; ca. 1926

Crossing the Bog River where it empties into Tupper Lake, this graceful concrete arch bridge, sheathed in stone, was built as part of road improvements to a long-gone recreation center at Horseshoe Lake as well as to the former American Legion Camp at Tupper Lake.

LO 10 DONNELLY'S SUNSET POINT CABINS
987 Deerland Road (NY 28N and 30); 1923 and later

Owned and operated by members of one family from the time Tom Rogers constructed the first components until 2006, this cluster of cabins was enlarged incrementally into the 1950s and has little changed since then.

LO 11 LONG VIEW LODGE
681 Deerland Road; 1929

Long View Lodge began as a tourist home run by Wallace and Mary Ann Emerson in the 1867 farmhouse built for his parents. The current building was erected in three months after the older one burned at the opening of the summer season in 1929. Four subsequent generations of the family operated the establishment over the next six decades.

BLUE MOUNTAIN LAKE

Town of Indian Lake, Hamilton County

BK 1 ADIRONDACK MUSEUM
9097 NY 28N and 30

The majority of the museum's extensive collections are housed in buildings of the mid-1950s and 1960s designed by a New York–based civil engineer, Walter Binger. The recent **visitor center** (1999–2000), designed by the Boston firm of Ann Beha Architects, forms a suitably impressive portal to the campus and an effective buffer to the parking deck. The museum grounds harbor a spectrum of 19th- and 20th-century structures—some original to the site, others moved there—that embodies examples of building no longer found elsewhere or seldom seen by the public. In recent years, too, a few interesting structures have been designed for the museum to serve as outdoor demonstration facilities.

Among buildings originally located on the site, the most important is the **Log Hotel**, erected for Tyler Merwin in 1876 as an annex to his Blue Mountain House and restored by the museum after it acquired the property in 1954. It affords a good sense of the pioneer hotels otherwise known only through old photographs. Adjacent is the **Artist's Cottage**, constructed around 1905 for painter Gustave Adolf Wiegand, who from about 1900 through the 1920s was available to hotel guests who wanted instruction. Below the hotel is the **rustic gazebo**, a 1988 replication of the late 19th-century structure on the site. On the hillside to the north lies **Bull Cottage**, built on the grounds for a minister, Clarence Bull, around 1899–1900, with large stone chimneys, split logs that retain their bark, and diamond-pane windows, all common features of rustic architecture at the turn of the 20th century. It was purchased by the museum in 1981. Directly above, the **Moodie Cottage** (ca. 1906), another residence built on the hotel grounds, is not yet publicly accessible.

Sunset Cottage, a small retreat sheathed in dazzling patterns of stickwork, was built in the 1880s at Camp Cedars, Frederick Clark Durant's camp at Forked Lake. All but this small structure at the camp was demolished by the 1950 blowdown. Cornelius Vanderbilt Whitney [LO 7] moved it to his Camp Deerlands thereafter. His widow, Mary Lou Whitney, donated it to the museum in 1995. Nearby, the **Reising Schoolhouse** (1905) was built in the Town of Ohio [Section 3] and operated until 1945. It was donated to the museum in 1987. Below, the **Buck Lake Club** is of recent vintage, constructed in the 1960s by Mike Virkler as a hunting camp on Buck Pond in the Town of Webb [Section 12]. It was given to the museum after the state acquired the leased land on which it stood in 1985. Behind the visitor center is a **fire tower** (1919) of a standardized design, but unusually low owing to the absence of vegetation

atop its original site on Whiteface Mountain [Section 7]. It was the first structure relocated to the museum grounds, in 1971.

To the east of Bull Cottage is the **Environmental Pavilion** (1988), a play on a polygonal gazebo, here greatly enlarged to accommodate school groups and other visitors. The architect, Thomas Chapin of Cambridge, New York, and a former employee of William G. Distin's successor firm, Wareham, De Lair, also designed the **Marion River Carry Pavilion** (1991), a muscular assemblage of log posts and trusses with iron chains as ties that shelters boats and the Marion River Railroad locomotive. Across the pond is a **lean-to** (1992), built by Tom Andrews as an exemplary illustration of structures common to camps of all sizes and a quintessential emblem of the Adirondacks.

The museum has never had a long-range plan for the acquisition of historic structures or for the replication of others. Those that have been moved to the site were determined on a case-by-case basis. Aside from the hotel annex and Wiegand's cabin, including historic structures was not part of the initial scheme. The limitations imposed by the property's size and terrain precluded siting these moved structures in a way suggestive of their original environments.

BK 2 HEMLOCK HALL LODGE AND COTTAGES
305 Maple Lodge Road, off NY 28N and 30; 1898 and later

Built as Camp Na-Wa-Da-Ha for Michael and Clara E. Paul of Philadelphia, this grand dwelling is a relatively early camp for Blue Mountain Lake. Sited high above the water, it bears more affinity to a sizable residence in one of Philadelphia's railroad suburbs from the late 19th century than the rustic compounds Durant was creating in the area. Hemlock Hall became a hostelry in 1948 and has in recent decades benefited from care by several generations of the Provost family.

BK 3 MINNOWBROOK LODGE CONFERENCE CENTER OF SYRACUSE UNIVERSITY
End of Maple Lodge Road; 1988–89, Schleicher-Soper, architects (Syracuse, N.Y.) (accessible by prior arrangement)

Camp Minnowbrook was the name first given to this property of nearly twenty-nine acres by Fred M. Kimball from Swampscott, Massachusetts, when he purchased it from the Blue Mountain Lake Land Company in 1904. Kimball used the property for hunting parties; buildings of any permanent sort were not erected until 1915–16. Nearly four decades later, Stewart Hollingshead, who had enjoyed the premises as a guest, purchased Minnowbrook as an executive retreat for his business, a New Jersey–based chemical company. The main lodge and kitchen burned three years later, in 1947. Hollingshead commissioned a new building, constructed of logs and designed by William G. Distin in the grand camp manner. Five years after its completion in 1948, Minnowbrook was deeded to Syracuse University as a conference center. It, too, burned, in 1988, and was replaced by the present building, a well-crafted and even more dramatic iteration of its predecessor.

BK 5 BLUE MOUNTAIN DESIGNS
8938 NY 30; 1895; 1968, probably Edward Larrabee Barnes, architect (New York); addition 1979

Constructed as Blue Mountain Lake's school in 1895, this modest two-classroom building remained in operation until 1967. It was extensively remodeled the following year to serve as the showroom of Blue Mountain Designs, founded in 1965 by Edith Mitchell and the Barklie McKee Henrys, summer residents from Princeton, New Jersey. This enterprise focused on selling crafts of quality fabricated in the region. The company's logo was designed by Charles Fauber of New York, and it is

BK 4 EPISCOPAL CHURCH OF THE TRANSFIGURATION
NY 28N and 30, opposite Cedar Lane; 1885, Manley N. Cutter, architect (New York)

Facing the lake, this rustic house of worship was built to serve patrons at the lake's hotels, many of whom arrived by boat. Its elementary form is enlivened by the use of slab-log sheathing. The original bellcote was replaced by the present tower probably in the early 20th century.

likely that a still relatively young Edward Larrabee Barnes drew plans for the renovations. Barnes contributed one of the first pieces exhibited, a coffee table; he and his wife designed andirons to be made locally and sold on the premises; and he also designed the Henrys' camp nearby. Within a few years he would become a major figure in architecture, designing museums, office buildings, and other work that won national acclaim.

BK 6 BLUE MOUNTAIN LAKE OUTFITTING (STEAMBOAT LANDING)
8913–21 NY 30; *late 1870s and later*

Inaugurated in 1879, William West Durant's Blue Mountain & Raquette Lake Steamboat Line was an essential component in his plans to make Blue Mountain Lake a major destination for summer visitors. At least portions of the smaller of the two main buildings in this complex were constructed early on as the baggage house for that service. The larger, adjacent building was erected around two decades later to serve a dual purpose. First it sheltered the construction of the line's largest craft, the twin-stacked, seventy-five-foot-long *Tuscarora*, and then it protected that vessel from the elements off-season.

The line's operation continued until 1930. Thereafter, Herbert A. Birrell, a company ticket agent, purchased the property and with his wife, Margaret, converted the building into a tourist hotel, called the Steamboat Landing, with a store at ground level. The Birrells added several cottages during the next decade. Later Herbert Birrell engaged in other businesses, becoming president of several major companies. But since the 1930s this one-of-a-kind conversion has experienced little physical change.

BK 7 POTTER'S COLONY HOTEL
8897 NY 30; *1937 and later*

Across the road from the site of Blue Mountain Lake Hotel lies another storied tourist facility, which was developed by Edgar C. Potter. He took over the holdings of that hotel's owner, John C. Holland, after the grand building burned in 1903. Early on Potter had a lakeside restaurant constructed on the site of the present building and converted guides' sleeping quarters into guest cabins. His replacement hotel burned in 1924, but he kept the lakeside development and the numerous older cottages on the hotel grounds operating. After the main lakeside building burned in 1936, Potter commissioned the current restaurant, which continued until recent years. The hotel cottages on the opposite side of NY 28 were demolished in the 1990s for new residential development. The future of the lakeside property remains uncertain.

BK 8 M. CALLAHAN & COMPANY GENERAL STORE
3445–49 NY 28; *ca. 1900s*

A year after Maurice Callahan began to work for William West Durant in 1895 he became the senior captain of the Blue Mountain & Raquette Lake Steamboat Line. Eight years later he rose to the superintendent's post and later purchased the company and served as its general manager. At a relatively early stage in this upward trajectory, between 1901 and 1911, Callahan erected this sizable emporium purveying general merchandise, groceries, pharmaceuticals, hardware, and building supplies. It continued this basic function into the late 20th century. Recently it has been rehabilitated, restoring many of its original features, but has yet to gain tenants.

BK 9 UNITED METHODIST CHURCH
3437 NY 28; *1888–89 and later*

Originally constructed as a non-denominational Christian Union and community library, this modest shingled building was converted in 1904 to its present use, with comparatively few physical alterations. Across the street at 3432 NY Route 28 is **St. Paul's Catholic Church** (1902–04).

BK 10 BLUE MOUNTAIN LAKE BOAT LIVERY
3435 NY 28; 1910

This unassuming edifice was built as the headquarters for what has become perhaps the oldest continually operating boat livery in the United States. Currently it harbors two 1916 excursion craft: *Neenykin*, built as a sixteen-passenger shuttle between Hyannis and Martha's Vineyard, Massachusetts, and the larger *Towahloondah*.

BK 11 THE HEDGES
End of Hedges Road, off NY 28; 1882 and later

The pioneer camp at Blue Mountain Lake was built for Colonel Hiram Duryea, president of the National Starch Company in New York. He purchased 266 acres on the lake's south side around 1880 and proceeded to develop a compound over the next two decades. The **main house**, erected in 1882, is of a type used for many dwellings of the post–Civil War period, one story capped by a mansard roof. Some of its rustic trappings may have been added as part of the numerous alterations the house has experienced. A **gazebo** was constructed about three years later; a **caretaker's residence** (**Upper House**) and **horse barn**, about 1890. A second residence (**Stone Cottage**) was built ca. 1900–03.

Duryea was killed by a deranged son in 1914; his other son, facing financial troubles, committed suicide several years later. Richard J. Collins, caretaker and superintendent of Sagamore Lodge [RL 7, Section 12], purchased The Hedges at auction in 1920, and developed the property as an informal hotel. A rustic **dining hall** was built around 1924–25 and eight **lakeside cottages** were erected in the 1930s. It was probably during the interwar decades, too, that a full second story was added to a portion of the main house. The Collins family ran the establishment until 1972. It remains in operation, as one of the few places where the public can find lodging in a vintage camp environment.

INDIAN LAKE
Town of Indian Lake, Hamilton County

IL 1 LAKE THEATER
6314 NY 39; 1937, Ward Grover Shippey, architect (Glens Falls, N.Y.)

Built as a seasonal movie theater on a relatively low budget, this modest building, as domestic as it is commercial in its character, reflects the area's small population, even in summer. The facility continued in its original capacity until 2004. After a sensitive rehabilitation, it reopened in 2008 as a year-round movie theater, performing arts venue, and community center.

IL 2 WILLIAM McCANE GENERAL STORE
6127 NY 30; late 19th century and later

This two-story, gable-end building is typical of many mercantile houses built in Adirondack communities around the turn of the 20th century. Here, the two-tier porch and large display windows are modifications likely dating to the 1910s or 1920s. Since then, the building has experienced little physical change. Recently it has been home to the Adventure Sports Rafting Company.

IL 3 NO VACANCY, SANDERS AND SALLY BERK CAMP
471 Lake Adirondack Road; ca. mid-1930s; alterations to cabin 2004–05, Sally Berk, architect (Washington, D.C.); tower addition 2012, Sally Berk and Albert, Righter &

Tittmann, architects (Boston)

After its purchase in 2001, a small one-story building was transformed by its new owners into a fanciful concoction that is fully in the spirit of the individualistic expression found in many Adirondack camps of the late 19th and early 20th centuries. Alterations to the original dwelling were designed by the co-owner, long an active preservationist in Washington, D.C., who was trained as an architect. For the large, three-story ("tower") addition she collaborated with Jacob Albert, partner in a firm nationally known for its elegant historicizing residential designs.

ued under a lease, with Oliver Hutchins the manager. The club was formed in 1948 by people who had enjoyed their sojourns to the place for some years.

In a clearing on land that slopes down to the river, the clubhouse gives a now rare sense of Adirondack retreats that were rustic in their simplicity, not their embellishment. Public access has only occurred since the land was acquired by the state for the Forest Preserve. A local initiative is under way to retain the building as a museum to this important genre of social organization.

IL 4 GOOLEY CLUB
End of Chain Lakes Road, 3.6 miles northeast of NY 28, 1-mile walk from road's end; 1927

Fishing and hunting clubs abound in the Adirondacks, sequestered along rivers and brooks as well as on lakeshores, often on leased land. Situated on the Indian River not far from its junction with the Hudson, this organization took its name from Mike and Oliver Gooley, who were long associated with the site. Between 1877 and 1893 the Gooleys ran Chain of Lakes Camp for Harve Bonnie of Pittsfield, Massachusetts. They subsequently acquired a farm nearby, where, now independently, they catered to hunters and fishermen. Soon they replaced the log house at what they dubbed Mouth of the Indian Farm with a wood-frame structure. After that building burned in 1927 they replaced it with the current lodge. Later, after Finch, Pruyn & Company purchased the land, the operation contin-

IL 5 INDIAN LAKE DAM
Indian Lake Dam Road, 3.5 miles off NY 30, via Big Brook Road and Jerry Savarie Road; 1898, George W. Rafter, engineer

A dam was first constructed at this location in 1845, during the area's initial period of settlement, to facilitate the flow of logs down the Indian River to the Hudson. Half a century later the Indian River Company was chartered to build a taller, masonry dam—one of the largest in the Adirondacks at that time—to develop a reservoir for drinking water and, no doubt, to make Indian Lake a more appealing resort. As a result, the lake became one of the major bodies of water in the area. Some camps and commercial establishments were developed along its shores, but it never became a major destination.

IL 6 TIMBERLOCK

NY 30, 9.4 miles south of NY 28, Sabael; ca. 1887 and later

Over a decade before construction of the new dam, logger David Farrington built a substantial log structure (now Timberlock's offices) as quarters for his crew. In 1899, following the lake's enlargement, now extending fifteen miles in length with eighty-five miles of shoreline, most of it still surrounded by wilderness, Farrington began to take in guests, building tent platforms to accommodate them. After purchasing the compound in 1922 Fred Garrett expanded the lodge and erected a number of cabins on the hillside formerly occupied by the tent platforms. Dick and Barbara Catlin acquired the business in 1964, making further additions, but capping the number of guests to seventy-five and maintaining the informal rusticity that had long characterized the establishment. It is now the only Adirondack commercial resort off the grid.

12

SOUTHWEST LAKES

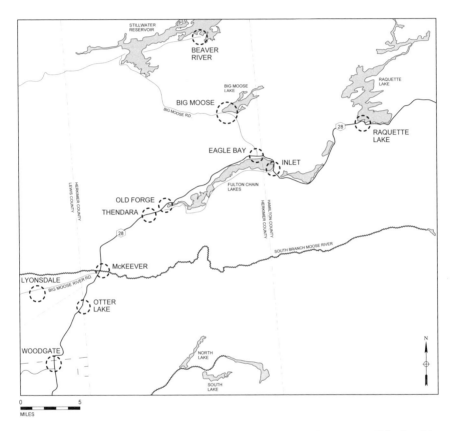

LIKE MANY OTHER PARTS OF THE WESTERN ADIRONDACKS, most of the land in this section, extending from Raquette Lake to White Lake, is uninhabited. Developed areas lie primarily on or near those lakes along the path of what is now NY 28, cutting across Hamilton, Herkimer, Lewis, and Oneida counties. Much of that area is linked by the Fulton Chain—from Eighth Lake, not far to the southwest from Raquette Lake, to First Lake, which terminates at Old Forge, a length of twenty-five miles. Of these, Fourth Lake is the biggest. The chain was created in 1850 by several dams along the Moose River as a means of supplying water to the Black River Canal, west of the Blue Line. Nonetheless, settlement was scarce before the latter decades of the 19th century. With a few exceptions, catering to those in search of recreation and leisure has formed the primary economic base. Early visitors came primarily for fishing and hunting in a wild environment. Toward the century's end several lakes boasted resort hotels, but none of these establishments approached

374

the scale or level of luxury offered by the finest ones at Blue Mountain Lake, the Saranac lakes, or Lake Placid. On the other hand, Raquette Lake became the nexus for some of the most ambitious camps erected in the Adirondacks. A rich array of rustic architecture was also created around Little Moose and other lakes in the large preserve of the Adirondack League Club, near Old Forge. Big Moose Lake was another focus of rustic design, for camps and small hotels alike. Camps of modest size, cabins, campgrounds, and motels are dispersed throughout the area, but even on well-traveled roads, the sense of remoteness amid a vast natural landscape is often present. In Oneida County, resort development around Otter Lake and White Lake was on a modest scale.

THE FIRST WHITE PEOPLE TO TRAVERSE THE AREA around Raquette Lake were trappers and others in search of abundant game. The earliest business established to accommodate hunters and fishermen was Wilbur's Raquette Lake House, a small, elementary wilderness hotel erected in 1857. The year after it closed, in 1873, a second Raquette Lake House opened on Kendall's Point. This venture was more commodious, but lasted only thirteen years before it burned. More typical was the Long Point camp of brothers Edward and Charles Bennett, where a small cabin and tents accommodated visitors (Thomas C. Durant among them). Edward Bennett built the lake's first frame hotel nearby in 1879–80, and after it burned two years later the establishment was replaced by one twice its size. Called Under the Hemlocks, Bennett's hostelry was an unembellished two-and-one-half-story frame building enveloped by a porch, accommodating forty to fifty guests. His younger brother got the upper hand when he purchased land across the lake at Constable Point and built The Antlers [RL 3], which opened in 1887 and long served as the area's finest hotel. Breaking from convention, it consisted of numerous relatively small buildings rather than a single large one. A third Raquette Lake House was built to the south for Glens Falls lumberman Patrick C. Moynehan in 1903, concurrent with his Adirondack Hotel at Long Lake [LO 5, Section 11].

During the same period the construction of substantial camps was fueled by William West Durant, who first visited Raquette Lake with his sister and father in 1876. By then Thomas C. Durant's Adirondack Company owned some 540,000 acres within what would become the park, more land than was held by the state at that time. The elder Durant considered Raquette Lake to be strategically important to gaining control of the central Adirondacks and profitably developing the company's vast landholdings. Most of the acreage surrounding the lake, however, remained in state ownership, and by the mid-1880s state officials were beginning to acquire more acreage through tax sales rather than allow private-sector interests to do so. Raquette Lake had become well known through William H. H. Murray's *Adventures in the Wilderness* (1869), and Durant realized the possibilities of attracting well-heeled seasonal residents. Soon after his initial stay at Raquette Lake, William West Durant began work on Camp Pine Knot [RL 6], on Long Point, near Edward Bennett's hotel. It was a place of pleasure, but also intended to serve as a catalyst for the lake's development as an elite resort. The venture was an instrument for Durant to eventually shape the character of the area's growth.

Well educated and well traveled, but inexperienced in gainful employment at age twenty-six, the younger Durant threw himself into creating a camp like no other, and by the time the second building campaign was completed in 1882, Pine Knot had received much publicity and praise. Even before then, Durant began creating other camps, most of them for members of his extended family. Camp Fairview (1879–84) on Osprey Island and Camp Cedars (begun 1880) and Little Forked Camp (by 1885), both on nearby Forked Lake, were all for cousins. Camp Stott (begun 1879) on Bluff Point was built for Frank Stott, whose daughter Durant married in 1884; and Echo Camp (ca. 1883), adjacent to Pine Knot, was for former Connecticut Governor Phineas Lounsbury. Durant's early camps transformed the meaning of the term from a place with a shelter, small cabin, or just tents, to one that could entail a retreat of considerable dimensions, diversions, and comforts—one with architectural embellishments rendered in a cultivated rustic fashion. He also succeeded in spurring many others to erect camps on the lake, from the remarkably eccentric Camp Inman (1890s) to the grand, sprawling camp for Lucy Carnegie, widow of Andrew Carnegie's brother (1902–03) at North Point.

North Point, Lucy Carnegie camp, Raquette Lake, 1902–03. (early 20th-century postcard)

Building on his momentum, Durant embarked on developing two of the largest camps in the Adirondacks, probably in the hopes that they would lure others to do the same. His 1,500-acre Camp Uncas (1893–95), several miles south of Raquette Lake, was sold to J. Pierpont Morgan in 1896. The previous year Durant sold Pine Knot to Collis P. Huntington, a former partner of his father's in building the transcontinental railroad. Durant then embarked on the 1,526-acre estate Sagamore [RL 7], in 1897, which he briefly occupied, but then sold to Alfred Gwynne Vanderbilt in 1901. Additionally he sold Lieutenant Governor Timothy Woodruff 1,500 acres for Kamp Kill Kare. To improve access Durant spearheaded constructing a spur of the New York Central Railroad from Old Forge to Raquette Lake. Funded by Huntington, Morgan, William C. Whitney, and William Seward Webb, the Raquette Lake Railway opened in 1899, greatly expediting the trip there and to Blue Mountain Lake. The infrastructure included space for parking private railroad cars, an amenity seldom available to the very rich in the Adirondacks. The line also generated a small hub for the otherwise dispersed community, where a large general store and Moynehan's hotel were built, and other services were provided [RL 2]. Among hamlets in the Adirondacks, Raquette Lake's center was unusual in that it was almost exclusively a staging ground for servicing seasonal residents whose habitations lay some distance afield.

Between Fourth Lake to the west and Fifth and Sixth lakes to the east, the small hamlet of Inlet has always been a service center for the Fulton Chain, but its complexion is historically quite different from Raquette Lake. Fourth Lake became a magnet for relatively modest resort hotels. Fred Hess is credited with starting the settlement during the 1870s when he built a cabin on Cedar Island to tend to an ailing friend. Soon it became an enclave of buildings catering to sportsmen. But the major impetus for resort development occurred in 1895, when a railroad line connected the New York Central (at a station also called Fulton Chain, later Thendara) to First Lake at Old Forge and steamboat service was inaugurated to Inlet. That

Steamer Clearwater, *servicing the Fulton Chain of Lakes. (early 20th-century postcard)*

year Hess sold his Cedar Island House, while developing the Inlet Inn, the lake's first hotel. Around the same time he created two other hostelries: Hess Camp and Hess House. The former was subsequently enlarged and remains in operation as The Woods Inn; the latter was also expanded as the Arrowhead. After it burned in 1913, the Arrowhead was replaced by a grander, four-story hotel of the same name, which lasted until 1962. To the west, the three-story Eagle Bay Hotel was erected shortly after 1900. On the lake's south shore rose the Neodak (ca. 1900; rebuilt 1920; burned 1966) and the Ara-Ho Hotel (1923), which continued to operate as Holl's Inn until recently. No other Adirondack community supported so many medium-sized resort facilities during the early 20th century.

Hess was also a guide for the short-lived Fulton Chain Club, which was organized in 1889 by five businessmen who purchased over 6,000 acres from Fourth to Seventh lakes. They intended to create a sequestered retreat along the lines of the Adirondack

Inlet Inn, 1895, burned 1913. (ca. 1900s photograph)

League Club, but the venture failed to attract a critical mass of investors and by the mid-1890s land began to be subdivided for individual camps. The Fulton Chain did attract a number of people who built such places during the early 20th century. While a few were quite grand, the majority of dwellings were more modest. Inlet village emerged as a cluster of stores catering to seasonal residents and vacationers, but also assumed the trappings of a permanent community, with a school and churches. Winter sports had become popular by the 1930s, with hockey games occurring regularly and a 660-foot, double-chute toboggan run (1935) on Fourth Lake.

Principal street (later NY 28), Inlet; Mary's Gift Shop at far right. (ca. 1920s postcard)

378

Higby Camp, Big Moose Lake, 1891, burned 1978. (early 20th-century postcard)

Resort development has also dominated the area around Big Moose Lake, still a remote place some four miles north of Fourth Lake. Jim Higby arrived in 1875 and established the first seasonal hunting and fishing camp for Philadelphian William Dutton the following year. William Dart built a similar outpost on nearby Dart's Lake in 1879, and Henry Covey did likewise at Big Moose in 1880. Other camps followed suit during the decade that followed. Dart built a log lodge in 1888; Higby did the same soon thereafter. Two substantial frame hotels, Lake View Lodge and the Hotel Glenmore, were erected in 1898 and 1899, respectively. More distinctive was The Waldheim [BG 3], begun in 1902 and configured more like many camps, with a modest lodge and cabins, than a resort hotel. Henry Covey's son Earl struck out on his own, designing, building, and operating Twitchell Lake Inn [BG 4] nearby in 1899. His work culminated in Covewood Lodge [BG 1] in 1924–25. Ultimately it was the tradition of vertical log camps and log hotels that shaped the character of development at Big Moose, rendering it the quintessential rustic resort.

If Earl Covey is revered at Big Moose, William Seward Webb is less well remembered for shaping that area as a resort community. He owned all the land around Big Moose and Twitchell lakes, acreage that he subdivided with covenants stipulating the land be used exclusively for "forestry, hotel, camp and cottage purposes." Many of the lots had 100-foot lake frontage. At Big Moose, especially, Webb proved to have had a greater direct impact on development than Durant at Raquette Lake. While not appearing to be part of a master plan Big Moose was among the largest single waterfront developments within the park before the mid-20th century.

The origins of Old Forge are much earlier. In 1798 John Francis, son-in-law of the legendary Providence merchant and industrialist John Brown, lost a valuable cargo he had been sent to deliver, but returned with a promissory note and mortgage on some 200,000 acres in the western Adirondacks. Another son-in-law, Charles Frederick Herreshoff, arrived in 1811 to make good on the unanticipated investment.

Herreshoff built a manor house near present-day Thendara and a forge (the source of the later community's name) along the Moose River. Frustrated attempts to develop the wilderness led to his suicide in 1819. Further initiatives to settle the area were few over the next half century. The Forge House was built in 1871 at the western end of First Lake to accommodate hunting and fishing parties. But it was the arrival of Webb's Mohawk & Malone (New York Central) Railroad some twenty years later that was the essential factor in developing Old Forge and the Fulton Chain of Lakes. The railroad's path lay to the west of Old Forge; the station, around which a small settlement grew, was also called Fulton Chain (renamed Thendara in 1920). From this point a two-mile spur line was constructed to the lakeshore in front of a now greatly expanded Forge House.

Forge House, Old Forge, 1870–71, 1890s, burned 1924. (early 20th-century postcard)

In the Old Forge area the railroad spawned logging as much as tourism into the early 20th century. Centered around the Fulton Chain station, this industry was spearheaded by William Scott deCamp, whose wife, Julia, had inherited some 18,000 acres purchased by her father, Lyman R. Lyon, from John Brown's descendants. After deCamp's death in 1905, son Lyon set his sights on resort development. He successfully petitioned to have the hamlet's name changed to Thendara (supposedly, rim of the forest in Iroquois), created a golf course nearby [OF 8], and formed a development company, Ga-Wan-Ka (the gathering place) for campsites along the Moose River. His principal project was Okara [OF 14], an enclave of modest dwellings built in the early 1920s around two small lakes to the southwest of Old Forge. DeCamp also sold a part of his land to Joseph Young, fresh from developing Hollywood, Florida, to create a North Country sequel on First Lake. Neither of these ventures had the decisive impact on Old Forge their promoters may have wished. Still, the community became a major converging ground for visitors to, and seasonal residents on, the Fulton Chain. After World War II Old Forge emerged as a popular tourist destination, spurred by ski hills and a children's theme park [OF 2], as well as lakeside activities. Motels emerged as the primary form of accommodation. First Lake was lined with modest cottages.

*　　*　　*　　*　　*

380

RAQUETTE LAKE

Town of Long Lake, Hamilton County

RL 1 BURKE'S MARINA AND CABINS
620 NY 28; ca. 1946 and later

Fredolin Burke invested his wartime savings in building this complex, which was mostly completed by decade's end. It remains owned and operated by the family, a prime example of small-scale recreation-oriented enterprises from the mid-20th century.

RL 2 RAQUETTE LAKE SUPPLY COMPANY GENERAL STORE
1 Main Street (CR 2) at lakeside; 1928–31, George Edwin Jackson, architect (Utica, N.Y.)

Dennis Dillon came to Raquette Lake in 1898, working as clerk in John Wheeler's store on Long Point. The operation was moved across the lake next to the head of the new Raquette Lake Railway in 1900. Nine years later Dillon organized the Raquette Lake Supply Company, taking over the store and also Moynehan's Raquette Lake House. A major fire destroyed the complex in 1927. Dillon had the store and warehouse rebuilt, but not the hotel. The store remains intact and is still operated by the family. Nowhere else in the Adirondacks does a single commercial enterprise figure so prominently in serving an entire community.

Just to the west on Main Street lies the **Dillon house** of the same date and by the same architect. Jackson may also have designed the **Casino**, which stands adjacent and long served as a community center.

In 1959 it was taken over by **St. William's Catholic Church**, just to the south, which was built in 1938–39 from funds donated by Mrs. Francis Garvin, J. P. Morgan, and John Callahan. The architect was one N. La Vante of Syracuse. To the north of this cluster lies the hamlet's **Library** (1930, altered), which was also designed by Jackson.

RL 3 EPISCOPAL CHAPEL OF THE LAKE
224 CR 2; 1927–28; addition 1967

Just before fire ravaged the commercial center, this modest house of worship, the first for Protestants in the hamlet, was constructed for year-round use. At the same time, it has much of the informality associated with resort buildings.

RL 4 THE ANTLERS
530 Antlers Road, via Browns Tract Road; 1887 and later (accessible by prior arrangement)

When it opened, Charles Bennett's establishment differed from other Adirondack resort hotels in its dispersed configuration. The Long Point camp he had run with his older brother may have inspired Bennett, but he avoided any of the rustic allusions cultivated by William West Durant. The **main lodge** could easily be confused for a sizable late 19th-century house, with parlor and dining room that served as major gathering places. Sleeping quarters were developed over the years in a variety of wood-frame **cabins**, all informally arranged around the site. At the lakeside a **casino** was erected around the turn of the 20th century as a hub where guests arrived and departed by boat. The building contained a small store with a gathering room above and wing for storing guideboats and canoes. As the hotel grew during the early 20th century a separate **dining pavilion** was erected. It remains today, moved to the adjacent girls' camp at 392 Antlers Road.

After Bennett's death in 1915, The Antlers was taken over by his sister Margaret. Five years later she sold it to the Cedar Island Corporation, which continued to make changes to the physical plant. In 1965, while some of the cottages were sold to private parties, the core of the property was acquired by the Faculty Student Association of the State University Teacher's College at Cortland (now SUNY Cortland), which continues to run it, along with Camp Pine Knot [RL 6], as part of the Center for Environmental and Outdoor Education. The college has been a good steward; much of Bennett's complex remains intact.

RL 5 RAQUETTE LAKE CHURCHES
(accessible by water)

Both the **Episcopal Church of the Good Shepherd** (1880) and **St. William's Catholic Church** (1890) were commissioned by William West Durant, the first for wealthy camp owners, the second primarily for his camp-building workforce that was quartered on Long Point. Both were designed by the prominent New York firm headed by J. C. Cady (J. C. Cady & Company; later Cady, Berg & See). The Catholic church is an especially spirited rendition of the Shingle Style, a mode then at its height of

popularity. Later it became a summer retreat for friars and priests. Now operated as a non-profit ecumenical retreat center, St. William's has recently undergone a meticulous restoration.

RL 6 CAMP PINE KNOT
Long Point, accessible by water; 1877–78, 1879–82, 1889–92, William West Durant, designer; later additions (accessible by prior arrangement)

Pine Knot was the proving ground for Durant to develop his vision of an Adirondack camp, and no less so for his workforce to create a rustic architecture that was also elegant and refined. The complex grew incrementally over several building campaigns, absent any evidence of a master plan. William's father, Thomas C. Durant, purchased the property from Charles Bennett in exchange for the elder Durant's securing titles to the land occupied by Bennett's camp.

The first phase entailed a one-story log **lodge**, configured as if a very large tent, but with a low-pitched roof, and broad eaves, loosely suggesting the form of a chalet. Two small log **cabins**, an open **dining pavilion** of cedar logs (now glazed), **kitchen building**, and platforms for two tents were also part of the ensemble. The

layout was informal, with most buildings set among the trees, but with enough clearing to allow visual ties with the lake—a balance between privacy and connectivity that would come to characterize many Adirondack camps. While rough by standards Durant would soon embrace, the experience of the camp nonetheless distinguished itself from the impermanent nature of those such as Bennett's. One commentator in 1877 queried whether "camping out … combined with the comforts and luxuries of city life" did not erode the sense "of some of those features which have always supposed to lend a charm to life in the wilderness."

Durant ignored such admonitions. Within a couple of years he greatly expanded the camp's infrastructure, with a **bath house, pump house, caretaker's cabin, guide's cabin, smokehouse, servant's cabin, blacksmith shop, carpenter's shop, well house**, and **carriagehouse**. Concurrently he built a rustic **houseboat**, the *Barque of Pine Knot* (now on land) for leisurely lake trips. This campaign culminated around 1882 with the rebuilding of the **lodge**, transforming it into what he called a "Swiss cottage." The log base, probably making use of some of the orig-

inal timber, supports a wood-frame second story, sheathed in stretched cedar bark—a veneer Durant would come to use increasingly often. The final building campaign entailed a rambling one-story cottage, again sheathed in cedar bark, for him and his family. As sizable as Pine Knot had become, Durant eschewed erecting a great lodge, instead maintaining the patterns of relatively modest-sized buildings informally sited. By this point, Pine Knot was well known through descriptions and prints; it was widely considered a model in concept if not in all of its particulars.

Durant sold Pine Knot to Collis P. Huntington in 1895. Around 1896–97, the new owner commissioned a large steel **water tower**—a concession to convenience over rusticity. He also added a substantial **recreation building** soon thereafter that was the most ornamentally rustic component of the camp. With flourishes fashioned from branches festooning the porch and a great bay window covered in birch bark and ornamental twigwork, it is entirely of log construction rather than wholly or partially sheathed. If the building was more conspicuous than earlier work, it was also set toward the rear edge of the compound. Given the close relationship between Durant and Huntington, which included financial backing, the former was likely involved in the conception.

After Huntington's death in 1900, the family did not use Pine Knot, but the camp was minimally maintained. Nearly half a century later, in 1948, the 200-acre property was transferred to the State University Teacher's College at Cortland (now SUNY Cortland), which continues to run it, together with The Antlers [RL 4], as part of the Center for Environmental and Outdoor Education. Several buildings fell victim to fire in 1983, and the college has added several others. Overall, however, the camp remains remarkably intact.

RL 7 SAGAMORE LODGE

End of Sagamore Road, off NY 28; 1897–99,
William West Durant, designer; later additions
(accessible through regularly scheduled tours)

If Pine Knot was Durant's grand experiment, Sagamore was the culmination of his camp-building career. The **lodge** itself brings the chalet idiom to a crescendo. In its mass and siting, this building approaches being a civic statement. Rising at the end of a circular driveway and blocking the lake view, the lodge is like a monument to wilderness conquest. This great wall of spruce-slab log sheathing (the building's length is too great for log construction) belies the fact that the lodge is far wider than it is deep and has no great spaces within. Flanking the drive at right angles are the **dining hall and kitchen** that are as understated as the lodge is imposing. Durant also built a large **service complex** to the west that included a barn, blacksmith shop, hen house, wood and tool sheds, vegetable cellar, and carriage shed.

Durant occupied Sagamore briefly; whether he had hoped to be its long-term resident is unclear. Whatever his intentions, he was forced to sell it in 1901 due to his increasingly precarious financial situation. The new owner, Alfred Gwynne Vanderbilt, added to the dining hall and commissioned a **casino** designed by William L.

Coulter, as well as a guest cottage, **Lakeside**, and a "**bachelor's hall**"—all around 1902. Vanderbilt apparently spent little time there from 1903 until he married Margaret Emerson McKim in 1911. Thereafter, a new building campaign was launched, which included another guest

cottage, **Wigwam**, and a **bowling alley** (both 1914); the "**men's camp**" in the service complex, as well as a **laundry building** (both 1914–15); and a **carpenter's shop** and **hydroelectric plant** (both 1915). Vanderbilt died with the sinking of the *Lusitania* four years later. His widow (remarried 1918; divorced 1928) continued to occupy Sagamore into the mid-20th century, entertaining extensively. She undertook numerous projects, including two additions to the dining hall (1924, ca. 1927), enlargements to Lakeside (ca. 1925, ca. 1940), and additional **cottages** for two of her children (ca. 1938).

In 1954 the property was given to Syracuse University for use as a conference center. The pending sale of the property in 1975 became a cause célèbre among the growing contingent of people concerned with the future of grand Adirondack camps.

The state's Department of Environmental Conservation was the only bidder, prompting fears that the camp would be lost under the forever wild provisions of the state constitution once the transfer occurred. The newly formed Preservation League of New York State worked with the DEC to find an outside party to buy the 7.5-acre area in which most of the buildings lay. That initiative succeeded with acquisition by the National Humanistic Education Center (now Sagamore Institute of the Adirondacks). However, the service complex was omitted from the sale and was imminently threatened with destruction. Sagamore and the Preservation League formed a coalition in 1983 to secure a swap of 200 acres of wild land for the ten acres occupied by the complex, necessitating an amendment to the state constitution. Both episodes served as a launching pad for activist preservation in the Adirondacks.

INLET

Town of Inlet, Hamilton County

IN 1 BRYNILSEN'S VIKING VILLAGE
2387 South Shore Road (CR 118); ca. 1890 and later

Around 1890 Melzer Aldrich built his house, The Homestead, on the shores of Fourth Lake, expanding it into a hotel, Camp Monroe, around 1895–97. Little changed, it is a rare surviving example of a small Adirondack resort from the period. In 1944 the property was purchased by Alexander Brynilsen, farmer and real estate agent, who added a number of cabins to the resort, all of which he designed and built with the assistance of his brother, Rolf, and son, Olaf. This team was also responsible for **St. Olaf's Church** (1953), which lies

directly across the road and was inspired by Norwegian stave churches. Still operated by the family, the compound bears the strong personal imprint of its creators.

IN 2 MARY'S GIFT SHOP
152 NY 28; ca. 1920s

This wood-frame mercantile building, once typical of emporia in the Adirondacks, has experienced little change. It was long occupied by the gift shop of Mary and Dan Decker and still retains that function.

IN 3 THE WOODS INN
148 NY 28; 1894 and later

Built as one of Fred Hess's several hostelries at Inlet, it was sold within a decade and probably not long thereafter substantially enlarged. In 1905 it was purchased by Philo Wood and renamed Wood Hotel. The establishment remained in continuous operation until 1989—one of the longest runs in the Adirondacks. After lying vacant for fifteen years it was refurbished and reopened in 2004. Along with Earl Covey's hotels at Big Moose [BG 1] and Twitchell [BG 4] lakes and the Ausable Club (formerly St. Hubert's Inn) at Keene Valley [KV 7, Section 7], this ranks among the least altered turn-of-the-20th-century resort hotels within the Blue Line. Adjacent to the east lie two well-preserved early 20th-century **cottage compounds** designed for seasonal use.

BIG MOOSE

Town of Webb, Herkimer County

BG 1 COVEWOOD LODGE
120 Covewood Lodge Road, off Big Moose Road (CR 1); 1924–25 and later, Earl Covey, designer and builder

A man of many talents, Earl Covey was as imaginative as he was resourceful. After successfully operating Twitchell Lake Inn [BG 4] for over two decades, he embarked on a new hotel venture, purchasing about fifty acres near his father's rustic hostelry, Camp Crag, in 1921. With eleven guest rooms Covewood Lodge is not large, but seems monumental with its lakefront elevation enunciated by three sets of paired trunk columns, each pair supporting a deck, with the spaces between left open. The main floor is raised one story above the ground and reached by a ceremonious stair—a baroque gesture in rock. On the south side the porch continues uninterrupted, its columns widely, but evenly, spaced, as if fragments from some primeval temple. While the building is of wood-frame construction, with a few steel I-beams (boxed in hollowed logs) spanning major spaces inside, the exterior has all the massiveness of a masonry building, its slabbed spruce vertical siding reinforcing a sense of monolithic solidity. A cottage

sheathed in half-logs was constructed at the same time; four more were added in 1926–28. As at Twitchell Lake Inn, the Covey family ran the resort. They sold the property in 1951, a year before Earl's death. The establishment remains in operation little changed.

BG 2 BIG MOOSE COMMUNITY CHAPEL
1544 Big Moose Road; 1928–30, burned; rebuilt 1930–31, Earl Covey, designer and builder

When a group of summer residents asked Covey to design and build a chapel, he agreed, but insisted it be constructed of stone instead of their preferred wood. Covey quarried much of the granite used for the walls himself, securing the services of a skilled stonecutter, Louis Panunzio, from Malone to dress and lay the pieces. Covey also selected the spruce logs for the framing, a modified form of cruck construction inspired by medieval English precedent. Instead of an altar in this nondenominational house of worship for year-round residents as much as seasonal ones, Covey built a sandstone fireplace, a feature he revered for its capacity to gather people together. The walls are faced in birch boards with cherry battens. Above the ends, these woods are used to striking effect in sunburst patterns.

Covey all but donated his labor to the project, which tragically burned as it was nearing completion. He was able to salvage some of the masonry, but otherwise had to rebuild the edifice entirely. Like Covewood

Lodge, the chapel possesses a stunning combination of forcefulness and naiveté. He considered it his best work.

BG 3 THE WALDHEIM

End of Martin Road, 1.6 miles from Big Moose Road; 1902–04 and later, Edward Joseph Martin and Charles Martin, designers and builders

The Waldheim is the best surviving example of a Big Moose pioneer family's rustic lodge with cottages. Brothers Edward Joseph (E. J.) and Charles Martin arrived in the early 1890s seeking construction work. They gained ample exposure to local precedent by doing jobs at Jim Higby's and William Dart's lodges. In 1901 they purchased a sizable parcel of land on the lake's north side, erecting the lodge in 1902–04 and several cottages and a dining pavilion in the following years. Like Covey at Twitchell Lake they were designers, builders, and proprietors. E. J. assumed full ownership in 1906. By 1920 the complex boasted eight cottages. More acreage was added fifteen years later. Most of the buildings are sheathed in split logs. They have changed little, set in a wooded landscape that gives a vivid sense of what such compounds were like a century ago.

BG 4 TWITCHELL LAKE INN

Twitchell Lake Road, 2.5 miles north of Big Moose Road; 1899 and later, Earl Covey, designer and builder

Covey's earliest independent work was also his most adventurous from a technical standpoint. For unknown reasons he used pit-sawed (i.e., hand-sawn) half-logs, six to eight inches in diameter, set vertically on a wood sill. This method is an unorthodox adaptation of palisade construction, setting logs vertically into the ground. The original building was modest in its dimensions, assuming the standard domestic form of a five-bay front. It was expanded significantly as the business prospered, transforming the principal (west) front

into a grand rustic ensemble, perched high above the lake. Cottages were added in the early 20th century, as were a boathouse, barn, and workshop. Covey built the last major addition in 1920. He not only undertook the construction, but did the electrical and plumbing work as well, his skills for which were self-taught.

Though not long, the road to Twitchell Lake has always been a poor one and heightens the sense of remoteness that still pervades. Covey erected a stone bridge along this route as a memorial to a son lost in World War I.

BG 5 NEW YORK CENTRAL RAILROAD STATION

2138 Big Moose Road; 1927

A temporary station was built here a year after the railroad arrived in 1892. The building that soon replaced it burned in 1927. This, the third facility on the site, is of a standardized design that seems to have changed little from those of the early 20th century. After railroad operations ceased in 1965, the building lay vacant for some years. It has been sensitively rehabilitated as a restaurant.

BEAVER RIVER

Town of Webb, Herkimer County

BV 1 NORRIDGEWOCK

Norridgewock Road; early 20th century (accessed by ferry or hotel boat [for guests] from Stillwater, just northeast of intersection of Big Moose and Stillwater roads)

Among Adirondack resorts, Norridgewock is probably the most difficult to access. When the first hotel by that name was built on the site in 1889, it was reached by Stillwater Road, an old military route. Four years earlier a low earthen dam had been created at Stillwater, one of several such projects intended to improve the water flow into the Black River Canal. A higher dam, erected in 1894, and yet another replacement, this time in concrete with a hydroelectric plant (extant, but not visible from any public road) was built in 1922–24. These projects flooded some 4,000 acres of timberland and cut Norridgewock off from any road. The establishment flourished nonetheless due to William Seward Webb's railroad, which passed directly in front of the building.

When the original hostelry burned it was quickly replaced by a larger building, which also incorporated the **former barn**, raising it a story and modifying it to accommodate guests. This segment of the complex and a simple two-story **annex** constructed to accommodate overflow remain more or less intact. Adjacent lies a one-and-one-half-story **section camp**, built for railroad maintenance workers, probably the last of its kind in the park. The second hotel was replaced by the current facility in 1964.

A number of small **cottages** from the late 19th and early 20th centuries exist in the vicinity, following the common practice of private parties building their own quarters to take advantage of proximity to a hotel. To the south a concrete arch **bridge**, probably dating to the 1910s or 1920s, connects to additional cottages. As a landscape, Beaver River is one of the most evocative of a remote, modest vacation enclave from the turn of the 20th century.

EAGLE BAY

EB 1 EPISCOPAL CHURCH OF ST. PETER-BY-THE-LAKE

4796–4800 NY 28; 1905, 1910, Christian J. Goodsell, designer and builder

William Seward Webb donated the land for this shingled church, which was built to serve seasonal residents. Like the Raquette Lake churches [RL 4], this one was originally accessible only by boat. Besides his accomplishments in the building art, Goodsell was a well-known guide. The adjacent **rectory** dates to 1912.

OLD FORGE and THENDARA

Town of Webb, Herkimer County

Though of modest size, the hamlet of Old Forge is among the most intensively visited tourist destinations in the Adirondacks. Like Lake George village it is easily accessed from population centers beyond the Blue Line. The commercial core and the strips that extend along NY 28 are foremost magnets for a seasonal trade. The contiguous hamlet of Thendara, by contrast, has been partly bypassed and retains some of the character of a railroad hub.

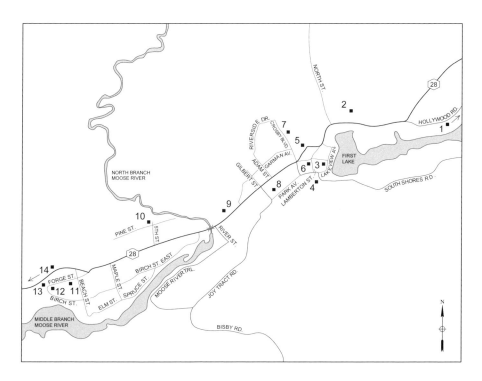

OF 1 HOLLYWOOD HILLS HOTEL
Hollywood Road (CR 216), .7 mile southwest of NY 28; 1933–34

Real estate entrepreneur Joseph Young, who had invested heavily in the development of Hollywood, Florida, managed to retain enough capital after the market there collapsed in 1926 to attempt another ambitious project where he believed demand remained strong. With the aid of investors in 1928 he purchased land along First Lake from Lyon deCamp for $1.156 million and began to survey a tract on the north shore, which he christened Hollywood Hills. With a staff he brought from Florida, Young established a sales office in Utica and began an aggressive promotional campaign, announcing that a 175-room hotel, eighteen-hole golf course, boardwalk, and dancehall would be completed by the spring of 1929. Young also imported a fleet of thirty-two buses from Florida to bring potential buyers from Syracuse, Rome, Rochester, Ilion, and Herkimer, as well as Utica. A beach and pier welcomed people who were transported by boat from Old Forge. The Depression slowed the development, but it did enjoy a brief resurgence when Young held an extravagant Fourth of July celebration in 1931 at a casino erected for the occasion. Over five years, Young sold around 1,400 small lots, ranging from $600 to $1,200, but few cottages were erected given the economic downturn.

Just before the event, Young decided to proceed with plans for a hotel, albeit on a smaller scale than originally envisioned.

389

He may have been inspired by Covey's work at Big Moose, for he determined that the structure would be made entirely of hand-hewn spruce logs harvested from nearby. The design was of an entirely different sort, however, one that Young claimed was inspired by a lodge he had seen in Canada. Two long wings flank an octagonal drum with a two-story public space in the middle of which rises an immense, freestanding, four-sided stone fireplace. Young died in February 1934, five months before work was completed. Creditors filed for involuntary bankruptcy the following year. The forty-eight-room hotel survived under a series of owners into the mid-20th century. Soon after he purchased the property in 1978–79, Timothy Noonan had the hotel converted into condominiums.

OF 2 ENCHANTED FOREST/WATER SAFARI

3183 NY 28; 1956 and later, Russell Patterson (New York), designer of original park; Charlie Gillette, designer of numerous later additions

This complex embodies three phases of amusement park development: a theme park based on nursery rhymes and fairy tales, a water park, and a family entertainment center. Old Forge merchant A. Richard Cohen (son of Moses A. Cohen and a member of the state authority charged with developing ski centers at Gore and Whiteface mountains) and two partners developed the park, hiring designer Russell Patterson to create concept paintings and prepare detailed studies for several of the structures. Patterson had become a famous illustrator during the 1920s; thereafter he designed sets for Twentieth-Century Fox and Paramount studios, display windows for Macy's, restaurant interiors, WAC uniforms, and, late in life, clear plastic umbrellas and rain gear.

Timothy Noonan, owner of a chain of liquor stores in Utica, bought the park in 1977, adding rides and increasing atten-

dance. Seven years later he opened two 350-foot flumes built by Dick Croul, one of the originators of the water slide. In 1986 the 700-foot Raging Rapids tube ride was added, joined by two other water rides in 1999. It has always been among the largest water parks in the state.

OF 3 FORGE MOTEL

South Shore Road, Park Avenue, Laureston and Fulton streets; 1952 and later

Before he began work on the Enchanted Forest, A. Richard Cohen undertook this venture, situated near the Forge House site, in an effort to rejuvenate tourism in the community. Forming a sweeping arc overlooking First Lake, the motel was expanded twice by the year of Enchanted Forest's opening. Cohen also developed a Howard Johnson's restaurant (still discernible as such) nearby on NY 28. Little changed; the motel continues to be a major draw.

OF 4 COTTAGE KENT, BERNARD HEMMER HOUSE

216 Park Avenue; 1930–31, Bernard Hemmer, designer and builder

After serving in World War I, Hemmer came to Old Forge for health reasons. He built and, along with his wife, operated the Hemmer Cottage Colony adjacent to the Town of Webb School [OF 8] into the 1950s. Each of the dozen cottages was given its own rustic design. Despite its name, Cottage Kent is somewhat Germanic in form and was designed in a manner at once fanciful and chaste in its use of slab log sheathing. Hemmer built it as a wedding present for his sister, but he and his

wife later occupied the premises. Most of the complex was purchased for school expansion during the 1960s. The last of the compound to remain, Cottage Kent, was acquired by the Town of Webb Historical Association, which moved it to its current site in 2002.

OF 5 THOMSON BLOCK-STRAND THEATER
3093 NY 28; 1922 and later

C. I. Thomson and his son, Ray, owners of the Forge House hotel, expanded their operations with an opera house flanked by stores and with offices above. The influx of summer visitors no doubt justified constructing one of the few such facilities in the Adirondacks. Faced with the loss of their hotel to fire in 1924, and without adequate insurance coverage, the Thomsons sold the still new theater to Walter D. Marks and A. J. Sardino of Syracuse, who undertook some interior remodeling and added dressing rooms for the performers in road shows and vaudeville acts whose programs were billed along with first-run movies. A decade later Marks added some Art Deco embellishments, including the marquee and entry doors, and changed the name to the Strand. Since 1992 the theater has been under new ownership, its fabric carefully maintained. Additional screens were added in 2000.

OF 6 OLD FORGE HARDWARE COMPANY GENERAL STORE
104 Fulton Street and Crosby Boulevard; 1922–23, George Edwin Jackson, architect (Utica); later additions

When Lithuanian-born peddler Moses Asher Cohen came to Old Forge in 1900 he had difficulty finding someone willing to rent him space. Two years later, as a successful businessman, he erected the largest, most elaborate building in what was still a rough-hewn boomtown. Opened in 1903, his new quarters provided hardware of all sorts and an ever-increasing variety of other goods. Fire destroyed the Cohen Block in 1922. When the emporium reopened in the current building a year later, it functioned as a general store. Cohen later took over Peter Rivet's dry goods and souvenir store at the block's eastern end. Son A. Richard Cohen erected the one-story section between the two during the mid-20th century. The original section retains much of its early 20th-century interior.

OF 7 MOSES A. COHEN HOUSE
220 Crosby Boulevard; ca. 1927–28, possibly George Edwin Jackson, architect (Utica); later alterations and additions

Cohen lived in Utica when his large store burned in 1922; thereafter he relocated to Old Forge, only a block away from his business. The size and reserved interpretation of Tudor motifs differentiate the dwelling from virtually all others in the hamlet, enunciating Cohen's prominent role as a merchant and also one of the largest landowners in the community. In 1976 the house was donated to the Old Forge Library, after which the porches were fully enclosed and other discreet exterior modifications made.

OF 8 TOWN OF WEBB SCHOOL
110 Gilbert Street (NY 28); 1912–13, Walter G. Frank, architect (Utica); additions 1926–27, O. L. Weldman, architect (New York); 1962–65, Moulton & Van Keuren, architects

(Syracuse); 1999–2000, Sear-Brown Group, architects (office location unknown)

Replacing a wood-frame school of 1907, the core of the current building is a robust classical pile that became less awkward with large lateral extensions of seamless design. In contrast, the one-story 1960s addition bears no physical relation to its forebear. The most recent portion, while rendered in a flashy modernist vocabulary, helps tie the ensemble together.

OF 9 NUTTY PUTTY
2931 NY 28, 1959–60; Meyer and Ida Cohen, designers and builders

Perhaps the oldest surviving amusement of its kind in the Adirondacks, Nutty Putty embodies the individualistic and elementary nature of miniature golf courses during the post–World War II era. Members of the Cohen family (no relation to Moses and A. Richard Cohen) continue to operate their well-maintained business.

OF 10 THENDARA GOLF CLUB
151 5th Street; 1920–21, Donald J. Ross, golf architect (Boston), Walter B. Hatch, associate; 1958 second nine holes added, William Harries, golf architect (New York)

Created during the heyday of country club development, Thendara was spearheaded by Lyon deCamp and Maurice Callahan, among others. One of their major target audiences were members of the Adirondack League Club, who, unlike their counterparts at the Ausable and Lake Placid clubs, had no course of their own. Designed by the foremost golf architect of the times, the course is among the most topographically varied and picturesque in the park. Harries's work of the 1950s was intended to be a seamless extension.

OF 11 WEBB TOWN HALL
120 Forge Street; 1900–01, Levi Deis, designer and builder

After the Town of Webb was formed in 1898 William Scott deCamp donated the

land and perhaps this building on the condition that it always be used as a town hall. Larger than most such facilities in the Adirondacks, it served multiple purposes. Besides town offices, it included a jail in the basement and a community hall upstairs. Dances, parties, theatrical performances, and even church services were held there into the mid-20th century. DeCamp's beneficence was likely in part motivated by his desire to have Thendara (then Fulton Chain) become the dominant center for the area. The designer and builder owned Deis & Son Lumber Company nearby. He also was responsible for St. Bartholomew's Catholic Church at Old Forge (1898) and built the second school at Big Moose.

OF 12 VAN AUKEN'S INN
108 Forge Street; 1893, Nelson C. Neice and E. Melville Moose, builders (Rome, N.Y.); later alterations and additions

Constructing hotels near railroad stations was a common practice in American towns and cities during the late 19th and early 20th centuries. Originally built as Mack's Hotel, this is an unusual survivor of its kind in the Adirondacks. It was moved across the tracks to the present site in 1905 due to the hazard caused by locomotive sparks. The building was sold to Charles Van Auken in 1908, when it was aggrandized with a two-tier porch, a portion of which is treated somewhat like a portico. The building may also have been enlarged at that time. It remains in operation as a bar, restaurant, and inn.

OF 13 NEW YORK CENTRAL RAILROAD STATION
Forge Street at NY 28; 1894

A conventional combination (freight and passengers) station of the period, this depot catered to the large number of passengers proceeding to and from the Fulton Chain and points east. The freight house was constructed two years later. Adjacent lies the **Foley Lumber Company** yard on the site of Deis's mill and yard. The New York Central suspended passenger service in 1965. Since 1994 the station has served the Adirondack Scenic Railroad, a seasonal tourist train running to and from Utica.

OF 14 OKARA
Entered on Okara Road, off NY 28; begun ca. 1920, H. van Buren Magonigle, architect (New York)

Lyon deCamp's grand vision of transforming the area into an archipelago of resorts went largely unrealized. This 640-acre enclave, developed around two small lakes southwest of Thendara, is the primary manifestation. For reasons unknown deCamp commissioned a distinguished New York architect to design the **cottages** and a filling station with motifs inspired by traditional Japanese dwellings, eschewing the rustic conventions by then popular in Adirondack resorts. The venture ranks among the early attempts to create a planned resort enclave for middle-income families. Good examples of the original houses can be seen at **107** and **204 Easka Road** and **148 Onekio Road**.

McKEEVER
Town of Webb, Herkimer County

MK 1 HAMLET REMNANTS

Named after William Seward Webb's railroad superintendent, Robert Townsend McKeever, this tiny settlement began as a camp for the line's construction in 1892. Located just beyond the confluence of the South and Middle branches of the Moose River, McKeever became the only place in this part of the Adirondacks to sustain industrial production on a substantial scale for a prolonged period. John A. Dix and his partners established the Moose River Lumber Company's mill there in 1894. Dix was also an investor in the Iroquois Paper Company, which built a pulp mill nearby and acquired the lumber mill in 1907. The plant was sold to the Gould Paper Company in 1924, the Rice Veneer Company in 1947, and finally the Georgia Pacific Company in 1956, only to close four years later. The **plant ruins** can be seen from the NY 28 bridge over the Moose River. The **New York Central Railroad station** (1908), just off NY 28 on the river's west side, ceased operating in the late 1950s, but has been sensitively adapted as a residence.

TOWN OF LYONSDALE
Lewis County

LY 1 MOOSE RIVER BRIDGE
Moose River Extension, just off Moose River Road; early 20th century

393

Moved to its present site during the 1930s, this Pratt truss bridge of standardized design is probably the sole survivor of its kind in the park that is still in use.

LY 2 SCHOOL
9892 Moose River Road; 1876

Once serving a small rural community, this schoolhouse was a cut above many counterparts elsewhere in the park. The tall, medieval-inspired windows and board-and-batten siding suggests that it may have been derived from a scheme by architect Philip Johonnot published in his *Country School Houses* of 1866. It now serves as a residence. Along Moose River Road to the west are good examples of modest summer cottages from the first half of the 20th century.

OTTER LAKE
Town of Forestport, Oneida County

OT 1 LIGHTHOUSE CABINS
NY 28 just west of Norton Road; early 1920s and later, Ray Duntz, designer

Development of the low-key resort community of Otter Lake began in the 1880s and was boosted by the railroad's arrival in 1892. This small compound was developed by Ray and Lucille Duntz, who came in 1922 and subsequently had a lakeside cabin built on the site. Additional cabins soon followed, four facing the lake and others built along a semi-circular drive. Capped by a homespun rendition of a lighthouse tower (with dormer windows) to attract the motorist's eye, the main building (1930) included a restaurant and store as well as office and owner's apartment. Duntz apparently built a model for this component, giving it to carpenters to execute the building. It remained in their ownership until 1961. Regrettably, the establishment has lain vacant for some years.

A range of **cottages** on Norton Road, just off NY 28, are good examples of the modest seasonal dwellings erected in the Adirondacks at the turn of the 20th century.

OT 2 OTTER LAKE COMMUNITY CHURCH
NY 28; 1861

Originally built in 1861 at Hawkinsville, New York, for a German Lutheran congregation, this building is a good example of the wood-frame rural Gothic ecclesiastical design developed and popularized by the celebrated New York architect Richard Upjohn. Abandoned in 1891, it survived for several decades until it was dismantled and reconstituted at Otter Lake in 1921 as a nondenominational house of worship.

WOODGATE

Town of Forestport, Oneida County

WT 1 ROUND LAKE CAMP

End of Round Lake Road, off NY 28; begun 1924 (accessible by prior arrangement)

Initiated by William J. Wiley, superintendent of the Masonic Home in Utica, Round Lake Camp was conceived as a summer refuge for the home's orphan children. The 472-acre Dallarmi farm, which dated from the mid-19th century, was purchased in December 1923, and during the following spring Masons and boys from the Masonic Home were at work repairing the existing farmstead and adapting it for its new use. Soon other Masonic Home orphans came as well. New buildings were constructed and the grounds were expanded to 1,573 acres by 1932.

Situated on a gently sloping hill facing Round Lake, the compound boasts an array of elegantly simple buildings, most, if not all, of which were constructed by Masons. Many also suggest the hand of an architect, whose identity, with one exception, remains unknown. Most buildings were constructed during the mid-to-late 1920s, including the **gatehouse**, **Ainsworth Cottage** (originally two dormitory buildings, joined at an early date), **Allen Cottage**, and the **infirmary**, all of which are low-slung, wood-frame structures with cobblestone veneers extending to the windowsill line—a homespun iteration of the earlier Prairie School in the Midwest. The **library** is built of cobblestones, as is the **Sarah Hill Wiley Memorial Chapel**, a medievalizing tribute to Wiley's mother built in 1928–29 from plans by Utica architects Kinne & Frank. To the west near the lakeshore lie the wood-frame **dining hall** and adjacent **guest dormitories** and **bandstand** as well as a cobblestone **gazebo**. Set in a pine grove, the campus also contains an array of whimsical stone sculptural pieces. With most of its components little altered, the place offers a vivid picture of a well-developed children's camp from the interwar decades.

ARCHITECTS, BUILDERS, AND DESIGNERS

MOST OF THE INDIVIDUALS PROFILED HERE LIVED AND PRACTICED in the Adirondacks year-round. But I have also included several figures who, while based in New York City, opened a branch office or were otherwise professionally active in the region as seasonal residents. I have not included Augustus D. Shepard (New York) or William Wicks (Buffalo), as their work was primarily at the Adirondack League Club and other locations that are not publicly accessible. Nor have I included current Adirondack-based architects whose work is not cited in the guide.

RONALD R. ALLWORK
(1905–77), Lake Placid

Based in New York, Ronald Allwork became a seasonal resident of Lake Placid after World War II and designed several residences as well as facilities for the Lake Placid Club between 1950 and 1970.

Born in Brooklyn, Allwork began working as a draftsman after graduating from Columbia University in 1930. Four years later he received his professional degree from Columbia's School of Architecture and soon found employment as an engineer for the American Radiator Company. He worked on the design of the Red Hook Houses in New York (1938–39) and opened his own office in 1941. Much of his time was spent preparing technical literature for journals (*Architectural Record*, *Pencil Points*) and company catalogues. After serving in the War Production Board's Plumbing and Heating Division, he reopened his office in 1946. Allwork continued his technical writing and took an increasingly active role in state and national professional organizations. In 1971 he was elected a Fellow in the American Institute of Architects for his "contribution to the advancement of the profession."

Designing buildings was really a sideline for Allwork, and most of these commissions were in Lake Placid. His style embraced the modernist penchant for openness and transparency, but also entailed a luxurious display of natural materials and reliance on some traditional forms. One of his first projects, the Golf House for the Lake Placid Club (1951, altered), led to many others for remodeling among affluent seasonal residents. Besides the club's Ski Loj (1962; demolished), he designed a large residence for Nettie Marie (Mrs. W. Alton) Jones on Placid Lake (1966) and a grand hillside residence for his family on Military Road (1963). Much of his work was done in collaboration with his first wife, Eleanor, an accomplished interior designer.

ALFRED C. BOSSOM
(1881–1965), Elizabethtown

At an early stage in his prolific architectural career, Alfred Bossom was engaged in two projects in the eastern Adirondacks: Meadowmount, a country estate in Lewis begun ca. 1906 [LE 6], and the reconstruction of Fort Ticonderoga begun in 1908 [TI 1]. While based in New York, he opened a branch office in Elizabethtown when both projects were under way, no doubt in the hope of securing additional work.

Born in London, the son of a stationer, Bossom attended the Regent Street Polytechnic and in 1899 took a position at the London County Council Architect's office while enrolling in evening classes at the Royal Academy. In 1903 he moved to the United States with George Crawley, a socially prominent amateur architect, who had received the promise of commissions from Henry Phipps, a partner in U.S. Steel. Bossom's experience in London proved valuable in designing a workers' housing complex in Pittsburgh. But it was his marriage in 1910 to Emily Bayne, daughter of the president of Seaboard National Bank, based in New York, that put his practice on a solid footing. Thereafter, and especially in the years following World War I, he designed banks (many of them office towers) in New York, New Jersey, Pennsylvania, Virginia, North Carolina, Louisiana, and Washington, D.C. The strong ties that Bossom's father-in-law, Samuel Bayne, had to the oil industry led to major commissions in Dallas, Galveston, and Houston. Bossom became a champion of skyscraper design in the United States. His *Building to the Skies: The Romance of the Skyscraper* (1934) posited Meso-American temples as a historical inspiration for the three-dimensional, sculptural forms.

Eight years earlier, Bossom returned to England with his wife and two sons, abandoning his architectural career. He joined the London County Council on its housing committee and subsequently was an alderman. He was elected to the House of Commons in 1931, a seat he held for twenty-eight years, until he received a life peerage.

FLOYD EMERY BREWSTER
(1888–?), Lake Placid

Though long forgotten, Brewster made a significant contribution to his hometown during the early years of his practice. Born in Lake Placid, Brewster received an architectural degree from Cornell University in 1912 and held a post-graduate scholarship from his alma mater the following year. Immediately thereafter, he established a firm (Brewster & Kennedy) with offices in Brooklyn as well as Lake Placid. Within two years he managed to secure three important commissions: the Bank of Lake Placid and the Masonic Lodge (both 1915–16) [LP 12], and the town hall (1916, altered). The economic effects of World War I led him to dissolve his practice and relocate to Riverside, California, where he taught architectural, mechanical, and freehand drawing at the Polytechnic High School. By March 1922 he had moved to Santa Barbara, his wife's former home, where he established a new practice that lasted at least until the late 1930s.

BRYAN BURKE
(b. 1945), Essex

Born at Fort Devens, Massachusetts, and raised in northern Vermont, Burke attended the U.S. Naval Academy, receiving a B.S. in 1966. During the next five years he was a member of the Submarine Service. He left the Navy to pursue an architectural career, receiving a B.Arch. from Harvard University's Graduate School of Design in 1974. After four years of working for firms in Cambridge, Massachusetts, and Burlington and Waitsfield, Vermont, he joined BOORA Architects in Portland, Oregon, as a designer. Between 1985 and 1998 he ran his own practice in Portland, moving to Essex, New York, in the latter year. Since then he has worked under the title of Premises Architecture + Design. He has also served as a visiting professor at the New Jersey School of Architecture in Newark (2008) and at the School of Architecture and Art at Norwich University in Northfield, Vermont (2011–14).

A committed modernist, Burke has proven quite varied in his approach to resolving a particular design in response to site, budget, and functional requirements. His work embodies not so much a strong personal style as a deft ability to adapt to the circumstances of each project. Among his Adirondack buildings are three very different residences in Essex County: the

MacDonald-Brown house (2003–05) [WD 10], Caboose House (2005–06) [BO 3], and Farkas-Scavo house (2011–12) [JA 9], as well as the Town of Dannemora Highway Department building (2010–13) [DN 3].

WILLIAM L. COULTER
(1865–1907), Saranac Lake

Coulter was probably the first architect to establish a professional practice in the Adirondacks. Although his career was brief, he developed a distinct style of rustic architecture that had a significant impact on seasonal work in the region. He also helped set a high standard for the design of year-round commercial, institutional, and residential architecture in Saranac Lake. Finally the firm he established endured for over a century, leaving an unparalleled regional legacy.

Born in Norwich, Connecticut, Coulter began to work for architects in New York when he was sixteen, taking courses at the Cooper Institute (now Cooper Union) at night. In 1893 he was hired by the prestigious firm of Renwick, Aspinwall & Renwick, only to contract tuberculosis two years later. He was sent to Montana to recuperate, but the defining move came in the spring of 1896 when he accompanied J. Lawrence Aspinwall to work on E. L. Trudeau's sanitarium at Saranac Lake [SL 38]. Both the location and Trudeau's approach to treatment proved beneficial. A year later, Coulter opened his own office and became so successful that in 1899 he constructed an office building—one of the first in the village that was thoroughly urban in its attributes—as an investment and as quarters for his burgeoning firm [SL 19]. The building was substantially enlarged two years later, and in 1905 Coulter took in a partner, Max Westhoff. Although tuberculosis claimed Coulter's life not long thereafter, he had laid an enduring foundation.

Coulter's most distinctive work was arguably for the huge camps he designed on the Saranac lakes, including Moss Ledge for Isabel Ballentine (1899); Knollwood Club, an enclave for six families, including Louis Marshall's (1899); Bull Point for Otto Kahn (1901–03); Prospect Point for Adolph Lewisohn (1902–04) [SN 2]; and Eagle Island for Levi Morton (1903) [SN 3]. He was responsible for several summer houses at Lake Placid [LP 18a and d] as well as residences for well-to-do tuberculosis patients in Saranac Lake [SL 37c, e, f, and h]. Beginning around 1900, he did a number of projects for the Lake Placid Club. Coulter also designed two seasonal churches, for the Presbyterians at Paul Smiths (1899) [PS 7] and the Episcopalians at Lake Placid (1898–1900) [LP 13].

EARL COVEY
(1876–1952), Big Moose

During a career that lasted over forty years, Covey proved to be among the most imaginative designers of rustic buildings in the Adirondacks. Born in Lewis County, New York, the son of a blacksmith, Covey moved with his family to Old Forge in 1885. It was there, apparently, that his father, Henry Covey, began to build as an additional source of income, erecting a "portable camp" on Third Lake in 1886. He constructed Camp Crag on Big Moose Lake, a base for hunting and fishing parties. Following his wife's death from tuberculosis in 1890, Henry Covey ran the establishment with his two sons. By the decade's end Earl Covey began work on a camp of his own on nearby Twitchell Lake [BG 4]. For the rest of his career, Earl combined the art of building with managing rustic hostelries of his own devising.

During the early 20th century Earl Covey built a number of camps on Big Moose Lake, while his wife and growing children ran the Twitchell Lake Inn. With her death in 1920, he lost interest in the business. Remarried in 1923, Covey began work on a new place, Covewood Lodge [BG 1], the following year. For over a decade the hotel flourished under the Coveys' management.

Always the avid outdoorsman, Covey was forced to scale back his demanding activities by 1937, leasing Covewood and moving to Florida for the winter. He suffered a stroke in 1949 and died three years later at Big Moose.

In his building, Covey drew from the pragmatic, extemporaneous, and sometimes whimsical work of the rugged camps created by his father and other pioneering guides at Big Moose Lake. He was prone to experiment with form, with the use of logs as structure, and with rustic decorative motifs. He proved equally adept working in masonry at the Big Moose Community Chapel (1928–31) [BG 2], his last major work. Largely self-taught, he took inspiration from the vernacular work of his adopted home, while he also had a decisive impact on Big Moose Lake's development as a distinctive resort.

WILLIAM G. DISTIN
(1884–1970), Saranac Lake

For nearly half a century Distin headed the firm founded by William L. Coulter and was likely the most prolific architect to practice in the Adirondacks. Born in Montreal, he moved to Saranac Lake with his parents in 1898. Distin graduated from high school two years later. From then until he entered Columbia University's School of Architecture in 1907, he worked as a draftsman for Coulter. During those six years, he gained experience in design, detailing, and supervising construction. In 1911 he left Columbia to work for a prominent Chicago architect, Solon S. Beeman, and attended classes at the Art Institute. Distin returned to Saranac Lake around 1912, rejoining Coulter's firm, now headed by Max Westhoff. He took leave during 1917–18 to work for the Construction Division of the U.S. Army in Washington. When Westhoff left the region in 1918, Distin took over the firm. During the 1920s he had an associate, Arthur Wilson, about whom little is known, and in 1952 Distin formed a partnership with Arthur Wareham.

Distin is best remembered for his grand rustic camps, most of them designed at the end of the era when such expansive retreats were commissioned: LaJeunesse for Henry H. Blagden (1930) and Wonundra for William Rockefeller (1930–33) on Upper Saranac Lake; Indian Pass and Last Chance ranches at North Elba; Debar Pond Lodge for Arthur Wheeler at Duane (1939–40) [DU 1]; and Minnowbrook for the Hollingshead company at Blue Mountain Lake (1947–48) [BK 3]. His greatest work is arguably that built for Walter and Katherine Hochschild at Eagle Lake (1937–38), an enormous lodge where log construction is treated with uncharacteristic dynamism. Distin also did extensive work for the Lake Placid Club and Northwood School [LP 20].

At the same time Distin was a generalist, and the bulk of his practice was devoted to a broad range of buildings used year-round. Churches, a bank, an airport terminal, courthouse additions, and houses were among the many types for which he prepared plans. The scope of his work ranged from the enormous arena for the 1932 Winter Olympic Games at Lake Placid (1931–32) [LP 6a], to wartime semi-detached houses for workers in Mineville (1942) [MV 1], to the somewhat loose reconstruction of Fort William Henry at Lake George (1954–55) [LG 7]. After the partnership with Wareham was established, Distin became less involved in the office's work; however, he remained a titular partner until his death at the age of eighty-six.

WILLIAM WEST DURANT
(1850–1934), Raquette Lake

For nearly a quarter century William West Durant was among the largest and most ingenious land developers in the Adirondacks. Probably his most enduring contribution was the creation of a rustic architecture that, directly or otherwise, became a paradigm for camps and other seasonal buildings throughout the region.

Durant had no preparation for his Adirondack enterprises. Born to privilege in Brooklyn, he was the son of Thomas C. Durant, financier and vice-president of the Union Pacific Railroad, who also built the first rail line into the Adirondacks. Son William spent much of his youth abroad in English schools and then at the University of Bonn. While touring in Africa, he was summoned to assist in developing the vast territory owned by his father's Adirondack Company. Durant's strategy was building camps, a type that he was instrumental in transforming from an elementary, largely open cluster of small shelters into a grand assemblage of special-purpose buildings that at once celebrated their rugged settings and provided an array of comforts and diversions. The initiative began at Raquette Lake with Camp Pine Knot (1877–78, 1879–82) [RL 6] and culminated at Sagamore Lodge (1897–99) [RL 7].

Elsewhere, Durant developed a country club and resort community of more modest proportions at Blue Mountain Lake. He contemplated creating a one-million-acre game park and developing projects as far as the Saranac lakes. Durant also invested heavily in infrastructure. Road improvements, a rail line from Old Forge to Raquette Lake, a short steamboat line, a golf course, churches, dams, channels, a telegraph line, and subdivisions were all part of his multi-pronged effort to make Raquette and Blue Mountain lakes accessible and attractive resorts. Durant's extravagant tastes and lack of business acumen began to undermine his endeavors within a half-dozen years of his father's death in 1885. For a while he benefited from the financial support of Collis P. Huntington, who had worked with the elder Durant in building the Transcontinental Railroad and who purchased Camp Pine Knot in 1895. Huntington helped underwrite Durant's grand schemes; however, after the railroad magnate's death in 1900, his heirs expressed no interest in continuing the relationship. Durant was also besieged with lawsuits from his sister and former wife. He was forced to declare bankruptcy in 1904 and did little of consequence up to his death thirty years later at age eighty-three.

DOUGLAS HASKELL
(1899–1979), North Elba

While he had no training as an architect and never established an architectural practice, Douglas Haskell was widely admired by members of that profession internationally for his many accomplishments as an architecture critic and editor. He also designed many components of the North Country School–Camp Treetops complex [NE 1], of which he was the partial owner and where he spent many summer months.

Born in Macedonia, the son of a Congregational missionary, Haskell was educated in German boarding schools before returning to his parents' native Ohio for high school and Oberlin College. After graduating in 1923 he worked for a college weekly and gradually developed an interest in architecture. He joined the staff of Creative Art in 1927. From 1931 to 1942 he was architecture critic for the Nation, producing the first regular column on the subject in the United States. For seven years he wrote for Architectural Record. In 1949 he became senior editor of Architectural Forum. During his fifteen-year tenure with that serial, he developed it into the most insightful and wide-ranging periodical in the field—addressing the concerns of builders, real estate developers, and clients as well as architects. No rival publication came close to matching its breadth, insights, and acuity of criticism.

To supplement his journalist income Haskell worked at Camp Treetops, beginning in 1925. He and his wife, Helen, became co-directors in 1928 and purchased the enterprise five years later. Helen's sister and her husband, Leonora and Walter Clark, joined them and subsequently

401

established North County School on part of the property in 1938. Haskell designed the main building, in part as a means of learning the processes of design and construction. Subsequently he designed a major addition (1942, 1946–47) as well as several other components of the school and camp. Even before work on the school began Haskell undertook an extensive transformation of the landscape to provide shelter, privacy, and definition to the campus. His approach was one of understatement. Buildings and landscape alike appear more as intuitive responses than carefully conceived designs. At the same time, they were developed with painstaking attention to matters of use, climate, topography, and setting. Haskell was the rare modernist who grasped the balance between pragmatism and whimsy that long characterized the region's best rustic architecture.

PAUL F. JAQUET
(1889–1951), Saranac Lake

For a brief period, Paul Jaquet enjoyed a promising career in the Adirondacks. Born in Soleure, Switzerland, he immigrated to the United States at a young age with his parents. Jaquet took classes in architecture at Philadelphia's Drexel Institute (now Drexel University) between 1907 and 1909 and gained additional experience by concurrently working in a succession of architectural offices. By 1910 he had acquired enough experience to work as senior draftsman for a Pittsburgh firm while taking graduate classes at Carnegie Institute of Technology (now Carnegie Mellon University). Between 1912 and 1914 he completed his formal education at the University of Pennsylvania and began working for the prominent Philadelphia firm of Mellor & Meigs. Jaquet probably suffered from tuberculosis and around 1914 came to Saranac Lake, where he found employment as senior draftsman for Scopes & Feustmann. In 1915 he married Marie Callanan, whose father co-

owned one of the region's largest building supply and construction firms. Jaquet subsequently worked for architects in Montreal and Minneapolis before returning to Saranac Lake, where he opened his own office in 1920.

Ill health forced Jaquet to terminate his practice six years later, but by February 1926 he was employed by Thompson, Holmes & Converse in Rochester, New York. Within a year he was back in Saranac Lake, again working for Scopes & Feustmann. His condition seems to have improved. In 1929 he was appointed to the state architect's office, where he was in charge of projects related to large institutional buildings. Nine years later he moved to Washington, D.C., as consulting architect to the Public Buildings Administration. His work in that capacity for the Department of State led to a transfer to that agency's Foreign Buildings Operations division, where he designed several embassies and legations in Central and South America. Jaquet's health deteriorated once more, leading to an early retirement in 1950, not long before his death.

While in Saranac Lake Jaquet designed a number of buildings for the Catholic church, including alterations to St. Elizabeth's Church in Elizabethtown (1922) [EL 15], Holy Name Church in Tupper Lake (1922–24) [TL 9], and, most notably, St. Bernard's School in Saranac Lake (1924–25) [SL 6]. He also designed a small schoolhouse in Keene (1921–22, altered), a new front for Leonard's department store (1922–23) [SL 20], and other buildings in Saranac Lake. Plans for the North Elba Town House (1927) [SL 5] were probably done after he had returned to work for Scopes & Feustmann.

ROCKWELL KENT
(1882–1971), Au Sable Forks

Widely known and admired for his paintings, prints, book illustrations, and graphic work, Kent was also a trained architect; he designed several buildings for family and friends in and around Au Sable Forks. Born in Tarrytown, New York, where his parents had a sizable country house, Kent attended Columbia University's School of Architecture. But not long before his 1904 graduation, he left the program to study under Robert Henri at the New York School of Art. He also continued to pursue architectural endeavors, working in the offices of McKim, Mead & White and Ewing & Chappell. He gained note as an architectural renderer for such prominent firms as Delano & Aldrich.

By 1920 Kent turned his attention to painting and the graphic arts. As his work gained substantial recognition and praise, he decided in 1927 to leave New York for the Adirondacks. The kind of rugged, wild landscape that he embraced in his art was a major attraction. At the same time, New York remained readily accessible by train, a connection essential to maintaining his career. Artists had been drawn to the region since the mid-19th century, but even those who established a base there—most famously Winslow Homer—did so on a strictly seasonal basis. Kent was the first of note to move to the region year-round.

After an extensive search, Kent and his wife secured a 200-acre farm along the banks of the Ausable River, a short distance south of Au Sable Forks. He designed a commodious dwelling, a large dairy barn, other service buildings, a manager's house, and a studio. Kent's style was rooted in practicality, but also fine craftsmanship—an unpretentious rendition of the Colonial Revival then popular. Kent found virtually all forms of architecture in the Adirondacks unappealing and was a fervent anti-modernist. Asgaard Farm, as Kent christened his new home (honoring the mythical farm of Norse gods), was a serious place of work—farming as well as art—but it was also a place for entertaining, where the Kents maintained ties with their many New York friends.

Kent made sketches for an extensive remaking of the house of his friend, lawyer O. Byron Brewster (1931) [EL 12], and more modest additions for another friend, poet Louis Untermeyer (ca. 1932), in Elizabethtown. His most ambitious project was for New York banker J. Cheever Cowdin (ca. 1931) a short distance from Asgaard Farm. Aside from minor changes to the farm, Kent designed little else save an unrealized American Legion hall in Au Sable Forks (1946) and a mundane replacement for his own house after it burned in 1969.

NILS EDWARD LUDEROWSKI
(b. 1942), Keene Valley

In recent decades Nils Edward Luderowski has been one of the few architects catering primarily to seasonal residents to maintain a year-round office in the Adirondacks. He has developed a personal style that is informed by a wide variety of historical and contemporary precedents and at the same time is well suited to the landscape of the region. Born in Washington, D.C., he moved to Sweden with his mother, Ulla af Ugglas, in 1949, where he attended the National College of Art, Craft, and Design (Konstfack) in Stockholm from 1965 to 1967. He then moved to New York, where he received a B.F.A. from the Pratt Institute in 1971. Luderowski worked for architects in Stockholm, Detroit, and New York before opening his own interior design firm in 1973. Twenty years later he established an architectural office in Keene Valley.

For nearly a quarter century Luderowski has maintained a design-oriented practice specializing in camps and other residences. Realized projects include work on Long, Upper Saranac, Tupper, Loon, Raquette, Placid, Mirror, and Spitfire lakes, as well as cottages at St. Huberts. He also was responsible for the sensitive rehabilitation of architect Kirkland Cutter's North Point, the 1902–03 Lucy Carnegie camp on Raquette Lake (2011), and additions to his own residence in Keene [KN 1]. His designs draw inspiration from strains of modernism in the

U.S. and Scandinavia, especially since 1950, while they also embody characteristics of the Shingle Style and the Arts and Crafts Movement. The whimsy that has characterized some of the best rustic architecture in the region for well over a century is evident in much of his work. At the same time, these designs embody a concern for practicality and livability that renders them thoroughly a part of the contemporary world.

ARTO MONACO
(1913–2003), Upper Jay

Arto Monaco's visions of fantasy had a major impact on the landscape of recreation in the Adirondacks from the structures he conceived for children's theme parks. His father had emigrated from Italy at the young age of fourteen, eventually opening a restaurant in Upper Jay. Rockwell Kent befriended the family and convinced father and son that the latter, a high-school dropout, should become an artist. Kent used his influence to get Arto Monaco enrolled at the Pratt Institute. After graduating in 1936, Monaco secured short-term employment at the studios of MGM, Warner Brothers, Walt Disney, and Paramount. During World War II he co-established the U.S. Army Signal Corps Training Aids Division. In that capacity he designed Annadorf, a mock Bavarian village in southern California, where soldiers could practice infiltration and street fighting.

With the return of peace, Monaco assisted Kent; went to Lake Arrowhead, California, to design a resort village; then worked in New York for the Ideal Toy Company. He soon started his own business, across from his father's restaurant, making wood toys for some of the nation's foremost department stores. In 1948 Julian Reiss commissioned him to design Santa's Workshop in Wilmington [WM 1]. A pioneering venture nationally, the theme park was inspired by Annadorf, but also rendered like a giant three-dimensional cartoon village. Reiss's second venture, Old McDonald's Farm at Lake Placid (opened 1953), which Monaco also designed, proved unsuccessful. Soon thereafter, his toy factory was closed and the building demolished for highway realignment.

In the spring of 1953 Monaco set out to develop his own park, which he called the Land of Makebelieve. Part fairytale village, part miniature Western town, the complex was located close to the Ausable River in Upper Jay. Like Santa's Workshop, the park thrived, and additions were made on a frequent basis. Monaco continued to make toys in a workshop on the premises. He also consulted extensively for Charles R. Wood, an entrepreneur who developed Storytown (1954) and Gaslight Village (1956) in Lake George, as well as for La Ronde, the amusement park at Expo 67 at Montreal. Repeated flooding at Upper Jay forced Monaco to close his beloved Land of Makebelieve in 1979, but he continued to make toys and consult on Wood's Great Escape, a consolidation of his earlier parks, where several of the Upper Jay structures were relocated. Monaco remained active until close to his death at age ninety.

BENJAMIN A. "BEN" MUNCIL
(1867–1930), Gabriels

Born into poverty, Ben Muncil managed to work his way up into prominence as a builder in the Gabriels–Paul Smiths area. He also made a distinctive contribution to rustic design that extends well beyond the places where he worked. A native of Vermontville, New York, Muncil was one of nine children, most of whom wound up in foster homes. He began to work tending babies when he was only five and at fourteen secured employment at a logging camp. Four years later he augmented his income as a guide at the Livingston camp on Upper St. Regis Lake. The Livingstons and other summer residents began to tap his carpentry skills. Soon in business for himself, Muncil married in 1890. Within a decade his daughter taught him how to read sufficiently well that he could become a full-fledged building contractor.

Muncil worked as a builder on a number of Upper St. Regis camps, including those of Whitelaw Reid, W. K. Vanderbilt, and Marjorie Merriweather Post. On Osgood Pond he built White Pine Camp (1907–08, 1911) [PS 2] and Northbrook Lodge (1919–20), whose owner commissioned him to design and construct a large farm complex to service the camp (1922) [GA 2]. Muncil's earliest known design was for the Brighton Town Hall (1914) [PS 1]. He also designed and built the Church of the Assumption (1922–23) [GA 3] nearby. His most distinctive trademark was what he termed "brainstorm" siding, where the bottom edge of each board is left rough. He apparently devised this pattern at White Pine Camp.

During the 1920s Muncil employed most male residents of Gabriels. He had his own lumber company and also established the Tupper Lake Furniture Company (1916). He was killed in his car at a railroad crossing in 1930.

SCOPES & FEUSTMANN
Saranac Lake

Founded in 1903, the firm headed by William Henry Scopes (1877–1964) and Maurice M. Feustmann (1870–1943) rivaled that run by William L. Coulter, Max Westhoff, and William G. Distin in the extent of its work in the northern Adirondacks. The office also became nationally recognized for hospital designs.

Scopes came from Albany to Trudeau's sanitarium in 1896 and soon developed an interest in architecture. While still a patient he began to take correspondence courses and apparently was for a short time enrolled at Columbia University's School of Architecture. Around 1900 he went to work for the Saranac Lake building firm of Branch & Callanan. Within a few years he was in practice, designing

the Fowler Block at Saranac Lake in 1900 [SL 17], a large house in the Highland Park subdivision (ca. 1902) [SL 37d], and the St. Armand Town Hall at Bloomingdale in 1903 [BM 1].

Feustmann also came to Saranac Lake for "the cure" in the late 1890s. Prior to that time, he had acquired an impressive portfolio. A native of Philadelphia, he graduated from the University of Pennsylvania in 1890 and completed architectural studies at the Royal Polytechnic Institute in Munich. Returning to Philadelphia in 1893, he worked for the nationally prominent firm of Cope & Stewardson. Feustmann must have met Scopes soon after coming to the Adirondacks. Following a relatively brief stay, Feustmann continued his treatment in the American Southwest. In 1903 Scopes asked him to enter into a partnership that lasted some three decades.

Winning the competition for the Reception Hospital (1903–05) [SL 28] launched the new firm on a trajectory as specialist in tuberculosis facilities. Among their works were the State Sanitarium at Pittsford, Vermont (1906); the Canandaigua Tuberculosis Hospital in New Hampshire (1915); and the William Wirt Winchester Hospital in New Haven, Connecticut (1915). Locally, they were responsible for numerous buildings at the Trudeau Sanitorium between 1924 and 1930 [SL 38 d–h] and the Will Rogers Memorial Hospital (1928–29) [SL 1]. In 1910 they began to develop cure cottages as part of what became known as Cottage Row [SL 36 a–f]. The firm was also responsible for several of Saranac Lake's most prominent buildings, including the Pontiac Theater (1917; burned), the Harrietstown Town Hall [SL 8], and the Hotel Saranac [SL 23] (both 1926–28).

The Depression dealt a fatal blow to the practice, which did little work after 1930. Feustmann died of heart disease in 1943. Scopes lived into his eighty-seventh year.

ARTHUR WAREHAM
(1904–2005), Saranac Lake

Like his predecessors in the firm founded by William L. Coulter, Wareham came with solid professional credentials. Born in Morrisville, Pennsylvania, he attended Brooklyn Technical High School and received his architectural degree from Pratt Institute in 1938. From then until American entry into World War II he worked in the office of Eggers & Higgins, the successor firm to that of John Russell Pope, in New York. After active duty Wareham was employed by the U.S. Public Health Service in Washington, D.C. He, too, came to Saranac Lake after contracting tuberculosis. When he joined the office then headed by William G. Distin is unclear, but the two entered a partnership in 1953 that lasted until 1970. The relationship appears to have been one of convenience; the two men did not collaborate on work. Wareham was a modernist, producing designs quite different from those of Distin and his generation. Wareham was responsible for several schools, including Lake Clear (1954–55) [LC 2] and the Trudeau Institute (1962–64) [SL 41] on Lower Saranac Lake.

MAX WESTHOFF
(ca. 1870–early 1950s), Saranac Lake

Following William L. Coulter's early death in 1906, Max Westhoff managed to retain the momentum of the practice for a decade. Born in Brooklyn, he was a member of the initial class at the Pratt Institute and worked for the prominent New York firm of Eidlitz & McKenzie. He moved to Saranac Lake in 1902, probably as a tuberculosis patient, and later joined Coulter's office. He became an associate two years later and a partner in 1905. For at least five years after Coulter's death Westhoff retained the firm name of Coulter & Westhoff, capitalizing on his deceased partner's reputation and suggesting continuity in the practice. Perhaps in search of greater job opportunities he moved to Springfield, Massachusetts,

in 1917, though he kept an interest in the Saranac Lake office, now run by William G. Distin, until 1920. Westhoff retired in 1935 and moved to Florida, where he died in the early 1950s.

Like Coulter, Westhoff received commissions from Melvil Dewey for the Lake Placid Club, and he designed the original components of Northwood School (1911–12) [LP 20]. His portfolio also included camps at Lower Saranac Lake, Big Moose Lake, and at Sunapee, New Hampshire, as well as cottages at the Saranac Inn. Among the several seasonal residences for which Westhoff prepared plans at Lake Placid, Camp Carolina (ca. 1913) is arguably the most accomplished. He also designed a variety of commercial and institutional buildings, including St. Bernard's Catholic Church (1910–11, burned), the St. Regis Hotel (1908, burned), and the Adirondack National Bank (1906–7, altered), all at Saranac Lake.

During the mid-1920s Horace Augustus Moses, founder of Strathmore Paper Company in Springfield, commissioned Westhoff to design three buildings in Moses's hometown of Ticonderoga: the Moses-Luddington Hospital (1923, demolished); the headquarters of the New York Historical Association (1925–26) [TI 21], a replica of the long-demolished Thomas Hancock house in Boston; and the multi-purpose Community Building (1927–29) [TI 4].

RUSSELL F. WHITEHEAD
(1884–1954), Westport

Whitehead's career was similar to that of Ronald Allwork. He was foremost a writer; what little architectural design he undertook was primarily in the Adirondack community where he was a seasonal resident. But, unlike Allwork, Whitehead was of an earlier generation and a staunch traditionalist.

Born in Trenton, New Jersey, Whitehead spent two years taking civil engineering courses at Princeton University, then attended Drexel Institute (now Drexel University), from which he graduated in 1903. Until 1910 he worked for several New York architectural offices, including Kirby, Petit & Green and Walker & Gillette. After a two-year study tour in Europe, he became an editor for *Architectural Record*. From 1913 to 1915 he was editor and part owner of another leading architectural journal, *The Brickbuilder*, which later became *Architectural Forum* (the journal that Haskell headed after World War II). For the next seventeen years Whitehead edited and published the *White Pine Series of Architectural Monographs* and then edited its successor, the *Monograph Series*. The latter two serials were widely considered to be the definitive source for pictorial information (photographs and measured drawings) on 18th- and early 19th-century American architecture.

For part of this period (1924–30), Whitehead conducted an architectural practice, Clark & Whitehead, officially based in New York (in Whitehead's apartment), but much of the work he did was in Westport, where he and his family spent summers. Besides extensively remodeling a mid-19th-century house for his residence (ca. 1920) [WP 11], Whitehead designed the community's yacht club (1927) and country club (1927–28) [WP 12]. He was also architect for the Westport Inn Realty Company. After World War II, Whitehead retired to Albuquerque, New Mexico. For his distinguished service in publishing, he was proposed as a Fellow in the American Institute of Architects, but died before his nomination could be considered.

BIBLIOGRAPHY

THESE CITATIONS ARE MOSTLY FOR HISTORICAL STUDIES published since 1945. A much more extensive bibliography, including suggestions for further reading, is available to AARCH members on the organization's website.

THEMATIC AND GENERAL HISTORIES

Agriculture and Industry

Gereau, Leonard A. *Tahawus Memories 1941–1963: The Story of a Unique Adirondack Hometown.* Saranac Lake, N.Y.: Hungry Bear, 2014.

Gooley, Lawrence P. *Lyon Mountain: The Tragedy of a Mining Town.* Peru, N.Y.: Bloated Toe Press, 2004.

Hardy, Philip J. "The Iron Age Community of the J. & J. Rogers Iron Company, Au Sable Forks, New York: 1825–1900." Ph.D. dissertation, Bowling Green State University, 1985.

Hochschild, Harold K. *Lumberjacks and Rivermen in the Central Adirondacks 1850–1950.* Blue Mountain Lake, N.Y.: Adirondack Museum, 1962.

———. *The Macintyre Mine—From Failure to Fortune.* Blue Mountain Lake, N.Y.: Adirondack Museum, 1962.

Hyde, Floy S. *Adirondack Forests, Fields, and Mines: Brief Accounts and Stories Concerning Lumbering, Forest-Related Products, Farm Specialties, and Mining, Yesterday and Today.* Lakemont, N.Y.: North Country Books, 1974.

McMartin, Barbara. *The Great Forest of the Adirondacks.* Utica, N.Y.: North Country Books, 1994.

———. *Hides, Hemlocks and Adirondack History: How the Tanning Industry Influenced the Region's Growth.* Utica, N.Y.: North Country Books, 1992.

Moravek, John Richard. "The Iron Industry as a Geographic Force in the Adirondack-Champlain Region of New York State, 1800–1971." Ph.D. dissertation, University of Tennessee, Knoxville, 1976.

Rosenquist, Valerie Beth. "The Iron Ore Eaters: A Portrait of the Mining Community of Moriah, New York." Ph.D. dissertation, Duke University, 1997.

Seely, Bruce E. "Blast Furnace Technology in the Mid-19th Century: A Case Study of the Adirondack Iron and Steel Company." *IA, Journal of the Society for Industrial Archeology* 7:1 (1981): 27–54.

Welsh, Peter C. *Jacks, Jobbers and Kings: Logging in the Adirondacks 1850–1950.* Utica, N.Y.: North Country Books, 1995.

Conservation and the Natural Environment

Keller, Jane Eblen. *Adirondack Wilderness: A Story of Man and Nature.* Syracuse: Syracuse University Press, 1980.

McMartin, Barbara. *The Adirondack Park: A Wildlands Quilt.* Syracuse: Syracuse University Press, 1999.

———. *Perspectives on the Adirondacks: A Thirty-Year Struggle by People Protecting Their Treasure.* Syracuse: Syracuse University Press, 2002.

Terrie, Philip G. *Contested Terrain: A New History of Nature and People in the Adirondacks.* 2nd ed. Syracuse: Syracuse University Press; Blue Mountain Lake: Adirondack Museum, 2008.

VanValkenburgh, Norman J. *The Forest Preserve of New York State in the Adirondack and Catskill Mountains: A Short History.* Schenectady: Adirondack Research Center, 1983.

Recreation

Anzalone, Jonathan David. "Creating a Modern Wilderness Playground: The Transformation of the Adirondack State Park, 1920–1980." Ph.D. dissertation, Stony Brook University, 2012

Bond, Hallie E., et al. *"A Paradise for Boys and Girls": Children's Camps in the Adirondacks.* Blue Mountain Lake, N.Y.: Adirondack Museum; Syracuse: Syracuse University Press, 2006.

Hirsch, Rose Ann. *Kiddie Parks of the Adirondacks.* Charleston, S.C.: Arcadia, 2006.

Martin, J. Peter. *Adirondack Golf Courses Past and Present.* 1987. Reprint, Lake Placid, N.Y.: Adirondack Golf, 1994.

Schlett, James. *A Not Too Greatly Changed Eden: The Story of the Philosophers' Camp in the Adirondacks.* Ithaca: Cornell University Press, 2015.

Woods, Lynn. "An Adirondack Auto Biography." *Adirondack Life,* June 1996, 34–43, 86–87.

———. "Meanwhile, Back at the Ranch: Wranglers, Rodeos and Riders in the Sky." *Adirondack Life,* June 1997, 38–47.

Transportation

Cameron, Duncan H. "Adirondack Railways: Historic Engine of Change." *Adirondack Journal of Environmental Studies* 19 (2013): 11–23.

Gove, Hill. *Logging Railroads in the Adirondacks.* Syracuse: Syracuse University Press, 2006.

Harter, Henry A. *Fairy Tale Railroad: The Mohawk and Malone—from the Mohawk, through the Adirondacks to the St. Lawrence.* Utica, N.Y.: North Country Books, 1979.

Hochschild, Harold K. *Adirondack Railroads, Real and Phantom.* Blue Mountain Lake, N.Y.: Adirondack Museum, 1962.

Shaughnessy, Jim. *Delaware & Hudson.* Syracuse: Syracuse University Press, 1997.

Other Studies

Adler, Jeanne Winston. *Early Days in the Adirondacks: The Photographs of Seneca Ray Stoddard.* New York: H. N. Abrams, 1997.

Barnhill, Georgia B. *Wild Impressions: The Adirondacks on Paper.* Blue Mountain Lake, N.Y.: Adirondack Museum; Boston: David R. Godine, 1995.

Bellico, Russell P. *Sails and Steam in the Mountains: A Maritime and Military History of Lake George and Lake Champlain.* 2nd ed. Fleischmanns, N.Y.: Purple Mountain Press, 2001.

Bogdan, Robert. *Adirondack Vernacular: The Photography of Henry M. Beach.* Syracuse: Syracuse University Press, 2003.

———. *Exposing the Wilderness: Early Twentieth-Century Adirondack Postcard Photographers.* Syracuse: Syracuse University Press, 1999.

De Sormo, Maitland C. *The Heydays of the Adirondacks.* Saranac Lake, N.Y.: Adirondack Yesteryears, 1974.

Donaldson, Alfred L. *A History of the Adirondacks,* 2 vols. 1921. Reprint, Fleischmanns, N.Y.: Purple Mountain Press, 1992.

Henry, Tom, et al. *Lake Champlain: An Illustrated History.* Jay, N.Y.: Adirondack Life, 2009.

Hotaling, Mary. *A Rare Romance in Medicine: The Life and Legacy of Dr. Edward Livingston Trudeau.* Saranac Lake, N.Y.: Historic Saranac Lake, 2016.

Jenkins, Jerry, with Andy Keal. *The Adirondack Atlas: A Geographic Portrait of the Adirondack Park.* Syracuse: Syracuse University Press; Blue Mountain Lake, N.Y.: Adirondack Museum, 2004.

McMartin, Barbara. *The Privately Owned Adirondacks: Sporting and Family Clubs, Private Parks and Preserves, Timberlands and Easements.* Canada Lake, N.Y.: Lakeview Press, 2004.

Podskoch, Martin. *Adirondack Civilian Conservation Corps Camps: History, Memories & Legacy of the CCC.* East Hampton, Conn.: Podskoch Press, 2011.

Tissot, Caperton. *Adirondack Ice: A Cultural and Natural History.* Saranac Lake, N.Y.: Snowy Owl Press, 2010.

ARCHITECTURE, ENGINEERING, FURNITURE, AND LANDSCAPE

Fire Towers

Laskey, Paul. *The Fire Observation Towers of New York State.* Ballston Spa, N.Y.: MLK Publishing, 2003.

Podskoch, Martin. *Adirondack Fire Towers: Their History and Lore, The Northern Districts.* Fleischmanns, N.Y.: Purple Mountain Press, 2005.

———. *Adirondack Fire Towers: Their History and Lore, The Southern Districts.* Fleischmanns, N.Y.: Purple Mountain Press, 2003.

Starr, Bill. "A Pictorial History of the Fire Towers in New York State." National Historic Lookout Register. http://www.nhlr.org/media/2972/new_york_fire_tower_pictorial_history_by_bill_starr_11-27-10.pdf.

Forts

Bellico, Russell P. *Empires in the Mountains: French and Indian War Campaigns and Forts in the Lake*

Champlain, Lake George, and Hudson River Corridor. Fleischmanns, N.Y.: Purple Mountain Press, 2010.

Charbonneau, André. "The Redoubt in New France: A Contribution to the History of Fortification in North America." Fort, The International Journal of Fortification and Military Architecture 18 (1990): 43–67 [Fort St. Frédéric]

Crego, Carl R. Fort Ticonderoga. Charleston, S.C.: Arcadia, 2004.

Figel, Richard. "The Second Building of Fort Ticonderoga," Adirondack Life, June 1978, 12–15. 46–49.

Furness, Gregory T. "Crown Point: An Outline History." America's Historic Lakes. www.historiclakes.org.

Westbrook, Nicholas. "Ticonderoga in Print: Prints from the Fort Ticonderoga Museum Collection." Imprint, Journal of the American Historical Print Collectors Society 26 (Spring 2001): 2–18.

Hotels, Motels, and Resort Complexes

Gates, William Preston. History of the Fort William Henry Hotel, Lake George, New York. Queensbury, N.Y.: by the author, 2004.

———. History of the Sagamore Hotel, Bolton Landing on Lake George, NY. Queensbury, N.Y.: by the author, 2001.

———. Lake George Hotels & Landings. Queensbury, N.Y.: by the author, 2010.

Metcalfe, Ann Breen. The Leland House: An Adirondack Innovator. Elizabethtown, N.Y.: Essex County Historical Society, 1994.

Tolles, Bryant F., Jr. Resort Hotels of the Adirondacks: The Architecture of a Summer Paradise, 1850–1950. Hanover, N.H.: University Press of New England, 2003.

Williams, Donald R. Adirondack Hotels and Inns. Charleston, S.C.: Arcadia, 2008.

Houses and Camps

Barrett, Charlotte K. A Visitor's Guide to Camp Santanoni. Keeseville, N.Y.: Adirondack Architectural Heritage, 2013.

Bridger, Beverly. Great Camp Sagamore: The Vanderbilts' Adirondack Retreat. Charleston, S.C.: History Press, 2012.

Engel, Robert, et al. Santanoni: From Japanese Temple to Life in an Adirondack Great Camp. 2nd ed. Keeseville, N.Y.: Adirondack Architectural Heritage, 2009.

Everest, Allan S. Pioneer Homes of Clinton County 1790–1820. Plattsburgh, N.Y.: Clinton County Historical Association, 1966.

Gilborn, Craig. Adirondack Camps: Homes Away from Home, 1850–1950. Blue Mountain Lake, N.Y.: Adirondack Museum; Syracuse: Syracuse University Press, 2000.

Hewitt, Mark Alan. "Living with Antiques: The Pavilion, Ticonderoga, New York." Antiques 134 (July 1988): 130–41.

Hislop, David. "Elegance Comes to Lake Champlain: Belden Noble's Greystone in Essex, New York." Nineteenth Century 24 (Spring 2004): 33–37.

Kaiser, Harvey H. Great Camps of the Adirondacks. Boston: David R. Godine, 1982.

Longstreth, Richard. "Protecting Artifice amid Nature: Camp Santanoni and the Adirondack Forest Preserve," in Public Nature: Scenery, History, and Park Design, edited by Ethan Carr, et al. Charlottesville: University of Virginia Press, 2013.

Malo, Paul. "A Home to Call Our Own." Adirondack Life, December 1997, 56–61. 79.

Montgomery, Gladys. An Elegant Wilderness: Great Camps and Grand Lodges in the Adirondacks. New York: Acanthus Press, 2011.

O'Brien, Kathryn E. The Great and the Gracious on Millionaires' Row. Utica, N.Y.: North Country Books, 1978.

Randl, Chad. "A List: The Kitschy Charms of Triangular Living." Adirondack Life, Collectors' Issue 2006, 56–63, 76.

Reiff, Daniel D. Historic Camps of Mt. Arab and Eagle Crag Lakes. Mount Arab, N.Y.: Mount Arab Preserve Association, 1995.

Sexton, R. W., ed. and comp. Camps in the Woods by Augustus D. Shepard, A.I.A. New York: Architectural Book Publishing Co., 1931.

Stock, John W. Litchfield Park: Stories from an Adirondack Great Camp. Blue Mountain Lake, N.Y.: Adirondack Museum, 2004.

Svenson, Sally. "Rockitecture: A Handful of Stone Boathouses Stand Sentinel on Adirondack Lakeshores." Adirondack Life, At Home in the

Adirondacks 2014, 54–59.

Woods, Lynn, et al. *Adirondack Style: Great Camps and Rustic Lodges*. New York: Rizzoli, 2011.

Other Studies

Brockway, Lucinda A. *A Favorite Place of Resort for Strangers: The King's Garden at Fort Ticonderoga*. Ticonderoga, N.Y.: Fort Ticonderoga, 2001.

Clifford, George E., et al. *Lake Champlain Lighthouses: An Illustrated Guide to the Historic Beacons*. Plattsburgh, N.Y.: Clinton County Historical Association, 1999.

Clinton Prison at Dannemora. Plattsburgh, N.Y.: Clinton County Historical Museum, 1987.

Engelhart, Steven. *Crossing the River: Historic Bridges of the Ausable River*. Keeseville, N.Y.: Friends of Keeseville, 1991.

Everest, Allan S. *Our North Country Heritage: Architecture Worth Saving in Clinton and Essex Counties*. Plattsburgh, N.Y.: Tundra Books, 1972.

Gallos, Philip L. *Cure Cottages of Saranac Lake: Architecture and History of a Pioneer Health Resort*. Saranac Lake, N.Y.: Historic Saranac Lake, 1985.

Gilborn, Craig. *Adirondack Furniture and the Rustic Tradition*. New York: Henry N. Abrams, 1987.

Longstreth, Richard. "Douglas Haskell's Adirondack Legacy: The Understated Campus of North Country School and Camp Treetops," in *Looking Beyond the Icons: Midcentury Architecture, Landscape, and Urbanism*. Charlottesville: University of Virginia Press, 2015.

Loughrey, Janet. *Gardens, Adirondack Style*. Camden, Maine: Down East Books, 2006.

MacKenzie, Mary, et al. *Main Street, Lake Placid: An Architectural and Historic Survey*. Lake Placid, N.Y.: Lake Placid Public Library, 2010.

McGowan, Robert Harold. *Architecture from the Adirondack Foothills*. Malone, N.Y.: Franklin County Historical and Museum Society, 1977.

Miller, Mara, et al. *Places of the Spirit: Sacred Sites of the Adirondacks*. Lake Placid, N.Y.: Lake Placid Center for the Arts and Humanities, 2003.

Randl, Chad. "Chalet Chic: The Alpine Influence in Adirondack Architecture." *Adirondack Life*, Collectors' Issue 2008, 48–55, 99–101.

Svenson, Sally. *Adirondack Churches: A History of Design and Building*. Keeseville, N.Y.: Adirondack Architectural Heritage, 2006.

Tissot, Caperton. *Saranac Lake's Ice Palace: A History of Winter Carnival's Crown Jewel*. Saranac Lake, N.Y.: Snowy Owl Press, 2012.

Zimmerman, Edward, et al. *Essex: An Architectural Guide*. Essex, N.Y.: Essex Community Heritage Organization, 1986.

ARCHITECTS, DESIGNERS, AND BUILDERS

Barrows, John E. "Earl Covey, Adirondack Builder." *Fine Homebuilding*, June–July 1987.

Bramen, Lisa. "Nils Luderowski: A Portfolio of This Keene Architect's Eclectic Designs." *Adirondack Life*, At Home in the Adirondacks 2015, 30–37.

Byrne, Peggy. "Arto Monaco and the Company He Keeps…" *Adirondack Life*, Fall 1971, 36–39.

Covey, Frances Alden. *The Earl Covey Story*. New York: Exposition Press, 1964.

De Sormo, Maitland C. *John Bird Burnham: Klondiker, Adirondacker, Eminent Conservationist* Saranac Lake, N.Y.: Adirondack Yesteryears, 1978.

Gilborn, Craig. *Durant: The Fortunes and Woodland Camps of a Family in the Adirondacks*. Sylvan Beach, N.Y.: North Country Books; Blue Mountain Lake, N.Y.: Adirondack Museum, 1981.

Hotaling, Mary B. "Architects and Builders in the Adirondacks." *Adirondack Architectural Heritage Newsletter* 1, no. 1 (May 1992): 5–8.

———. "Ben Muncil, Master Builder." *Adirondack Architectural Heritage Newsletter* 6, no. 1 (June 1997): 1, 3.

———. "Framing a Legacy: How a Century-Old Architectural Firm Defended the Regional Style." *Adirondack Life*, April 1997, 33–39.

———. "Isaac Perry, Craftsman-Architect." *Adirondack Architectural Heritage Newsletter* 9, no. 1 (Summer 2000): 1, 3–4.

———. "Max Westhoff, Revival-Style Architect." *Adirondack Architectural Heritage Newsletter* 8, no. 1 (June 1999): 4, 11.

———. "Scopes and Feustmann, Saranac Lake Architects." *Adirondack Architectural Heritage Newsletter* 7, no. 1 (June 1998): 1, 3.

———. "W. L. Coulter, Architect." *Adirondack Architectural Heritage Newsletter* 4, no. 2 (December 1995): 1, 3.

Lynch, Tom, "The Shippey Family: Adirondack Architect and Builders." *Adirondack Architectural Heritage Newsletter* 12, no. 2 (Winter 2003–04): 1, 3–4.

MacKinnon, Anne. "Arto Monaco: From Tinseltown to Land of Makebelieve, Portrait of Upper Jay's Old Master." *Adirondack Life*, June 2001, 58–66, 71–72.

———. "A Home to Live and Breathe: The Adirondack Architecture of Rockwell Kent." *Adirondack Life*, April 1993, 34–39, 58–59, 66–67, 71.

Roberts, Russell B. "Architect-Author William S. Wicks." *Adirondack Architectural Heritage Newsletter* 6, no. 2 (December 1997): 1, 6.

COMMUNITIES

Barlow, Jane A., ed. *Big Moose Lake in the Adirondacks: The Story of the Lake, the Land, and the People.* Big Moose Lake, N.Y.: Big Moose Lake History Project; Syracuse: Syracuse University Press, 2004.

Bauerschmidt, Shawn R. *Star Lake.* Charleston, S.C.: Arcadia, 2006.

Clothier, Rachael A. *Corinth.* Charleston, S.C.: Arcadia, 2009.

Cohen, Linda, and Sarah Cohen. *Old Forge and the Fulton Chain of Lakes.* Charleston, S.C.: Arcadia, 2011.

———, et al. *Old Forge: Gateway to the Adirondacks.* Charleston, S.C.: Arcadia, 2003.

Collins, Clifford. *A Century—Mining for Souls, 1875–1975.* n.p.: by the parishes of St. Bernard's, St. Michael's, and Memorial Methodist churches, 1975. [Lyon Mountain and Standish]

Collins, Geraldine. *The Brighton Story: Being the History of Paul Smith's, Gabriels and Rainbow Lake.* Lakemont, N.Y.: North Country Books, 1977.

Corbett, Theodore. *The Making of American Resorts: Saratoga Springs, Ballston Spa, Lake George.* New Brunswick, N.J.: Rutgers University Press, 2001.

Deker, Randy. *The Sacandaga Valley.* Charleston, S.C.: Arcadia, 2000.

DeMarsh, Arnold W. *Indian Lake, Hamilton County.* Charleston, S.C.: Arcadia, 2007.

De Sormo, Maitland C. *Summers on the Saranacs.* Saranac Lake, N.Y.: Adirondack Yesteryears, 1980.

Gates, William Preston. *Old Bolton on Lake George, NY.* Queensbury, N.Y.: by the author, 2006.

Glenn, Morris F. *The Story of Three Towns: Westport, Essex and Willsboro, New York.* Ann Arbor: Braun-Brumfield, 1977.

Hadley-Luzerne Historical Society. *Hadley and Lake Luzerne.* Charleston, S.C.: Arcadia, 2002.

Halm, Gale J., and Mary H. Sharp. *Lake George.* Charleston, S.C.: Arcadia, 2000.

Harste, Nancy. *Greetings from Schroon Lake: A Postcard History of an Adirondack Community.* Schroon Lake, N.Y.: Town of Schroon Bicentennial Committee, 2004.

Hastings, John T. *Around Warrensburg.* Charleston, S.C.: Arcadia, 2009.

Hislop, David Conrad. *Essex on Lake Champlain.* Charleston, S.C: Arcadia, 2009.

Historic Saranac Lake LocalWiki. http://localwiki .net/hsl.

Hochschild, Harold K. *An Adirondack Resort in the Nineteenth Century: Blue Mountain Lake, 1870–1900, Stagecoaches and Luxury Hotels.* Blue Mountain Lake, N.Y.: Adirondack Museum, 1988.

———. *Life and Leisure in the Adirondack Backwoods.* Blue Mountain Lake, N.Y.: Adirondack Museum, 1988. [Raquette Lake]

Kammer, James M. *Around Raquette Lake.* Charleston, S.C.: Arcadia, 2007.

Kapusinski, George T. *Huletts Landing on Lake George.* Charleston, S.C.: Arcadia, 2008.

Kopp, Jon. *Tupper Lake.* Charleston, S.C.: Arcadia, 2012.

LaForest, Shirley, and Morris F. Glenn. *Whallonsburg, New York, Agricultural Heritage Area.* Essex, N.Y.: Town of Essex, 2001.

McMartin, Barbara. *Caroga: An Adirondack Town Recalls Its Past.* 1976. Reprint, Caroga, N.Y.: Town of Caroga, 1998.

———. "Ironville." *Adirondack Life*, August 1982, 24–25, 48–49.

Nolan, Margaret, ed. and comp. *Black Brook, Ausable Forks: Yesterday, Today, Tomorrow.* Elizabethtown, N.Y.: Denton Publications, 1977.

Page, Kyle M., and Anderson Falls Heritage Society. *Around Keeseville.* Charleston, S.C.: Arcadia, 2015.

Plunz, Richard, ed. *Two Adirondack Hamlets in*

History: Keene and Keene Valley. Fleischmanns, N.Y.: Purple Mountain Press; Keene Valley, N.Y.: Keene Valley Library Association, 1999.

Provoncha, Fred V. *Ticonderoga*. Charleston, S.C.: Arcadia, 2013.

Reflections and Recollections of the Town with a Past, Warrensburgh, New York. Glens Falls, N.Y.: Greenwood, 2002.

Scheffler, William L., and Frank Carey. *Big Moose Lake, New York, in Vintage Postcards*. Charleston, S.C.: Arcadia, 2000.

Silver Bay Association: A Pictorial History 1900–1935. Silver Bay, N.Y.: Silver Bay Association, 1992.

Simmons, Louis J. *"Mostly Spruce and Hemlock": Historical Highlights of Tupper Lake and the Town of Altamont*. 1976. Reprint, with Index by Carol Payment Poole, Saranac Lake, N.Y.: Hungry Bear, 2009.

Smalley, Carol Parenzan. *Around Caroga Lake, Canada Lake, and Pine Lake*. Charleston, S.C.: Arcadia, 2011.

Smeby, Susan Thomas. *Cranberry Lake and Wanakena*. Charleston, S.C.: Arcadia, 2002.

Stansfield, Dean S. *Lake Placid*. Charleston, S.C.: Arcadia, 2002.

———. *North Elba and Whiteface Mountain*. Charleston, S.C.: Arcadia, 2003.

Suprenant, Neil. *Saranac Lake*. Charleston, S.C.: Arcadia, 2014.

Timm, Ruth. *Raquette Lake: A Time to Remember*. Utica, N.Y.: North Country Books, 1989.

Viestenz, Jacqueline A., and Frank Edgerton. *Moriah and Port Henry in the Adirondacks*. Charleston, S.C.: Arcadia, 2013.

Weaver, Anne E., and Beverly Hoffman. *Lake Pleasant and Speculator in the Adirondacks*. Charleston, S.C.: Arcadia, 2010.

Wilmington Historical Society. *Wilmington and the Whiteface Region*. Charleston, S.C.: Arcadia, 2013.

CLUBS AND PRESERVES

Ackerman, David H. *Lake Placid Club, 1895–1980: An Illustrated History*. Lake Placid, N.Y.: Lake Placid Educational Foundation, 1998.

Bergmann, Carl, et al. *Life at an Adirondack Inn: The Story of One Hundred Years of the Irondequoit Club Inn and Its Owner, the Piseco Company*. Piseco, N.Y.: Irondequoit Inn, n.d.

Comstock, Edward, Jr., ed. *The Adirondack League Club, 1890–1990*. Old Forge: N.Y.: Adirondack League Club, 1990.

Pilcher, Edith. *Up the Lake Road: The First Hundred Years of the Adirondack Mountain Reserve*. Keene Valley, N.Y.: Adirondack Mountain Reserve, 1987.

Potter, Orlando B. III, and Donald Brandreth Potter. *Brandreth: A Band of Cousins Preserves the Oldest Adirondack Family Enclave*. Bennington, Vt.: Two Loon Media, 2011.

INDEX

THE LISTING BELOW INCLUDES MANY PERSONS WHO HAVE significantly contributed to the history of the Adirondacks. I have listed those individuals and companies that have helped shape the region physically into seven categories: **architects, builders, engineers, golf architects, landscape architects, manufacturers of buildings and structures**, and **real estate developers**. There is also a separate category for **artists**. References to individual buildings, structures, and landscapes are by type (that is, function). Transportation modes are listed under **highways, railroads**, and **steamboats, ferry boats and water transportation companies**. In addition to a category, **industrial plants and industries**, ones exist for **iron mining and manufacturing, logging and lumbering, mining** (generally), **paper making, quarrying**, and **tanning**. Categories are also provided for the **conservation** of natural resources and for **historic preservation**. A page number in bold indicates that an image appears on that page.

INDEX

427